# SPORTS LAW

## THE ESSENTIALS

Steven J.J. Weisman

SENIOR LECTURER, LAW, TAXATION, AND FINANCIAL PLANNING
BENTLEY UNIVERSITY

© 2018 LEG, Inc. d/b/a West Academic
    444 Cedar Street, Suite 700
    St. Paul, MN 55101
    1-877-888-1330

West, West Academic Publishing, and West Academic are trademarks of West Publishing Corporation, used under license.

Printed in the United States of America

**ISBN:** 978-1-63460-486-4

This book is dedicated to Olivia, Remington, Chase, Taylor, Delaney and Hutch.

# Table of Contents

# Table of Cases

# SPORTS LAW

## THE ESSENTIALS

# Introduction

Grantland Rice was correct in 1941 when he said that in sport the important thing is not whether you win or lose, but how you play the game. However, the laws that govern how the games are played are far different today when sports law deals with issues Grantland Rice could not have imagined.

The one constant is change and nowhere has change been faster and more profound than in sports law as it attempts to regulate a sporting world filled with new developments, such as fantasy sports, gender issues, concerns of disabled athletes, performance enhancement that is moving beyond drugs to genetic manipulation and more. This book looks at all of the traditional areas of sports law including college sports, professional contracts and labor law, but it also follows sports law's increased involvement with stadium financing, the use of advanced analytics, sports gambling and other new areas of concern.

This book is an eye opening introduction to the many complex aspects of sports law today.

In this book, you will find discussions of issues such as:

• The changing economic structure of college sports brought through a confluence of factors including tremendous amounts of money poured into college sports by television and sporting goods marketers.

- The oddity of colleges taking in millions of dollars from sports, yet, for the most part their sports programs, operate at a deficit.

- The radical changes in college scholarships and increased recognition of the rights of college athletes.

- How E sports continue to become a larger part of the sports landscape.

- The expansion of women's sports through Title IX and the many myths associated with Title IX.

- Complex issues related to sexuality such as hyperandrogenism and transgender as they relate to the world of sports.

- The long history of financial problems encountered by Olympic host cities.

- How much a role politics have played in the Olympics.

- The increased opportunities in the United States and in international competition for disabled athletes and the controversial standards of disability.

- The intricate and complex provisions of professional sports contracts for all of the major professional sports.

- The tremendous attention focused on policing the use of performance enhancing drugs and the future of gene alteration and other emerging methods of scientifically affecting athletic performance as well as a discussion of the complicated ethical issues involved.

- Criminal and tort law as it applies to sports including product liability law and class actions involving issues such as concussion danger and liability.

- The expanding role of labor law in both amateur and professional sports including a detailed analysis of "Deflategate" and its larger meaning in labor law as it applies to sports.

- The burgeoning area of intellectual property in sports including consideration trademark issues and copyrighting touchdown dances and catchphrases.

- The role of agents in professional sports.

- Endorsement contracts for athletes and coaches including morality provisions.

- Social media restrictions for college and professional athletes and consideration of First Amendment rights.

- The dramatic expansion of sports gambling and its effect on sports.

- How fantasy sports have evolved into the multimillion dollar market they have become.

- The increasing role of analytics and technology in sports including the ethical and legal questions that are accompanying their increased use.

- How stadium financing for professional sports teams is accomplished by local and state governments and the effects on taxpayers.

Sports law is dynamically evolving to meet this changing world of sports in our society. This book will show you how.

# Labor and Antitrust Law

## LABOR LAW

Antitrust laws prohibit agreements or practices that restrict business competition to the detriment of consumers. These laws ban abusive behavior by businesses that dominate markets. Most antitrust laws are federal in nature so the federal government is given jurisdiction when the businesses participate in interstate commerce. Antitrust laws and regulations help insure competition which goes to the essence of a free economy.

Under antitrust law, workers are able to organize unions to bargain collectively on behalf of individual workers to achieve a Collective Bargaining Agreement that deals with working conditions. While such collective bargaining limits the rights of individual workers, it increases the overall bargaining power of workers through bargaining as a collective unit.

## ANTITRUST LAWS

The first antitrust law was the Sherman Antitrust Act of 1890 which prohibited monopolies that harmed consumers. The law prohibited agreements or practices that unduly restricted free competition between businesses. This legislation was followed by the Clayton Act of 1914 which exempted labor unions from being considered monopolies even though they regulated working conditions. Later, the Norris LaGuardia Act of 1932 permitted employees to organize as a collective bargaining unit without violating the law. This law represented a balancing of the rights of individual employees with the best interests of all the employees of a particular employer and while for most companies the bargaining power of individual employees is not very strong when contrasted with the bargaining power of a union representing all of the workers, in the realm of professional athletics, the bargaining power of the superstars of the respective sports would exceed that of the union representing all of the players, however, for the betterment of all of the athletes in a particular sport, collective bargaining is how all of the major professional team sports operate.

## THE PER SE RULE AND THE RULE OF REASON

Under the *per se* rule, a labor practice is considered a violation of antitrust law if it is an inherently unreasonable restraint of trade. As was stated in the NCAA v. Board of Regents of the University of Oklahoma, 468 U.S. 85 (1984), "Per se rules are invoked when surrounding circumstances make the likelihood of anticompetitive conduct so great as to render unjustified further examination of the challenged conduct." This is both a flexible and vague standard.

The other primary rule for determining violations of antitrust law is the rule of reason. It too is a vague and flexible standard by which the anti-competitive aspects of a particular practice are balanced against the pro-competitive benefits. In the Mackey case discussed later in this chapter, the Rule of Reason was discussed indicating that "The focus of an inquiry under the Rule of Reason is whether the restraint imposed is justified by legitimate business purposes, and is no more restrictive than necessary." Mackey v. NFL, 543 F2d 606 (1976).

# COLLEGE FOOTBALL ANTITRUST ISSUES

The NCAA's control over college football was challenged on antitrust grounds in 1984 by the University of Oklahoma in a case that ultimately was decided by the Supreme Court. NCAA v. Board of Regents of the University of Oklahoma 468 U.S. 85 (1984). At the time of the lawsuit, the NCAA limited television appearances of schools to no more than four national and six regional televised games over a two year period.

Justice John Paul Stevens wrote on behalf of the Supreme Court, "There can be no doubt that the challenged practices of the NCAA constitute a 'restraint of trade.' " However he went on to explain that not all restraints of trade were necessarily unreasonable restraints of trade and only unreasonable restraints of trade were illegal under antitrust law.

Justice Stevens determined that a central governing body was necessary for proper operation of college sporting events so the per se standard was not appropriate for determining whether a violation of antitrust law existed. The standard that was to be used was the rule of reason standard. Due to the fact that the NCAA plan did plainly restrain trade, it was up to the NCAA to prove that such restraint was reasonable. One of the arguments presented by the NCAA to justify its television restrictions was that it was necessary to enhance the competitiveness of college football, however, Justice Stevens in essence ruled that if it ain't broke don't fix it, indicating that there was no need to protect the market against non-existent competitors. He further dismissed the NCAA's arguments that the television restrictions were necessary in order to protect the live attendance at games saying, "The NCAA's argument that its television plan is necessary to protect live attendance is not based on a desire to maintain the integrity of college football as a distinct and attractive product, but rather on a fear that the product will not prove sufficiently attractive to draw life attendance when faced with competition from televised games."

The vote in favor of the University of Oklahoma was 7–2 and it is interesting to note that among the two dissenters was Justice Byron White who during his college football playing days was known as Whizzer White. Justice White also has the distinction of being the only Supreme Court Justice ever to lead the National Football League in scoring which he did as a running back for the Pittsburgh Pirates (now Steelers) in 1938. While White acknowledged in his dissent that superficially collegiate athletic competitions were similar to professional sporting competitions, he emphasized that the purpose of professional sports were to earn profits while the objective of college sports was to incorporate them into an educational goal in which he believed the restrictions placed by the NCAA were reasonable.

Perhaps unknowingly, White may have correctly predicted the state of college football today in which huge television contracts from networks such as ESPN are driving forces of the game even dictating when a game will be played.

In 2015 the college football playoffs alone brought in 400 million dollars in revenues with the top five conferences having television contacts as follows:

1. ACC television contracts 212 million dollars;

2. Big 12 television contracts 162 million dollars;

3. Pac-12 television contracts 215 million dollars;

4. Big 10 television contracts 279 million dollars

5. SEC television contracts 347 million dollars.[1]

In his dissent, White wrote, "While it would be fanciful to suggest that colleges are not concerned about the profitability of their

---

[1]   "5 College Conferences That Bring in Over $250 Million" Sports Cheat Sheet, Jason Alsher, January 4, 2017.

ventures, it is clear that other, non-commercial goals play a central role in their sports programs. . . . The NCAA's member institutions have designed their competitive athletic programs to be a vital part of the educational system. . . Deviations from this goal produced by a persistent and perhaps inevitable desire to 'win at all costs,' have in the past led, and continue to lead, to a wide range of competitive excesses that prove harmful to students and institutions alike. . . The fundamental policy underlying the NCAA's regulatory program, therefore, is to minimize such deviations and 'to maintain intercollegiate athletics as an integral part of the educational program that the athlete as an integral part of the student body and, by so doing, retain a clear line of demarcation between college athletics and professional sports. The NCAA, in short exits primarily to enhance the contribution made by amateur athletic competition to the process of higher education as distinguished from realizing maximum return on it as an entertainment commodity."

He went on to say, "When these values are factored into the balance, the NCAA's television plan seems eminently reasonable. Most fundamentally, the plan fosters the goal of amateurism by spreading revenues among various schools and reducing the financial incentives toward professionalism."

It is, of course, interesting to note that while today's college football can hardly be called an amateur sport, the profits are essentially reaped not by the players, but the colleges themselves.

## NCAA v. BOARD OF REGENTS OF UNIV. OF OKLA.

United States Supreme Court
468 U.S. 85 (1984)

Held:

The NCAA's television plan violates 1 of the Sherman Act.

(a) While the plan constitutes horizontal price fixing and output limitation, restraints that ordinarily would be held "illegal per se," it would be inappropriate to apply a per se rule in this case where it involves an industry in which horizontal restraints on competition are essential if the product is to be available at all. The NCAA and its members market competition itself—contests between competing institutions. Thus, despite the fact that restraints on the ability of NCAA members to compete in terms of price and output are involved, a fair evaluation of their competitive character requires consideration, under the Rule of Reason, of the NCAA's justifications for the restraints. But an analysis under the Rule of Reason does not change the ultimate focus of the inquiry, which is whether or not the challenged restraints enhance competition.

(b)   The NCAA television plan on its face constitutes a restraint upon the operation of a free market, and the District Court's findings establish that the plan has operated to raise price and reduce output, both of which are unresponsive to consumer preference. Under the Rule of Reason, these hallmarks of anticompetitive behavior place upon the NCAA a heavy burden of establishing an affirmative defense that competitively justifies this apparent deviation from the operations of a free market. The NCAA's argument that its television plan can have no significant anticompetitive effect since it has no market power must be rejected. As a matter of law, the absence of proof of market power does not justify a naked restriction on price or output and, as a factual matter, it is evident from the record that the NCAA does possess market power.

(c)   The record does not support the NCAA's proffered justification for its television plan that it constitutes a cooperative "joint venture" which assists in the marketing of broadcast rights and hence is procompetitive. The District Court's contrary findings undermine such a justification.

(d)   Nor, contrary to the NCAA's assertion, does the television plan protect live attendance, since, under the plan, games are televised during all hours that college football games are played. Moreover, by seeking to insulate live ticket sales from the full spectrum of competition because of its assumption that the product itself is insufficiently attractive to draw live attendance when faced with competition from televised games, the NCAA forwards a justification that is inconsistent with the Sherman Act's basic policy. "The Rule of Reason does not support a defense based on the assumption that competition itself is unreasonable." National Society of Professional Engineers v. United States, 435 U.S. 679, 696.

(e) The interest in maintaining a competitive balance among amateur athletic teams that the NCAA asserts as a further justification for its television plan is not related to any neutral standard or to any readily identifiable group of competitors. The television plan is not even arguably tailored to serve such an interest. It does not regulate the amount of money that any college may spend on its football program or the way the colleges may use their football program revenues, but simply imposes a restriction on one source of revenue that is more important to some colleges than to others. There is no evidence that such restriction produces any greater measure of equality throughout the NCAA than would a restriction on alumni donations, tuition rates, or any other revenue-producing activity. Moreover, the District Court's well-supported finding that many more games would be televised in a free market than under the NCAA plan, is a compelling demonstration that the plan's controls do not serve any legitimate procompetitive purpose.

707 F.2d 1147, affirmed.

STEVENS, J., delivered the opinion of the Court, in which BURGER, C. J., and BRENNAN, MARSHALL, BLACKMUN, POWELL, and O'CONNOR, JJ., joined. WHITE, J., filed a dissenting opinion, in which REHNQUIST, J., joined, post, p. 120.

JUSTICE STEVENS delivered the opinion of the Court.

The University of Oklahoma and the University of Georgia contend that the National Collegiate Athletic Association has unreasonably restrained trade in the televising of college football games. After an extended trial, the District Court found that the NCAA had violated 1 of the Sherman Act 1 and granted injunctive relief. 546 F. Supp. 1276

(WD Okla. 1982). The Court of Appeals agreed that the statute had been violated but modified the remedy in some respects. 707 F.2d 1147 (CA10 1983). We granted certiorari, 464 U.S. 913 (1983), and now affirm.

There can be no doubt that the challenged practices of the NCAA constitute a "restraint of trade" in the sense that they limit members' freedom to negotiate and enter into their own television contracts. In that sense, however, every contract is a restraint of trade, and as we have repeatedly recognized, the Sherman Act was intended to prohibit only unreasonable restraints of trade.

It is also undeniable that these practices share characteristics of restraints we have previously held unreasonable. The NCAA is an association of schools which compete against each other to attract television revenues, not to mention fans and athletes. As the District Court found, the policies of the NCAA with respect to television rights are ultimately controlled by the vote of member institutions. By participating in an association which prevents member institutions from competing against each other on the basis of price or kind of television rights that can be offered to broadcasters, the NCAA member institutions have created a horizontal restraint—an agreement among competitors on the way in which they will compete with one another. A restraint of this type has often been held to be unreasonable as a matter of law. Because it places a ceiling on the number of games member institutions may televise, the horizontal agreement places an artificial limit on the quantity of televised football that is available to broadcasters and consumers. By restraining the quantity of television rights available for sale, the challenged practices create a limitation on output; our cases have held that such limitations are unreasonable restraints of trade. Moreover, the District Court found that the minimum aggregate price in fact operates to preclude any price negotiation between broadcasters and institutions, thereby constituting horizontal price fixing, perhaps the paradigm of an unreasonable restraint of trade.

Horizontal price fixing and output limitation are ordinarily condemned as a matter of law under an "illegal per se" approach because the probability that these practices are anticompetitive is so high; a per se rule is applied when "the practice facially appears to be one that would always or almost always tend to restrict competition and decrease output." Broadcast Music, Inc. v. Columbia Broadcasting System, Inc., 441 U.S. 1, 19–20 (1979). In such circumstances a restraint is presumed unreasonable without inquiry into the particular market context in which it is found. Nevertheless, we have decided that it would be inappropriate to apply a per se rule to this case. This decision is not based on a lack of judicial experience with this type of arrangement, on the fact that the NCAA is organized as a nonprofit entity, or on [468 U.S. 85, 101] our respect for the NCAA's historic role in the preservation and encouragement of intercollegiate amateur athletics. Rather, what is critical is that this case involves an industry in which horizontal restraints on competition are essential if the product is to be available at all.

As Judge Bork has noted: "[S]ome activities can only be carried out jointly. Perhaps the leading example is league sports. When a league of professional lacrosse teams is formed, it would be pointless to declare their cooperation illegal on the ground that there are no other professional lacrosse teams." R. Bork, The Antitrust Paradox 278 (1978). What the NCAA and its member institutions market in this case is competition itself—contests between competing institutions. Of course, this would be completely ineffective if there were no rules on which the competitors agreed to create and define the competition to be marketed. A myriad of rules affecting such matters as the size of the field, the number of players on a team, and the extent to which physical violence is to be encouraged or proscribed, all must be agreed upon, and all restrain the manner in which institutions compete. Moreover, the NCAA seeks to market a particular brand of football—college football. The identification of this "product" with an academic tradition differentiates college football from and makes it more popular than professional sports to which it might otherwise be comparable, such as, for example, minor league baseball. In order to preserve the character and quality of the "product," athletes must not be paid, must be required to attend class, and the like. And the integrity of the "product" cannot be preserved except by mutual agreement; if an institution adopted such restrictions unilaterally, its effectiveness as a competitor on the playing field might soon be destroyed. Thus, the NCAA plays a vital role in enabling college football to preserve its character, and as a result enables a product to be marketed which might otherwise be unavailable. In performing this role, its actions widen consumer choice—not only the choices available to sports fans but also those available to athletes—and hence can be viewed as procompetitive.

Broadcast Music squarely holds that a joint selling arrangement may be so efficient that it will increase sellers' aggregate output and thus be procompetitive. See 441 U.S., at 18–23. Similarly, as we indicated in Continental T. V., Inc. v. GTE Sylvania Inc., 433 U.S. 36, 51–57 (1977), a restraint in a limited aspect of a market may actually enhance marketwide competition. Respondents concede that the great majority of the NCAA's regulations enhance competition among member institutions. Thus, despite the fact that this case involves restraints on the ability of member institutions to compete in terms of price and output, a fair evaluation of their competitive character requires consideration of the NCAA's justifications for the restraints.

Our analysis of this case under the Rule of Reason, of course, does not change the ultimate focus of our inquiry. Both per se rules and the Rule of Reason are employed "to form a judgment about the competitive significance of the restraint." National Society of Professional Engineers v. United States, 435 U.S. 679, 692 (1978). A conclusion that a restraint of trade is unreasonable may be "based either (1) on the nature or character of the contracts, or (2) on surrounding circumstances giving rise to the inference or presumption that they were intended to restrain trade and enhance prices. Under either branch of the test, the inquiry is confined to a consideration of impact on competitive conditions."

Per se rules are invoked when surrounding circumstances make the likelihood of anticompetitive conduct so great as to render unjustified further examination of the challenged conduct. But whether the ultimate finding is the product of a presumption or actual market analysis, the essential inquiry remains the same—whether or not the challenged restraint enhances competition. Under the Sherman Act the criterion to be used in judging the validity of a restraint on trade is its impact on competition.

Because it restrains price and output, the NCAA's television plan has a significant potential for anticompetitive effects. The findings of the District Court indicate that this potential has been realized. The District Court found that if member institutions were free to sell television rights, many more games would be shown on television, and that the NCAA's output restriction has the effect of raising the price the networks pay for television rights. Moreover, the court found that by fixing a price for television rights to all games, the NCAA creates a price structure that is unresponsive to viewer demand and unrelated to the prices that would prevail in a competitive market. And, of course, since as a practical matter all member institutions need NCAA approval, members have no real choice but to adhere to the NCAA's television controls.

The anticompetitive consequences of this arrangement are apparent. Individual competitors lose their freedom to compete. Price is higher and output lower than they would otherwise be, and both are unresponsive to consumer preference. This latter point is perhaps the most significant, since "Congress designed the Sherman Act as a 'consumer welfare prescription.' " Reiter v. Sonotone Corp., 442 U.S. 330, 343 (1979). A restraint that has the effect of reducing the importance of consumer preference in setting price and output is not consistent with this fundamental goal of antitrust law. Restrictions on price and output are the paradigmatic examples of restraints of trade that the Sherma Act was intended to prohibit. See Standard Oil Co. v. United States, 221 U.S. 1, 52–60 (1911). At the same time, the television plan eliminates competitors from the market, since only those broadcasters able to bid on television rights covering the entire NCAA can compete. Thus, as the District Court found, many telecasts that would occur in a competitive market are foreclosed by the NCAA's plan.

Petitioner argues, however, that its television plan can have no significant anticompetitive effect since the record indicates that it has no market power—no ability to alter the interaction of supply and demand in the market. We must reject this argument for two reasons, one legal, one factual.

As a matter of law, the absence of proof of market power does not justify a naked restriction on price or output. To the contrary, when there is an agreement not to compete in terms of price or output, "no elaborate industry analysis is required to demonstrate the anticompetitive character of such an agreement." Professional Engineers, 435 U.S., at 692. Petitioner does not quarrel with the District Court's [468 U.S. 85, 110] finding that price and output are not responsive to demand. Thus the plan is inconsistent with the Sherman Act's command that price and supply be responsive to consumer preference. We have never required proof of market power in such a case. This naked restraint on price and output requires some competitive justification even in the absence of a detailed market analysis.

As a factual matter, it is evident that petitioner does possess market power. The District Court employed the correct test for determining whether college football broadcasts constitute a separate market— whether there are other products that are reasonably substitutable for televised NCAA football games. Petitioner's argument that it cannot obtain supracompetitive prices from broadcasters since advertisers, and hence broadcasters, can switch from college football to other types of programming simply ignores the findings of the District Court. It found that intercollegiate football telecasts generate an audience uniquely attractive to advertisers and that competitors are unable to offer programming that can attract a similar audience.

These findings amply support its conclusion that the NCAA possesses market power. Indeed, the District Court's subsidiary finding that advertisers will pay a premium price per viewer to reach audiences watching college football because of their demographic characteristics is vivid evidence of the uniqueness of this product. Moreover, the District Court's market analysis is firmly supported by our decision in International Boxing Club of New York, Inc. v. United States, 358 U.S. 242 (1959), that championship boxing events are uniquely attractive to fans and hence constitute a market separate from that for nonchampionship events. Thus, respondents have demonstrated that there is a separate market for telecasts of college football which "rest[s] on generic qualities differentiating" viewers. Times-Picayune Publishing Co. v. United States, 345 U.S. 594, 613 (1953). It inexorably follows that if college football broadcasts be defined as a separate market—and we are convinced they are—then the NCAA's complete control over those broadcasts provides a solid basis for the District Court's conclusion that the NCAA possesses market power with respect to those broadcasts. "When a product is controlled by one interest, without substitutes available in the market, there is monopoly power." United States v. E. I. du Pont de Nemours & Co., 351 U.S. 377, 394 (1956).

Thus, the NCAA television plan on its face constitutes a restraint upon the operation of a free market, and the findings of the District Court establish that it has operated to raise prices and reduce output. Under the Rule of Reason, these hallmarks of anticompetitive behavior place upon petitioner a heavy burden of establishing an affirmative defense which competitively justifies this apparent deviation from the operations of a free market. See Professional Engineers, 435 U.S., at 692–696. We turn now to the NCAA's proffered justifications.

Throughout the history of its regulation of intercollegiate football telecasts, the NCAA has indicated its concern with protecting live attendance. This concern, it should be noted, is not with protecting live attendance at games which are shown on television; that type of interest is not at issue in this case. Rather, the concern is that fan interest in a televised game may adversely affect ticket sales for games that will not appear on television.

Although the NORC studies in the 1950's provided some support for the thesis that live attendance would suffer if unlimited television were permitted, the District Court found that there was no evidence to support that theory in today's market. Moreover, as the District Court found, the television plan has evolved in a manner inconsistent with its original design to protect gate attendance. Under the current plan, games are shown on television during all hours that college football games are played. The plan simply does not protect live attendance by ensuring that games will not be shown on television at the same time as live events.

There is, however, a more fundamental reason for rejecting this defense. The NCAA's argument that its television plan is necessary to protect live attendance is not based on a desire to maintain the integrity of college football as a distinct and attractive product, but rather on a fear that the product will not prove sufficiently attractive to draw live attendance when faced with competition from televised games. At bottom the NCAA's position is that ticket sales for most college games are unable to compete in a free market television plan protects ticket sales by limiting output—just as any monopolist increases revenues by reducing output. By seeking to insulate live ticket sales from the full spectrum of competition because of its assumption that the product itself is insufficiently attractive to consumers, petitioner forwards a justification that is inconsistent with the basic policy of the Sherman Act. "[T]he Rule of Reason does not support a defense based on the assumption that competition itself is unreasonable." Professional Engineers, 435 U.S., at 696.

Petitioner argues that the interest in maintaining a competitive balance among amateur athletic teams is legitimate and important and that it justifies the regulations challenged in this case. We agree with the first part of the argument but not the second.

Our decision not to apply a per se rule to this case rests in large part on our recognition that a certain degree of cooperation is necessary if the type of competition that petitioner and its member institutions seek to market is to be preserved. It is reasonable to assume that most of the regulatory controls of the NCAA are justifiable means of fostering competition among amateur athletic teams and therefore procompetitive because they enhance public interest in intercollegiate athletics. The specific restraints on football telecasts that are challenged in this case do not, however, fit into the same mold as do rules defining the conditions of the contest, the eligibility of participants, or the manner in which members of a joint enterprise shall share the responsibilities and the benefits of the total venture.

The NCAA does not claim that its television plan has equalized or is intended to equalize competition within any one league. The plan is nationwide in scope and there is no single league or tournament in which all college football teams compete. There is no evidence of any intent to equalize the strength of teams in Division I-A with those in Division II or Division III, and not even a colorable basis for giving colleges that have no football program at all a voice in the management of the revenues generated by the football programs at other schools. The interest in maintaining a competitive balance that is asserted by the NCAA as a justification for regulating all television of intercollegiate football is not related to any neutral standard or to any readily identifiable group of competitors. [468 U.S. 85, 119]

The television plan is not even arguably tailored to serve such an interest. It does not regulate the amount of money that any college may spend on its football program, nor the way in which the colleges may use the revenues that are generated by their football programs, whether derived from the sale of television rights, the sale of tickets, or the sale of concessions or program advertising. The plan simply imposes a restriction on one source of revenue that is more important to some colleges than to others. There is no evidence that this restriction produces any greater measure of equality throughout the NCAA than would a restriction on alumni donations, tuition rates, or any other revenue-producing activity. At the same time, as the District Court found, the NCAA imposes a variety of other restrictions designed to preserve amateurism which are much better tailored to the goal of competitive balance than is the television plan, and which are "clearly sufficient" to preserve competitive balance to the extent it is within the NCAA's power to do so. And much more than speculation supported the District Court's findings on this score. No other NCAA sport employs a similar plan, and in particular the court found that in the most closely analogous sport, college basketball, competitive balance has been maintained without resort to a restrictive television plan.

Perhaps the most important reason for rejecting the argument that the interest in competitive balance is served by the television plan is the District Court's unambiguous and well-supported finding that many more games would be televised in a free market than under the NCAA plan. The hypothesis that legitimates the maintenance of competitive balance as a procompetitive justification under the Rule of Reason is that equal competition will maximize consumer demand for the product. The finding that consumption will materially increase if the controls are removed is a compelling demonstration that they do not in fact serve any such legitimate purpose.

The NCAA plays a critical role in the maintenance of a revered tradition of amateurism in college sports. There can be no question but that it needs ample latitude to play that role, or that the preservation of the student-athlete in higher education adds richness and diversity to intercollegiate athletics and is entirely consistent with the goals of the Sherman Act. But consistent with the Sherman Act, the role of the NCAA must be to preserve a tradition that might otherwise die; rules that restrict output are hardly consistent with this role. Today we hold only that the record supports the District Court's conclusion that by curtailing output and blunting the ability of member institutions to respond to consumer preference, the NCAA has restricted rather than enhanced the place of intercollegiate athletics in the Nation's life. Accordingly, the judgment of the Court of Appeals is

Affirmed.

# COLLECTIVE BARGAINING

Collective bargaining requires management and unions to negotiate in good faith on matters of compensation and working conditions. If an agreement cannot be worked out by management and the union, both sides have options. The owners have the right to lock out the players while the players have the right to strike. In both instances, the result is the same in professional sports, namely the games do not go on and it becomes a matter of which side is better able to weather the loss of income that comes about as a result of a work stoppage. However, unique to professional sports is another option of the players which they have exercised periodically although rarely to a conclusive result and that is to decertify their union and accuse the respective sports league, be it the NFL, MLB, NBA, or NHL of being in violation of antitrust laws. This is not an option that is available to a union, so in order to exercise this option, players' unions have had to be decertified in order for individual players to pursue this option.

The combination of short careers and little opportunity for alternative employment by professional athletes in the event of a strike or a lockout generally tilts the balance of power disproportionately in favor of the team owners rather than the players.

---

## QUESTION

1. Why is the option of players' unions to decertify such a significant option for players during a labor dispute?

# PROFESSIONAL SPORTS LEAGUES AS MONOPOLIES

Professional sports will always be susceptible to claims that they are in violation of antitrust laws because they are generally monopolies. However, not all monopolies are necessarily violations of antitrust laws. As Steve Balmer of Microsoft proclaimed, "We don't have a monopoly. We have market share. There's a difference." And indeed there is a difference. A company that has a monopoly and whose actions do not harm consumers is not violating antitrust law. Today the major professional sports in the United States, professional football, professional basketball, professional baseball and professional hockey are all essentially monopolies although in the latter half of the 20th century, the NFL, NBA and NHL all faced challenges from new professional leagues that challenged the monopolies of the established professional leagues. In the case of the American Football League (AFL) it merged with the NFL as did the American Basketball Association (ABA) with the NBA and the World Hockey League (WHL) with the NHL.

With the exception of baseball, the courts have specifically ruled that the other professional sports are specifically subject to the antitrust laws. Radovich v. National Football League, 352 U.S. 445 (1957) and Boston Professional Hockey Association v. Cheevers, 348 F. Supp. 261 (D. Mass. 1972) and Washington Professional Basketball Corp. v. NBA, 147 F. Supp. 154 (S.D.N.Y. 1956).

However, the courts have recognized that professional sport leagues are not typical businesses and that there is a need for the individual teams to work jointly through a central league administration in order to achieve success. As the Supreme Court said in American Needle, Inc. v. NFL, 560 U.S. 183 (2010) "The fact that the NFL teams share an interest in making the entire league successful and profitable, and that they must cooperate in the production and scheduling of games, provides a perfectly sensible justification for making a host of collective decisions."

# PROFESSIONAL BASEBALL

Baseball was ruled to be exempt from antitrust laws by the Supreme Court in the landmark case of Federal Base Ball Club of Baltimore, Inc. vs. National League of Professional Base Ball Clubs et al., 259 U.S. 200 (1922). This was a case brought by the owner of the Baltimore Terrapins, a professional baseball team from the Federal League which was disbanded in 1915. While the owners of most of the other Federal League teams were bought out by the owners of other professional baseball teams, the Terrapins were not and the owner sued the National League and the American League, accusing them of conspiring to destroy the Federal League and monopolize baseball in violation of federal antitrust law. At trial the defendants were found liable and assessed damages (the legal term for the money ordered by a court in a civil action) in the amount of $80,000. However, the Clayton Antitrust Act provided for triple damages so the total amount awarded to the plaintiff was $240,000, which to put it into perspective would be 19.6 million dollars in today's money. However, on appeal the decision of the lower court was overturned whereupon the plaintiff appealed to the Supreme Court which upheld the overturning of the district court verdict. The basis for this unanimous Supreme Court decision was that federal antitrust laws such as the Sherman Act and the Clayton Act required that the businesses be involved with interstate commerce for the laws to apply.

Writing for the unanimous Supreme Court, Justice Oliver Wendell Holmes, Jr. said, "the business is giving exhibitions in base ball, which are purely state affairs." Federal Base Ball Club of Baltimore, Inc. v. National League of Professional Base Ball Clubs, et al, 259 U.S. 200 (1922) Justice Holmes reasoned that although the scheduling and playing of games included travel across state lines, such travel was incidental to the business of baseball and that the games were essentially intrastate events. In truth, in 1922, the National League and American League were primarily umbrella organizations that arranged schedules and established the rules of the game, however, the business was entirely local with no revenue sharing between teams, no national radio and television contracts, no national sponsors and no national licensing contracts. Baseball, or as it was referred to then "base ball," was considered more a game than a business. This exemption from antitrust laws still exists today for baseball although no other professional sport has this status which is a remnant from another era.

# TOOLSON V. NEW YORK YANKEES

Baseball returned to the Supreme Court in 1953 in the case of Toolson v. New York Yankees, 346 U.S. 356 (1953). George Toolson was a minor league pitcher in the New York Yankees farm system. The Yankees were loaded with talent, which made it difficult for a minor leaguer to make the major league roster, however, even after his contract had expired, a standard provision of MLB since its inception was the "reserve clause" which prevented a player from negotiating a contract with another professional baseball team even after his contract had expired. Frustrated with his situation, Toolson sued the Yankees arguing that the reserve clause was an illegal restraint of trade that violated federal antitrust laws. He lost in both the initial District Court and Court of Appeals, following which he appealed to the U.S. Supreme Court.

The business of baseball had changed considerably since the Supreme Court's 1922 decision in which the Supreme Court ruled that antitrust laws did not apply to professional baseball. An interstate highway system enabled fans to readily cross state borders to attend games and radio and early television broadcasts of games brought new revenues to the "game" of baseball. Despite the significant changes in how Major League Baseball operated in 1953 as compared to how it was operated in 1922, by a vote of 7–2 the Supreme Court ruled against Toolson in a decision written in a single paragraph:

"In Federal Baseball Club of Baltimore v. National League of Professional Baseball Clubs this Court held that the business of providing public baseball games for profit between clubs of professional baseball players was not within the scope of the federal antitrust laws. Congress has had the ruling under consideration, but has not seen fit to bring such business under these laws by legislation having prospective effect. The business has thus been left for thirty years to develop on the understanding that it was not subject to existing antitrust legislation. The present cases ask us to overrule the prior decision and, with retrospective effect, hold the legislation applicable. We think that, if there are evils in this field which now warrant application to it of the antitrust laws, it should be by legislation. Without reexamination of the underlying issues, the judgments below are affirmed on the authority of Federal Baseball Club of Baltimore v. National League of Professional Baseball Clubs, supra, so far as that decision determines that Congress had no intention of including the business of baseball within the scope of the federal antitrust laws."

The longer and eloquent dissent by Justice Burton clearly pointed out the problems with the majority's ruling when he wrote:

"Whatever may have been the situation when the Federal Baseball Club case was decided in 1922, I am not able to join today's decision, which, in effect, announces that organized baseball in 1953 still is not engaged in interstate trade or commerce. In the light of organized baseball's well known and widely distributed capital investments used in conducting competitions between teams constantly traveling between states, its receipt and expenditures of large sums transmitted between states, its numerous purchases of materials in interstate commerce, the attendance at its local exhibitions of large audiences often traveling across state lines, its radio and television activities which expand its audiences beyond state lines, its sponsorship of interstate advertising, and its highly organized 'farm system' of minor league baseball clubs, coupled with restrictive contracts and understandings between individuals and among clubs or leagues playing for profit throughout the united States and even in Canada, Mexico, and Cuba, it is a contradiction in terms to say that the defendants in the cases before us are not engaged in interstate trade or commerce as those terms are used in the Constitution of the United States and in the Sherman Act." 346 U.S. 358.

"Conceding the major asset which baseball is to our Nation, the high place it enjoys in the hearts of our people and the possible justification of special treatment for organized sports which are engaged in interstate trade or commerce, the authorization of such treatment is a matter within the discretion of Congress. Congress, however, has enacted no express exemption of organized baseball from the Sherman Act, and no court has demonstrated the existence of an implied exemption from that Act of any sport that is so highly organized as to amount to an interstate monopoly or which restrains interstate trade or commerce. In the absence of such an exemption, the present popularity of organized baseball increases, rather than diminishes, the importance of its compliance with standards of reasonableness comparable with those now required by law of interstate trade or commerce. It is interstate trade or commerce, and, as such, it is subject to the Sherman Act until exempted." 346 U.S. 364.

# FLOOD V. KUHN

The next major case involving baseball's antitrust status came in 1969 in the case of Flood v. Kuhn, 407 U.S. 258 (1972). Curt Flood was an All Star outfielder for the St. Louis Cardinals when late in his career, he was traded to the Philadelphia Phillies following the 1969 baseball season. Then Flood did the unthinkable. For both personal and business reasons he refused to be traded and challenged the reserve clause found in all MLB contracts which prevented him from negotiating with another team. The reserve clause permitted teams to renew a contract for a period of one year following the end of the previous contract. Therefore if a team and a player could not agree on a contract, the team could bind the player to continue to play for the same salary for year after year.

The reserve clause had a long and storied history in professional baseball and was found in the earliest of professional baseball contracts as team owners feared players being able to negotiate with other teams at the expiration of their contracts would drive up team payrolls and reduce team profits. This type of collusion had been ruled to be an illegal restraint of trade and a violation of antitrust laws in other industries.

Because it takes years for a case to weave its way through the court system, Flood sought an injunction to allow him to negotiate with any team while the lawsuit was pending. His requests for an injunction were denied and rather than report to the Phillies, Flood sat out a full year losing considerable salary before signing with the Washington Senators in 1971 who had bought his rights from the Phillies, however his return to baseball after a year off at an advanced age for a baseball player was not successful and he retired less than a month into the season.

The Supreme Court's 5–3 decision in Flood v. Kuhn upholding the legality of the reserve clause and leaving intact baseball's exemption from antitrust laws is indeed an odd one. Justice Harry Blackman, writing for the majority even admitted that major league baseball at that time was engaged in interstate commerce. By the time of the Flood decision, the Supreme Court had already ruled that the NFL and the NBA were subject to antitrust laws in the case of Radovich v. National Football League, 352 U.S. 445 (1957) and Haywood v. National Basketball Association, 401 U.S. 1204 (1971).

In the Court's opinion, Justice Blackmun indicated in bullet points:

"1. Professional baseball is a business and it is engaged in interstate commerce." Thus the Court recognized that the basis for its decisions in Federal Baseball and Toolson no longer applied.

"2. With its reserve system enjoying exemption from the federal antitrust laws, baseball is, in a very distinct sense, an exception and an anomaly. Federal Baseball and Toolson have become an aberration confined to baseball." Here the Court specifically recognized its own inconsistencies in applying the law differently to other professional sports without providing a logical reason for so doing.

"3. Even though others might regard this as 'unrealistic, inconsistent or illogical,' see Radovich, 352 U.S. at 452, the aberration is an established one, and one that has been recognized not only in Federal Baseball and Toolson, but in Shubert, International Boxing, and Radovich, as well, a total of five consecutive cases in this Court. It is an aberration that has been with us now for half a century, one heretofore deemed fully entitled to the benefit of stare decisis, and one that has survived the Court's expanding concept of interstate commerce. It rests on a recognition and an acceptance of baseball's unique characteristics and needs.

4. Other professional sports operating interstate—football, boxing, basketball and presumably, hockey and golf are not so exempt." Here the Court actually states the well-founded criticism of its decision as being unrealistic, inconsistent and illogical, but does little to defend its position other than to say that this is an aberration, which is merely to say that this is a mistake without correcting the mistake. To reference the Federal Baseball case as a ruling that deserves to be relied upon merely because it is an old case is to miss the point that the Federal Baseball case, being fact specific, dealt with professional baseball at a time when, at least arguably, it did not involve interstate commerce, which was the key element of the decision while the court in Flood specifically recognized that baseball in 1972 was certainly engaged in interstate commerce and therefore should have been subject to antitrust laws. Justice Blackmun's opinion compounds the confusion when he gives absolutely no reason for treating other professional sports as subject to antitrust laws while exempting baseball.

Ultimately, Blackmun concluded by saying:

"Accordingly, we adhere once again to Federal Baseball and Toolson and to their application to professional baseball. We adhere also to International Boxing and Radovich and to their respective applications to professional baseball and professional football. If there is any inconsistency or illogic in all of this, it is an inconsistency and illogic of long standing that is to be remedied by the Congress and not by this Court. If we were to act otherwise, we would be withdrawing from the conclusion as to congressional intent made in Toolson and from the concerns as to retrospectivity therein expressed. Under these circumstances, there is merit in consistency, even though some might claim that beneath that consistency is a layer of inconsistency."

"And what the Court said in Federal Baseball in 1922 and what it said in Toolson in 1953, we say again here in 1972: the remedy, if any is indicated, is for congressional, and not judicial action."

Thus despite admitting to inconsistencies in its positions in recognizing that baseball does business in interstate commerce and that the Court specifically chose to treat all other professional sports differently by applying the antitrust rules to them, the Court still decided that action in regard to baseball should be deferred to Congress.

The dissenting opinion of Justice Douglas clearly pointed out what he believed were errors in the decision of the Court:

"This Court's decision in Federal Baseball Club v. National League made in 1922 is a derelict in the stream of the law that we, its creator, should remove. Only a romantic view of a rather dismal business account over the last 50 years would keep that derelict in midstream."

"Baseball is today big business that is packaged with beer, with broadcasting, and with other industries. The beneficiaries of the Federal Baseball Club decision are not the Babe Ruths, Ty Cobbs and Lou Gehrigs. The owners, whose records many say reveal a proclivity for predatory practices do not come to us with equities. The equities are with the victims of the reserve clause. I use the word 'victims' in the Sherman Act sense, since a contract which forbids anyone to practice his calling is commonly called an unreasonable restraint of trade."

"There can be no doubt 'that were we considering the question of baseball for the first time upon a clean slate' we would hold it to be subject to federal antitrust regulation. Radovich v. National Football League, 352 U.S. 445, 452. The unbroken silence of Congress should not prevent us from correcting our own mistakes."

In his dissent Justice Marshall said:

"This is a difficult case because we are torn between the principle of stare decisis and the knowledge that the decisions in Federal Baseball Club v. National League, 259 U.S. 200 (1922) and Toolson v. New York Yankees Inc., 346 U.S. 356 (1953) are totally at odds with more recent and better reasoned cases."

## ANDY MESSERSMITH

Andy Messersmith was an outstanding pitcher for the Los Angeles Dodgers who in 1975 demanded a no-trade provision in the contract he was negotiating with the Dodgers. Both sides would not budge during their negotiations so the Dodgers exercised their rights under the reserve clause and renewed Messersmith's contract. At the end of the season, Messersmith took the position that he was a free agent and could sign a contract with any team that he wished. The Dodgers' position was that pursuant to the reserve clause, he was legally bound to the Dodgers. The Major League Baseball Players Association (MPBA) filed a grievance on behalf of Messersmith which, in accordance with the CBA, was to be heard by Peter Seitz, the Impartial Arbitrator designated exclusively by the owners. Actually, the arbitration board that heard grievances was composed of three arbitrators, however one arbitrator was a union representative who always ruled in favor of the player, one representative was the owners' representative who always ruled on behalf of the owners and the remaining arbitrator was the Chairman and Impartial Arbitrator, Peter Seitz. Like most arbitrators, Seitz tried to convince the parties to settle the matter themselves, but was unsuccessful in this instance.

The argument of the Dodgers was that when Messersmith's contract was renewed in 1975 pursuant to the reserve clause, every term of the contract was renewed including the right of the club to choose to extend the contract the next year, which was the essence of the reserve clause as it had been operating since the 1880s. Seitz, however, interpreted the contract differently. His interpretation was that the contract only allowed for a single one year extension and that to interpret the contract otherwise was to make the option perpetual. For this to be the case, Seitz reasoned, the intention to do so would have to be clearly and unmistakably stated in the contract. Therefore, by playing pursuant to the one year contract extension without signing a new contract, Messersmith was free of any further obligation to the Dodgers and ruled to be the first free agent in MLB history.

While Seitz position is legally sound, it is interesting to note that it reflects an evolution of recognition of rights because under Seitz' interpretation, one would have thought that other players in all the years since the earliest application of the reserve clause would have played out their one year option year and become free agents the next year.

The reaction of MLB to the ruling was swift. Commissioner Bowie Kuhn immediately fired Peter Seitz as the permanent neutral arbitrator. MLB also appealed the decision of Seitz to federal court. As with other appeals of administrative hearing decisions, the appeals court in this case was not primarily concerned with evaluating the evidence, but merely focused its attention on evaluating the process for fundamental fairness. In this case, the owners were appealing the decision of Peter Seitz in interpreting the contract which is exactly what he was supposed to do. Being displeased with his interpretation was not a viable basis for appeal. After the Eighth Circuit Court of Appeals upheld Seitz's ruling (Kansas City Royals Baseball Corporation et al. v. Major League Baseball Players Association, 532 F.2d 615 (1976), and following a lockout of the players during the 1976 Spring Training, the owners and the players negotiated a free agency policy as part of the new CBA by which players became eligible for free agency after six years in the major leagues.

## KANSAS CITY ROYALS BASEBALL CORPORATION V. MAJOR LEAGUE BASEBALL PLAYERS ASSOCIATION

United States Court of Appeals, Eighth Circuit
532 F.2d 615 (1976)

Before GIBSON, CHIEF JUDGE, and HEANEY and STEPHENSON, CIRCUIT JUDGES.

HEANEY, CIRCUIT JUDGE.

The owners of the twenty-four Major League Baseball Clubs seek reversal of a judgment of the District Court for the Western District of Missouri. The court refused to set aside and ordered enforced an arbitration panel's award rendered in favor of the Major League Baseball Players Association. The arbitration panel was established pursuant to a collective bargaining agreement between the Club Owners and the Players Association. The award relieved pitcher Andy Messersmith of any contractual obligation to the Los Angeles Dodgers, and pitcher Dave McNally of any similar obligation to the Montreal Expos. It directed the Dodgers and Expos to remove Messersmith and McNally, respectively, from their reserve or disqualified lists. It ordered the American and National Leagues to inform and instruct their member clubs that the provisions of Major League Rule 4–A (reserve list rule) and Rule 3(g) (no-tampering rule) do not inhibit, prohibit or prevent such clubs from negotiating or dealing with Messersmith and McNally with respect to employment.

We hold that the arbitration panel had jurisdiction to resolve the dispute, that its award drew its essence from the collective bargaining agreement, and that the relief fashioned by the District Court was appropriate. Accordingly, we affirm the judgment of the District Court.

The Supreme court articulated the legal principles applicable to the arbitration of labor disputes in the *Steelworkers* trilogy, and recently reaffirmed them in *Gateway Coal Co. v. United Mine Workers of America,* 414 U.S. 368, 94 S.Ct. 629, 38 L.Ed.2d 583 (1974).

A party may be compelled to arbitrate a grievance only if it has agreed to do so. Gateway Coal Co. v. United Mine Workers of America, supra; *United Steelworkers of America v. Warrior & Gulf Navigation Co.,* 363 U.S. 574, 80 S.Ct. 1347, 4 L.Ed.2d 1409 (1960); *International Union, Etc. v. I.T. & T.,* 508 F.2d 1309 (8th Cir. 1975); *Laundry, Dry Cleaning & Dye House Workers International Union, Local 93 v. Mahoney,* 491 F.2d 1029 (8th Cir.), *cert. denied,* 419 U.S. 825, 95 S.Ct. 42, 42 L.Ed.2d 49 (1974). The question of arbitrability is thus one of contract construction and is for the courts to decide. *See, e. g., Wiley & Sons v. Livingston,* 376 U.S. 543, 84 S.Ct. 909, 11 L.Ed.2d 898 (1964); *General Drivers & Helpers Union, Local No. 554 v. Young & Hay Transportation Co.,* 522 F.2d 562 (8th Cir. 1975).

In resolving questions of arbitrability, the courts are guided by Congress's declaration of policy that arbitration is the desirable method for settling labor disputes. *See* § 203 of the Labor-Management Relations Act, 29 U.S.C. § 173(d). Accordingly, a grievance arising under a collective bargaining agreement providing for arbitration must be deemed arbitrable "unless it may be said with positive assurance that the arbitration clause is not susceptible of an interpretation that covers the asserted dispute. Doubts should be resolved in favor of coverage." *United Steelworkers of America v. Warrior & Gulf Navigation Co., supra,* 363 U.S. at 582–583, 80 S.Ct. at 1353, 4 L.Ed.2d at 1417, *cited with approval in Gateway Coal Co. v. United Mine Workers of America, supra,* 414 U.S. at 377–388, 94 S.Ct. at 636–637, 38 L.Ed.2d at 592 and *Laundry, Dry Cleaning & Dye House Workers International Union, Local 93 v. Mahoney, supra,* 491 F.2d at 1032.

Consistent with these principles, a broad arbitration provision may be deemed to exclude a particular grievance in only two instances: (1) where the collective bargaining agreement contains an express provision clearly excluding the grievance involved from arbitration; or (2) where the agreement contains an ambiguous exclusionary provision and the record evinces the most forceful evidence of a purpose to exclude the grievance from arbitration. *See United Steelworkers of America v. Warrior & Gulf Navigation Co., supra; Gateway Coal Co. v. United Mine Workers of America, supra; Laundry, Dry Cleaning & Dye House Workers International Union, Local 93 v. Mahoney, supra.*

If it is determined that the arbitrator had jurisdiction, judicial review of his award is limited to the question of whether it "draws its essence from the collective bargaining agreement." *United Steelworkers of America v. Enterprise Wheel & Car Corp.,* 363 U.S. 593, 597, 80 S.Ct. 1358, 1361, 4 L.Ed.2d 1424, 1428 (1960), *cited with approval in General Drivers & Helpers Union, Local No. 554 v. Young & Hay Transportation Co., supra,* 522 F.2d 567–568 *and International Union, Etc. v. White Motor Corp.,* 505 F.2d 1193, 1197 (8th Cir. 1974), *cert. denied,* 421 U.S. 921, 95 S.Ct. 1588, 43 L.Ed.2d 789 (1975). We do not sit as an appellate tribunal to review the merits of the arbitrator's decision.

We turn first to the question of the jurisdiction of the panel to arbitrate the Messersmith-McNally grievances.

We begin with the proposition that the language of Article X of the 1973 agreement is sufficiently broad to require arbitration of the Messersmith-McNally grievances. We think this clear because the disputes involve the interpretation of the provisions of agreements between a player or the Players Association and a club or the Club Owners. The grievances require the construction of agreements manifested in paragraphs 9(a) and 10(a) of the Uniform Player's Contract.

9.(a)   The Club and the Player agree to accept, abide by and comply with all provisions of the Major League Agreement, the Major League Rules, the Rules or Regulations of the League of which the Club is a member, and the Professional Baseball Rules, in effect on the date of this Uniform Player's Contract, which are not inconsistent with the provisions of this contract or the provisions of any agreement between the Major League Clubs and the Major League Baseball Players Association, provided that the Club, together with the other Clubs of the American and National Leagues and the National Association, reserves the right to modify, supplement or repeal any provision of said Agreement, Rules and/or Regulations in a manner not inconsistent with this contract or the provisions of any then existing agreement between the Major League Clubs and the Major League Baseball Players Asociation [sic].

10.(a) On or before December 20 (or if a Sunday, then the next preceding business day) in the year of the last playing season covered by this contract, the Club may tender to the Player a contract for the term of that year by mailing the same to the Player at his address following his signature hereto, or if none be given, then at his last address of record with the Club. If prior to the March 1 next succeeding said December 20, the Player and the Club have not agreed upon the terms of such contract, then on or before 10 days after said March 1, the Club shall have the right by written notice to the Player at said address to renew this contract for the period of one year on the same terms, except that the amount payable to the Player shall be such as the Club shall fix in said notice; provided, however, that said amount, if fixed by a Major League Club, shall be an amount payable at a rate not less than 80% of the rate stipulated for the next preceding year and at a rate not less than 70% of the rate stipulated for the year immediately prior to the next preceding year.

Although we find that the grievances are arbitrable under Article X standing alone, we cannot ignore the existence of Article XV, which provides, *inter alia,* that the agreement "does not deal with the reserve system."

The provisions of the Uniform Player's Contract and the Major League Rules cited above are among the many contract provisions and rules which together constitute the reserve system. In fact, the Club Owners maintain that they are the very "core" or "heart" of the reserve system. The Club Owners argue that Article XV removed grievances arising out of the cited clauses from the coverage of Article X, and that when the agreement is read as a whole, as it must be, the Messersmith-McNally grievances are not arbitrable.

The District Court rejected this argument. It recognized that the agreement must be construed as a whole, but concluded that Article XV could not be interpreted to exclude any grievances from the procedures set forth in Article X.

We find the question more difficult than did the District Court. We cannot say that Article XV, on its face, constitutes a clear exclusionary provision. First, the precise thrust of the phrase "this Agreement does not deal with the reserve system" is unclear. The agreement incorporates the provisions which comprise the reserve system. Also, the phrase is qualified by the words "except as adjusted or modified hereby." Second, the impact of the language "This Agreement shall in no way prejudice the position * * * of the Parties" is uncertain. Third, the "concerted action" which the parties agree to forego does not clearly include bringing grievances. Fourth, Article XV affords no basis for the Club Owners' distinction between the "core" and the periphery of the reserve system. Finally, Article X(A)(1), which declares certain disputes non-grievable, is silent as to the reserve system. We find, however, that Article XV creates an ambiguity as to whether the grievances here involved are arbitrable. Accordingly, we must look beyond the face of the agreement and determine whether the record as a whole evinces the most forceful evidence of a purpose to exclude these grievances from arbitration. *See United Steelworkers of America v. Warrior & Gulf Navigation Co., supra.*

We cannot say, on the basis of the evidence discussed above, that the record evinces the most forceful evidence of a purpose to exclude the grievances here involved from arbitration.

(a) The 1968 agreement clearly permitted the arbitration of grievances relating to the reserve system. It, therefore, cannot be said that the Club Owners never consented to the arbitration of such grievances. The Club Owners might have argued that they agreed to arbitrate such grievances because the Commissioner of Baseball was designated as the arbitrator, and that he, recognizing the importance of the reserve system to baseball, would interpret the disputed provisions to allow perpetual control by a Club Owner over its players. That argument, however, was not advanced before either the arbitration panel, the District Court or this Court. Moreover, the argument would not be particularly flattering to any Commissioner of Baseball.

(b) Article XIV, the predecessor to Article XV, was suggested by the Players Association for rather specific purposes and the Club Owners clearly did what they could to preserve their right to argue that the reserve system remained a part of the collective bargaining agreement. Indeed, if the Club Owners' counterproposals with respect to Article XIV had been accepted, the reserve system would clearly have remained subject to arbitration.

Article XV was clearly designed to accomplish the same purposes as Article XIV. If in accomplishing these purposes the players had clearly agreed to exclude disputes arising out of the operation of the reserve system from arbitration, the Messersmith-McNally grievances would not be arbitrable For the reasons discussed in this opinion, however, no such agreement can be found.

(c) From 1970 to 1973, a number of grievances concerning the reserve system were submitted to arbitration. The Club Owners raised no jurisdictional objections. While this fact alone is not of controlling significance, because the grievances submitted did not go to what the Club Owners regard as the "core" or "heart" of the reserve system, the submission of grievances relating to the reserve system is certainly a fact that detracts from the Club Owners' contention that the parties clearly understood Article XIV to mean that grievances relating to the reserve system would not be subject to arbitration.

(d)   The fact that Marvin Miller may have given assurances, during the 1970 negotiations, that the players would not grieve over house rules cannot be viewed as the most forceful evidence of a purpose to exclude the Messersmith-McNally grievances from arbitration. First, there is some dispute in the record as to whether Miller made such a statement. Second, assuming he did, the term "house rules" is ambiguous. Third, and we think most important, the weight of the evidence, when viewed as a whole, does not support the conclusion that Article XV was intended to preclude arbitration of any grievances otherwise arbitrable.

(e)   The essence of the Club Owners' arguments on the question of arbitrability was perhaps best articulated in the testimony of Larry McPhail, President of the American League, in which he stated: "Isn't it fair to say that our strong feelings on the importance of the core of the reserve system would indicate that we wouldn't permit the reserve system to be within the jurisdiction of the arbitration procedure?" The weaknesses in this argument have been previously discussed in paragraphs (a), (b) and (c) above. We add only that what a reasonable party might be expected to do cannot take precedence over what the parties actually provided for in their collective bargaining agreement.

The Club Owners contend that even if the arbitration panel had jurisdiction, the award must be vacated. They argue that the award exceeded the scope of the panel's authority by "fundamentally altering and destroying the Reserve System as it historically existed and had been acquiesced in by the Association."

As we have previously noted, our review of the merits of an arbitration panel's award is limited. The award must be sustained so long as it "draws its essence from the collective bargaining agreement." *United Steelworkers of America v. Enterprise Wheel & Car Corp., supra,* 363 U.S. at 597, 80 S.Ct. at 1361, 4 L.Ed.2d at 1428; *cited with approval in General Drivers & Helpers Union, Local No. 554 v. Young*

*& Hay Transportation Co., supra,* 522 F.2d at 567–568 *and International Union, Etc. v. White Motor Corp., supra, 505 F.2d at 1197.*

The nub of the Club Owners' argument is that both they and the Players Association understood the reserve system to enable a club to perpetually control a player, that this understanding was reflected in the 1973 agreement, and that the arbitration panel was without authority to alter the agreed upon operation of the reserve system.

We cannot agree that the 1973 collective bargaining agreement embodied an understanding by the parties that the reserve system enabled a club to perpetually control a player. First, the agreement contained no express provision to that effect. Second, while there is evidence that the reserve system operated in such a manner in recent years, the record discloses that various Players Association representatives viewed the system as allowing a player to become a free agent by playing under a renewed contract for one year.

Moreover, it can be argued that the arbitration panel's award did not "alter" the reserve system. To the extent that the reserve system did enable a club to perpetually control a player, it was not necessarily by virtue of successive invocations of the renewal clause, or application of the reserve list and no-tampering rules in the absence of a contractual obligation. Other provisions operate to deter a player from "playing out his option," as is evidenced by the fact that few players have done so. On this basis, it may be said that the arbitration panel's decision did not change the reserve system, but merely interpreted various elements thereof under circumstances which had not previously arisen.

The 1973 agreement empowered the arbitration panel to "interpret, apply or determine compliance with the provisions of agreements" between the players and the clubs. We find that the arbitration panel did nothing more than to interpret certain provisions of the Uniform Player's Contract and the Major League Rules. We cannot say that those provisions are not susceptible of the construction given them by the panel. Accordingly, the award must be sustained.

CONCLUSION

We hold that the arbitration panel had jurisdiction to hear and decide the Messersmith-McNally grievances, that the panel's award drew its essence from the collective bargaining agreement, and that the relief fashioned by the District Court was appropriate. Accordingly, the award of the arbitration panel must be sustained, and the District Court's judgment affirmed. In so holding, we intimate no views on the merits of the reserve system. We note, however, that Club Owners and the Players Association's representatives agree that some form of a reserve system is needed if the integrity of the game is to be preserved and if public confidence in baseball is to be maintained. The disagreement lies over the degree of control necessary if these goals are to be achieved. Certainly, the parties are in a better position to negotiate their differences than to have them decided in a series of arbitrations and court decisions. We commend them to that process and suggest that the time for obfuscation has passed and that the time for plain talk and clear language has arrived. Baseball fans everywhere expect nothing less.

This Court's mandate affirming the judgment of the District Court shall issue seven days from the date this opinion is filed. Our previous order staying enforcement of the District Court's decree shall continue in effect until the issuance of the mandate.

# CURT FLOOD ACT

Congress did finally act on this matter and out of deference to the pioneering position taken by Curt Flood called its October 1998 law the Curt Flood Act which made the rules restricting player movement in baseball subject to antitrust laws, however, this issue was now moot as the rules of free agency had already been determined by MLB through collective bargaining spurred by the decision in the case of Andy Messersmith. However, the Curt Flood Act specifically did not apply to minor league players who still could be subjected to the reserve clause and, quite significantly, did not apply to the ability of teams to relocate without league approval.

# RELOCATION OF PROFESSIONAL SPORTS FRANCHISES

It is not just players who have had antitrust disputes with team owners. Team owners have also had antitrust disputes with the leagues themselves, most often over a team owner wanting to move the team to another city. Al Davis the owner of the NFL Oakland Raiders sued the NFL and won an antitrust lawsuit in 1982 after the NFL would not let him move the Raiders from Oakland to Los Angeles. Following his victory in court, Davis moved the team to Los Angeles only to later return to Oakland.

The threats of lawsuits led to more movements, such as the LA Rams to St. Louis, and the Cleveland Browns to Baltimore. Since 1971 seven NFL teams have moved, eight NBA teams have moved and nine NHL teams have moved to new cities.

The ability of a team to relocate at its own discretion came to the forefront again when the Oakland Athletics wanted to move to San Jose and signed an option to build a stadium in San Jose. In 2013, the city of San Jose sued Major League Baseball challenging MLB's antitrust exemption that allowed MLB to prevent the Athletics from moving to San Jose unless three fourths of the other owners agreed. The lawyers for San Jose argued that preventing the Athletics from moving to San Jose was harmful to consumers and only benefited the San Francisco Giants, a competing baseball team. The Ninth Circuit Court of Appeals ruled that "Only Congress and the Supreme Court are empowered to question Flood's continued vitality and with it, the fate of baseball's singular and historic exemption from the antitrust laws" City of San Jose vs. Office of the Commissioner of Baseball, 776 F. 3d (2015). In 2015, the Supreme Court without comment refused to take the case leaving the opinion of the Ninth Circuit Court of Appeals as the controlling decision.

# NFL UNION HISTORY

John Mackey was the first president of the NFLPA following the merger of the American Football League (AFL) and the National Football League (NFL). His involvement as a labor leader stemmed from his own experience as he spoke of "What most people don't know is that my commitment stemmed mostly from one incident in which the NFL in which I was handed a piece of paper, a contract and was told to sign it. Of course I didn't, and from that moment of youthful pique evolved the fight by NFL players to choose for whom they work."[2]

In 1972 he, as the lead plaintiff and fourteen other present and former NFL players filed a lawsuit against the NFL challenging the Roselle Rule, named after then NFL commissioner Pete Rozelle. Under the Rozelle Rule, the commissioner was empowered to award compensation to a team that lost a player to free agency if the teams were unable to agree upon compensation. Following a fifty-five day trial, the judge ruled that the Rozelle Rule was a per se violation of antitrust laws and an improper restriction on free agency. The Per se rule in antitrust law is that if an action is inherently unreasonable and anticompetitive, it is a violation of antitrust law. Mackey's lawyers argued that the requirement that a team losing a player to free agency had to provide "fair and equitable" compensation as determined by the commissioner rendered free agency meaningless because teams were dissuaded from bidding for free agents due to the cost of having to provide compensation to the player's former team. While the Appeals Court failed to agree that the Rozelle Rule violated the Per se rule, it did conclude that the Rozelle Rule violated the Rule of Reason and therefore constituted a violation of antitrust law.

Following the final decision of the Appeals Court, the players settled with the league, however, a year after the court's decision in the Mackey case, the NFLPA and the owners entered into a CBA which

---

[2]  "John Mackey Dies at 69: Helped Revolutionize N.F.L." New York Times, Richard Goldstein, July 7, 2011.

included a modified version of the Rozelle Rule. True free agency did not come to the NFL until the 1990s.

## MACKEY V. NATIONAL FOOTBALL LEAGUE

United States Court of Appeals, Eighth Circuit
543 F.2d 606 (1976)

Mandatory Subject of Bargaining.

Under § 8(d) of the National Labor Relations Act, 29 U.S.C. § 158(d), mandatory subjects of bargaining pertain to "wages, hours, and other terms and conditions of employment. . . ." *See NLRB v. Borg-Warner Corp.,* 356 U.S. 342, 78 S.Ct. 718, 2 L.Ed.2d 823 (1958). Whether an agreement concerns a mandatory subject depends not on its form but on its practical effect. *See Federation of Musicians v. Carroll,* 391 U.S. 99, 88 S.Ct. 1562, 20 L.Ed.2d 460 (1968). Thus, in *Meat Cutters v. Jewel Tea, supra,* the Court held that an agreement limiting retail marketing hours concerned a mandatory subject because it affected the particular hours of the day which the employees would be required to work. In *Teamsters Union v. Oliver,* 358 U.S. 283, 79 S.Ct. 297, 3 L.Ed.2d 312 (1959), an agreement fixing minimum equipment rental rates paid to truck owner-drivers was held to concern a mandatory bargaining subject because it directly affected the driver wage scale.

In this case the district court held that, in view of the illegality of the Rozelle Rule under the Sherman Act, it was "a nonmandatory, illegal subject of bargaining." We disagree. The labor exemption presupposes a violation of the antitrust laws. To hold that a subject relating to wages, hours and working conditions becomes nonmandatory by virtue of its illegality under the antitrust laws obviates the labor exemption. We conclude that whether the agreements here in question relate to a mandatory subject of collective bargaining should be determined solely under federal labor law. *Cf. Meat Cutters v. Jewel Tea, supra.*

On its face, the Rozelle Rule does not deal with "wages, hours and other terms or conditions of employment" but with inter-team compensation when a player's contractual obligation to one team expires and he is signed by another. Viewed as such, it would not constitute a mandatory subject of collective bargaining. The district court found, however, that the Rule operates to restrict a player's ability to move from one team to another and depresses player salaries. There is substantial evidence in the record to support these findings. Accordingly, we hold that the Rozelle Rule constitutes a mandatory bargaining subject within the meaning of the National Labor Relations Act.

Bona Fide Bargaining.

The district court found that the parties' collective bargaining history reflected nothing which could be legitimately characterized as bargaining over the Rozelle Rule; that, in part due to its recent formation and inadequate finances, the NFLPA, at least prior to 1974, stood in a relatively weak bargaining position vis-a-vis the clubs; and that "the Rozelle Rule was unilaterally imposed by the NFL and member club defendants upon the players in 1963 and has been imposed on the players from 1963 through the present date."

On the basis of our independent review of the record, including the parties' bargaining history as set forth above, we find substantial evidence to support the finding that there was no bona fide arm's-length bargaining over the Rozelle Rule preceding the execution of the 1968 and 1970 agreements. The Rule imposes significant restrictions on players, and its form has remained unchanged since it was unilaterally promulgated by the clubs in 1963. The provisions of the collective bargaining agreements which operated to continue the Rozelle Rule do not in and of themselves inure to the benefit of the players or their union. Defendants contend that the players derive indirect benefit from the Rozelle Rule, claiming that the union's agreement to the Rozelle Rule was a *quid pro quo* for increased pension benefits and the right of players to individually negotiate their salaries. The district court found, however, that there was no such *quid pro quo,* and we cannot say, on the basis of our review of the record, that this finding is clearly erroneous.

In view of the foregoing, we hold that the agreements between the clubs and the players embodying the Rozelle Rule do not qualify for the labor exemption. The union's acceptance of the status quo by the continuance of the Rozelle Rule in the initial collective bargaining agreements under the circumstances of this case cannot serve to immunize the Rozelle Rule from the scrutiny of the Sherman Act.

ANTITRUST ISSUES.

We turn, then, to the question of whether the Rozelle Rule, as implemented, violates § 1 of the Sherman Act, which declares illegal "every contract, combination * * * or conspiracy, in restraint of trade or commerce among the several States." 15 U.S.C. § 1. The district court found the Rozelle Rule to be a *per se* violation of the Act. Alternatively, the court held the Rule to be violative of the Rule of Reason standard.

Rule of Reason.

The focus of an inquiry under the Rule of Reason is whether the restraint imposed is justified by legitimate business purposes, and is no more restrictive than necessary. *See Chicago Board of Trade v. United States, supra; Worthen Bank & Trust Co. v. National BankAmericard Inc., supra.*

In defining the restraint on competition for players' services, the district court found that the Rozelle Rule significantly deters clubs from negotiating with and signing free agents; that it acts as a substantial deterrent to players playing out their options and becoming free agents; that it significantly decreases players' bargaining power in contract negotiations; that players are thus denied the right to sell their services in a free and open market; that as a result, the salaries paid by each club are lower than if competitive bidding were allowed to prevail; and that absent the Rozelle Rule, there would be increased movement in interstate commerce of players from one club to another.

We find substantial evidence in the record to support these findings. Witnesses for both sides testified that there would be increased player movement absent the Rozelle Rule. Two economists testified that elimination of the Rozelle Rule would lead to a substantial increase in player salaries. Carroll Rosenbloom, owner of the Los Angeles Rams, indicated that the Rams would have signed quite a few of the star players from other teams who had played out their options, absent the Rozelle Rule. Charles De Keado, an agent who represented Dick Gordon after he played out his option with the Chicago Bears, testified that the New Orleans Saints were interested in signing Gordon but did not do so because the Bears were demanding unreasonable compensation and the Saints were unwilling to risk an unknown award of compensation by the Commissioner. Jim McFarland, an end who played out his option with the St. Louis Cardinals, testified that he had endeavored to join the Kansas City Chiefs but was unable to do so because of the compensation asked by the Cardinals. Hank Stram, then coach and general manager of the Chiefs, stated that he probably would have given McFarland an opportunity to make his squad had he not been required to give St. Louis anything in return.

In support of their contention that the restraints effected by the Rozelle Rule are not unreasonable, the defendants asserted a number of justifications. First, they argued that without the Rozelle Rule, star players would flock to cities having natural advantages such as larger economic bases, winning teams, warmer climates, and greater media opportunities; that competitive balance throughout the League would thus be destroyed; and that the destruction of competitive balance would ultimately lead to diminished spectator interest, franchise failures, and perhaps the demise of the NFL, at least as it operates today. Second, the defendants contended that the Rozelle Rule is necessary to protect the clubs' investment in scouting expenses and player developments costs. Third, they asserted that players must work together for a substantial period of time in order to function effectively as a team; that elimination of the Rozelle Rule would lead to increased player movement and a concomitant reduction in player continuity; and that the quality of play in the NFL would thus suffer, leading to reduced spectator interest, and financial detriment both to the clubs and the players. Conflicting evidence was adduced at trial by both sides with respect to the validity of these asserted justifications.

The district court held the defendants' asserted justifications unavailing. As to the clubs' investment in player development costs, Judge Larson found that these expenses are similar to those incurred by other businesses, and that there is no right to compensation for this type of investment. With respect to player continuity, the court found that elimination of the Rozelle Rule would affect all teams equally in that regard; that it would not lead to a reduction in the quality of play; and that even assuming that it would, that fact would not justify the Rozelle Rule's anticompetitive effects. As to competitive balance and the consequences which would flow from abolition of the Rozelle Rule, Judge Larson found that the existence of the Rozelle Rule has had no material effect on competitive balance in the NFL. Even assuming that the Rule did foster competitive balance, the court found that there were other legal means available to achieve that end—e. g., the competition committee, multiple year contracts, and special incentives. The court further concluded that elimination of the Rozelle Rule would have no significant disruptive effects, either immediate or long term, on professional football. In conclusion the court held that the Rozelle Rule was unreasonable in that it was overly broad, unlimited in duration, unaccompanied by procedural safeguards, and employed in conjunction with other anticompetitive practices such as the draft, Standard Player Contract, option clause, and the no-tampering rules.

We agree that the asserted need to recoup player development costs cannot justify the restraints of the Rozelle Rule. That expense is an ordinary cost of doing business and is not peculiar to professional football. Moreover, because of its unlimited duration, the Rozelle Rule is far more restrictive than necessary to fulfill that need.

We agree, in view of the evidence adduced at trial with respect to existing players turnover by way of trades, retirements and new players entering the League, that the club owners' arguments respecting player continuity cannot justify the Rozelle Rule. We concur in the district court's conclusion that the possibility of resulting decline in the quality of play would not justify the Rozelle Rule. We do recognize, as did the district court, that the NFL has a strong and unique interest in maintaining competitive balance among its teams. The key issue is thus whether the Rozelle Rule is essential to the maintenance of competitive balance, and is no more restrictive than necessary. The district court answered both of these questions in the negative.

We need not decide whether a system of inter-team compensation for free agents moving to other teams is essential to the maintenance of competitive balance in the NFL. Even if it is, we agree with the district court's conclusion that the Rozelle Rule is significantly more restrictive than necessary to serve any legitimate purposes it might have in this regard. First, little concern was manifested at trial over the free movement of average or below average players. Only the movement of the better players was urged as being detrimental to football. Yet the Rozelle Rule applies to every NFL player regardless of his status or ability. Second, the Rozelle Rule is unlimited in duration. It operates as a perpetual restriction on a player's ability to sell his services in an open market throughout his career. Third, the enforcement of the Rozelle Rule is unaccompanied by procedural safeguards. A player has no input into the process by which fair compensation is determined. Moreover, the player may be unaware of the precise compensation demanded by his former team, and that other teams might be interested in him but for the degree of compensation sought.

Judge Frank emphasized the harshness of a rule in the field of professional baseball similar to the Rozelle Rule:

As one court, perhaps a bit exaggeratedly, has put it, "While the services of these baseball players are ostensibly secured by voluntary contracts a study of the system as * * * practiced under the plan of the National Agreement, reveals the involuntary character of the servitude which is imposed upon players by the strength of the combination controlling the labor of practically all of the players in the country. * * *" [I]f the players be regarded as quasi-peons, it is of no moment that they are well paid; only the totalitarian-minded will believe that high pay excuses virtual slavery.

In sum, we hold that the Rozelle Rule, as enforced, unreasonably restrains trade in violation of § 1 of the Sherman Act.

CONCLUSION.

In conclusion, although we find that non-labor parties may potentially avail themselves of the nonstatutory labor exemption where they are parties to collective bargaining agreements pertaining to mandatory subjects of bargaining, the exemption cannot be invoked where, as here, the agreement was not the product of bona fide arm's-length negotiations. Thus, the defendants' enforcement of the Rozelle Rule is not exempt from the coverage of the antitrust laws. Although we disagree with the district court's determination that the Rozelle Rule is a *per se* violation of the antitrust laws, we do find that the Rule, as implemented, contravenes the Rule of Reason and thus constitutes an unreasonable restraint of trade in violation of § 1 of the Sherman Act.

We note that our disposition of the antitrust issue does not mean that every restraint on competition for players' services would necessarily violate the antitrust laws. Also, since the Rozelle Rule, as implemented, concerns a mandatory subject of collective bargaining, any agreement as to inter-team compensation for free agents moving to other teams, reached through good faith collective bargaining, might very well be immune from antitrust liability under the nonstatutory labor exemption.

It may be that some reasonable restrictions relating to player transfers are necessary for the successful operation of the NFL. The protection of mutual interests of both the players and the clubs may indeed require this. We encourage the parties to resolve this question through collective bargaining. The parties are far better situated to agreeably resolve what rules governing player transfers are best suited for their mutual interests than are the courts. *See Kansas City Royals v. Major League Baseball Players*, 532 F.2d 615, 632 (8th Cir. 1976). However, no mutual resolution of this issue appears within the present record. Therefore, the Rozelle Rule, as it is presently implemented, must be set aside as an unreasonable restraint of trade.

With the exception of the district court's finding that implementation of the Rozelle Rule constitutes a *per se* violation of § 1 of the Sherman Act and except as it is otherwise modified herein, the judgment of the district court is AFFIRMED. The cause is remanded to the district court for further proceedings consistent with this opinion."

---

John Mackey went on to a Hall of Fame career, however, he died at age 69 having suffered from CTE and dementia for many years prior to his death that his family believed was caused by concussions suffered while playing football. Following his death in 2011 his brain was donated to the BU Center for the Study of Traumatic Encephalopathy. His family filed a wrongful death lawsuit against the NFL in 2013 related to his brain injuries.

# LABOR HISTORY OF THE NBA

The first president of the NBA players' union upon its inception in 1954 was Boston Celtics future Hall of Famer Bob Cousy. The NBPA became the first union to represent players in one of the major professional sports. At the time that the union was formed, the NBA provided no pension, no per diem costs while on the road, no minimum wage and no health benefits. The average annual salary was $8,000. While the union was formed in 1954, the NBA initially refused to recognize it and summarily dismissed all but one of Cousy's initial demands including abolishment of the $15 whispering foul which NBA referees were permitted to assess for players whispering to each other during the game. In today's NBA where trash talking has been elevated to an art, it is hard to imagine such an infraction. The only demand agreed to was for the payment of two weeks of back salary to six players for the Baltimore franchise which had gone out of business.

It took a threat of a strike and the possibility of the NBPA affiliating with the AFL-CIO in 1957 to induce the NBA to agree to discussions with the now formally recognized NBPA. As a result of their negotiations, the whispering fine was abolished, the players were to receive a $7 per diem payment and a number of other minor concessions were made.

Progress was slow for the NBPA until the 1964 NBA All Star Game which was a momentous occasion as it was to be nationally televised for the first time. The players refused to play unless specific demands were met including most prominently, the establishment of a pension plan, the formal recognition of the NBPA as the exclusive bargaining agent for the players and an increase in the per diem to $8 dollars per day, an increase of one dollar since it was first instituted in 1957. Both sides engaged in a standoff until literally minutes before the game when NBA President Walter Kennedy personally guaranteed that their demands including a pension plan would be met. The tip off of the game ended up being delayed by ten minutes.

Players' salaries rose dramatically with the birth of the American Basketball Association in 1967 and its competition for players. The NBA's response was to consider a merger of the two leagues at which time NBA players, led by then union president Oscar Robertson filed an antitrust lawsuit attempting to block any merger. In addition, the players took the opportunity to include a complaint against the NBA's reserve clause which bound a player to his original team for life with no opportunity for free agency. The NBPA successfully obtained a restraining order to block any merger which compelled the owners to negotiate with the union over these issues in a new CBA. Bargaining from the superior position provided by their restraining order, the NBPA was able to negotiate the abolishment of the reserve clause and get modified free agency. In return for settling and dismissing their lawsuit the players got benefits including increased salaries averaging $200,000 per year, increased pension benefits, medical and dental coverage, life insurance and a reasonable per diem.

The 1983 CBA instituted the dramatic steps of revenue sharing and a salary cap by which the players received 53% of league revenues. The salary cap instituted, as now, was a soft cap with numerous exceptions.

In February of 1987 the NBPA and the owners began collective bargaining toward a new CBA. The primary concerns of the players at that time were the salary cap, which they wanted eliminated, the college draft and the right of first refusal, which the players believed limited their options in free agency. With the negotiations stalled and the expiration of the old CBA only a week away, a group of nine players including NBPA president Junior Bridgman filed a class action antitrust lawsuit against the NBA and its individual franchises. With little progress being accomplished, the players increased the pressure on the NBA by starting the nuclear option which was a vote to decertify the union thereby enabling the players to bring an action alleging that the structure of the NBA violated antitrust laws. Ultimately, the players and the owners came to an agreement on a new six year CBA on April 26, 1988 which included a reduction of the draft to only two rounds and, most importantly to the players, eliminating the right of first refusal after a player has competed his second contract with unrestricted free agency for veteran players and a reduction of the college draft to three rounds in 1988 and two rounds thereafter.

The year 1995 brought more tension between the players and the owners. Following the completion of the 1995 playoffs, the owners locked out the players for the first time in league history. The prime concern of the owners at that time was their perceived need to reduce salaries. The players again were ready to go the route of decertification and an antitrust challenge in the courts believing that their legal position challenging the manner in which the league operated was strong. It apparently worked because the threat of the lawsuit was sufficient to bring movement to the negotiations that ended up with something for both sides. The owners got the elimination of many of the myriad of salary cap exceptions that had resulted in team payrolls soaring. The owners also were able to get a rookie wage scale with predetermined salaries. The players kept one of the most important exceptions to the salary cap which has come to be known as the Bird exception, named after Boston Celtics player Larry Bird. Under the Bird exception, a team is allowed to exceed the salary cap without any penalty in order to sign its own free agents. This exception can work for both sides as it increases the chances that a superstar player will be highly paid without any financial incentive to be lured to another team thereby making it easier for teams to keep their own star players who have come to establish the team's identity. The players also were able to negotiate into the new CBA a provision eliminating all restrictions on free agency once a player's initial contract has expired.

Unhappy with the last CBA in regard to the high payrolls, the owners exercised their option in the CBA to terminate the agreement at the conclusion of the 1997–1998 season. When negotiations went nowhere, the owners locked the players out on July 1, 1998. The goal of the owners was to get a hard cap in order to reduce their payroll costs. The negotiations stretched out without a resolution into the new league year and the NBA initially cancelled the pre-season games and later the first two months of the season. Finally as the date was approaching when it was deemed unavoidable to cancel the entire season, the players and the owners came to an agreement in January of 1999 with a reduced fifty game season to start in February.

Although the owners did not get their desired hard cap, a number of other provisions intended to reduce payrolls were adopted.

The year 2011 brought labor unrest again to professional basketball with the owners locking out the players on July 1, 2011 after the expiration of the 2005 CBA. The lockout lasted 161 days and resulted in a shortened 66 game season. The primary issues were the salary cap and the luxury tax. According to the owners, 22 of 30 teams had lost money the previous season and overall the league was losing 300 million dollars per year. The owners wanted to reduce the players' share of total revenues from 57% to 43%, institute a hard salary cap and increase the luxury tax. Following the same pattern of recent years, little progress was made until the pressure was put on the owners by the NBPA dissolving and an antitrust lawsuit against the league being filed by a group of NBA players. Ultimately, the players and owners agreed on the players' share of revenues being reduced to a low of 49% during the term of the new CBA, a flexible salary cap and harsher luxury tax provisions.

# AGE RULES IN PROFESSIONAL SPORTS

Although it may seem hard to imagine today, in the earlier years of the NBA, players were not eligible to be drafted into the NBA until after they had graduated college or four years after their class graduated high school. This generally meant that players went to college and played four years before they entered the NBA.

The first change in that rule involved Spencer Haywood, a star on the 1968 U.S. Olympic team (at a time when only amateur basketball players played on the U.S. Olympic team) who left the University of Detroit after his second year to play for the Denver Rockets in the American Basketball Association (ABA) under a hardship exemption provided for in the rules of the upstart ABA to permit such players, whom the NBA would have considered underage, to play professional basketball. Since the ABA and NBA did not merge until 1976, the ABA operated under different rules than the NBA at the time the Denver Rockets signed Haywood. When he turned 21, Haywood repudiated his ABA contract alleging fraud and signed a contract with the then Seattle Supersonics of the NBA, however, the Supersonics signed Haywood to an NBA player contract within four years of Haywood's high school graduation thereby prompting the NBA to threaten to invalidate the contract and issue sanctions to the Supersonics.

Haywood's response to the threats was to join with the Seattle Supersonics team in a lawsuit against the NBA alleging that the action of the NBA was a per se violation of antitrust law. The NBA's action, Haywood alleged amounted to an illegal group boycott and the NBA draft rules were per se violations of antitrust law. Due to the fact that lawsuits can take years to make their way through the court, Haywood asked for a temporary injunction while the case was in the courts to allow him to play. In order to be successful in his request for such an injunction, Haywood had to prove that he was likely to win his case and that if he were not granted the injunction to allow him to play while the case was pending, he would be irreparably harmed. The federal district court ruled in his favor indicating:

"If Haywood is unable to continue to play professional basketball for Seattle, he will suffer irreparable injury in that a substantial part of his playing career will have been dissipated, his physical condition, skills and coordination will deteriorate from lack of high-level competition, his public acceptance as a super star will diminish to the detriment of his career, his self-esteem and his pride will have been injured and a great injustice will be perpetrated on him."

The NBA appealed the case to the Ninth Circuit of Appeals which issued a stay of the injunction from which was ultimately appealed to the Supreme Court which on March 1, 1971 ruled that the injunction would stand and Haywood could play for the Supersonics. 401 U.S. 1204 (1971).

Soon after the Supreme Court decision, the league and Haywood settled the case permitting him to play in the NBA.

In response to the Haywood lawsuit, the NBA established an exception to its four years from high school graduation rule for players who could show an economic hardship if they had to wait four years from their high school graduation to be eligible to play professional basketball in the NBA. Then in 1976, the hardship rule was replaced by a new standard by which any player could be eligible to play in the NBA, but would, by doing so, lose his eligibility to play college basketball which merely meant that if a player, such as LeBron James chose to go directly to the NBA from high school, he would not be able to compete in college basketball if his NBA career did not work out.

Now we are in the era of the "one and done" whereby players are not eligible for the NBA draft until one year after their high school class graduates. Various proposals to change this are often being considered including one to require players accepting college basketball scholarships to play two years of college basketball before they can enter the NBA.

The present NBA rule setting a minimum age of nineteen years before a player can be drafted into the NBA was made a part of the CBA agreement in 2005 and while not a popular concession by the players, was one that in return for the players received other concessions during the negotiation of the CBA. NBA Commissioner Adam Silver has indicated that he would like to see the minimum age raised to twenty. The NBPA has already stated that they will most likely be making this an issue in the next CBA. The concern on behalf of the players is that their careers are short and taking away a year of a player's career causes significant harm to him. In addition, the risk of a career ending injury during a required one year college basketball career is always hanging over the head of the player.

A study by Ramogi Huma, of the National College Players Association and Ellen Staurowsky a professor of Sports Management at Drexel University concluded that the potential financial cost to a potential top ten draft pick in the NBA is more than 1.6 million dollars for that lost year not including the money the player could have earned by endorsements.[3]

It has been argued that the reason for the minimum age requirements is to benefit the NCAA and the NBA at the expense of the players. The value to the NCAA is quite apparent. Its largest money maker is March Madness, its annual national championship tournament. Diluting the talent pool of the tournament by permitting the best players to go directly from high school to the NBA could dramatically alter the quality of the tournament play. As for the NBA, it benefits from the minimum age rule by having an extra year for young players to develop and to monitor and evaluate their skills against higher levels of competition. From a strict financial standpoint, having a minimum age also delays by a year the time when an athlete in his prime can become a free agent. The minimum age also protects the NBA from its own talent evaluating mistakes. While many people may focus on the stellar careers of Kevin Garnett, Kobe Bryant and LeBron James who went to the NBA directly from high school, the careers of many players such as Kwame Brown, the only direct from high school player to have been chosen with the first pick in the draft, were often busts. During his thirteen year NBA career Brown averaged 6.6 points per game and 5.5 rebounds per game.

## NFL AGE RULES

The rules for declaring oneself eligible for professional sports are regulated by the various professional leagues. The National Football League requires an athlete to have been out of high school for three years in order to be eligible for the NFL draft.

Maurice Clarett was a star freshman running back for Ohio State when it won the national football championship in 2002, however, after being suspended by Ohio State for filing a false police report, he

---

3    Huma, R., & Staurowsky, E. J. (2012). The $6 billion heist: Robbing college athletes under the guise of amateurism. A report collaboratively produced by the National College Players Association and Drexel University Sport Management.

declared himself eligible for the NFL draft and sued the NFL challenging the rule requiring him to wait three years from graduating high school to be eligible for the NFL draft. At trial, Judge Shira Scheindlin ruled that the NFL's rules preventing Clarett from being eligible for the NFL draft were invalid as violations of anti-trust law, however, her decision was later overruled by the Court of Appeals in an opinion written by now Supreme Court Justice Sonia Sotomayor. Meanwhile, Mike Williams, a USC sophomore football player upon hearing of Clarett's initial court victory also declared himself eligible for the NFL draft and hired an agent. Following the appeals court decision, both Clarett and Williams were banned from playing college football for declaring themselves draft eligible and hiring agents. Although Clarett, never played in an NFL game, Williams waited out his one year before he would be eligible for the NFL draft, was chosen as a number one draft pick in the 2005 NFL draft and played five years in the NFL.

## CLARETT V. NATIONAL FOOTBALL LEAGUE
United States Court of Appeals, Second Circuit
369 F.3d 124 (2004)

"Because the major source of the parties' factual disputes is the relationship between the challenged eligibility rules and the current collective bargaining agreement governing the terms and conditions of employment for NFL players, some elaboration on both the collective bargaining agreement and the eligibility rules is warranted. The current collective bargaining agreement between the NFL and its players union was negotiated between the NFL Management Council ("NFLMC"), which is the NFL member clubs' multi-employer bargaining unit, and the NFL Players Association ("NFLPA"), the NFL players' exclusive bargaining representative. This agreement became effective in 1993 and governs through 2007. Despite the collective bargaining agreement's comprehensiveness with respect to, inter alia, the manner in which the NFL clubs select rookies through the draft and the scheme by which rookie compensation is determined, the eligibility rules for the draft do not appear in the agreement.

At the time the collective bargaining agreement became effective, the eligibility rules appeared in the NFL Constitution and Bylaws, which had last been amended in 1992. Specifically, Article XII of the Bylaws ("Article XII"), entitled "Eligibility of Players," prohibited member clubs from selecting any college football player through the draft process who had not first exhausted all college football eligibility, graduated from college, or been out of high school for five football seasons. Clubs were further barred from drafting any person who either did not attend college, or attended college but did not play football, unless that person had been out of high school for four football seasons. Article XII, however, also included an exception that permitted clubs to draft players who had received "Special Eligibility" from the NFL Commissioner. In order to qualify for such special eligibility, a player was required to submit an application before January 6 of the year that he wished to enter the draft and "at least three NFL seasons must have elapsed since the player was graduated from high school." The Commissioner's practice apparently was, and still is, to grant such an application so long as three full football seasons have passed since a player's high school graduation. Appellant's Brief, at 7 n. 3."

". . . on the merits of Clarett's antitrust claim, the district court found that the eligibility rules were so "blatantly anticompetitive" that only a "quick look" at the NFL's procompetitive justifications was necessary to reach the conclusion that the eligibility rules were unlawful under the antitrust laws. Id. at 408. The NFL had argued that because the eligibility rules prevent less physically and emotionally mature players from entering the league, they justify any incidental anticompetitive effect on the market for NFL players. Id. In so doing, according to the NFL, the eligibility rules guard against less-prepared and younger players entering the League and risking injury to themselves, prevent the sport from being devalued by the higher number of injuries to those young players, protect its member clubs from having to bear the costs of such injuries, and discourage aspiring amateur football players from enhancing their physical condition through unhealthy methods. Id. at 408–09. The district court held that all of these justifications were inadequate as a matter of law, concluding that the NFL's purported concerns could be addressed through less restrictive but equally effective means. Id. at 410. Finding that the eligibility rules violated the antitrust laws, the district court entered judgment in favor of Clarett, and, recognizing that this year's draft was then just over two months away, issued an order deeming Clarett eligible to participate in the draft."

"Our decisions in Caldwell, Williams, and Wood all involved players' claims that the concerted action of a professional sports league imposed a restraint upon the labor market for players' services and thus violated the antitrust laws. In each case, however, we held that the non-statutory labor exemption defeated the players' claims. Our analysis in each case was rooted in the observation that the relationships among the defendant sports leagues and their players were governed by collective bargaining agreements and thus were subject to the carefully structured regime established by federal labor laws. We reasoned that to permit antitrust suits against sports leagues on the ground that their concerted action imposed a restraint upon the labor market would seriously undermine many of the policies embodied by these labor laws, including the congressional policy favoring collective bargaining, the bargaining parties' freedom of contract, and the widespread use of multi-employer bargaining units. Subsequent to our decisions in this area, similar reasoning led the Supreme Court in Brown v. Pro Football, Inc., 518 U.S. 231, 116 S.Ct. 2116, 135 L.Ed.2d 521 (1996), to hold that the non-statutory exemption protected the NFL's unilateral implementation of new salary caps for developmental squad players after its collective bargaining agreement with the NFL players union had expired and negotiations with the union over that proposal reached an impasse. We need only retrace the path laid down by these prior cases to reach the conclusion that Clarett's antitrust claims must fail."

"Clarett argues that he is physically qualified to play professional football and that the antitrust laws preclude the NFL teams from agreeing amongst themselves that they will refuse to deal with him simply because he is less than three full football seasons out of high school. Such an arbitrary condition, he argues, imposes an unreasonable restraint upon the competitive market for professional football players' services, and, because it excludes him from entering that market altogether, constitutes a per se antitrust violation. The issue we must decide is whether subjecting the NFL's eligibility rules to antitrust scrutiny would "subvert fundamental principles of our federal labor policy." Wood, 809 F.2d at 959. For the reasons that follow, we hold that it would and that the non-statutory exemption therefore applies."

"Although the NFL has maintained draft eligibility rules in one form or another for much of its history, the "inception of a collective bargaining relationship" between the NFL and its players union some thirty years ago "irrevocably alter[ed] the governing legal regime." Caldwell, 66 F.3d at 527. Our prior cases highlight a number of consequences resulting from the advent of this collective bargaining relationship that are relevant to Clarett's litigation. For one, prospective players no longer have the right to negotiate directly with the NFL teams over the terms and conditions of their employment. That responsibility is instead committed to the NFL and the players union to accomplish through the collective bargaining process, and throughout that process the NFL and the players union are to have the freedom to craft creative solutions to their differences in light of the economic imperatives of their industry. Furthermore, the NFL teams are permitted to engage in joint conduct with respect to the terms and conditions of players' employment as a multi-employer bargaining unit without risking antitrust liability. The arguments Clarett advances in support of his antitrust claim, however, run counter to each of these basic principles of federal labor law.

Because the NFL players have unionized and have selected the NFLPA as its exclusive bargaining representative, labor law prohibits

Clarett from negotiating directly the terms and conditions of his employment with any NFL club, see NLRB v. Allis-Chalmers Mfg. Co., 388 U.S. 175, 180, 87 S.Ct. 2001, 18 L.Ed.2d 1123 (1967), and an NFL club would commit an unfair labor practice were it to bargain with Clarett individually without the union's consent, see Medo Photo Supply Corp. v. NLRB, 321 U.S. 678, 683, 64 S.Ct. 830, 88 L.Ed. 1007 (1944). The terms and conditions of Clarett's employment are instead committed to the collective bargaining table and are reserved to the NFL and the players union's selected representative to negotiate. Allis-Chalmers Mfg. Co., 388 U.S. at 180, 87 S.Ct. 2001."

"As a permissible, mandatory subject of bargaining, the conditions under which a prospective player, like Clarett, will be considered for employment as an NFL player are for the union representative and the NFL to determine. Clarett, however, stresses that the eligibility rules are arbitrary and that requiring him to wait another football season has nothing to do with whether he is in fact qualified for professional play. But Clarett is in this respect no different from the typical worker who is confident that he or she has the skills to fill a job vacancy but does not possess the qualifications or meet the requisite criteria that have been set. In the context of this collective bargaining relationship, the NFL and its players union can agree that an employee will not be hired or considered for employment for nearly any reason whatsoever so long as they do not violate federal laws such as those prohibiting unfair labor practices, 29 U.S.C. § 201 et seq., or discrimination, 42 U.S.C. § 2000e et seq. See Reliance Ins. Cos. v. NLRB, 415 F.2d 1, 6 (8th Cir.1969) ("[Employer is usually free to] pick and choose his employees and hire those he thinks will best serve his business interests."). Any challenge to those criteria must "be founded on labor rather than antitrust law." Caldwell, 66 F.3d at 530."

"The threat to the operation of federal labor law posed by Clarett's antitrust claims is in no way diminished by Clarett's contention that the rules were not bargained over during the negotiations that preceded the current collective bargaining agreement. The eligibility rules, along with the host of other NFL rules and policies affecting the terms and conditions of NFL players included in the NFL's Constitution and Bylaws, were well known to the union, and a copy of the Constitution and Bylaws was presented to the union during negotiations. Given that the eligibility rules are a mandatory bargaining subject for the reasons set out above, the union or the NFL could have forced the other to the bargaining table if either felt that a change was warranted. See NLRB v. Katz, 369 U.S. 736, 743, 82 S.Ct. 1107, 8 L.Ed.2d 230 (1962). Indeed, according to the declaration from the NFLMC's Vice President for Labor Relations, Peter Ruocco, this is exactly what the NFL did."

"The disruptions to federal labor policy that would be occasioned by Clarett's antitrust suit, moreover, would not vindicate any of the antitrust policies that the Supreme Court has said may warrant the withholding of the non-statutory exemption. This is simply not a case in which the NFL is alleged to have conspired with its players union to drive its competitors out of the market for professional football. See Pennington, 381 U.S. at 665, 85 S.Ct. 1585. Nor does Clarett contend that the NFL uses the eligibility rules as an unlawful means of maintaining its dominant position in that market. See Allen Bradley Co., 325 U.S. at 809, 65 S.Ct. 1533 ("The primary objective of all the Anti-trust legislation has been to preserve business competition and to proscribe business monopoly."). This lawsuit reflects simply a prospective employee's disagreement with the criteria, established by the employer and the labor union, that he must meet in order to be considered for employment. Any remedies for such a claim are the province of labor law. Allowing Clarett to proceed with his antitrust suit would subvert "principles that have been familiar to, and accepted by, the nation's workers for all of the NLRA's [sixty years] in every industry except professional sports." Caldwell, 66 F.3d at 530. We, however, follow the Supreme Court's lead in declining to "fashion an antitrust exemption [so as to give] additional advantages to professional football players that transport workers, coal miners, or meat packers would not enjoy." Brown, 518 U.S. at 249, 116 S.Ct. 2116."

---

## QUESTION

1.     Should a union be able to negotiate terms of employment on behalf of athletes who are not members of the union and have no vote in the determination of those terms?

# NHL AND MLB AGE RULES

The NHL and MLB operate under systems by which players can go directly from high school to professional hockey in the NHL and professional baseball in MLB, however, it is interesting to note that the NCAA makes little money from college hockey and college baseball and therefore does not have the same incentive to keep these athletes in college for a year.

Baseball has its own minor league system for which it covers the cost. However, the minor league system for professional football and basketball is the NCAA which is operated at no cost to the NFL and NBA. They get a minor league system paid for by colleges. The colleges and universities make large amounts of money and the players get only scholarship compensation.

The rules for the age of players are negotiated with the players' unions of the respective sports which is ironic since the young athletes are not members of the unions when their rights are bargained away.

---

## QUESTIONS

1.     What are the purposes behind the paternalistic rules in professional sports regarding age?

2.     If athletes with short athletic careers do not wish to delay their entrance into professional sports why should they be prevented from doing so?

# MAJOR LEAGUE BASEBALL COLLECTIVE BARGAINING AGREEMENT

In 2016, a new CBA was agreed to by the owners and the players with little animosity. The minimum salary for Major League Baseball players was raised in the 2016 CBA from $507,500 in 2016 to $535,000 in 2017; $545,000 in 2018 and $555,000 in 2019. A cost of living adjustment would be applied to arrive at the minimum salaries in 2020 and 2021.

Among the benefits in the new CBA are provisions for full time chefs and registered dieticians on staff for each team to help improve clubhouse meal nutrition. In addition, all teams are required to provide a sports psychologist available to the players as an indication of the increased recognition of the mental stresses placed on MLB players.

Drug protocols were strengthened with the number of random in-season urine tests increased from 3,400 to 4,800 and the number of off-season tests increasing from 350 to 1,550 to make sure that every player will have at least one random off-season urine test each season. Human Growth Hormone (HGH) testing can only be done by a blood test. The new CBA provides for an increase in the number of random blood tests from 260 to 500 and the number of off-season random blood tests increasing from 140 to 400. Significantly, arbitrators, under the 2016 CBA, have increased authority and discretion in determining suspensions for use of performance enhancing drugs including the ability to reduce the penalties based upon mitigating circumstances in each case.

Chewing tobacco sometimes known as smokeless tobacco was banned in all stadiums where its use was banned by local laws or ordinances. In addition, new players joining MLB teams for the first time will be prevented from using smokeless tobacco on the field at every stadium.

Teams exceeding the Competitive Balance Tax, more commonly known as the Luxury Tax (195 million in 2017), under the 2016 CBA are required to pay an increased amount with the tax rate for first time offenders of the Luxury Tax paying a tax rate of 20%, second time offenders pay a tax rate of 30% and third or more offenders pay a 50% tax rate. In addition, to as an incentive to further reduce spending by the biggest offenders such as the Yankees an additional surcharge for payrolls between 20 and 40 million of 12% is added to the Luxury Tax of the offending team and if a team exceeds the luxury cap threshold by more than 40 million dollars the surcharge rises to 45%. Further disincentive to exceeding the salary cap came in a new provision in the CBA beginning in 2018 where teams will lose positions in the MLB amateur draft if they exceed the Luxury Tax.

During the negotiations, the owners dropped their demand for an International Draft largely as a result of the opposition of Hispanic players. However, in its place is a hard cap for signing of international players, which represents the first hard cap in MLB history through the setting up of a hard cap signing bonus pool. A hard cap represents a firm limitation of the amount of money that can be spent on player contracts.

## NBA COLLECTIVE BARGAINING AGREEMENT

The year 2016 also brought a new seven year CBA between the NBA and the National Basketball Players Association (NBPA). The CBA which provides for either party to be able to opt out of the agreement after six years, divides basketball-related income (BRI) 51% to the players and 49% to the owners so long as expected specified levels of BRI are met. The major source of revenue for players and owners is television contracts, most notably the nine year 2.1 billion dollar contract with ESPN and Turner Sports. The definition of BRI includes apparel sales, stadium signs, and other basketball related income. While the percentage of BRI that the players received under the CBA in 2011 was 57%, the dramatic increase in BRI resulted in the money the players received in 2017 at a lower 51% BRI figure to still be 1.5 billion dollars more than the players received in 2011. The new CBA increased the rookie salary scale, the veteran minimum salaries and specific free agent salary exceptions by approximately 45%. In addition, the owners and the players both agreed to jointly fund a new life long health insurance plan for former players with at least three years of NBA service. The biggest item left unchanged, however, was the rule limiting eligibility for the NBA draft to nineteen year olds at least one year after their high school graduation year.

# WORK STOPPAGES

There have been a number of significant work stoppages in professional sports over the years including:

1.    In 1979 a strike of MLB umpires went from opening day to May 18th when, under tremendous pressure, in a game where the officials perhaps play a more significant role than in any other professional team sport, MLB agreed to increase the salaries, travel per diem and vacation time for the umpires.

2.    The MLB players' strike during the 1981 season resulted in the cancellation of more than 700 games. The key issue was how free agency would be structured with a compromise being reached that included free agency being restricted to players with at least six years of major league experience.

3.    In 1982, the NFL players' union went on a strike that shortened the season that year to 9 games and ended with the players receiving increased regular season and playoff pay, however five years later, the NFL players' union went on strike again after the first two games of the 1987 season, causing the cancellation of NFL games for week three of the season, however this time the owners hired replacement players who played the next three regular scheduled games much to the consternation of fans throughout the country. The strike was far

from a unified action by the players with approximately 15% of the players including stars such as Mark Gastineau, Randy White, Joe Montana and Doug Flutie crossing the picket lines to play. Attendance plummeted with the smallest number of people attending a replacement game in Philadelphia where only 4,074 people attended. The strike's main issue was the league's free agency policy.

For five years after the 1987 strike, the players worked without a collective bargaining agreement and instead resorted to the courts. When a collective bargaining agreement was finally obtained it contained the first salary cap.

4.     The 1992 NHL players' strike lasted a mere ten days during the 1992 season. Ultimately the strike was settled with a new two year collective bargaining agreement that included increased playoff bonuses and an increase in the length of the season. Just three years later the NHL had another work stoppage, however, this time it was the owners locking out the players from October 1, 1994 to January 11, 1995. The lockout ended with the owners getting a rookie salary cap and free agency restrictions.

5.     MLB players struck again on August 12, 1994 in a strike that lasted until April 2, 1995 and actually resulted in no World Series being played. The strike was caused by a disagreement over the owners' proposal for a salary cap and restrictions on free agency. During the strike, the owners suspended free agency and salary arbitration, which action, the players argued successfully in court, was illegal. Federal Judge and now Supreme Court Justice Sonia Sotomayor ordered the owners to reinstate free agency and salary arbitration at which point the strike was settled and the players went back to work (or play).

6.     The last of the major professional sports' leagues to have a work stoppage was the NBA when the owners locked out the players during the 1998–1999 season. The lockout which began technically during the summer of 1998 extended until January 20, 1999. The

ultimate settlement of this labor dispute included limits on the maximum salaries for player as well as a rookie wage scale.

7.    With NHL teams spending 76% of their income on player salaries, team owners were unhappy with their Collective Bargaining Agreement and wanted to install a hard salary cap limiting the amount that teams could pay their players so in September of 2004 they locked the players out when no agreement on a new CBA could be reached. As the sides continued to be unable to reach any kind of a resolution, NHL Commissioner Gary Bettman cancelled the entire season in February of 2005 which resulted in the only time that one of the American major professional sports leagues lost an entire season due to a labor dispute. The lost season also resulted in the only time since 1919 that the Stanley Cup, one of the most iconic sports trophies in history was not awarded. Ultimately the players union and the owners agreed on a new CBA during the summer of 2005 in which the owners got their much desired salary cap and the players ended up getting little in return.

8.    One of the most bitter labor disputes in professional sports was the 2011 lockout of NFL players that went on for four and a half months. At that time the NFL was incredibly profitable. According to Forbes Magazine, the average NFL team was worth 1.04 billion dollars at that time with teams' revenues increasing during the 2010 season by 4% over the previous season to 261 million dollars.[4]

However, the team owners were not happy with a salary cap that required them to pay players 51% of the total revenues and wanted a reduction of that figure. The players were willing to reduce that amount to 50%, but that was not satisfactory to the owners who locked out the players in order to induce the players to accept a lower figure for a new CBA. Eventually, they settled on 47% and 48% for the period of the new CBA. In order to increase revenues, the owners also wanted, but did not get an increase in the length of the season by

---

[4]    "The NFL's Most Valuable Teams," Kurt Badenhausen, Forbes Magazine, September 7, 2011.

two additional games which was strongly objected to by the players due to concerns about the effects on their health and safety brought about by an extended season.

The NFL owners had been planning for a possible lockout or strike for some time prior to 2011 and even negotiated television contract extensions for less money in 2009 and 2010 that would pay the owners 4 billion dollars in 2011 regardless of whether the games were played or not. The NFLPA challenged the validity of the television contracts on the basis that when the NFL negotiated the broadcasting rights contracts in 2009 and 2010 they violated an agreement with the players that required the NFL to make a good faith effort to maximize revenue for the players. The players argued that the contracts were negotiated in a manner to provide the NFL owners with greater leverage in the event of a labor lockout. Initially, pursuant to the CBA, the matter was decided by a special master, however, Federal District Court Judge David Doty ruled that the special master erred in concluding that the NFL can act as a self-interested conglomerate, instead of being required to negotiate contracts for the mutual benefit of the players and the owners. According to Judge Doty, "The record shows that the NFL undertook contract renegotiations to advance its own interests and harm the interests of the players." Judge Doty also wrote in his opinion that the NFL "consistently characterized gaining control over labor as a short-term objective and maximizing revenue as a long-term objective. . . advancing its negotiating position at the expense of using best efforts to maximize total revenues for the joint benefit of the NFL and the players."[5]

Although the decision of Judge Doty provided some impetus for a new CBA, it did not happen in the days following Judge Doty's decision and on March 11th the NFLPA rejected the owner's latest offer and took the dramatic step of decertifying as a union. The

---

[5]   Order, Reggie White et al. v. NFL et al., U.S. District Court, District of Minnesota Civil No. 4–92–906 (DSD).

lockout began in earnest on March 12th. Immediately following the lockout and no longer prevented from doing so by having a certified union representing the players, a group of players including high profile quarterbacks Tom Brady, Peyton Manning and Drew Brees filed an antitrust lawsuit against the NFL. Because antitrust claims cannot be made against an employer by a union representing the employees, it was necessary to dissolve the union for such a claim to be made in court by the players as individuals and on a class action basis. In their complaint the players asked for an injunction against the lockout. After court ordered negotiations to resolve the case failed, Judge Susan Nelson ruled in favor of the players' and ended the lockout, however, the players' victory was short lived as the owners successfully appealed to the 8th Circuit Court of Appeals where the injunction against the lockout was lifted. Eventually in late July the owners and the players agreed upon the terms of a new CBA thereby saving the season. The new CBA included a hard salary cap with the players receiving 47% of league revenues.

# DEFLATEGATE

Ever since the Watergate scandal that brought down the presidency of Richard Nixon in 1974, it appears that almost every scandalous event becomes labeled with "gate" and the labor dispute that has come to be known as "deflategate" is no exception. It was hard for many people unfamiliar with labor law to understand that as the case developed through the courts, the factual issues of whether or not New England Patriots quarterback Tom Brady was involved in some manner with the deflating of footballs used in the AFC championship game against the Indianapolis Colts was of little interest to the federal court judges ruling on this matter. Instead the focus was on the process and whether it was sufficiently fair to comply with established labor law.

The New England Patriots played the Indianapolis Colts at the Patriots' Gillette Stadium in the AFC Championship Game on the evening of January 18, 2015. The game itself was not much of a contest with the Patriots totally overwhelming the Colts by a score of 45–7, but the controversy that began in that game continued for a year. According to the NFL's investigation known as the Wells report, prior to the beginning of the game, the Colts had indicated to the NFL league office that they suspected that the Patriots were underinflating their game balls.[6]

NFL rules require footballs to be inflated to a pressure between 12.5 and 13.5 pounds per square inch (psi). Some NFL quarterbacks prefer under-inflated balls because they are considered to be easier to grip and throw, particularly in cold or rainy weather. Since 2006, all NFL teams provide their own game balls to use on offense. Just about the only time that an opposing team will handle their opponent's game ball is after a fumble recovery or interception and so it was during the Patriots-Colts game. During the first half of the game, Patriots quarterback Tom Brady threw a ball which was intercepted by Colts linebacker, D'Qwell Jackson who took the ball with him to the sideline to keep as a souvenir. Following the interception, a Colt's equipment manager measured the ball pressure and notified NFL officials that it was under-inflated. The second half of the game was played with balls that met NFL requirements. The Patriots went on to score 28 points in the second half while shutting out the Colts to make the final score 45–7. It is interesting to note, as was done in the Wells report, that Tom Brady's passing improved in the second half while using the higher inflated footballs. When the game ended, the investigation began.

Five days after the game, the NFL hired New York lawyer Ted Wells to investigate the matter. After four months, Wells submitted his 243 page report concluding that the balls had been tampered with and that it was "more probable than not" that Brady was aware that the Patriots equipment staff purposely deflated the game balls. The report also concluded that neither Coach Bill Belichick nor members of his

---

6    "Investigative Report Concerning Footballs Used During the AFC Championship Game on January 18, 2015" Paul, Weiss, Rifkind, Wharton & Garrison LLP. Theodore V. Wells, Jr., Brad S. Karp and Lorin L. Reisner, May 6, 2015.

staff were aware of the situation. The two people identified by Wells as the probable culprits were locker-room attendant Jim McNally and equipment manager John Jastremski. Again, using the standard of "more probable than not" Wells determined that they deliberately deflated the footballs used in the game.

The standard of proof, "more probable than not" equates to the "preponderance of the evidence" standard used in civil actions as contrasted with the higher "beyond a reasonable doubt" standard used in criminals cases. It is interesting to note that the NFL's use of the standard of "more probable than not" goes back to 2008 when in response to criticism of the handling of the investigation into the New England Patriots improperly videoing their rivals that came to be known as "Spygate," the NFL changed its standard of proof for competitive violations to the lesser standard of "more probable than not" from a standard of conclusive proof.

Wells relied heavily on a scientific analysis done by the consulting company Exponent which was supported by Princeton Physics professor Daniel Marlow that concluded that no environmental or physical factors could explain the reduced air pressure of the balls used by the Patriots. This scientific analysis came under extreme criticism for being faulty and biased, most notably by Robert F. Young (an admitted Patriots fan) who filed an amicus brief with the federal court when the federal court was reviewing the Commissioner's determination. The amicus brief clearly indicated the flaws in Exponent's analysis and provided scientific explanations for the natural deflation of the balls.[7]

Young's position was supported in an op-ed piece for WBUR-FM by New York Law School Professor Robert Blecker, a self-described Patriots detractor[8].

---

[7] NFL Management Council v. NFL Players Association, Case No 15–cv–596 (RMB)(JCF) Robert F. Young's Amicus Curiae in Opposition to the NFL's Motion to Confirm Arbitration Award.

[8] "DeflateGate, And the Patriots' False Appearance of Guild" WBUR Cognoscenti, Robert Blecker, August 31, 2015.

More importantly, MIT professor John Leonard posted a one and a half hour lecture on YouTube in which he debunked the analysis and conclusion of Exponent and concluded "If I had to stake my reputation and my career on it, the Patriots balls match the Ideal Gas Law prediction and I don't why people can't get that."

On May 11, 2015, the response of the Commissioner to the Wells report was to suspend Tom Brady for the first four games of the next NFL season and the Patriots were fined a million dollars and forfeited their first-round pick in the 2016 NFL draft and its fourth round pick in the 2017 draft.

Part of the reason for the harshness of the penalty to Brady was as described by the NFL Executive President Troy Vincent in his letter to Brady, "With respect to your particular involvement, the report established that there is substantial and credible evidence to conclude you were at least generally aware of the actions of the Patriots' employees involved in the deflation of the footballs and that it was unlikely that their actions were done without your knowledge. Moreover, the report documents your failure to cooperate fully and candidly with the investigation, including by refusing to produce any relevant electronic evidence (emails, texts, etc.), despite being offered extraordinary safeguards by the investigators to protect unrelated personal information and by providing testimony that the report concludes was not plausible and contradicted by other evidence."[9]

Three days after the issuance of the Commissioner's ruling, on behalf of Brady, the NFLPA filed an appeal, pursuant to their rights under the CBA. The NFLPA requested that the appeal be heard by a neutral arbitrator, but the NFL determined that Commissioner Roger Goodell, would preside over the appeal. After the ten hour appeal hearing was concluded, Commissioner Goodell upheld the suspension indicating that a critical factor in his decision was Brady's

---

[9]    "NFL Releases Statement on Patriots' Violations" Press Release, National Football League, May 11, 2015.

destruction of his cell phone. The next day the NFLPA appealed the Commissioner's decision into the federal court.

Tom Brady also responded to Commissioner Goodell's ruling by issuing a statement on his Facebook page:

"I am very disappointed by the NFL's decision to uphold the 4 game suspension against me. I did nothing wrong, and no one in the Patriot's organization did either. Despite submitting to hours of testimony over the past 6 months, it is disappointing that the Commissioner upheld by suspension based upon a standard it was "probable" that I was "generally aware" of misconduct. The fact is that neither I, nor any equipment person, did anything of which we have been accused. I also disagree with yesterday's narrative surrounding my cellphone. I replaced my broken Samsung phone with a new iPhone 6 AFTER my attorneys made it clear to the NFL that my actual phone device would not be subjected to investigation under ANY circumstances. As a member of a union, I was under no obligation to set a new precedent going forward, nor was I made aware at any time during Mr. Wells' investigation, that failing to subject my cell phone to investigation would result in ANY discipline.

Most importantly, I have never written, texted, emailed to anybody at anytime, anything related to football air pressure before this issue as raised at the AFC Championship game in January. To suggest that I destroyed a phone to avoid giving the NFL information it requested is completely wrong. To try and reconcile the record and fully cooperate with the investigation after I was disciplined in May, we turned over detailed pages of cell phone records and all of the emails that Mr. Wells requested. We even contacted the phone company to see if there was any possible way we could retrieve any/all of the actual text messages from my old phone. In sort, we exhausted every possibility to give the NFL everything we could and offered to go thru the identity for every text and phone call during the relevant time."

The NFLPA appealed on Tom Brady's behalf to the Federal District Court. NFL League Mgt. Council v. NFL Players Association, 125 F. Supp. 3d 449—District Court SD New York 2015.

The bases for appeals to court to overturn an arbitration decision are quite limited. Federal law found in 9 USC Section 10(a) lists them:

"1.  where the award was procured by corruption, fraud or undue means;

2.  where there was evident partiality or corruption in the arbitrators, or either of them;

3.  where the arbitrators were guilty of misconduct in refusing to postpone the hearing, upon sufficient cause shown, or in refusing to hear evidence pertinent and material to the controversy; or of any other misbehavior by which the rights of any party have been prejudiced; or

4.  where the arbitrators exceeded their powers, or so imperfectly executed them that a mutual, final, and definite award upon the subject matter submitted was not made."

Essentially, courts have the ability to overturn the decision of an arbitrator (referred to in the statutes as the "award") when there is a lack of fundamental fairness or due process.

The NFLPA, on behalf of Brady argued that the due process and fairness procedures established in the CBA and the NFL rules as well as basic "industrial due process" were violated in the commissioner's handling of this case. In addition, the union argued that the NFL violated the established practices followed by the NFL in the past referred to as "the law of the shop."

Although it was not particularly significant for the court's rulings, it is interesting to note that nowhere in the NFL's Wells Report or rulings was there any direct evidence that Tom Brady was involved in any manner in the deflating of footballs. The farthest that the Wells Report went was to say, "it is more probable than not that Tom Brady (the quarterback of the Patriots) was at least generally aware of the inappropriate activities of McNally and Jastremski involving the release of air from Patriots game balls."

Much had been made about the refusal of Tom Brady to provide his cell phone although in a telephone press conference, Ted Wells said, that Brady "answered every question I put to him. He did not refuse to answer any questions in terms of the back and forth between Mr. Brady and my team. He was totally cooperative." "And I want to be crystal clear. I told Mr. Brady and his agents, I was willing not to take possession of the phone. I said, 'I don't want to see any private information.' I said, 'Keep the phone. You and the agent, Mr. Yee, you can look at the phone. You give me documents that are responsible to this investigation and I will take you at your word that you have given me what's responsive.' And they still refused."[10]

The refusal to provide the phone, upon advice of counsel, was a normal disagreement regarding the extent of the authority of the Commissioner's office to demand the phone. As for the destroying of the phone, it was acknowledged that Brady on a regular basis cycled his phones and for understandable security reasons destroyed the older phones. However, what often went unsaid as this case played out in the media was that Brady's attorneys offered the Commissioner to provide the names of everyone with whom Brady had communicated with on his phone with the Commissioner then able to compel a search of those phones for text messages from Brady. The NFL did not have a right pursuant to league rules and the CBA to the contents of Brady's phone and Brady, under advice of counsel exercised his right to refuse the request for his phone. Ironically when the NFL hired former FBI director Robert Mueller to investigate the league's handling of the Ray Rice domestic abuse case Commissioner Goodell refused to provide his personal cell phone to Mueller.

The basis for the NFLPA arguments against the NFL's actions against Brady included the inappropriateness of punishing Brady

---

[10] "Transcript of Ted Wells conference call," Boston Herald, Adam Kurkjian, May 12, 2015.

under a new standard of culpability defined as "general awareness" of alleged misconduct of others as a basis for punishing Brady; the inability to suspend Brady since the league's player policy for actions related to tampering with the football would have been limited to a fine; the use of the league's Competitive Integrity Policy as a basis for punishing Brady where that policy only applies to individual teams and not players; and that even if Brady were deemed to have been guilty of non-cooperation, a response to non-cooperation had previously only been fines and not suspensions.

The NFL Players Association's appeal on behalf of Tom Brady was heard initially by Judge Richard Berman in the Federal District Court for the Southern District of New York 15 Civ. 5916 and 15 Civ. 5982 (2015).

On September 3, 2015 Judge Berman overturned the ruling of Commissioner Goodell.

Judge Berman wrote, "The Court is fully aware of the deference afforded to arbitral decisions, but nevertheless, concludes that the Award should be vacated. The award is premised upon several significant legal deficiencies, including (A) inadequate notice to Brady of both his potential discipline (four game suspension) and his alleged misconduct; (B) denial of the opportunity for Brady to examine one of two lead investigators, namely NFL Executive Vice President and General Counsel, Jeff Pash; and (c) denial of equal access to investigative files including witness interview notes."

"The Court finds that Brady had no notice that he could receive a four-game suspension for general awareness of ball deflation by others or participation in any scheme to deflate footballs, and non-cooperation with the ensuing Investigation. Brady also had not notice that his discipline would be the equivalent of the discipline imposed upon a player who used performance enhancing drugs."

Judge Berman noted how "rightly or wrongly, a sharp change in sanctions or discipline can often be seen as arbitrary and as an impediment rather than an instrument of change."

Judge Berman further noted "It is the 'law of the shop' to provide professional football players with (advance) notice of prohibited conduct and of potential discipline." Judge noted as precedent for this position a 1991 case involving Cleveland Brown wide receiver Reggie Langhorne who refused to accept assignment to the team practice squad and, as a result, was heavily fined without any notice that his actions could result in such a fine. Coincidentally, the coach of the Cleveland Browns at that time was Bill Belichick.

Judge Berman concluded "Brady had no notice that such conduct was prohibited, or any reasonable certainty of potential discipline stemming from such conduct."

Additionally, Judge Berman also ruled that the Commissioner's denying of Brady's lawyer the opportunity to question Jeff Pash, the co-lead investigator of the report, which Judge Berman referred to as the Wells-Pash Investigation seriously prejudiced Brady as did the refusal of Commissioner Goodell to have access to the files used in the preparation of the supposedly independent Pash-Wells Investigation while the NFL was given full access to those files. Judge Berman wrote that "Commissioner Goodell had 'the affirmative duty. . . to insure that relevant documentary evidence in the hands of one party is fully and timely made available to the other party."

Following Judge Berman's decision in favor of Tom Brady, the NFL, in turn, appealed Judge Berman's decision to a three judge panel of the Federal Second Circuit Court of Appeals and its appeal was successful as by a vote of 2–1 the panel voted to reinstate the NFL's punishment of Tom Brady.

The opinion of the court reinforced that arbitration done in accordance with the terms and provisions of the CBA is given extreme deference. NFL Management Council v. NFLPA et al, 820 F. 3d. 527 (2016) As Judge Parker wrote in the majority opinion, "The basic principle driving both our analysis and our conclusion is well established: a federal court's review of labor arbitration awards is narrowly circumscribed and highly deferential—indeed, among the most deferential in the law. Our role is not to determine for ourselves whether Brady participated in a scheme to deflate footballs or whether the suspension imposed by the Commissioner should have been for three games or five games or none at all. Nor is it our role to second-guess the arbitrator's procedural rulings. Our obligation is limited to determining whether the arbitration proceedings and award met the minimum legal standards established by the Labor Management Relations Act, 29 U.S.C. section 141 et seq. (the 'LMRA'). We must simply ensure that the arbitrator was 'even arguably construing or applying the contract and acting within the scope of his authority' and did not 'ignore the plain language of the contract.' United Paperworks Int'l Union v. Misco, Inc., 484 U.S. 29, 38 (1987). These standards do not require perfection in arbitration awards. Rather, they dictate that even if an arbitrator makes mistakes of fact or law, we may not disturb an award so long as he acted within the bounds of his bargained-for authority."

The rules for arbitration are generally provided for as a part of the Collective Bargaining Agreement and consequently, the standards to be followed and the respective authority of the parties involved can vary considerably from what may be the standards in other CBAs. In the NFL CBA the powers of the Commissioner in this regard were quite broad. As the Court wrote in its opinion:

"Here the authority was especially broad. The commissioner was authorized to impose discipline for, among other things 'conduct detrimental to the integrity of, or public confidence, in the game of professional football.' In their collective bargaining agreement, the players and the League mutually decided many years ago that the Commissioner should investigate possible rule violations, should impose appropriate sanctions, and may preside at arbitrations challenging his discipline. Although this tripartite regime may appear unorthodox, it is the regime bargained for and agreed upon by the parties, which we can only presume they determined was mutually satisfactory."

The Court went on to say that Article 46 of the Collective Bargaining Agreement "gives the Commissioner broad authority to deal with conduct he believes might undermine the integrity of the game. The Commissioner properly understood that a series of rules relating to uniforms and equipment does to repeal his authority vested in him by the Association to protect professional football from detrimental conduct."

In responding to the Judge Berman's initial decision that the NFL's refusal to allow its General Counsel Jeff Pash to testify at the arbitration concerning his role in the preparation of the Wells Report was reversible error, the judge wrote "It is well settled that procedural questions that arise during arbitration, such as which witnesses to hear and which evidence to receive or exclude, are left to the sound discretion of the arbitrator and should not be second guessed by the courts." This reflects a common position taken by many courts that arbitrators have immense discretion in the determination of the rules of evidence they will follow so long as they are acting consistent with the terms of the arbitration as set out in the CBA.

In the last paragraph of the judges' opinion they dealt with the issue of the alleged lack of impartiality of the Commissioner in ruling in this case and again looked at the case through the provisions of the CBA saying "Here, the parties contracted in the CBA to specifically allow the Commissioner to sit as the arbitrator in all disputes brought pursuant to Article 46, Section 1(a). They did so knowing full well that the Commissioner had the sole power of determining what constitutes 'conduct detrimental,' and thus knowing that the Commissioner would have a stake both in the underlying discipline and in every arbitration brought pursuant to Section 1(a). Had the parties wished to restrict the Commissioner's authority they could have fashioned a different agreement."

Essentially what the judges said to the NFLPA was that you made your bed and now you have to lie in it. It certainly can be expected that the power of the Commissioner to act in future arbitrations will be an issue that the players' union will want to revisit.

The dissenting judge at the appeals court was Chief Justice Robert Katzmann who wrote:

"Article 46 of the Collective Bargaining Agreement between the NFL Players Association (the 'Association') and the NFL Management Council requires the Commissioner to provide a player with notice of the basis for any disciplinary action and an opportunity to challenge the discipline in an appeal hearing. When the Commissioner, acting in his capacity as an arbitrator, changes the factual basis for the disciplinary action after the appeal hearing concludes, he undermines the fair notice for which the Association bargained, deprives the player of an opportunity to confront the case against him, and, it follows, exceeds his limited authority under the CBA to decide 'appeals' of disciplinary decisions."

"Additionally, on a more fundamental level, I am troubled by the Commissioner's decision to uphold the unprecedented four-game suspension. The Commissioner failed to even consider a highly relevant alternative penalty and relied, instead, on an inapt analogy to the League's steroid policy. This deficiency, especially when viewed in combination with the shifting rationale for Brady's discipline, leaves me to conclude that the Commissioner's decision reflected 'his own brand of industrial justice.' United Steelworkers of Am. v. Enter. Wheel & Car Corp., 363 U.S. 593, 597 (1960)."

"With regard to the first step, Article 46 of the CBA vests the Commissioner with exceptional discretion to impose discipline for 'conduct detrimental,' but it checks that power by allowing the player to challenge that discipline through an 'appeal.' Joint App. at 345–46. IN deciding the appeal, the arbitrator may decide whether the misconduct charged actually occurred, whether it was actually 'detrimental' to the League, and whether the penalty imposed is permissible under the CBA. But the arbitrator has no authority to base his decision on misconduct different from that originally charged. When he does so, the arbitrator goes beyond his limited authority, and the award should be vacated."

In particular, Judge Katzmann referred to the Commissioner's consideration of allegations that first appeared in the Commissioner's appeal decision, but not in the Wells report about Brady providing "inducements and rewards" supporting a scheme by Patriots' personnel to tamper with the game balls which he found to be a material change as to the alleged misconduct of Brady. Judge Katzmann indicated in his dissent that he believed the Commissioner exceeded his authority when he based the discipline ordered on facts not included in the Wells report.

Judge Katzmann also went on to deal with the issue of the punishment saying:

"Yet, the Commissioner failed to even mention, let alone explain, a highly analogous penalty, an omission that underscores the peculiar nature of Brady's punishment. The League prohibits the use of stickum, a substance that enhances a player's grip. Under a collectively bargained-for Schedule of Fines, a violation of this prohibition warrants an $8,268 fine in the absence of aggravating circumstances. Given that both the use of stickum and the deflation of footballs involve attempts at improving one's grip and evading the referees' enforcement of the rules, they would seem a natural starting point for assessing Brady's penalty. Indeed, the League's justification for prohibiting stickum—that it 'affects the integrity of the competition and an give a team an unfair advantage,' Joint App. at 384 (League Policies for Players)—is nearly identical to the Commissioner's explanation for what he found problematic about the deflation—that it 'reflects an improper effort to secure a competitive advantage in, and threatens the integrity, of, the game,' Special App. at 57.

Notwithstanding these parallels, the Commissioner ignored the stickum penalty entirely. This oversight leaves a noticeable void in the Commissioner's decision, and in my opinion, the void is indicative of the ward's overall failure to draw its essence from the CBA."

"In sum, the Commissioner's failure to discuss the penalty for violations of the prohibitions on stickum, the Commissioner's strained reliance on the penalty for violations of the League's steroid policy, and the Commissioner's shifting rationale for Brady's discipline, together, leave me with the firm conviction that his decision in the arbitration appeal was based not on his interpretation of the CBA, but on 'his own brad of industrial justice.' Enter. Wheel & Car Corp., 363 U.S. at 597."

In the concluding paragraphs of his dissent, Judge Katzmann wrote:

"The Commissioner's authority is, as the majority emphasizes, broad. But it is not limitless, and its boundaries are defined by the CBA. Here, the CBA grants the Commissioner in his capacity as arbitrator only the authority to decide 'appeals,' that is whether the initial disciplinary decision was erroneous. The Commissioner exceeded that limited authority when he decided instead that Brady could be suspended for four games based on misconduct found for the first time in the Commissioner's decision. This breach of the limits on the Commissioner's authority is exacerbated by the unprecedented and virtually unexplained nature of the penalty imposed. Confirming the arbitral award under such circumstances neither enforces the intent of the parties nor furthers the 'federal policy that federal courts should enforce [arbitration] agreements. . . and that industrial peace can best be obtained only in that way.' Textile Workers Union of Am. v. Lincoln Mills of Ala., 353 U.S. 448, 455 (1957).

I end where I began. The Article 46 appeals process is designed to provide a check against the Commissioner's otherwise unfettered authority to impose discipline for 'conduct detrimental.' But the Commissioner's murky explanation of Brady's discipline undercuts the protections for which the NFLPA bargained on Brady's and others' behalf. It is ironic that a process designed to ensure fairness to all players has been used unfairly against one player."

Somewhat ironically, in the Fall of 2016, the New York Giants complained to the NFL offices that balls used by the Pittsburgh Steelers in a game against the Giants on December 4, 2016 were underinflated. In this case, no action was taken by the NFL Commissioner's office ostensibly because control of the balls was done by the referees, however, it also could be considered a tacit admission that indeed, as many scientists had concluded balls naturally deflate in colder temperatures and there was no evidence of wrongdoing by the NE Patriots in general and Tom Brady in particular in regard to the Deflategate game, particularly when there were no pregame measurements of the balls in the Patriots' game against the Colts to compare against the balls deemed to be underinflated during the course of the first half of that game.

# SYNOPSIS

1.    Antitrust laws prohibit agreements or practices that restrict business competition to the detriment of consumers.

2.    The first antitrust law was the Sherman Antitrust Act of 1890 that prohibits monopolies that harm consumers. The law prohibits agreements or practices that unduly restrict free competition between businesses.

3.    The Clayton Act of 1914 exempted labor unions from being considered monopolies even though they regulate working conditions.

4.    The Norris LaGuardia Act of 1932 permits employees to organize as a collective bargaining unit without violating the law.

5.    Under the *per se* rule, a labor practice is considered a violation of antitrust law if it is as inherently unreasonable restraint of trade.

6.    The rule of reason is another standard for determining antitrust violations by which the anti-competitive aspects of a particular practice are balanced against the pro-competitive benefits.

7.   Collective bargaining requires management and unions to negotiate in good faith on matters of compensation and working conditions.

8.   Professional sports will always be susceptible to claims that they are in violation of antitrust laws because they are generally monopolies.

9.   Not all monopolies are violations of antitrust law.

10.  The Supreme Court ruling that determined that professional baseball was exempt from antitrust laws has never been overturned by the Supreme Court.

11.  The Supreme Court upheld the constitutionality of the reserve clause in the 1953 case of Toolson v. New York Yankees.

12.  The Reserve Clause was successfully challenged in the arbitration hearing of MLB pitcher Andy Messersmith.

13.  The federal court ruling on the dispute commonly known as Deflategate was determined solely on the applicability of the arbitration rules used without any consideration of whether or not balls were tampered with.

14.  In the case of NCAA v. Board of Regents of the University of Oklahoma, 468 U.S. 85 (1984) the Supreme Court ruled that the NCAA rules limiting televised coverage of football games was a violation of antitrust law.

15.  The NFL's Rozelle rule was successfully challenged by NFL players, however, a modified version of the rule was included in the next collective bargaining agreement between the players and NFL owners.

16.  Age limits set by professional sports leagues limiting when an athlete may play professional sports have been upheld in litigation against professional sports leagues.

# Professional Sports Contracts

All of the major professional sports leagues have standard contracts with terms primarily determined through the Collective Bargaining Agreements negotiated with their respective players' unions. Many of the terms of the standard contracts for the NBA, MLB, NFL and NHL are similar; however, there are some striking differences as well. In addition, permissible variations are allowed with limitations for the contracts of individual players in each league.

## NBA

The National Basketball Association (NBA) first signed a Collective Bargaining Agreement (CBA) with the players' union, the NBA Players Association in 1968. Many of the provisions of the standard NBA Uniform Players Contract are determined by the CBA.

## NBA STANDARD CONTRACT

The length of the contract may be for a single season or multiple years although it is unusual for a contract length to exceed ten years. Under the terms of the standard contract, the team is responsible for the costs of room, board and travel expenses on the road. It is common for teams to have a clause requiring a player to be in good physical condition. Most often this includes weight restrictions. This provision was used most notably when Vin Baker's contract was terminated in 2004 by the Boston Celtics for his failure to keep himself in first-class condition as required by a term of the standard NBA contract. At the time that the Celtics terminated Baker's contract, he had 2 ½ years remaining on his contract with 35 million dollars of salary remaining. Baker had been suspended previously for violating the terms of his alcohol treatment program. The position of the Celtics was based upon Baker's alcoholism. The termination of the contract was appealed by the NBA Players Association and the case was settled prior to arbitration under terms not disclosed.

If a player is compelled to retire due to medical reasons, the balance of his contract is required to be paid although the payment of the salary is generally covered by insurance.

## QUESTIONS

1.     Is alcoholism a disease such that it should not qualify as a basis for terminating a player's contract for failing to maintain himself in good physical condition?

2.     Should the failure of a player to maintain himself in good physical condition as grounds for termination of a contract be limited to an intentional failure or neglect by the player?

# NO TRADE CLAUSES

Although in theory the NBA allows no trade clauses, only players who have played in the NBA eight years of which four are with their present club are eligible for no trade clauses in their contracts and even then only when the clause is negotiated into a new contract as compared with a contract extension. It is for this reason that in a league with 446 players only six qualified under this standard in 2015. Another 22 players qualified for no trade clauses under a specific exception written into the most recent Collective Bargaining Agreement (CBA) that provides for a restricted free agent to be able to negotiate a no trade clause in his contract, but even then only for the first year of a new contract. However, as is obvious from these numbers, particularly when you consider that the average NBA career is only five years in duration, no trade clauses are not common by any means in the NBA.

## QUESTION

1.    Do the conditions required to qualify for a no-trade clause in an NBA player's contract render no-trade clauses meaningless?

# CONDUCT

Section 5 of the standard player's contract entitled "Conduct" has numerous interesting provisions including the following:

"(b) the Player agrees: (i) to give his best services, as well as his loyalty to the Team, and to play basketball only for the Team and its assignees; (ii) to be neatly and fully attired in public; (iii) to conduct himself on and off the court according to the highest standards of honesty, citizenship and sportsmanship; and (iv) not to do anything that is materially detrimental or materially prejudicial to the best interests of the Team or the League."

"(e) The Player agrees that if the Commissioner, in his sole judgment, shall find that the Player has bet, or has offered or attempted to bet, money or anything of value on the outcome of any game participated in by any team which is a member of the NBA, the Commissioner shall have the power in his sole discretion to suspend the player indefinitely or to expel him as a player for any member of the NBA, and the Commissioner's finding and decision shall be final, binding, conclusive and unappealable."

It is interesting to note in Section 5(b) that the standards to which the player must adhere are quite subjective, such as the standard of the highest standards of sportsmanship, however, Section 17 of the standard contract provides that any disputes arising between the player and the team as a result of differing interpretation of the contract will be resolved through arbitration as provided for in the

CBA. It is further interesting to note, however, that when it comes to allegations of gambling, the Commissioner can make a determination as to whether a violation of the contract has occurred in his sole judgment and then, with not uncommon legalese, this power is reinforced and emphasized through the use of the description of the Commissioner's determination as being "final, binding, conclusive and unappealable." Gambling and particularly the specter of "point shaving" and the "fixing" of games is considered by the NBA to be such a threat to the integrity of the game, that the Commissioner's authority is absolute on this matter.

All professional sports leagues and teams are exceedingly conscious of public relations and their public image. In the NBA a player can be fined for making a statement deemed to be detrimental to the best interests of basketball or the NBA. Players also can be fined for publicly criticizing another player, coach, arena's sponsors or advertisers.

## QUESTIONS

1.    What is the justification for the determination of the Commissioner in regard to an individual player being guilty of gambling to be unappealable?

2.    Do rules limiting players' rights to make statements critical of other players, coaches, arena sponsors or advertisers violate the players' rights of free speech pursuant to the First Amendment to the United States Constitution?

# PROHIBITED ACTIVITIES

The standard contracts for all professional sports contain provisions prohibiting players from participating in certain activities that can pose a substantial risk to the player of harm that could result in his inability to play his sport and the standard NBA contract is no exception. Section 12 of the NBA standard contract provides:

"The Player and the team acknowledge and agree the Player's participation in certain other activities may impair or destroy his ability and skill as a basketball player, and the Player's participation in any game or exhibition of basketball other than at the request of the Team may result in injury to him. Accordingly, the Player agrees that he will not, without the written consent of the Team, engage in any activity that a reasonable person would recognize as involving or exposing the participant to a substantial risk of bodily injury including, but not limited to: (i) sky-diving, hang gliding, snow skiing, rock or mountain climbing (as distinguished from hiking), rappelling, and bungee jumping; (ii) any fighting, boxing, or wrestling; (iii) driving or riding on a motorcycle or moped; (iv) riding in or on any motorized vehicle in any kind of race or racing contest; (v) operating an aircraft of any kind; (vi) engaging in any other activity excluded or prohibited by or under any insurance policy which the Team procures against injury, illness or disability to or of the Player, or death of the Player, for which the Player has received written notice from the Team prior to the execution of this Contract; . . . Nothing contained herein shall be intended to require the Player to obtain the written consent of the Team in order to enable the Player to participate in, as an amateur, the sports of golf, tennis, handball, swimming, hiking, softball, volleyball, and other similar sports that a reasonable person would not recognize as involving or exposing the participant to a substantial risk of bodily injury."

Notably, Michael Jordan while with the Chicago Bulls had a provision in his contact, often referred to as a "love of the game" clause that allowed him to play in any basketball games he wished.

## QUESTIONS

1. Are the rules of the NBA and other sports leagues in restricting participation in activities deemed to be risky excessive and a violation of the players' personal liberty and privacy?

2. What is the justification for such rules?

# PROMOTIONAL ACTIVITIES

All professional sports are forms of entertainment. Public relations and image are an essential part of these businesses. Therefore the standard NBA contract provides for specific duties of the player to participate in promotional activities. Section 13 of the standard NBA contract provides as follows:

"(c) Upon request, the Player shall consent to and make himself available for interviews by representatives of the media conducted at reasonable times.

(d)   In addition to the foregoing. . . the Player agrees to participate, upon request, in all other reasonable promotional activities of the Team, the NBA, and any League-related entity. For each such promotional appearance made on behalf of a commercial sponsor of the Team, the Team agrees to pay the Player $2,500 or, if the Team agrees, such higher amount that is consistent with the team's past practice and not otherwise unreasonable."

## QUESTIONS

1.   Is the requirement of a player to give interviews to the media a violation of his individual rights particularly when limitations are placed on the player's speech?

2.   Should a player's duty to his team pursuant to his contract be limited merely to playing and not require that he perform promotional activities on behalf of the team?

# TERMINATION

Although the standard NBA contract may not be terminated by the team for any reason not specifically provided for in the CBA or no reason, as may be done with NFL contracts, the standard NBA contract still provides the teams with broad authority to terminate contracts of their players. Section 13 of the standard NBA contract provides:

"(a) The Team may terminate this Contract upon written notice to the Player if the Player shall:

(i)    At any time, fail, refuse or neglect to conform his personal conduct to standards of good citizenship, good moral character (defined here to mean not engaging in acts of moral turpitude, whether or not such acts would constitute a crime), and good sportsmanship, to keep himself in first class physical condition or to obey the Team's training rules:

(ii)   at any time commit a significant and inexcusable physical attack against any official or employee of the Team or the NBA (other than another player) or any person in attendance at any NBA game or event, considering the totality of the circumstances, including (but not limited to) the degree of provocation (if any) that may have led to the attack, the nature and scope of the attack, the Player's state of mind at the time of the attack, and the extent of any injury resulting from the attack:

(iii)  at any time, fail in the sole opinion of the Team's management to exhibit sufficient skill or competitive ability to qualify to continue as a member of the Team; . . ."

Subsection (i) is what is commonly referred to in entertainment and sports contracts as a "morals clause" which is generally a broadly worded contract provision that enables the employer to terminate the contract of the employee for conduct that includes conduct that is not related to the employee's performance of his job. Because of the perceived importance of public approval of sports and media personalities to the financial success of their employers, these contract provisions are quite common. Employers want them written as broadly as possible while employees want them written as narrowly as possible, particularly when it comes to interpreting the vague, but commonly used term "moral turpitude." This term is generally understood to mean an offense that is considered morally reprehensible instead of merely being a technical infraction of civil or criminal law. The interpretation of the term differs from era to era and locality to locality. Where at one time a drunk driving offense was considered a crime of moral turpitude it is unlikely that such an interpretation would be upheld today. Crimes of a sexual nature, such as rape or child abuse would, by today's standards, certainly qualify as conduct that constitutes moral turpitude. It is important to note that the standard NBA contract does not require that the acts of moral turpitude ultimately result in a criminal conviction for such conduct to be considered a violation of the contract which could result in the termination of the contract.

## QUESTIONS

1.   Are the rights of the team to terminate a player's contract as provided for in Section 13(a)(i) too broad? Are these rights fair?

2.   Are the rights of the team to terminate a player's contract as provided for in section 13(a)(iii) too broad and too subjective?

# MISCONDUCT

The standard NBA player contract incorporates specific provisions of the NBA constitution into section 35 of the standard player contract including:

"(c) If in the opinion of the Commissioner any act or conduct of a Player at or during an Exhibition, Regular Season, or Playoff game has been prejudicial to or against the best interests of the Association or the game of basketball, the Commissioner shall impose upon such Player a fine not exceeding $50,000 or may order for a time the suspension of any such Player from any connection or duties with Exhibition, Regular Season, or Playoff games, or he may order both such fine and suspension.

(d) The Commissioner shall have the power to suspend for a definite or indefinite period, or to impose a fine not exceeding $50,000, or inflict both such suspension and fine upon any Player who, in his opinion, (i) shall have made or caused to be made any statement having or that was designed to have, an effect prejudicial or detrimental to the best interests of basketball of the Association or of a Member, or (ii) shall have been guilty of conduct that does not conform to standards of morality or fair play, that does not comply at all times with all federal, state, and local laws, or that is prejudicial or detrimental to the Association."

# NBA RULES

The NBA rules which apply to how the game is played also govern player conduct during the course of a game. Among the rules are:

"e.  Cursing or blaspheming an official shall not be considered the only cause for imposing technical fouls. Running tirades, continuous criticism or griping may be sufficient cause to assess a technical. Excessive misconduct shall result in ejection from the game."

The rules do not provide guidance as to the proper amount of misconduct before it can result in ejection from the game. It also is interesting to note the elevated position that officials are given by the rules since blasphemy is generally defined as speaking irreverently of God.

# COMPENSATION

Bonuses can be a significant part of a player's compensation. Although bonuses are not allowed for winning a particular game or series, teams often include bonuses in players' contracts for total wins for the season or the team's final position in the league standings.

# TEAM RULES

In addition to rules established by the league, individual teams will also have rules and policy handbooks consistent with the CBA that deal with matters such as attendance at practices, personal grooming, manner of dress, treatments of injuries, travel logistics, complementary game tickets, curfew, personal conditioning, violence, drugs and gambling.

A typical provision found in one team's policy handbook provides that trips over an hour will be by airplane and first class when available. "On trips under one hour or when it is more feasible and deemed necessary to take a bus, we shall do so. Anyone objecting this will be subjected to a fine. NO COMPLAINTS WILL BE TOLERATED."

By team policy, wives, girlfriends or other friends in general are not permitted to travel with the team during the regular season and guests including spouses may stay in hotel rooms while the team is playing on the road without advance permission of the head coach. For one team, violation of the overnight guest rule carries the ridiculously low fine of $50.

A typical curfew provision found in NBA team rules is 12:30 a.m. on the night before a game. If there is more than a day between games, the curfew is 2:30 a.m.

## QUESTION

1.   Are curfews for professional athletes an unreasonable restraint of their personal liberty?

# SALARY CAP

The NBA like the NFL, MLB and NHL has a salary cap that is incorporated into the Collective Bargaining Agreement (CBA), however, unlike the NFL salary cap which must be rigidly adhered to by each team, the NBA salary cap is riddled with exceptions which in theory are intended to make it easier for teams to keep their own stars under contract. Among the many exceptions are the mid-level exception which allows a team the ability to sign one player to a contract equal to the average NBA salary even if the contract would put the team over the salary cap; the Larry Bird exception which allows a team to exceed the salary cap to resign its own free agents for the maximum league salary for up to five years; the early bird exception for which free agents qualify after playing two years without changing teams; the nonbird exception which allows teams to resign players to contracts for as long as 6 years at 120% of their previous year's salary or 120% of the league minimum salary, whichever is greater; the traded player exception and the disabled player exception. And even after utilizing all of these exceptions, a team may still exceed the salary cap so long as it pays a luxury tax to the league.

The determination of the salary cap is made based upon the NBA's Basketball Related Income (BRI) which includes national television rights and other sources of revenue. Under the present CBA the players receive between 49% and 51% of the BRI depending upon if the BRI either exceeds or falls short of projections. Under the former CBA, the players received 57% of BRI.

A common misconception is that all teams in the NBA pay their players the full amount of the salary cap. In recent years financially strapped teams paid somewhat less. Under the present CBA, however, all teams are required to spend at least 90% of the salary cap on players' salaries. Just as some teams spent under the salary cap, other teams, most commonly, the New York Knicks, the Los Angeles Lakers and the Dallas Mavericks, even after considering all of the various exceptions, still exceeded the salary cap. Unlike the NFL where a team is not permitted to exceed the salary cap, in the NBA, a team exceeding the salary cap is merely required to pay a luxury tax of one dollar for every one dollar their salaries exceed the luxury tax threshold.

In the 2015–2016 NBA season the salary cap was 70 million dollars and the luxury tax threshold was 84.74 million dollars. During the previous season, by far the largest luxury tax was paid by the Brooklyn Nets who paid $19,978,360 as a luxury tax to the league. The other teams paying a luxury tax in the 2014–2015 NBA season were the Cleveland Cavaliers, the Indiana Pacers, the New York Knicks and the Oklahoma City Thunder.

NBA salaries increased dramatically during the 2016 off season due to dramatically increased television revenue. ESPN and Turner Broadcasting agreed to pay the NBA 24 billion dollars for a nine year contract which was an increase of approximately 180% over the previous broadcasting rights contract. This is due partly to the popularity of NBA basketball, but also reflects the value of live sporting events which are among the few television shows that are consistently watched live with their attendant commercials rather than recorded or watched in some other format where commercials may be deleted. With a salary cap projected to be 107 million dollars for the 2017–2018 season primarily due to the increased television revenues and teams being required to spend at least 90% of the cap on players' salaries, free agent contacts are soaring for even players not considered to be among the NBA elite as exemplified by the 153 million dollar five year contract of Mike Conley of the Memphis Grizzlies.

# MAJOR LEAGUE BASEBALL

Major League Baseball is the oldest of the American professional sports and has a long history both on the field and in the courtrooms. The present Uniform Player's Contract reflects the most recent CBA between Major League Baseball and the player's union.

# UNIFORM PLAYER'S CONTRACT FOR MLB

An interesting provision found in the uniform player's contract is found in section 3.(a) entitled Loyalty, which reads as follows:

"The Player agrees to perform his services hereunder diligently and faithfully, to keep himself in first-class physical condition and to obey the Club's training rules, and pledges himself to the American public and to the Club to conform to high standards of personal conduct, fair play and good sportsmanship."

The uniform player's contract, similar to the contracts for other professional sports requires the player to cooperate in promotional activities as described in sections 3.(b) and 3.(c). which are entitled respectively Baseball Promotion and Pictures and Public Appearances which read as follows:

"In addition to his services in connection with the actual playing of baseball, the Player agrees to cooperate with the Club and participate in any and all reasonable promotional activities of the Club and Major League Baseball, which, in the opinion of the Club, will promote the welfare of the Club or professional baseball, and to observe and comply with all reasonable requirements of the Club respecting conduct and service of its team and tis players, at all times, whether on or off the field."

"The player agrees that his picture may be taken for still photographs, motion pictures or television at such times as the Club may designate and agrees that all rights in such pictures shall belong to the Club and may be used by the Club for publicity purposes in any manner it desires. The player further agrees that during the playing season he will not make public appearances, participate in radio or television programs or permit his picture to be taken or write or sponsor newspaper or magazine articles or sponsor commercial products without the written consent of the Club, which shall not be withheld except in the reasonable interests of the Club or professional baseball."

Similar to provisions found in other major professional sports contracts, the uniform player's contract requires the player to represent to the Club as to his ability and condition in sections 4.(a) and 4.(b) which read as follows:

"The Player represents and agrees that he has exceptional and unique skill and ability as a baseball player; that his services to be rendered hereunder are of a special, unusual and extraordinary character which gives them peculiar value which cannot be reasonably or adequately compensated for in damages at law, and that the player's breach of this contract will cause the Club great and irreparable injury and damage. The player agrees that, in addition to other remedies the Club shall be entitled to injunctive and other equitable relief to prevent a breach of this Contract by the player, including among others, the right to enjoin the Player from playing baseball for any other person or organization during the term of his contract."

"The player represents that he has no physical or mental defects known to him and unknown to the appropriate representative of the Club which would prevent or impair performance of his services."

Also similar to the provisions found in the standard NBA player's contract prohibiting the player from participating in certain other sporting or other activities that could threaten his MLB career, Section 5.(b) provides as follows:

"The Player and the Club recognize and agree that the player's participation in certain other sports may impair or destroy his ability and skill as a baseball player. Accordingly, the Player agrees that he will not engage in professional boxing or wrestling; and that, except with the written consent of the Club, he will not engage in skiing, auto racing, motorcycle racing, sky diving, or in any game or exhibition of football, soccer, professional league basketball, ice hockey or other sport involving a substantial risk of personal injury."

The uniform player's contract also provides for the conditions under which the Club may terminate the contract in section 7.(b) which reads as follows:

"The Club may terminate this contract upon written notice to the Player (but only after requesting and obtaining waivers of this contract from all other Major League Clubs) if the Player shall at any time:

(1) Fail, refuse or neglect to conform his personal conduct to the standards of good citizenship and good sportsmanship or to keep

himself in first-class physical condition or to obey the Club's training rules; or

(2) Fail in the opinion of the Club's management, to exhibit sufficient skill or competitive ability to qualify or continue as a member of the Club's team; or

(3) Fail refuse or neglect to render his services hereunder or in any other manner materially breach this contract."

Interestingly, section 7.(c) provides that if a player's contract is terminated by the Club, "the Player shall be entitled to receive an amount equal to the reasonable traveling expenses of the Player, including first-class jet air fare and meals en route, to his home city."

# NO TRADE CLAUSES

Unlike the NBA, major league baseball teams may include no trade clauses in their contracts although they are certainly not the norm. A no trade clause can be earned by a player through ten years of service in MLB with at least the last five with his current team or it can be negotiated by any player and his Club into their contract. MLB players also sometimes negotiate limited no trade clauses indicating the teams to which the player could not be traded and the ones to which the player would agree to be traded. Certainly players are desirous of the security provided by being able to refuse to be traded to a team in another city and having to uproot their families. The no trade clause also provides the player with leverage to get more money if his present team wishes to trade him. In 2010, Toronto Blue Jays pitcher Roy Halladay used such leverage by only agreeing to a trade to the Philadelphia Phillies if they would give him a three year sixty million dollar contract extension.

## QUESTIONS

1. Should all players have the right to no trade clauses in their contracts?

2.    If a player signs a contract to play for a particular team, should the team have to get his permission to trade him to another team?

# COMPENSATION

In addition to their basic salaries, MLB players' contracts will often have bonus provisions. Late in his career, pitcher Roger Clemens' contract with the Houston Astros included a bonus of 1.4 million dollars based on the Astros season attendance figures. Bonuses for personal performance achievements while common in football are not allowed in professional baseball, however, players can receive bonuses for appearance related matters, such as innings pitched or games played. Award based bonuses such as cash payments for being named to the All Star Team, receiving a Golden Glove award for being an exceptional fielder or votes received in the Most Valuable Player (MVP) balloting are common.

# MLB SALARY ARBITRATION

Salary arbitration was first instituted in 1974 after being negotiated into the Collective Bargaining Agreement. At the time it was considered a major victory for the players with the owners agreeing to it as a way of avoiding, at least for a while, free agency. Owners pay league minimum salaries to players during their first three year contracts. Generally, players with three years of experience, but less than six years of experience at the major league level are eligible to file for salary arbitration. After six years of service, the player becomes a free agent.

At the end of a successful player's initial three year contract, it is not unusual for a player to receive a substantial raise in his next contract. Chris Carter of the Houston Astros received an annual salary of $510,000 in 2014. In 2015, when he became eligible for salary arbitration he signed a contract raising his salary to $4,175,000.

Unlike arbitrators in other situations outside of baseball who generally are free to find a middle ground between the positions of the two sides involved in a dispute, MLB salary arbitrators are required to accept either the salary proposed by the player or the salary proposed by the team. This encourages both sides to make a more reasonable offer in order to avoid having their offers deemed by the arbitrators as too extreme.

The arbitration panel is made up of three arbitrators agreed upon by the team owners and the players' union. According to the standard set in the CBA, the determination of salary by the arbitrators is based upon the "quality of the player's contribution to his club during the past season." In making that determination, the arbitrators consider the following factors:

1. Overall performance—statistical analysis;

2. Length and consistency of the player's career;

3. Record of past compensation;

4. Existence of any physical or mental deficiencies;

5. Leadership qualities and public attraction;

6. Recent performance of the club both in league standings and attendance.

In addition, the arbitrators also compare salaries of other similar players and evidence of special accomplishments of the player in deciding which figure they will rule is correct.

The arbitrators are specifically not permitted to consider the following matters in making their decision:

1. The financial position of the player and the team;

2. Press comments, or testimonials other than recognized annual player awards such as League MVP;

3. Offers made by either side made prior to arbitration;

4. Non baseball salaries.

## QUESTION

1.    Should baseball arbitrators be permitted to consider the financial position of the team in making his or her decision?

———————

Most often, even after filing for arbitration, the team and the player will come to a settlement and avoid the actual arbitration hearing. In 2015 there were only 14 hearings with the owners winning eight times and the players six. Between 1974 when the first salary arbitration hearings were held and 2015 the players won 42.34% of the arbitration hearings and the owners won 57.66%. During that time, the Tampa Bay Rays won 100% of the six salary arbitration hearings with which they were involved while the Detroit Tigers at 30% have the lowest winning percentage for the twenty salary arbitration hearings with which they have been involved.

# NATIONAL HOCKEY LEAGUE

# STANDARD PLAYERS CONTRACT (SPC)

Similar to the contracts for the other major professional sports, the SPC for the National Hockey League (NHL) provides for the player to both cooperate in public relations activities on behalf of the team and comport his personal conduct with league standards. Section 2 reads in part that the player agrees:

"(d) to cooperate with the Club and participate in any and all reasonable promotional activities of the Club which will in the opinion of the Club promote the welfare of the Club and to cooperate in the promotion of the League and professional hockey generally.

(e)    to conduct himself on and off the rink according to the highest standards of honesty, morality, fair play and sportsmanship, and to refrain from conduct detrimental to the best interest of the Club, the League or professional hockey generally."

Section 7 of the SPC also closely mirrors similar provisions found in the standard contracts for other professional sports in regard to prohibited outside activities. It reads as follows:

"7. The Player and the Club recognize and agree that the Player's participation in other sports may impair or destroy his ability and skill as a hockey player. Accordingly the Player agrees that he will not during the period of this SPC or during any period when he is obligated under this SPC to enter into a further SPC with the Club engage or participate in football, baseball, softball, hockey, lacrosse, boxing, wrestling or other athletic sport without the written consent of the Club, which consent will not be unreasonably withheld."

Section 8 of the SPC deals with the player's personal rights of publicity and reads:

"8. (a)    The Club recognizes that the Player owns exclusive rights to his individual personality, including his likeness. The player recognizes that the Club owns exclusive rights to its name, emblems and uniform which the player wears as a hockey player for the Club.

The Player herby irrevocably grants to the Club during the period of this SPC and during any period when he is obligated under this SPC to enter into a further SPC with the Club the right to permit or authorize any firm, person or corporation to take and make use of any still photographs, motion pictures or electronic (including television) images of himself in uniform and agrees that thereafter all rights in such photographs, pictures and images (including the right to identify him by name) shall belong to the Club exclusively for the purposes of telecasts, film or video documentaries or features, advertisements and promotions of the Club's games, use by the media for reportorial purposes, game programs, yearbooks, magazines and the like, and purposes in which the focus is on the Club or game and not the individual Player.

The Club hereby irrevocably grants to the Player during the period of this SPC and thereafter the right to use the name of the Club (but not the emblem or uniform unless otherwise agreed) to identify himself, truthfully, as Player of the Club, past or present."

Section 9 of the SPC deals with bonuses:

"9. It is mutually agreed that the Club will not pay, and the Player will not accept from any person, any bonus or anything of value for winning or otherwise attempting to affect the outcome of any particular game or series of games except as authorized by the League By-Laws."

The NHL rules for bonuses are quite different from those of the other professional sports. Bonuses are only available on entry-level contracts. The length of a player's first contract depends upon the age of the player on September 15th of the year in which he signs his initial NHL contract. If he is between the ages of 18 and 21, his contract is for three years. If he is between the ages of 22 and 23 his contract is for two years. If he is 24 years old when he signs his contract, his contract is for one year. If he is classified as European and between the ages of 25 and 27 his entry level contract is also of a one year duration. Interestingly, the CBA classifies anyone playing hockey outside of North America as European.

Bonuses can either be signing bonuses limited to 10% of the player's overall salary that he receives as an advance of that salary, games played bonuses or performance bonuses. Performance bonuses may include provisions for ice time, goals and plus/minus, which is a measure of how many goals are scored by the player's team as compared to goals allowed by the player's team while the player is on the ice. Under the present CBA total bonuses cannot exceed $850,000.

Although generally contract bonuses paid to the player by his team are limited to entry level contracts, the league itself pays bonuses to the top five players for the various post season awards, such as the Hart, Norris or Vezina awards or if he places in the top ten players in the league in various offensive or goaltending categories. The Hart Trophy is given to the MVP for the regular season; the Norris Trophy is given to the top defenseman for the regular season and the Vezina Trophy is given to the top goalie for the regular season. Further, the individual teams themselves may give bonuses to players for earning these awards.

# CONTRACT TERMINATION

Pursuant to the CBA, section 13 of the SPC provides for the Club to have the ability to terminate the contracts of individual players by putting the player on unconditional waivers and giving him his unconditional release from his contract. This is done by giving the player notice that the team intends to buy-out his contract pursuant to terms provided for in the CBA. The waiver period is limited each year to between June 15th and June 30th unless the start of the period is delayed if the Stanley Cup Final extends beyond June 15th. Slightly different time periods apply if the Club or player had previously selected salary arbitration.

Under the terms of the SPC, the amount that the player is paid is dependent upon his age at the time of the termination of the contract. If the player is less than 26 years old, he gets one third of the compensation remaining on his contract. If the player is 26 years old or older at the time of termination of the contract, he gets two thirds of the compensation remaining on his contract. Upon the contract being terminated, the player immediately becomes an Unrestricted Free Agent and may sign with any other team, however, if while on unconditional waivers another team claims him, his prior team is relieved of the obligation to buy out his contract.

Teams also have the right to terminate a contract if, as provided in section 14 of the SPC if the player shall:

"9. (a)    fail, refuse, or neglect to obey the Club's rules governing training and conduct of Players, if such failure, refusal or neglect should constitute a material breach of this SPC."

Interestingly and quite unique in professional sports to NHL contracts, the final section of the SPC states;

"Les parties ont par les presents exprime leur volonte expresse que ce contrat soit redige en anglais. The parties hereby state their expressed wish that this SPC be drafted in the English language."

---

**QUESTION**

1.    What is the purpose of the final section of the SPC written both in French and in English?

# STANDARD CLUB RULES

Among the more interesting of the Standard Club Rules provided for in the CBA are:

1.    "Alcohol consumption is absolutely prohibited on Club flights, in airports or in any hotel in which the Club is staying, unless specifically authorized by the Head Coach or General Manager. In all other cases, alcohol consumption must be sensible. If a Player has been drinking and has a vehicle with him, the Club shall reimburse him for his cab fare home without questions or retribution."

2.    "Gambling on any NHL Game is prohibited."

5.    "Players are required to wear jackets, ties and dress pants to all Club games and while traveling to and from such games unless otherwise specified by the Head Coach or General Manager."

8.    "Personal agents or personal advisors shall not be permitted in the dressing room at any time."

9.    "The use of tobacco products while in the presence of fans in any arena or while attending any team function is prohibited."

10.   "All members of the media are to be treated with courtesy. Media Regulations agreed to by the NHL and NHLPA must be strictly adhered to."

11.   "Fans are to be treated with respect and courtesy. Autograph requests in the vicinity of Club facilities should not be unreasonably denied."

12. "All Players shall adhere to the Club's curfew policy."

## QUESTION

1. Do the dress requirements and tobacco use requirements improperly infringe upon the individual rights of players?

# PROFESSIONAL FOOTBALL CONTRACTS

Professional football players generally have the shortest careers of all professional athletes. Regardless of whether you accept the figure of 6 years as indicated by the NFL or 3.3 years as indicated by the NFL Players' Association, it is still a short career. It is a dangerous and violent sport that presents many health risks including risks of injuries that manifest themselves years after a player's career is done. In many basic ways, NFL player contracts are different from those in the NHL, NBA or MLB, most notably in the general absence of guaranteed contracts.

# SALARY CAP

The NFL salary cap came about as a result of the Collective Bargaining Agreement (CBA) signed in 1993 and was made effective for the 1994 season. The initial salary cap in 1994 was 34.6 million dollars. In 2017 this amount had risen to 167 million dollars. A salary cap sets a maximum amount of money that each team can spend on players' contracts during a single season. It is the same amount for each team and is intended to prevent richer teams from outspending less financially strong teams and hiring all of the best players. Since the salary cap is the same for all teams and no team is permitted to go over the salary cap, the competitive balance of the NFL is enhanced. A minimum salary requirement was first put into the 2013 CBA which requires the teams collectively to spend at least 95% of the salary cap amount. If they fail to do so, the shortfall must be paid directly to the players.

The salary cap is calculated each year based upon a percentage of what is referred to in the CBA as "All Revenues" (AR) of the teams during the league year. Under the present CBA, this figure is 48.5%. All Revenues is a slight misnomer since it does not include all sources of revenue for NFL teams and the league, but it does include ticket sales from regular season, preseason and postseason games, which specifically includes the lucrative tickets sale revenues from luxury suites and premium seating. Among the most lucrative revenue sources that also are included in the AR are media contracts including television, radio, Internet, cable and satellite rights. AR also includes merchandise sales and naming rights for stadiums.

For salary cap purposes, a player's salary has three elements. The first is the player's base salary for the year; the second is bonuses received by the player such as signing bonuses and roster bonuses; and the third relates to the performance bonuses the player receives.

Bonuses are amortized over the entire duration of the contract for salary cap purposes. For instance, Andrew Luck, the first pick in the 2012 NFL draft signed a four year contract for 22.1 million dollars of which 14.5 million dollars was a guaranteed bonus. However, for salary cap purposes, his bonus was amortized over the four years of the contract so 3.625 million dollars of the bonus was counted against the Indianapolis Colts' salary cap for each of the four years of his contract. Unlike contracts in other professional sports an NFL player's contract can be terminated at any time with or without cause. Thus a player signing a four year contract is not guaranteed that he will be paid for four years. However, if a player's contract is terminated prior to the end of the contract, the entire amount of the remaining unamortized signing bonus is counted in that year's salary cap which puts the team in the less advantageous position of having less money to spend on players because a portion of its salary cap is allocated to a player not on the team.

If a player chooses to retire with years still remaining on his contract, any remaining unamortized amount of his present contract's signing bonus is included in that year's salary cap. However, it is now common for NFL players' contracts to include a clause informally referred to as the Barry Sanders Rule by which if a player retires or refuses to play for a team, the player is required to repay the portion of his signing bonus attributable to the remaining years on his contract. This provision is named after NFL Hall of Fame running back Barry Sanders who played his entire career for the Detroit Lions, but retired while still at the height of his skills because the Lions would not agree to trade him to a team with better prospects of winning. Two years prior to his retirement, Sanders signed a six year contract with the Lions that included an 11 million dollar signing bonus. Upon his retirement, the Lions demanded that Sanders return 5.5 million dollars of the bonus. An arbitrator ruled that Sanders had to repay the 5.5 million dollars sought by the Lions. Prior to the arbitrator making his ruling, Sanders had offered to return the 5.5 million dollars asked for by the Lions if they would release him from his contract thereby permitting him to sign with the team of his choosing, however, the Lions refused.

Salaries for long term contracts may not include an annual increase in salary for subsequent years of more than 30% over the salary of the previous year. This was done to close the loophole by which teams attempted to avoid the salary cap by backloading contracts and pushing larger amounts of a player's salary to the latter years of his contract.

The 2011 CBA included a rookie salary cap for the first time. Compensation for rookies is based on a combination of the league's salary cap and the Rookie Compensation Pool, which limits the total amount each team can spend on a first year player's salary and initial standard four year contract. The amount each team can spend on rookie contracts is dependent upon their total number of draft picks in the particular year and how high or low those picks are in each round. Thus teams picking earlier in the draft or who have accumulated additional picks through trades are allotted more money for signing rookie players. Each drafted first year player signs a four year contract. Undrafted players may only be signed in their first contract for a maximum of three years which enables an unsigned player who establishes himself in the league to be eligible for free agency sooner.

Unlike other professional sports with salary caps, the NFL salary cap is a "hard cap" which means that no team may exceed the salary cap. Every player contract must be approved by the NFL League Office before it is legally binding. If the NFL League Office determines that a contract would violate the salary cap, it will not be approved. Other professional sports leagues, such as the NBA and MLB operate with "soft caps" which set limits on total salaries that can be avoided either through a myriad of complicated exemptions, as is found in the NBA or luxury taxes found in both the NBA and MLB for teams that choose to exceed the salary cap.

---

**QUESTIONS**

1.    Is the NFL's version of the salary cap responsible for the league perhaps being the most competitive professional sports league?

2.    Does a rookie salary cap unfairly discriminate against first year players?

# CONTRACTS

As with all professional sports, individual contracts must comply with the provisions of the collective bargaining agreement (CBA) negotiated between the player's union and the owners of the teams. As with all professional sports, the CBA sets the terms and conditions of employment of players as well as the rules by which the league operates. Individual player contracts may, however, be amended if done in a manner consistent with the collective bargaining agreement.

Unlike other professional sports contracts, an NFL contract can generally be cancelled by the team at any time for any reason. Therefore a player signing a four year contract is not guaranteed that he will be paid as provided for in the contract for four years. The NFL is the only major professional sports organization that does not guarantee its contracts. The only money guaranteed to the player is his initial signing bonus. It has been estimated that approximately 57% of the compensation paid to NFL players is guaranteed mostly through the payment of signing bonuses although some players with greater bargaining power have negotiated contracts with significant amounts of guaranteed salaries.

In addition, the salaries of NFL players are significantly less than the salaries of Major League Baseball players or NBA players while their average length of career is significantly shorter. Coupled with the fact that their contracts can generally be terminated at any time by the owners without having to pay the remaining years salaries, it is apparent that NFL players are at a distinct disadvantage when it comes to compensation when compared to other professional athletes.

Why is this so?

As with so many questions, the answer is, it is about the money. While the NFL produces the most money of any professional sport, the number of players on each team is considerably more. There are 53 players on an NFL team and with 32 teams in the NFL, the total number of players in the NFL is 1,696. Comparatively, NBA teams are made up of 15 players on 30 teams for a total of 450 players throughout the entire NBA.

During CBA negotiations the owners have steadfastly resisted any discussion of fully guaranteeing contracts and the players' union has not been strong enough to make this an issue during collective bargaining. However, pursuant to the CBA, the contracts of the first nineteen picks in the draft which are four year contracts with an additional option to the team to extend the duration of the contract for one more year are fully guaranteed for the four or five year duration of their initial contract. It is true though that the majority of players are, indeed, effectively playing with one year, unguaranteed contracts.

A major reason for the owners' resistance to guaranteed contracts is the nature of the game. It is a far more violent game than the other professional sports and results in a large number of serious injuries, making owners resistant to signing players to contracts that would pay their players even if they were unable to perform or perform at dramatically reduced levels due to injuries recognized as a part of the game.

## ROOKIE CONTRACTS

The CBA also provides for minimum salaries to be paid to players based upon their time in the NFL. Under the present CBA a rookie's minimum annual salary in 2017 is $465,000. In 2018 it will rise to $480,000. In 2017 the minimum salary for a player with one years of experience in the NFL was $540,000, with two years of experience $615,000, with three years of experience $690,000, with between four and six years of experience $775,000, with between seven and nine years of experience $900,000 and the minimum salary for players with ten or more years of experience was $1,000,000. These figures do not include signing bonuses, roster bonuses or likely to be earned incentives. Pursuant to the CBA, all rookie contracts are for four years. According to the NFL Players Association the average length of the career of an NFL player is only 3.3 years, however according to the NFL League office's statistics based upon the length of career of players who are on the roster on the opening day of the season, the average length of an NFL career is six years. Either way, for the average and even non-average player, a significant portion of his career compensation is tied to the initial contract he signs when his bargaining power is greatly diminished. In addition, teams have an option for a fifth year in the initial contracts of first round draft choices. This option must be exercised by the team after the third year of the contract.

Under the rookie wage rules instituted in the 2011 CBA, the first ten picks in the first round of the draft receive a salary of the average of the top ten players at their position. Picks 11–32 of the first round receive a salary of the average of the pay of the top 3 through 25 players at their position.

The essential format for the standard NFL player's contract is a mere twenty-five paragraphs, however, the devil (or angel, in some circumstances) is in the details and the details about bonuses and performance incentives can be found in addendums to the contract which can add as much as twenty or more pages to the standard contract.

# STANDARD CONTRACT PROVISIONS

The NFL and all professional sports are dependent on media coverage and publicity which is why one standard contract provision found in all NFL player contracts states, "Player will cooperate with the news media and will participate upon request in reasonable activities to promote the Club and the League." The standard contract further provides "Player hereby grants to Club and the League, separately and together, the right and authority to use, and to authorize others to use solely as described below, his name, nickname, initials, likeness, image, picture, photograph, animation, persona, autograph/signature (including facsimiles thereof), voice, biographical information and/or any and all other identifying characteristics (collectively, "Publicity Rights") for any and all uses or purposes that publicize and promote NFL Football, the League or any of its member clubs. . ."

Another particularly important provision found in all NFL player contracts deals with the integrity of the game. It reads, "Player therefore acknowledges his awareness that if he accepts a bribe or agrees to throw or fix an NFL game; fails to promptly report a bribe offer or an attempt to throw or fix an NFL game; bets on an NFL game; knowingly associates with gamblers or gambling activity; uses or provides other players with stimulants or other drugs for the purpose of attempting to enhance on-field performance; or is guilty of any other form of conduct reasonably judged by the League Commissioner to be detrimental to the League. . . The commissioner will have the right. . . to fine player. . . to suspend player. . . or to terminate this contract."

In order to prevent players from participating in activities deemed dangerous that could injure them and cause them to be unable to play professional football, the standard player contract contains a provision that provides that the player will not "engage in any activity other than football which may involve a significant risk of personal injury." Giants' defensive end Jason Pierre-Paul suffered severe hand damage including the loss of a finger in a Fourth of July fireworks accident, however it happened at a time when his contract had tolled and he was in the midst of negotiations with the New York Giants so this contract provision did not apply. Ultimately, he signed a contract in which the largest part of the contract was tied to incentives related to playing time and the number of sacks he records.

Physical conditioning is, of course, a major prerequisite for playing in the NFL and the standard contract specifically provides:

"Player represents to Club that he is and will maintain himself in excellent physical condition. Player will undergo a complete physical examination by the Club physician upon request, during which physical examination Player agrees to make full and complete disclosure of any physical or mental condition known to him which might impair his performance under this contract and to respond fully and in good faith when questioned by the Club physician about such condition. If Player fails to establish or maintain his excellent physical condition to the satisfaction of the Club physician, or make the required full and complete disclosure and good faith responses to the Club physician, then Club may terminate this contract."

The standard contract also provides that if a player is injured during the course of a season and unable to play for the remainder of the season, the team must continue to pay him under his contract for the remainder of the season in which his injury occurs, however, the team can then terminate the remainder of any multi-year contract without owing the player any further compensation.

# BONUSES

Bonuses are the most significant part of an NFL player's compensation largely because few contracts are guaranteed and thus the team can terminate a player's contract at any time during the term of the contract without having to pay the player anything further despite the fact that there may be years left on the player's contract. Bonuses, on the other hand, are guaranteed money generally paid in a lump sum. It is common for many players to be paid the minimum salaries according to their years of service as provided for in the CBA with the vast part of their earnings and potential earnings coming in the form of their bonuses. Thus a large part of an NFL player's compensation comes in the form of incentive bonuses based on either the particular player's specific achievements, team achievements or both.

Bonuses are divided into two categories, namely Likely to be Earned (LBTE) and Not Likely to be Earned (NLTBE). Performance bonuses which are classified as "Likely to be Earned", such as playing in a specific number of games during the season, are included in the team's calculations for purposes determining compliance with the salary cap. Performance bonuses that are earned but were classified as "Not Likely to be Earned" are not included in salary cap calculations for the year in which they are earned, but are subtracted from the team's salary cap for the next season.

Roster bonuses are a common form of NFL bonuses. Merely being on the team at a specific time designated in the contract will trigger the payment of a bonus. Roster bonuses during the off season are the most beneficial to the player. For example, if a player has a bonus that results in a payment if he is on the team on the second day of the

League Year which begins on March first of each year, which is the second day of the free agency period, he is paid a lump sum of money that is his to keep even if he gets cut by the team during the course of the season. This is particularly beneficial to the player because it forces the team to make an often substantial financial commitment to him early in the season, which provides some level of job security. In addition, if the team determines that it is not willing to make such a financial commitment to the player and terminates his contract, it puts the player in a better position to catch on with another team early in the free agency period when teams generally have more money available to sign new players.

Bonuses for participating in off season workout programs serve both the players and the teams. Participation in off season workouts is not mandatory, so by tying participation in these workouts to cash bonuses, the teams induce their players to participate in the workouts and the players get substantial cash payments. For example, in 2016, Julian Edelman of the New England Patriots earned a $250,000 bonus for participating in off season workouts.

A common area of bonuses relates to weight restrictions for lineman as an incentive to them to not put on excessive weight. For example, in 2016 Marcus Cannon of the New England Patriots earned a $100,000 bonus by meeting weight restrictions three times during the 2016 season. Other bonuses may relate to performance such as the number of total catches for a receiver or number of yards rushed for a running back. Examples of this include New England Patriots running back LeGarrette Blount who in 2016 earned an extra $750,000 in bonus payments for meeting nine separate rushing yard bonus levels between 700 yards and 1,100 yards. Blount finished the 2016 season with 1,161 yards rushing. Julian Edelman's 2016 contract provided for a $500,000 bonus if he achieved any of four goals regarding yards receiving, receptions, touchdowns and a Super Bowl title. Edelman achieved three of the four goals and thereby received the $500,000 bonus payment.

Participation in a certain percentage of offensive plays or defensive plays, referred to as snaps is another common criterion for bonuses. In 2016, defensive lineman Alan Branch of the New England Patriots earned $500,000 in bonuses by meeting bonus levels of 50% of defensive snaps for which he received a $250,000 bonus and 55% of defensive snaps for which he received an additional $250,000 bonus. Branch played 59.5% of the Patriots' defensive snaps during the season. Had he played in 65% of the defensive snaps, he would have received another $250,000 bonus.

Coming into the last game of the 2015 NFL season, Dallas Cowboys linebacker Sean Lee merely needed to play in the game to collect a two million dollar bonus tied to his playing in 80% of the Cowboys' defensive snaps. However, Lee, who had a hamstring injury going into the game, chose not to play in the game because he determined he would not have been as effective as he needed to be. According to Lee, "I'm not going to disrespect my teammates and my coaches and be out there not playing the right way."[1] By not playing in the game, the percentage of defensive snaps in which he played for the season dropped to 77% thereby losing him the two million dollar bonus.

# WONDERLIC TEST

The NFL Scouting Combine uses many techniques to evaluate whether a football player has the physical and mental abilities necessary to succeed in the NFL. This information is used by the teams to determine whether or not they will draft a particular college football player and how highly they rate him in regard to his position in the draft. Each year, at the NFL's Scouting Combine, players seeking to be chosen in the NFL draft undergo tests of their physical abilities including a 40 yard dash, bench press, vertical jump and broad jump, but also tests of their mental abilities, most notably through the Wonderlic test. The Wonderlic test is a test of cognitive

---

[1]   "Sean Lee gives up $2 million because playing injured wasn't fair to his team" Mark Sandritter, sbnation, January 3, 2016.

ability that was developed in the 1930s by Eldon Wonderlic and used by many companies to help predict successful job performance. It first was used by the Dallas Cowboys in the 1960s and later by the then Baltimore Colts. By the late 1970s most NFL teams used the test and in 2007 it became a standard test administered to all prospective NFL players at the NFL Scouting Combine. The test does not relate to football knowledge and is not a math test or reading comprehension test. Rather it is intended to evaluate a player's ability to think and solve problems. Due to the complexity of offenses and defenses in the NFL, such skills can be important to success in the NFL. The test has been criticized over the years as being racially and culturally biased, but whether those accusations are valid or not has not been conclusively determined and the test continues to be used by NFL teams. The highest possible score is a 50 for the twelve minute, fifty question test. The average score for an NFL player taking the test has been reported to be 20.[2]

Since its first use by the NFL, only one player, Cincinnati Bengals receiver and punter Pat McInally who attended Harvard University has received a perfect score of 50. It has also been reported that Harvard quarterback Ryan Fitzpatrick scored a 48, taking only nine minutes to complete the test. In the 1984 book, "The New Thinking Man's Guide to Pro Football," Paul Zimmerman wrote that the highest average scores by position were led by offensive tackles with a score of 26, followed by centers at 25, quarterbacks at 24, offensive guards at 23, tight ends at 22, safeties and middle linebackers at 21, defensive linemen and outside linebackers at 19, cornerbacks at 18, wide receivers and fullbacks at 17 and halfbacks at 16. No NFL team will ever indicate how it specifically utilizes the test and the weight it gives to the test, however, after more than forty years of general use, it remains a staple of the evaluation of potential NFL players.

---

[2]  "The Five Best, Five Worst Wonderlic Scores in NFL History" Bleacher Report, Jeffrey Schmidt, April 4, 2012.

# FREE AGENCY

After three years in the league, a player can become a restricted free agent upon the expiration of his contract. Although he has the right to then negotiate a new contract with any other team in the NFL, his previous team retains the right to match the new team's offer and keep the player under the terms of the contract offered to the player by the other team. If the former team chooses not to match the offer to its player by a new team, the former team receives compensation from the new team in the form of a draft choice.

After four years in the league, a player can become an unrestricted free agent upon the expiration of his contract and can sign a new contract with any other team in the league without the new team having to pay any form of compensation to the player's former team.

# FRANCHISE PLAYER

Another unique provision of the NFL in regards to players' contracts is the designation by a team of a Franchise Player. The CBA provides for each team to name a single potential free agent player as a Franchise Player. A Franchise Player is required to sign a one year contract with his team for the greater of either the average of the top five salaries in the league for the position he plays or 120% of his prior salary. While it would seem that being paid a salary equal to the average of the top five salaries for the position played by the player would be desirable, players generally do not favor being named a Franchise Player because there is no bonus factored into the payment to the player which can dramatically reduce his total compensation. For the 2017 season the franchise figures were as follows:

Quarterback: $21.268 million dollars

Running Back: $12.120 million dollars

Wide Receiver: $15.682 million dollars

Tight End: $9.780 million dollars

Offensive Lineman: $14.271 million dollars

Defensive End: $16.934 million dollars

Defensive Tackle: $13.387 million dollars

Linebacker: $14.550 million dollars

Cornerback: $14.212 million dollars

Safety: $10.896 million dollars

Punter/Place Kicker: $4.835 million dollars

While this may seem clear, it turned out to be far from clear when in 2014 the New Orleans Saints and their All Pro receiver Jimmy Graham disagreed as to whether he was a tight end or a wide receiver. Although Graham lined up as either a wide receiver or in the backfield as a slot back rather than as a tight end on 67% of the plays in which he participated the previous year, the Saints argued that his position was that of tight end. In 2014, whether he was a tight end or a wide receiver would have meant a difference of more than five million dollars in salary if he was declared to be a Franchise Player by the Saints. In their contract negotiations with Graham, the Saints tagged Graham as their Franchise Player and Graham appealed the designation pursuant to his rights under the CBA. The arbitrator ruled in favor of the Saints. However, the Saints and Graham continued their negotiations after the arbitrators ruling and ultimately, rather than being declared a Franchise Player, Graham and the Saints came to an agreement on a contract that made Graham the highest paid tight end in the NFL.

# TRANSITION PLAYER

In addition to designating one of its players who would otherwise be eligible for free agency as a Franchise Player, each team also has the right to designate one of its players who would otherwise be eligible for unlimited free agency as a Transition Player. This designation provides the team with a right to match the offer of any other team that makes an offer to the player. Unlike with restricted free agency, if the player designated as a Transition Player signs with another team and his former team decides not to match the offer of the new team, the former team does not receive any form of compensation from the new team. In return for the designation as a Transition Player, the player must be offered a one year contract by his present team equal to the average of the top ten salaries of players in the league for his position or 120% of his previous salary, whichever is greater.

In 2017 the Transition player salaries were as follows:

Quarterback: $21.588 million dollars

Running Back: $12.755 million dollars

Wide Receiver: $15.795 million dollars

Tight End: $9.865 million dollars

Offensive Lineman: $14.829 million dollars

Defensive End: $16.988 million dollars

Defensive Tackle: $14.770 million dollars

Linebacker: $15.287million dollars

Cornerback: $15.095 million dollars

Safety: $11.691 million dollars

Punter/Place Kicker $4.946 million dollars

# RENEGOTIATIONS

Both players and management have incentives to renegotiate contracts. Players may believe that they have played at a higher level than what they are presently being paid while teams may desire to renegotiate a contract to either reduce compensation or adjust the contract for purposes of the salary cap. It is quite common for teams to tell players who have multiple years left on their contracts that they are being overpaid and that if they do not agree to renegotiate and restructure their contract, they will be released outright. This is one reason why when considering the true value of an NFL player's contract, you should never look at the salaries that are provided for in future years of the contract particularly in the latter years of a long multi-year contract. The true measure of an NFL contract is how much money is guaranteed either through the signing bonus or guaranteed salary, which is far more the exception than the rule.

A lesson in how a restructured contract can work to the benefit of both the player and the team is illustrated by New England Patriots' quarterback Tom Brady's contract renegotiations prior to the 2012 season. Under the terms of his renegotiated contract, Brady agreed to reduce his 2012 salary from 5.75 million dollars to $950,000. The team, however agreed to take that remaining 4.8 million dollars and add it to a 6 million dollar bonus due Brady merely for being on the roster to make his bonus at the start of the 2012 season 10.8 million dollars. Thus Brady still received the same amount of money, however by changing the characterization of the money paid to him, money was freed up for the team for salary cap purposes since bonuses are amortized over the remaining years of the contract for salary cap purposes leaving the team with 7.2 million dollars more money to pay players and remain under the salary cap for the upcoming season.

# WORLD WRESTLING ENTERTAINMENT

Professional wrestling as performed by World Wrestling Entertainment (WWE) formerly known as the World Wrestling Federation (WWF) until it lost an intellectual property lawsuit to the World Wildlife Federation (WWF) is popular worldwide with hundreds of live events each year throughout the world culminating in its annual Wrestlemania extravaganza.

Spoiler alert: If you are old enough to read this book, you learned long ago that professional wrestling bouts are not true athletic contests, but rather scripted events that include choreographed athletic maneuvers, which although scripted certainly require significant athletic talent. Although it was generally known that professional wrestling matches were not actual legitimately contested athletic events, it was not until 1989 that the WWE publicly stated that its product was sports entertainment rather than pure sports. The reason for this public acknowledgement of what had already been generally known was strictly to avoid taxes from state athletic commissions that taxed athletic events.

Just as there are standard contracts in other professional sports so are there standard contracts for the WWE, however, since the wrestlers competing in the WWE are considered independent contractors and are not represented by a union, there is no Collective Bargaining Agreement (CBA) and the contract terms and provisions are largely dictated by the WWE although some individual wrestlers will be in a better bargaining position to negotiate more favorable contracts for themselves.

# WWE CONTRACT

The initial "Premises" section of the contract clearly states many of the key elements of the relationship between the WWE and the individual wrestler which reads as follows:

"WHEREAS, PROMOTER IS DULY LICENSED, as required, to conduct professional wrestling exhibitions and is actually engaged in the business of organizing, publicizing, arranging, staging and conducting professional wrestling exhibitions and/or events, as defined below, throughout the world and of representing professional wrestlers in the promotion and exploitation of a professional wrestler's name, likeness, personality and character; and

WHEREAS, PROMOTER, has established a nationwide network of television stations, which regularly broadcast PROMOTER's wrestling programs for purposes of publicizing PROMOTER's professional wrestling exhibitions and/or events, as defined below, and PROMOTER has established a network of cable television organizations which regularly broadcast PROMOTER's professional wrestling exhibitions on a pay-per-view basis; and in addition thereto,

PROMOTER has developed and produced certain other television programs, which are also used to publicize, display and promote PROMOTER's professional wrestling exhibitions; and

WHEREAS, PROMOTER's business operations afford WRESTLER opportunities to wrestle and obtain public exposure which will increase the value of his wrestling services and his standing in the professional wrestling community and entertainment industry; and

WHEREAS, WRESTLER is duly licensed, as required, to engage in professional wrestling exhibitions and/or Events as defined below, and is actually engaged in the business of performing as a professional wrestler; and

WHEREAS, WRESTLER is a performing artist and the professional wrestling exhibitions arranged by PROMOTER constitute demonstrations of wrestling skills and abilities designed to provide athletic-styled entertainment to the public, and such professional wrestling exhibitions and Events constitute entertainment and are not competitive sports; and

WHEREAS, WRESTLER desires PROMOTER to arrange professional wrestling exhibitions and/or events, as defined below, for WRESTLER and to assist WRESTLER in obtaining public exposure through live exhibitions, television programs, public appearances, and in merchandising activities or otherwise;"

A critical element of the contract is found in section 2.3 which reads as follows:

"2.3 WRESTLER's appearance, performance and work product in any and all of the Events and/or Programs shall be deemed work for hire; and notwithstanding the termination of this Agreement, PROMOTER shall own in perpetuity, all Programs and all of the rights, results, products and proceeds in and to, or derived from the Events and Programs (including without limitation all incidents, dialogue, characters, actions, routines, ideas, gags, costumes or parts of costumes, accessories, crowns, inventions, championship, title or other belts (if applicable), and any other tangible or intangible materials written, composed, submitted, added, improvised, or created by or for WRESTLER in connection with appearance at the Events and/or in the Programs) and PROMOTER may obtain copyright and/or trademark and/or any other legal protection therefor, now known or hereinafter discovered, in the name of PROMOTER and/or on behalf of PROMOTER's designee."

# INTELLECTUAL PROPERTY

Intellectual property is a major part of the standard WWE contract. In section 3 of the standard contract the wrestler assigns to the WWE any "service marks, trademarks, and/or distinctive and identifying indicia, including ring name, nickname, likeness, personality, character, caricatures, voice, signature, props, gestures, routines, themes, incidents, dialogue, actions, gags, costumes or parts of costumes, accessories, crowns, inventions, championship, title or other belts (if applicable), and any other items of tangible or intangible property written, composed, submitted, added, improvised, created and/or used by or associated with WRESTLER's performance in the business of professional wrestling or sports entertainment. . . are hereby assigned to and shall belong to PROMOTER, in perpetuity, with PROMOTER retaining all such ownership rights exclusively throughout the world notwithstanding any termination of this Agreement." However, Section 7 of the standard contract provides for payments to the wrestler of 25% of the net receipts received from the sale of products utilizing the particular wrestler's intellectual property as described above.

# WRESTLER'S OBLIGATIONS

Section 9 of the contract deals with the wrestler's obligations. Some pertinent provisions are:

"9.2 WRESTLER shall be responsible for WRESTLER's own training, conditioning, and maintenance of wrestling skills and abilities, as long as they do not interfere with WRESTLERS's appearance at scheduled events as follows:

(a) WRESTLER shall establish his own training program, shall select time of training, duration of training, exercises, pattern of exercise and other actions appropriate to obtaining and maintaining physical fitness for wrestling. WRESTLER shall select his own training apparatus, including mats, weights, machines and other exercise paraphernalia. WRESTLER is responsible for supplying his own training facilities and equipment, whether by purchase, lease, license, or otherwise.

(b) WRESTLER shall establish his own method of physical conditioning, shall select time for conditioning, duration of conditioning and form of conditioning. WRESTLER shall select time for sleep, time for eating, and time for any other activities. WRESTLER shall select his own foods, vitamins and other ingested items, excepting illegal and/or controlled substances and drugs.

9.3 WRESTLER shall be responsible for providing all costumes, wardrobe, props and make-up necessary for the performance of WRESTLER's services at any Event and WRESTLER shall bear all costs incurred in connection with his transportation to and from any such EVENTs (except those transportation costs which are covered by PROMOTER's then current travel Policy), as well as the costs of food consumed and hotel lodging utilized by WRESTLER in connection with his appearance at such Events.

9.4 WRESTLER shall use best efforts in employing WRESTLER's skills and abilities as a professional wrestler and be responsible for developing and executing the various details, movements, and maneuvers required of wrestlers in a professional wrestling exhibition.

9.5 WRESTLER shall take such precautions as are appropriate to avoid any unreasonable risk of injury to other wrestlers in any and all Events. These precautions shall include, without limitation, pre-match review of all wrestling moves and maneuvers with wrestling partners and opponents; and pre-match demonstration and/or practice with wrestling partners and opponents to insure familiarity with anticipated wrestling moves and maneuvers during a wrestling match. In the event of injury to WRESTLER, and/or WRESTLER's partners and opponents during a wrestling match, WRESTLER shall immediately signal partner, opponent and/or referees that it is time for the match to end; and WRESTLER shall finish the match forthwith so as to avoid aggravation of such injury.

9.6 WRESTLER shall use best efforts in the ring in the performance of wrestling services for a match or other activity, in order to provide an honest exhibition of WRESTLER's wrestling skills and abilities, consistent with the customs of the professional wrestling industry; and WRESTLER agrees all matches shall be finished in accordance with the PROMOTER's direction. Breach of this Section 9.6 shall cause a forfeiture of any payment due WRESTLER pursuant to SECTION 7 of this Agreement and all other obligations of PROMOTER to WRESTLER hereunder shall entitle PROMOTER to terminate this Agreement, but such breach shall not terminate PROMOTER's licenses and other rights under this Agreement."

# EMPLOYEE BENEFITS

The wrestlers of the WWE are specifically designated within the standard contract as independent contractors rather than employees even though the WWE directs much of the manner in which they perform their job. If the wrestlers were considered employees, the WWE as an employer would be responsible for the withholding of income taxes, payment of worker's compensation insurance and numerous other legal requirements of employers. The general rule followed by the IRS and others is that a person is an independent contractor rather than an employee if the person paying the worker has the right to control or direct only the result of the work and not what will be done and how it will be done. Under this definition it would appear that professional wrestlers should be considered employees rather than independent contractors, however, the WWE standard contract emphasizes the position of the WWE, as shown in the following paragraphs from the standard contract, that the wrestlers are independent contractors thereby reducing the responsibilities of the WWE as the employer.

## QUESTION

1. Should professional wrestlers be considered independent contractors?

---

"9.11    WRESTLER shall be responsible for payment of all of WRESTLER's own Federal, state or local income taxes, all social security, FICA and FUTA taxes, if any, as well as all contributions to retirement plans and programs or other supplemental income plan or program that would provide WRESTLER with personal or monetary benefits upon retirement from professional wrestling.

9.12 (a)    WRESTLER shall be responsible for his own commercial general liability insurance, worker's compensation insurance, professional liability insurance, as well as any excess liability insurance, as he deems appropriate to insure, indemnify and defend WRESTLER with respect to any and all claims arising out of WRESTLER's own acts, transactions, or conduct as a professional wrestler.

(b) WRESTLER acknowledges that the participation and activities required by WRESTLER in connection with his performance in a professional wrestling exhibition may be dangerous and may involve the risk of serious bodily injury including death. WRESTLER knowingly and freely assumes full responsibility for all such inherent risks as well as those due to the negligence of the PROMOTER or other wrestlers.

(c) WRESTLER hereby releases, waives and discharges promoter from all liability to wrestler and covenants not to sue promoter for any and all loss or damage on account of injury to their person or property or resulting in serious or permanent injury to WRESTLER or WRESTLER's death, whether caused by the negligence of PROMOTER or other wrestlers under contract to PROMOTER"

"9.13 (a) WRESTLER may at his election obtain health, life and/or disability insurance to provide benefits in the event of physical injury arising out of WRESTLER's professional activities; and WRESTLER acknowledges that PROMOTER shall not have any responsibility for such insurance or payment in the event of physical injury arising out of WRESTLER's professional activities.

(b) In the event of physical injury arising out of WRESTLER's professional activities, WRESTLER acknowledges that WRESTLER is not entitle to any worker's compensation coverage or similar benefits for injury, disability, death or loss of wages; and WRESTLER shall make no claim against PROMOTER for such coverage or benefit."

---

## QUESTION

1.    Should wrestling promoters be able to avoid liability to wrestlers for their negligence as provided for in Section 9.12(b) of the standard contract?

# MORALS CLAUSE

Similar to the clauses found in other professional athlete contracts, the WWE standard contract contains the following morals clause in section 9.14.

"9.14    Wrestler shall act at all times with due regard to public morals and conventions during the term of this Agreement. If Wrestler shall have committed or shall commit any act or do anything that is or shall be an offense or violation involving moral turpitude under Federal, state or local laws, or which brings WRESTLER into public disrepute, contempt, scandal or ridicule or which insults or offends the community or any employee, agent, or affiliate of PROMOTER or which injures WRESTLER's reputation in PROMOTER's sole judgment, or diminishes the value of WRESTLER's professional wrestling services to the public or PROMOTER, then at the time of any such act, or any time after PROMOTER learns of such act, POMOTER shall have the right to fine WRESTLER in an amount to be determined by PROMOTER; and PROMOTER shall have the right to suspend and/or terminate this Agreement forthwith."

# DRUG POLICY

The drug policy in the WWE is one of the toughest in professional sports. It not only requires that all wrestlers be initially screened for drugs, but even provides in section 10.2(d) as follows:

"(d) In addition to the foregoing, WRESTLER acknowledges and agrees that PROMOTER shall have the right at any time during the Term to have WRESTLER submit to a drug screening, at such times and places as PROMOTER shall determine in its sole discretion. WRESTLER further agrees that the cost and expense of such drug screening shall be borne by WRESTLER and PROMOTER shall have the right to deduct such cost and expense from any and all compensation due WRESTLER without further notice to WRESTLER."

Violation of the WWE's drug policy is, under the terms of the contract, a breach of the contract and can result in termination of the contract as an option to the WWE.

In addition, in section 10.3 the WWE reserves the right without limitation to have the wrestler examined by a doctor of the WWE's choosing at any time during the term of the contract.

# TERMINATION

Similar to an NFL player contract, a professional wrestler's contract can be terminated by the WWE with or without cause by providing ninety days written notice. The contract can also be terminated by the mutual consent of the WWE and the wrestler. However, according to the standard WWE contact, the WWE retains the rights to the wrestler's intellectual property forever although the same payments to the wrestler for use of his intellectual property provided for within the contract also continue.

# CONFIDENTIALITY

In a unique provision of the contract, the wrestler is required to keep confidential items, such as "story lines, scripts, story boards or ideas, routines, gags. . ."

# PROFESSIONAL CHEERLEADERS

The era of cheerleaders in professional sports began in 1972 when the Dallas Cowboys introduced the first Dallas Cowboy Cheerleaders. These cheerleaders were recruited from models that unfortunately, lacked the athletic skills necessary for cheerleading. Later the team hired Texie Waterman, the owner of a Dallas dance studio to choose and train its cheerleaders and the rest is history.

NFL cheerleaders generally range in age from 18 to 36 years old although there is no upper age limit. It is not a full-time job and most, until recently were considered independent contractors or even volunteers.

Traditionally, NFL cheerleaders have been designated by their employing teams as independent contractors. The designation by NFL teams of their cheerleaders as independent contractors is particularly troublesome when you consider that the key difference between an independent contractor and an employee is the degree of control over the employee and the NFL teams had extraordinary invasive rules and regulations to which the cheerleaders had to adhere not only while performing their job, but off the field as well with strict rules as to not gaining weight, rules on who they could date, not being able to endorse products and not even being able to accept modeling, acting or other entertainment industry employment without the written consent of the team. The reason that the teams wished to designate the cheerleaders as independent contractors is that by so doing, they were able to avoid paying minimum wage and benefits.

Lacy Thibodeaux was a cheerleader for the NFL Oakland Raiders. Before cheering for the Raiders, Thibodeaux had been a cheerleader with the NBA's Golden State Warriors where she was paid for practices as well as games and had her expenses reimbursed. However as an Oakland Raiders' cheerleader she was paid a mere $125 per game and did not receive any payment until the end of the season. Neither did the team pay for travel expenses, attendance at mandatory promotional events nor calendar photo shoots. Dissatisfied with the working conditions, Thibodeaux filed a class action lawsuit against the Oakland Raiders for labor law violations alleging that the Raiders failed to pay minimum wage, illegally deducted fines for minor infractions such as being late for a practice, failed to reimburse necessary business expenses and only paid the cheerleaders once at the end of the season. The case was settled in September of 2014 for 1.25 million dollars to be divided between 90 Oakland Raider cheerleaders, known as the Raiderettes from the 2010 through 2013 football seasons. Pursuant to the settlement the Raiders also agreed to comply with both state and federal labor laws. In 2015, the state of California took this further and enacted legislation that designated cheerleaders as employees rather than independent contractors as the NFL teams generally designated their cheerleaders. This requires the teams to provide time for meals, paid sick leave, and perhaps most important, minimum wage.

Following Thibodeaux's filing of her class action lawsuit against the Oakland Raiders, cheerleaders for other NFL teams followed her lead and initiated litigation. According to the lawsuit filed by the Cincinnati Bengals' cheerleaders, they were paid $2.85 per hour while the lawsuit filed by the Tampa Bay Buccaneers' cheerleaders alleged that they were paid less than $2 per hour and received nothing for required community appearances and charity events. The Buccanneers' cheerleaders later settled their lawsuit for $825,000.

# SYNOPSIS

1.  The Collective Bargaining Agreements for each of the major professional sports leagues, the NFL, NBA, MLB and NHL provide the terms of the standard player contract in that sport.

2.  Variations within limits are allowed in the contracts of individual players.

3.  The standard NBA, MLB, NFL and NHL contracts require players to maintain themselves in good physical shape as a condition of the contract.

4.  Although no-trade clauses are allowed in theory in NBA contracts, they are so severely limited by the conditions required for a player to be eligible for one that they are extremely rare.

5.  The standard NBA, MLB, NFL and NHL contracts have broad provisions governing the conduct of players off the court.

6.  The standard NBA, MLB, NFL and NHL contracts prohibit specific off court activities of players that the leagues deem puts the player at an unreasonable risk of becoming injured.

7.  The standard NBA, MLB, NFL and NHL contracts require the player to cooperate with media coverage of the player and the team for which he plays as well as participate in promotional activities of the team.

8.  The standard NBA, MLB, NFL and NHL contracts contain morals clauses.

9.  NBA salaries are governed by a salary cap that has many complex exceptions.

10. MLB contracts may include no-trade clauses which, although not common, are more attainable than NBA no-trade clauses.

11. MLB contracts are subject to a salary cap, however, MLB teams exceeding the salary cap are required to pay a luxury tax.

12. MLB contracts are subject to salary arbitration.

13. Bonus provisions in NHL players' contracts are substantially limited.

14. Professional wrestling contracts classify the wrestlers as independent contractors.

15. Professional wrestling is described in its contracts as athletic styled entertainment.

16. The contracts of professional wrestlers contain significant intellectual property rights limitations of the wrestlers.

17. Professional cheerleaders had traditionally been classified as independent contractors and often significantly underpaid.

18. The NFL has a "hard" salary cap that may not be exceeded under any circumstances by individual teams.

19. The NFL salary cap is determined through the collective bargaining process. Rookies have their own specific salary cap.

20. NFL player contracts are the only contracts in professional sports that can be terminated by the team at any time without cause.

21. Bonuses play a large part of the compensation of an NFL player.

22. The NFL has provisions for restricted and unrestricted free agency.

# CHAPTER THREE

# Agents

## INTRODUCTION

Agency law has existed for hundreds of years. Under agency law one person is authorized to act on behalf of another person. Agents have an important role to play in professional sports today. The careers of professional athletes are short and the opportunities for maximizing financial gain from their athletic skills are correspondingly often limited While the standard player contracts for each of the major professional sports leagues, the NFL, NHL, NBA and MLB are determined by the leagues' respective Collective Bargaining Agreements, there is still much that is left to be negotiated on behalf of individual athletes who need the knowledge and skills of agents to represent them in this process. Effective agents must have not just negotiating skills but also knowledge of the complex rules regarding salary caps found in all professional sports, but particularly the NFL, which strictly forbids teams from spending over a specific amount on players' compensation. In addition, agents will generally act on behalf of their clients in other business and financial related ventures.

## HISTORY

Although the modern era of sports agency is generally thought to have originated in the 1960s, the seeds were first sewn in 1925 when University of Illinois football star Red Grange, known in his playing days as the Galloping Ghost, hired theatrical producer Charles Pyle to represent him in his negotiations with the Chicago Bears of the fledgling National Football League with whom he signed one day after completing his college football career at the University of Illinois. The signing of this national hero was a tremendous step for professional football which, at that time, was not the hugely popular sport of today. The contract Pyle negotiated was noteworthy on several fronts. The size of his compensation was incredible for that era. At a time when most professional football players were paid no more than a hundred dollars per game, Grange was paid a guaranteed salary of $3,000 per game and a percentage of the paid attendance. He was such a huge draw that the Bears last game before Grange joined the team was watched by 7,500 fans while in the first Bears game in which he played the stadium was filled with 36,000 fans, many of whom didn't even have seats. Foreshadowing the full service sports agents of today, Pyle also negotiated product endorsements and even movie roles for Grange.

For many years, however, the Reserve Clauses in professional sports contracts by which players were tied to their teams for their entire careers limited the negotiating power of athletes and reduced somewhat the value of having an agent. In addition, there was a general resistance by team owners to dealing with agents.

With the advent of free agency, spurred by the 1975 case of Andy Messersmith in which the Reserve Clause was initially struck down in a Major League Baseball arbitration hearing and then through a series of court decisions and ultimately through collective bargaining, free agency came to all professional sports. The NFL adopted free agency rules in 1992. The NHL adopted free agency rules in 1995 and the NBA became the last of the major professional sports leagues to adopt free agency rules in 1996. Once free agency became a permanent fixture of professional sports, the role of agents in guiding players through free agency became prominent.

# BASIS OF AGENCY LAW

All agency law is based on the fiduciary relationship between the agent and the client, which is goes to the essence of the relationship and is implied by law in all agency relationships. A fiduciary relationship was described by Supreme Court Justice Benjamin Nathan Cardozo as "something stricter than the morals of the marketplace. Not honesty alone, but the very punctilio of an honor the most sensitive is then the standard of behavior." Meinhard v. Salmon, 164 N.E. 545 (1928). It is a special relationship of trust and confidence where the agent owes the highest standard of loyalty to his or her client and must avoid any conflict of interest.

Some of the specific services provided by sports agents are:

1. Negotiating the terms of his or her client's contract with the team, which can include issues of compensation, salary, bonuses, guarantees, no-trade clauses and length of contract.

2. Representing the athlete in commercial endorsements, speaking engagements and other activities intended to maximize the value of the client's "right of publicity."

3. Performing public and media relations duties.

4. Marketing the athlete to other teams when he or she becomes eligible for free agency.

5. Representing the athlete in matters of club or league discipline pertaining to violation of team or league rules or regulations.

Financial management is not generally a part of the services specifically provided by the agent who negotiates the player's contract to play for a particular team, however, agents will often direct their clients to the proper accountants, lawyers, investment advisers and other financial professionals needed to provide tax advice, estate planning and financial planning. Good agents will also assist in helping the athlete transition from a short career in professional sports to life after his or her playing days are over.

One need not be a lawyer to be a sports agent, but many agents are lawyers. There is no typical, formal education program for sports agents. Most have college degrees. Those who attend college earn degrees in a variety of related fields, including legal studies, political science, sociology, and sports management.

# VICTIMS OF FINANCIAL DISTRESS AND BANKRUPTCY

A disturbing fact is that despite often earning millions of dollars during their playing careers, significant numbers of former players find themselves in serious financial distress and even bankruptcy shortly after their athletic careers have ended According to an often quoted 2009 article in Sports Illustrated, within two years after retirement from the NFL, 78% of former players have either declared bankruptcy or are in serious financial distress as well as 60% of former NBA players within five years of their retirement.[1]

Some examples include:

NFL Hall of Famer Warren Sapp who over the course of his thirteen year career earned 82 million dollars, but within five years of retiring filed bankruptcy in 2012.

Vince Young, who during the course of his eight year NFL career earned 64 million dollars in salary and endorsements, yet filed bankruptcy in 2014 within two years of leaving the NFL.

Antoine Walker, who earned 108 million dollars in salary during his thirteen year NBA career, but ended up bankrupt in 2010, two years after his retirement due to bad investments and a lavish lifestyle for himself, his entourage and family.

NBA Hall of Famer, Allen Iverson, earned 154.5 million dollars in salary during his fourteen year NBA career, but lost it all through an expensive lifestyle. However, he was saved financially by Reebok

---

[1]  "How and Why Athletes Go Broke," Sports Illustrated Vault, Pablo S. Torre, March 23, 2009.

where he has a lifetime endorsement contract with thirty million dollars in trust for him that he cannot access until 2030.

Heavyweight Boxing Champion, Mike Tyson earned 400 million dollars over his career, but declared bankruptcy in 2003.

According to sports agent Leigh Steinberg the main reason so many former NFL players run into financial difficulties upon retirement are:

1.   Lack of good financial advice encompassing, budgeting, tax issues and sound investment strategies;

2.   Divorce and child support payments;

3.   Supporting of large entourages of hangers on including family and friends.

4.   Failing to understand how short their careers are;

5.   Failing to plan for life after their careers are over.[2]

A common thread of many athletes who suffer financial distress upon their retirement from professional sports is living an exorbitant life styles and failing to recognize that their high earning years are limited by the short careers of many professional athletes particularly NFL players. According to one study, the average NBA career is 4.8 years, the average MLB career is 5.6 years, the average NHL career is 5.5 years and the average NFL career is a mere 3.5 years.

A notable example of an athlete living within his means is that of NE Patriots tight end Rob Gronkowski, who in his initial five years in the NFL saved his entire salary of more than 16 million dollars. As he indicated in his autobiography, "It's Good to be Gronk"

"To this day, I still haven't touched one dime of my signing bonus or NFL contract money. I live off my marketing money and haven't blown it on any big-money expensive cars, expensive jewelry or tattoos and still wear my favorite pair of jeans from high school."

---

[2]   "5 Reasons Why 80% of Retired NFL Players Go Broke," Forbes Magazine, Leigh Steinberg, February 9, 2015.

While the attraction of some players to high risk investments such as restaurants and nightclubs have contributed to the financial distress of many players, others have become victims of fraudulent investment advisers. For example, the victims of convicted Ponzi schemer Robert Allen Stanford included many professional athletes including professional baseball player, Jacoby Ellsbury.

According to the NFL players association at least 78 players lost more than 42 million dollars between 1999 and 2002 due to trusting financial advisers who scammed them.[3]

A part of the fiduciary duty of an agent is to avoid any personal conflicts of interest. An agent must not use his position as the athlete's agent to his own financial advantage without the knowledge and consent of the athlete. In 2008, agent Bill Henkel negotiated a memorabilia contract for NFL running back LaDamian Tomlinson that, unknown to Tomlinson, provided for a kickback of $75,000 to Henkel for recommending the company to Tomlinson. Henkel pleaded guilty to criminal charges of criminal deprivation of property and attempted criminal deprivation of property in regard to the kickback scheme.

In 2002 and 2004, agent William "Tank" Black was convicted of defrauding his clients out of 12 million dollars through a pyramid scheme by taking advantage of their trust in him combined with their lack of investment experience.

Hedge fund manager Kirk Wright was convicted of 47 counts of fraud and money laundering related to the defrauding of his clients out of more than 150 million dollars. Many of his clients were NFL players.

---

[3] "Financial Fraud is One of the Biggest Off-Field Challenges to NFL Players," National Sports Law Institute Newsletter, Volume 21, Number 4, Laurence M. Landsman, October-December 2010.

## QUESTIONS

1.    Is it part of the agent's fiduciary responsibility to his or her client to play a greater role in protecting the future financial security of his or her client?

2.    Should all sports agents be required to be licensed lawyers because the various state bar associations would have greater oversight over the manner in which they practiced and ethics rules are already in place?

# UNION CERTIFICATION OF SPORTS AGENTS

While no law requires any specific qualifications in order to act as a sports agent, the various professional sports unions have enacted requirements that must be met in order to represent one of their members. The unions of professional baseball players, basketball players, football players and hockey players each require that agents be certified by the particular union in order to represent athletes in their particular sport. Prior to certifying an agent, the union will do a background check on the prospective agent which includes an investigation of the applicant's criminal record, bankruptcy filings and possible charges of fraud. Agents can also be suspended or disciplined for failure to comply with union promulgated regulations regarding agent actions such as providing paying a player to induce him to sign with the agent, offering money or other things of value to the family of a prospective client to induce them into recommending the agent, or otherwise providing false or misleading information to the player.

# NBA AGENT RULES

In order to serve as an agent of an NBA player, an agent has to be certified by the National Basketball Players Association. The standard NBA agent contract as provided by the NBA Players Association provides that if a player is paid the minimum salary as determined by the Collective Bargaining Agreement (CBA), the agent gets no more than a 2% commission. If the agent obtains a higher than the CBA indicated minimum salary, the agent's commission can be as high as 4%. The standard NBA agent contract requires the agent to be responsible for his expenses incurred in representing his or her client; however, he can be reimbursed for travel and communications expenses. Both the athlete and the agent each have the right to terminate the agency contract upon fifteen days' notice. The NBA requires that all agents be college graduates. An agent who represents NBA players is not allowed to represent an NBA coach or general manager who participates in salary negotiations. Agents are specifically prohibited from paying players to induce them to hire the agent. This rule has been abused many times in the past, particularly as it related to agents luring college players into signing agency contracts by providing payments to the athletes or their families.

---

**QUESTIONS**

1.    Why should college graduation be a requirement to act as a sports agent?

2.    What are the reasons behind the NBA's rule prohibiting agents from representing players and coaches or general managers who may control their salaries?

# NFLPA AGENT RULES

The National Football League Players Association (NFLPA) requires agents to be college graduates although exceptions are permitted. Agents must be certified by the union, which requires them to attend an NFLPA sponsored seminar and pass a written examination. If the prospective agent fails to pass the exam in two consecutive years, the agent is not allowed to take the exam for the next five years. The fees an agent receives for representing a client in contract negotiations with an NFL team are regulated by the NFLPA and capped at 3% of the contract payments or 2% for franchise designated players, transition designated players or restricted free agents. Unlike in the

NBA, agents for NFL players can represent NFL coaches. NFL agency contracts can be terminated by either the player or the agent on five days' notice. If a player fires his agent during the course of negotiations and his new agent completes negotiations for a new contract by which the player is paid more than what the previous agent had negotiated, the new agent is only paid a commission on the amount by which the new compensation package exceeds the compensation package negotiated by the previous agent while the previous agent receives a commission based upon the value of the initially negotiated contract. Agents are not permitted to offer money to athletes to induce them into signing agency contracts with them.

## QUESTION

1.    Should all players' agents be required to pass an exam in order to be certified as an agent and, if so, what knowledge should such exam test?

# MLB

As in all of the professional spots, in order to act as a player's agent in Major League Baseball, an agent must be certified by the players' union, in this case, the Major League Baseball Players Association (MLBPA). The MLBPA does not require that agents be college graduates and does not regulate the fee to be paid by the player to his agent, however, union rules require that no player is responsible for a fee or commission to be paid to his agent that leaves him with less than the minimum salary as provided for in the MLB Collective Bargaining Agreement, which in 2016 was $507,500 per year.

# NCAA AGENCY RULES

The rules governing agents and college athletes are of tremendous importance because NCAA regulations provide that the mere hiring of an agent terminates the amateur standing of a collegiate athlete and his or her ability to participate in NCAA competitions. However, there is an exception to this rule by which a college athlete is allowed to retain an agent to represent him or her in negotiations with a professional sports team and even play as a professional athlete in that particular sport so long as he or she does not play that sport in college. For instance, Chris Weinke played professional minor league baseball in the Toronto Blue Jays organization before returning to Florida State University where he was ineligible to play collegiate baseball, but eligible to play collegiate football which he did, leading Florida State to the National Championship while he earned the Heisman Trophy.

## QUESTION

1.   Should merely hiring an agent who can assist a player in determining whether it makes financial sense for a player to stay in school or declare himself eligible for the professional drafts be sufficient to lose his or her NCAA amateur standing.

# NEED FOR REGULATION

Time and time again, the problem of players being represented by agents while playing NCAA sports has come back to haunt college players and their schools, such as when UMass basketball star Marcus Camby was found to have hired an agent while still competing in college basketball, which resulted in the University of Massachusetts having its 1996 Final Four appearance removed from the record books.

Unscrupulous agents have been offering money not just to college athletes, but even to high school athletes in an effort to lure them as clients. The presence of agents in high schools increased in the late 1990s when high school students, such as Kevin Garnett in 1995, were allowed to go directly into the NBA upon completion of their high school careers. Even with the change in the minimum age for eligibility being changed by the NBA to not permit a high school student to enter the NBA draft until a year after his class' high school graduation, agents continue to maintain contacts with high school athletes. Some agents even sponsor summer basketball teams. Summer basketball coaches have become registered agents and end up representing players from their teams.

Unscrupulous agents hire college students known as "runners" who will contact student athletes at their schools and offer money and other inducements to student-athletes on behalf of the agents seeking to be hired to represent the student-athlete while hiding their relationship with the athlete, which would, if exposed, result in the disqualification of the athlete from NCAA competition.

## SPARTA

The federal law that deals with sports agency is The Sports Agent Responsibility and Trust Act of 2004 commonly referred to as SPARTA.

SPARTA makes it unlawful for an agent to directly or indirectly solicit a student athlete for representation by making false promises or providing false information to the student athlete. The agent is also prohibited from providing anything of value to the student athlete or anyone, such as a family member who may be associated with the student athlete. This specifically includes a prohibition from loaning money or co-signing a loan to benefit a student athlete.

SPARTA is not only concerned with protecting the rights of student athletes and their eligibility to play college sports, but also with protecting colleges and universities from NCAA repercussions if it is determined that a college's or university's student-athletes become disqualified from participating in NCAA sports due to being declared ineligible due to violating NCAA rules by signing with an agent.

SPARTA requires all agency contracts with student athletes contain the following boldfaced disclosure:

"Warning to Student Athlete: If you agree orally or in writing to be represented by an agent now or in the future, you may lose your eligibility to compete as a student athlete in your sport. Within 72 hours after entering into this contract or before the next athletic event in which you are eligible to participate, whichever occurs first, both you and the agent by whom you are agreeing to be represented must notify the athletic director of the educational institution at which you are enrolled, or other individual responsible for athletic programs at such educational institution that you have entered into an agency contract."

Jurisdiction over enforcement of SPARTA is given to the Federal Trade Commission (FTC) which has the authority to regulate "unfair and deceptive acts and practices in connection with the contact between an athlete agent and a student-athlete."

# UAAA

In addition to SPARTA, forty states have enacted regulations of sports agents with thirty-eight of them adopting some form of the Uniform Athlete Agents Act (UAAA). The Uniform Athletes Agents Act (UAAA) was drafted in 2000 by the National Conference of Commissioners on Uniform State Laws, a non-profit organization made up of commissioners from each of the states to develop laws to provide uniformity in specific areas of the law, such as the Uniform Commercial Code. Included in the UAAA is the requirement that sports agents register in each state where they may contact a student athlete as well as the state where they live. Variations in law from state to state can make it complicated for an agent to comply with the law in every state in which he or she may do business.

Criminal punishments vary from state to state. West Virginia law provides for a penalty of a year in prison for an agent failing to register and up to three years in prison for providing false information to a student athlete while in Texas the potential penalty for engaging in conduct that jeopardizes a student athlete's eligibility to play college athletics is up to ten years in prison.

Pursuant to the UAAA, agents are prohibited from doing any of the following activities:

1.    Giving any materially false or misleading information or making a materially false promise or representation.

2.    Furnishing, directly or indirectly, anything of value to a student-athlete before the student-athlete enters into the agency contract. This is intended to apply to the use of "runners."

3.    Furnishing, directly or indirectly, anything of value to any individual other than the student-athlete or another registered athlete agent.

The UAAA was intended to specifically deal with agent conduct when seeking to represent student athletes. A notable flaw in the UAAA and the state enacted versions of the UAAA is that it deals only with the recruiting and representing of student athletes and does not deal with the obligations and responsibilities of agents to athletes after the athlete has become a professional athlete.

---

## QUESTIONS

1.    Should sports agency law be uniform in all of the states?

2.    Should sports agency law define the obligations and responsibilities of agents to athletes after the athlete has become a professional athlete?

# EXAMPLES OF STATE LAWS

## Alabama

Alabama, home to perennial college football power, University of Alabama has been particularly vigilant in enforcing its version of the UAAA and has brought criminal charges against agents for failing to register with the state as required by the Alabama enacted version of the UAAA. Most states that have enacted their own versions of the UAAA have not been as active as Alabama in policing the registration of sports agents.

The Alabama version of the UAAA states that an agent may not:

*"(1) Give any materially false or misleading information or make a materially false promise or representation. (2) Furnish, directly or indirectly, any thing of value to a student-athlete before the student-athlete enters into the agency contract. (3) Furnish, directly or indirectly, any thing of value to any individual other than the student-athlete or another registered athlete agent.* [Alabama Code § 8–26A–14(a)]. It also goes on to state that a student-athlete may not, *(2) Accept anything from an athlete agent without first entering into a contract in conformity with this chapter.* (Alabama Code § 8–26A–14(d))."

Alabama law also significantly provides for punishment of both any student-athlete as well as any agent violating the law with penalties of up to twenty years in prison for violations of the law by agents and community service penalties for student athletes violating the law. In addition, the Alabama law, Alabama Code § 8–26A–16(B) provides for universities and colleges harmed by the actions of agents violating the law to be able to bring civil legal actions against such agents where the schools may have suffered financial losses due to the actions of the agents.

### Arkansas

In 2011 Arkansas increased its penalties for violations of its version of the UAAA to include financial penalties of up to $250,000 for each felony classified violation. The previous limit had been $50,000.

In addition to SPARTA's 72 hour notification rule, Arkansas law now requires agents to notify a college's or university's athletic director before even contacting an athlete.

# NOTABLE SPORTS AGENTS

## Bob Wolfe

Bob Wolfe was one of the original sports agents from the 1960s. While representing his first sports client, Boston Red Sox pitcher Earl Wilson, the resistance by teams to players being represented by agents was so strong that Wolfe was not even allowed by the Red Sox to be in the room where negotiations between Wilson and the Red Sox went on. Instead, in an era prior to cellphones, Wilson had to excuse himself at important junctures in the negotiations to call Wolfe for guidance on the phone.

Word of how effective an agent and lawyer Wolfe was spread and he soon represented a long list of prominent athletes including Larry Bird, Joe Montana and Julius Erving. Wolfe's style of negotiating was firm, but non-adversarial, always trying to arrive at contracts that were win-win contracts good for both parties while still strongly advocating for his clients. He even wrote a book entitled "Friendly Persuasion." Unlike many agents of the time, Wolfe refused to renegotiate contracts for his clients while their previous contracts were still in force. This caused a number of his clients, such as Julius Erving to terminate their relationships, but Wolfe believed as a matter of principle that if you make a contract you should honor that contract.

## Mark McCormack

McCormack was a highly skilled collegiate golfer at the College of William & Mary in which capacity he met and played against Wake Forest golfer Arnold Palmer. It was his personal relationship with Palmer from those early days that led to McCormack's representation of Palmer and then other golfers following McCormack's graduation from Yale Law School. From golf, McCormack expanded his coverage of sports to tennis, skiing, track and field, professional baseball and professional football. The hallmark of McCormack's representation of his clients through his company IMG was that IMG would manage all areas of their clients' lives, leaving the athletes to focus on their sport while every other area of their lives, including investments, taxes, marketing and money management were competently taken care of by IMG.

## David Falk

David Falk specialized in representing professional basketball players. In the 1984 NBA draft he did not represent Akeem Olajuwon who was the first overall pick in the NBA draft by the Houston Rockets nor did he represent the second pick in the draft, Sam Bowie who was chosen by the Portland Trailblazers He did, however, represent Michael Jordan, the third pick in the draft and the two of them had a tremendous mutually profitable history together. In the year 2000, Falk had at least one player on all but two of the NBA teams.

Perseverance is an essential defining characteristic of David Falk. While in college, he called sports agent Donald Dell on the phone seventeen times during a three hour period until Dell finally took his call and told Falk that he had no job to offer him, to which Falk responded that he would work for free. Falk began his work an unpaid intern while in law school. Upon graduation in 1975 he began working full time for Dell at the princely salary of $13,000 a year.

In the 1980s, only Kareem Abdul Jabbar had a shoe endorsement contract worth more than a $100,000. In 1982 Falk negotiated a 1.2 million dollar endorsement contract for James Worthy of the Los Angeles Lakers with New Balance.

Until Michael Jordan left the University of North Carolina in 1984, he had always worn Adidas shoes off the court and Converse while playing for Coach Dean Smith at North Carolina because that is the company that paid Smith for his endorsement. Nike offered Jordan an endorsement contract that would pay him $250,000 plus a percentage of shoe sale revenues for his own personalized line of shoes. Adidas offered a flat $500,000 as payment for his endorsement. Falk convinced Nike to raise its offer to $500,000, but in so doing the percentage of revenues was taken off the table. This was a rare misstep by Falk who in effect was not betting on the value of his client. The Nike contract also gave Nike the option to terminate the contract if specific sales figures were not reached or if Jordan failed to make the NBA All Star team during his first three years. Nike's projected revenues for the shoe sales were three million dollars for the first four years. In 1985 alone, Nike earned 130 million dollars from sales of Air Jordan shoes. In 1997 while represented by Falk, Jordan signed a thirty million dollar endorsement contract with Nike.

Even working under the NBA Players Association's rule limiting agent's compensation to 4%, in one six day period in 1996, Falk negotiated six contracts for Michael Jordan, Alonzo Mourning, Juwan Howard, Kenny Anderson, Dikembe Mutombo and Lee Mayberry worth more than $335,000,000 resulted in commissions to him of thirteen million dollars. However, it is important to note that the 4% limit on agent commissions only applies to commissions derived from player contract negotiations with the player's team. Negotiations for endorsement contracts and other contracts carry no limitation. The commission of Falk and other agents for endorsement contracts can be as high as 20%

## Drew Rosenhaus

In 1989, at the age of 22 Rosenhaus became the youngest registered sports agent. He has negotiated more than a billion dollars' worth of NFL contracts for clients such as Rob Gronkowski of the New England Patriots. He obtained many of his early clients through his close ties to the University of Miami which he attended between 1984 and 1987. While a student at the University of Miami he met many University of Miami football players through his work as an academic tutor.

In 2003, University of Miami star running back Willis McGahee suffered a knee injury in the National Championship Game at the Fiesta Bowl that appeared to end his professional football career before it ever began. Rosenhaus offered to represent McGahee as an agent and waive his entire commission if McGahee was not chosen in the first round of the NFL draft which was occurring only a few months later During McGahee's rehab, Rosenhaus managed a massive publicity campaign to convince NFL general managers' of his client's ability to play successfully in the Fall. McGahee was picked by the Buffalo Bills in the first round and received a sixteen million dollar contract. McGahee's prolonged physical rehabilitation resulted in him missing the next NFL season, however, a year later, fully recovered from his injury, he rushed for more than a 1,000 yards in his first year in the NFL.

## Leigh Steinberg

Steinberg's first client was a classmate of his at the University of California, Berkeley, Quarterback Steve Bartkowski in 1975. Other notable clients have included Hall of Fame quarterbacks Steve Young and Warren Moon.

Steinberg required all of his clients to have a provision in their NFL contracts through which the athletes would contribute some of their compensation to their hometown, high school, college, national charities or foundations. His clients have donated six hundred million dollars to charities. Ahead of his time, he also organized panels of neurologists to discuss the issue of the dangers of concussions long before the issue was one debated in the mainstream.

Movie lore is that Steinberg was the agent who formed the basis of the title character in the Tom Cruise movie, "Jerry Maguire" and that Director Cameron Crowe while following Steinberg during the Spring 1993 NFL owners meeting heard one of Steinberg's clients utter some form of the phrase that became immortalized in the movie as "show me the money."

In 2001 two of his colleagues broke off and formed their own agency taking half of the agency's clients with them. Lawsuits followed. Initially Steinberg won a 45 million dollar judgment, but eventually the case was settled outside of court for an undisclosed amount. From the top of the world to starting over after battles with former colleagues, bankruptcy, divorce and alcoholism, Steinberg regained his sobriety in 2010 and reentered the world of sports agents.

## Scott Boras

One of the more controversial sports agents of recent times is Scott Boras, a former minor league baseball player who has represented many MLB star players including Max Scherzer, Jacoby Ellsbury, and Alex Rodriguez. Boras played in the minor league systems of the St. Louis Cardinals and Chicago Cubs who paid for his tuition to attend the University of Pacific Law School. His initial clients came from the ranks of former teammates. He is particularly knowledgeable in baseball and always comes exceptionally prepared with extensive statistics to any negotiation or salary arbitration. He also is creative. In 2004 when representing Red Sox catcher, Jason Varitek in negotiations with the Boston Red Sox, he argued for a no-trade clause which the Red Sox were adamantly against both on principle and because they had a contract with four other players including Manny Ramirez which stipulated that if the Red Sox included a no-trade clause in any of their players' contracts, these players would automatically have no trade clauses included in their contracts. Boras responded to this concern by persuading the team to change its policy regarding no-trade contracts to one where only if a player had eight years of service with the Red Sox, would he be eligible for a no-trade contract. This change in policy made Varitek along with pitcher Tim Wakefield, the only players eligible for such treatment.[4]

The annals of baseball are filled with stories of overworked young pitchers whose careers are shortened due to injuries. While a common misconception is that the overhand throwing motion used by major league pitchers is an unnatural motion, recent studies have shown that far from being unnatural, the motion developed actually was an evolutionary development. However, according to Glenn Fleisig, the research director of the American Sports Medicine Institute, "What's not natural is throwing a hundred pitches from a mound every fifth

---

[4]  "It's Now Captain Varitek" Hartford Courant, David Heuschkel, December 25, 2004.

day. That amount of throwing at that intensity is not natural." It can also lead to serious injuries particularly to young pitchers.[5]

According to Jeff Zimmerman of Baseball Heat Maps, MLB pitchers lost 18,000 days to injury in 2015 which was a 33% increase since 2005. In addition, in 2015 101 professional baseball pitchers had Ulnar Collateral Ligament Reconstruction (UCLR) surgery, more commonly referred to as Tommy John Surgery as contrasted with less than half of that number ten years earlier according to Jon Roegele of Hardball Times. Ulnar Collateral Ligament Reconstruction surgery is a surgical procedure by which the ulnar collateral ligament in the elbow is replaced with a tendon from somewhere else in the patient's body. This procedure was first done on Los Angeles Dodgers pitcher, Tommy John whose name has been forever linked with the surgery.[6]

Boras has repeatedly tried to influence both his clients, who often wish to continue to pitch even when their health may be jeopardized as well as the major league clubs for which they pitch who might be more concerned with the short term benefits of overworking a particular pitcher rather than the long term benefit to the athlete and the team by a more measured response.

Boras' client Stephen Strasburg was the first pick in the 2009 amateur draft of the Washington Nationals, a team in dire need of pitching and whose intention was to work him into their starting rotation as soon as possible. However, Boras' research indicated that pitchers in their early 20s who pitched extensively at the major league level rarely had long careers. Boras was able to convince Nationals' management to exercise restraint in the number of innings he would pitch early in his career. In the 2012 season, Boras' recommendation was a limit of 160 innings for the season for Strasburg. Despite the perceived need for Strasburg to pitch, the Nationals agreed to shut him down for the season in September of 2012 after pitching 159 1/3 innings which

---

[5]   "Scientists Unlock Mystery in Evolution of Pitchers," NY Times, James Gorman, June 26, 2013.

[6]   "Scott Boras Will Save You Now." ESPN the Magazine, Sam Miller, March 18, 2016.

while in the short run may have looked questionable was in the long run better for both the team and the player.

## SYNOPSIS

1.    Agents serve their clients in multiple ways beyond negotiating their contracts with professional teams.

2.    Despite earning millions of dollars during their playing careers, many professional athletes find themselves in financial distress soon after their playing careers are completed.

3.    The unions for each of the major professional sports provide for a certification process for agents before an agent can represent a player in the particular sport.

4.    The hiring of an agent by a college athlete terminates his or her amateur standing and ability to play an NCAA sport with some minor exceptions.

5.    SPARTA is the federal law that regulates sports agents and deals primarily with the duty to avoid misrepresentations and requires specific disclosures be included in all agency contracts.

6.    The Uniform Athletes Agents Act has been enacted in most states, but may differ from state to state in regard to the specific provisions of the versions enacted in each state.

# CHAPTER FOUR

# Endorsements

The modern era of sports endorsements began when young professional golfer Arnold Palmer turned to a former college golfing opponent Mark McCormack, then a lawyer, to help with establishing Palmer as a worldwide brand. From $6,000 worth of endorsements in 1960, their first year together, to $500,000 worth of endorsements in the second year, the burgeoning market for athlete endorsements was born. Right up until his death and well into his retirement, Palmer continued to earn 25 million dollars per year from endorsements for companies such as Callaway and Rolex.

American companies pay billions of dollars each year to leagues, teams, athletes and coaches for endorsements of their products.

Why would companies pay so much money?

Famous athletes increase brand recognition and are believed by sponsors to create a positive impression for their products by the transference of positive feelings felt toward particular athletes to their products. A particular athlete can also help the brand develop an identifiable personality. Athletes with reputations for excellence can also bring that perception to the product. In addition, endorsers can also provide the company greater public visibility and recognition as well as distinguish them from their competitors.

Popular athletes also can provide an element of excitement to an otherwise dull product. Athletes with winning personalities can continue to endorse products even after they have completed their playing careers as shown by Michael Jordan and Shaquille O'Neal.

# EXAMPLES OF ENDORSEMENT CONTRACTS

In 2003 Soccer superstar David Beckham signed a lifetime contract with Adidas that paid him an initial 80 million dollars with an additional 80 million dollars to be paid over his lifetime. As further compensation, however, he also receives money for promotional work and a percentage of Adidas' profits. The Adidas money along with his other endorsements earned him 75 million dollars in 2014, his first full year of retirement, which is more than he had earned in any year during which he played soccer.

George Foreman, the charismatic boxer sold his name and endorsement of the George Foreman Grill to Salton, Inc. for 23.5 million dollars in stock and five annual cash payments of 22.75 million dollars. Prior to selling his name, Foreman had been paid 60% of the profits on grill sales.

Between prize money and endorsements including his initial five year 40 million dollar endorsement deal with Nike that he signed upon becoming a professional golfer, Tiger Woods became the first professional athlete to cross the billion dollar amount for total earnings.

Coca Cola in 2003 signed eighteen year old LeBron James to a 12 million dollar endorsement contract before he ever played a minute in the NBA. In addition, Nike also signed James to a 90 million dollar endorsement contract promptly upon becoming the first player chosen in the 2003 NBA draft just after having graduated high school. Now, Lebron James has a lifetime Nike contract of 30 million dollars a year plus a share of shoe sales.

In 2016 Forbes listed Jamaican Gold Medal Olympic sprint champion Usain Bolt as number 32 on the list of world's highest earning athletes. Between June of 2015 and June of 2016 he earned 32.5 million dollars which is more than any other sprinter had ever earned in a single year. Among his endorsement contracts are Hublot, Virgin Media, Nissan and Visa, however, his biggest endorsement contract is with Puma which pays him 9 million dollars per year.

# NIKE

Of the top twenty-five highest paid athletic endorsement contracts, twelve of them are with Nike.

Nike dominates the athletic shoe market with a market share of more than 90%. It also has the greatest number of NBA players endorsing its shoes including LeBron James who has a lifetime contract with Nike. However, as a good example of the value of an endorsement for shoe sales, original Nike endorser and NBA superstar Stephen Curry switched his endorsement to Under Armour, a new comer to the world of basketball shoes in 2013 when his initial Nike endorsement contract ended. Nike, which was paying Curry 2.5 million dollars per year for his endorsement declined to match the 3 million dollar offer made to him by Under Armour. The immense popularity of Curry translated into shoe sales with the Under Armour shoes carrying his name bringing in 160 million dollars in sales in 2016 which is more than the signature shoes of every other player in the NBA including LeBron James.

# WHO EARNS ENDORSEMENTS?

While well-known, popular athletes such as Michael Phelps will earn millions in endorsements, according to the USA Track & Field Foundation of the top ten athletes in their events 80% are paid less than $50,000 a year in sponsorships and endorsements. In addition, if their rankings within their event drop, often their payments drop as well with many athletes' sponsorships terminated if their performances are not deemed worthy.

# MICHAEL JORDAN

Michael Jordan may be the most successful endorser of all time endorsing a wide range of products from those associated directly with athletics such as Nike or Gatorade to those merely connecting with the good will associated with him as a personality such as Hanes and Presbyterian Healthcare.

When Michael Jordan came back from his initial retirement from basketball, the five companies whose products he was endorsing had a 2% increase in the value of their stock.[1]

# PUBLIC IMAGE

Athletic excellence, however, is not all it takes for an athlete to be a valuable endorser. He or she must be likable. Even before rumors of steroid abuse surfaced against baseball superstar Barry Bonds, his perceived surly personality made him an anathema to companies seeking athletes for endorsements.

The public image and perception of an athlete's character is critical to commercial success. When the public starts to think negatively about the athlete, companies will drop the athlete. There is a long list of athletes who lost endorsement contracts due to scandal although in the case of Tiger Woods, the loss was not permanent.

Associating with a particular athlete will always carry some degree of risk. Young athletes may exhibit a degree of immaturity that can be harmful to the image of the company he or she is endorsing. The public perception of the athlete can change for numerous reasons including merely the erosion of the athlete's skills. However, the athlete can also become involved with a scandal that changes the public perception of the athlete. Regardless of the reason for the change in public perception of an athlete, sponsors are wary of

---

[1] "Athletic Endorsements and Their Effect on Consumers' Attitudes and Consumption," National Sporting Goods Association Management Conference Presentation, Dr. Karla McCormick 2013.

negative feelings about a disgraced or no longer superior athlete being transferred to perceptions of their products.

According to the research of Victor Stango and Christopher Knittel of the UC Davis Graduate School of Management Nike, Gatorade, Accenture, AT&T, Tiger Woods PGA Golf (Electronic Arts), Gillette (Proctor and Gamble), TLC Laser Eyes Centers and Golf Digest and other sponsors of Tiger Woods lost five to twelve billion dollars of shareholder value in the thirteen trading days following the car crash at his home that started a sex scandal and December 17th a week after Tiger temporarily left the PGA tour. As might be expected the sports related companies, Tiger Woods PGA Tour Golf, Gatorade and Nike had their stock drop the most at 4.3%.[2]

# PROVISIONS OF TYPICAL ENDORSEMENT CONTRACTS

A typical endorsement contract will require the athlete to make public appearances on behalf of the company as well as endorse the product. After two to six appearances, the contracts will generally provide for further compensation for additional appearances. The player agrees that his or her name and likeness can be used for marketing specific items, such as shoes or sports gear as well as related products. Pursuant to the contract, the player will agree not to wear a competitor's sports gear, shoes or other products in public. Along with the base compensation provided for in the contract, many contracts will provide for additional bonus payments based upon various achievements such as being named to the All-Star team or MVP.

An important provision in shoe contracts is a waiver of tort liability on the part of the athlete so that should the athlete suffer a foot injury or other injury that might be attributable to wearing the endorsed

---

[2] "Celebrity Endorsements, Firm Value and Reputation Risk: Evidence from the Tiger Woods Scandal," U.C. Davis Graduate School of Management, Christopher R. Knittel and Victor Stango, February 9, 2012.

shoe, the athlete waives the right to hold the shoe company responsible for such injury.

Because the image of the athlete is important to the company paying the athlete for his or her endorsement, there will often be provisions within the endorsement contract prohibiting the athlete from endorsing or promoting weapons, alcoholic beverages or tobacco products.

---

**QUESTION**

1.    Why are liability waivers important in an endorsement contract?

# MORALITY CLAUSE

Another critical provision found in all endorsement contracts is the morality clause. Companies invest tremendous amounts of money in athletes in return for their endorsement. Should the athlete's conduct harm the reputation of the company and his or her endorsement go from being a valuable asset to negatively affecting the company and its sales due to the public's change in perception of the athlete, morality clauses provide a method for the company to terminate the contract and sever their relationship if they deem it necessary. Professional golfer John Daly lost his endorsement contract with Wilson after a number of drinking binges. In 1991 he had signed a 10 million dollar contract with sporting goods company Wilson to endorse their golf equipment. In the wake of drinking binges that culminated in his wrecking of a hotel room at a golf tournament from which Daly withdrew, the morality clause in his contract was exercised and his Wilson endorsement contract was terminated in 1997. Later that same year, Daly signed an endorsement contract with golf equipment maker Callaway that had a narrowly written morality clause that included gambling and excessive drinking as grounds for terminating the contract which was invoked two years later. Kmart terminated professional golfer Fuzzy Zoeller's endorsement contract following comments considered racist about Tiger Woods and Woods himself lost many endorsement contracts following personal marital troubles.

One of the more unusual instances of the invoking of the morality clause occurred in 2000 when Mike Borkowski, a NASCAR driver for the AT&T Broadband team drove into two other cars during the course of a race causing the other cars to crash. Although this type of behavior is not unusual in a NASCAR race, AT&T terminated Borkowski's endorsement contract in part because of television broadcasting of the event which referred to the AT&T car as the responsible party for the crashes. The narrowly written morality clause provided for termination of the contract if Borkowski were to commit "any act or become involved in any situation or occurrence tending to bring AT&T into public disrepute, contempt, scandal or ridicule... or reflecting unfavorably on AT&T, or its name, reputation, public image or products."[3]

There is no standard morality clause. Certainly, criminal infractions are grounds to terminate contracts pursuant to the morality clause, but even behavior that merely puts the athlete or company into disrepute or behavior considered immoral can be the basis for a morality clause. Morality clauses are not uniform and the respective bargaining power of the company and the athlete can influence the specific wording of the morality clause. The athlete will want, as much as possible, language limiting the breadth of the morality clause to a criminal conviction for a crime involving moral turpitude, an old term used often to describe sex crimes in particular, while the company will want the morality clause to be written as broadly as possible such as to provide the company with the ability to terminate the contract in the event of any actions of the athlete bring him and the company into public disrepute as interpreted by the company in its sole discretion.

In 1999, professional basketball player Chris Webber won a 2.61 million dollar judgment from Fila which had terminated his

---

[3] "Jocks on the Rocks," Westword, Eric Dexheimer, January 18, 2001.

endorsement contract after he was charged with possession of marijuana while on a promotional trip for the company. Webber's lawyers successfully argued that his particular morality clause only provided for termination in the event of the conviction of a crime and the nature of Webber's offense was not that of a crime because marijuana had been decriminalized in Puerto Rico where the charges originated and his infraction was merely one that resulted in an administrative fine. Therefore, they argued, the offense did not constitute a crime and could not be used as the basis for terminating the contract pursuant to the morality clause in Webber's endorsement contract. This case illustrates the critical importance of the precise language used in an endorsement contract's morality clause.

On the other hand, in 1997, Converse terminated professional basketball player Latrell Sprewell's endorsement contract after he choked his coach P.J. Carlesimo, an infraction that also resulted in his being suspended from the NBA for 68 games. Sprewell sued Converse alleging that Converse had improperly terminated his endorsement contract, but the court ruled in favor of Converse.

## RASHARD MENDENHALL

NFL running back Rashard Mendenhall signed an endorsement contract with Hanesbrand, the parent company of Champion, a maker of sports apparel in 2008 upon his entering the NFL as the first round choice of the Pittsburgh Steelers. Two years later he signed a contract extension valued at more than a million dollars. However in 2011, shortly after Osama bin Laden's was shot to death by Navy Seals, Mendenhall tweeted a series of tweets questioning the general celebratory reaction of most Americans to bin Laden's death as well as even questioning the attacks on the World Trade Center of 9/11. Within three days, Hanesbrand terminated the endorsement contract pursuant to the morality clause contained in the endorsement contract. Mendenhall responded to the termination of his endorsement contract by suing Hanesbrand for a million dollars alleging breach of contract. According to Mendenhall, there was not sufficient evidence to warrant the invoking of the morality clause to terminate the contract. Hanesbrand filed a Motion for a Judgment on the Pleadings whereby Hanesbrand believed that no trial was necessary to come to a determination on this matter because all of the evidence required by the court to rule on the matter was contained in the Plaintiff's Complaint and the Defendant's Answer. The position of Hanesbrand was that the morality clause was specific enough to leave it up to the sole discretion of Hanesbrand to determine if Mendenhall had breached the terms of the contract and therefore there were no issues of fact requiring a trial. The Federal District Court did not grant the motion although it did recognize that Hanesbrand had the right to interpret the morality clause. However, the court also ruled that a trial would be necessary to determine whether or not Hanesbrand interpreted the contract and the morality clause in good faith. Based on this decision, Mendenhall would have had a difficult time winning his case at trial. Ultimately, Hanesbrand and Mendenhall settled the lawsuit without disclosing the terms of the settlement.

## MENDENHALL V. HANESBRANDS, INC.

United States District Court, M.D. North Carolina
856 F.Supp.2d 717 (2012)

### I.    Factual Background

Taking as true the facts alleged in the Complaint, the Court will recount the relevant background facts surrounding Plaintiff's claim against Defendant. Mr. Mendenhall is a professional athlete in the National Football League ("NFL") and is employed as a running back by the Pittsburgh Steelers. (Complaint ¶ 1). In May 2008, Mr. Mendenhall and Hanesbrands, a Maryland corporation with its principal place of business located in Winston-Salem, North Carolina, entered into a Talent Agreement (the "Talent Agreement"). (Under the terms of the Talent Agreement, Hanesbrands would use the services of Mr. Mendenhall to advertise and promote Hanesbrands' products sold under the Champion trademark. The Talent Agreement was for a three-year term, beginning on May 1, 2008, and expiring on April 30, 2011.

In August 2010, the parties executed an "Amendment and Extension of Hanesbrands Inc. Talent Agreement" (the "Extension Agreement"), which extended the term of the Talent Agreement for an additional four years, until April 30, 2015. In addition to extending the term of the Talent Agreement, the Extension Agreement modified Section 17(a) of the Talent Agreement. (Under the original terms of Section 17(a) as stated in the Talent Agreement:

If Mendenhall is arrested for and charged with, or indicted for or convicted of any felony or crime involving moral turpitude, then HBI shall have the right to immediately terminate this Agreement.

Pursuant to Section 3(a) of the Extension Agreement, the terms of Section 17(a) were modified to state the following:

If Mendenhall commits or is arrested for any crime or becomes involved in any situation or occurrence (collectively, the "Act") tending to bring Mendenhall into public disrepute, contempt, scandal, or ridicule, or tending to shock, insult or offend the majority of the consuming public or any protected class or group thereof, then we shall have the right to immediately terminate this Agreement. HBI's decision on all matters arising under this Section 17(a) shall be conclusive.

On May 2, 2011, Plaintiff issued the following tweets regarding Osama bin Laden, whose death had been announced by President Obama on May 1, 2011:

What kind of person celebrates death? It's amazing how people can HATE a man they never even heard speak. We've only heard one side . . .

I believe in God. I believe we're ALL his children. And I believe HE is the ONE and ONLY judge.

Those who judge others, will also be judged themselves.

For those of you who said we want to see Bin Laden burn in hell and piss on his ashes, I ask how would God feel about your heart?

There is not an ignorant bone in my body. I just encourage you to # think @dkller23 We'll never know what really happened. I just have a hard time believing a plane could take a skyscraper down demolition style.

In response to the May 2, 2011 tweets noted above, Plaintiff received some comments in support and some comments opposed to his views. On May 4, 2011, "[i]n response to some negative reaction" to the May 2, 2011 tweets, Mr. Mendenhall issued the following explanation:

I appreciate those of you who have decided to read this letter and attain a greater understanding of my recent twitter posts. I see how they have gotten misconstrued, and wanted to use this outlet as a way to clear up all things that do not truthfully represent myself, what I stand for personally, and any organization that I am a part of.

First, I want people to understand that I am not in support of Bin Laden, or against the USA. I understand how devastating 9/11 was to this country and to the people whose families were affected. Not just in the US, but families all over the world who had relatives in the World Trade Centers. My heart goes out to the troops who fight for our freedoms everyday, not being certain if they will have the opportunity to return home, and the families who watch their loved ones bravely go off to war. Last year, I was grateful enough to have the opportunity to travel over seas and participate in a football camp put on for the children of U.S. troops stationed in Germany. It was a special experience. These events have had a significant impact in my life.

"What kind of person celebrates death? It's amazing how people can HATE a man they have never even heard speak. We've only heard one side . . ."

This controversial statement was something I said in response to the amount of joy I saw in the event of a murder. I don't believe that this is an issue of politics or American pride; but one of religion, morality, and human ethics. In the bible, Ezekiel 33:11 states, "Say to them, 'As surely as I live, declares the Sovereign LORD, I take no pleasure in the death of the wicked, but rather that they turn from their ways and live. Turn! Turn from your evil ways . . .'" I wasn't questioning Bin Laden's evil acts. I believe that he will have to face God for what he has done. I was reflecting on our own hypocrisy. During 9/11 we watched in horror as parts of the world celebrated death on our soil. Earlier this week, parts of the world watched us in horror celebrating a man's death.

Nothing I said was meant to stir up controversy. It was my way to generate conversation. In looking at my timeline in its entirety, everything that I've said is with the intent of expressing a wide array of ideas and generating open and honest discussions, something I believe we as American citizens should be able to do. Most opinions will not be fully agreed upon and are not meant to be. However, I believe every opinion should be respected or at least given some thought. I apologize for the timing as such a sensitive matter, but it was not meant to do harm. I apologize to anyone I unintentionally harmed with anything that I said, or any hurtful interpretation that was made and put in my name.

It was only meant to encourage everyone reading it to think.

In a letter dated May 5, 2011, and addressed to Rob Lefko, one of Mr. Mendenhall's representatives at Priority Sports and Entertainment, Hanesbrands' Associate General Counsel, L. Lynette Fuller-Andrews, indicated that it was Hanesbrands' intent to terminate the Talent Agreement effective Friday, May 13, 2011, pursuant to Paragraph 17(a) of the Agreement. On May 6, 2011, Hanesbrands issued a public statement to ESPN, stating the following:

Champion is a strong supporter of the government's efforts to fight terrorism and is very appreciative of the dedication and commitment of the U.S. Armed Forces. Earlier this week, Rashard Mendenhall, who endorses Champion products, expressed personal comments and opinions regarding Osama bin Laden and the September 11 terrorist attacks that were inconsistent with the values of the Champion brand and with which we strongly disagreed. In light of these comments, Champion was obligated to conduct a business assessment to determine whether Mr. Mendenhall could continue to effectively communicate on behalf of and represent Champion with consumers.

While we respect Mr. Mendenhall's right to express sincere thoughts regarding potentially controversial topics, we no longer believe that Mr. Mendenhall can appropriately represent Champion and we have notified Mr. Mendenhall that we are ending our business relationship. Champion has appreciated its association with Mr. Mendenhall during his early professional football career and found him to be a dedicated and conscientious young athlete. We sincerely wish him all the best.

In a series of correspondence between Mr. Mendenhall's representative at Priority Sports and Entertainment and Hanesbrands' Associate General Counsel, Mr. Mendenhall contended that Hanesbrands had no legal basis for terminating the Talent Agreement and Extension. In contrast, Hanesbrands contended that Mr. Mendenhall's May 2, 2011 tweets regarding the death of Osama bin Laden and the events of September 11, 2001, met the standard set forth in Section 17(a) of the Talent Agreement and Extension and therefore Hanesbrands was within its right to terminate the Agreement.

Defendant, in its Motion for Judgment on the Pleadings, contends that it was within its rights under the express terms of Section 17(a) to terminate the Talent Agreement and Extension with Mr. Mendenhall pursuant to Section 17(a) of the Agreement. Hanesbrands argues that its decision on all matters arising under Section 17(a) are to be deemed conclusive pursuant to the Section's express terms. It is for these reasons that Hanesbrands moves for Judgment on the Pleadings [Doc. #11], asserting that "[b]ecause the undisputed terms of the

Talent Agreement vested Hanesbrands with the conclusive authority to terminate its contractual relationship with Mr. Mendenhall once it determined that his controversial and offensive statements tended to bring him into public disrepute, contempt, scandal or ridicule, or tended to shock, insult, or offend the majority of the consuming public, Mr. Mendenhall's breach of contract claim fails as a matter of law." In the alternative, Defendant requests that the Court dismiss Plaintiff's Complaint for failure to state a claim.

As to the third element, that is, as to Plaintiff's contention of non-performance by Defendant, Plaintiff has alleged that "by [Hanesbrands'] actions purporting to terminate the Talent Agreement and Extension under Section 17(a), and by its failure and refusal to pay amounts due Mr. Mendenhall, Defendant Hanesbrands is in breach of the Talent Agreement and Extension." As previously noted, pursuant to Section 17(a) of the Talent Agreement and Extension, Hanesbrands had the right to immediately terminate the Agreement, "[i]f Mendenhall commits or is arrested for any crime or becomes involved in any situation or occurrence tending to bring Mendenhall into public disrepute, contempt, scandal or ridicule, or tending to shock, insult or offend the majority of the consuming public or any protected class or group thereof." (Complaint, Ex. B at 4). Plaintiff does not allege that the morals clause in Section 17(a) is unenforceable as a general matter. Rather, Plaintiff alleges that Hanesbrands' action in purporting to terminate the Talent Agreement and Extension pursuant to Section 17(a), based on Plaintiff's May 2, 2011 tweets regarding Osama bin Laden, was "unreasonable, violates the express terms of the Talent Agreement and Extension, is contrary to the course of dealing between the parties with regard to Mr. Mendenhall's use of Twitter to freely express opinions on controversial and non-controversial subjects, [and] violates the covenant of good faith and fair dealing implied in every contract."

As it relates to the reasonableness of Hanesbrands' action, implied in all contracts governed by New York law "is a covenant of good faith and fair dealing in the course of contract performance," which requires parties exercising discretion under the contract "not to act arbitrarily or irrationally in exercising that discretion." *Dalton v. Educ. Testing Serv.,* 87 N.Y.2d 384, 389, 639 N.Y.S.2d 977, 663 N.E.2d 289 (1995) (finding that "within the implied obligation of each promisor to exercise good faith are any promises which a reasonable person in the position of the promisee would be justified in understanding were included" and that where the contract contemplates the exercise of discretion, the covenant of good faith and fair dealing "includes a promise not to act arbitrarily or irrationally in exercising that discretion"); *Fishoff v. Coty Inc.,* 634 F.3d 647, 653 (2d Cir.2011); *Sveaas v. Christie's Inc.,* 452 Fed.Appx. 63, 66 (2d Cir.2011). Courts have "equated the covenant of good faith and fair dealing with an obligation to exercise ... discretion reasonably and with proper motive, ... not ... arbitrarily, capriciously, or in a manner inconsistent with the reasonable expectations of the parties." *Fishoff,* 634 F.3d at 653 (quoting *In re Kaplan,* 143 F.3d 807, 819 (3d Cir.1998) (internal quotation marks omitted)). The "duty of good faith and fair dealing, however, is not without limits, and no obligation can be implied that would be inconsistent with other terms of the contractual relationship." *Dalton,* 87 N.Y.2d at 389, 639 N.Y.S.2d at 979–80, 663 N.E.2d 289. A "breach of the duty of good faith and fair dealing is considered a breach of contract." *Fishoff,* 634 F.3d at 653.

In the present case, the Court finds that to the extent that the Talent Agreement and Extension provides Hanesbrands with discretionary termination rights under Section 17(a), that discretion is subject to the implied covenant of good faith and fair dealing. As such, Hanesbrands' exercise of any such discretion, under the implied covenant of good faith and fair dealing, would include a promise on Hanesbrands' part not to act arbitrarily, irrationally or unreasonably in exercising that discretion.

In alleging that Hanesbrands acted unreasonably, Plaintiff's Complaint includes factual allegations that Hanesbrands, in a letter dated May 5, 2011, purported to terminate the Talent Agreement and Extension pursuant to Section 17(a) of the Agreement, while at the same time issuing a public statement to ESPN on May 6, 2011, which indicated that Hanesbrands ended its business relationship with Mr. Mendenhall for another reason, that being because it strongly disagreed with Mr. Mendenhall's comments. Since Section 17(a) is applicable only to the extent that Mr. Mendenhall became involved in an act that tended to "bring [him] into public disrepute, contempt, scandal or ridicule," or tended "to shock, insult or offend the majority of the consuming public or any protected class or group thereof," mere disagreement with Mr. Mendenhall's comments would not have triggered Hanesbrands' termination rights under Section 17(a). Therefore, from Plaintiff's factual allegations, the Court can reasonably infer that Defendant's actions in purporting to terminate the Talent Agreement and Extension pursuant to Section 17(a), may have been unreasonable, in light of the covenant of good faith and fair dealing, if such action was based on mere disagreement with Plaintiff's statements rather than on the applicability of Section 17(a)'s standard, as alleged by Plaintiff.

However, Defendant, in its Memorandum in Support of its Motion for Judgment on the Pleadings, contends that "Defendant had the right to terminate the contract as a result of the backlash caused by [Plaintiff's] outrageous statements." Defendant also contends that there was well-documented negative public reaction to Plaintiff's May 2, 2011 statements and that "Plaintiff's statements caused an almost instantaneous public uproar." In support of its contention, Defendant attached to its Answer select news reports relating to Mr. Mendenhall's May 2, 2011 tweets. The Court notes that for the purposes of a motion for judgment on the pleadings, documents attached to the Answer are part of the pleadings and may be considered by the Court without converting the motion to one for summary judgment only if the documents are central to Plaintiff's claim and the authenticity is not challenged. In this case, Plaintiff challenges the authenticity of the news reports that were attached to Defendant's Answer. Therefore, the news reports that are attached to Defendant's Answer are not properly before the Court for the purposes of a motion for judgment on the pleadings, and the Court will not convert Defendant's Motion to one for summary judgment. As such, the Court finds that it is not appropriate at this stage of the proceedings to consider the news reports attached to Defendant's Answer.

Nevertheless, Defendant contends that even without reference to the news reports, the undisputed facts support dismissal of this action. Specifically, Defendant contends that Plaintiff admits in the Complaint that: 1) after posting the 9/11 Tweets, he received 'negative reaction' and comments 'opposed' to his views; 2) his statements were 'controversial'; and 3) Plaintiff "apparently received enough criticism or ridicule in the two days that followed his posting of the 9/11 Tweets that he felt the need to post a public 'clarification' to attempt to mollify anyone he had 'unintentionally harmed' by his statements."

Therefore, the Court finds that a dispute of fact exists between the parties as to the nature of the public's response to Plaintiff's May 2, 2011 tweets. Furthermore, based on Plaintiff's allegations, the Court finds that, at this early stage of the proceedings, Plaintiff has stated at the very least a plausible claim for breach of contract based on the implied covenant of good faith and fair dealing. To find otherwise would require the Court to impermissibly draw inferences in Defendant's favor. To resolve this matter, a factual determination as to the nature of the public's response is necessary in order to assess whether the public's response to Plaintiff's May 2, 2011 tweets could reasonably be characterized in a manner that would trigger Hanesbrands' right to terminate the Agreement under Section 17(a)'s standard, which applied only to acts that tended to "bring [Mr. Mendenhall] into public disrepute, contempt, scandal, or ridicule," or tended "to shock, insult, or offend the majority of the consuming public." When, as in this case, there exists a material dispute of fact, such a determination goes beyond the scope of a motion for judgment on the pleadings, and therefore judgment as a matter of law is not appropriate at this stage of the proceedings. Therefore, Defendant's Motion for Judgment on the Pleadings will be DENIED.

---

## QUESTIONS

1.    How would you write a morality clause if you represented an athlete and how would it differ from one that you would write if representing a company paying for his or her endorsement?

2.    What should a company be required to provide as evidence of its good faith in terminating an endorsement contract based upon violation of a morality clause?

# COMPANY RESPONSE

Even if a company has grounds for terminating an athlete's endorsement contract due to a violation of the morality clause, it will not necessarily take that step, but rather evaluate each case individually based upon its perception of the public reaction and the perceived level of damage, if any, to the company. At this point the company has three possible options:

1.    Issue a press release condemning the actions, but supporting the athlete;

2.    Decline public comment while waiting to see whether the matter will be a lasting concern;

3.    Terminate the contract if they conclude that the athlete poses a serious determent to their image and their sales.

In making the decision as to whether to continue to employ a particular athlete as an endorser of their product, companies are most concerned with the response and attitudes of their customers to the particular offense and to the athlete. How much good will the athlete has accumulated and how much coverage the particular embarrassing event received or continues to receive in the news are major factors in the decision making by companies. Companies often count on the fading of the public's attention to various negative incidents. In some instances, without precisely proclaiming it, a company may be pleased with an edgier image if the company believes this will translate into greater sales.

Russian tennis star Maria Sharapova was suspended by the International Tennis Federation for two years from competition due to her failing a drug test that detected Melodonium a heart medication only recently banned by the International Tennis Federation. Upon appeal the Court of Arbitration for Sport reduced her penalty by nine months ruling that she was unaware that the drug had been added to the list of banned substances only a few months before her test showed the presence of the drug which is used by some athletes believing it improves blood flow and improves the athlete's recovery while training. Sharapova had been using the drug since 2006 for what she said was a range of health issues. The combination of an offense not considered to be of a significant performance enhancing drug nature combined with generally continuing public favorability of Sharapova caused sponsors such as Avon, Evian, Head and most importantly Nike to stand by her.

In a stunning example of how public perceptions can change, Michael Vick, while quarterback of the Atlanta Falcons was convicted of operating an illegal dog fighting operation and served 21 months in federal prison. As one would expect, he promptly lost all of his valuable endorsement contracts, however upon emerging from prison he successfully rejoined the NFL and was the 2010 Comeback Player of the Year while playing for the Philadelphia Eagles. The combination of excellent play and genuine contrition made him the first athlete ever to be dropped by Nike and then rehired as an endorser which they did in 2011.

The reactions of different companies will be dependent upon the product, to whom they sell the product and their corporate culture. In 2009, the British Tabloid, News of the World, published a photograph of Olympic swimming champion Michael Phelps showing him smoking marijuana through a bong three months after he had won eight gold medals at the 2008 Beijing Olympic Games. As a result of the notoriety, Kellogg's the makers of Kellogg's Corn Flakes breakfast cereal upon whose box, Michael Phelps image had appeared, immediately dropped him as an endorser, however, the Subway sandwich shop chain maintained its relationship with him, correctly determining that their customers would not be offended by Phelps smoking marijuana. He apologized for "using bad judgment" and was suspended from competition by American swimming authorities for five months. Kellogg's chose to end its relationship with him, stating his behavior was not consistent with the image of Kellogg's as a family brand.

Speedo, another product endorsed by Phelps issued the following statement:

"Speedo would like to make it clear that it does not condone such behavior and we know Michael truly regrets his action. . . Michael is a valued member of the Speedo team and a great champion. We will do all that we can to support him and his family." Thus the company still supported Phelps after determining the value of his public perception for excellence was not too negatively affected by his out of the water behavior.[4]

NBA superstar Kobe Bryant was accused of rape in 2003. Bryant held a press conference with his wife at his side and tearfully admitted that he had sex with a 19 year old hotel employee but claimed that it was consensual. Ultimately the criminal case was dropped and a civil case was settled with a confidentiality agreement as to the amount of any payment. As a result of the incident McDonalds, Nutella and Coca-Cola ended their relationships with Bryant. Nike continued the relationship, but did not feature him in any advertising for two and a half years. Since then he has somewhat reclaimed his image.

---

[4]    Journal of Advertising Research September 2011.

## QUESTIONS

1.    How does a company determine its response to an incident likely to put its endorsing athlete in a bad light?

2.    How does a company determine when to invoke the morality clause in a contract of an endorsing athlete and should the criteria they use be the same for all endorsing athletes?

# RYAN LOCHTE

American swimmer Ryan Lochte's story about being robbed at a gas station in Brazil in the early morning hours after an evening of partying became one of the biggest stories of the 2016 Summer Olympics in Rio and an obsession of the media. Lochte initially said that he and some other swimmers were pulled over by criminals posing as policemen who pointed guns at them and took their money. His story changed as videos emerged contradicting his version of what happened, at which point Lochte famously said that due to being intoxicated he "over-exaggerated" his story. The public and the media which had initially been sympathetic and supportive of his plight turned on him as the facts changed.

Of interest is that the common misconception held by many in the public was that Lochte and the other swimmers had vandalized a bathroom at the gas station before being confronted by armed security guards. The truth, which was largely overlooked by many in the public, was that while Lochte and his fellow swimmers did urinate on an outside wall of the gas station when they could not get into the bathroom, they in no way vandalized the bathroom. As he returned to his taxi, Lochte did pull down a poster from a wall, however, his version of a gun being pointed at him and the other swimmers and money demanded was indeed accurate. In any event, the public perception is what matters to advertisers so in an exercise of quick damage control, Ralph Lauren and other Lochte sponsors promptly exercised their rights under the morals clauses in their endorsement contracts and terminated the contracts. Speedo issued the following statement:

"While we have enjoyed a winning relationship with Ryan for over a decade and he has been an important member of the Speedo team, we cannot condone behavior that is counter to the values this brand has long stood for. We appreciate his many achievements and hope he moves forward and learns from this experience."

Yet within a few weeks, other sponsors saw opportunity to pick up a high profile endorser at a bargain price. Pine Bros a cough drop company entered into an endorsement contract with him saying "just as Pine Bros. is forgiving to your throat, the company asks the public for a little forgiveness for an American swimming legend." Lochte followed this up with a new endorsement contract with a crime prevention device maker, Robocopp.

## OTHER ATHLETES LOSING ENDORSEMENTS

Lance Armstrong, an American cyclist was an iconic figure as both a cancer survivor and winner of the Tour de France a record seven consecutive times. However, when he was ultimately exposed as a liar and user of numerous banned substances he lost all of his endorsement contracts including eight of them in a single day in 2012 at a cost to him of an estimated 150 million dollars.

Aaron Hernandez, a successful tight end for the New England Patriots lost both of his endorsement contracts with Cytosport, the maker of Muscle Milk and Puma when he first became under suspicion of murder. He was later convicted of murder and committed suicide in prison.

Boxer Manny Pacquiao's endorsement contract was terminated by Nike following anti-gay comments made in an interview by Pacquiao. The response of Nike was swift, issuing a statement in which they indicated that they found his views "abhorrent and reiterated Nike's long standing support of the LGBT community."

# OLYMPIC RULES

Since 1991 the by-laws of Rule 40 of the Olympic charter prohibit athletes from advertising their own particular sponsors during the Olympic Games. It reads "no competitor, team official or other team personnel who participates in the Olympic Games may allow his person, name, picture or sports performances to be used for advertising purposes during the Olympic Games."

"Use of a Participant's image for advertising purposes during the Rio 2016 Olympic Games

Rule 40 of the Olympic Charter:

What you need to know as a Participant

Are you an athlete, coach/trainer or official participating in the Rio 2016 Olympic Games? If so, read the following document to learn more about Rule 40.

Bye-law 3 to Rule 40 of the Olympic Charter (commonly referred to in this context as "Rule 40") states that: "Except as permitted by the IOC Executive Board, no competitor, coach, trainer or official who participates in the Olympic Games may allow his person, name, picture or sports performances to be used for advertising purposes during the Olympic Games."

The Olympic Charter is the guiding document for the entire Olympic Movement. It defines the mission and role of the International Olympic Committee (IOC), National Olympic Committees (NOCs) and International Federations (IFs). It also provides rules for the organisation and administration of the Olympic Games, as well as guidance on disciplinary procedures and other governance issues.

1.    What is the purpose of Rule 40?

Rule 40 is in place for various reasons, including:

•    To preserve the unique nature of the Olympic Games by preventing overcommercialisation.

•    To allow the focus to remain on the athletes' performance.

•    To preserve sources of funding, as 90 per cent of the revenues generated by the IOC are distributed to the wider sporting movement. This means that USD 3.25 million every day goes to the development of athletes and sports organisations at all levels around the world.

2.    Who does Rule 40 apply to?

Athletes, coaches/trainers and officials participating in the Rio 2016 Olympic Games.

3.    When does Rule 40 apply? During the Olympic Games period from 27 July until 24 August 2016 (nine days prior to the Opening Ceremony until three days after the Closing Ceremony of the Rio 2016 Olympic Games).

4.    As a Participant, can my personal sponsor launch an advertising campaign during the period of the Rio 2016 Olympic Games?

Yes, if they are Olympic sponsors.

No, if they are not an Olympic sponsor as the advertising campaign would then be seen as benefiting from the appeal of the Olympic Games.

Support from the business community, including Olympic sponsors, who acquire exclusive rights, is crucial to the staging of the Games and the operations of every organization within the Olympic Movement. Revenue generated by commercial partnerships accounts for more than 40 per cent of Olympic revenues and partners provide vital technical services and product support to the entire Olympic Movement, in particular to provide the best possible conditions for athletes.

Olympic sponsors are: TOP Partners for international rights; NOC local sponsors for national rights; Rio 2016 Olympic Games sponsors for host territory rights.

5. Can my personal sponsors continue running an existing campaign during the period of the Rio 2016 Olympic Games?

Advertising by your sponsors—who are not Olympic sponsors—may in principle continue during the period of the Olympic Games, subject to the following:

• NOCs may decide to restrict or prohibit advertising subject to the territory's applicable laws and regulations

• The advertising must not create any impression of a commercial connection with any Olympic property and in particular the Olympic Games

• Applications to advertise must be submitted for approval to the NOC or IOC

6. Can my personal sponsors refer to my performance or my participation at the Rio 2016 Olympic Games?

Yes, if they are Olympic sponsors.

If they are not Olympic sponsors, the use of certain terms related to the Olympic Games alongside the Participant's name or image is not permitted, whether it is an existing campaign or not. See below for examples:

Olympic, Olympics, Games, Olympiad, Olympiads "Citius, Altius, Fortius"

Any use of other Olympic-related terms in such a way as to imply an association with the Olympic Games, depending upon context, is not permitted. Please see the examples below. For a full list of terms and further details please contact your NOC.

2016, Rio or Rio de Janeiro, Gold or Silver or Bronze, Medal, Performance, Sponsors, Victory, Summer, Games

7.    How do I apply for my personal sponsors' advertising during the period of the Rio 2016 Olympic Games?

Athletes must initiate the application process.

Step 1 Check your NOC's position Step 2 If your NOC permits advertising by your sponsor, complete and submit the application form

—    for a national campaign in your NOC's territory: to your NOC

—    for a national campaign in another NOC's territory: to the NOC in question

—    for an international campaign: to the IOC

Step 3 Wait for feedback

—    NOC or IOC expected to provide an answer within 21 calendar days

—    No response after 21 days means the request is deemed approved

8.    When should I send my application?

As soon as possible to ensure that your application is reviewed in a timely manner.

9.    Can my agent, coach or personal sponsor apply in my name?

Yes, but your signature is required. Application forms are available from:

—    your NOC

—    athletes@olympic.org

—    Athletes' Hub from 2016

10.    Who is responsible for implementing Rule 40?

The implementation of Rule 40 in each country is the responsibility of the NOC of the relevant territories or the Rio 2016 Olympic Games Organising Committee.

NOCs may have additional requirements in relation to Rule 40 and its implementation. Local laws may also impact how Rule 40 is implemented in a specific country or territory. Please contact your NOC for further details.

11.   What happens if I breach Rule 40 guidelines?

If the IOC/NOC is made aware of a potential breach of Rule 40, it will investigate and handle each case individually depending on the circumstances. Potential sanctions by the IOC as per the Olympic Charter or by the respective NOC, depending on its regulations, may apply.

12.   Who should I contact for further information?

Contact your NOC for further information. If they are in doubt regarding specific questions, they will contact the IOC.

13.   Can I also contact the IOC Athletes' Commission directly?

Yes. You can write to them for any athlete-related questions, advice and information at athletes@olympic.org."[5]

---

Rule 40 was designed to enhance and protect the value of the sale by the IOC of official sponsorships for the Olympic Games. This rule works, however, to the detriment of the individual athletes who are prevented from advertising their particular sponsor's products during the Olympic Games, thereby diminishing the exposure and value of their endorsement to their sponsor. The IOC's response to this concern was to permit companies sponsoring individual athletes, but who are not official sponsors of the Olympic Games to use the athletes in advertising during the Olympic Games, but not permit them to use the name "Olympic Games" or similar terms. For extremely well-known athletes, such as Michael Phelps and his endorsement of the sportswear company Under Armour, this is not a

---

[5]   "Use of a Participant's image for advertising purposes during the Rio 2016 Olympic Games: Rule 40 of the Olympic Charter: What you need to know as a Participant," International Olympic Committee.

problem, however, for many lesser known Olympic athletes the inability to mention the Olympic Games dramatically reduces the value of the endorsement and hence the amount they are paid.

In 2015 American Olympic 800 meter track athlete Nick Symmonds sued the U.S. Olympic Committee and USA Track and Field, the national organization that controls track and field in the United States, alleging that their requirement that at the Olympic trials and at Olympic competition only the logo of Nike, the official apparel company of the United States Olympic Committee was a violation of anti-trust law and possibly put him in violation of his contract with his own endorsement contract with Brooks Running, the company with which he had a personal endorsement contract.

The Federal District Court for Oregon dismissed the lawsuit in 2016 saying in part,

"The logo restrictions in this case directly implicate USOC's ability to generate revenue for the United States Olympic Team; allowing any company to advertise on competitor apparel would unduly interfere with USOC's fundraising mission. First, the Regulations prevent a dilution of the Olympic brand. The Regulations permit the USOC and USATF to play a gatekeeping function which preserves the exclusivity—and thus value—of the Olympic symbols and name. By strictly limiting the advertisements that can appear on the field of competition itself, the Defendants can control the use of the Olympic brand and preserve the integrity of their primary fundraising mechanism. Second, the Regulations bolster the value of USOC's and USATF's corporate sponsorships. If, instead of purchasing an official sponsorship through USATF, would-be advertisers could instead place their logos directly on high-profile athletes, the value of these corporate sponsorships would necessarily decrease. Accordingly, the Regulations are necessary to implement the clear intent of Congress and to make the ASA's statutory scheme work. Without them,

USOC's revenue-generating capabilities would be compromised in a way that is plainly repugnant to the text and purpose of the Act."[6]

---

## QUESTION

1.    Do you agree with the court's decision? Should individual athletes be permitted at the Olympics to wear sports apparel with the logo of companies that are not official sponsors of the Olympics?

# SYNOPSIS

1.    Endorsements of products by athletes are lucrative contracts for both the athlete and the company whose product the athlete is endorsing.

2.    Endorsement contracts will generally contain liability waivers by the athlete.

3.    Endorsement contracts will generally contain morality clauses which can vary from contract to contract depending on the relative bargaining strength of the parties.

4.    Whether a company will invoke the morality clause depends on a multitude of factors.

5.    A company is required by law to exercise good faith in invoking a morality clause.

6.    Athletes participating in the Olympic Games have significant limitations on their ability to obtain individual endorsement contracts.

---

[6]    Gold Medal LLC v. USA Track & Field et al., U.S. District Court, District of Oregon, Civ. No. 6:16–cv–00092–MC, May 11, 2016.

# College Sports

College sports are extremely popular and ingrained in our culture. Five hundred thousand athletes play college sports in the United States. According to a survey by Harris Interactive, approximately 45% of Americans follow college sports while 29 million people attended a college sporting event in 2014. Approximately 80 million people watch the NCAA Men's Division I basketball tournament and the billion dollars' worth of television commercials included in the television coverage. The Tournament has come to be known as March Madness, a term trademarked by the NCAA. The United States is unique in the world in having high level sports competition done by colleges which are largely regulated by the NCAA. March Madness represents the greatest source of profits to the NCAA. In 2015 the NCAA received approximately 900 million dollars in March Madness related revenue, primarily from its broadcast rights contracts with CBS. More than two-thirds of the NCAA's revenues come from the March Madness basketball tournament.

## IT'S ABOUT THE MONEY

In 2016, CBS Sports and Turner Broadcasting paid 8.8 billion dollars to the NCAA to extend its rights to the NCAA men's basketball tournament for eight more years to 2032. The previous fourteen year contract ran through 2024 at a total cost of 10.8 billion dollars. Turner broadcasts the games on its TBS, TNT and truTV networks. Trying to anticipate the media landscape many years in the future is obviously difficult, but the contract also includes live streaming rights. According to the terms of the contract, the national championship game will alternate between CBS and TBS.

Rutgers joined the Big Ten conference in 2014 and has not been very competitive in most sports as exemplified by a 2016 football loss to Michigan by a score of 78–0. However, the numbers that really count in college football are the numbers of dollars and in that regard, Rutgers joining the Big Ten is a win for Rutgers and for the league itself. Each year, Rutgers receives ten million dollars in conference revenue, which will be increasing in upcoming years to more than forty million dollars per year derived primarily by television revenues. With Big Ten conference teams, such as Ohio State and Michigan, primarily based in the central part of the United States, the addition of Rutgers, the state university of New Jersey brought with it an additional eight million homes in the metropolitan New York City to the Big Ten Network television coverage with significant increases in advertising revenue.

In 2010 the Southeastern Conference (SEC) became the first athletic conference to bring in a billion dollars in athletic related revenues from tickets sales, merchandising, licensing, but primarily television contacts.

In addition to the broadcasting revenues, the NCAA also sells what it refers to as corporate partnerships whereby companies are designated as official partners of the NCAA and are allowed to use the NCAA logo in their advertising. These partnerships sell for approximately ten million dollars each.

The colleges themselves also profit from March Madness. Merely playing in the tournament in a first round game has resulted in schools recently receiving 1.7 million dollars. Teams that make it to the Sweet Sixteen receive payments of 5 million dollars and schools making it to the Final Four have received 8.3 million dollars.

In 2015 the College Football Playoff bowl games paid 505.9 million dollars to the colleges and universities playing in the 39 post season games and their conferences. It should be noted, however, that FBS schools participating in the NCAA playoffs also spent 100.2 million dollars as expenses of their participation. However, this is still a substantial profit. The amounts paid to the schools also represented an increase of 196 million dollars from what was received by the post season playing schools in the previous 2013–2014 season, the last without a playoff system. Under the playoff system used in the 2014–2015 season, the top four teams chosen by a selection committee participated in two semi-final bowl games with the winners of these two teams playing for the national title. Previously under the old BCS system, the two top teams chosen by polls and computer rankings competed for the national championship.

# THE ROLE OF CONFERENCES

Division I college sports is ruled by individual conferences, the most significant of which are the five conferences that bring in the largest revenues, namely the Pacific 12 Conference (Pac 12), the Southeastern Conference (SEC), the Big Ten Conference, The Big 12 Conference and the Atlantic Coast Conference (ACC), which collectively are often referred to as the "Power Five."

# BUSINESS MODEL

Although revenues earned by college sports continue to rise, the expenses are increasing even more rapidly. According to financial information provided by the 50 public institutions in the Power Five conferences, their total revenues rose by 304 million dollars in 2015, however, their expenses rose by 332 million dollars. "Can College Athletics Continue to Spend Like This" Erik Brady, USA Today April 17, 2016.

For the 178 public schools in Division I of the NCAA that are not members of the Power Five conferences, revenues increased by 199 million dollars, but expenses increased by 218 million dollars.

# BUDGETS

Only twelve of the NCAA's top 230 athletic programs are self-sufficient. Texas A&M ran a profit of $83,295,225 in 2015. Texas, Ohio State, LSU, Oklahoma, Tennessee, Penn State,, Kentucky, Arkansas, South Carolina and Nebraska also were profitable, but to a lesser extent, however, the large majority of NCAA college sports programs run at losses that need to be made up through a combination of student fees, which are sometimes buried within the student bills and not readily apparent, government subsidies and university subsidies. This comes at a time when costs are rising as there is increased pressure to increase the value of scholarships as well as allow athletes to share in intellectual property rights. In addition concussion lawsuits and other costly litigation also represent possible area of greater costs to colleges and universities in the future.

As a cost cutting measure, in recent years Division One schools have dropped hundreds of varsity teams. Between 2007 and 2012, Division One schools cut 205 varsity sports. Men's tennis, gymnastics and wrestling, in particular, have been the victims of athletic budget constraints.

So why do schools continue to pour money into often unprofitable sports programs? In some instances it is a matter of prestige. Tied to that however, is what has come to be known as the "Flutie effect," named after Heisman Trophy winning Boston College quarterback, Doug Flutie. Doug J. Chung, Harvard Business School Assistant Professor of Marketing attributed a 30% increase in college applications at Boston College to the exploits of Flutie. In addition, successful sports programs spur on alumni donations in amounts not reflected in athletic department revenues.

A major exception to the rule that Division I athletic programs are not self-supporting is Ohio State University, which has one of the biggest athletic budgets in the country. In 2015, its athletic budget was almost 114 million dollars. Ohio State fields 26 varsity sport teams including riflery and synchronized swimming. The only two sports that are financially profitable at Ohio State are football and men's basketball, with football in 2015 making a profit of more than 40 million dollars and men's basketball returning a profit of more than 14 million dollars. These sports are so profitable that they not only help fund the other men's and women's sports including an expensive women's ice hockey program, but in 2015 the athletic department actually turned over millions dollars of excess funds back to the University.

The pressure to come up with money to fund athletic programs also leads college football powers, such as Ohio State and Alabama to schedule games with schools with weaker football programs who are paid upwards of a million dollars or more to bring their football team to the football power's campus for a game in which they will be trounced. With so much money on the line in bowl games and the college football playoffs, every win is precious and carries with it the potential for big financial payoffs for the football powers while for the schools with the lesser programs, these games bring much needed funds to help keep the school's athletic department afloat. In 2012 Savannah State accepted an $860,000 payout to lose to Oklahoma State by a score of 84–0.

## STUDENT FEES

USA Today did a study of the relationship between student fees and college athletic budgets in 2010 using revenue and expense reports filed by colleges with the NCAA. It found that during the 2008–2009 school year, students in 222 Division One public schools paid more than 795 million dollars in student fees to supplement school athletic budgets. Student fees generally cover a range of activities including health care; however, USA Today found that the largest amount of mandatory student fees went to cover shortfalls in athletic department budgets. In return, students often received either free or reduced cost tickets to school sporting events. According to USA Today, "At least six schools—all in Virginia—charged each of their students more than $1,000 as an athletics fee for the 2008–2009 school year. That ranged from 10% to more than 23% of the total tuition and mandatory-fee charges for in-state students."

Often those athletic fees were not clearly indicated on students' bills. According to USA Today's study 15 of the 20 colleges with the highest student athletic fees failed to disclose their fees either on students' bills or University websites.

The relationship between often undisclosed student athletic fees and the cost of operating college athletics was also a concern of the Knight Commission on Intercollegiate Athletics in its 2010 report entitled "Restoring the Balance: Dollars, Values, and the Future of College Sports." In that report the Knight Commission recommended making student fees more transparent and open. According to Commission co-chairman, William E. Kirwan, "At a time when the cost of attendance at college is going up at a very high rate, it is a matter of transparency and fairness and equity that people out to know what they're spending their money on. . . . I think that this is a way of bringing pressure to bear—this transparency and this exposure of revenues and expenditures—and beginning to put a hold on, to tamp down, the rate of increase (of spending) in intercollegiate athletics."

# SPONSORSHIP AGREEMENTS

Corporate sponsorships, particularly by athletic apparel companies are a major source of funding for college sports. In 2016, Under Armour signed a 15 year 280 million dollar contract with UCLA. Nike which has dominated the athletic apparel field in the past signed a 15 year contract with Ohio State earlier in 2016 for 252 million dollars. Also, in 2016, UCLA and Under Armour entered into the biggest college sports sponsorship contract ever made worth an estimated 280 million dollars in cash and sporting gear over fifteen years. The attractiveness of college sports for marketing by sports apparel companies, particularly the big three of Under Armour, Nike and Adidas have turned college sponsorships into a bidding war to land the most popular and visible schools such as Notre Dame with Under Armour and Michigan, Texas and Ohio State with Nike.

Tom Izzo, the Michigan State basketball coach is paid $400,000 per year to endorse Nike, while the Nike contract of Duke coach Mike Krzyzewski is estimated to be a multi-million dollar contract.

For their money, the athletic sponsors get increased visibility on multiple levels. The Nike contract with the University of Alabama requires not just athletes but even upper-level administrators to wear Nike gear in public so that if university officials including the president of the university are playing golf, they must wear Nike golf shoes. While most apparel company sponsorship agreements require the athletic department employees to wear the apparel of the sponsoring company, the contract provision that other university employees in positions unrelated to sport are required to wear such garb is somewhat unusual.

In addition the logos of Nike, Adidas and Under Armour sponsors appear on the uniforms of players as well as in various places around the stadiums.

In 2014, Under Armour, whose founder and CEO was a former football player for the University of Maryland signed a ten year contract with the University of Maryland under which it pays the school 33 million dollars in cash and athletic apparel. In addition, Under Armour tests new products including ungrabbable shirts for football uniforms in conjunction with the University. "Under Armour Seeks to do for Maryland What Nike Did for Oregon," Marc Tracy, NY Times August 25, 2015.

## COACHES' SALARIES

Coaches' salaries in Division One football and men's basketball programs are quite high, particularly when compared to their unpaid student-athletes. In 2015, the average college football coach's salary reached two million dollars. Ten years ago it was $950,000.

In 2017 Nick Saban, the successful coach of the University of Alabama football team signed a three year contract extension to his existing contract which pays him 11.25 million dollars for the 2018 football season. Saban's contract, which now extends through 2025 provides for payments of 65 million dollars plus incentive bonuses that could reach as high as $700,000 each year of the contract. To put this into perspective the Governor of Alabama is paid $105,000 per year and the University of Alabama President is paid $611,000. However, perhaps we should remember the words of Babe Ruth who when asked in 1930 about his earning a salary of $80,000 per year while President Herbert Hoover was paid $75,000 annually responded that he had a better year than the President.

In fact, in most states, the college basketball and football coaches at the state universities are the highest paid state employees. It also should be noted, however, that much of the source of Division One football and basketball coaches' salaries comes from multimedia and marketing rights. Funds received from radio and television contracts, shoe contracts and money paid from booster clubs provide much of a Division One coach's revenue. The amounts paid to the coach are often justified by the argument much of the money being derived from media and marketing contracts, however, with overall athletic programs at the majority of Division I schools running in the red even at big time schools, it can seem odd that coaches are paid as much as they are.

Additional perks coaches receive may include the use of private jets, low interest home loans, annuities, luxury suites at school stadiums and vacation homes. Approximately 10% of college coaches even receive a percentage of ticket revenues.

Bonuses often form a major part of the compensation packages of Division One football and basketball coaches. In 2014 Missouri football coach Gary Pinkel achieved seven bonuses provide for in his contract that brought him an additional $900,000, the most of any Division One football coach that year.

Some successful coaches eschew bonuses. Hall of Fame Kentucky men's basketball coach, John Calipari, whose previous contact with the University of Kentucky provided for six annual bonuses that could reach as much as $750,000 agreed to eliminate all bonuses in his 2015 contract extension with the exception of a $50,000 bonuses related to his team's academic performance. Calipari's contact extension did, however make him the highest paid college basketball coach with a seven year contract worth 52.5 million dollars. It should be noted that Calipari has earned his academic performance bonus in each of the years since his contract extension was signed. In a sport where academic performance has often not lived up to athletic performance, the University of Kentucky basketball team scored a perfect 1.000 APR for the past three years, according to the NCAA. The Academic Progress Rate (APR) is determined through consideration of academic eligibility, retention and graduation of players.

Despite these large coaching salaries, the money earned by top flight programs in some instances more than covers the salaries and other operating expenses of the sport in college basketball where Coach Mike Kryzewski's program results in a profit of 12.8 million dollars to Duke University, Rick Pitino's program results in a profit of 4.6 million dollars to the University of Louisville and John Calipari's program results in a 7.7 million dollar profit to the University of Kentucky. "College Basketball Coaches and their Slam Dunk Salaries" Erik Sherman, Fortune Magazine March 21, 2015.

# NCAA

The National Collegiate Athletic Association (NCAA) is a non-profit association of more than 1,200 member colleges and universities which regulates college sports. The NCAA divides schools into three separate divisions, namely Division I, Division II and Division III. Division I schools generally consist of the largest schools with the biggest budgets while Division III schools are generally the smallest schools with the smallest budgets. In fact, Division III schools do not even provide athletic scholarships to their athletes.

Division I schools alone field 6,000 teams on which more than 170,000 athletes compete. Overall, the NCAA regulates 89 different championships in 23 sports across its three divisions.

Uniquely, Division I football is divided into two subgroupings. The first subgroup of the larger, higher revenue producing schools is called the Football Bowl Subdivision (FBS). These schools are, as the name implies, eligible to participate in post season bowl games and the playoff for the national championship. The other subgroup of schools with less financial investment in their football programs is called the Football Championship Subdivision (FCS) and has its own playoff for its own national championship.

# HISTORY OF THE NCAA

The first intercollegiate American football game occurred on November 6, 1869 when Rutgers beat Princeton by a score of 6–4. In its early days, football was particularly brutal with 25 collegiate football players killed during the 1905 season. Coupled with the brutality of the sport was widespread corruption that led to calls to abolish football. President Theodore Roosevelt, a former collegiate boxer, called a White House meeting attended by representatives of Harvard, Princeton and Yale, the leading football colleges of that era in an effort to come up with a plan to save college football. As a result of the meeting, the three schools issued a public statement in which they acknowledged that college sports needed to change in order to survive and the seeds for the NCAA were first planted with 68 schools forming the Intercollegiate Athletic Association (IAA), later renamed the NCAA.

College sports became increasingly popular in the 1920s and rapidly evolved into a big business. While we may often think of recruiting improprieties as being a recent phenomenon, it was common during the 1920s for college football players to be paid as much as $10,000 which translates to close to about $90,000 in today's dollars. Colleges openly paid players and provided them with no-show jobs. In 1939 freshman football players at the University of Pittsburgh actually went on strike because they were getting paid less than upper class members of the team. A 1929 report of the Carnegie Foundation found that 81 of 112 schools surveyed ignored NCAA rules regarding compensation of players. In 1948 the NCAA enacted the "Sanity Code," which was intended to eliminate such financial abuses and limit payments to athletes to scholarships awarded entirely on the basis of financial need. Under the Sanity Code, student athletes' compensation was limited to free tuition and one free meal per day during the sport season.

The penalty for violating the Sanity Code was total expulsion from NCAA membership, which, in effect was banishment from participating in intercollegiate sports. The Sanity Code was not popular with NCAA member schools, in large part because of the harshness of the sole penalty for violation. The Sanity Code was repealed in 1951. While the Sanity Code was in effect 27 schools were investigated on suspicion of violating the Sanity Code, but none was ever determined to have violated the Sanity Code although in the cases of seven schools investigated in the second year of the Sanity Code, a majority of the NCAA schools voted to find the schools in violation of the Sanity Code. A two-thirds vote was required to find a school in violation of the Sanity Code so no sanctions were ever issued.

Things started to change with the hiring of Walter Byers as NCAA executive director in 1951. In his first year at the helm he engineered a suspension of then defending NCAA men's basketball national champion University of Kentucky basketball team, coached by the legendary Adolph Rupp, for the upcoming 1952 and 1953 season on the basis of a point shaving gambling scandal. Unlike the enforcement of the Sanity Code which required a two-thirds majority of all schools to act in response to violations, Byers was able to act through a small infractions board. This action solidified his power.

The next major development in the evolution of college sports was the increased interest in televising games, particularly college football. Television was in its infancy in the 1950s and instead of recognizing the marketing and advertising potential of this new medium, the NCAA was more concerned about what it perceived as the danger of lost stadium ticket sales as a result of televising games. As a result, in 1951 the NCAA member schools voted 161 to 7 to prohibit the televising of games with the exception of a few games selected by the NCAA. The NCAA initially limited televised games to one televised game each Saturday. In addition, it ruled that no college football team could participate in more than one televised regular season game per year. Initially, the revenues derived from each game televised were divided between the NCAA and the two teams playing in the particular game. In 1952 NBC paid 1.4 million dollars to the NCAA for the rights to broadcast an eleven game football season with the NCAA keeping 12% of this sum and the rest being divided equally among all of the NCAA member schools. In these early years of televised football, the television networks paid more for the rights to college football games than for the rights to televise professional football.

As the popularity of college football rose in the 1970s and 1980s, the larger football schools resented sharing the television revenues that they generated. In 1979 a group of 61 of the larger football schools formed their own College Football Association and negotiated their own contract with NBC totally separate from the NCAA. The proposed contract was to be a four year contract at a cost of 180 million dollar. The response of the NCAA was strong and swift. The NCAA ruled that any college negotiating its own television contract apart from the NCAA would be banned from not just participating in NCAA sanctioned football games, but in addition would be banned from all athletic competitions regulated by the NCAA. The Board of Regents of the University of Oklahoma and the University of Georgia Athletic Association responded by suing the NCAA arguing that the NCAA's actions were an illegal restraint of trade and violated antitrust law. Both the Federal District Court and later the Circuit Court of Appeals ruled in favor of the colleges against the NCAA. Ultimately, the case went to the Supreme Court where by a vote of 7–2 the Supreme Court also ruled in favor of the colleges and determined that the actions of the NCAA violated anti-trust law. Interestingly, one of the two dissenting justices and the author of the dissenting opinion was Justice Byron White, who wrote that the NCAA's television regulations were reasonable and intended "to keep university athletics from becoming professionalized to the extent that profitmaking objectives would overshadow educational objectives." He also wrote that "More generally, in my view, the television plan reflects the NCAA's fundamental policy of preserving amateurism and integrating athletics and education." What makes Justice White's perspective most interesting is that Byron White or "Whizzer" White as he was referred to while playing both collegiate and professional football is the only Supreme Court Justice to have played both collegiate football and later professional football. In fact, Justice White was a three time All-Pro selection and led the NFL in scoring two years. However, despite his knowledge of football, his knowledge of the workings of collegiate football and its economic underpinnings was based more on the game as played during the 1930s when he played college football than the 1980s.

## STUDENT ATHLETE

Although the NCAA requires that Division I student-athletes spend no more than 20 hours per week on their sport during the playing season and no more than 8 hours per week during the off season, this rule is routinely and openly ignored. The rule itself, however, has numerous illogical exceptions that render the rule meaningless as administrative meetings, weight lifting, conditioning, viewing of game film and rehabilitation exercises are not counted in determining the 20 hours. A NCAA survey in 2006 found that athletes generally spend 45 hours a week on their sport during the season. A similar NCAA survey in 2011 found that 70% of Division I football players and 69%

of men's basketball players dedicated as much time to their sport out of season as during the playing season.

The men's basketball championship playoffs referred to as March Madness started out as a two week tournament and has evolved into a month long event with games spread out around the country requiring student-athletes to play, practice, travel and attend media events at a time that for most colleges is a critical time of the semester, between midterm examinations and final exams.

In 2014, the presidents of the PAC 12 Conference sent a joint letter critical of the NCAA to other member schools urging reforms and asserting the "need to reassert the academic primacy of our mission." Specifically, the presidents suggested that scholarships be guaranteed "for enough time to complete a bachelor's degree, provided that the student remains in good academic standing"; "decrease the time demands placed on the student-athlete in season and correspondingly enlarge the time available for studies and full engagement in campus life by doing the following: Prevent the abuse of the organized 'voluntary' practices to circumvent the limit of 20 hours per week. More realistically assess the time away from campus and other commitments during the season including travel time." The presidents also suggested that the schools "similarly decrease time demands out of season by reducing out-of-season competition and practices and by considering shorter seasons in specific sports."

Much of the justification of the NCAA's power and regulations has been is its stated desire to protect the integrity of the concept of the "student-athlete" and while this may appear to be a worthy goal, the facts seem to belie the NCAA's statements. Article 2.2 of the NCAA's Constitution provides the "Principle of Student-Athlete Well-Being" which states that "intercollegiate athletics programs shall be conducted in a manner designed to protect and enhance the physical and educational well-being of student-athletes." According to Walter Byers, a former NCAA Executive Director, the term "student-athlete" was created in 1964 in an effort to avoid adverse court decisions based upon athletes being considered as employees. The term "student-athlete" first appeared in a legal decision when the widow of Fort Lewis A & M football player Ray Dennison filed for worker's compensation payments following his death in a college football game. Was he an employee of the university? Students being paid for performing services under a work-study job at the school library would be considered employees for worker's compensation purposes. Should a college football player being compensated through a scholarship be similarly considered an employee for worker's compensation purposes? The Colorado Supreme Court determined that Dennison was not an employee and his widow was not entitled to worker's compensation benefits.

Kent Waldrep, a Texas Christian University football player paralyzed in a 1974 football game against the University of Alabama also sued for Workers Compensation benefits and while initially the Texas Workers Compensation Commission ruled that he was an employee and entitled to benefits, this ruling was overturned on appeal. Waldrep v. Texas Employers Insurance Association, 21 S.W.3d 692 (2000). The case was not finally resolved by the courts until twenty-six years after Waldrep was injured. Most interesting is the conclusion of the court in which although it ruled against Waldrep's Worker's Compensation claim appeared to recognize the tremendous differences between college football as it was played when Waldrep was injured in 1974 and the big business into which it had already evolved in 2000.

Excerpts from the case:

"In August 1972, Waldrep enrolled at TCU. In October 1974, while playing football for TCU against the University of Alabama, Waldrep was critically injured. He sustained a severe injury to his spinal cord and was paralyzed below the neck. Today, Waldrep has no sensation below his upper chest. In 1991, Waldrep filed a workers' compensation claim for his injury. The Commission entered an award in his favor. TEIA appealed this decision to the district court. In a trial de novo, a jury found that Waldrep was not an employee of TCU at the time of his injury. The district court rendered judgment in favor of TEIA."

"On the facts of this record, any contract of hire must have been a contract whereby TCU hired Waldrep to attend the university, remain in good standing academically, and play football. However, if Waldrep played football for pay, he would have been a professional, not an amateur. The evidence reflects that the actions of both Waldrep and TCU were consistent with a joint intention that Waldrep be considered an amateur and not a professional. It is undisputed that before Waldrep signed the Letter of Intent and Financial Aid Agreement, both he and TCU understood that his recruitment and future football career at TCU would be governed by and subject to the rules of the NCAA. The record indicates that the NCAA's policies and rules in effect at that time exhibited a concerted effort to ensure that each school governed by these rules made certain that student-athletes were not employees. Indeed, the rules declared that the fundamental policy of the NCAA was "to maintain intercollegiate athletics as an integral part of the educational program and the athlete as an integral part of the student body, and, by so doing, retain a clear line of demarcation between college athletics and professional sports." NCAA Manual at 5. Following its policy, the evidence reflects that the NCAA rules made the principle of amateurism foremost and established several requirements to ensure that the student-athlete would not be considered a professional. For example, the NCAA had strict rules against student-athletes taking pay for participation in sports, and student-athletes were ineligible to participate if they were receiving or had received a salary from a professional sports organization.

Additionally, the record reflects that Waldrep and TCU did not treat the financial aid Waldrep received as 'pay' or 'income.' First, as previously noted, the NCAA rules provided that student-athletes would be ineligible if they used their skill for pay in any form; however, that same rule goes on to state that 'a student-athlete may accept scholarships or educational grants-in-aid from his institution' as these benefits do not conflict with the NCAA rules. As the NCAA rules were based upon a principle of amateurism and strictly prohibited payment for play, these two provisions together indicate that the NCAA and its participating institutions did not consider the acceptance of financial aid from the institution to be 'taking pay.' Moreover, the rules provided that any financial aid that exceeded tuition and fees, room and board, required course-related supplies and books, and incidental expenses of fifteen dollars per month would be considered 'pay' for participation in intercollegiate athletics. TCU gave Waldrep financial aid for these items but nothing more, indicating that TCU did not intend to pay Waldrep for his participation. Of equal significance, TCU never placed Waldrep on its payroll, never paid him a salary, and never told him that he would be paid a salary. There is no evidence that Waldrep expected a salary. No social security or income tax was withheld from Waldrep's grant-in-aid. See Continental Ins. Co. v. Wolford, 526 S.W.2d 539, 540 (Tex.1975) (withholding taxes is indicia of employee status). Waldrep never filed a tax return reporting his financial aid. See Anchor Cas. Co. v. Hartsfield, 390 S.W.2d 469, 470 (Tex.1965); Mayo v. Southern Farm Bureau Cas. Ins. Co., 688 S.W.2d 241, 243 (Tex.App.-Amarillo 1985, writ ref'd n.r.e.).

The evidence further reflects that Waldrep and TCU intended that Waldrep participate at TCU as a student, not as an employee. During the recruitment process, TCU never told Waldrep that he would be an employee, and Waldrep never told TCU that he considered himself to be employed. Moreover, a basic purpose of the NCAA, which governed Waldrep's intercollegiate football career, was to make the student-athlete an integral part of the student body. See NCAA Manual at 5. According to the NCAA rules, "[a]n amateur student-athlete is one who engages in athletics for the education, physical, mental and social benefits he derives therefrom, and to whom athletics is an avocation." Of importance is the evidence that Waldrep was aware when he signed the Letter of Intent and Financial Aid

Agreement that he would still receive financial aid even if hurt or unable to play football, as long as he complied with the rules of the Southwest Conference. Thus, TCU could not 'fire' Waldrep as it could an employee. See Mayo, 688 S.W.2d at 243. In addition, when Waldrep signed the agreements, he still had to meet the scholastic requirements for athletic awards and qualify for admission to TCU in order to enroll and participate in the football program. Waldrep testified that he knew when he signed the agreements that in order to play football at TCU he would have to maintain certain academic requirements as a student. Thus, his academic responsibilities dictated whether he could continue to play football.

Financial-aid awards are given to many college and university students based on their abilities in various areas, including music, academics, art, and athletics. Sometimes these students are required to participate in certain programs or activities in return for this aid. But, as the Supreme Court of Indiana observed, '[s]cholarship recipients are considered to be students seeking advanced educational opportunities and are not considered to be professional athletes, musicians or artists employed by the [u]niversity for their skill in their respective areas.' Rensing v. Indiana State Univ. Bd. of Trustees, 444 N.E.2d 1170, 1174 (Ind.1983).

Although the record in this case contains facts from which the jury could have found that Waldrep and TCU were parties to a contract of hire, there is also probative evidence to the contrary. Viewing the evidence in the light most favorable to the jury's verdict, we hold that the record before us reflects more than a mere scintilla of evidence that Waldrep was not in the service of TCU under a contract of hire."

"CONCLUSION

In conclusion, we note that we are aware college athletics has changed dramatically over the years since Waldrep's injury. Our decision today is based on facts and circumstances as they existed almost twenty-six years ago.

We express no opinion as to whether our decision would be the same in an analogous situation arising today; therefore, our opinion should not be read too broadly. Having disposed of all of the issues before us, we affirm the district court's judgment."

# THE O'BANNON CASE

Ed O'Bannon, a former college basketball player for UCLA was the lead plaintiff in a 2009 lawsuit against the NCAA and Electronic Arts, Inc., the maker of a college basketball video game sanctioned by the NCAA. In the lawsuit he alleged that his name and image were used improperly in violation of his intellectual property rights.

One of the unlikely leading figures behind the bringing of the O'Bannon case was Sonny Vaccaro who had for many years represented Nike and later Adidas in negotiating shoe contracts with college coaches. It was Vacarro who met with attorney Michael Hausfeld and persuaded him to take on the NCAA. Vacarro also recruited Ed O'Bannon, who was then working as a car dealer to serve as the lead plaintiff.

Vacarro may be most famous for his testimony before the Knight Commission in 2001. At the time, Vacarro worked for Adidas and was asked by Bryce Jordan, the President Emeritus of Penn State, "Why should a university be an advertising medium for your industry? To which Vacarro replied, "They shouldn't sir. You can be very moral and righteous in asking that question, sir, but there's not one of you in this room that's going to turn down any of our money. You're going to take it. I can only offer it."[1]

After the Ninth Circuit Court of Appeals issued a ruling, shown below, against EA Sports in the case, it settled with the plaintiffs and agreed to pay $60,000,000. EA Sports also stopped making video games based on college basketball and football. Although NCAA rules prohibit players' names from appearing in video games, the

---

[1]   New York Times, February 12, 2016, Joe Nocera and Ben Strauss "A Reformed 'Sneaker Pimp' Takes On the NCAA".

avatars appearing in these video games licensed by the NCAA were based upon real college athletes from their heights and weights to the color of their uniforms reflecting the colleges attended by the real athletes. For instance, one avatar was a left handed quarterback with the identical height and weight of Tim Tebow wearing the uniform colors of the University of Florida While the avatar may not have had Tebow's name on the back of his jersey, it was clear who the avatar was intended to represent.

## IN RE NCAA STUDENT-ATHLETE NAME & LIKENESS LICENSING LITIGATION

United States Court of Appeals, Ninth Circuit
724 F.3d 1268 (2013)

Before: SIDNEY R. THOMAS and JAY S. BYBEE, CIRCUIT JUDGES, and GORDON J. QUIST, SENIOR DISTRICT JUDGE.

### OPINION

BYBEE, CIRCUIT JUDGE:

In this case, we must balance the right of publicity of a former college football player against the asserted First Amendment right of a video game developer to use his likeness in its expressive works.

Samuel Keller was the starting quarterback for Arizona State University in 2005 before he transferred to the University of Nebraska, where he played during the 2007 season. EA is the producer of the *NCAA Football* series of video games, which allow users to control avatars representing college football players as those avatars participate in simulated games. In *NCAA Football,* EA seeks to replicate each school's entire team as accurately as possible. Every real football player on each team included in the game has a corresponding avatar in the game with the player's actual jersey number and virtually identical height, weight, build, skin tone, hair color, and home state. EA attempts to match any unique, highly identifiable playing behaviors by sending detailed questionnaires to team equipment managers. Additionally, EA creates realistic virtual versions of actual stadiums; populates them with the virtual athletes, coaches, cheerleaders, and fans realistically rendered by EA's graphic artists; and incorporates realistic sounds such as the crunch of the players' pads and the roar of the crowd.

EA's game differs from reality in that EA omits the players' names on their jerseys and assigns each player a home town that is different from the actual player's home town. However, users of the video game may upload rosters of names obtained from third parties so that the names do appear on the jerseys. In such cases, EA allows images from the game containing athletes' real names to be posted on its website by users. Users can further alter reality by entering "Dynasty" mode, where the user assumes a head coach's responsibilities for a college program for up to thirty seasons, including recruiting players from a randomly generated pool of high school athletes, or "Campus Legend" mode, where the user controls a virtual player from high school through college, making choices relating to practices, academics, and social life.

In the 2005 edition of the game, the virtual starting quarterback for Arizona State wears number 9, as did Keller, and has the same height, weight, skin tone, hair color, hair style, handedness, home state, play style (pocket passer), visor preference, facial features, and school year as Keller. In the 2008 edition, the virtual quarterback for Nebraska has these same characteristics, though the jersey number does not match, presumably because Keller changed his number right before the season started.

The California Supreme Court formulated the transformative use defense in *Comedy III Productions, Inc. v. Gary Saderup, Inc.,* 25 Cal.4th 387, 106 Cal.Rptr.2d 126, 21 P.3d 797 (2001). The defense is "a balancing test between the First Amendment and the right of publicity based on whether the work in question adds significant creative elements so as to be transformed into something more than a mere celebrity likeness or imitation." *Id.* 106 Cal.Rptr.2d 126, 21 P.3d at 799. The California Supreme Court explained that "when a work contains significant transformative elements, it is not only especially worthy of First Amendment protection, but it is also less likely to interfere with the economic interest protected by the right of publicity." *Id.* 106 Cal.Rptr.2d 126, 21 P.3d at 808.

. . . we conclude that EA's use of Keller's likeness does not contain significant transformative elements such that EA is entitled to the defense as a matter of law. The facts of *No Doubt* are very similar to those here. EA is alleged to have replicated Keller's physical characteristics in *NCAA Football,* just as the members of No Doubt are realistically portrayed in *Band Hero.* Here, as in *Band Hero,* users manipulate the characters in the performance of the same activity for which they are known in real life—playing football in this case, and performing in a rock band in *Band Hero.* The context in which the activity occurs is also similarly realistic—real venues in *Band Hero* and realistic depictions of actual football stadiums in *NCAA Football.* As the district court found, Keller is represented as "what he was: the starting quarterback for Arizona State" and Nebraska, and "the game's setting is identical to where the public found [Keller] during his collegiate career: on the football field." *Keller v. Elec. Arts, Inc.,* No. C 09–1967 CW, 2010 WL 530108, at *5 (N.D.Cal. Feb. 8, 2010).

EA argues that the district court erred in focusing primarily on Keller's likeness and ignoring the transformative elements of the game as a whole. Judge Thomas, our dissenting colleague, suggests the same. *See* Dissent at 1285. We are unable to say that there was any error, particularly in light of *No Doubt,* which reasoned much the same as the district court in this case: "that the avatars appear in the context of a videogame that contains many other creative elements[ ] does not transform the avatars into anything other than exact depictions of No Doubt's members doing exactly what they do as celebrities." *No Doubt,* 122 Cal.Rptr.3d at 411. EA suggests that the fact that *NCAA Football* users can alter the characteristics of the avatars in the game is significant. Again, our dissenting colleague agrees. *See* Dissent at 1286–87. In *No Doubt,* the California Court of Appeal noted that *Band Hero* "d[id] not permit players to alter the No Doubt avatars in any respect." *Id.* at 410. The court went on to say that the No Doubt avatars "remain at all times immutable images of the real celebrity musicians, in stark contrast to the 'fanciful, creative characters' in *Winter* and *Kirby.*" *Id.* The court explained further:

[I]t is the differences between *Kirby* and the instant case . . . which are determinative. In *Kirby,* the pop singer was portrayed as an entirely new character—the space-age news reporter Ulala. In *Band Hero,* by contrast, no matter what else occurs in the game during the depiction of the No Doubt avatars, the avatars perform rock songs, the same activity by which the band achieved and maintains its fame. Moreover, the avatars perform those songs as literal recreations of the band members. That the avatars can be manipulated to perform at fanciful venues including outer space or to sing songs the real band would object to singing, or that the avatars appear in the context of a videogame that contains many other creative elements, does not transform the avatars into anything other than exact depictions of No Doubt's members doing exactly what they do as celebrities.

EA urges us to adopt for right-of-publicity claims the broader First Amendment defense that we have previously adopted in the context of false endorsement claims under the Lanham Act: the *Rogers* test. *See Brown v. Elec. Arts,* 724 F.3d at 1239–41, 2013 WL 3927736, at *1–2 (applying the *Rogers* test to a Lanham Act claim brought by former NFL player Jim Brown relating to the use of his likeness in EA's *Madden NFL* video games).

*Rogers v. Grimaldi* is a landmark Second Circuit case balancing First Amendment rights against claims under the Lanham Act. 875 F.2d 994 (2d Cir.1989). The case involved a suit brought by the famous performer Ginger Rogers against the producers and distributors of *Ginger and Fred,* a movie about two fictional Italian cabaret performers who imitated Rogers and her frequent performing partner Fred Astaire. *Id.* at 996–97. Rogers alleged both a violation of the Lanham Act for creating the false impression that she endorsed the film and infringement of her common law right of publicity. *Id.* at 997.

The *Rogers* court recognized that "[m]ovies, plays, books, and songs are all indisputably works of artistic expression and deserve protection," but that "[t]he purchaser of a book, like the purchaser of a can of peas, has a right not to be misled as to the source of the product." *Id.* "Consumers of artistic works thus have a dual interest: They have an interest in not being misled and they also have an interest in enjoying the results of the author's freedom of expression." *Id.* at 998. The *Rogers* court determined that titles of artistic or literary works were less likely to be misleading than "the names of ordinary commercial products," and thus that Lanham Act protections applied with less rigor when considering titles of artistic or literary works than when considering ordinary products. *Id.* at 999–1000. The court concluded that "in general the Act should be construed to apply to artistic works only where the public interest in avoiding consumer confusion outweighs the public interest in free expression." *Id.* at 999. The court therefore held:

In the context of allegedly misleading titles using a celebrity's name, that balance will normally not support application of the [Lanham] Act unless the title has no artistic relevance to the underlying work whatsoever, or, if it has some artistic relevance, unless the title explicitly misleads as to the source or the content of the work.

In this case, EA argues that we should extend this test, created to evaluate Lanham Act claims, to apply to right-of-publicity claims because it is "less prone to misinterpretation" and "more protective of free expression" than the transformative use defense. Although we acknowledge that there is some overlap between the transformative use test formulated by the California Supreme Court and the *Rogers* test, we disagree that the *Rogers* test should be imported wholesale for right-of-publicity claims. Our conclusion on this point is consistent with the Third Circuit's rejection of EA's identical argument in Hart. *See Hart*, 717 F.3d at 154–58. As the history and development of the *Rogers* test makes clear, it was designed to protect consumers from the risk of consumer confusion—the hallmark element of a Lanham Act claim. *See Cairn v. Franklin Mint Co.*, 292 F.3d 1139, 1149 (9th Cir.

2002). The right of publicity, on the other hand, does not primarily seek to prevent consumer confusion. *See Hart*, 717 F.3d at 158 ("[T]he right of publicity does not implicate the potential for consumer confusion. . . ."). Rather, it primarily "protects a form of intellectual property [in one's person] that society deems to have some social utility." *Comedy III*, 106 Cal. Rptr.2d 126, 21 P.3d at 804. As the California Supreme Court has explained:

Often considerable money, time and energy are needed to develop one's prominence in a particular field. Years of labor may be required before one's skill, reputation, notoriety or virtues are sufficiently developed to permit an economic return through some medium of commercial promotion. For some, the investment may eventually create considerable commercial value in one's identity.

The right of publicity protects the *celebrity*, not the *consumer*. Keller's publicity claim is not founded on an allegation that consumers are being illegally misled into believing that he is endorsing EA or its products. Indeed, he would be hard-pressed to support such an allegation absent evidence that EA explicitly misled consumers into holding such a belief. *See Brown v. Elec. Arts*, 724 F.3d at 1242–43, 2013 WL 3927736, at *4 (holding under the *Rogers* test that, since "Brown's likeness is artistically relevant to the [*Madden NFL*] games and there are no alleged facts to support the claim that EA explicitly misled consumers as to Brown's involvement with the games," "the public interest in free expression outweighs the public interest in avoiding consumer confusion"). Instead, Keller's claim is that EA has appropriated, without permission and without providing compensation, his talent and years of hard work on the football field. The reasoning of the *Rogers* and *Mattel* courts—that artistic and literary works should be protected unless they explicitly mislead consumers—is simply not responsive to Keller's asserted interests here. *Cf. Hart*, 717 F.3d at 157 ("Effectively, [EA] argues that [Hart] should be unable to assert a claim for appropriating his likeness as a football player precisely because his likeness was used for a game about football. Adopting this line of reasoning threatens to turn the right of publicity on its head.'").

California has developed two additional defenses aimed at protecting the reporting of factual information under state law. One of these defenses only applies to common law right-of-publicity claims while the other only applies to statutory right-of-publicity claims. *Montana v. San Jose Mercury News, Inc.,* 34 Cal.App.4th 790, 40 Cal.Rptr.2d 639, 640 (1995). Liability will not lie for common law right-of-publicity claims for the "publication of matters in the public interest." *Id.* at 640–41. Similarly, liability will not lie for statutory right-of-publicity claims for the "use of a name, voice, signature, photograph, or likeness in connection with any news, public affairs, or sports broadcast or account, or any political campaign." Cal. Civ.Code § 3344(d). Although these defenses are based on First Amendment concerns, *Gill v. Hearst Publ'g Co.,* 40 Cal.2d 224, 253 P.2d 441, 443–44 (1953), they are not coextensive with the Federal Constitution, *New Kids on the Block v. News Am. Publ'g, Inc.,* 971 F.2d 302, 310 n. 10 (9th Cir.1992), and their application is thus a matter of state law.

EA argues that these defenses give it the right to "incorporate athletes' names, statistics, and other biographical information" into its expressive works, as the defenses were "designed to create 'extra breathing space' for the use of a person's name in connection with matters of public interest." Keller responds that the right of publicity yields to free use of a public figure's likeness only to the extent reasonably required to report information to the public or publish factual data, and that the defenses apply only to broadcasts or accounts of public affairs, not to EA's *NCAA Football* games, which do not contain or constitute such reporting about Keller.

California courts have generally analyzed the common law defense and the statutory defense separately, but it is clear that both defenses protect only the act of publishing or reporting. By its terms, § 3344(d) is limited to a "broadcast or account," and we have confirmed that the common law defense is about a publication or reporting of newsworthy items. *Hilton,* 599 F.3d at 912. However, most of the discussion by California courts pertains to whether the subject matter of the communication is of "public interest" or related to "news" or "public affairs," leaving little guidance as to when the communication constitutes a publication or reporting.

We think that, unlike in *Gionfriddo, Montana,* and *Dora,* EA is not publishing or reporting factual data. EA's video game is a means by which users can play their own virtual football games, not a means for obtaining information about real-world football games. Although EA has incorporated certain actual player information into the game (height, weight, etc.), its case is considerably weakened by its decision not to include the athletes' names along with their likenesses and statistical data. EA can hardly be considered to be "reporting" on Keller's career at Arizona State and Nebraska when it is not even using Keller's name in connection with his avatar in the game. Put simply, EA's interactive game is not a publication of facts about college football; it is a game, not a reference source. These state law defenses, therefore, do not apply.

Under California's transformative use defense, EA's use of the likenesses of college athletes like Samuel Keller in its video games is not, as a matter of law, protected by the First Amendment. We reject EA's suggestion to import the *Rogers* test into the right-of-publicity arena, and conclude that state law defenses for the reporting of information do not protect EA's use.

# CONTINUATION OF THE O'BANNON CASE FOLLOWING THE EA SETTLEMENT

Following the settlement of EA Sports with the plaintiffs, the case continued against the NCAA. After trial, Federal Judge Claudia Wilken ruled that the NCAA's scholarship regulations constituted an unreasonable restraint of trade in violation of anti-trust law. She did, however, indicate that the schools could put a limit on the amount of money that a football or basketball player could receive while a student, but that the limit could not be less than the full cost of attending the school. In Judge Wilken's ruling, she suggested that colleges could share some of the profits derived from college athletics to increase the value of scholarships or even pay players through a trust fund from which athletes could receive payments after completing their college careers. According to Judge Wilken, placing a $5,000 per year per player ceiling on such payments would not violate antitrust laws. The NCAA adamantly opposed the suggestion of such a trust fund although a number of NCAA member schools responded to the court's decision by increasing the amount of their scholarships to the full cost of attending their institutions.

## O'BANNON APPEAL

On appeal, the Ninth Circuit Court of Appeals gave something to both the plaintiffs and the NCAA. Most importantly, the Appeals Court upheld Judge Wilken's ruling that the NCAA's rules regarding amateurism violated antitrust law and agreed that colleges should be able to compensate athletes up to the full cost of attending their schools. However, the NCAA won a partial victory when the three judge panel overruled Judge Wilken's provision for trusts that could provide up to $5,000 per year for name, image and likeness rights to college athletes. The Appeals Court was troubled by providing trust fund payments for name, image and likeness rights that were unrelated to educational expenses. Critics of the decision, however, questioned the inherent fairness of colleges and universities earning billions of dollars and coaches earning millions of dollars from the efforts of college athletes while the players whose efforts form the basis for which these riches are derived receive comparatively little in return.

# O'BANNON V. NATIONAL COLLEGIATE ATHLETIC ASSOCIATION

United States Court of Appeals, Ninth Circuit
802 F.3d 1049 (2015)

Before: SIDNEY R. THOMAS, CHIEF JUDGE, JAY S. BYBEE, CIRCUIT JUDGE and GORDON J. QUIST, SENIOR DISTRICT JUDGE.

Partial Concurrence and Partial Dissent by CHIEF JUDGE THOMAS.

## OPINION

BYBEE, CIRCUIT JUDGE:

We conclude that the district court's decision was largely correct. Although we agree with the Supreme Court and our sister circuits that many of the NCAA's amateurism rules are likely to be procompetitive, we hold that those rules are not exempt from antitrust scrutiny; rather, they must be analyzed under the Rule of Reason. Applying the Rule of Reason, we conclude that the district court correctly identified one proper alternative to the current NCAA compensation rules—*i.e.,* allowing NCAA members to give scholarships up to the full cost of attendance—but that the district court's other remedy, allowing students to be paid cash compensation of up to $5,000 per year, was erroneous. We therefore affirm in part and reverse in part.

### a. Anticompetitive effects

At the first step of the Rule of Reason, the court found that the NCAA's rules have an anticompetitive effect on the college education market. Were it not for those rules, the court explained, schools would compete with each other by offering recruits compensation exceeding the cost of attendance, which would "effectively lower the price that the recruits must pay for the combination of educational and athletic opportunities that the schools provide." *Id.* at 972. The rules prohibiting compensation for the use of student-athletes' NILs are thus a price-fixing agreement: recruits pay for the bundles of services provided by colleges with their labor and their NILs, but the "sellers" of these bundles—the colleges—collectively "agree to value [NILs] at zero." *Id.* at 973. Under this theory, colleges and universities behave as a cartel—a group of sellers who have colluded to fix the price of their product.

The court found in the alternative that the college education market can be thought of as a market in which student-athletes are sellers rather than buyers and the schools are purchasers of athletic services. In the court's alternative view, the college education market is a monopsony—a market in which there is only one buyer (the NCAA schools, acting collectively) for a particular good or service (the labor and NIL rights of student-athletes), and the colleges' agreement not to pay anything to purchase recruits' NILs causes harm to competition. *Id.* at 973, 991.

(1) *Amateurism.* The NCAA argued to the district court that restrictions on student-athlete compensation are "necessary to preserve the amateur tradition and identity of college sports." *Id.* It contended that amateurism had been one of the NCAA's core principles since its founding and that amateurism is a key driver of college sports' popularity with consumers and fans. *Id.* at 999–1000.

The district court rejected the NCAA's contention that it had a "longstanding commitment to amateurism," concluding instead that the NCAA's definition of amateurism was "malleable," changing frequently over time in "significant and contradictory ways." *Id.* at 1000. The court suggested that, even today, the NCAA's definition of amateurism is inconsistent: although players generally cannot receive compensation other than scholarships, tennis players are permitted to accept up to $10,000 in prize money before enrolling in college, and student-athletes are permitted to accept Pell grants even when those grants raise their total financial aid package above their cost of attendance. *Id.* It thus concluded that amateurism was not, in fact, a "core principle[ ]" of the NCAA. *Id.*

The district court was not persuaded that amateurism is the *primary* driver of consumer demand for college sports—but it did find that amateurism serves some procompetitive purposes. The court first concluded that consumers are primarily attracted to college sports for reasons unrelated to amateurism, such as loyalty to their alma mater or affinity for the school in their region of the country. *Id.* at 977–78. It also found much of the NCAA's evidence about amateurism unreliable. For example, the NCAA provided a survey conducted by Dr. J. Michael Dennis, a "survey research expert," which purported to show that Americans "generally oppose[ ] the idea of paying college football and basketball players." *Id.* at 975. The court deemed the Dennis survey "unpersuasive" for a couple reasons, one of which was that it believed the survey's initial question skewed the results by priming respondents to think about *illicit* payments to student-athletes rather than the possibility of allowing athletes to be paid. *Id.*

But the district court ultimately found that the NCAA's "current understanding of amateurism" plays some role in preserving "the popularity of the NCAA's product." *Id.* at 1005. It found that the NCAA's current rules serve a procompetitive benefit by promoting this understanding of amateurism, which in turn helps preserve consumer demand for college sports.

### c.   Less restrictive alternatives

Having found that the NCAA had presented two procompetitive justifications for "circumscribed" limits on student-athlete compensation—*i.e.,* increasing consumer demand for college sports and preventing the formation of a "wedge" between student-athletes and other students—the court proceeded to the third and final step of the Rule of Reason, where it considered whether there were means of achieving the NCAA's procompetitive purposes that were "substantially less restrictive" than a total ban on compensating student-athletes for use of their NILs. *Id.* at 1004–05.

The court held that the plaintiffs had identified two legitimate, less restrictive alternatives to the current NCAA rules: (1) allowing schools to award stipends to student-athletes up to the full cost of attendance, thereby making up for any "shortfall" in their grants-in-aid, and (2) permitting schools to hold a portion of their licensing revenues in trust, to be distributed to student-athletes in equal shares after they leave college. *Id.* at 1005–06. The court determined that neither of these alternatives to the total ban on NIL compensation would undermine the NCAA's procompetitive purposes. The court also held that it would be permissible for the NCAA to prohibit schools from funding these stipends or trusts with anything other than revenue derived from the use of players' NILs. *Id.* at 1005.

After entering judgment for the plaintiffs on their antitrust claims, the district court permanently enjoined the NCAA from prohibiting its member schools from (1) compensating FBS football and Division I men's basketball players for the use of their NILs by awarding them grants-in-aid up to the full cost of attendance at their respective schools, or (2) paying up to $5,000 per year in deferred compensation to FBS football and Division I men's basketball players for the use of their NILs, through trust funds distributable after they leave school. The NCAA timely appealed, and we have jurisdiction under 28 U.S.C. § 1291.

## B.  *Procompetitive Effects*

As discussed above, the NCAA offered the district court four procompetitive justifications for the compensation rules: (1) promoting amateurism, (2) promoting competitive balance among NCAA schools, (3) integrating student-athletes with their schools' academic community, and (4) increasing output in the college education market. The district court accepted the first and third and rejected the other two.

Although the NCAA's briefs state in passing that the district court erred in failing to "credit all four justifications fully," the NCAA focuses its arguments to this court entirely on the first proffered justification—the promotion of amateurism. We therefore accept the district court's factual findings that the compensation rules do not promote competitive balance, that they do not increase output in the college education market, and that they play a limited role in integrating student-athletes with their schools' academic communities, since we have been offered no meaningful argument that those findings were clearly erroneous.

But, as *Board of Regents* demonstrates, not every rule adopted by the NCAA that restricts the market is necessary to preserving the "character" of college sports. We thus turn to the final inquiry—whether there are reasonable alternatives to the NCAA's current compensation restrictions.

## C. *Substantially Less Restrictive Alternatives*

The third step in the Rule of Reason analysis is whether there are substantially less restrictive alternatives to the NCAA's current rules. We bear in mind that—to be viable under the Rule of Reason—an alternative must be "virtually as effective" in serving the procompetitive purposes of the NCAA's current rules, and "without significantly increased cost." *Cnty. of Tuolumne v. Sonora Cmty. Hosp.*, 236 F.3d 1148, 1159 (9th Cir.2001) (internal quotation marks omitted). We think that plaintiffs must make a strong evidentiary showing that its alternatives are viable here. Not only do plaintiffs bear the burden at this step, but the Supreme Court has admonished that we must generally afford the NCAA "ample latitude" to superintend college athletics.

The district court identified two substantially less restrictive alternatives: (1) allowing NCAA member schools to give student-athletes grants-in-aid that cover the full cost of attendance; and (2) allowing member schools to pay student-athletes small amounts of deferred cash compensation for use of their NILs. *O'Bannon*, 7 F.Supp.3d at 1005–07. We hold that the district court did not clearly err in finding that raising the grant-in-aid cap would be a substantially less restrictive alternative, but that it clearly erred when it found that allowing students to be paid compensation for their NILs is virtually as effective as the NCAA's current amateur-status rule.

## 1. Capping the permissible amount of scholarships at the cost of attendance

The district court did not clearly err in finding that allowing NCAA member schools to award grants-in-aid up to their full cost of attendance would be a substantially less restrictive alternative to the current compensation rules. All of the evidence before the district court indicated that raising the grant-in-aid cap to the cost of attendance would have virtually no impact on amateurism: Dr. Mark Emmert, the president of the NCAA, testified at trial that giving student-athletes scholarships up to their full costs of attendance would not violate the NCAA's principles of amateurism because all the money given to students would be going to cover their "legitimate costs" to attend school. Other NCAA witnesses agreed with that assessment. *Id.* at 983. Nothing in the record, moreover, suggested that consumers of college sports would become less interested in those sports if athletes' scholarships covered their full cost of attendance, or that an increase in the grant-in-aid cap would impede the integration of student-athletes into their academic communities. *Id.*

The NCAA, along with fifteen scholars of antitrust law appearing as *amici curiae,* warns us that if we affirm even this more modest of the two less restrictive alternative restraints identified by the district court, we will open the floodgates to new lawsuits demanding all manner of incremental changes in the NCAA's and other organizations' rules. The NCAA and these *amici* admonish us that as long as a restraint (such as a price cap) is "reasonably necessary to a valid business purpose," it should be upheld; it is not an antitrust court's function to tweak every market restraint that the court believes could be improved.

We agree with the NCAA and the *amici* that, as a general matter, courts should not use antitrust law to make marginal adjustments to broadly reasonable market restraints. The particular restraint at issue here, however—the grant-in-aid cap that the NCAA set below the cost of attendance—is not such a restraint. To the contrary, the evidence at trial showed that the grant-in-aid cap has no relation whatsoever to the procompetitive purposes of the NCAA: by the NCAA's own standards, student-athletes remain amateurs as long as any money paid to them goes to cover legitimate educational expenses.

Thus, in holding that setting the grant-in-aid cap at student-athletes' full cost of attendance is a substantially less restrictive alternative under the Rule of Reason, we are not declaring that courts are free to micromanage organizational rules or to strike down largely beneficial market restraints with impunity. Rather, our affirmance of this aspect of the district court's decision should be taken to establish only that where, as here, a restraint is *patently and inexplicably* stricter than is necessary to accomplish all of its procompetitive objectives, an antitrust court can and should invalidate it and order it replaced with a less restrictive alternative.

A compensation cap set at student-athletes' full cost of attendance is a substantially less restrictive alternative means of accomplishing the NCAA's legitimate procompetitive purposes. And there is no evidence that this cap will significantly increase costs; indeed, the NCAA already permits schools to fund student-athletes' full cost of attendance. The district court's determination that the existing compensation rules violate Section 1 of the Sherman Act was correct and its injunction requiring the NCAA to permit schools to provide compensation up to the full cost of attendance was proper.

## 2. Allowing students to receive cash compensation for their NILs

In our judgment, however, the district court clearly erred in finding it a viable alterative to allow students to receive NIL cash payments untethered to their education expenses. Again, the district court identified two procompetitive purposes served by the NCAA's current rules: "preserving the popularity of the NCAA's product by promoting its current understanding of amateurism" and "integrating academics and athletics." *O'Bannon*, 7 F.Supp.3d at 1005; *see also Board of Regents*, 468 U.S. at 117, 104 S.Ct. 2948 ("It is reasonable to assume that most of the regulatory controls of the NCAA are justifiable means of fostering competition among amateur athletic teams and therefore procompetitive because they enhance public interest in intercollegiate athletics."). The question is whether the alternative of allowing students to be paid NIL compensation unrelated to their education expenses, is "virtually as effective" in preserving amateurism as *not* allowing compensation. *Cnty. of Tuolumne*, 236 F.3d at 1159 (internal quotation marks omitted).

We cannot agree that a rule permitting schools to pay students pure cash compensation and a rule forbidding them from paying NIL compensation are both *equally* effective in promoting amateurism and preserving consumer demand. Both we and the district court agree that the NCAA's amateurism rule has procompetitive benefits. But in finding that paying students cash compensation would promote amateurism as effectively as not paying them, the district court ignored that not paying student-athletes is *precisely what makes them amateurs*.

Having found that amateurism is integral to the NCAA's market, the district court cannot plausibly conclude that being a poorly-paid professional collegiate athlete is "virtually as effective" for that market as being as amateur. Or, to borrow the Supreme Court's analogy, the market for college football is distinct from other sports markets and must be "differentiate[d]" from professional sports lest it become "minor league [football]." *Bd. of Regents*, 468 U.S. at 102, 104 S.Ct. 2948.

Aside from the self-evident fact that paying students for their NIL rights will vitiate their amateur status as collegiate athletes, the court relied on threadbare evidence in finding that small payments of cash compensation will preserve amateurism as well the NCAA's rule forbidding such payments. Most of the evidence elicited merely indicates that paying students large compensation payments would harm consumer demand more than smaller payments would—not that small cash payments will preserve amateurism. Thus, the evidence was addressed to the wrong question. Instead of asking whether making small payments to student-athletes served the same procompetitive purposes as making no payments, the evidence before the district court went to a different question: Would the collegiate sports market be better off if the NCAA made small payments or big payments? For example, the district court noted that a witness called by the NCAA, Bernard Muir, the athletic director at Stanford University, testified that paying student-athletes modest sums raises less concern than paying them large sums. The district court also relied on Dr. Dennis's opinion survey, which the court read to indicate that in the absence of the NCAA's compensation rules, "the popularity of college sports would likely depend on the size of payments awarded to student-athletes." *O'Bannon*, 7 F.Supp.3d at 983. Dr. Dennis had found that payments of $200,000 per year to each athlete would alienate the public more than would payments of $20,000 per year. *Id.* at 975–76, 983. At best, these pieces of evidence indicate that small payments to players will impact consumer demand less than larger payments. But there is a stark difference between finding that small payments are less harmful to the market than large payments—and finding that paying students small sums is virtually as effective in promoting amateurism as not paying them.

Finally, the district court, and the dissent, place particular weight on a brief interchange during plaintiffs' cross-examination of one of the NCAA's witnesses, Neal Pilson, a television sports consultant formerly employed at CBS. Pilson testified that "if you're paid for your performance, you're not an amateur," and explained at length why paying students would harm the student-athlete market. Plaintiffs then asked Pilson whether his opinions about amateurism "depend on the level of the money" paid to players, and he acknowledged his opinion was "impacted by the level." When asked whether there was a line that "should not be crossed" in paying players, Pilson responded "that's a difficult question. I haven't thought about the line. And I haven't been asked to render an opinion on that." When pressed to come up with a figure, Pilson repeated that he was "not sure." He eventually commented that "I tell you that a million dollars would trouble me and $5,000 wouldn't, but that's a pretty good range." When asked whether deferred compensation to students would concern him, Pilson said that while he would not be as concerned by deferred payments, he would still be "troubled by it."

So far as we can determine, Pilson's offhand comment under cross-examination is the sole support for the district court's $5,000 figure. But even taking Pilson's comments at face value, as the dissent urges, his testimony cannot support the finding that paying student-athletes small sums will be virtually as effective in preserving amateurism as not paying them. Pilson made clear that he was not prepared to opine on whether pure cash compensation, of any amount, would affect amateurism. Indeed, he was never asked about the impact of giving student-athletes small cash payments; instead, like other witnesses, he was asked only whether big payments would be worse than small payments. Pilson's casual comment—"[I] haven't been asked to render an opinion on that. It's not in my report"—that he would not be troubled by $5,000 payments is simply not enough to support the district court's far-reaching conclusion that paying students $5,000 per year will be as effective in preserving amateurism as the NCAA's current policy.

The difference between offering student-athletes education-related compensation and offering them cash sums untethered to educational expenses is not minor; it is a quantum leap. Once that line is crossed, we see no basis for returning to a rule of amateurism and no defined stopping point; we have little doubt that plaintiffs will continue to challenge the arbitrary limit imposed by the district court until they have captured the full value of their NIL. At that point the NCAA will have surrendered its amateurism principles entirely and transitioned from its "particular brand of football" to minor league status. *Bd. of Regents*, 468 U.S. at 101–02, 104 S.Ct. 2948. In light of that, the meager evidence in the record, and the Supreme Court's admonition that we must afford the NCAA "ample latitude" to superintend college athletics, *Bd. of Regents*, 468 U.S. at 120, 104 S.Ct. 2948, we think it is clear the district court erred in concluding that small payments in deferred compensation are a substantially less restrictive alternative restraint. We thus vacate that portion of the district court's decision and the portion of its injunction requiring the NCAA to allow its member schools to pay this deferred compensation.

By way of summation, we wish to emphasize the limited scope of the decision we have reached and the remedy we have approved. Today, we reaffirm that NCAA regulations are subject to antitrust scrutiny and must be tested in the crucible of the Rule of Reason. When those regulations truly serve procompetitive purposes, courts should not hesitate to uphold them. But the NCAA is not above the antitrust laws, and courts cannot and must not shy away from requiring the NCAA to play by the Sherman Act's rules. In this case, the NCAA's rules have been more restrictive than necessary to maintain its tradition of amateurism in support of the college sports market. The Rule of Reason requires that the NCAA permit its schools to provide up to the cost of attendance to their student athletes. It does not require more.

We vacate the district court's judgment and permanent injunction insofar as they require the NCAA to allow its member schools to pay student-athletes up to $5,000 per year in deferred compensation. We otherwise affirm. The parties shall bear their own costs on appeal.

# SCHOLARSHIPS

College athletes are often supported by scholarships funded partly by the NCAA and the balance by the college itself. Division I and II schools offer athletic scholarships; however, Division III schools do not. The Division I Ivy League, as a league policy does not offer athletic scholarships, however Ivy League schools offer financial aid and a skilled athlete attending an Ivy League university will not have to go into debt to finance his or her education.

In 2015, in response to the O'Bannon case, representatives of the 65 colleges that make up what are referred to as the Big 5 conferences, the Atlantic Coast Conference, the Big Ten Conference, the Big Twelve Conference, the Pac 12 Conference and the Southeastern Conference approved a rule enabled by a recent change of NCAA rules permitting its member schools to add additional funds to their student aid to make up the difference between the value of the scholarship and the full cost of attendance at the schools. The vote at the NCAA to allow additional cost of attendance benefits was 79–1 with Boston College being the only school to vote against the proposal on the grounds that allowing such additional aid would further segregate student-athletes from the rest of the student population who would not be eligible for such additional aid. Formerly, the maximum financial aid package could cover tuition, fees, room and board and books, but now can include other expenses related to attending the schools such as travel and cell phone bills. The present amount of the increased scholarships is averaging between $5,000 and $7,000.

College scholarships had traditionally not been guaranteed for all four years and could even have been rescinded if the athlete became injured and unable to compete. In 2014, the Big Ten became the first conference to provide for scholarships to cover the entire term of the athlete's enrollment at the school and even allow athletes who left school prematurely to come back and finish their degrees on scholarship. Then in a historic vote in 2015, multi-year scholarships became the rule throughout college sports. In addition, since 2015 schools can no longer choose to not renew a student's scholarship for athletic reasons. Previously most scholarships had to be renewed annually and students were sometimes pressured to giving up scholarships if their level of athletic success was not considered sufficient.

# ELIGIBILITY

In order to be deemed eligible for a college scholarship, the athlete must register at the end of his or her junior year of high school with a clearinghouse in order to prove that he or she is both an amateur and academically eligible based upon his or her high school grade point average and scores on standardized tests. It is not unusual for high school athletes to hire videographers to produce high quality videos touting them as an athlete which are sent to schools which the athlete wishes to attend. You can find on YouTube such videos used by Super Bowl winning quarterback Tom Brady when he was seeking a college football scholarship.

Along with the NCAA eligibility regulations, each school is permitted to establish its own eligibility rules. In 2011 Brigham Young University basketball player Brandon Davies was suspended for violating his school's honor code due to having premarital sex. Davies did not contest the suspension and apologized to his teammates. The BYU honor code requires all students to "be honest, live a chase and virtuous life. . . use clean language" and abstain from alcohol, tobacco, tea, coffee and drugs. It also bars gambling, use of pornography and homosexual behavior, though "feelings or attraction" are allowed.

The NCAA has set specific rules regarding eligibility to participate in NCAA sanctioned college athletics which include regulations pertaining to years of participation, academic performance and transfer rules. In addition there are specific rules prohibiting receiving benefits from an agent or even entering into oral or written agreements with an agent.

A college athlete has five years in which to complete his or her four years of participation in college sports. The fifth year is called the red shirt year. College athletes often use that year to recover from an injury, physically grow, gain maturity or wait for someone ahead of them on the depth chart to leave school. Many freshman athletes, in particular are redshirted for these reasons. While redshirting, an athlete is still enrolled at the college, attends classes and is permitted to practice with his or her team, however, he or she may not participate in actual games or athletic contests.

When the Arizona State football coach approached a young Pat Tillman with the idea of redshirting in order to give him time to achieve greater physical maturity, Tillman responded "I've got things to do with my life. You can do whatever you want with me, but in four years I'm gone." In fact, Tillman only stayed at Arizona State for the 3.5 years it took him to graduate summa cum laude with a 3.84 GPA. The coach decided not to redshirt Tillman who went on to become the Pac 10's defensive player of the year and then a star for the NFL's Phoenix Cardinals before quitting football in response to the attacks of 9/11, turning down a 3.6 million dollar, three year contract to join the army and becoming an Army Ranger. He was later killed by friendly fire in Afghanistan, the only NFL player to die in combat in 34 years.

Because many college students including varsity athletes graduate in four years, it is not uncommon for redshirted athletes to graduate in four years and then compete one more year while taking graduate school courses. Atlanta Falcon quarterback Matt Ryan and Seattle Seahawks quarterback Russell Wilson both took this route.

The rules governing college athletes transferring from one school to another are somewhat complicated. An athlete transferring from a Division One football, basketball or hockey program is generally required to sit out a year before becoming eligible to compete for his or her new school. Although the athlete is not able to immediately compete upon transferring, he or she may practice with the team and still is able to receive the benefits of a scholarship. This year is often referred to as an "academic year-in-residence." The purpose of the rule is to prevent luring of athletes from one program to another.

Spike Albrecht, a point guard on the University of Michigan basketball team was granted medical redshirt status after missing most of the 2016 season following hip surgery. With one year left of eligibility he was told by Coach John Beilein that his scholarship would not be renewed leaving Albrecht with no other option but to transfer to another school if he wanted to compete in his final year of eligibility. Generally, undergraduates must sit out a year following a transfer unless the school that they are leaving agrees to waive that requirement. The rule is somewhat less onerous for a student who has completed his or her undergraduate degree and is transferring to a school where he or she will enroll as a graduate student and can become immediately eligible to play. However, the school from which the athlete is transferring can still block the ability of a transferring graduate student athlete to play an NCAA sport at the new college or university. And that is just what happened to Albrecht when the University of Michigan refused to permit him to transfer to another Big 10 school. Fortunately, following considerable uproar about the unfairness of the Draconian decision of the University of Michigan, the school changed its position and allowed Albrecht to play wherever he chose whereupon he chose Purdue, a Big 10 school.

The fundamental unfairness of colleges and universities which cannot prevent a coach from breaking his or her contract and moving to another school, but are allowed to limit the ability to transfer of a college athlete who may be transferring because the coach who recruited him and for whom he or she wishes to play has gone to another school is now being challenged in a class action filed by Steve Berman.

# RECRUITING

Jim Harbaugh, the football coach of the University of Michigan was criticized in 2016 for some of his recruiting tactics which, it should be understood, are not tactics practiced just by Harbaugh, but also by most other successful college coaches.

The criticism of Harbaugh started when one of his recruits, Rashad Weaver, classified as a three star recruit decommitted from the Michigan 2017 team to which he had committed seven months earlier. College football recruits are classified by a star system of between two and five stars with five stars being the highest classification. What prompted Weaver to decommit, however was that he was told that he was no longer guaranteed a scholarship. When criticized in the media for promising a young athlete a scholarship and then changing the school's commitment to the athlete, Harbaugh was unapologetic saying that the team is a meritocracy and that the burden is on the high school athletes committing to Michigan to maintain their status to meet the athletic and scholastic standards of the university. It is not uncommon for a high school athlete to commit to a school as a sophomore and then not develop either athletically or scholastically sufficient for the school to uphold its end of the bargain. There is no penalty for colleges that withdraw scholarship offers so there is no disincentive to college coaches to offer more scholarships initially than they ultimately provide. Certainly a high school athlete who has not maintained his academic or athletic skills bears some responsibility for losing a scholarship, but he also is the only one who suffers if a college merely chooses to replace a three star recruit with a four star recruit. The athlete loses his scholarship at the last minute and has stopped communicating with other schools that might have been inclined to offer him a scholarship.

## OVERSIGNING

The NCAA limits the number of scholarships that may be offered by colleges in each sport. In addition, each conference may have its own rules that can be more restrictive than those of the NCAA. The NCAA limits Football Bowl Subdivision football schools to signing no more than 85 scholarships with 25 of those scholarships allocated to high school students who sign National Letters of Intent during the official signing period between National Signing Day and May 31st of each year. Oversigning occurs when a school either signs too many new high school recruits such that they bring their total number of scholarship athletes on the team to more than 85 or if they sign more than 25 high school students to National Letters of Intent. The NCAA however permits oversigning of up to 28 National Letters of Intent. Part of the reason the NCAA permits oversigning of high school recruits is the implicit recognition that some of those initial scholarship offers will indeed be withdrawn before the student-athlete ever enrolls in the college or university, as illustrated by the actions of coaches such as Jim Harbaugh.

From the coach's perspective, just as airlines overbook flights because they have come to reasonably expect a number of people will not show up for a scheduled flight for which they have purchased a ticket, not all high school students offered scholarships will actually enroll in the college. A player may end up not being academically eligible and without oversigning, the team may not have another player to meet that particular need. A player may also change his mind or commit an infraction that would make him ineligible. Unfortunately, because some schools may not take away their commitment to an incoming freshman until late in the summer it can be impossible for the athlete to find another school that can offer him a scholarship at that late date.

Of course, it isn't just football that goes through such machinations to keep its awarding of scholarships in line with NCAA and conference rules. College basketball teams are limited to thirteen scholarships. In an interesting example of how schools manage to get around these limitations, heading into the 2010–2011 college basketball season the University of Louisville basketball team found itself with sixteen scholarship players. Three of Coach Rick Pitino's seniors, two of whom were starters from the previous season's squad, agreed to give up their scholarships and go back to the status of walk-ons, student athletes who try out for the team without a scholarship, which is how the three all came originally to the University of Louisville. In this case, the two returning starting players and captains of the team, Kyle Kuric and Chris Smith were not dependent upon their scholarships to pay for the cost of attending the University of Louisville. Kuric's parents were a neurosurgeon and a nurse practitioner and Smith was the younger brother of NBA professional basketball player, J.R. Smith who had already paid for his younger brother's cost of attending the university during the 2009–2010 season in which Chris Smith was not able to play due to his having to sit out the season as a transfer student.

Grayshirting is the name for the practice of a football recruit deferring enrollment in the university until January to receive the scholarship they were promised in an effort to keep the numbers of scholarships for the team down to the required number during the season. In other instances a recruit may enroll in the school but defer his scholarship until the next calendar year so long as he is not enrolled as a full time student, meaning taking fewer than 12 credit hours. Therefore although he is still on campus, paying his own way and not participating in some team activities, his scholarship is put off until the next year in regard to being counted against NCAA imposed limits. Other times schools will encourage a player to attend a junior college.

Despite criticism, University of Alabama Coach Nick Saban who signed 133 recruits in five years indicated, "We have never gotten rid of a player because of his physical ability." He went on to say, "Any player that has left this program prematurely has created his own exit route. . . He's created his own conditions for leaving, if that makes any sense, whether they're academic in terms of not doing what he needs to do academically, whether there's some violation in terms of team rule or policy, whatever it is. Some of these things we're not allowed to comment on."

Schools have also been accused of extensively using medical hardship scholarships where not warranted to cover up and avoid NCAA rules. They also have been accused of releasing players for violation of team rules, a wide ranging category that some have argued is used to dismiss underperforming athletes while star athletes who have actually committed greater violations of team rules or even crimes manage to retain their positions on the teams.

It has been suggested that if scholarships were guaranteed for four years, the practice of oversigning could be reduced. Since 2012 Individual schools now have the ability to offer such scholarships, but not all do although all of the schools in the Power 5 conferences offer four year scholarships.

# AMATEUR STANDING

College sports are, by definition, amateur, but the definition of amateur is by no means simple and, in fact is not consistent across the entire spectrum of "amateur" athletics. In its regulations the NCAA defines an amateur athlete as "one who participates in competitive physical sports only for the pleasure and the physical, mental, moral and social benefits directly derived therefrom." An athlete may be an amateur as determined by the United States Olympic Committee (USOC), but not for purposes of the NCAA.

Once a student has hired an athletic agent or declared himself or herself eligible for professional sports drafts, according to the NCAA, he or she become ineligible to play NCAA sanctioned college sports.

In 1974 the NCAA rules were amended to permit a professional athlete in one sport to participate in a different sport as an amateur collegiate athlete. For example, Chris Weinke was a professional baseball player for the Toronto Blue Jays in their minor league system before giving up on professional baseball and enrolling as a 25 year old freshman at Florida State University where he played quarterback on Florida State's football team, leading them to a national championship in his Junior year and winning the Heisman Trophy in his Senior year in 2000 as the oldest athlete ever to do so.

On the other hand, Jeremy Bloom was an Olympic and professional World Cup skier when he enrolled at the University of Colorado to play football. Concerned that the NCAA might rule that he would be ineligible to play college football, he sought an injunction to permit him to play college football although he received prize money for skiing as well as money for modeling and endorsements. Bloom argued that his skiing prize money as well as his endorsement compensation from companies such as Under Armour and modeling money did not relate at all to his playing college football and, in fact, he had these sources of funds well before he enrolled at the University of Colorado. The NCAA, however, distinguished salary an athlete would receive as a professional baseball player, for example, from prize money he won as a skier. According to the NCAA, receiving prize money and endorsement pay violated the NCAA's rules about earning money based on athletic ability. Had he been paid a salary rather than receiving prize money for skiing, the NCAA would have approved his application to play college football. In fact, most professional skiers make the bulk of their income from endorsements rather than actual prize money. Judge Hale ruled in favor of the NCAA in the case, denying the injunction although he was openly sympathetic to Bloom.

In his opinion, Judge Hale wrote,

"Here the NCAA had an opportunity to recognize and support a World Cup champion and an Olympic competitor by supporting his future success—by leaving doors open rather than closing them. . . Mr. Bloom is truly an amateur athlete in football with only dreams of even receiving playing time. . . The NCAA is missing an opportunity to promote amateurism on the one hand, and the opportunity to support the personal and football and non-athletic growth of a student athlete on the other.

Mr. Bloom is the epitome of an amateur who wishes to live out his dream of playing college football for the University of Colorado without abandoning the once-in-a-lifetime future opportunities he has. I would like to see him live out those dreams. I would like to be able to find a legal basis for me to be able to enjoin the NCAA. However, I cannot find a sound legal basis that would allow me to do so."

The courts traditionally defer to the rules and administrative decisions of organizations such as the NCAA in the regulation of athletics. In this case the judge ruled that the rules were rationally related to the NCAA's stated purposes and that they were not arbitrarily and capriciously applied and therefore reluctantly he ruled in favor of the NCAA.

Olympic swimmer Katie Ledecky put off entering Stanford University on a swimming scholarship until she had finished competing in the 2016 Summer Olympics in Rio. By agreeing, however, to accept a swimming scholarship at Stanford, she had to agree to give up endorsements and paid appearance opportunities that could have brought her more than a million dollars. The question is, as always, how is her sport harmed by her being able to make money from her talents? A college football player is not allowed to make money from football related endeavors and still compete in NCAA sanctioned competition, yet a musician in the marching band playing at half time can use his or her musical talents off campus and be paid whatever the market will pay. What is the difference?

# EARLY AMATEUR RETIREMENT

In addition to the three games that make up the college football national championship playoffs to determine a national champion there are thirty eight other bowl games, many of which are of lesser prestige particularly with so many teams qualifying for what used to be an elite group. In 2016, 20% of the teams playing in the post season bowl games did not even have winning records. This drop in the quality and even perception of these games may have contributed in 2016 to a few high profile college football players, most notably Christian McCaffrey of Stanford and Leonard Fournette of LSU deciding not to play in their teams' bowl games. While the bowl promoters and the schools make money from the bowl games, the players are not compensated at all for participating in these games and run the risk of being injured and losing out on millions of dollars in NFL contract money. In 2015 Jaylon Smith of Notre Dame, who had been projected as a top five NFL draft pick which would have earned him a contract worth more than 20 million dollars, tore the anterior cruciate ligament in his knee while playing in the Fiesta Bowl which resulted in his not being drafted until the second round by the Dallas Cowboys for a contract valued at 6 million dollars. He did not even play in the 2016 NFL season as he spent his entire rookie year rehabilitating his knee. Making up somewhat for his injury, Smith was paid $850,000 from a loss of value insurance policy that paid him when his NFL draft status went down due to his knee injury.

In the 2017 NFL draft, Jake Butt of the University of Michigan who was the 2016 Mackey Award winner as the best tight end in college football was originally projected as a high second round choice, but was not picked until the fifth round, due primarily to his suffering a serious injury in the 2016 postseason Orange Bowl however he too had a loss of value insurance policy that paid him $543,000. While this may seem to be a considerable amount of money, had Butt been chosen in the second round, as originally projected, Butts would have received a contract with approximately 4 million dollars in guaranteed money as contrasted to the $380,000 of guaranteed money he received as the first pick in the fifth round of the draft.

## E-SPORTS

Video game competitions also known as E-Sports have become highly competitive intercollegiate sports. More than 10,000 students play in organized intercollegiate video game competitions which are more than double the number that play Division One basketball. In 2014 Robert Morris University became the first college to offer scholarships to E-Sports players. Now twenty-five schools offer college scholarships for E-Sports players.

Robert Morris University competes in the Collegiate Star League which is made up of more than a hundred colleges and universities including Arizona State, Boston College, Brown University, Columbia University, Cornell University, Duke, Florida State, George Washington University, Georgetown, Johns Hopkins and Harvard.

E-sports are not governed by the NCAA such that Blizzard Entertainment, a video game developer flew eight finalists from colleges around the country to Seattle for a tournament with scholarship prize money, which would not be allowed in NCAA regulated sports. Other video game companies sponsor similar competitions with cash prizes.

In 2014, Riot Games, the maker of the popular League of Legends video game hosted the first intercollegiate championships for the League of Legends video game won by a team of five students from the University of Washington in front of a large crowd and 169,000 more people watching online. Prizes of $7,500 in scholarship funds were awarded to each member of the winning team.

In 2015, 1,600 schools competed in League of Legends leading up to the final four teams from four regions competing for the North American Collegiate Championships (NACC) title and $30,000 in scholarships. In 2016, the NACC changed its name to uLoL Campus Series with 32 teams from four regions.

In 2017, the Big Ten Network and Riot Games began a joint venture in which twelve of the fourteen schools that make up the Big Ten Conference competed in a two month season League of Legends competition. Only Penn State and Nebraska did not participate in the competition. Teams consisted of six players who had to be full time students and who would each receive $5,000 in scholarship funds paid by Riot.

In addition to organized collegiate competition, the NBA has recognized the value of E-sports and is the first professional sports league to sponsor an e sports league, the NBA 2K eLeague. In conjunction with Take-Two Interactive Software Inc., a manufacturer of video games, each of the thirty NBA teams is able to create its own NBA basketball E game team to compete for substantial cash prizes. Just as participation in the NBA is limited to players who have been drafted by the individual NBA teams, so is participation in the E sport version of NBA basketball limited to those players drafted by the participating NBA franchises. Teams choose five players to represent the team in regular season play and playoffs culminating in a championship game played in an NBA arena. The avatars of the real players will resemble the drafted players with, of course, no restriction on size or gender. Individual games will be broadcast both online and on television during the regular NBA season. The worldwide marketing potential of NBA sanctioned E sport competition is tremendous.

## QUESTIONS

1.  Are E-Sports legitimate sports?

2.  Should the NCAA regulate E-Sports?

3.  Do you think E-Sports will flourish as professional competitions and would the relationship with professional sports leagues such as the NBA create a symbiotic situation?

# SCANDALS

It is about the money. That simple phrase could describe the crux of the problem with college athletics as ruled by the NCAA.

In 1989 the Knight Commission on Intercollegiate Athletics was formed by the John S. and James L. Knight Foundation in response to years of scandals in college sports. The commission was made up of distinguished members of the academic, athletic and journalism communities. In the years since its first report in 1991 entitled, "Keeping Faith with the Student Athlete" the commission has issued two more reports and continues to be a voice for reform in college athletics.

In its initial 1991 report, the Knight Commission noted that the problem was not of recent origin. It stated, "As far back as 60 years ago, another major American foundation—the Carnegie Foundation for the Advancement of Teaching—had published a study on college athletics which concluded that recruiting had become corrupt, professionals had replaced amateurs, education was being neglected and commercialism reigned." However, as the report noted, "The problem had become even worse in the intervening years because the millions of dollars television was pouring into college athletics had raised the stakes—and put an even higher premium on winning."

The commission found that in the 1980s 109 colleges and universities had been disciplined by the NCAA. Additionally, the Knight Commission noted that a third of present and former professional football players polled indicated that they had accepted illegal payments while they participated in intercollegiate athletics.

Also according to the Knight Commission "In the typical Division I college or university, only 33% of basketball players and 37.5% of football players graduate within five years. Overall graduation rates for all student-athletes (men and women) in Division I approach graduation rates for all students in Division I according to the NCAA—47% of all student—athletes in Division I graduate in five years. . . . About two-thirds of the student-athletes in big-time revenue-producing sports have not received a college degree within five years of enrolling at their institution."

According to the first Knight Commission report on Intercollegiate Athletics, "Power struggles for control of big-time football, revenue distribution, and other matters reflect a culture dominated by competitive rather than academic concerns and one that often ignores the welfare of the athletes representing their institutions."

Over the years the intense pressure to succeed in collegiate sports has resulted in numerous schools becoming involved in scandals. Academic fraud, which is specifically outlawed by the NCAA's Operating Bylaw 19 is considered extremely serious by the NCAA and some of its heaviest actions have been against schools found guilty of academic fraud.

In 1989 a basketball player at Miami University received an A in a course taught by his coach. The player needed the A in order to maintain his academic eligibility. Despite the fact that the athlete received an A for his work in the course, the athlete did not complete the class work and did not participate in class.

Between 1990 and 1993 the head baseball coach at Southwest Texas State University gave grades of A to six baseball players who were enrolled in a class he taught although none of the players ever attended the class or participated in any other way.

Between 1993 and 1999 at least 18 University of Minnesota athletes had take-home exams and hundreds of assignments done for them by faculty and staff including a secretary in the athletics department and a tutor assigned to provide assistance to the athletes. Even this was not enough to maintain the grades of some athletes so various members of the athletic department intimidated professors and staff into changing grades for athletes in order to maintain academic eligibility.

In 2009 Florida State was put on probation by the NCAA and had football scholarships taken away by the NCAA for widespread academic cheating involving ten sports. NCAA investigators found instances of 61 Florida State athletes cheating while taking online exams between the Fall of 2006 and the Summer of 2007 or receiving inappropriate assistance from athletic department staffers who provided exam question answers to the athletes or even, in some instances typed term papers for the athletes. Academic fraud is taken extremely seriously by the NCAA and Florida State's failure to properly monitor such unethical conduct was deemed a major violation.

The most serious NCAA sanction against a school for violating NCAA rules was the imposition of the so-called "death penalty" on Southern Methodist University's football team. SMU was found guilty of a number of offenses, most notably the maintaining of a slush fund created by the team's boosters to pay players to induce them to attend SMU from the 1970s through 1986. According to NCAA investigators, 13 players had been paid a total of $61,000 from the slush fund established by SMU boosters, including a prominent

Dallas real estate developer, who had played football for SMU between 1969 and 1971. The "death penalty" included the cancelling of the entire 1987 football season and the taking away of 45 football scholarships over the next two years. This was the only time that the NCAA has ever forced a school to cancel a school's football season. Although SMU was permitted by the NCAA to play in 1988, the damage to the football team brought about through the death penalty imposition made it impossible for SMU to field a team in 1988 and the school made the decision to forego football for that year. Over the next twenty years following the imposition of the death penalty against SMU, the school's football team had just one winning season.

In retrospect the tremendous damage done to the SMU football program by the imposition of the death penalty has made the NCAA hesitant to issue this extreme sanction although it still maintains the power to do so. John Lombardi, the President of the University of Florida in 2002 summed up what many people involved in college sports thought when he said, "SMU taught the committee that the death penalty is too much like the nuclear bomb. It's like what happened after we dropped the atom bomb in World War II. The results were so catastrophic that now we'll do anything to avoid dropping another one."

In 2010 the storied athletic department at the University of Southern California (USC) received one of the NCAA's most serious penalties in recent years. Among the long list of penalties imposed on USC was the banning of its football team from post season competition for two years and the banning of its basketball team from post season competition for one year. In addition they also were publicly reprimanded and censured, lost basketball and football scholarships and were put on probation for four years.

The investigation that prompted the action by the NCAA stemmed from the recruiting and paying of two star athletes: Reggie Bush, the winner of the 2005 Heisman Trophy, which he later returned in response to the allegations of his receiving gifts and benefits in violation of NCAA rules and basketball star O.J. Mayo who went on to play in the NBA. The primary charges against USC were that they were negligent in their oversight of the athletic programs. According to the NCAA's ruling "Universities may not hide their heads in the sand and purport to treat all programs and student-athletes similarly when it comes to the level of scrutiny required. NCAA members including USC, invest substantial resources to compete in athletics competition at the highest levels, particularly in football and men's basketball. They must commit comparable resources to detect violations and monitor conduct."

A constant issue in NCAA investigations is the NCAA's lack of true judicial power. It does not have the authority to subpoena witnesses or compel testimony. Many people involved in or subject to NCAA investigations including notably Derek Rose of the University of Memphis have declined to be interviewed by NCAA investigators.

# LOUISVILLE SANCTIONS

In 2015 Katina Powell, a self-described escort described in her book "Breaking Cardinal Rules: Basketball and the Escort Queen" about being hired to provide sexual favors to basketball recruits at the University of Louisville. The book caused an immediate uproar. The University of Louisville promptly initiated an investigation that concluded that a former basketball staffer, Andre McGee paid for the services to recruits as alleged in the book. Prior to the NCAA taking any action, Louisville imposed significant sanctions upon itself including banning the basketball team from postseason play in the 2015–2016 season and reducing its number of scholarships for 2016–2017. The university's investigation did not find knowledge or fault in head coach Rick Pitino. However, in June of 2017, the NCAA finished its own investigation which resulted in additional penalties including putting the school on four years of probation, but also found fault with Coach Pitino for failing to monitor the basketball program. Pitino was suspended by the NCAA for the first five

Atlantic Coast Conference Games in the 2017–2018 season. Both the University of Louisville and Rick Pitino appealed the NCAA's ruling.

---

## QUESTION

1.   What is the extent of the responsibility of a college coach to monitor his or her sports program for NCAA rules compliance?

# MCCANTS AND RAMSAY V. NCAA AND UNIVERSITY OF NORTH CAROLINA

One of the most significant cases exposing hypocrisy and exploitation of college athletes was brought in 2015 by two former University of North Carolina athletes, Rashanda McCants, a women's basketball player and Devon Ramsay, a football player in which they argued that they and other athletes at UNC were deprived of a proper education by the UNC administration and that the NCAA was negligent in not monitoring the situation better. The allegations against the NCAA were dismissed early by the judge on the ground that it had not breached any duty to the student-athletes, but the case against UNC continued.

As stated in the lawsuit, "This case arises out of the NCAA and UNC's abject failure to safeguard and provide a meaningful education to scholarship athletes who agreed to attend UNC—and take the field—in exchange for academically sound instruction." Particularly in the light of the NCAA's constant defense of its failing to provide to athletes a share of funds received by the NCAA and its member schools derived from college athletics and its marketing by touting the extreme value of the education provided to college athletes, this allegation appears particularly egregious.

According to the lawsuit, between 1989 and 2011 UNC guided college athletes into sham "paper classes" that did not even have to attend and, except for an exceedingly small number of classes, were not even taught by regular UNC faculty members.

The lawsuit accuses UNC of wrongdoing, but also indicates that the problem is certainly not limited to UNC, when it states, "Yet it is the schools, the conferences, and the NCAA that are engaging in exploitation, subverting the educational mission in the service of the big business of college athletics—and then washing their hands of college athletes once they have served their purpose."

In regard to the classes into which they were guided by the university, both lead plaintiffs argued that they were not aware that the class was academically unsound and that their work was neither supervised, graded or reviewed by a UNC faculty member.

The classes that were the focus of the scandal were irregular courses offered in the Department of African and Afro-American Studies (AFAM). The classes did not require the student to attend a class meeting or do any work other than a single term paper. The courses were managed by the AFAM office secretary who graded the papers generously regardless of the quality of the work. The courses were taught and administered without the involvement of any faculty members. They became known as "paper classes."

A particularly popular paper class was third level Swahili which met the school's foreign language requirement although the course which again only required a single term paper about Swahili culture be submitted and permitted the paper to be written entirely in English.

In 2015, the University of North Carolina settled a lawsuit with Mary Willingham, the former athletics literary counselor who exposed the university's 20 year history of academic fraud by paying her $335,000. For five years, Willingham was vilified by the University which accused her of lying, however she persisted in her accusations and ultimately, the University hired an independent investigator, Ken Wainstein in 2014 who confirmed everything Willingham had said.

The two people behind the paper classes, Julius Nyang'oro who headed the AFAM department and his office secretary Deborah Crowder indicated that their motivation in establishing these classes according to the Wainstein report was to assist students who were struggling with the academic rigor of the University of North Carolina and particularly "that subset of student-athletes who came to campus without adequate academic preparation."

UNC's own investigative report found 3,000 students, mostly varsity athletes took what were referred to as "paper classes" that involved little teaching and less effort.[2]

As the report indicated, "These paper classes were also very popular among student-athletes and especially those from the 'revenue sports' of football and men's basketball. Approximately 1, 871 of the 3,933 total enrollments between 1999 and 2011 were student-athletes, of whom 1,189 were members of the football and men's basketball teams. In percentage terms, that means that 47.6% of the paper class enrollments were student-athletes and 24.5% were football or basketball players. By comparison, approximately 4% of the Chapel Hill student body are student-athletes in any given year and approximately 0.6% are football players."

The report went on to say that "It was common knowledge among student-athletes that it was the norm to receive an A or B in the paper classes, regardless of the quality of their submitted papers—an understanding that was borne out by the fact that grades in the paper classes were 10% higher than those awarded in the regular AFAM courses."

# THE KNIGHT COMMISSION REPORT OF 2001

The 2001 Knight Commission report entitled "A Call to Action: Reconnecting College Sports and Higher Education published in 2001 stated "We find that the problem of big-time college sports have grown rather than diminished. The most glaring elements of the problems outlined in this report—academic transgressions, a financial

---

[2]    "Investigation of Irregular Classes in the Department of African and Afro-American Studies at the University of North Carolina at Chapel Hill" Kenneth L. Wainstein, A. Joseph Lay III, Colleen Depman Kukowski, October 16, 2014.

arms race, and commercialism—are all evidence of the widening chasm between higher education's ideals and big-time college sports."

In this scathing report it found "the ugly disciplinary incidents, outrageous academic fraud, dismal graduation rates, and uncontrolled expenditures surrounding college sports reflect what the (University of Michigan President James J. Duderstadt) and others have rightly characterized as 'an entertainment industry' that is not only the antithesis of academic values but 'is corrosive and corruptive to the academic enterprise." Indeed President Duderstadt had stated that the "current (NCAA) model is built on the exploitation of young student athletes—they live in poverty, less than half will ever get a college degree (and those that do usually get a meaningless degree), and they put their future health at great risk—all for the obscene wealth of coaches, (athletic directors) presidents, the NCAA, the networks and others."

The report further found "Big-time athletic departments seem to operate with little interest in scholastic matters beyond the narrow issue of individual eligibility. They act as though the athletes" academic performance is of little moment. The historic and vital link between playing field and classroom is all but severed in many institutions... Athletes are often admitted to institutions where they do not have a reasonable chance to graduate. They are athlete-students brought into the collegiate mix more as performers than aspiring undergraduates. Their ambiguous academic credentials lead to chronic classroom failures or chronic coverups of their academic deficiencies."

# THE KNIGHT COMMISSION REPORT OF 2010

In the Knight Commission's 2010 report entitled, "Restoring the Balance—Dollars, Values and the Future of College Sports" they concluded that much had improved since the time of the earlier Knight reports, however, when the NCAA touts its graduation rates even saying that 65% of student-athletes graduate compared to 63% of other college students, these figures can be misleading. Statistics on women athletes boost the NCAA figures as do the higher graduation rates for student-athletes playing sports such as tennis, golf, lacrosse and soccer. Figures from the College Sports Research Institute still found that FBS football players graduated at a rate of 19.7% less than the general student population while Division One men's basketball players graduated at a rate 20.6% less than the general student population.

Further compounding this problem are the student-athletes who manage to graduate with concentrations of studies into which they are steered, such as "general studies" that leave even the graduating athletes unprepared to find a good job.

# STUDENT ATHLETE UNION

In 2014 a regional office of the NLRB ruled that football players on scholarship at Northwestern University were to be considered employees under the National Labor Relations Act and consequently could organize a union for purposes of collective bargaining. The ruling was based on considering the scholarships received by the players as compensation for the work performed as collegiate athletes. The decision also focused on the extensive control over the lives of scholarship athletes exercised by their coaches including training, monitoring players' behavior and the requirement of adherence to NCAA rules and even the control over the private lives of the athletes including posts on social media and use of alcohol as well as limitations on outside employment.

Northwestern appealed the decision to the full NLRB which unanimously dismissed the players' petition to unionize and be recognized as employees. On narrow legal grounds that the great majority of FBS schools were public colleges and universities over which the NLRB did not have jurisdiction, the NLRB dismissed the petition even though Northwestern was and is a private institution.

Notably, however, the NLRB avoided actually ruling on the question as to whether student athletes were to be considered employees.

In a press release, the NLRB wrote

"August 17, 2015

Washington, D.C.—In a unanimous decision, the National Labor Relations Board declined to assert jurisdiction in the case involving Northwestern University football players who receive grant-in-aid scholarships. The Board did not determine if the players were statutory employees under the National Labor Relations Act (NLRA). Instead, the Board exercised its discretion not to assert jurisdiction and dismissed the representation petition filed by the union.

In the decision, the Board held that asserting jurisdiction would not promote labor stability due to the nature and structure of NCAA Division I Football Bowl Subdivision (FBS). By statute the Board does not have jurisdiction over state-run colleges and universities, which constitute 108 of the roughly 125 FBS teams. In addition, every school in the Big Ten, except Northwestern, is a state-run institution. As the NCAA and conference maintain substantial control over individual teams, the Board held that asserting jurisdiction over a single team would not promote stability in labor relations across the league.

This decision is narrowly focused to apply only to the players in this case and does not preclude reconsideration of this issue in the future."[3]

The significance of this case cannot be overstated and may harken a new era in the recognition of the legal rights of college athletes.

## SYNOPSIS

1.   College sports can be extremely lucrative to the NCAA and the individual colleges and universities.

---

[3]   NLRB Office of Public Affairs "Board Unanimously Decides to Decline Jurisdiction in Northwestern Case" August 17, 2015.

2.   The NCAA regulates college sports.

3.   Most of the NCAA budget comes from income attributable to "March Madness," the NCAA men's college basketball championship.

4.   During the early part of the 20th century college athletes were often paid far in excess of tuition, room and board.

5.   The NCAA's rules limiting televising of college football games were ruled by the Supreme Court to be violations of anti-trust law.

6.   The O'Bannon case resulted in video games using the images of college athletes being stopped and colleges providing enhanced scholarship amounts to college athletes.

7.   The term "student-athlete" was created by the NCAA in order to avoid responsibility for injuries suffered by college athletes during intercollegiate athletic events.

8.   Despite the large amounts of money earned as a result of college athletics, most college athletic programs are not self-supporting.

9.   Student fees subsidize a large amount of the cost of college athletics.

10.   College coaches are paid large salaries.

11.   The NCAA has established rules disqualifying a college athlete from participating in NCAA sporting events if the athlete has hired an agent.

12.   The NCAA has specific rules regarding eligibility to participate in college sports including academic requirements.

13.   While NCAA rules permit a professional athlete in one sport to play a different sport in college, such an athlete is not eligible to compete in NCAA sports if the source of the athlete's compensation in the other sport is prize money.

14.   Numerous scandals have occurred in college sports involving improper payments to athletes and academic fraud.

15. Controversy continues as to whether college athletes should be considered employees.

# CHAPTER SIX

# Olympics

The most prominent international sporting events are the Summer and Winter Olympics, held every four years. The Olympics are governed by the International Olympic Committee and 28 International Federations that control the various sports in which Olympic competition is held.

Presently 206 countries participate in the Olympics which is more than the number of countries in the United Nations which is only 193. This is due to the fact that "countries" such as Puerto Rico, Bermuda and Hong Kong have their own Olympic teams.

Initially only amateurs were allowed to participate in the Olympics with the exception of fencers who were allowed to compete even if they were professional fencers. After years of abuse of the amateur rules by many countries and out of recognition that the rules were seriously outdated particularly in Eastern Bloc countries where amateurs, such as the Soviet Olympic Hockey Team were entirely state sponsored, the rules were changed. Presently, the determination as to allowing professional participation is made by the international federation for the specific sport that it governs. In 2016 for the first time professional boxers were allowed to compete in the Olympics.

## HISTORY

The original Olympic Games began in 776 BC in Greece and were held every four years thereafter for more than a thousand years. Many of the original events related to military skills of the time such as the hoplitodomia, a race of twenty-five athletes who ran more than four hundred yards wearing full armor while carrying shields weighing thirty pounds.

Chariot racing, wrestling and javelin throwing were other military skill competitions found in the original Olympics.

The marathon is the name of the 26 mile 385 yard race that concludes each modern Olympic Summer Games. According to legend, Philippides, a Greek warrior was sent from the victorious battlefield at Marathon to Athens, a distance of 26 miles 385 yards away to announce the defeat of the Persians in September of 490 BC. According to legend, upon completing his run, Philippides proclaimed "we have won" and then promptly keeled over dead. The marathon was not a part of the original Olympic Games, but was included in the modern Olympics when they were revived in Athens in 1896 in an attempt to find an exciting event to exemplify the ancient glory of Greece.

Politics has always been a part of human endeavors and the early Olympics were no exception. In 67 AD, the Roman Emperor Nero competed with a ten horse team in the four horse chariot race. Thrown from his chariot during the course of the event and unable to complete the race, he was still proclaimed the winner on the basis that he would have won the race had he been able to continue.

Despite the political overtones, the spirit of athletic competition was exemplified by the truce that was declared among the often warring Greek City-States during the times of the Olympic Games when athletes from each of the cities were guaranteed safe passage to and from the games and all City-State wars were temporarily halted.

Cheating and performance enhancing drugs which are not uncommon in the modern day Olympic Games were also a part of the original Olympics. Wrestlers would cover their skin with olive oil to make them difficult to grab. Bribery of officials and athletes was common. This pattern is not much different than what occurred in the 2002 Winter Games in Salt Lake City when a French judge gave Russian pairs skaters higher marks than warranted in return for favors from the Russian judges.

However, cheaters were dealt with somewhat more harshly at the original Olympic Games where cheaters were both fined and publicly flogged. In addition their names were engraved in statues lining the roads to the Olympic stadiums. During the Olympics of 388 BC, Eupolus a boxer from Thessaly bribed three of his opponents to let him win. When the plot was uncovered all four were whipped, fined and statues bearing their names were erected.

Similar to the banning of nations or teams for violating rules such as the banning of the Russian track and field team from the 2016 Rio Summer Games for PED violations, in 420 BC, Sparta was banned from the games for violating a peace treaty. However, a Spartan athlete, posing as an athlete from Thebes, entered and won the chariot race. When the truth was discovered, he was whipped and his victory taken from him.

The modern Olympic Games have grown from forty-three events in nine sports in the 1896 Olympic Games in Athens to four hundred different events in the Summer and Winter Olympic Games. The only events to have been included in every modern Olympic Games are the 100 meter, 400 meter, 800 meter and 1,500 meter runs, 110 meter hurdles, running high jump, running long jump, triple jump, shot-put, discus, pole vault, 1,500 meter freestyle swimming, foil fencing, saber fencing and the marathon.

The 1896 Athens Olympics had 241 competitors, all of whom were men.

In the 1900 Paris Olympics the number of events grew to 95 in 18 sports and included events such as Live (not for long) Pigeon Shooting where the gold medal was won by Leon de Lunden of Belgium who killed 21 pigeons.

In Paris, the number of men competing increased to 975 men and 22 women took part in the modern Olympics for the first time. American Margaret Abbott won the Women's Golf gold medal without being aware that she was competing in the Olympics. She thought she had entered a local tournament. Golf was an Olympic sport in the 1900 and 1904 Olympics only to be removed as an Olympic sport until the 2016 Rio games. Similarly Rugby was an Olympic sport between 1900 and 1924 only to reemerge at the 2016 Rio Olympics in the quicker 7 person format.

The 1912 Olympic Games were held in Stockholm. The number of male competitors rose to 2,359 and the number of women competitors increased to 48. Following Sweden's decision to ban boxing from the Olympic games as morally objectionable, the International Olympic Committee changed the rules such that the sports to be included in the games would be determined by the IOC and not the host country, however, the host country is now allowed to pick demonstration sports to be included at their Olympics. Tennis, which later went on to become a recognized Olympic sport was a demonstration sport at the 1984 Los Angeles Olympic Games along with baseball. Curling was a demonstration sport at the 1988 Calgary Winter Olympic Games and bowling was a demonstration sport at the 1988 Seoul Summer Olympic Games.

The Winter Olympics began in 1924 and originally were held in the same year as the Summer Olympics until 1994 when they went on their own four year cycle resulting in there being either a Winter or Summer Olympic Game every two years.

In the 1928 Amsterdam Olympics 135 women competed in various events including, for the first time, the women's 800 meters track event which, following reports of the collapse of a number of runners at the end of the race, was then banned from the Olympics due to concerns about the health of women athletes until it was reintroduced in 1960. This paternalistic vestige of protecting women from exhausting events persisted for many years. World Record Holder

Katie Ledecky could not swim the 1,500 meter race in the 2016 Rio Olympics because that event was only open to men. The 1,500 meter swimming race for women was added as an Olympic event for the 2020 Summer Olympics.

The 1948 London Olympic Games were the first to be broadcast on television, however, the television signals did not reach the United States and few people in the UK at that time actually had television sets. Approximately 4,000 athletes from 59 countries participated in the London Games.

The 1960 Rome Olympics brought wide-spread television coverage to the Olympic Games, changing them forever. Live broadcasts were done throughout Europe and film was flown to America where it was seen "only" hours old. At the Rome Olympics the number of male competitors increased to 4,727 and the number of women dramatically increased to 611.

The 1964 Tokyo Olympics brought the first gender testing of female athletes.

The 1968 Mexico City Olympics brought the first disqualification for drug use. Hans-Gunnar Liljenwall, a Swedish pentathlete became the first Olympic athlete to lose a medal for failing a drug test. In his case, the banned substance was alcohol. While the idea of alcohol as a performance enhancing drug may seem odd, the justification for it being a banned substance was that in some events it could be used to relax the athlete and reduce stress thereby giving an unfair advantage. Alcohol is now banned only in Archery.

The 1984 LA Olympics saw American Joan Benoit win the initial running of the women's marathon. A lawsuit brought against the IOC in an effort to include the women's 5,000 meter and 10,000 meter runs in the Olympics failed. Four years later, however, the women's 10,000 meter run became an Olympic event, eight years before the women's 5,000 meter run also was included in the Olympics. Largely as a result of the vision of Los Angeles Olympic organizer Peter Uberoff, the 1984 Summer Olympic Games which utilized existing structures, extensive corporate sponsorships and increased television revenue became the first Olympics to earn a profit, earning 223 million dollars.

# CHOOSING A CITY

Choosing the host cities for the Olympics has become a difficult task as the International Olympic Committee (IOC) application process has distinct requirements that require much spending by the host country merely to apply. Numerous cities have dropped out of consideration to host the Olympics due to the high cost of becoming an Olympic host city. Merely putting in a bid can be an expensive undertaking with Chicago estimated to have paid as much as 100 million dollars in its failed application to host the 2016 Summer Games. The bidding process takes approximately seven years. Host cities are responsible for the entire costs incurred in putting on the Games in their city although the International Olympic Committee provides some small financial contributions.

Security costs have increased tremendously in the years following the terrorist attacks at the 1972 Munich Olympics in which eleven Israeli athletes were killed and in the wake of the attacks of September 11, 2001. The budget for security at the 2000 Sydney Summer Games was 250 million dollars, however four years later at the 2004 Olympic Games in Athens, the security budget increased to more than 1.6 billion dollars.

One of the major costs incurred in putting on any Olympic Games is housing. The IOC requires that host cities for Summer Olympic Games must have secure housing for 15,000 athletes as well as 40,000 tourists attending the games. The demand for these housing units after the games are finished does not generally continue. For example, 40% of Lillehammer, Norway's hotels went bankrupt in the five years after it hosted the 1994 Winter Olympic Games when tourism did not increase to levels sufficient to support the hotels.

Large stadiums as well as numerous smaller sporting venues for the myriad of Olympic events generally have to be built by the city hosting the Olympics and rarely translate into increased use by the local population when the Olympic Games are completed. In addition, the opening and closing ceremonies have turned into extremely expensive spectacles that may not merit the funds expended.

The Olympics have a history of creating buildings and infrastructure that are later abandoned. The Sochi 2014 Winter Games cost an estimated 51 billion dollars for the construction of stadiums, hotels and other infrastructure which, barely a year after the Olympics, were largely decaying and empty. The Rio de Janeiro 2016 Summer Games is the most recent example of abandoned buildings and promises of improved infrastructure left unfulfilled.

Cities seeking to host the Olympics will usually commission studies that indicate tremendous future financial benefits for the hosting cities that generally don't materialize. Increased tourism and lasting economic benefit although often cited in these studies rarely seem to occur.

Such claims are based on the idea that the Games can serve as a tourist attraction, as well as increase the visibility of a city to business leaders around the world. The model of the frugal and profitable 1984 Los Angeles Olympics is often invoked as are the 1992 Barcelona Games, which contributed to the revival of the city. Barcelona may have done the best job of taking the Olympics as an opportunity to make long lasting improvements to the host city. A blighted industrial waterfront area was developed into an esplanade with affordable housing in 1992 as a part of the Games. But there is little evidence that the Olympics increase tourism or attract new investment. Huge spending for a single event that is over in a matter of weeks has not proven to be a positive financial strategy for host cities. While host cities and the countries in which they are located spend money on expensive infrastructure including highways and airports, those same improvements could be done in a financially more efficient manner if these improvements were built independent of the Olympics without the additional costs of having to build extensive stadiums and athletic facilities that historically have not provided long term benefits to the host cities and countries. To a large part, the Los Angeles Olympics were financially successful because existing athletic facilities were used and new construction of stadiums and other athletic venues was avoided.

While Olympic television revenues can be significant, the International Olympic Committee takes 70% of broadcast revenues. Revenues derived from tourists and ticket sales, while significant are never sufficient to make the games profitable.

Many Olympics have lost considerable money such as the 1976 Montreal Olympics which may have lost the most. It took thirty years for Montreal to pay off its 1.5 billon dollar debt from the 1976 Olympic Games.

Almost uniformly, the cost of the games has exceeded the original budgets for Olympic Games since 1968. The 2012 London Summer Olympics which were originally budgeted at no more than 5 billion dollars ended up costing 15 billion dollars which is not unusual for Olympic costs in recent years.

A possible solution to the problem of the great financial cost to host cities would be to have a permanent site such as Athens for the Summer Games.

Along with having the Olympics permanently sited in Athens or some other permanent site, other suggestions have included having a city host the games for two consecutive Olympics over eight years which would serve as an incentive for host cities to be more judicious in their construction of necessary infrastructure. Another interesting proposal is for a city to host the Games and then host them again twelve years later which would provide also serve as an incentive to make the infrastructure more permanent.

## QUESTION

1.   How could the choice for future Olympic host cities be done in a more economical basis?

# BIDDING TO HOST THE OLYMPICS

For many years, the industrialized countries of the Western World provided most of the host cities. From the start of the modern Olympic Games in 1896 until 1998, more than 90% of the host cities were in Western Europe, the United States, Canada, Australia and Japan. In recent years, however, the games have opened up to countries with emerging economies such as the 2016 Rio Olympics in Brazil. The international prestige that comes with hosting the Olympic Games may be important to a city and country seeking to emerge into a larger position on the world economic stage.

The 1970s witnessed a decline in enthusiasm among cities willing to host the Games. After having been initially awarded the 1976 Winter Olympics, voters in Denver in 1972 rejected a $5 million bond referendum that was to have been used to finance the Games, resulting in the International Olympic Committee rescinding its award of the 1976 Games to Denver.

Following the financial debacle of the 1976 Montreal Olympics, Los Angeles was the only city that bid for the 1984 Summer Games. Taking advantage of its superior bargaining position, the Los Angeles Olympic Organizing Committee was able to substantially dictate the terms of its bid to the International Olympic Committee. For example, it did not offer to build glitzy new facilities, but rather utilized the area's existing sports infrastructure, including the 60-year old Los Angeles Coliseum for the hallmark track and field events as well as the opening and closing ceremonies. The Los Angeles Olympic Organizing Committee also became the first to extensively finance the games through corporate sponsorships. The focus on keeping costs down resulted in total expenditures for the Games of a "mere" $546 million ($1.27 billion in 2016 dollars), less than one-fourth of what was spent by Montreal eight years earlier. The 1984 Los Angeles Olympics managed to become one of the only profitable Games in Olympic history, with a final profit of $232.5 million. The example of Los Angeles led numerous cities to consider Olympic bids in the hope of duplicating Los Angeles' success. For a time, the increased interest of cities to host the Olympic Games made the competition to host the games more intense and expensive.

Not only did the competition among cities to host create a bidding environment prone to bribery and corruption, but in an effort to impress and influence the International Olympic Committee, bidders proposed spectacular expensive sporting venues such as Beijing's Bird's Nest and the London Aquatics Centre. The initial estimated cost of the National Olympic Stadium in Tokyo, which would be the primary stadium for the Tokyo 2020 Summer Olympics, was two billion dollars. Due to public outrage at the exorbitant cost, the plans were scrapped and a less costly stadium was commissioned.

Increasingly, cities are beginning to realize the financial challenges of hosting the Olympics may be too high a price to pay for the privilege. Twelve cities bid for the 2004 Summer Games, however only five bid for the 2020 games and only two competed for the 2022 Winter Games.

Many cities including Boston have cancelled bids because of lack of political and public support, often due to the extreme expense as cited by Rome in withdrawing from consideration for the 2024 Olympic Games.

Six bids were submitted for the 2022 Winter Olympics although four were withdrawn within a year, leaving Almaty the capital of Kazakhstan and Beijing, China as the only two cities competing to host the Games. Ultimately, in 2015 the games were awarded to Beijing. Among the cities that dropped their initial bids was Oslo, Norway citing the high financial cost of the games and the lack of public support which to a great extent related to the ultimate cost to Norwegian taxpayers.

Being financially successful, however, may not necessarily be a prime motivation behind many Olympic bids as the Olympics have served as international recognition of a country's increased status on the world stage as exemplified by the Tokyo 1964 Olympics, Munich 1972 Olympics and Beijing 2008 Olympics.

Interestingly, according to a 2009 study by Andrew K. Rose, an economist at the University of California, Berkeley, and Mark M. Spiegel, an economist at the Federal Reserve Bank of San Francisco (Andrew K. Rose & Mark M. Spiegel, "The Olympic Effect" National Bureau of Economic Research, Working Paper No. 14854) the economies of host cities and the countries in which they are located often improved following the hosting of an Olympic Games, however, most notably, their research also indicated that the economies of countries that had lost bids to host the Olympics also had improved economies in the years following their rejected bids which leads to the conclusion that it is not the Olympics that spurs on the economy of these cities, but that cities with already improving economies become the candidates to host the Olympic Games. In fact, cities and countries that are unsuccessful in their bids to host the Olympic Games may actually experience larger gains in their economies as a result of not having the increased debt and building of unnecessary stadiums that come with a winning Olympic bid.

Even before Boston and Hamburg's withdrawals as applicant cities for the 2024 Summer Olympic Games, and only two cities applying to host the 2022 Winter Olympic Games, the International Olympic Committee had been considering major changes to its strategic vision in regard to hosting Olympic Games. Its Olympic Agenda 2020, which was unanimously passed at the IOC's 127th Session in Monaco in December 2014, included 40 recommendations for reform, many of which promoted increased economic sustainability for host cities.

The recommendations recognize the economic problems encountered by host cities and seek to provide a guideline for reform. Specifically, they propose to:

1)    shape the bidding process as an invitation;

2)    evaluate bid cities by assessing key opportunities and risks;

3)    reduce the cost of bidding;

4)    include sustainability in all aspects of the Olympic Games;

5)    include sustainability within the Olympic Movement's daily operations; and

6)    reduce the cost and reinforce the flexibility of Olympic Games management (IOC 2014a).

In addition, Olympic Agenda 2020 seeks to reduce corruption by increasing transparency. These are merely recommendations and how they will be implemented largely remains to be seen. The International Olympic Committee has not yet had a full bidding process done pursuant to the new guidelines, but already it appears some cities are following the recommendations. Los Angeles, which emerged as the U.S. bid city for 2024 after the withdrawal of the Boston bid, has proposed using existing college dormitories at UCLA and the University of Southern California for athlete housing during the Game which would eliminate more than $1 billion in costs for an athletes' village from their original plans. The response of the IOC to the new bids will indicate if the IOC intends to follow its own recommendations or will retreat to the former preference for elaborate and expensive Olympics.

# OLYMPIC SPORTS

BMX bicycle racing has been an Olympic sport since 2008 and is one of a number of sports sometimes referred to as extreme sports of more recent vintage that are popular with younger people, a key television demographic, that have made their way into the present day Olympics. Many of these sports have become Winter Olympic sports including ski halfpipe, ski slopestyle, snowboard slopestyle and snowboard parallel slalom. The 2020 Tokyo Olympic Games will include skateboarding, sport climbing, surfing and three-on-three basketball played with one basket as often done in playground basketball.

More and more, a major consideration in adding new events is the popularity to broad television audiences around the world. NBC Universal in 2014 paid 7.75 billion dollars for the exclusive broadcast rights to six Olympic Games between 2022 and 2032. The IOC is always cognizant as to how particular sports will appeal to the interests of a wide viewing audience.

In 2016, the International Olympic Committee recognized the sports of cheerleading and the combat sport Muay Thai which is a first step toward the inclusion of these sports in future Olympics. The international governing bodies for these sports have until 2019 to apply for inclusion in the Olympics. Also in 2016, the IOC accepted skateboarding, surfing and sport climbing to be included in the 2020 Summer Olympic Games in Tokyo as the IOC continues to attempt to appeal to the interests of younger sport fans around the world.

The Global Gaming League has strongly advocated for including video games in the Olympics. A move has been on for years to bring pole dancing into the Olympics and while the image of this sport in the United States may be more of an activity associated with strip clubs, pole fitness or vertical dancing is a serious sport throughout much of the world. The sport itself has a rule book including compulsory moves and scoring rules as well as banning movements done "in an overtly erotic manner." Recent world championships included a hundred competitors from approximately two dozen countries.

For a sport to qualify to be included in the Olympics, it generally needs to be played in at least 75 countries on four continents for men's sports and 40 countries and three continents for women's sports, have an internationally recognized governing body recognized by the IOC, standardized judging and have its own world championship. In addition, no motor sports may be considered for

Olympic recognition. Once a sport passes that initial screening, a majority vote is required to be placed on the Recognized Sports List.

Some of the sports to be dropped over the years include the standing high jump, the standing long jump, tug of war (an event contested in the original ancient Olympic Games), rope climbing, motor boat racing and rugby. It is interesting to note that years before the introduction of the Paralympics, American George Eyser won the rope climbing gold medal in the 1904 Olympics despite having only one leg, having lost a leg in a train accident.

Another sport discontinued after being a demonstration sport in the 1928 St. Moritz, Switzerland Olympics was Skijoring which involves a competitor on skis being pulled by a horse.

Wrestling, which had been an original sport of the ancient games, was removed as a sport by a 2013 vote of the IOC while at the same meeting the IOC voted to retain the modern pentathlon. Although it may appear to be an anachronism today the Modern Pentathlon, a sport which combines pistol shooting, fencing, 200 meter freestyle swimming, horse jumping and a 3 kilometer has been a continuous Olympic sport since 1912.

At the 2012 London Olympic Games only 26 countries even had participants competing in the modern pentathlon while at the same Olympics, wrestling medals were awarded to athletes from 29 different countries. Further, while public interest is a paramount factor in the inclusion and exclusion of sports in the Olympics, almost twice as many people watched the wrestling competition on television as compared to the modern pentathlon. The response to the banning of wrestling, which was not to take effect until 2020, was swift. The International Federation Internationale des Luttes Associees (FILA) the governing body of international wrestling promptly changed its rules in an effort to modernize the sport, following which wrestling was readmitted to the Olympics before its exclusion could even take effect. In an unusual move, the effort to reintroduce wrestling had the support of the United States, Russia and

Iran which hardly agree on anything. Among the rule changes were the dropping of two weight classes for men and the adding of two weight classes for women. In addition, in order to make the matches more exciting, rules were changed rewarding more aggressive play and punishing more passive wrestlers.

# SCANDALS

Scandals have been a constant feature of the modern Olympic Games. Often the scandals involved bribery such as that of IOC members by members of the organizing committee for the Salt Lake City Winter games in 2002 which resulted in four members resigning and six being expelled.

Perhaps the best known Olympic scandal involved the pairs' figure skating competition at the 2002 Winter Olympics in Salt Lake City, Utah. In the figure skating pairs competition, Elena Berezhnaya and Anton Sikharulidze of Russia were awarded the Gold medal over the Canadian pair of Jamie Sale and David Pelletier although it appeared to both the viewing public and expert observers the Canadian pair had clearly won the competition. Questions as to a possible conspiracy and wrong doing focused on the French judge Marie-Reine Le Gougne who reportedly had been pressured by the French skating organization to vote for the Russian pair regardless of the quality of their skate. The public outrage was so intense that an immediate investigation was done by the International Skating Union which was completed within a couple of days and resulted in the Russian pair being allowed to keep their gold medals since there was no evidence of any wrongdoing on their part, however, the Canadian pair was also awarded gold medals and a new award ceremony was done. This did not end the controversy, however and after further investigation over the course of the next two months, LeGougne as well as Didier Gailhaguet, the President of the French Ice Sports Federation were suspended by the ISU for three years and barred from the 2006 Winter Olympics. Allegedly the actions of LeGougne were done as a part of a deal by which the French skaters competing in the ice dance competition would get the votes of the Russian judges in return for the French judges voting for the Russian skaters in the pairs competition.

# UNDERAGE CHINESE GYMNASTS SCANDAL

At the 2008 Olympics the Chinese women's gymnastics team had a number of competitors who appeared younger than the minimum eligibility age of sixteen years. Jiang Yuyuan, Yang Yilin and He Kexin in particular appeared to be quite young. He Kexin was only 4 feet 8 inches tall and weighed a mere 72 pounds. Chinese officials denied that the athletes were underage, pointing to evidence such as He's passport although numerous other official records indicated she was 14 at the time of the 2008 Olympics. This was not the first time Chinese underage athletes had falsified records in order to compete in gymnastics. In the 2000 Sydney games, Yang Yun won a bronze medal in the uneven bars event and although her passport indicated she was 16 at the time of the Olympics, in truth she was 14. In 2010, following an investigation, the IOC ordered China to return the women's team bronze medal because one of its gymnasts, Dong Fangxiao was only 14 at the time of the Sydney 2000 Games. The medal instead went to the American gymnastics team which had finished in fourth place.

The minimum age requirement was raised from 15 to 16 in 1997 by the International Gymnastics Federation in order to protect the health of young athletes. Prior to 1981 the minimum age was 14.

## QUESTION

1.   Is the minimum age rule for gymnastics paternalistic or necessary for the health of competing athletes?

# OKSANA CHUSOVITINA

In an era where 22 year old Ally Raisman of the United States was referred to as grandma by her American gymnastic teammates in Brazil at the 2016 Summer Olympics, Oksana Chusovitina stands out. The 2016 Rio Olympics were her seventh Olympic Games. Competing at 41 years old, the mother of a seventeen year old son (older than many of her competitors, including the two 16 year old gymnasts who competed before her and after her in the Vault Final in which Ms. Chusovitina placed seventh overall) has competed for the Soviet Union, Germany and her native Uzbekistan. She won a gold medal in the team competition representing the Soviet Union at the 1992 Barcelona games. Although she finished seventh in the vault at Rio, she was one of only two gymnasts to attempt the Produnova vault, a vault so difficult that it is sometimes referred to as the vault of death.

# POLITICS

Despite the fact that the modern Olympics represent the ideal of people from countries around the world joining together free of politics to participate in a grand international sports festival, politics has played a major part in the Olympics from the first modern Olympic games at Athens in 1896 when Germany and France were initially reluctant to participate due to lingering ill will going back to the Franco-Prussian war of more than twenty years earlier.

Turkey, Hungary, Austria, Germany and Bulgaria were banned from the 1920 Antwerp, Belgium Olympics for their role in World War I. The Antwerp Olympic Games were the first to be held following the end of World War I. Germany was also barred from participating in the 1924 Olympic Games although the other four countries were welcomed back.

American participation in the 1936 Berlin Olympics was hotly debated in the United States with many people viewing participation in the Olympics as support of Germany's Nazi policies. Ultimately the

United States decided to join the Games. Adolph Hitler saw the 1936 Olympics as an opportunity to display the superiority of the Aryan race to the world, however, the most outstanding athlete of the games was African-American Jesse Owens who won four gold medals. It is interesting to note, however, that racial segregation in the United States was still strictly observed in 1936 and while Owens was allowed to stay in the same hotels as white members of the United States Olympic team while in Germany, he had to stay in segregated hotels in many parts of the United States. Following the Olympics, after a parade for him down the streets of New York that ended with a reception in his honor at the Waldorf Astoria hotel in New York City, Owens was not allowed to enter the hotel through the front entrance, but had to go in through a freight elevator to get to the event honoring him.

The 1948 Olympics in London continued the political traditions of the supposedly non-political Olympic Games when the IOC banned Japan and Germany from participating in the games due to their role in World War II which had ended three years earlier.

The 1956 Melbourne Olympics was the first Olympic Games to be boycotted. The Netherlands, Spain and Switzerland refused to send teams as a protest of the Soviet Union's bloody suppression of the Hungarian revolution earlier that year. At the Melbourne Games, a Water Polo game between the Soviet Union and Hungary turned into a major international incident. With Hungary leading 4–0 and the match becoming increasingly violent in front of a loud pro-Hungarian crowd, the officials stopped the match and awarded the victory to Hungary which went on to win the Gold medal.

China boycotted the 1956 Melbourne Games due to the IOC's recognition of Taiwan and did not return to the Olympic Games until 1980. Meanwhile, in their own political statement, Egypt, Iraq and Lebanon boycotted the Games as a protest of Israel's invasion of the Sinai.

The IOC banned the participation of South Africa from the 1960 Rome Olympic Games due to its racial apartheid policies. South Africa did not return to the games until 1992.

Chapter 5 of the Olympic charter states, "No kind of demonstration or political, religious or racial propaganda is permitted in the Olympic areas." At the 1968 Mexico City Games American sprinters Tommie Smith and John Carlos who had won the gold medal and bronze medal respectively in the 200 meter dash gave a black power salute wearing black gloves during the medal ceremony. The response of the crowd at the stadium was loud boos and IOC President Avery Brundage ordered both athletes expelled from the Olympics. It is sometimes overlooked that the third man on the podium, silver medal winner Peter Norman, a white Australian wore the badge of the Olympic Project for Human Rights as a show of solidarity with his fellow medal winners. The Olympic Project for Human Rights was an organization of which Tommie Smith and John Carlos were two of the founders that protested racial segregation and racism in sports.

In 1972 and 1976 many African countries threatened to boycott the Olympics if South Africa and Rhodesia were not banned due to their apartheid policies. They also wanted New Zealand banned from the Olympics because New Zealand sent a touring rugby team to South Africa even though rugby was not an Olympic sport. The IOC did not ban New Zealand and consequently 22 African countries boycotted the 1976 Olympics. Taiwan withdrew from participation in the games after China pressured Canada to deny Taiwan status to compete in the games.

In 1980 sixty five countries including the United States boycotted the Moscow Olympics due to the Soviet Union's invasion of Afghanistan resulting in only 80 countries competing in the Games, the lowest number of participating countries since 1956. Four years later the Soviet Union led a boycott of the Los Angeles 1984 Olympics that included 14 Eastern Bloc countries. Notably, gymnastic power Romania did not join the 1984 boycott.

The 1992 games in Barcelona were the first games to be played since the end of the cold war and the breakup of the Soviet Union. Latvia, Lithuania and Estonia competed as independent countries for the first time and the other countries that formerly had made up the Soviet Union competed as the Unified Team. West Germany and East Germany competed as a single team for the first time since 1964 and now apartheid-free South Africa was welcomed back to the games for the first time in 32 years.

# FINANCIAL SUPPORT

American Olympic athletes are generally funded by the USOC and the national governing body of their particular sport.

The United States Olympic Committee determines its financial support of the various sports according to the likelihood of the sport winning medals at the Olympics. Training can be expensive and the U.S. Olympic Committee does not receive government funding from the federal government.

The Track and Field Athletes Association a union of American track and field athletes reported in 2012 that half of its athletes who were in the top 10 in their respective events made less than $15,000 per year including prize money and endorsements while only 20% made more than $50,000 per year. Athletes not in the top ten in their events receive limited financial support.

# BONUSES

Russian athletes in the Olympics winning gold medals have been awarded the equivalent of $60,000 and additional amounts for world records. This is why Russian weightlifter Vasily Alexiev would attempt world record attempts only by the slightest of weights in order to constantly set new world records and receive commensurate bonuses. One of the greatest weight lifters of all time, the Soviet superheavyweight won the Olympic Gold medal in 1972 and 1976. During the course of his career he set 80 world records between 1970 and 1977. Because he would receive a cash bonus whenever he broke a world record, Alekseyev would never attempt to break the world record by more than 0.5 kg (1.1 pounds) thereby enabling him to continually break the world record and continually receive cash bonuses. Following his example, Ukrainian pole vaulter Sergey Bubka, who won the 1983 World Championships at age 19 broke the world record for the pole vault thirty-five times by the slightest of amounts during the course of his career receiving cash bonuses from not only the Soviet Union, but also sponsors such as Nike.

South Korean athletes have an additional incentive to win an Olympic medal because Korean medal winning athletes are exempt from having to do military service which is required universally of all able bodied men.

The United States Olympic Committee (USOC) also awards cash prizes to Olympic and Paralympic medal winners. In 2016, the prize money was $25,000 for a gold medal, $15,000 for a silver medal and $10,000 for a bronze medal. Prior to 2016, these bonuses were subject to income tax.

In 2016 following the 2016 Rio Summer Olympic Games a law was passed by Congress to eliminate the tax on cash awards paid by the United States Olympic Committee to medal winning athletes as well as the tax on the value of the medals themselves which are valued at $600 for gold medals, $300 for silver medals and minimal value for the bronze medal.

The law was made retroactive so athletes from the 2016 Olympics and Paralympics did not owe income tax on their medals or the cash prizes awarded. Formerly the winnings were taxed as ordinary income for federal income tax purposes. The law was passed with only one vote against the proposal in the House of Representatives and unanimously in the Senate. The argument in favor of the law was that Olympians and Paralympians spend years in expensive training and often earn little money while they train. However, the law does not apply to athletes, such as Michael Phelps who earn at least a million dollars per year.

Wrestling is not a sport where its athletes generally become household names and earn major endorsement contracts, however it has its own bonus program. In an effort to both recognize the hard work that goes into training to be an Olympic wrestler as well as to provide money to enable talented wrestlers to support themselves while competing, a group of former wrestlers including successful businessmen Michael E. Novogratz and David Barry started the Living the Dream Medal Fund in 2009 which awards substantial cash prizes to Olympic and World Championship medal winning wrestlers. At the 2016 Olympics, one male wrestler and one female American wrestler, Kyle Snyder and Helen Maroulis each earned $250,000 for their Gold medal victories.

# WOMEN AND GAYS IN THE OLYMPICS

The IOC voted to allow women to compete in the 1924 Olympics. Turkey, Japan, France and the United States all voted against permitting women to compete. However, merely permitting women to compete in the Olympics did not mandate particular countries to include women athletes on their national teams. It was not until 2012 that the women athletes first competed for Saudi Arabia at the Olympics.

In 2014 Olympic Principle 6 which deals with discrimination was amended to include sexual orientation as a protected class. It now reads:

"The enjoyment of the rights and freedoms set forth in this Olympic Charter shall be secured without discrimination of any kind, such as race, colour, sex, sexual orientation, language, religion, political or other opinion, national or social origin, property, birth or other status."

# KATIE LEDECKY

Nineteen year old Katie Ledecky, one of the stars of the 2016 Rio Olympics after winning Gold medals in the 200 meter, 400 meter and 800 meter freestyle events and a silver medal in the 4 × 100 meter freestyle relay didn't even get to swim in her best event, the 1,500 meter freestyle at the Rio Olympics because although the event is recognized by FINA the sports federation governing international swimming, the event was not included in the Olympics where the longest event a woman competitor can swim in was the 800 meter freestyle. For years male swimmers at the Olympics swam the same events as the female swimmers with the one exception of the 800 meter freestyle, which was exclusively a women's event and the 1,500 meter freestyle which was exclusively a men's event until 2017 when the IOC voted to include a men's 800 meter freestyle and a women's 1,500 meter freestyle for the first time at the 2020 Olympics. Various arguments were made as to why until now there was no 1,500 meter freestyle event for women in the Olympics. Some of the arguments were that adding the race would make too many events, the race was boring or the paternalistic argument that women couldn't swim as far as men, but none of the arguments were sound. The race was certainly no more boring for women than the 1,500 event already being competed in by men and as for women being unable to compete in this event, Katie Ledecky's times for the event met the men's Olympic qualifying time and would have beaten many of the male's competing in the event. Now men and women will swim the same races for the first time in the 2020 Tokyo Summer Olympic Games.

## QUESTION

1.    Would equality of the sexes in the Olympics require that men and women each compete in the exact same events?

# RUSSIA AND THE 2016 RIO OLYMPIC GAMES

Shortly before the 2016 Rio Olympics the McLaren Investigation Report for the World Anti-Doping Agency (WADA) was released in which details of the large scale state sponsored performance enhancing drug program of Russia were made public.

The IOC left it up to the various international sports federations to initially determine whether a country's team in a particular sport would be banned, such as had already done by track and field's ruling body the International Association of Athletic Federation which banned the Russian track and field team in June of 2016 based on earlier reports of widespread state sponsored Russian performance enhancing drug use. Only a single Russian track and field athlete who had trained entirely outside of Russia and passed all drug tests was allowed to compete in the 2016 Rio Games. Russian Rowers were particularly hit hard with only six members of the 28 person rowing team allowed to participate. This is particularly noteworthy because it was not due to the athletes failing drug tests, but because of irregularities in the Moscow drug lab.

The Russian archery, badminton, tennis, triathlon, table tennis, volleyball, beach volleyball, equestrian and fencing teams were all permitted to compete. The judo federation of which Russian President Vladimir Putin is the honorary president also said all athletes could compete. A total of 118 of the 389 Russian Olympic team athletes were banned from the 2016 Rio Olympics.

President Putin's response to the doping scandal and banning of large numbers of Russian athletes was to initially claim that Russia was the victim of double standards of shortsighted politicians although after the Olympics, Russia acknowledged widespread performance enhancing drug violations among its athletes while continuing to deny that it was state sponsored.

# COMPETING FOR ANOTHER COUNTRY

Pole vaulter Giovanni Lanaro was born and raised in California, but competed for Mexico in the Rio Olympics in 2016. His mother was born in Mexico and the Mexican Olympic Committee merely requires a Mexican heritage to compete for Mexico. Other Americans with ancestors in other countries competing for those countries include David Torrence for Peru, Alexi Pappas for Greece and Peter Callahan for Belgium.

Chapter 6 of the Olympic charter acknowledges that indeed the games are "competitions between athletes in individual or team events and not between countries." In fact, the IOC does not even keep an official medal count by countries. However, the athletes are selected by national Olympic committees. Rule 41 of the Olympic charter requires that "Any competitor in the Olympic Games must be a national of the country of the NOC which is entering such competitor."

The Olympic charter requires that if someone has already competed for their native country in international competition, they must wait three years before they can compete for another country. However, this rule is generally waived by the athlete's country of birth thereby making it quicker for such athletes to compete as nationals of other countries. The key is to be eligible for dual citizenship which is now allowed in many countries around the world thereby eliminating the need to renounce their citizenship in the country of their birth in order to compete for another country. Some countries such as Japan, China and India make it very difficult to obtain citizenship after birth with often strict language and residency requirements. Other countries make it easy. American Kylie Dickson competed for Belarus in the 2016 Olympics although she had no family connection to the country and hadn't even ever been in the country at the time of her becoming a member of its Olympic gymnastics team.

Half of the Azerbaijan Olympic team at the 2012 Olympics was made up of naturalized citizens.

While many American athletes compete for other countries when, due to the intense competition, they are unable to make the American team, the United States has also rushed through EB-1 visas for a Kenyan born distance runner and a Chinese born table tennis player.

Table Tennis or Ping Pong, by which it is often known, has been an Olympic sport since 1988. China has dominated the event in the years since then, winning 32 of the 36 gold medals awarded through the Rio Olympics of 2016. China dominates the sport so much that there are many world class Table Tennis athletes born in China who are unable to make the Chinese Olympic team and so they immigrate to other countries and play for them. At the Rio Olympics, Chinese born Table Tennis athletes played for 21 of the 56 countries competing in Table Tennis not including China. While it is not unusual for a few foreign born athletes to move to and compete for other countries, approximately one third of the Table Tennis athletes at the Rio Olympics were not born in the countries they represented.

Making the matter even more complicated is the fact that there are limits on the number of athletes a country can send in each event. Xu Xin of China was ranked third in the world in table tennis, but was also ranked third in China and thereby ineligible to compete in the singles competition where only two competitors can be sent by each country. He did, however, make the Chinese Olympic team as a competitor in the team table tennis competition.

## QUESTIONS

1.   If indeed Olympic competition is, as indicated in the Olympic charter, between athletes and not between countries, is it appropriate for athletes to compete for countries other than ones in which they were born?

2.   Should athletes be able to compete for a country other than their native country only if they are unable to earn a position on their native country's team in order to avoid athletes becoming mercenaries?

# SYNOPSIS

1.   The Olympics are governed by the International Olympic Committee and 28 International Federations governing various sports.

2.   Women first participated in the Olympics at the Paris 1900 Olympics.

3.   Host cities are chosen by the IOC through competitive bidding.

4.   Long term financial benefits of hosting an Olympic Games are extremely rarely achieved.

5.   Reforms to provide for greater financial transparency and reducing the costs of hosting Olympics are being implemented.

6.   The sports that make up the Olympics have continuously evolved in an effort to stay relevant.

7.   Scandals and political controversies have been a constant feature of the Olympics.

8.   Athletes receive financial support from their national Olympic Committees as well as often receiving cash prizes from their respective governments for medal winning performances.

9.   Individual athletes compete for countries with which they have had little connection.

# CHAPTER SEVEN

# Horse Racing

Horse racing is perhaps the oldest sport in world history. Its origins can be traced back to 1500 BC in ancient Egypt and it continues to have worldwide popularity today, sparked most recently by the Triple Crown winning year of American Pharoah in 2015. Race horses are great athletes with an average stride of 24.6 feet and able to achieve speeds of 44 miles per hour.

The operation of the horse racing industry is decentralized. It has no national governing body. It is regulated exclusively by state associations with varying rules regarding track surfaces, medications and all other aspects of the industry.

## EARLY HISTORY

Chariot races were a part of the original Olympic Games. Thousands of spectators attended races at the Circus Maximus in Rome. In the late 1600s and early 1700s British monarchs bred their own mares (female horses) with speedy Arabian and Turkish stallions (male horses) and the sport of kings was born. In fact, all of the thoroughbred race horses of today can trace their heritage back to the three Arabian and Turkish stallions, Byerley Turk, Darley Arabian and Godolphin Barb brought to England during that time. The first public race track opened in London in 1174 and American colonists brought their love of horse racing to the new world where thoroughbred horse racing became quite popular. The first major thoroughbred racing track in America was built in Saratoga Springs, New York where the track constructed in 1863 still stands. Races of high quality horses are hosted there each summer. In the early years of racing in the colonies, jockeys were often African Americans, but eventually they were forced out of racing until the latter part of the 20th century. Present day jockeys include men and women as well as people of all nationalities and races.

# OWNERSHIP

Race horses can be purchased for as little as $10,000, which was the price for 2014 Kentucky Derby and Preakness winner California Chrome. They also can be bought for as much as the 64 million dollar purchase price for 2000 Kentucky Derby winner Fusaichi Pegasus.

The most common business model for race horse ownership today is for the horses to be owned by syndicates of investors who share in the expenses and the profits. This makes the cost of horse ownership more affordable to individual investors who may not have the necessary funds to pay for the significant costs of maintaining and training a thoroughbred race horse. The syndicates are generally done in the form of a limited liability company. Each year, the costs required to maintain the horse are divided between the owners of the shares in the limited liability company.

# MAJOR RACES

Each year the public's attention becomes fixed on the three Triple Crown races, the Kentucky Derby, the Preakness and the Belmont. These races are limited to three year old horses. However, horses get stronger and faster as they get older and the best of horses are often horses older than three years of age. The annual Breeders' Cup World Championship races which occur over two days culminating with the Breeders' Cup Classic in which the finest horses race to determine which horse really is the best of them all, is the true World Series of horseracing.

# FAMOUS HORSES

## Seabiscuit

Many people are familiar with Seabiscuit through the best-selling book and movie about him. Seabiscuit was a late bloomer. As a two year old, he raced 35 times and won only five times. Seabiscuit did not begin to succeed on the track until well into his third racing season when he was bought by Charles Howard who also brought in Tom Smith as a new trainer and Red Pollard as a new jockey. Howard bought Seabiscuit in a claiming race, which is a common type of race in which each of the horses running in the race may be "claimed" or purchased for a specified amount.

Seabiscuit's jockey Red Pollard was as unusual as the horse he rode. Pollard was a former boxer who was blind in one eye and at 5 feet 7 inches tall, far bigger than the typical jockey. However, Pollard had an indescribable mental connection to the horse, a trait shared by many successful jockey-horse combinations in history. Between 1936 and 1940 Seabiscuit dominated all competition on the track with his career highlight being his victory in a one on one match race with East Coast bred Triple Crown winner and Horse of the Year, War Admiral. During the Great Depression, Seabiscuit was a popular folk hero. When he finally retired after six years of racing he had won 33 races and set 16 track records. Claimed for a mere $7,500 by Howard, he earned $437,730 during his long career.

## Secretariat

Secretariat, often affectionately referred to as Big Red won the Triple Crown in 1973 culminating with his victory in the Belmont, the final Triple Crown race, by an astonishing 31 lengths setting a record that stands to this day. During his career, he had 16 victories in 21 races and only once, in his very first race, finished lower than third. During the course of his career, he earned $1,316.808. He was tremendously popular and was even named by ESPN as one of its top 100 athletes of the 20th Century, coming in at number 35 and the only non-human on the list.

Secretariat was euthanized in 1989 after suffering from the painful hoof disease laminitis. An autopsy was performed in which the size of his heart was found to be enormous, which could explain his ability to run at such great speed over long distances.

According to Dr. Thomas Swerczek, the veterinarian who performed the autopsy,

"We were all shocked. I've seen and done thousands of autopsies on horses, and nothing I'd ever seen compared to it. The heart of the average horse weighs about nine pounds. This was almost twice the average size and a third larger than any equine heart I'd ever seen. And it wasn't pathologically enlarged. All the chambers and the valves were normal. It was just larger. I think it told us why he was able to do what he did."[1]

As with all great horses, Secretariat was closely connected to his jockey, Ron Turcotte who won more than 3,000 races in his career that ended when he was paralyzed following being thrown from a horse in a race in 1978.

## Funny Cide

Funny Cide became the first New York bred horse to win the Kentucky Derby in 2003. Funny Cide was also the first gelding to win the Derby since 1929. A gelding is a castrated horse which means that the horse will never be used for breeding purposes. Since much of the money made in modern day horse racing is based upon the value of the horse for breeding purposes, the decision to geld a horse is not made lightly. Gelding a horse will generally result in the horse being more calm and easier to work with; however, if the horse is expected to become a big winner on the track, the horse will generally not be

---

[1]   "Pure Heart: The thrilling life and emotional death of Secretariat," William Nack, Sports Illustrated January 2, 2015.

gelded. The decision to geld a horse is made while the horse is still quite young and if the horse is predicted to be a winner on the track, the owners will not geld the horse. Funny Cide was purchased by his first owners for a mere $12,500. As a two year old, Funny Cide was sold for $75,000 to a consortium of ten friends from upstate New York who called their group, Sackatoga Stable. Entering the 2003 Kentucky Derby, Funny Cide was a 13–1 long shot, but went on to not only win that race, but also the Preakness that year by an incredible 9 ¾ lengths. Heading into the Belmont, the third "jewel" of the Triple Crown, there was great anticipation that Funny Cide could accomplish the difficult feat of winning the Triple Crown. However, Funny Cide came in third behind Empire Maker and Ten Most Wanted. Both of those horses who beat Funny Cide in the Belmont came into the race better rested due to both of them skipping the Preakness, the second leg of the triple crown races, which allowed them to come into the Belmont fresher.

While successful ungelded stallions are usually retired and sent to make their money breeding after their three year old racing campaign or shortly thereafter with owners unwilling to risk injury to the horse that could cause them to lose out on the large money earned through breeding successful race horses, Funny Cide was a gelding with no breeding career in his future so he continued to race until the ripe age of seven after which he retired, having earned $3,529,412.

## Rags to Riches

Rags to Riches' short career consisted of only seven races of which she won five earning 1.3 million dollars in winnings. Most notably, in 2007 she became the first filly (female horse) to win the Belmont in more than a hundred years in a thrilling race against Horse of the Year, Curlin.

The success of fillies racing against male horses has been limited. Only three fillies have ever won the Kentucky Derby. Part of the reason for this may be that, with notable exceptions such as Zenyatta, male horses are generally bigger and stronger. It has been hypothesized that female horses naturally defer to male horses during the course of a race, but there is no evidence and no studies confirming that commonly held belief.

Following the end of her racing career, Rags to Riches is earning considerable money as a brood mare, by which horse owners pay considerable funds to breed their stallions with her.

## Zenyatta

Perhaps the most successful female racing horse of all time, Zenyatta won the first 19 races of her career with the only blemish on her record being a photo finish loss at the 2010 Breeders' Cup Classic which is the premier race each year. A year earlier she had won the same race. Zenyatta was renowned for consistently falling far behind in the early stages of races only to make incredible runs to victory late in the races. Over the course of her career she earned $7,034,580 and is earning large amounts of money as a brood mare. However, she has had little success early in her breeding career with two of her four foals (baby horses) having died. One died from a lung disease and the other died in a farm accident. Her other two foals have not been early winners on the track, but it is still too early to see if she will be able to pass on her successful racing genetics.

## American Pharoah

In 2015, American Pharoah became the first Triple Crown Winner in 37 years. He capped his racing year by winning the prestigious Breeders' Cup Classic in 2015 becoming the first horse in history to win the three Triple Crown races and the Breeders' Cup Classic race in the same year. Over the course of his 11 race career, he won 9 races and earned $8,650,000. He is now retired to stud where he is presently earning 30 million dollars per year in stud fees because of the great demand for his services in the hope that he will be able to pass on his ability to win to his offspring.

# BETTING

The pari-mutuel system of betting on horse races originated in France in the 1860s. Under this system the odds of winning are calculated, after the track takes its fee, based upon the relative amounts bet on the horses with the more money bet on a particular horse lowering the odds and the payouts to winners.

The most common bets are bets on the horse to win, in which the person making the bet is paid if the horse wins, comes in second or third; to place, in which the person making the bet is paid if the horse comes in second or third; and to show, in which the person making the bet is paid if the horse comes in third.

Additionally, there are what are referred to a "exotic" bets such as:

Exacta—Picking the first two finishers in the correct order

Trifecta—Picking the first three finishers in the correct order

Superfecta—Picking the first four finishers in the correct order

Daily Double—Picking the winners in two consecutive races

Pick 3, 4 or 6—Picking the winners in that particular number of consecutive races

# JOCKEYS

Many of the jockeys in the early years of horseracing in America were African Americans although discrimination forced many out of riding until the latter part of the 20th century. Now, African American jockeys, Latinos and women can all be found in the ranks of jockeys. In addition to their essential riding skills, the mental connection and empathy with their favorite horses contributes substantially to the success of a jockey.

In 2015 when he won the Triple Crown, jockey Victor Espinoza's gross earnings were more than $800,000. The top 10 jockeys earned more than $750,000 that year. Jockeys are generally independent contractors rather than employees with their earnings based almost exclusively on the success of their rides. Most jockeys struggle to earn a living. The top 100 earning jockeys take home 57% of the purse money earned by all riders. Generally jockeys only get paid about $100 per ride although they can ride a number of different horses in a single day of racing. In addition, they receive 10% of the purse if they ride the winning horse. If they ride a horse that comes in second, third or fourth, they receive 5% of the purse. However, as independent contractors, jockeys are responsible for their own expenses which include having to pay their agents and equipment valets around 35% of what they earn thereby reducing their ultimate pay. In addition, jockeys pay for their own transportation, lodging and food as well as their own health insurance. The average pay for the 1,300 jockeys outside of the top 100 is approximately $37,000 per year.

Jockeys begin working as young as 14 as exercise riders for horse trainers. The minimum age for obtaining a jockey's license is 16. Most weigh less than 110 pounds with a level of body fat that sometimes can be as low as 2%. To put that into perspective, cycling and gymnastic athletes are not allowed to compete with a body fat percentage of less than 5%. Many jockeys suffer from malnutrition and dehydration which coupled with their low weight and body fat percentage puts excessive strain on their internal organs. Jockeys will resort to unhealthy techniques including starvation diets, diuretics, saunas and laxatives to maintain low body weight which can lead to many health problems. Weight requirements differ depending upon the race and the track, however generally the amount of weight that a horse is allowed to carry will range between 112 pounds and 126 pounds which not only includes the jockey, but also the weight of all of the equipment, which usually weighs around 7 pounds. There has been little support within the horse racing industry to raise the allowable weights of jockeys with the reason often given that increased jockey weights would be detrimental to the health of the horses, however, exercise riders who work out the horses every day are generally much heavier than jockeys.

## QUESTION

1.    Should weight and body fat rules be instituted for jockeys similar to other sports such as gymnastics?

# WHIPS

The use of the whip or as it is sometimes referred to euphemistically, the crop, is quite controversial. Is it cruel to use a whip? Does it hurt the horse? Does it make the horse go faster? There is a distinct dearth of scientific studies about the use of the whip in thoroughbred racing. The one significant paper, "An Investigation of Racing Performance and Whip Use by Jockeys in Thoroughbred Racing" concluded,

"To summarize, the results of this study show that jockeys in more advanced placings at the 400 and 200 m positions before the post in races whip their horses more frequently. To gain the advantageous placings at 400 m positions, no horses were whipped while between the 400 and 200 m positions only half were whipped. On average, they achieved higher speeds when there was no whip use, and the increased whip use was most frequent in fatigued horses. That increased whip use was not associated with significant maintenance of velocity as a predictor of superior race placing at the finish of the race. Further studies with on-board sensors of gait characteristics are required to study responses to whipping in individual horses.

The authors conclude that under an ethical framework that considers costs paid by horses against benefits accrued by humans, these data make whipping tired horses in the name of sport very difficult to justify. However, it is worth noting that other ethical frameworks would not condone the practice even if it did, contrary to the findings of this study, cause horses to run faster."[2]

---

[2]    "An Investigation of Racing Performance and Whip Use in Jockeys in Thoroughbred Races," David Evans, Paul McGreevy, PLoS One 2011; 6(1) e15622, January 27, 2011.

Regardless, the use of the whip is firmly entrenched in American thoroughbred racing although in recent years, greater attention has been given to limiting its use and making the use more humane.

In an effort to make the whip less painful, New York has issued regulations that limit the size of the whip and the use of a flap at the end of the whip that is intended not to sting the horse, but to make a popping sound that gets the horse's attention. Regulations limit not only where the horse may be struck, but the excessive use of the whip although there are no universal regulations that precisely define what it means to be excessive. In New York the horse may be struck five times in succession without pause while in California the horse may only be struck once before seeing if the horse responds before striking the horse again.

An example of recent regulation is the NY Racing Regulation Section 4035.9 which reads:

## 9 CRR-NY 4035.9NY-CRR

## OFFICIAL COMPILATION OF CODES, RULES AND REGULATIONS OF THE STATE OF NEW YORK

TITLE 9.   EXECUTIVE DEPARTMENT

SUBTITLE T.   NEW YORK STATE GAMING COMMISSION

CHAPTER I.   DIVISION OF HORSE RACING AND PARI-MUTUEL WAGERING

SUBCHAPTER A.   THOROUGHBRED RACING

ARTICLE 1.   RULES OF RACING

PART 4035.   RULES OF THE RACE

4035.9    Use of riding crops.

(a)   All riding crops are subject to inspection and approval by the stewards and the clerk of scales.

(1)   Riding crops shall have a shaft and a flap and will be allowed in flat racing including training only as follows:

(i)   maximum weight of eight ounces;

(ii)  maximum length including flap of 30 inches;

(iii) minimum diameter of the shaft of three-eighths inch; and

(iv) shaft contact area must be smooth, with no protrusions or raised surface, and covered by shock absorbing material that gives a compression factor of at least one-millimeter throughout its circumference.

(2)   The flap is the only allowable attachment to the shaft and must meet these specifications:

(i)   length beyond the end of the shaft a maximum of one inch;

(ii)  width a minimum of 0.8 inch and a maximum of 1.6 inches;

(iii) no reinforcements or additions beyond the end of the shaft;

(iv) no binding within seven inches of the end of the shaft; and

(v)   shock absorbing characteristics similar to those of the contact area of the shaft.

(b)   In all races where a jockey will not ride with a whip, an announcement shall be made over the public address system of such fact.

(c)   Although the use of a whip is not required, any jockey who uses a whip during a race is prohibited from whipping a horse:

(1)   on the head, flanks or on any other part of its body other than the shoulders or hind quarters;

(2)   during the post parade or after the race except when necessary to control the horse;

(3)   excessively or brutally causing welts or breaks in the skin;

(4)   when the horse is clearly out of the race or has obtained its maximum placing; or

(5)   persistently even though the horse is showing no response under the whip.

(d)   Correct uses of the whip are:

(1)   showing horses the whip before hitting them;

(2)   using the whip in rhythm with the horse's stride; and

(3)   using the whip as an aid to maintain a horse running straight.

9 CRR-NY 4035.9

Current through July 31, 2016.

---

## QUESTIONS

1.   Should whips be permitted to be used on race horses and, if so, should they be regulated?

2.   If whip regulations are enacted, what should they include?

# TRACK SURFACES

Races are run on three different types of surfaces, namely turf, which is grass; dirt, the most common surface; and artificial turf, which was initially developed for greater horse safety although whether it achieves that goal is somewhat controversial. Statistically, the number of horse fatalities at racetracks in California dropped by 40% in the first three years that California horse racing authorities required California racetracks to switch from dirt to synthetic tracks. During that time the number of fatalities went down from 3.09 per 1,000 starts to 1.70. Critics of artificial turf have argued, however, that synthetic tracks increase soft tissue injuries. The United States has the dubious distinction of leading the world in thoroughbred deaths. In Europe and elsewhere where races are conducted more frequently on turf and where also stricter medication rules are enforced, racehorse deaths are much less frequent including in Australia where racehorse deaths occur at a rate of 0.44 per 1,000 starts.

However, despite apparent safety benefits, the use of artificial turf remained controversial and not favored among the horse racing industry. Increased hind leg injuries to horses, objections of jockeys saying the surface was too hard when they fell and difficulties of the artificial tracks in handling rain led to a relaxation of the rule by California authorities permitting racetracks who installed the artificial surfaces to revert back to dirt. Now not a single major racetrack in America uses the synthetic surfaces.

## QUESTION

1.   Should track surfaces be mandated to provide for the greatest degree of safety for horses and jockeys?

# BREEDING

More than 35,000 young horses, called foals are born each year so the odds of one of these becoming a Triple Crown winning horse are long indeed. The breeding season begins on February 14th each year (is it a coincidence that it begins on Valentine's Day?) and runs through July with the baby horses, known as foals being born between the next January through June. The gestation period for a horse is 342 days. Retired race horses will go to breeding farms such as Three Chimneys in Kentucky which could be characterized as a boutique breeding farm with only eight stallions. For a fee, the farm will syndicate the breeding rights to interested investors. For instance, 2004 Kentucky Derby winner Smarty Jones' breeding rights were syndicated into 60 shares with the horse owner keeping half of the shares. The sixty shares were valued at 39 million dollars. His initial stud fee in 2005 was $100,000. Two years later, the year before the first of his initial foals raced he was bred 114 times. However, as time went on and his offspring began to race, it became apparent that he was not able to pass on his greatness on the track to his offspring and his stud fee dropped all the way to $7,500.

All horses use January 1st as their birthday and they are on the racetrack and competing as two year olds with the most prestigious races being the races in the Breeders' Cup limited to two year old horses. Winners of the Breeders' Cup Juvenile or the Juvenile Fillies (restricted to female horses) often become the favorites for the next year's Kentucky Derby and Oaks, a race run at Churchill Downs in Kentucky restricted to female horses on the day prior to the Kentucky Derby.

Female horses, such as Zenyatta are certainly desirable for breeding, however, unlike male stallions that can be bred more than a hundred times in a year, a mare (female horse) can only be bred once per year.

Horses are bred for speed, but too often they are delicate and break down. Two horses a day break down at racetracks around the country and are euthanized. Although horses' skeletal systems are still developing until they are four years old, thoroughbreds are raced at two years of age. Horses are not bred for long, productive careers, but rather for speed. The thin legs bred into today's racehorses are valued for the speed which enables a racehorse to clear the starting gate, but leaves the horses prone to leg injuries. Speedy horses with genetically thin legs are bred with other speedy horses with genetically thin legs making them even more prone to injury and likely to break down.[3]

In her essay for the Humane Education Network in 2011 entitled "A Dying Legacy: Thoroughbred Racing" Amanda Kowalczyk suggests that the solution to the increasing vulnerabilities of the race horses of today is to change the breeding industry by requiring the breeding of the fragile, but speedy racehorses so prized by buyers with sturdier, stronger horses, such as Dutch warmbloods, a sturdier breed of horse used primarily and successfully in show jumping competitions.

Unfortunate occurrences, such as the euthanizing of the filly Eight Belles on the track of the 2008 Kentucky Derby after finishing a gallant second to winner Big Brown happen too often due to the highly desired speed traits that increase the vulnerabilities of the horses to injury. The goal of many horse owners is to win a Triple Crown race and then retire the horse and make their biggest profits through breeding rights. The nineteen years breeding career of Storm

---

3    Lubrano, Alfred. "Horse Racing Is Still Saddled by Cruelty Issue." Philadelphia Inquirer [Philadelphia] 27 May 2006. SIRS. Web. 2 Feb. 2011.

Cat included a period where his superior genetics were such that between 2002 and 2007, his stud fee was $500,000 for each horse he sired. During that period he sired 1,392 horses.

During the five month breeding season a prime stud, such as Triple Crown winner American Pharoah will be bred two or even three times a day. With his stud fee in his first year of breeding in 2016 at $200,000 to impregnate a mare, the total amount American Pharoah earned from breeding in just his first year was more than 30 million dollars, a figure that far exceeds the 8.65 million dollars earned by American Pharoah in his active racing career.

But just because a horse has a great name and a great track record does not make him a great breeder. Cigar, one of the greatest horses of all times who at one point in his career won 16 consecutive races and earned more than ten million dollars in his racing career ended up being sterile and did not breed a single offspring.

A more unusual case was that of War Emblem, the Kentucky Derby and Preakness winner in 2002. Shortly after the Triple Crown racing season was over, he was sold to a Japanese breeder for 17.7 million dollars, however, although War Emblem was not sterile, he was particularly choosy with the mares he was supposed to impregnate. He rejected most of the mares provided to him for mating purposes, producing only four foals in his first year of breeding, forty in his second year and then only two in his third year of breeding. In 2010 he rejected 295 of the 300 mares with which he was supposed to breed. By 2012 he was only bred with three mares and none of those mares became pregnant. After his owners gave up on War Emblem as a stud, he was sent back to a retirement farm in the United States, however, once again, his tendencies came back to haunt him. Regulations require all stallions entering the United States from a foreign country to be tested for equine metritis by test breeding with two mares. While quarantined for a month, War Emblem rejected all of the mares brought to him for breeding whereupon the only way he was allowed to stay in the United States was to be gelded.

No one knows whether a great race horse will pass on the traits necessary to win on the track until the horse has been bred for a few seasons. However, no horse has had a greater effect on today's horses than Native Dancer. Native Dancer was born in 1950 and had an outstanding career on the track. As a three year old he narrowly lost the Kentucky Derby, but went on to win both the Preakness and the Belmont, the other two legs of the Triple Crown. He retired after winning twenty-one races. The one blemish on his otherwise perfect record was his Kentucky Derby second place finish. His retirement was prompted by foot and lower leg injuries. However, once his career on the track was finished, his breeding career off the track began. He fathered 247 foals during his breeding career including a number of racing champions; however, he was not considered a top breeder until after his death when the correlation between his blood lines and winning became more apparent including thirteen straight Kentucky Derby winners and Triple Crown winner Affirmed. All in all, 75% of American thoroughbred racehorses can now trace their lineage back to Native Dancer. The present most valuable breeding stud, Storm Cat, who is a descendant of Native Dancer had a mediocre racing career himself, but his ability to sire winning horses has brought his price per breeding up to an astounding $300,000. In Kentucky, which is the hub for racehorse breeding, the average stallion will be bred approximately 60 times in a year.

Horse racing is an expensive sport. The average prices of one year olds at auctions are now more than $100,000 while two year olds can sell for as much as sixteen million dollars. With such money invested, horse owners are looking to buy horses with what appear to be the best chances of winning as shown by their lineage. However, just as inbreeding among royal families in the past led to an increase in otherwise rare diseases so have flaws such as Native Dancer's foot problems been passed on to new generations of horses and while the health issues in the new champions become more and more apparent, the fact that they are champions, albeit for short periods makes these speedy horses with inbred flaws attractive to owners looking for champions who can then be made into breeders of champions. Where at one time durability was a desired trait for a racehorse that would run for many years, the business model of today's racing business is generally to run the horse as a two year old and a three year old and then retire the horse.

Swimming against this tide, however, was successful horse owner Jess Jackson who had made millions of dollars in the wine industry with his Kendall-Jackson wines and then took his money and successfully went into the horse racing business. Rather than follow the conventional wisdom of limiting his horse buying to horses at American auctions with popular blood lines, Jackson went around the world to Europe, South America and Africa to find horses free of steroids and excessive medication who had been bred for greater durability in the hope of winning with and then breeding a new, healthier and stronger line of horses. His death in 2011 ended his efforts to build a better racehorse.

## QUESTIONS

1.    Are racehorses being bred to win races or bred to be sold to breed?

2.    Should the breeding of racehorses be regulated and, if so, in what manner?

# DRUGS

Drugs are not just an issue in human sports competitions such as baseball, football, basketball and hockey, but in horse racing as well. Misuse of drugs starts early in the life of a racehorse soon after they are weaned when often they are given steroids to make them more muscular and enhance their appearance in advance of a sale as a yearling (a horse between the age of one and two). Unfortunately, the artificially stimulated muscle puts a strain on their still developing bones while they are racing as two year olds.

Big Brown, the 2008 Kentucky Derby winner was using the steroid Stanozolol at the time of his win. At the time of his Derby win, the use of this and other steroids were completely legal in Kentucky. According to his trainer, the drugs were not administered to the horse in an effort to increase the muscle mass of Big Brown, but rather to increase the horse's appetite and brighten his coat. At that time only 12 of the 38 states where thoroughbred horse racing is done had banned steroids. Due, however, to greater public attention to the problem of the drugging of racehorses, more and more states are now either banning the use of steroids or limiting their use to more than thirty to forty-five days prior to a race. Kentucky rules still permit the use of Stanozolol but not within 60 days of race.

Horse racing does not have a single national governing body, but rather is controlled by individual state racing commissions New regulations are intended to meet concerns that pain medications and anti-inflammatory drugs have been given to horses to that would mask serious underlying problems such that they would not be found in pre-race inspections thereby enabling horses to race when they would be endangering their health. For instance, cortisone shots can reduce the pain, while doing nothing to reduce the underlying problems which would only get worse by running in a race when not healthy.

Prior to Pennsylvania banning steroid use in racehorses, tests showed that approximately 2/3 of all race horses tested positive for steroids.

The National Thoroughbred Racing Association, a voluntary association of racetracks, owners, breeders and others involved in the horse racing industry issued a Code of Standards in April of 2016 that included the following rule regarding the administering of steroids to horses.

"C. Exogenous Anabolic Steroids

Racetrack Member shall prohibit the use of exogenous anabolic steroids in training and in competition in a manner consistent with the ARCI model rule ARCI–011–020(I), based on RMTC recommendations. To the extent the regulatory authorities do not so regulate exogenous steroids, Members shall advocate the adoption of such rules by the regulatory authority. If, however, after a reasonable period of time, a Member's advocacy fails to achieve passage of the amendment necessary to bring the contrary legislative or regulatory enactment into conformity with the Code, such failure shall result in revocation of current Accreditation, awarding of Provisional Accreditation or denial of future Accreditation."

The ARCI is the Association of Racing Commissioner International. Below is reproduced their model rule approved March 24, 2016.

ARCI–011–020(I)

"ARCI–011–020    Medications and Prohibited Substances

Upon a finding of a violation of these medication and prohibited substances rules, the stewards shall consider the classification level of the violation as listed in at the time of the violation in the Uniform Classification Guidelines of Foreign Substances as promulgated by the Association of Racing Commissioners International and impose penalties and disciplinary measures consistent with the recommendations contained therein. The stewards shall also consult with the official veterinarian to determine if the violation was a result of the administration of a therapeutic medication as documented in a veterinarian's Medication Report Form received per ARCI–011–010 (C). The stewards may also consult with the laboratory director or other individuals to determine the seriousness of the laboratory finding or the medication violation Penalties for all medication and drug violations shall be investigated and reviewed on a case by case basis. Extenuating factors include, but are not limited to:

(1)   The past record of the trainer, veterinarian and owner in drug cases;

(2)   The potential of the drug(s) to influence a horse's racing performance;

(3)   The legal availability of the drug;

(4)   Whether there is reason to believe the responsible party knew of the administration of the drug or intentionally administered the drug;

(5)   The steps taken by the trainer to safeguard the horse:

(6)   The probability of environmental contamination or inadvertent exposure due to human drug use;

(7)   The purse of the race;

(8)   Whether the drug found was one for which the horse was receiving a treatment as determined by the Medication Report Form;

(9)   Whether there was any suspicious betting pattern in the race, and:

(10) Whether the licensed trainer was acting on the advice of a licensed veterinarian. As a result of the investigation, there may be mitigating circumstances for which a lesser or no penalty is appropriate for the licensee and aggravating factors, which may increase the penalty beyond the minimum.

A.   Uniform   Classification   Guidelines   The   following   outline describes the types of substances placed in each category. This list shall be publicly posted in the offices of the official veterinarian and the racing secretary.

(1)   Class 1

Opiates, opium derivatives, synthetic opioids, psychoactive drugs, amphetamines, all United States Drug Enforcement Agency (DEA) Schedule I drugs and many Schedule II drugs. Also found in this class are drugs that are potent stimulants of the central nervous system. Drugs in this class have no generally accepted medical use in the racing horse and their pharmacologic potential for altering the performance of a racing horse is very high.

(2)   Class 2

Drugs placed in this category have a high potential for affecting the outcome of a race. Most are not generally accepted as therapeutic agents in the racing horse. Many are products intended to alter consciousness or the psychic state of humans, and have no approved or indicated use in the horse. Some, such as injectable local anesthetics, have legitimate use in equine medicine, but should not be found in a racing horse. The following groups of drugs placed are in this class:

(a)  Opiate partial agonists, or agonist-antagonists;

(b)  Non-opiate psychotropic drugs. These drugs may have stimulant, depressant, analgesic or neuroleptic effects;

(c)  Miscellaneous drugs which might have a stimulant effect on the central nervous system (CNS);

(d)  Drugs with prominent CNS depressant action;

(e)  Antidepressant and antipsychotic drugs, with or without prominent CNS stimulatory or depressant effects;

(f)  Muscle blocking drugs that have a direct neuromuscular blocking action;

(g)  Local anesthetics that have a reasonable potential for use as nerve blocking agents (except procaine); and

(h)  Snake venoms and other biologic substances, which may be used as nerve blocking agents.

(3)  Class 3

Drugs placed in this class may or may not have an accepted therapeutic use in the horse. Many are drugs that affect the cardiovascular, pulmonary and autonomic nervous systems. They all have the potential of affecting the performance of a racing horse. The following groups of drugs are placed in this class:

(a)  Drugs affecting the autonomic nervous system that do not have prominent CNS effects, but which do have prominent cardiovascular or respiratory system effects. Bronchodilators are included in this class;

(b) A local anesthetic that has nerve blocking potential but also has a high potential for producing urine residue levels from a method of use not related to the anesthetic effect of the drug (procaine);

(c) Miscellaneous drugs with mild sedative action, such as the sleep inducing antihistamines;

(d) Primary vasodilating/hypotensive agents;

(e) Potent diuretics affecting renal function and body fluid composition; and

(f) Anabolic and/or androgenic steroids and other drugs

(4) Class 4 Drugs in this category comprise primarily therapeutic medications routinely used in racing horses. These may influence performance, but generally have a more limited ability to do so. Groups of drugs assigned to this category include the following:

(a) Non-opiate drugs that have a mild central analgesic effect;

(b) Drugs affecting the autonomic nervous system that do not have prominent CNS, cardiovascular or respiratory effects

(A) Drugs used solely as topical vasoconstrictors or decongestants

(B) Drugs used as gastrointestinal antispasmodics

(C) Drugs used to void the urinary bladder

(D) Drugs with a major effect on CNS vasculature or smooth muscle of visceral organs.

(E) Antihistamines which do not have a significant CNS depressant effect (This does not include H1 blocking agents, which are listed in Class 5);

(c) Antihistamines that do not have a significant CNS depressant effect. This does not include H2 blocking agents, which are in Class 5.

(d) Mineralocorticoid drugs;

(e) Skeletal muscle relaxants;

(f) Anti-inflammatory drugs. These drugs may reduce pain as a consequence of their anti-inflammatory action

(A) Non-Steroidal Anti-Inflammatory Drugs (NSAIDs;

(B) Corticosteroids (glucocorticoids); and

(C) Miscellaneous anti-inflammatory agents.

(g) Less potent diuretics;

(h) Cardiac glycosides and antiarrhythmic agents.

(A) Cardiac glycosides;

(B) Antiarrhythmic agents (exclusive of lidocaine, bretylium and propranolol); and

(C) Miscellaneous cardiotonic drugs.

(i) Topical Anesthetics—agents not available in injectable formulations;

(j) Antidiarrheal drugs;

(k) Miscellaneous drugs.

(A) Expectorants with little or no other pharmacologic action;

(B) Stomachics; and

(C) Mucolytic agents.

(5) Class 5

Drugs in this category are therapeutic medications for which concentration limits have been established by the racing jurisdictions as well as certain miscellaneous agents. Included specifically are agents that have very localized actions only, such as anti-ulcer drugs and certain antiallergenic drugs. The anticoagulant drugs are also included.

B. Penalties

(1) In issuing penalties against individuals found guilty of medication and drug violations a regulatory distinction shall be made between the detection of therapeutic medications used routinely to treat

racehorses and those drugs that have no reason to be found at any concentration in the test sample on race day.

(2)  The stewards or the commission will use the penalty guidelines schedule contained in these rules as a starting place in the penalty stage of the deliberations for a rule violation for any drug listed in the Association of Racing Commissioners International Uniform Classification Guidelines for Foreign Substances.

(3)  If a licensed veterinarian is administering or prescribing a drug not listed in the RCI Uniform Classification Guide lines for Foreign, the identity of the drug shall be forwarded to the official veterinarian to be forwarded to the Drug Testing Standards and Practices Committee of the Association of Racing Commissioners International for classification. Page 291 The Association of Racing Commissioners International Model Rules of Racing Version 6.2 Approved by ARCI Members March 24, 2016.

(4)  Any drug or metabolite thereof found to be presenting a pre or post-race sample which is not classified in the most current RCI Uniform Classification Guidelines for Foreign Substances shall be assumed to be a RCI Class 1 Drug and the trainer and owner shall be subject to those penalties as set forth in schedule "A" unless satisfactorily demonstrated otherwise by the Racing Medication and Testing Consortium, with a penalty category assigned.

(5)  The penalty categories and their related schedules, if applicable, shall be on the following criteria:

(a)  Whether the drug is approved by the U.S. Food and Drug Administration for use in the horse;

(b)  Whether the drug is approved by the U.S. Food and Drug Administration for use in any species;

(c)  Whether the drug has any legitimate therapeutic application in the equine athlete;

(d)  Whether the drug was identified as "necessary" by the RMTC Veterinary Advisory Committee;

(e) Whether legitimate, recognized therapeutic alternatives exist, and;

(f) The current RCI Classification of the drug."

# DRUG LIMITATIONS

Under regulations now in effect, Stanozolol can only be used for medicinal purposes and, under present Kentucky regulations, may not be administered to a horse within sixty days of racing. Stanozolol is one of only three steroids that are allowed for medicinal purposes in lower dosages. All other steroids are banned.

Clenbuterol is another problematic pharmaceutical drug. Short term use of Clenbuterol can assist in managing respiratory diseases; but when given in large amounts for extended periods of time it can build muscle. However, given in this manner it can also cause serious health problems. Several states now restrict its use. A typical restriction prohibits the drug being administered no later than 21 days prior to a race.

Butazolidin and other similar drugs are used to reduce the pain of a horse's injury, but also serve to mask the pain such that the horse can continue to run and risk further injury. A 2012 study in New York ordered by Governor Andrew Cuomo found that more than half of the twenty-one race horses that were euthanized at New York's Aqueduct Racetrack that year might have been saved if racing authorities had more closely monitored their health and limited the use of drugs administered primarily for the purpose of having the horses run on the track rather than for their health. Pain medications and anti-inflammatory drugs in particular can mask serious problems during pre-race inspections of horses for soundness. The investigation found that it appeared veterinarians and racing officials were more interested in getting horses into money generating races rather than whether the horses were healthy enough to race.[4]

---

[4] New York Task Force on Racehorse Health and Safety, Official Report, Investigation of Equine Fatalities at Aqueduct 2011–2012 Fall/Winter Meet.

According to Howard B. Glaser, New York's Director of State Operations, "At the New York Racing Association, concern of the health of the horses finished a distant second to economics." As a result of the report, New York initiated health and safety reforms.[5]

---

**QUESTION**

1.    Does thoroughbred racing need a national governing body?

# SYNOPSIS

1.    Horse racing is the world's oldest sport.

2.    Race horses are generally owned by syndicates of owners.

3.    Jockeys are independent contractors responsible for their own expenses.

4.    Jockeys race at unhealthy weights and fat percentages.

5.    Often the biggest money derived from a race horse is the horse's breeding rights.

6.    Due to the emphasis on short careers with early retirement of race horses to the breeding farm, the emphasis in breeding has been on creating fast, but vulnerable horses that are not sturdy.

7.    Drug use on race horses has been a significant issue.

8.    There is no national governing authority for thoroughbred racing.

9.    The use of the whip on horses by jockeys is very controversial.

---

5    "Probe: Racehorse deaths avoidable," UPI, September 28, 2012.

# Gender and Sports

## TITLE IX

Title IX is the primary federal law that deals with sex discrimination in sports. Title IX of the 1972 Education Amendments provides that no one on the basis of sex shall be excluded from participation in or denied the benefit of or discriminated against in any education program that receives federal financial assistance. Although the language of the law speaks of education programs, its primary focus has been on equal opportunity for women in the area of athletics.

The law does not apply to single sex schools, the military academies and religious colleges. Title IX induces colleges and universities to comply with its anti-discrimination rules by making the receipt of federal funds contingent upon compliance. This is often called the power of the purse and is a way the federal government is able to enforce rules in areas it would otherwise not have jurisdiction. This was done with the drinking age of 21 whereby states that failed to increase their drinking age for alcoholic beverages to 21 would have lost federal highway funds.

Sex discrimination results in limited opportunities for women to participate in organized sports. Discrimination occurs in school regulations that may exclude women and girls from participating in particular sports such as football to rules which, although not specifically intended to be discriminatory, are applied in a manner that discriminates against women. However, the failure to provide funding for women's sports in general is perhaps the most significant form of discrimination.

The importance of women's sports goes beyond mere equality of opportunity. A higher percentage of women college athletes graduate when compared to other students including male athletes. In addition, research has shown that women high school athletes are less likely to use drugs or become pregnant than non-athletes and more likely to graduate than non-athletes.

Although the opportunities for women athletes have increased dramatically in the years since Title IX was first passed, the opportunities for women, while improving are certainly not yet equal to the opportunities for men.

# REGULATIONS

The Department of Education enforces Title IX and is authorized to issue appropriate regulations.

The regulations specifically address athletics at 34 C.F.R. §§ 106.37(c) and 106.41. The regulation at issue in this case, 34 C.F.R. § 106.41 (1995), provides:

"(a) General. No person shall, on the basis of sex, be excluded from participation in, be denied the benefits of, be treated differently from another person or otherwise be discriminated against in any interscholastic, intercollegiate, club or intramural athletics offered by a recipient, and no recipient shall provide any such athletics separately on such basis.

(b) Separate teams. Notwithstanding the requirements of paragraph (a) of this section, a recipient may operate or sponsor separate teams for members of each sex where selection of such teams is based upon competitive skill or the activity involved is a contact sport. However, where a recipient operates or sponsors a team in a particular sport for members of one sex but operates or sponsors no such team for members of the other sex, and athletic opportunities for members of that sex have previously been limited, members of the excluded sex must be allowed to try-out for the team offered unless the sport involved is a contact sport. For the purposes of this part, contact sports include boxing, wrestling, rugby, ice hockey, football, basketball and other sports the purpose or major activity of which involves bodily contact.

(c) Equal Opportunity. A recipient which operates or sponsors interscholastic, intercollegiate, club or intramural athletics shall provide equal athletic opportunity for members of both sexes. In determining whether equal opportunities are available the Director will consider, among other factors:

(1) Whether the selection of sports and levels of competition effectively accommodate the interests and abilities of members of both sexes;

(2) The provision of equipment and supplies;

(3) Scheduling of games and practice time;

(4) Travel and per diem allowance;

(5) Opportunity to receive coaching and academic tutoring;

(6) Assignment and compensation for coaches and tutors;

(7) Provision of locker rooms, practice and competitive facilities;

(8) Provision of medical and training facilities and services;

(9) Provision of housing and dining facilities and services;

(10) Publicity.

In 1979, regulations were enacted to clarify the operation of Title IX 44 Fed.Reg. 71,413–71,423 (1979). The Policy Interpretation established tests and factors to be considered in determining compliance with Title IX. These have been referred to as the Three Prong Tests for determining compliance with Title IX. The regulations read:

"(1) Whether intercollegiate level participation opportunities for male and female students are provided in numbers substantially proportionate to their respective enrollments; or

(2) Where the members of one sex have been and are underrepresented among intercollegiate athletes, whether the institution can show a history and continuing practice of program expansion which is demonstrably responsive to the developing interest and abilities of the members of that sex; or

(3) Where the members of one sex are underrepresented among intercollegiate athletes, and the institution cannot show a continuing practice of program expansion such as that cited above, whether it can be demonstrated that the interests and abilities of the members of that sex have been fully and effectively accommodated by the present program."

# DIFFERENT APPROACHES TO RESOLVING DISCRIMINATION

There are three approaches to resolving issues of discrimination against women in the opportunity to compete in sports. The three are separate but equal, mixed competition and component approach. Separate but equal was determined by the Supreme Court to be inherently unequal when applied to issues of racial discrimination in education, but it is a viable option for providing opportunity for women in sports by having separate teams on which to compete against other women. However, merely having a separate women's basketball team, for example, does not mean that the women are receiving equal opportunity. They should also receive equal coaching, equipment, and access to facilities, for example. Separate but equal is less concerned with the precise numbers of athletic programs that exist, but rather the equality of the opportunity.

Mixed competition in sports comes in two varieties. In one, men and women compete directly against each other without regard to sex. Equestrian events, for example, provide for men and women to compete against each other even at the Olympic level. In addition, some sports will have mixed events where men and women will form a team and compete against other teams of mixed sex athletes. Tennis and figure skating are two such sports that compete in this fashion. Mixed competition is generally not done in sports where physical contact between the competing athletes is a part of the sport.

The third approach is the component approach where a single team will be composed of a men's team and a women's team of the same sport, such as swimming or track and field where the winner is determined by the total scores of both the men's and women's components of the overall team.

An interesting recent development involves new mixed medley swimming relays which are done with four swimmers, two of each sex on a team. Each team determines which strokes in the mixed medley of swimming strokes their individual swimmers will swim. Such mixed relays were added in 2015 to international swimming competitions and will be first introduced into the Olympics at the 2020 Tokyo Olympic Games as will a 4 × 400 meter running relay of two men and two women per team on the track.

## FINANCIAL ISSUES

Money is, of course, a major concern to all college and university athletic departments and fewer than 7% of Division I sports programs earn a profit according to a 2010 NCAA study so finding a way to maximize the athletic opportunities for all college athletes regardless of sex is a challenging task.

A common misunderstanding of Title IX is that it requires schools to spend the same amount on men's and women's sports. The law does not require this and it certainly is not found to be true in college athletic programs around the country. However, this disparity in spending is not necessarily discriminatory primarily because some men's sports, particularly football are much more expensive to operate than women's sports. The truth is that at just about every school, more is spent on men's sports. Schools are allowed to spend differently on different sports; however the spending itself cannot be done in a discriminatory fashion.

Another common misunderstanding is the belief that Title IX has resulted in men's sports having to be dropped by colleges and universities in order to comply with Title IX. A telling example is Rutgers University's elimination of the men's tennis team in 2006 while spending $175,000 on hotel rooms for the men's football team for the night before home games which was more than the entire budget for men's tennis.

Sports such as men's wrestling which has been discontinued at many colleges may have been sacrificed for budgetary reasons, but it is not because the money had to be used for women's sports. Between 1984 and 1988 enforcement of Title IX was suspended when it was deemed not to apply to school athletic departments. During that four year period, 53 colleges dropped wrestling programs which is an average of over 13 per year. Between 1988, when Title IX was once again applied to college athletic programs, and 2000 only 56 schools dropped wrestling programs which is an average of less than 5 a year so it is apparent that the financial reasons for dropping men's wrestling were not caused by women's sports. More often the money saved by dropping wrestling and other non-revenue sports primarily went into expensive men's collegiate football and basketball programs.

Football and men's basketball are the favored sports by colleges and universities regardless of whether the sport is a money maker or a money glutton. They consistently receive the largest amounts of college athletic budgets. As indicated in an article in the Cycle 3 2012 edition of the PIT Journal, approximately 80% of athletic funding of Division I colleges and universities goes to the football and basketball programs leaving only about 20% for all of the other sports both men's and women's. Title IX is not the culprit when it comes to eliminating men's sports teams. It is the allocation of funds to football and basketball that is the primary reason.[1]

Data compiled by the NCAA Revenues and Expenses of Divisions I and II Intercollegiate Athletics Programs showed how much money was spent per male athlete among Division I schools. The data indicated that Division I colleges spent about $38,895 per football player and about $78,846 per male basketball player. This was compared to an average of $8,442 that was spent on male athletes participating in every other sport.[2]

# COMPLIANCE

One way for schools to bring themselves into compliance with the requirements of Title IX is to meet the proportionality test by which they provide athletic opportunities proportionate to the number of each sex attending the college or university. The proportionality test is the standard used when evaluating the legitimacy of programs being cut. Schools, however, also can comply with Title IX by continually increasing the opportunities for athletes of the underrepresented sex to participate in athletics. This can help reduce what could be seen as the Draconian effects of enforcing the proportionality test, however, when athletic teams are discontinued by schools only the proportionality test is applied.

The courts generally prefer colleges to pick their own route to gender equality.

---

## QUESTIONS

1.   Do women want to compete in college sports as much as men do?

2.   Does proportionality punish men unnecessarily?

    1   "False Assumptions: Why Title IX is not to Blame for Changes in Men's Athletics" Angell Wescott, PIT Journal, Cycle 3, 2012.
    2   Marburger, Daniel R., and Hogshead-Makar, Nancy. "Is Title IX Really to Blame for the Decline in Intercollegiate Men's Nonrenevue Sports Symposium: Title IX at Thirty." Marquette Law Sports Review 14.1 (2003–2004): 65–94. Web.

3.    Should there be some consideration of a level of interest by women and men in sports rather than a Draconian number?

# COHEN V. BROWN

In 1991 Brown University had 15 women's athletic teams and 16 men's athletic teams which would appear to provide equal opportunity for men and women athletes. However, primarily due to the size of the men's football team, the actual numbers of athletes participating on these teams were 566 men and 328 women which translated to the total athlete population being 63% men and 37% women. In order to save money Brown decided to eliminate women's volleyball and gymnastics along with men's water polo and golf. Although the funding cuts were somewhat more from women's teams than the men's teams, the relative numbers of men and women athletes remained the same. However, using a proportionality standard, the women at Brown represented 48% of the total student population, but only 37% of the athletes, thereby making Brown not in compliance with Title IX. A number of women at Brown brought a class action against Brown alleging violations of Title IX. Ultimately, the courts agreed that Brown was not in compliance with Title IX and ruled that the women's gymnastics and volleyball programs could not be eliminated.

## COHEN V. BROWN UNIVERSITY
United States Court of Appeals, First Circuit
101 F.3d 155 (1996)

"This suit was initiated in response to the demotion in May 1991 of Brown's women's gymnastics and volleyball teams from university-funded varsity status to donor-funded varsity status. Contemporaneously, Brown demoted two men's teams, water polo and golf, from university-funded to donor-funded varsity status. As a consequence of these demotions, all four teams lost, not only their university funding, but most of the support and privileges that accompany university-funded varsity status at Brown."

"Brown's decision to demote the women's volleyball and gymnastics teams and the men's water polo and golf teams from university-funded varsity status was apparently made in response to a university-wide cost-cutting directive. *Cohen I,* 809 F.Supp. at 981. The district court found that Brown saved $62,028 by demoting the women's teams and $15,795 by demoting the men's teams, but that the demotions "did not appreciably affect the athletic participation gender ratio." *Cohen III* at 187 n. 2.

Plaintiffs alleged that, at the time of the demotions, the men students at Brown already enjoyed the benefits of a disproportionately large share of both the university resources allocated to athletics and the intercollegiate participation opportunities afforded to student athletes. Thus, plaintiffs contended, what appeared to be the even-handed demotions of two men's and two women's teams, in fact, perpetuated Brown's discriminatory treatment of women in the administration of its intercollegiate athletics program."

"Applying § 1681(b), the prior panel held that Title IX "does not mandate strict numerical equality between the gender balance of a college's athletic program and the gender balance of its student body." *Cohen II,* 991 F.2d at 894. The panel explained that, while evidence of a gender-based disparity in an institution's athletics program is relevant to a determination of noncompliance, "a court assessing Title IX compliance may not find a violation *solely* because there is a disparity between the gender composition of an educational institution's student constituency, on the one hand, and its athletic programs, on the other hand." *Id.* at 895."

"Brown simply ignores the fact that it is required to accommodate fully the interests and abilities of the underrepresented gender, not because the three-part test mandates preferential treatment for women *ab initio,* but because Brown has been found (under prong one) to have allocated its athletics participation opportunities so as to create a significant gender-based disparity with respect to these opportunities, and has failed (under prong two) to show a history and continuing practice of expansion of opportunities for the underrepresented gender. Brown's interpretation conflates prongs one and three and distorts the three-part test by reducing it to an abstract, mechanical determination of strict numerical proportionality. In short, Brown treats the three-part test for compliance as a one-part test for strict liability."

"Brown has contended throughout this litigation that the significant disparity in athletics opportunities for men and women at Brown is the result of a gender-based differential in the level of interest in sports and that the district court's application of the three-part test requires universities to provide athletics opportunities for women to an extent that exceeds their relative interests and abilities in sports. Thus, at the heart of this litigation is the question whether Title IX permits Brown to deny its female students equal opportunity to participate in sports, based upon its unproven assertion that the district court's finding of a significant disparity in athletics opportunities for male and female students reflects, not discrimination in Brown's intercollegiate athletics program, but a lack of interest on the part of its female students that is unrelated to a lack of opportunities."

"We view Brown's argument that women are less interested than men in participating in intercollegiate athletics, as well as its conclusion that institutions should be required to accommodate the interests and abilities of its female students only to the extent that it accommodates the interests and abilities of its male students, with great suspicion. To assert that Title IX permits institutions to provide fewer athletics participation opportunities for women than for men, based upon the premise that women are less interested in sports than are men, is (among other things) to ignore the fact that Title IX was enacted in order to remedy discrimination that results from stereotyped notions of women's interests and abilities."

"Interest and ability rarely develop in a vacuum; they evolve as a function of opportunity and experience. The Policy Interpretation recognizes that women's lower rate of participation in athletics reflects women's historical lack of opportunities to participate in sports. *See* 44 Fed.Reg. at 71,419 ("Participation in intercollegiate sports has historically been emphasized for men but not women. Partially as a consequence of this, participation rates of women are far below those of men.").''

"Finally, the tremendous growth in women's participation in sports since Title IX was enacted disproves Brown's argument that women are less interested in sports for reasons unrelated to lack of opportunity. *See, e.g.,* Mike Tharp et al., *Sports crazy! Ready, set, go. Why we love our games,* U.S. News & World Report, July 15, 1996, at 33–34 (attributing to Title IX the explosive growth of women's participation in sports and the debunking of "the traditional myth that women aren't interested in sports")."

"As explained previously, Title IX as it applies to athletics is distinct from other anti-discrimination regimes in that it is impossible to determine compliance or to devise a remedy without counting and comparing opportunities with gender explicitly in mind. Even under the individual rights theory of equal protection, reaffirmed in *Adarand,* ____ U.S. at ____, 115 S.Ct. at 2112 (the equal protection guarantee "protect[s] persons, not groups"), the only way to determine whether the rights of an individual athlete have been violated and what relief is necessary to remedy the violation is to engage in an explicitly gender-conscious comparison. Accordingly, even assuming that the three-part test creates a gender classification that favors women, allowing consideration of gender in determining the remedy for a Title IX violation serves the important objective of "ensur[ing] that in instances where overall athletic opportunities decrease, the actual opportunities available to the underrepresented gender do not." *Kelley,* 35 F.3d at 272. In addition, a gender-conscious remedial scheme is constitutionally permissible if it directly protects the interests of the disproportionately burdened gender. *See Hogan,* 458 U.S. at 728, 102 S.Ct. at 3338 ("In limited circumstances, a gender-based classification favoring one sex can be justified if it intentionally and directly assists members of the sex that is disproportionately burdened.")."

"Under Brown's interpretation of the three-part test, there can never be a remedy for a violation of Title IX's equal opportunity mandate. In concluding that the district court's interpretation and application of the three-part test creates a quota, Brown errs, in part, because it fails to recognize that (i) the substantial proportionality test of prong one is only the starting point, and not the conclusion, of the analysis; and (ii) prong three is not implicated unless a gender-based disparity with respect to athletics participation opportunities has been shown to exist. Where such a disparity has been established, the inquiry under prong three is whether the athletics interests and abilities of the underrepresented gender are fully and effectively accommodated, such that the institution may be found to comply with Title IX, notwithstanding the disparity.

Of course, a remedy that requires an institution to cut, add, or elevate the status of athletes or entire teams may impact the genders differently, but this will be so only if there is a gender-based disparity with respect to athletics opportunities to begin with, which is the only circumstance in which prong three comes into play. Here, however, it has not been shown that Brown's men students will be disadvantaged by the full and effective accommodation of the athletics interests and abilities of its women students.

"The district court itself pointed out that Brown may achieve compliance with Title IX in a number of ways:

It may eliminate its athletic program altogether, it may elevate or create the requisite number of women's positions, it may demote or eliminate the requisite number of men's positions, or it may implement a combination of these remedies. I leave it entirely to Brown's discretion to decide how it will balance its program to provide equal opportunities for its men and women athletes. I recognize the financial constraints Brown faces; however, its own priorities will necessarily determine the path to compliance it elects to take."

"It is clearly in the best interest of both the male and the female athletes to have an increase in women's opportunities and a small decrease in men's opportunities, if necessary, rather than, as under Brown's plan, *no* increase in women's opportunities and a *large* decrease in men's opportunities. Expanding women's athletic opportunities in areas where there is proven ability and interest is the very purpose of Title IX and the simplest, least disruptive, route to Title IX compliance at Brown."

"There can be no doubt that Title IX has changed the face of women's sports as well as our society's interest in and attitude toward women athletes and women's sports. *See, e.g.,* Frank DeFord, *The Women of Atlanta,* Newsweek, June 10, 1996, at 62–71; Tharp, *supra,* at 33; Robert Kuttner, *Vicious Circle of Exclusion,* Washington Post, September 4, 1996, at A15. In addition, there is ample evidence that increased athletics participation opportunities for women and young girls, available as a result of Title IX enforcement, have had salutary effects in other areas of societal concern. *See* DeFord, *supra,* at 66."

"One need look no further than the impressive performances of our country's women athletes in the 1996 Olympic Summer Games to see that Title IX has had a dramatic and positive impact on the capabilities of our women athletes, particularly in team sports. These Olympians represent the first full generation of women to grow up under the aegis of Title IX. The unprecedented success of these athletes is due, in no small measure, to Title IX's beneficent effects on women's sports, as the athletes themselves have acknowledged time and again. What stimulated this remarkable change in the quality of women's athletic competition was not a sudden, anomalous upsurge in women's interest in sports, but the enforcement of Title IX's mandate of gender equity in sports."

# WHAT ABOUT CONTACT SPORTS?

When there is no women's team for a particular non-contact sport, the courts have generally allowed women to compete on the men's team, however Title IX does permit a school to deny women the ability to try out for a men's team that is a contact sport. Legendary college football coach Duffy Daugherty said, "Football isn't a contact sport, it's a collision sport. Dancing is a contact sport." Contact sports have been defined to include boxing, rugby, ice hockey, football and even basketball. Some courts have even included baseball and soccer as contact sports. On the other hand a school can choose to allow women to play on men's contact sport teams and if they do, they must not discriminate against the women trying out for such teams.

# HEATHER MERCER V. DUKE

Heather Mercer had been an all-state kicker on her high school football team in New York. She tried out as a freshman for the Duke University football team in 1994, but did not make the team. She did, however become the team manager and participated in off season conditioning programs with the team. She also attended practices with the kickers. In April of 1995 she kicked the winning field goal in an intra-squad scrimmage. Following the game, it was announced Mercer would be a member of the varsity football team for the upcoming Fall 1995 football season. However, Duke Coach, Fred Goldsmith later reversed his decision and refused to allow her to participate in the preseason camp or even be in uniform and sit on the sidelines during games. During practices she was given fewer opportunities to practice. In addition, the coaches made sexist comments to her such as asking her why she was interested in football rather than beauty pageants. Eventually at the start of the 1996 season she was dismissed from the team although the kickers kept on the team were no more qualified than she was. She sued under Title IX and was awarded a dollar in compensatory damages, but 2 million dollars in punitive damages as well as having her attorney's fees paid in the amount of $388,799. However, on appeal in 401 F. 3d 199 (2005) the punitive damage award of 2 million dollars was overturned because there was no provision under Title IX for the use of private actions to enforce Title IX. The Court ultimately awarded attorney's fees of $349,243.96.

In 2001, following in the wake of Heather Mercer, Ashley Martin, a kicker for Jacksonville State University became the first women to participate and score in a Division 1-AA football game. In 2003 Katie Hnida of the University of New Mexico, became the first woman to score in a Division 1-A football game.

## MERCER V. DUKE UNIVERSITY

United States Court of Appeals, Fourth Circuit
190 F.3d 643 (1999)

OPINION

Appellant Heather Sue Mercer challenges the federal district court's holding that Title IX provides a blanket exemption for contact sports and the court's consequent dismissal of her claim that Duke University discriminated against her during her participation in Duke's intercollegiate football program. For the reasons that follow, we hold that where a university has allowed a member of the opposite sex to try out for a single-sex team in a contact sport, the university is, contrary to the holding of the district court, subject to Title IX and therefore prohibited from discriminating against that individual on the basis of his or her sex.

I.

Appellee Duke University operates a Division I college football team. During the period relevant to this appeal (1994–98), appellee Fred Goldsmith was head coach of the Duke football team and appellant Heather Sue Mercer was a student at the school.

Before attending Duke, Mercer was an all-state kicker at Yorktown Heights High School in Yorktown Heights, New York. Upon enrolling at Duke in the fall of 1994, Mercer tried out for the Duke football team as a walk-on kicker. Mercer was the first-and to date, only-woman to try out for the team. Mercer did not initially make the team, and instead served as a manager during the 1994 season; however, she regularly attended practices in the fall of 1994 and participated in conditioning drills the following spring.

In April 1995, the seniors on the team selected Mercer to participate in the Blue-White Game, an intrasquad scrimmage played each spring. In that game, Mercer kicked the winning 28-yard field goal, giving the Blue team a 24–22 victory. The kick was subsequently shown on ESPN, the cable television sports network. Soon after the game, Goldsmith told the news media that Mercer was on the Duke football team, and Fred Chatham, the Duke kicking coach, told Mercer herself that she had made the team. Also, Mike Cragg, the Duke sports information director, asked Mercer to participate in a number of interviews with newspaper, radio, and television reporters, including one with representatives from "The Tonight Show."

Although Mercer did not play in any games during the 1995 season, she again regularly attended practices in the fall and participated in conditioning drills the following spring. Mercer was also officially listed by Duke as a member of the Duke football team on the team roster filed with the NCAA and was pictured in the Duke football yearbook.

During this latter period, Mercer alleges that she was the subject of discriminatory treatment by Duke. Specifically, she claims that Goldsmith did not permit her to attend summer camp, refused to allow her to dress for games or sit on the sidelines during games, and gave her fewer opportunities to participate in practices than other walk-on kickers. In addition, Mercer claims that Goldsmith made a number of offensive comments to her, including asking her why she was interested in football, wondering why she did not prefer to participate in beauty pageants rather than football, and suggesting that she sit in the stands with her boyfriend rather than on the sidelines.

At the beginning of the 1996 season, Goldsmith informed Mercer that he was dropping her from the team. Mercer alleges that Goldsmith's decision to exclude her from the team was on the basis of her sex because Goldsmith allowed other, less qualified walk-on kickers to remain on the team. Mercer attempted to participate in conditioning drills the following spring, but Goldsmith asked her to leave because the drills were only for members of the team. Goldsmith told Mercer, however, that she could try out for the team again in the fall.

On September 16, 1997, rather than try out for the team again, Mercer filed suit against Duke and Goldsmith, alleging sex discrimination in violation of Title IX of the Education Amendments of 1972, 20 U.S.C. §§ 1681–1688, and negligent misrepresentation and breach of contract in violation of North Carolina law. Duke and Goldsmith filed a motion to dismiss for failure to state a claim under Title IX, and, after discovery was completed, Duke and Goldsmith filed additional motions for summary judgment and a motion to dismiss for lack of subject-matter jurisdiction. On November 9, 1998, the district court granted the motion to dismiss for failure to state a claim under Title IX, and dismissed the state-law claims without prejudice, refusing to exercise supplemental jurisdiction over those claims. The district court declined to rule on any of the other outstanding motions. The district court subsequently denied Mercer's motion to alter judgment.

From the district court's order dismissing her Title IX claim for failure to state a claim upon which relief can be granted and its order denying the motion to alter judgment, Mercer appeals.

II.

Title IX prohibits discrimination on the basis of sex by educational institutions receiving federal funding. See 20 U.S.C. § 1681(a) ("No person in the United States shall, on the basis of sex, be excluded from participation in, be denied the benefits of, or be subjected to discrimination under any education program or activity receiving

Federal financial assistance."). Soon after enacting Title IX, Congress charged the Department of Health, Education, and Welfare (HEW) with responsibility for developing regulations regarding the applicability of Title IX to athletic programs. See Pub.L. No. 93–380, § 844, 88 Stat. 484 (1974). Acting upon that charge, HEW duly promulgated 34 C.F.R. § 106.41, which reads in relevant part as follows:

Athletics.

(a)   General. No person shall, on the basis of sex, be excluded from participation in, be denied the benefits of, be treated differently from another person or otherwise be discriminated against in any interscholastic, intercollegiate, club or intramural athletics offered by a recipient, and no recipient shall provide any such athletics separately on such basis.

(b)   Separate teams. Notwithstanding the requirements of paragraph (a) of this section, a recipient may operate or sponsor separate teams for members of each sex where selection for such teams is based upon competitive skill or the activity involved is a contact sport. However, where a recipient operates or sponsors a team in a particular sport for members of one sex but operates or sponsors no such team for members of the other sex, and athletic opportunities for members of that sex have previously been limited, members of the excluded sex must be allowed to try out for the team offered unless the sport involved is a contact sport. For the purposes of this part, contact sports include boxing, wrestling, rugby, ice hockey, football, basketball and other sports the purpose or major activity of which involves bodily contact.

34 C.F.R. § 106.41(a)–(b). The district court held, and appellees contend on appeal, that, under this regulation, "contact sports, such as football, are specifically excluded from Title IX coverage." We disagree.

Subsections (a) and (b) of section 106.41 stand in a symbiotic relationship to one another. Subsection (a) establishes a baseline prohibition against sex discrimination in intercollegiate athletics, tracking almost identically the language in the parallel statutory provision prohibiting discrimination by federally funded educational institutions. In addition to generally barring discrimination on the basis of sex in intercollegiate athletics, subsection (a) specifically prohibits any covered institution from "provid[ing] any such athletics separately on such basis."

Standing alone, then, subsection (a) would require covered institutions to integrate all of their sports teams. In order to avoid such a result-which would have radically altered the face of intercollegiate athletics-HEW provided an explicit exception to the rule of subsection (a) in the first sentence of subsection (b), allowing covered institutions to "operate or sponsor separate teams for members of each sex where selection for such teams is based upon competitive skill or the activity involved is a contact sport." By its terms, this sentence permits covered institutions to operate separate teams for men and women in many sports, including contact sports such as football, rather than integrating those teams.

The first sentence of subsection (b), however, leaves unanswered the question of what, if any, restrictions apply to sports in which a covered institution operates a team for one sex, but operates no corresponding team for the other sex. HEW addressed this question in the second sentence of subsection (b).

This second sentence is applicable only when two predicate criteria are met: first, that the institution in question "operates or sponsors a team in a particular sport for members of one sex but operates or sponsors no such team for members of the other sex," and second, that "athletic opportunities for members of that sex have previously been limited." In this case, appellees do not dispute that athletic opportunities for women at Duke have previously been limited, and thus we assume that the second condition has been met. Further, we assume, without deciding, that Duke operated its football team "for members of one sex"-that is, for only men-but did not operate a separate team "for members of the other sex," and therefore that the first condition has also been satisfied. Thus, insofar as the present appeal is concerned, we consider the predicate conditions to application of the sentence to have been met.

Provided that both of the conditions in the protasis of the second sentence of subsection (b) have been met, the apodosis of the sentence requires that "members of the excluded sex must be allowed to try out for the team offered unless the sport involved is a contact sport." The text of this clause, on its face, is incomplete: it affirmatively specifies that members of the excluded sex must be allowed to try out for single-sex teams where no team is provided for their sex except in the case of contact sports, but is silent regarding what requirements, if any, apply to single-sex teams in contact sports. As to contact sports, this clause is susceptible of two interpretations. First, it could be read to mean that "members of the excluded sex must be allowed to try out for the team offered unless the sport involved is a contact sport, in which case the anti-discrimination provision of subsection (a) does not apply at all." Second, it could be interpreted to mean that "members of the excluded sex must be allowed to try out for the team offered unless the sport involved is a contact sport, in which case members of the excluded sex need not be allowed to try out."

Appellees advocate the former reading, arguing that HEW intended through this clause to exempt contact sports entirely from the coverage of Title IX. We believe, however, that the latter reading is the more natural and intended meaning. The second sentence of subsection (b) does not purport in any way to state an exemption, whether for contact sports or for any other subcategory, from the general anti-discrimination rule stated in subsection (a). And HEW certainly knew how to provide for a complete exemption had it wished, Congress itself having provided a number of such exemptions in the very statute implemented by the regulation. Rather, the sentence says, and says only, that covered institutions must allow members of an excluded sex to try out for single-sex teams in non-contact sports. Therefore, the "unless" phrase at the end of the second clause of the sentence cannot (logically or grammatically) do anything more than except contact sports from the tryout requirement that the beginning of the second clause of the sentence imposes on all other sports.

Contrary to appellees' assertion, this reading of the regulation is perfectly consistent with the evident congressional intent not to require the sexual integration of intercollegiate contact sports. If a university chooses not to permit members of the opposite sex to tryout for a single-sex contact-sports team, this interpretation respects that choice. At the same time, however, the reading of the regulation we adopt today, unlike the one advanced by appellees, ensures that the likewise indisputable congressional intent to prohibit discrimination in all circumstances where such discrimination is unreasonable-for example, where the university itself has voluntarily opened the team in question to members of both sexes-is not frustrated.

We therefore construe the second sentence of subsection (b) as providing that in non-contact sports, but not in contact sports, covered institutions must allow members of an excluded sex to try out for single-sex teams. Once an institution has allowed a member of one sex to try out for a team operated by the institution for the other sex in a contact sport, subsection (b) is simply no longer applicable, and the institution is subject to the general anti-discrimination provision of subsection (a). To the extent that the Third Circuit intended to hold otherwise in Williams v. School Dist. of Bethlehem, Pa., 998 F.2d 168, 174 (3d Cir.1993), with its lone unexplained statement that, "[i]fit is determined that [a particular sport] is a contact sport, no other inquiry is necessary because that will be dispositive of the title IX claim," we reject such a conclusion as inconsistent with the language of the regulation.

Accordingly, because appellant has alleged that Duke allowed her to try out for its football team (and actually made her a member of the team), then discriminated against her and ultimately excluded her from participation in the sport on the basis of her sex, we conclude that she has stated a claim under the applicable regulation, and therefore under Title IX. We take to heart appellees' cautionary observation that, in so holding, we thereby become "the first Court in United States history to recognize such a cause of action." Br. of Appellees at 20. Where, as here, however, the university invites women into what appellees characterize as the "traditionally all-male bastion of collegiate football," id. at 20 n. 10, we are convinced that this reading of the regulation is the only one permissible under law.

The district court's order granting appellees' motion to dismiss for failure to state a claim is hereby reversed, and the case remanded for further proceedings.

REVERSED AND REMANDED

## QUESTION

1.   Is it paternalistic and wrong to permit schools to prevent women from playing contact sports with men or is it a realistic rule?

# FIELD HOCKEY

Although throughout the world, field hockey is played by men, it is primarily a women's game in the United States which creates the problem of boys wanting to play field hockey in high school when the only teams available are girls' teams. Massachusetts, Maine and California are states that have allowed boys to play on girls teams in high school.

Some have argued that boys are physically dominant and change the tenor of the games they play. Bradley Bell at fourteen years old was 5 feet 10 inches tall and 220 pounds when he played on the Amherst-Pelham Regional High School Junior Varsity field hockey team in Massachusetts in 2001. He was born in South Africa where he played field hockey before moving to the United States. In addition, there is the question of whether a boy taking a position on a high school field hockey team takes away an athletic opportunity from a girl thereby reducing the athletic opportunities for females. On the other hand if athletic opportunity should not be denied because of gender, arguably a boy who has no boys' field hockey team on which to play should be able to play on the girls' team.

Thirteen year old Keeling Pilaro was initially allowed to play field hockey as a member of his Southampton New York high school's team, but his eligibility was later taken away when he was deemed to be too skilled. Pilaro who won all conference honors was banned pursuant to a New York regulation that permitted administrators to ban particular boys from girls' teams if the boy's participation "would have a significant adverse effect upon the opportunity of females to participate successfully." Pilaro who was born in the United States but grew up (although not that much since in the eighth grade when he was banned from playing on the field hockey team he was only 4 feet 9 inches tall and weighed 82 pounds) in Ireland where field hockey is played regularly by males. Pilaro had been allowed to play for the two previous years by administrators who conditioned his eligibility on it being renewed each year depending upon the facts. Although his size did not result in him being banned, his skills did.

# WILLIAMS V. SCHOOL DISTRICT OF BETHLEHEM

In one of the rare cases to go to a federal appeals court, John Williams was initially permitted to play high school field hockey. The school district in denying his eligibility to play field hockey had argued that field hockey was a contact sport and therefore the school could limit participation by sex. The school district argued that although according to the rules of the game, field hockey was not a contact sport with bodily contact a violation of the rules of the game, such contact regularly occurred during competitive games. In regard to the argument that boys would dominate the sport and take away opportunities for girls, the court looked at the fact that few boys expressed any interest in the sport and so the concern did not appear to be based on fact. Williams v. School District of Bethlehem, 998 F. 2d 168 (1993).

On appeal, however, the district court decision was overturned and Williams did not get to play.

## WILLIAMS V. SCHOOL DIST. OF BETHLEHEM, PA.

United States District Court, E.D. Pennsylvania
799 F.Supp. 513 (1992)

### MEMORANDUM

Troutman, Senior District Judge.

Plaintiff John Williams is a male student at Liberty High School in the Bethlehem School District. In August, 1990, at age 14, John Williams and another male student tried out for the school's field hockey team, which participates in an interscholastic schedule of games. Williams was selected for the junior varsity squad as a goalie and began practicing with the team. He was issued equipment and a team uniform. At the end of August, however, the school district notified the coach that boys are not permitted to play on the girls' field hockey team and ordered that Williams neither practice with the team nor participate in the games.

The instant action by Sarah and Wayne Williams to restore their son to the Liberty High School field hockey team was commenced on October 5, 1990, accompanied by a Motion for Preliminary Injunction. Subsequently, on October 15, 1990, plaintiff filed a Motion for Temporary Restraining Order. That motion was joined with the preliminary injunction motion and heard on October 16, 1990. The preliminary injunction/temporary restraining order was denied on the record upon the Court's conclusion that plaintiffs had failed to prove irreparable harm, a necessary element of the emergency equitable relief sought in the motions. (Hearing Transcript, Doc. # 8, at 51).

Thereafter, the case proceeded through discovery and the parties were able to reach a partial compromise for the 1991 field hockey season whereby John Williams was permitted to practice with the team but not permitted to play in the interscholastic games. Presently before the court is plaintiffs' motion for summary judgment, which should dispose of the case in time for the 1992 scholastic field hockey season.

Plaintiffs assert that the defendant's exclusion of John Williams from the girls' field hockey team, which effectively bars him from playing that sport since there is no school field hockey team for boys, violates Title IX of the Education Amendments of 1972, (20 U.S.C. § 1681, *et seq.*), and its implementing regulations, the Pennsylvania Constitution, specifically the Equal Rights Amendment thereof, and both the Equal Protection and Due Process clauses of the Fourteenth Amendment to the United States Constitution.

It is undisputed that the defendant school district limits player participation on the field hockey team to female students and that John Williams was dismissed from his position on the Liberty High School junior varsity field hockey team only because of that school district policy. Thus, it is undisputed that John Williams has been prevented from playing interscholastic field hockey solely on the basis of his gender. The ultimate issue before the Court, therefore, is whether the school district's action was proper in light of the laws applicable to gender classifications in scholastic athletic programs. We will begin our consideration of this issue with plaintiffs' federal statutory claims, and will address defendant's arguments that disputed issues of material fact preclude summary judgment as such arguments become relevant to the legal issues.

## I.  Title IX of The Education Amendments of 1972

Pursuant to 20 U.S.C. § 1681(a), popularly known and hereafter referred to as Title IX, students are protected from gender discrimination in educational programs and activities which receive federal financial assistance. Plaintiffs here contend that the Bethlehem

School District athletic programs are subject to the Title IX prohibition against discrimination on the basis of sex and that the defendant's announced policy of preventing males from player participation on the field hockey team, which is designated as a girls' sports team, violates that statute.

Defendant first argued that Title IX is inapplicable in that its athletic programs do not receive federal financial assistance, but now concedes that the Civil Rights Restoration Act of 1987, 20 U.S.C. § 1687, specifies that Title IX is fully operative when any part of an educational program or any local or state educational entity receives federal financial assistance. Defendant, therefore, further concedes that its argument concerning the applicability of Title IX has been vitiated insofar as that argument was based upon the absence of federal money for its athletic programs. (*See,* Addendum to Brief of Defendant in Opposition to Plaintiff's Summary Judgment Motion, Doc. # 26 at 2). Defendant continues to argue, however, that its policy of prohibiting boys from playing on the field hockey team does not violate Title IX in that field hockey is a contact sport and athletic opportunities for boys have not previously been limited in the Bethlehem School District. (*Id.*).

These arguments arise from the defendant's interpretation of the portion of Title IX's implementing regulations which address athletic programs, found at 34 CFR § 106.41. In subparagraph (a) thereof, the rule states the general proposition that,

No person shall, on the basis of sex, be excluded from participation in, be denied the benefits of, be treated differently from another person or otherwise be discriminated against in any interscholastic, intercollegiate, club or intramural athletics offered by the recipient, and no recipient shall provide any such athletics separately on such basis.

This general rule is qualified by subparagraph (b), however, to permit separate teams under certain conditions, *i.e.,*

Notwithstanding the requirements of paragraph (a) of this section, a recipient may operate or sponsor separate teams for members of each sex where selection for such teams is based upon competitive skill or the activity involved is a contact sport. However, where a recipient operates or sponsors a team in a particular sport for members of one sex but operates or sponsors no such team for members of the other sex, and athletic opportunities for members of that sex have previously been limited, members of the excluded sex must be allowed to try-out for the team offered unless the sport is a contact sport. For purposes of this part, contact sports include boxing, wrestling, rugby, ice hockey, football, basketball and other sports the purpose or major activity of which involves bodily contact.

As is obvious from the plain language of the applicable regulation, the defendant cannot lawfully exclude boys from the field hockey team unless we determine that field hockey is a contact sport, and that boys' athletic opportunities have not been previously limited, since a boys' field hockey team is not offered. Pursuant to § 106.41(b), the school district is required to permit boys to try-out for a girls' team if there is no boys' team for the particular sport, which is here admitted, if the sport is not a contact sport *and* if athletic activities for the excluded sex, here the boys, have previously been limited.

Despite defendant's vigorous attempt to create an issue of fact for trial concerning whether field hockey is a contact sport, we conclude that it is not for purposes of the athletic regulations under Title IX. In the first instance, a number of contact sports are enumerated in § 106.41(b), including ice hockey. The omission of field hockey suggests that this sport was not recognized as a contact sport when the rule was drafted.

Second, the rules of play for high school field hockey define as a violation or foul virtually every activity on the field which involves bodily contact between field hockey players or between a player's body and the ball, as well as practices which could lead to bodily contact or which threatens such contact, *e.g.,* raising the stick during play and hitting the ball in a manner which might cause it to be propelled through the air. (*See,* Exhibit J to Plaintiffs' Motion for Summary Judgment, Doc. # 13). It defies logic to conclude that bodily contact is a purpose or major activity of field hockey when a team may be penalized not only when its players or a ball hit by one of its players contacts another player, but also when such contact is threatened or likely.

Finally, although it is clear from the affidavits of experienced players and coaches given on behalf of both sides that some bodily contact will inevitably occur in the heat of a field hockey game, none of the affiants asserted that bodily contact is the purpose or a major activity of field hockey. Thus, we conclude that field hockey is not a contact sport as that term is defined in § 106.41(b) of the regulations implementing Title IX.

Next, we must determine whether the second Title IX criterion supports the defendant's policy of excluding boys from the field hockey team by considering whether athletic opportunities for males, the sex excluded from the field hockey team, have previously been limited. Defendant assumes, without presenting any evidence in support thereof, that athletic opportunities for boys at Liberty High school have not been limited. The evidence, however belies that unsupported conclusion.

In testimony concerning past limitations of athletic opportunities, the defendant's Director of Athletic Plant Management, Dominic Villani, referred to the situation in the late sixties and early seventies when girls had limited athletic opportunities. Now, however, according to Villani, the defendant is proud of having equalized athletic opportunity by creating an equal number of teams for boys and girls at Liberty High School and by permitting girls to tryout for all of the boys' teams as well as all of the girls' teams. (*See,* Doc. # 8 at 20, 31).

In fact, the record demonstrates that as a consequence of this plan for expanding opportunities for girls in athletics, such opportunities are now limited for boys and have been since 1973 when the new athletic policies were implemented. (*Id.*). In an effort to comply with Title IX, the defendant has established at Liberty High School ten sports teams which are exclusively for girls, ten teams designated as boys' teams but for which the girls may also try-out, and two teams designated as co-ed. (Thus, since the new policies were implemented, boys have been permitted to try-out for twelve teams, while girls could try-out for all twenty-two teams offered at Liberty High School. (*Id.*). Moreover, a girl who is good enough could play on a boys' team for which there is no comparable girls' team, such as wrestling, as well as on a boys' team in a sport for which there is also a girls' team, such as basketball. On the other hand, a boy such as the plaintiff in this case, who wishes to play a non-contact sport for which a boys' team is not offered, may not try-out or play for the girls' team.

The question arises whether, after at least eighteen years of giving girls more athletic opportunities than offered to the boys, the defendant can reasonably base its athletic policies upon the assumption that boys have not "previously" been denied opportunities in athletics, and, therefore, whether the defendant can maintain an exclusively girls' team for a non-contact sport when no comparable boys' team exists. It appears to the Court that the term "previously" refers to a reasonable time in the past, and does not hearken back to the beginning of interscholastic athletic programs. In addition, it is reasonable to construe the term "previously" to include current limitations on athletic opportunities. Thus, it further appears that where there has been at least eighteen years of limitations on athletic opportunities for boys and that such limitations are presently in force, the Title IX requirement of previous limitation on athletic participation for the excluded sex has been met.

We conclude, therefore, that, in this instance, defendant is violating Title IX by excluding boys from the field hockey team since there is no boys' team for that sport, field hockey is a non-contact sport and the excluded sex, males, have previously been denied athletic opportunities.

The only other evidence concerning the general interest of boys in playing field hockey in the Bethlehem School District suggests that Villani's speculation is nothing more than a baseless attempt to justify a discriminatory policy. Villani himself testified that there is insufficient interest among boys to justify an attempt to organize a boys' field hockey team in the district. (Moreover, it is obvious that this lack of interest among boys does not arise from lack of opportunity for boys to familiarize themselves with the sport, since the school district offers a coed field hockey program at the junior high level. Finally, Villani testified that even if the Bethlehem School District offered a boys' field hockey team, there would be no other teams against which to compete. Thus, it appears that lack of interest in field hockey among boys is common. This inference is supported by the affidavit of Lynn Ralston, Director of Development of the Field Hockey Association of America, who stated that because field hockey has traditionally been perceived as a women's sport, the biggest obstacle in promoting the sport generally lies in convincing boys that they can play. (Exh. B to Plaintiffs' Motion for Summary Judgment, Doc. # 13).

It appears from all of the foregoing facts and reasonable inferences to be drawn therefrom that there is a demonstrated lack of interest in playing on girls' teams in general among males at Liberty High School, as well as a general lack of interest among males in playing field hockey at all.

Moreover, defendant's assertion that permitting boys to play on the girls' field hockey team would certainly deprive at least one girl of the opportunity to play is likewise unsupported by the evidence. First, according to the uncontradicted testimony of the Liberty High School field hockey coach, Martin Romeril, girls' interest in field hockey fluctuates. (Exh. D to Doc. # 13 at 25). In one season, there were only eleven girls on the junior varsity squad, barely enough to field a team. (*Id.*). Thus, in any given year, it is possible that the presence of one or more boys on the field hockey team could enhance girls' opportunities to play by assuring that there are sufficient players on the team.

Second, the coach testified that it was his policy to permit all potential players who try-out for the team to join, and to play in the games, at least on the junior varsity level. (*Id.*, at 41). As a general proposition, therefore, defendant's assertion that having even one boy on the field hockey team would absolutely diminish opportunities for girls to play is based upon speculation and assumptions of a worst case scenario rather than upon experience or reasonable expectations.

We conclude that the evidence of record establishes that defendant's fears concerning the purported potential of boys to dominate the field hockey team to the detriment of girls' athletic opportunities are completely unfounded or so ephemeral as to be insufficient justification for a policy which discriminates against boys in order to protect equal athletic opportunities for girls. With respect to this issue, defendant has relied entirely upon opinions which have no identifiable underlying factual support as its basis for asserting that disputed issues of material fact preclude summary judgment, or upon undisputed facts which are immaterial to the asserted interest. It is completely unnecessary, *e.g.,* to determine the extent of the physiological differences between boys and girls at the high school level. Although, on average, such differences may be substantial, that fact is not material to the defendant's position in light of the lack of evidence supporting defendant's assertions that permitting boys on the field hockey team would lead to dramatic increase in the number of boys who wish to play field hockey and thereby reduce opportunities for girls to play. Likewise, although the question whether the average physiological differences between boys and girls might give boys a competitive advantage over girls in playing field hockey could be considered a disputed issue of fact, it is immaterial for the same reason.

We further conclude that it is unnecessary to determine the extent to which alternatives to banning boys from the girls' field hockey team would be feasible as a means to further the defendant's interest in maintaining equal athletic opportunities since there is no evidence to support the proposition that permitting boys to play for the field hockey team would impact that interest.

## IV. Summary

Since we have concluded that defendant's policy of banning boys from the field hockey team at Liberty High School on the basis that it is a designated girls' team is unsupportable under Title IX of the Education Amendments of 1972, and, in addition, that it violates both the Equal Protection clause of the United States Constitution and the Pennsylvania Equal Rights Amendment, we will enter judgment in favor of the plaintiffs and order that John Williams be permitted to participate in field hockey at Liberty High School on the same basis as female students.

## WILLIAMS V. SCHOOL DISTRICT OF BETHLEHEM, PA.

United States Court of Appeals, Third Circuit
998 F. 2d 168 (1993)

The School District does not dispute that John Williams was excluded from the Liberty High School field hockey team solely on the basis of sex. It argues instead that its policy prohibiting boys from being members of the girls' field hockey team falls within both of the exceptions set forth in subsection (b), that which provides that a team may exclude members of one sex if the sport is "a contact sport" and that which requires try-outs by members of the excluded sex only when "athletic opportunities for members of that sex have previously been limited."

The text of subsection (b) provides that notwithstanding the general requirements of subsection (a), a recipient may operate or sponsor separate teams for members of each sex where selection for such teams is based upon competitive skill or the activity involved is a contact sport. However, where a recipient operates or sponsors a team in a particular sport for members of one sex but operates or sponsors no such team for members of the other sex, and athletic opportunities for members of that sex have previously been limited, members of the excluded sex must be allowed to try-out for the team offered unless the sport involved is a contact sport. For purposes of this part, contact sports include boxing, wrestling, rugby, ice hockey, football, basket-ball and other sports the purpose or major activity of which involves bodily contact.

Under the regulation, a school has the general obligation to make athletic opportunities available to boys and girls. Insofar as this obligation applies to sponsorship of sports teams, the regulation expressly contemplates situations where there will be some accommodation other than making each team equally open to both sexes. As the Sixth Circuit has explained, the provisions of title IX grant flexibility to the recipient of federal funds to organize its athletic program as it wishes, so long as the goal of equal athletic opportunity is met. *See Yellow Springs Exempted Village School Dist. Bd. of Educ. v. Ohio High School Athletic Ass'n*, 647 F.2d 651, 656 (6th Cir.1981).

The regulation does not preclude a school from maintaining a team for one sex only. Indeed, the *Policy Interpretation* specifically states that "In the selection of sports, the regulation does not require institutions to integrate their teams nor to provide exactly the same choice of sports to men and women." 44 Fed.Reg. at 71,417–18. The touchstone of the regulation is to "effectively accommodate[ ] the interests and abilities of male and female athletes" so that individuals of each sex have the opportunity "to have competitive team schedules which equally reflect their abilities." *Id.* at 71,418. The regulation requires a school to permit a member of the excluded sex to try out for the single-sex team only if the athletic opportunities of the excluded sex have previously been limited. Even if they have been so limited, exclusion is permitted if the sport involved is a contact sport. The contact sport exception is thus the broadest exception recognized to the overarching goal of equal athletic opportunity.

1.   Contact Sport

Because field hockey is not one of the sports expressly specified in the regulation as a contact sport, whether it can be so deemed depends on whether it is a sport "the purpose or major activity of which involves bodily contact." 34 C.F.R. § 106.41(b). Our task in reviewing the grant of summary judgment is to ascertain whether the party against whom judgment was granted created a genuine issue of material fact. *Martin v. United Way,* 829 F.2d 445, 452 (3d Cir.1987).

In support of their motion for summary judgment on the contact sport prong of the title IX inquiry, plaintiffs introduced the affidavits of four experts, each of whom concluded that field hockey is not a contact sport. In her affidavit, Lynn Ralston, Director of Development and Marketing for the Field Hockey Association of America, stated that "[f]ield hockey is technically, and according to the national and international rules which govern the play of the game, a non-contact sport." App. at 182. The affidavits of John Greer, Chairman of the Umpire Association of the Field Hockey Association of America, Richard Purser, U.S.A. National Coach of the Men's Field Hockey team, and Richard Kentwell, U.S.A. National and Olympic field hockey coach, and World Cup and Olympic field hockey umpire, included the same conclusion. All of these experts relied on the rules of play for field hockey promulgated by the National Federation of State High School Associations, which provide that almost all bodily contact or threatened bodily contact between players is a violation or foul.

In opposition to plaintiffs' summary judgment motion, the School District offered the affidavit of its expert, Vonnie Gros, Head Coach of the women's interscholastic field hockey team at Ursinus College in Collegeville, Pennsylvania. Gros was also Head Coach of the United States Women's Olympic Field Hockey Team from 1977 to 1984, of the women's teams at West Chester State University for thirteen years, and of the women's teams at Princeton University for four years. She has played on women's as well as coed teams. Based on her thirty years' experience with the sport, Gros concluded that field hockey is a contact sport. Gros explained that the major activities of the sport of field hockey include running up and down the field attempting to score a goal or preventing the other team from doing so. She stated that these activities "inevitably produce and involve bodily contact," App. at 79, even though such contact is a violation of the rules of play. She concluded that field hockey is a contact sport because bodily contact "regularly occurs throughout the course of any competitive game." App. at 79.

The School District also relied on the testimony of Dominic Villani, Director of Athletics at Liberty High School, given at the hearing on a temporary restraining order. Villani stated that, based on his twenty-seven years of experience as a physical educator and as a coach, field hockey is "definitely" a contact sport. App. at 30. Villani explained that a field hockey player is "going to use any skills and natural attributes of power, speed and strength . . . to get to that ball. And because of the nature of the game, there is going to be contact. There is contact." App. at 30.

In holding that the School District had not created a factual dispute and that, as a matter of law, field hockey is not a contact sport, the district court relied on the fact that field hockey is not mentioned in the list of contact sports in the regulation, even though ice hockey is included, and that there are blanket prohibitions against bodily contact in the National Federation rules. The court dismissed the affidavit of Vonnie Gros as containing a legal conclusion. Although the court acknowledged that some bodily contact may occur during field hockey play, it found that such contact was "incidental" only. Finally, the court stated that "none of the affiants asserted that bodily contact *is* the purpose or *a major activity* of field hockey." App. at 63 (emphasis added).

All of the parties agree that the "purpose" of field hockey, unlike boxing, wrestling, or football, does not involve bodily contact. We focus, therefore, on the alternative definition. We conclude that the district court erred in granting summary judgment on the basis of the record before it.

We note first that the district court may have misapprehended the legal inquiry. The regulation defines a contact sport as one "the purpose or major activity of which *involves* bodily contact." There is a subtle but important distinction between whether a major activity of field hockey "involves bodily contact" (the regulation's language) or whether bodily contact "is the purpose or major activity *of* field hockey," the language used by the district court and the plaintiffs. *See* App. at 63; Appellees' Brief at 12, 13. The district court's inquiry as to the major activity suggests that bodily contact can be deemed a "major activity" of a sport only if it is sanctioned activity. We believe that limiting the inquiry in that way would be duplicative of the "purpose" inquiry. Instead, the "major activity" prong takes into account the realities of the situation on the playing field.

Gros's affidavit and Villani's testimony raised an issue of material fact about whether a major activity of field hockey does indeed involve bodily contact. We see no reason why the district court labeled Gros's affidavit as a legal conclusion, inasmuch as Gros gave a reasoned explanation for her view in light of the realities of play, whereas the affidavits on behalf of Williams merely asserted a conclusion without any reference to actual activity during play.

It is not insignificant that the National Federation rules, introduced by the School District, require mouth protectors and shin guards, prohibit spiked shoes, require that artificial limbs be padded, and prohibit wearing jewelry. These rules suggest that bodily contact does in fact occur frequently and is expected to occur during the game.

2.   Previously Limited Athletic Opportunities

If it is determined that field hockey is a contact sport, no other inquiry is necessary because that will be dispositive of the title IX claim. Even if a sport is not a contact sport, and there is no team for the other sex in that sport, the implementing regulation requires that members of the excluded sex be permitted to try out for a single-sex team only if their athletic opportunities have "previously been limited." 34 C.F.R. § 106.41(b). In interpreting that language, the district court considered the composition of the athletic program at Liberty High School, which mirrors the team offerings in the School District of Bethlehem overall. The court compared the number of teams for boys and those for girls, noting that as of 1989, each of the two high schools in the School District has had ten boys' teams, ten girls' teams, and two coed teams. The court found that athletic opportunities for girls have surpassed those of boys because girls are permitted to try out for all twenty-two teams whereas boys may try out for only twelve, and it thus concluded that athletic opportunities for boys have "previously been limited."

Plaintiffs argue that even if we find that athletic opportunities for boys at Liberty High School have not been limited, the School District would still be in violation of title IX because it is clear that opportunities for boys in the sport of field hockey have previously been limited. Plaintiffs thus would interpret the regulation's inquiry with respect to prior opportunities as sports-specific, in this case focusing on boys' opportunities in a traditionally female sport. This reading of the regulation language was adopted by the court in *Gomes v. Rhode Island Interscholastic League,* 469 F.Supp. 659, 664 (D.R.I.) (holding that exclusion of boy from girls' volleyball team impermissible because boys' opportunities had been limited in that sport), *vacated as moot,* 604 F.2d 733 (1st Cir.1979).

We believe that the contrary interpretation adopted by the New York and New Hampshire courts is more persuasive. In *Mularadelis v. Haldane Central School Board,* 74 A.D.2d 248, 427 N.Y.S.2d 458, 461–64 (1980), the court looked at the phrase at issue in the context of the entire regulation. The court noted that the first clause expressly refers to a "particular sport" ("where a recipient operates or sponsors a team in a particular sport"), and the second clause uses broad and general language, defining the inquiry as whether "athletic opportunities" for members of the excluded sex have previously been limited. *Id.* If Congress had intended the inquiry into "athletic opportunities" to be limited to a "particular sport," it would have so stated, particularly since the phrase "particular sport" was used earlier in the same sentence. *Id.*

This analysis convinced the Superior Court of New Hampshire, which adopted it in *Gil v. New Hampshire Interscholastic Athletic Association,* No. 85–E–646, slip op. at 31–32. We agree. As the School District argues, if the plaintiffs' construction were adopted, there could never be a situation in a non-contact sport in which a team was limited to a single sex without a corresponding team for the other sex because, by definition, the opportunities in that particular sport will be limited for the excluded sex. It would mean that boys will always be able to argue that they had previous limited athletic opportunities just because certain sports have traditionally been considered women's sports, such as field hockey. This would render nugatory the purpose of the phrase in question, which was intended to authorize single-sex teams in certain circumstances.

We believe the district court was correct in implicitly rejecting the plaintiffs' sports-specific interpretation, and in looking instead to the overall athletic opportunities.

We conclude, however, that the district court applied a flawed analysis in holding as a matter of law that athletic opportunities for boys were previously limited at Liberty High School because girls have been able to try out for more teams than boys for almost two decades. The mere opportunity to try out for a team, which the district court found tipped the balance in favor of girls in the School District, is not determinative of the question of "previously limited" athletic opportunities under title IX. "Athletic opportunities" means real opportunities, not illusory ones. If, to satisfy title IX, all that the School District were required to do was to allow girls to try out for the boys' teams, then it need not have made efforts, only achieved in 1989, to equalize the numbers of sports teams offered for boys and girls.

The School District produced evidence that its decision in or about 1975 to allow girls the right to try out for all twenty-two teams did not equalize athletic opportunities between the sexes. Dominic Villani testified: "I don't believe that the fact that girls are allowed to try out for boys['] sports would help any problem of inequality. In the 27 years I have been in this business, I believe I have seen two girls that had tried out for a given sport and at best were carried on the team. It did not displace any boys." App. at 28. He concluded that "when you have girls involved in boys['] sports with respect to displacing someone, you are talking about the exception. And exceptions are very, very few." App. at 28–29.

Whether the opportunity for girls to try out for a boys' team is a realistic athletic opportunity with respect to that particular sport may turn on whether there are real and significant physical differences between boys and girls in high school. There was conflicting evidence introduced by the parties on this issue.

Plaintiffs offered evidence to show that the physical differences between boys and girls of high school age are negligible. In opposition, the School District offered the affidavit of its expert, Evan G. Pattishall III, M.D., Assistant Professor of Pediatrics at the Medical School of Pennsylvania State University, who testified that high school boys on average have "greater height, weight, total body strength, upper body st[r]ength and aerobic capacity . . . [as well as] a greater quantity of lean body mass . . . [which translate into] a greater ability to create explosive and sustained muscle power and sustained physical activity." App. at 82.

It follows that in determining whether boys' athletic opportunities at Liberty have previously been limited, the factfinder must decide whether meaningful physiological differences between boys and girls of high school age negate the significance of allowing girls to try out for boys' teams but not allowing the reverse.

Because the district court erred in finding dispositive the mere opportunity for girls to try out without acknowledging that the School

District had created a material issue of fact as to the effect of that opportunity, we will reverse the grant of summary judgment on the plaintiffs' title IX claim and remand for further factual development on the issue whether athletic opportunities for boys have previously been limited.

In this connection, we must note that although title IX and the regulation apply equally to boys as well as girls, it would require blinders to ignore that the motivation for promulgation of the regulation on athletics was the historic emphasis on boys' athletic programs to the exclusion of girls' athletic programs in high schools as well as colleges. *See, e.g., Cohen*, 991 F.2d at 892. Indeed, the *Policy Interpretation* notes that "[p]articipation in intercollegiate sports has historically been emphasized for men but not women." 44 Fed.Reg. at 71,419. With specific reference to high school athletics, the *Policy Interpretation* states: "During the period from 1971–1978 . . . the number of female participants in organized high school sports increased from 294,000 to 2,083,000—an increase of over 600 percent." *Id.* This growth was reflected in increased athletic participation of women on the campuses of the nation's colleges and universities. *Id.* Despite this increased participation, the *Policy Interpretation* reflects concern over the effect of prior discrimination. The *Policy Interpretation* requires continued affirmative steps, which "[i]n most cases . . . will entail development of athletic programs that substantially expand opportunities for women to participate and compete at all levels." *Id.* at 71,414. Thus it is clear that the obligation of an educational institution in complying with the requirements of title IX in interscholastic athletics cannot be measured simply by comparing the number of teams available to each sex, but instead must turn on "[w]hether disparities of a substantial and unjustified nature exist in the benefits, treatment, services, or opportunities afforded male and female athletes in the institution's program as a whole." *Id.* at 71,417.

## QUESTIONS

1.  Do you agree with the initial court decision in the Williams case or the Appeals Court decision and why?

2.  Is and should Title IX truly gender neutral?

# GENDER AND THE OLYMPICS

The history of male athletes participating as women is a long one. Stella Walsh was a gold medal Olympian in the 100 meter dash in the 1932 Olympics and a silver medal winner in the 1936 Olympics who lived her entire life as a woman and even was married for a short time. In 1980, she was killed tragically in a robbery at a shopping mall and an autopsy revealed male genitalia as well as both male and female chromosomes.

Gender testing first was done in the 1960s at a time when it was thought that the Soviet Union, East Germany and other Soviet bloc countries might have had men athletes competing as women. The significant use of steroids that altered the physical appearance of many of East Germany's women athletes in particular contributed to this suspicion.

Sex testing was first done at the 1966 European Track and Field Championships in Budapest and the test was a visual parade before a panel of gynecologists. All of the women tested passed the test; however, it was noteworthy that not every woman competitor submitted to the tests. Notably missing were dominant Soviet sister athletes Tamara and Irina Press who between 1959 and 1965 won five Olympic gold medals and set 26 world records. The Press sisters surprisingly retired prior to the championships.

Starting in 1967, the IOC used a chromosome test to determine the gender of an athlete. Simply speaking if the person had one X and one Y chromosome, the athlete was considered male while an athlete with two X chromosomes were considered female. The test was done with a scrape of a few skin cells from the inside of the athlete's cheek which was then used to determine if there were two X chromosomes. However, nature is not so simple. Some men have an extra X chromosome and some women are missing an X chromosome.

In 1967, Polish sprinter Ewa Klobukowska was banned from women's competitions for failing the chromosome test where just a year earlier she had passed the parade test.

At the 1968 Mexico City Olympics, the chromosome test was used to determine the sex of an athlete in Olympic competition.

As time went on the tests were criticized not merely for being an invasion of privacy, but out of a recognition that the definition of what it is that makes a person a woman is not as simple as it may initially appear. For while most people are easily classified as a man or a woman, there are others with physical aspects of both sexes. The IOC stopped using chromosome based sex verification tests at the Olympics before the 2000 Sydney Games because they were determined to be both unscientific and unethical.

Santhi Soundarajan a middle distance runner from India won a silver medal at the 2006 Asia Games which was taken back when she failed a gender test.

The essential problem is that there is no true definition of what it is to be a man or a woman. The question then becomes whether it is ethical to compel someone to prove their sex, when there is no precise definition of what it is to be a man or a woman.

In 2012 The IOC enacted regulations prior to the London 2012 Olympics to measure testosterone as a determiner as to whether an athlete would be allowed to participate as a female athlete.

The regulations indicated that "Competitions at the 2012 London Olympic Games are conducted separately for men and women (with the exception of certain events). Human biology, however, allows for forms of intermediate levels between the conventional categories of male and female, sometimes referred to as intersex. Usually, intersex athletes can be placed in the male or female group on the basis of their legal sex. However, as explained below, intersex female athletes with elevated androgen production give rise to particular concern in the context of competitive sports, which is referred to as 'female hyperandrogenism.'

In general, the performance of male and female athlete may differ mainly due to the fact that men produce significantly more androgenic hormones than women and, therefore, are under stronger influence of such hormones. Androgenic hormones have performance-enhancing effects, particularly on strength, power and speed, which may provide a competitive advantage in sports. This is one of the reasons why the exogenous administration of such hormones and/or the promotion of the endrogenous production to these hormones are banned under the Word Anti-Doping Code, to which the IOC is a signatory."

"In order to help protect the dignity and privacy of the athlete concerned, requests for investigations, information gathered during investigations, result of investigations and decisions regarding a case (or potential case of female hyperandrogenism, shall be kept confidential and not released or made public by the IOC."[3]

Testing was initiated only if the matter was brought up by a chief medical officer of a national Olympic committee or a member of the IOC's medical commission.

The Olympics had struggled for some time with the issue of what defined a person as a woman. Dutee Chand, a female Indian sprinter was suspended in 2014 by the International Association of Athletics Federations, the governing organization for international track and field for hyperandrogenism. Chand appealed the decision arguing that the regulations discriminated unlawfully against female athletes with a naturally occurring physical characteristic and were based upon flawed factual assumptions about the relationship between testosterone and athletic performance. On appeal, the Court of Arbitration for Sport

---

3    "IOC Regulations on Female Hyperandrogenism—Games of the XXX Olympiad in London, 2012" Medical and Scientific Department IOC, June 22, 2012.

agreed with her Chand's argument and overturned the suspension indicating that the IAAF had not proven that women with naturally occurring high levels of testosterone had a competitive advantage.

In its ruling the court ruled, "The IAAF has not discharged its onus of establishing that the Hyperandrogenism Regulations are necessary and proportionate to pursue the legitimate objective of organizing competitive female athletics to ensure fairness in athletic competition. Specifically, the IAAS has not provided sufficient scientific evidence about the quantitative relationship between enhanced testosterone levels and improved athletic performance in hyperandrogenic athletes. In the absence of such evidence, the panel is unable to conclude that hyperandrogenic female athletes may enjoy such a significant performance advantage that it is necessary to exclude them from competing in the female category."

The court's ruling reflected the realization that the determination of sex is not entirely clear, but is rather a part of a spectrum saying "Although athletic events are divided into discrete male and female categories, sex in humans is not simply binary." The Court went on to say that "As it was put during the hearing: 'Nature is not neat.' There is no single determinant of sex." However, the Court did recognize the need for standards saying "Nevertheless, since there are separate categories of male and female competition, it is necessary for the IAAF to formulate a basis for the division of athletes into male and female categories for the benefit of the broad class of female athletes. The basis chosen should be necessary, reasonable and proportionate to the legitimate objective being pursued."[4]

The Court suspended the IAAF's Hyperandrogenism Regulations for two years and gave the IAAF until July of 2017 to present new scientific evidence in support of their position.

---

[4]   Interim Arbitral Award, Court of Arbitration for Sport, CAS 2014/A/3759 Dutee Chand v. Athletics Federation of India (AFT) & The International Association of Athletics Federations (IAAF).

Interestingly, the response of the IOC to the ruling was that the regulation should be reinstated, but that the athlete should be then eligible to compete in male competition. This seems odd in that the particular athlete such as Dutee Chand anatomically is a woman and identifies herself as such. Why should her sex be solely determined by the amount of a naturally occurring hormone?

Indeed hyperandrogenism is not "normal," however, the physical makeup of many athletes that may give them a competitive edge is not normal. Athletes with higher levels of hemoglobin occurring naturally are not punished for this "abnormality." Eero Mantyranta, a cross country skier who won seven Olympic medals including three gold medals had a genetic mutation that increased his hemoglobin level 50% higher than the average man's, however, he was not punished for his genetic mutation or variation.

Nor, as Dutee Chand argued in her appeal, has it been proven that higher levels of testosterone were any more of a factor toward athletic success in women as better nutrition, better coaching, better training facilities or other genetic variations. Kenyan runners come from a country where they train at high altitudes which increases their ability to utilize oxygen more effectively. Anyone participating in the Olympics is by definition, exceptional from the general population or they would not be there. They are the best of the best.

# CASTER SEMENYA

Caster Semenya, an outstanding South African female runner was compelled to undergo sex tests after winning the Gold Medal in the 800 meter race at age 18 at the World Championships in 2009.

Following her victory at the 2009 World Championships, Semenya was required to undergo gender testing and although the results of the testing, consistent with International Association of Athletics Federations (IAAF) policy were not made public, reports were that she had proved to be intersex. At the time of gender testing, Semenya was not even told she was undergoing gender testing, but thought she was taking a routine drug test. Following the tests, the (IAAF) banned her from competing as a woman. An athlete failing gender testing was faced at that time with either not competing as a woman, undergoing surgical procedures to remove internal testes or undergoing hormone replacement therapies. Hormone replacement therapies are quite problematic and carry possible side effects of increased likelihood of developing breast cancer, ovarian cancer, strokes or heart attacks.

Ultimately, Semenya was permitted to compete in the 2012 London Olympics. Ironically, the Russian woman Mariya Savinova who beat her in the 2012 London Olympics tested positive for performance enhancing drugs and was stripped of her gold medal.

Semenya has not been accused of taking banned substances and Olympic and international sports officials have not "accused" her of being a man, however, there was still a concern voiced by some women athletes that allowing her to compete with a testosterone advantage was not fair. It was not a level playing field. But is the playing field ever level? Aren't all Olympic athletes generally genetic exceptions to be able to reach that pinnacle of athletic success? Where does the line get drawn and on what basis? Does that mean that anyone who declares themselves a woman can compete as a woman? Might this lead countries to attempt to recruit hyperandrogenic athletes or is this a case of as Mark Twain said, "I have had a lot of worries in my life, most of which never happened."

And while Semenya's dominated her event at the Rio Olympics, winning the 800 meters in a time of 1:55.28, beating second place finisher Francine Niyonsaba of Burundi by 1.21 seconds, Semenya's time was a full two second less than the world record in the event set by Jarmila Kratochvilova of Czechoslovakia in 1983. Further indicative of the fact that being a dominating athlete does not mean that there is some unfair genetic advantage is the case of Katie Ledecky. It is interesting to contrast Semenya's performance with that of American Swimmer Katie Ledecky who won the 800 meter freestyle event in a world record time of 8:06.68 beating second place finisher Jazz Carlin of the UK by more than 11.38 seconds. Neither performance enhancing drugs nor any obvious genetic mutations appeared to contribute to Ledecky's dominance.

According to Dr. Myron Genel in an article in the JAMA, entitled "The Olympic Games and Athletic Sex Assignment":

"It is increasingly evident that many factors, aside from sex and hormone milieu—favorable genetics, height, muscle type, economic opportunities, access to facilities and skilled coaching among them—contribute to competitive success in sport. With respect to genetics, factors on the Y chromosome controlling for height, lean body mass, and other favorable sports-related characteristics may account for an overrepresentation of successful athletes with disorders of sex development in elite sports than their frequency in the general population. Genetic conditions that enhance performance in sport include congenital mutations of the erythropoietin receptor gene leading to high levels of hemoglobin, which does not disqualify athletes. There is no fundamental difference between congenital disorders leading to elevated testosterone levels, functional or not, and an erythropoietin receptor mutation leading to high hemoglobin. The emerging participation of transgender athletes adds further complexity. However, all of these biological differences are minuscule compared with the suspected use of performance-enhancing substances."

"Given the recognized 10% to 20% difference in athletic performance between sexes, it is not unreasonable to separate most competition by sex, certainly at the elite level embodied in the Olympic Games, even though, inevitably, doing so would be arbitrary. However, with the passage of time and the recurring public spectacle of young women, often from less-developed areas of the world, having their underlying biology indiscriminately scrutinized in the world media, it has become evident that the hyperandrogenism policies are no more salutary than earlier attempts to define sharp sex boundaries. In that respect, much more must be done to adequately inform all stakeholders—participating athletes, sports officials, team physicians, the media, fans and the public at large—regarding the complexity and fluidity of factors that contribute to competitive success as well as to sex or gender identity. One of the fundamental recommendations published almost 25 years ago that athletes born with a disorder of sex development and raised as females be allowed to compete as women remains appropriate."[5]

# TRANSGENDER ATHLETES

While issues relating to transgender people became more public in 2016, particularly regarding laws in the United States relating to the use of bathrooms by transgender individuals, the issues related to transgender people were not much considered or even thought about until recently and thus most sports federations did not have regulations related to transgender athletes.

The IOC first enacted guidelines regarding transgender athletes in 2003. Under those regulations athletes transitioning from one sex to another could not compete in international athletic competition until they had sex reassignment surgery and at least two years of hormone therapy. In 2016 the IOC substantially revised their guidelines for transgender athletes and now indicate that surgery is no longer a requirement for a transgender athlete to participate in competitions under the gender of his or her choice. Transgender athletes transitioning from female to male are eligible to compete as men without any restrictions. A Transgender athlete transitioning from male to female will need to prove that her testosterone levels are below 10 nmol/L (10 nanomols per liter) for at least twelve months prior to her first competition as a woman. Generally, it takes anywhere from a year to two years to reach that level following the start of hormonal therapy. Further the transgender athlete transitioning from male to female must maintain a level of

---

    [5]  "The Olympic Games and Athletic Sex Assignment," Myron Genel MD, Joe Leight Simpson, MD, Albert de la Chapelle, MD, PhD, JAMA 2016:316(13):1359–1360.

testosterone below 10 nmol/L in order to remain eligible for competition as a female.

# SYNOPSIS

1.    Title IX of the 1972 Education Amendments provides that no one shall on the basis of sex be excluded from participation in or denied the benefit of or discriminated against in any education program that receives federal financial assistance. Although the language of the law speaks of education programs, its primary focus has been on equal opportunity for women in the area of athletics.

2.    There are three approaches to resolving issues of discrimination against women in the opportunity to compete in sports. The three are separate but equal, mixed competition and component approach.

3.    There are ten factors considered in determining whether an institution is in compliance with Title IX. The most important are:

a.    Whether the selection of sports and the levels of competition effectively accommodates both the interest and the abilities of both sexes;

b.    Provisions for equipment and athletic supplies with quality being more important than mere quantity;

c.    Scheduling of games and practice time;

d.    Travel and per diem allowances while traveling;

4.    A common misunderstanding of Title IX is that it requires schools to spend the same amount on men's and women's sports.

5.    Title IX arguments have been used to further the efforts of boys to play on girls' field hockey teams.

6.    When there is no women's team for a particular non-contact sport, the courts have generally allowed women to compete on the men's team, however Title IX does permit a school to deny women the ability to try out for a men's team that is a contact sport. On the other hand if the school chooses to allow women to play on men's

contact sport teams they must not discriminate against the women trying out for such teams.

7.    Sex testing was first done at the 1966 European Track and Field Championships in Budapest and the test was a visual parade before a panel of gynecologists.

8.    Starting in 1967 the IOC used a chromosome test to determine the gender of an athlete.

9.    Human biology allows for forms of intermediate levels between the conventional categories of male and female, sometimes referred to as intersex.

10.   Usually, intersex athletes can be placed in the male or female group on the basis of their legal sex.

11.   Intersex female athletes with elevated androgen production give rise to particular concern in the context of competitive sports, which is referred to as "female hyperandrogenism."

12.   Transgender athletes transitioning from female to male are eligible to compete in the Olympics as men without any restrictions.

13.   A transgender athlete transitioning from male to female must prove that her testosterone levels are below 10 nmol/L (10 nanomols per liter) for at least twelve months prior to her first competition as a woman.

# CHAPTER NINE

# Disabled Sports

Participation in organized sports is not limited to people without physical or intellectual disabilities. The value of being able to compete in sports for a disabled person goes beyond the rehabilitative aspect. According to the authors of a 2012 study entitled "Accessibility of sports facilities for persons with reduced mobility and assessment of their motivation for practice" found in Volume 41 of the academic journal "Work," "Doing sports is an invaluable instrument of intervention for disabled persons. On an individual level, sport can contribute to the improvement of the physical condition, psychomotor development (improvement of postural control, motor coordination, balance), cognitive development, promoting a sense of wellbeing and balance, preventing states of depression, reducing irritability and aggressiveness. On a social level sports also fosters the integration of disabled people by focusing on their abilities instead of on their difficulties."[1]

## HISTORY

The history of organized sports for disabled people began in 1911 with the first "Cripples Olympiad" which was, at the time, a societally acceptable term for the physically impaired. Despite a name which would appear to be demeaning to us today, the Cripples Olympiad

---

[1] Accessibility of sports facilities for persons with reduced mobility and assessment of their motivation for practice. Maria Manuel Sa et al, Work 41 (2012).

was a popular success. Its first star was Welshman Walter William Francis, a disabled athlete with an extreme limp who became celebrated for his winning efforts in running and wrestling events. He also competed outside of the Cripples Olympics in other sports such as rugby and even swam the fifteen mile Welsh Channel.

The most prominent international competition for disabled Olympics is the Paralympics where athletes from around the world with physical, visual or intellectual disabilities compete. However, international sporting competitions are also held, such as the Deaflympics for deaf athletes, the Special Olympics for adults and children with intellectual disabilities and the World Dwarf Games for athletes affected by dwarfism.

Eugene Rubens-Alcais, a deaf French athlete pioneered the first International Silent Games for the hearing impaired in 1924 which later became the Deaflympics. Like the Paralympics, the Deaflympics are officially sanctioned by the International Olympic Committee and are held every four years.

The Special Olympics grew out of summer events in the 1950s and early 1960s begun by Eunice Kennedy Shriver to enable the participation of intellectually disabled children in organized sports. By 1968, the Special Olympics had grown to an international event with a thousand intellectually disabled athletes from 26 American states and Canada participating. More than 7,500 athletes from 164 countries competed in the 12th Special Olympics World Summer Games held in Shanghai, China in 2007. Currently, more than 4.2 million intellectually disabled athletes participate in 70,000 sanctioned Special Olympics events around the world each year.

Sports for the disabled have progressed to the point where there are even professional disabled sports.

Wheelchair tennis has its own professional circuit under the International Tennis Federation and offers prize money of more than two million dollars. Wheelchair tennis has been a part of the U.S. Open since 1991, the Australian Open since 2002, and the French

Open since 2007. Out of a concern that the grass surface at Wimbledon made wheelchair singles too difficult only doubles were part of wheelchair tennis between 2006 and 2016, however, in 2016 singles tennis came to Wimbledon along with prize money to the wheelchair players of $259,000.

# PARALYMPICS

Dr. Ludwig Guttman, a neurologist who worked with victims of spinal injuries, initiated the Stoke Mandeville Games named for the hospital in England where he worked in 1948. These games evolved from rehabilitation programs for injured and wheel chair bound World War II veterans. The Stoke Mandeville Games became the modern day Paralympics in 1960 although the name Paralympics was not officially used until 1988.

The first official Paralympics was held in Rome in 1960 with 400 athletes from 23 countries competing in Rome, the site of that year's Summer Olympic Games. Since that time, the Paralympics have been held every four years in the same year as the Summer Olympic Games and since the 1988 Seoul, South Korea Summer Olympic Games, the Paralympics have been held in the same city as the Summer Olympics using the same facilities. The first Winter Paralympic Games were held in 1976 in Sweden. The 1976 Sweden Winter Paralympic Games were the first games in which multiple classes for athletes with differing levels of disabilities were used.

The Paralympics are governed by the International Paralympic Committee which oversees 176 national Paralympic committees and various international disabled sports federations.

Athletes with intellectual disabilities first competed in the Paralympics in 1996, however, they were excluded from competition after the 2000 Sydney Paralympics when it was discovered that ten gold winning Spanish basketball players had faked their disabilities. In 2013 Vernando Martin Vicente, the President of the Spanish Federation for Mentally Handicapped Sports was convicted of fraud, fined $7,766 and ordered to return $204,728 in government funds distributed to the cheating athletes as a prize by the Spanish government in recognition of their Paralympic Gold Medal. The outrage following this incident was so great, that intellectually disabled athletes were excluded from competing in the Paralympics until 2012 when intellectually disabled athletes were readmitted to the games subject to rigorous eligibility tests.

# PARALYMPIC STANDARDS FOR LEVEL OF IMPAIRMENT

In order to level the playing field so that the least impaired athlete does not win every competition, para-athletes compete in categories based upon their level of impairment.

The first and most important step is the determination as to whether the athlete fits into one of the ten eligible impairment classifications.

The ten eligible impairment types are:

1. Impaired muscle power, such as those caused by spinal cord injuries.

2. Impaired passive range of movement, such as arthrogryposis, a condition of congenital joint contractures. Acute conditions such as arthritis are not considered eligible impairments.

3. Limb deficiency, such as total or partial absence of bones or joints as a result of a traumatic incident such as an accident or an illness, such as bone cancer.

4. Leg Length difference, such as bone shortening in one leg due to congenital deficiency or trauma.

5. Short Stature, reduced standing height due to abnormal dimensions of bones of upper and lower limits or trunk.

6. Hypertonia, abnormal increase in muscle tension and a reduced ability of a muscle to stretch due to a neurological condition, such as cerebral palsy, brain injury or multiple sclerosis.

7. Ataxia, lack of coordination of muscle movements due to a neurological condition such as cerebral palsy, brain injury or multiple sclerosis.

8. Athetosis, generally characterized by unbalanced involuntary movements and a difficulty in maintaining a symmetrical posture due to a neurological condition, such as cerebral palsy, brain injury or multiple sclerosis.

9. Visual impairment, vision is impacted by either an impairment of the eye structure, optical nerves or optical pathways or the visual cortex.

10. Intellectual impairment, a limitation in intellectual functioning and adaptive behavior as expressed in conceptual, social and practical adaptive skills, which originates before the age of 18.

Although these are the ten eligible impairment types, each Paralympic sport's international federation makes its own rules as to what constitutes eligible impairments and how severe they must be to qualify in order to be eligible to compete. Because the skills required in different sports may vary significantly, it is left up to the individual sport's governing body to determine the precise disability criteria for their respective sports based on scientific evidence and research. Different disabilities may have varying impacts on different sports such that an athlete could be determined to be sufficiently disabled and impaired to qualify for participation in one sport and not in another.

A key element and one that has been controversial at times is that the impairment and disability must be of a permanent nature.

Once an athlete is deemed eligible for participation, there is a further classification of specific classes to promote greater fairness in competition by grouping athletes with similar limitations of activity for competition. While some sports, such as power lifting only have one class, running events which include athletes meeting the standards of all ten impairments has 52 separate classes to achieve greater fairness of competition. So, for instance, an athlete with a mental disability will not compete against a double amputee athlete.

Due to the fact that some conditions may indeed change over time, whether for better or worse, Paralympians are often reclassified numerous times during their careers. Disabled athletes are required to apply for reclassification when changes of their conditions occur.

# VICTORIA ARLEN

American Victoria Arlen spent three years in a vegetative state due to an autoimmune disorder. When she became regained consciousness, her legs were paralyzed due to a neurological condition called transverse myelitis. She turned to swimming and became a multi medal winner at the London 2012 Summer Paralympic games. Arlen competed in London under review status which meant she would need to be reevaluated each year. She won a gold medal and three silver medals. She also set a world record in her class in the 100 meter race. However, later she was ruled ineligible to compete in the 2016 Rio Summer Paralympics despite the fact that her legs were still paralyzed following a ruling by the International Paralympic Committee that she had "failed to provide conclusive evidence of a permanent eligible impairment."[2]

According to Arlen "Being penalized for maybe having a glimmer of hope of one day being able to walk again is beyond sad."[3]

The Committee however stood by their ruling that athletes have to be permanently impaired to compete in the Paralympics. Monique van der Vorst of the Netherlands won two silver medals in handcycling at the 2008 Paralympics in Beijing while suffering apparently from muscular dystrophy, however, two years later after having spent thirteen years in a wheelchair, she was able to walk and given a new diagnosis for her previous disease. Now it was diagnosed as

---

[2]    IPC Statement on USA swimmer Victoria Arlen, December 8, 2013.

[3]    "Swimmer Is Fighting a Ruling: She Is Not Disabled Enough," Sarah Lyall, New York Times, September 26, 2013.

conversion disorder, a psychiatric condition in which patients suffer inexplicable neurological symptoms.

When van der Vorst regained her ability to walk, the International Paralympic Committee investigated whether or not van der Vorst had initially intentionally misrepresented her condition and concluded that she had not. They wrote

"Over the course of her Paralympic career Monique presented for classification on several occasions with supportive medical evidence of muscular dystrophy and pain-related clinical manifestation. On this basis she was allocated a sport class to compete in handcycling. Only in late 2012 did the Head of the Spinal Cord Injury Unit at the American Centre for Rheumatology and Rehabilitation diagnose her with Conversion Disorder."[4]

## QUESTIONS

1.    Should a disabled athlete have to demonstrate that he or she is permanently disabled in order to compete in the Paralympics or should a disability present at the time of the competition be sufficient?

2.    What is the rationale behind requiring an athlete to be permanently disabled to compete in the Paralympics?

# DISABILITY OR ADVANTAGE?

In 1984, Neroli Fairhall, a female New Zealand archer who was paralyzed below the waist in a motorcycle accident at age 25 competed in the 1984 Summer Olympics in Los Angeles. She also competed in four Paralympics during her successful career. At the 1982 Commonwealth Games in Brisbane, Australia, she not only became the first disabled athlete to compete in the Commonwealth Games, but even won a gold medal. During a press conference, however, she was asked whether the windy conditions were helpful or

---

[4]    "IPC Concludes looking into van der Vorst case," Press Release of International Paralympic Committee, April 6, 2013.

a hindrance to her while shooting from a wheelchair to which she responded, "I don't know. I've never shot standing up."[5]

Wheel chair athletes are not permitted to compete against able bodied runners in the Marathon. Their high tech vehicles provide a significant advantage as illustrated by the finishing times of wheel chair athletes competing in wheel chair marathons on the same courses as non-disabled athletes. South African Ernst van Dyke won the Boston Marathon with a time of one hour and 18 minutes in 2004. Timothy Cherigat of Kenya won the men's division for able bodied athletes that year in a time of two hours and ten minutes.

Disabled athletes have competed at both the Olympics and Paralympics in archery, table tennis, swimming and equestrian competitions. No disabled athlete, as of yet, has won a medal in both the Olympics and Paralympics. However, American George Eyser has the distinction of having won an Olympic gold medal in gymnastics while competing with a wooden leg at the 1904 Olympic Games in St. Louis.

South African Oscar Pistorius in 2012 became the first double-leg amputee to compete at both the Olympics and the Paralympics. Pistorius had set disabled world records on the track in the 100, 200 and 400 meter events. At the London 2012 Summer Olympic, he managed to beat several non-disabled competitors in his qualifying heats. With advancements of technology, questions were raised about a possible unfair advantage Pistorius might have had over non-disabled runners due to his two prosthetic racing legs.

IAAF rules require amputee athletes to prove that that their prosthesis does not offer an advantage.

"Rule 144.3d

(d)   the use of any mechanical aid, unless the athlete can establish on the balance of probabilities that the use of an aid would not provide

---

5   "Neroli Fairhall" New Zealand Olympic Committee Website 2017.

him with an overall competitive advantage over an athlete not using such aid."

It is important to note that present technology for carbon fiber legs such as worn by Oscar Pistorius is not so advanced that the carbon fiber legs do not also provide disadvantages as well. Initial acceleration at the start of the race is less efficient and his knees do not flex as well as non-disabled runners.

Pistorius was initially declared ineligible to compete in the 2008 Beijing Summer Olympics, but appealed to the Court of Arbitration for Sport which overturned the ban on his competing, indicating that the initial decision declaring him ineligible for Olympic competition did not factor in the disadvantages presented by Pistorius' carbon fiber legs. While Oscar Pistorius was permitted by the IOC to compete in the 2012 London Summer Olympics, a few years later German long jumper Markus Rehm who won the Paralympic gold medal in 2012 in London applied to compete in the Summer Olympics in Rio in 2016. Rehm who lost his lower right leg in a boating accident when he was a teenager also uses a carbon fiber prosthesis.

To support his application to compete in the 2016 Summer Olympics, Rehm commissioned a study conducted by universities in Germany, the United States and Japan. The study concluded, however, that while the start of his run in the long jump is less efficient due to his prosthesis, the jump itself is increased by the technology of the prosthesis.

After being rejected from the 2016 Summer Olympics, Rehm competed in the 2016 Summer Paralympics where his gold medal effort would have placed him fifth in the non-disabled Olympics.

## QUESTIONS

1.   Do prosthetic legs merely level the playing field for a disabled athlete or are they the equivalent of technological performance enhancements that provide an unfair advantage?

2.   In order to be allowed to compete against able-bodied athletes, should athletes with prosthetics have the burden of proving they do not have an unfair advantage or should international sporting organizations have to prove that there is an advantage in order to disqualify the athlete from such competition?

# FINANCIAL SUPPORT OF PARALYMPIANS

American Olympic athletes are generally funded by the United States Olympic Committee (USOC) and the national governing body of their particular sport while American Paralympians are funded almost entirely by the USOC. The United States Olympic Committee has said that it determines its financial support of the various sports according to the likelihood of the sport winning medals at the Olympics.

In 2007, members of the American Paralympic track and field team were paid stipends of between $1,000 and $2,000 to train while Olympic track and field athletes generally received between $10,000 and $15,000. Cash bonuses are also paid by the USOC to gold medalists. American Olympic gold medalists received $25,000 however, Paralympian gold medalists only received $5,000.

Tony Iniguez an American 1,500 meter wheelchair racer for the United States Paralympic team unsuccessfully sued the United States Olympic Committee in 2003 for discrimination arguing that it was illegal for the American Olympic Committee to provide less financial support to Paralympic athletes than Olympic athletes. In the UK and Canada, financial support for training is provided to athletes based entirely on their level of international achievement in their support regardless of whether they are an Olympic athlete or a Paralympic athlete.

Iniquez lost at both the Federal District Court level and the U.S. Court of Appeals where the courts ruled that the USOC is not required to provide equal funding to disabled athletes and those without disabilities competing in the Paralympics and Olympics respectively. However, the concerns of Iniquez were shared by the District Court judge who wrote, "Do I decry a culture that relegates Paralympians to second-class status in the quality of support they receive from the U.S.O.C.? Emphatically yes."[6]

The defense of the U.S.O.C. is one plainly rooted in the financial realities of sport. The USOC argues that it receives little, if any, financial support from the federal government and so it must allocate its support to the teams and athletes that will bring the best financial return to keep the programs going. For instance, Team Handball had a dramatic reduction in the funds it received from the USOC which almost put their sport into bankruptcy with the reduction in funds having nothing to do with athletes being able-bodied or disabled.

In addition, the USOC further emphasized the dramatic growth in financial support for disabled athletes in recent years from 3 million dollars in 2004 to 11.4 million dollars in 2012 representing a percentage increase much greater than any increase in support for the non-disabled athletes.

## HOLLONBECK V. UNITED STATES OLYMPIC COMMITTEE

United States Court of Appeals, Tenth Circuit
513 F.3d 1191 (2008)

### Background

The USOC is a federally-chartered corporation that has exclusive jurisdiction over U.S. participation in three athletic competitions: the

---

6    "Paralympic Athletes Add Equality to Their Goals" Alan Schwarz, New York Times, September 5, 2008.

Olympic Games, the Paralympic Games, and the Pan American Games. 36 U.S.C. §§ 220502, 220503(3)(A). Under the Ted Stevens Olympic and Amateur Sports Act ("ASA") as amended, id. §§ 220501–220529, Congress has charged the USOC to "obtain for the United States, the most competent amateur representation possible in each event of the Olympic Games, the Paralympic Games, and the Pan-American Games." Id. § 220503(4).

The first Paralympic Games were held in 1960. Now the Paralympic Games immediately follow the Olympic Games in the same host city and involve between 1,100 and 4,000 athletes. Plaintiffs are all elite paralympic athletes who have competed in at least one Paralympic Games. Plaintiffs are wheelchair racing paralympians. U.S. Paralympians have been very successful compared to their Olympic counterparts with 42% of the Paralympians winning medals in 2000 and 75% winning medals in 2002 (compared to 16% of Olympians winning medals in both 2000 and 2002). Aplt.App. at 241.

To achieve its mission under the ASA, the USOC provides Athlete Support Programs which include various types of grants, tuition assistance, and health insurance benefits. The criterion that the USOC uses to distribute the benefits under its Resource Allocation Policy is that the applicant must be an athlete who is "eligible to represent the United States and who intend[s] to compete, if selected, in the next Olympic or Pan American Games." Id. at 110.

Plaintiffs challenge the USOC's policy of providing Athlete Support Programs only to Olympic team members, to the exclusion of Paralympic team members, as violating § 504 of the Rehabilitation Act. The district court consolidated two separate cases for oral argument which the parties and the court agreed raise identical legal issues under Title III of the Americans with Disabilities Act ("ADA"), and § 504 of the Rehabilitation Act: Hollonbeck v. USOC, No. 07–1053, on a motion to dismiss; and Shephard v. USOC, No. 07–1056, on cross-motions for summary judgment. The district court ruled for the USOC on the Title III and § 504 claims in both cases and entered final judgment pursuant to Fed.R.Civ.P. 54(b) on those claims. Prior to our disposition, Mr. Shepherd and the USOC stipulated to the dismissal of the appeal in 07–1056 pursuant to Fed. R.App. P. 42(b). Plaintiffs Hollonbeck, Iniguez, and Heilveil only appeal the district court's dismissal of their § 504 claims.

On appeal, Plaintiffs argue that (1) the relevant universe for analysis should be all amateur athletes over which the USOC has responsibility; (2) they are "otherwise qualified" for the Athlete Support Programs; (3) the USOC's policy discriminates against them; and (4) the USOC's policy has the effect of screening out amateur athletes with disabilities.

Discussion

We review the grant of a motion for summary judgment de novo, applying the same standard as the district court. Timmerman v. U.S. Bank, N.A., 483 F.3d 1106, 1112–13 (10th Cir.2007). Summary judgment is appropriate if "there is no genuine issue as to any material fact and the movant is entitled to judgment as a matter of law." Fed.R.Civ.P. 56(c). We review the grant of a Rule 12(b)(6) motion to dismiss de novo as well, considering whether the complaint contains "enough facts to state a claim to relief that is plausible on its face." Bell Atlantic Corp. v. Twombly, 550 U.S. 544, 127 S.Ct. 1955, 1974, 167 L.Ed.2d 929 (2007). All facts alleged in the Hollonbeck complaint are assumed to be true in reviewing the motion to dismiss. The parties stipulated to a set of facts in Shepherd for the purpose of the cross-motions for summary judgment. Aplee. Br. at 5 n. 1. Because the facts are undisputed, we consider whether Plaintiffs state a claim or whether the USOC is entitled to judgment as a matter of law.

Section 504 of the Rehabilitation Act states: "No otherwise qualified individual with a disability shall, solely by reason of her or his disability, be excluded from the participation in, be denied the benefits of, or be subjected to discrimination under any program or activity receiving Federal financial assistance." 29 U.S.C. § 794(a). A prima facie case under § 504 consists of proof that (1) plaintiff is handicapped under the Act; (2) he is "otherwise qualified" to participate in the program; (3) the program receives federal financial assistance; and (4) the program discriminates against plaintiff. Powers v. MJB Acquisition Corp., 184 F.3d 1147, 1151 (10th Cir.1999).

Plaintiffs first argue that the relevant universe for analysis is all amateur athletes over which the USOC has responsibility, and the district court erred in restricting its discrimination analysis to the Olympics. Plaintiffs argue that the ASA's use of the term "amateur athlete" and § 504's definition of "program or activity," in light of the history of the definition and precedent applying Title IX, compel an analysis of the USOC programs for Olympic, Pan American, and Paralympic athletes as a whole. Thus, Plaintiffs argue that we should compare the USOC's treatment of all amateur athletes, no matter the competition in which they compete.

The ASA defines "amateur athlete" to be "an athlete who meets the eligibility standards established by the national governing body or paralympic sports organization for the sport in which the athlete competes." 36 U.S.C. § 220501(b)(1). In 1998, the ASA was amended to give the USOC jurisdiction and responsibility over United States participation in the Paralympic Games in addition to the Olympic and Pan American Games. See 36 U.S.C. § 220503; S.Rep. 105–325 (1998). However, the ASA as amended does not direct the USOC's activities in any detail with respect to Olympic or Paralympic athletes other than requiring it to "obtain the most competent amateur representation possible in each event" of the three competitions. 36 U.S.C. § 220503(4). The mere use of the term "amateur athlete" in the statute does not enlarge the relevant universe to include all athletes under the USOC's purview.

The cases that Plaintiffs rely upon also do not support analyzing the USOC's three programs as a whole. First, Plaintiffs rely on Klinger v. Department of Corrections, where women prisoners sued the Nebraska Department of Corrections under Title IX for failing to provide equal educational opportunities for male and female prisoners. 107 F.3d 609, 611 (8th Cir.1997). The prisoners compared the educational opportunities available at their facility with the opportunities available at one specific male facility. Id. at 612. The court rejected the comparison holding that Title IX requires comparison of opportunities for male and female prisoners within the entire prison system taking into account the objective differences between the two populations and other relevant penological and security considerations. Id. at 615–16.

Plaintiffs' reliance on Klinger to alter § 504's definition of "program or activity" is misplaced. The case only holds that, under Title IX, the comparison between only the female facility and one specific male facility is not meaningful. See id. 615–16. A meaningful comparison requires viewing the jails in the context of the security, penological, and size differences among the various facilities. This holding does not support Plaintiffs' theory, and the reasoning in Klinger contradicts Plaintiffs' argument. The court noted that differences in programs between jails are permissible when considering the different circumstances in each jail. See id. at 616. Thus, the case's reasoning suggests that the USOC's three programs should only be compared considering the significant distinctions between each program in purpose, scope, success, and all other relevant differences.

Plaintiffs also rely on two ADA cases to suggest an analysis of the USOC as a whole: Rodde v. Bonta, 357 F.3d 988 (9th Cir.2004), and Concerned Parents to Save Dreher Park Center v. City of West Palm Beach, 846 F.Supp. 986 (S.D.Fla.1994). Both cases are readily distinguishable because they involve the consolidation of services for the disabled at a single facility and then cancellation of those services. See Rodde, 357 F.3d at 998 (noting these similarities in these two cases). These cases did not involve separate programs with separate eligibility requirements-they involved the provision of health and recreation services and the cancellation of those services for the disabled on a county-wide basis. Cf. Does 1–5 v. Chandler, 83 F.3d 1150, 1155 (9th Cir.1996) (concluding that a Hawaii general assistance program is functionally two programs-one for needy families and one for the needy disabled-and holding that "[t]he ADA does not require equivalent benefits in different programs"). Nothing in the analysis of these two cases supports a conclusion that the USOC's programs should be analyzed as a whole.

The additional Title IX precedent cited by Plaintiffs is not applicable here because it is based on a regulatory framework unique to the Title IX context. Title IX regulations recognize that separation based on gender may be necessary thus requiring an institution-wide analysis to determine whether a Title IX violation has occurred. See e.g., 34 C.F.R. § 106.41(b), (c); Roberts v. Colo. State Bd. of Agric., 998 F.2d 824, 829–32 (10th Cir.1993). Therefore, the relevant universe for analysis under § 504 is the individual programs under the USOC's umbrella. Plaintiffs must show that they are otherwise qualified for the Athlete Support Programs and that the program discriminates against them.

Second, Plaintiffs argue that they are "otherwise qualified" for the Athlete Support Programs because they are amateur athletes under the ASA. A plaintiff is "otherwise qualified" under the Rehabilitation Act if he "is able to meet all of a program's requirements in spite of his [disability]." Se. Cmty. Coll. v. Davis, 442 U.S. 397, 406, 99 S.Ct. 2361, 60 L.Ed.2d 980 (1979). Normally, if a plaintiff is unable to meet a program's requirements, a court must consider whether reasonable modifications or accommodations may be made that do not fundamentally alter the program. See Sch. Bd. of Nassau County, Fla. v. Arline, 480 U.S. 273, 288 n. 17, 107 S.Ct. 1123, 94 L.Ed.2d 307 (1987); Alexander v. Choate, 469 U.S. 287, 300, 105 S.Ct. 712, 83 L.Ed.2d 661 (1985). Plaintiffs' argument requires us to accept a premise that we already rejected, namely, that the relevant universe for analysis is all amateur athletes. In the alternative, Plaintiffs contend that the requirement of being on the Olympic team is not an "essential eligibility requirement" to qualify for the Athlete Support Programs. 28 C.F.R. § 41.32(b). Plaintiffs argue that the USOC could open the benefits to Paralympic athletes and that doing so would further the USOC's program as a whole. However, § 504 is not the vehicle to compel discretionary acts of administrators absent discrimination.

Third, Plaintiffs argue that the USOC's policy of excluding Paralympic athletes from Athlete Support Programs is both facially discriminatory and discriminatory by proxy. Even if Plaintiffs were "otherwise qualified" for the benefits, the USOC's policy does not discriminate against Plaintiffs by reason of their disability. First, Plaintiffs err in contending that the eligibility requirements for the Athlete Support Programs are intentionally discriminatory. The criterion that the USOC uses to distribute the benefits under its Resource Allocation Policy is that the athlete must be "eligible to represent the United States and intend to compete, if selected, in the next Olympic or Pan American Games." The policy, on its face, clearly does not contain an explicit requirement of not being disabled. Cf. Bangerter v. Orem City Corp., 46 F.3d 1491, 1500 (10th Cir.1995) (considering a city zoning ordinance for group homes for the disabled that "facially single[d] out the handicapped and appl[ied] different rules to them").

Plaintiffs also contend that the program discriminates against Paralympic athletes by proxy as the policy specifically excludes Paralympic athletes and the term "Paralympic athletes" is a proxy for amateur athletes with disabilities. The designation of "Olympic athlete" as a requirement for Athlete Support Programs is not a proxy for non-disabled athletes because there is no fit between being an Olympic athlete and not being disabled. The requirement of being an Olympic athlete is not "directed at an effect or manifestation of a handicap." McWright v. Alexander, 982 F.2d 222, 228 (7th Cir.1992). Thus, the requirement to be an Olympic athlete to be eligible for the Athlete Support Programs is not discriminatory to Paralympic athletes "by reason of [their] disability." See 29 U.S.C. § 794(a).

Fourth, Plaintiffs argue that the USOC's policy has the effect of screening out amateur athletes with disabilities. Plaintiffs' argument appears to allege that the USOC's policy impermissibly creates a disparate impact on disabled athletes, thus violating § 504. The Supreme Court has held that disparate impact, by itself, does not state a prima facie case under § 504. Choate, 469 U.S. at 299, 105 S.Ct. 712. Rather, actionable disparate impact requires analysis of whether the individual is otherwise qualified and whether reasonable accommodations may provide meaningful access. See id. at 299–301, 105 S.Ct. 712. Plaintiffs raise no additional argument here that we do not address above.

The dissent concludes that Plaintiffs are "otherwise qualified" for the Athlete Support Program because § 504 defines "program or activity" to include "all of the operations of" a covered entity. 29 U.S.C. § 794(b). However, Congress included the phrase "all of the operations of" a covered entity in § 504 to ensure that § 504 applies to an institution as a whole once any part of the institution receives federal funds. See supra note 2; see also DeVargas v. Mason & Hanger-Silas Mason Co., 911 F.2d 1377, 1384–85 (10th Cir.1990). The phrase does not create a parity requirement across an institution's individual programs (unlike the requirements under the specialized Title IX regulations). Further, the dissent's reading of the statute would change the eligibility requirements set by the USOC-being an Olympic team member-altering the nature of the program. Courts are not free to rewrite eligibility requirements but must analyze whether a plaintiff is "otherwise qualified" against the requirements set by the covered entity. See Davis, 442 U.S. at 413–14, 99 S.Ct. 2361 (rejecting a challenge to a nursing program because the requested modifications would have fundamentally altered the purposes and eligibility requirements of the program set by the college). Courts must ask whether reasonable modifications or accommodations may be made that do not fundamentally alter the program, see Choate, 469 U.S. at 300, 105 S.Ct. 712, or whether the requirement is not an "essential eligibility requirement" to qualify for the benefits or program, 28 C.F.R. § 41.32(b).

The dissent also argues that only extending the benefits at issue to Olympic athletes "has a discriminatory effect" against Paralympic athletes. However, disparate impact, by itself, does not state a prima facie case under § 504. Choate, 469 U.S. at 299, 105 S.Ct. 712. Further, our holding clearly does not permit denying benefits on the basis of gender, as the dissent suggests, because such a classification would be facially discriminatory. Here, the classification is facially neutral and is not "directed at an effect or manifestation of a handicap" as required for proxy discrimination. McWright, 982 F.2d at 228.

We sympathize with Plaintiffs' efforts to obtain benefits similar to those received by their Olympic counterparts. However, we cannot modify the Rehabilitation Act to reach a result in their favor absent statutory or regulatory authority to import, wholesale, Title IX regulations and precedent into § 504. See Choate, 469 U.S. at 293 n. 7, 105 S.Ct. 712. Plaintiffs should seek a remedy with the legislative or executive branches, not the courts.

AFFIRMED.

I respectfully dissent. Section 504 of the Rehabilitation Act provides that a qualified individual with a disability may not, solely because of his disability, be "excluded from the participation in, be denied the benefits of, or be subjected to discrimination under any program or activity receiving Federal financial assistance." 29 U.S.C. § 794(a). What the statute forbids is exactly what has occurred and is occurring here. This defiance of plain legislative intent is crystal-clear from the congressional statement that the Paralympics are "the Olympics for disabled amateur athletes." S.Rep. No. 105–325 at 2, 1998 WL 604018 (1998).

The issues presented.

A prima facie case under section 504 requires proof (1) that the plaintiff has a disability; (2) that plaintiff is otherwise qualified to participate in the program; (3) that the program receives federal money; and (4) that the program discriminated against the plaintiff. Powers v. MJB Acquisition Corp., 184 F.3d 1147, 1151 (10th Cir.1999). In these appeals it is not contested that Plaintiffs have disabilities and that the USOC receives federal money. Therefore, the questions before us are whether the Plaintiffs are "otherwise qualified" to participate in the program and whether the USOC discriminated against the Plaintiffs.

The plaintiffs are qualified to participate in the program.

Quite obviously, this court cannot answer the first question without determining what "the program" is in this case. Indeed, resolution of these appeals turns on whether the USOC is operating one "program" or separate programs, one for the disabled and one for the able-bodied. The clear answer to that question has been provided by Congress. Section 504 defines "program or activity" to include "all of the operations of" the covered entity. 29 U.S.C. § 794(b). Plaintiffs are qualified to participate in the program; they are recognized as elite paralympic athletes whose competition in the Paralympic Games is, Congress has mandated, to be promoted by the USOC.

Thus, this case can and should be resolved by simple application of the plain language of the statute, and this court should reverse the judgment of the district court. The majority reaches the wrong result because its analysis goes off the track at the outset by failing to follow the statutory definition of "program." As noted by the majority, Congress specifically amended the Rehabilitation Act and other statutes to broaden the definition of "program or activity." Maj. op. at 1195, n. 1. But the majority inexplicably ignores the definition, insisting that the definition is of no moment because it is undisputed in this appeal that the Act "applies to all of the USOC's programs." Id. (emphasis added).

This use of the plural reveals the circular nature of the majority's analysis. The underlying issue (easily resolved by the plain language of the statute) is whether, in examining the USOC's challenged activities, we should consider the USOC as operating a single program or several separate ones. The majority incorrectly assumes-there is certainly no explanation for the approach-that we are dealing with separate programs. And it is only by ignoring the statutory definition and making this assumption of dealing with separate programs that the majority is able to assert that the unequal treatment afforded to the Plaintiffs is permissible.

Not only does the majority ignore the statutory definition of "program," but its assumption that separate programs are involved exonerates the USOC for doing just what the Supreme Court instructs must not be done-defining the benefit "in a way that effectively denies otherwise qualified handicapped individuals the meaningful access to which they are entitled." Alexander v. Choate, 469 U.S. 287, 301, 105 S.Ct. 712, 83 L.Ed.2d 661 (1985).

The USOC's program discriminates against the plaintiffs.

Plaintiffs are subject to discrimination by being denied access to benefits that are provided to Olympic and Pan American Games athletes who are not disabled. The USOC's practice of providing health insurance and other benefits to Olympic and Pan American Games athletes, but not Paralympic athletes, clearly has a discriminatory effect. Section 504 prohibits not only intentional discrimination but, I am satisfied, also the use of criteria or methods of administration such as those involved here that have the effect of subjecting people with disabilities to discrimination. 28 C.F.R. § 41.5 1(b)(3)(1). See also Alexander v. Choate, 469 U.S. at 299, 105 S.Ct. 712.

Denying benefits to Plaintiffs because they are athletes training for the Paralympic Games, and not the Olympic or Pan American Games, is a proxy for discriminating against them because of their disabilities. The majority's assertion that "there is no fit between being an Olympic athlete and not being disabled," maj. op. at 1196, demonstrates the faulty aim of its analysis. Presumably the majority would not countenance the denial of equal benefits based on gender. Yet, if such blatant discrimination existed, even then it could be said that there was "no fit" between being an Olympic athlete and being male. The USOC has shown four examples in one hundred years of disabled athletes who have competed in the Olympics or Pan

American Games. The exceptions prove the rule: The policy of awarding benefits to athletes training for the Olympics or the Pan American Games while excluding those training for the Paralympic Games discriminates against the disabled. The reason that courts inquire about the "fit" between a practice and a class of protected individuals is because the fact that a practice does not discriminate against every member of a protected class is not sufficient to show that members of the protected class have the meaningful access to which they are entitled. See Lovell v. Chandler, 303 F.3d 1039, 1054 (9th Cir.2002).

For these reasons I am compelled to respectfully but emphatically dissent.

KELLY, CIRCUIT JUDGE.

## QUESTION

1.    Should American disabled athletes receive the same level of financial support from the USOC as able bodied athletes?

# RUSSIAN PARALYMPIC TEAM BANNED FROM 2016 SUMMER OLYMPICS

The IOC is authorized to do drug tests for up to ten years following the games in which the samples are taken. Urine samples used for the testing are stored in laboratory freezers in Switzerland where newer, up to date testing methods can be applied to samples that may have previously been able to avoid detection under procedures used at the time of the initial testing.

The first round of recent retests occurred in May of 2016 when it was disclosed that reanalysis of 53 athletes from more than a dozen countries showed evidence of performance enhancing drugs from the 2008 and 2012 games. The second round of retesting brought the total number of athletes found to have used performance enhancing drugs that had previously gone undetected to 98.

In 2016, just over a month before the 2016 Paralympic Games in Rio de Janeiro, the International Paralympic Committee (IPC) banned Russian disabled athletes from participating in the 2016 Paralympic Games in Rio de Janeiro. The ban came as a result of an investigation prompted by the whistle blowing of Russia's former antidoping lab director. The investigation found at least 35 performance enhancing drug violations by Russian Paralympians that had been covered up by Russian officials since 2011. In addition 19 doping samples from the Sochi 2014 Winter Paralympics were found to have evidence of performance enhancing drugs.

Russia unsuccessfully appealed the decision to the Court of Arbitration for Sport (CAS). In the banning of all athletes from Russia, the IPC went even further than the IOC which primarily left the decision to ban athletes to the various international sports federations governing the specific sports. Athletes who had never failed a drug test were summarily banned from the games.

According to the statement of the IPC:

"The decision was taken unanimously by the IPC Governing Board as a result of NPC Russia's inability to fulfil its IPC membership responsibilities and obligations.

The International Paralympic Committee (IPC) has suspended the Russian Paralympic Committee with immediate effect due to its inability to fulfil its IPC membership responsibilities and obligations, in particular its obligation to comply with the IPC Anti-Doping Code and the World Anti-Doping Code (to which it is also a signatory).

After evaluating all of the evidence before it, and allowing the Russian Paralympic Committee to present its case both in writing and in person, the IPC Governing Board unanimously determined that the Russian Paralympic Committee is unable to ensure compliance with and the enforcement of the IPC's Anti-Doping Code and the World Anti-Doping Code within its own national jurisdiction. These obligations are a fundamental constitutional requirement for all National Paralympic Committees (NPCs), and are vital to the IPC's ability to ensure fair competition and to provide a level playing field for all Para athletes around the world.

In line with the IPC's Suspension Policy, the Russian Paralympic Committee now has 21 days (28 August) to appeal the decision.

The effect of the suspension is that the Russian Paralympic Committee loses all rights and privileges of IPC membership. In particular, a member is not entitled to be heard, except with respect to their suspension, or to vote at meetings of members, and/or to enter athletes in competitions sanctioned by the IPC, and/or to participate in IPC activities. Consequently, the Russian Paralympic Committee will not be able to enter its athletes in the Rio 2016 Paralympic Games.

Sir Philip Craven IPC President, said: "This decision has placed a huge burden upon all our shoulders, but it's a decision we've had to take in the best interests of the Paralympic Movement.

Ultimately, as the global governing body for the Paralympic Movement, it is our responsibility to ensure fair competition, so that athletes can have confidence that they are competing on a level playing field. This is vital to the integrity and credibility of Paralympic sport, and in order to achieve this it is fundamental that each member abides by the rules.

Since the publication of the McLaren Report on 18 July our priority has been to establish the full facts in respect of Para sport. A decision of this magnitude must be evidence based and not influenced by the many and varied views of other people or organizations outside of the IPC and the Paralympic Movement.

In particular, we have taken the necessary time to ask further questions of Professor McLaren and his investigation team, to await the results of samples undergoing further forensic examination and to invite the Russian Paralympic Committee to present its case to the IPC and enter into dialogue with the IPC Governing Board.

With the full facts to hand, we were deeply saddened to find that the State-sponsored doping programme that exists within Russian sport regrettably extends to Russian Para sport as well.

"Tragically this situation is not about athletes cheating a system, but about a State-run system that is cheating the athletes. The doping culture that is polluting Russian sport stems from the Russian government and has now been uncovered in not one, but two independent reports commissioned by the World Anti-Doping Agency.

Our decision is driven by the need to hold our members accountable for their obligations. On the basis of the evidence we have, in the current environment our member the Russian Paralympic Committee cannot comply with the IPC's Anti-Doping Code and the World Anti-Doping Code. Those obligations are crucial to the IPC's guarantee of fair competition for all.

I believe the Russian government has catastrophically failed its Para athletes. Their medals over morals mentality disgusts me. The complete corruption of the anti-doping system is contrary to the rules and strikes at the very heart of the spirit of Paralympic sport. It shows a blatant disregard for the health and well-being of athletes and, quite simply, has no place in Paralympic sport. Their thirst for glory at all costs has severely damaged the integrity and image of all sport, and has certainly resulted in a devastating outcome for the Russian Paralympic Committee and Para athletes.

I have deep sympathy for Russian Para athletes who will miss out on the Rio 2016 Paralympic Games. They are part of a broken system and we sincerely hope that the changes that need to happen, do happen. Russia has some top-quality athletes across all sports and we look forward to the day when we can welcome the Russian Paralympic Committee back as a member safe in the knowledge that it is fulfilling all its obligations in order to ensure a level playing field for all.

Since opening suspension proceedings against the Russian Paralympic Committee on 22 July, the IPC has, among other things taken the following steps:

Step 1—Further investigation of the "disappearing positive samples"

• The McLaren Report identified 35 samples related to Paralympic sport where a liaison person within the Moscow Laboratory notified the Deputy Minister of Sport Yury Nagornykh following a positive screen result. Following this notification, samples were marked either as QUARANTINE or SAVE. Such actions are a direct breach of both the World Anti-Doping Code and the IPC Anti-Doping Code.

• Following a request from the IPC on Monday 18 July, Professor McLaren provided the names of the 35 athletes associated with the 35 samples on Thursday 21 July, together with the dates the samples were provided, the possible substance the athletes tested positive for, the sample code numbers and whether the sample had been marked QUARANTINE or SAVE.

• On Saturday 6 August, the investigation team provided the IPC with an additional 10 samples, relating to nine athletes, which were part of the "disappearing positive" methodology. In total the IPC now has information on 45 samples relating to 44 athletes.

• From these data, the IPC determined in what sports the 44 athletes compete, with the exception of one individual that has not been identified yet.

• Our research revealed that 17 of the 45 samples originate from athletes who participate in sports that are either not on the Paralympic programme or whose international federations are not recognised by the IPC.

• This leaves 27 samples that are related to athletes in eight Para sports that are part of the current Paralympic sport programme. Five of the eight sports are summer sports whilst three are winter sports.

- Some of the Para sports associated with the 27 samples are ones that the IPC governs as an International Federation, whilst others are non-IPC sports that are governed by other International Federations.

- At least 11 of the 27 Para sport athlete samples were marked SAVE by the Moscow Laboratory. This means that positive samples from these Para athletes were subsequently reported as a negative, and the athletes faced no punishment.

- Professor McLaren believes, that as with all sports listed in the report, there are likely to be even more samples that were included in the "disappearing positive" methodology.

Step 2—Testing of 21 samples from the Sochi 2014 Paralympic Winter Games

- Although not directly referred to in the McLaren Report, the IPC now has evidence that the sample swapping regime that operated during the Sochi 2014 Olympic Winter Games in the Sochi laboratory was also in operation during the Sochi 2014 Paralympic Winter Games.

- In total, the IPC sent 21 samples from seven Russian athletes who competed at Sochi 2014 to London for further forensic examination. These samples were selected by the investigation team on an intelligence-led basis, together with a small number of additional samples chosen by the IPC.

- Upon receipt, the laboratory found that two samples had sediment in the cap which meant they could not be tested, leaving 19 samples that could be properly examined.

- Of the 19 samples, forensic examination established that the caps of 18 samples showed scratches and marks that were consistent with those found on the Sochi 2014 Olympic Winter Games samples.

- DNA analysis confirms the clean urine which was swapped comes from the same athlete.

• According to the McLaren investigation team, the bottles examined are a representative sample that indicates Paralympic athletes were included in the broader doping scheme. They believe that further investigations will uncover many more samples involved in this programme.

• Now that these data have corroborated the claim that this State directed scheme has involved Russian Paralympic athletes, the IPC plans to reanalyse every Russian sample from the Sochi 2014 Paralympic Games in the coming months.

• The IPC is also seeking further advice from the IPC Anti-Doping Committee and WADA on what measures can be taken to address the athletes associated with these samples, including results management.

Step 3—Meeting with the Russian Paralympic Committee

• In accordance with the IPC's Suspension Policy, the IPC provided sufficient time to allow the Russian Paralympic Committee to present their case to the IPC.

• On Friday 29 July, the Russian Paralympic Committee provided written submissions to the IPCGoverning Board for consideration.

• On Wednesday 3 August, a seven-person delegation from the Russian Paralympic Committee visited the IPC's headquarters in Bonn, Germany, to additionally present their arguments in person before the IPC Governing Board.

• Twelve of the IPC Governing Board members—six of which are Paralympians—participated in the three-hour meeting which also provided an opportunity for both parties to enter dialogue and ask and answer questions of each other.

• After this meeting, the IPC Governing Board convened for a further two hours to discuss the evidence it had before it.

• Questions that could not be fully answered in the meeting were responded to within 24 hours in writing.

Slot redistribution and next steps

Following the decision, the IPC is now working with the relevant International Federations to determine how the 267 slots Russian athletes had secured across 18 sports for Rio 2016 can potentially be redistributed to other NPCs. A final decision will not be taken on redistributing these slots until after the outcome of any potential appeal by the Russian Paralympic Committee is decided.

The IPC also will now begin developing the steps the Russian Paralympic Committee will need to take to meet its membership obligations. By rule, the Russian Paralympic Committee's suspension will be lifted immediately following the Governing Board's determination that the member is once again able to meet its membership obligations in full."[7]

## QUESTION

1. Was it fair for the IPC to ban the entire Russian Paralympic team from the 2016 Summer Paralympics?

# RIGHTS OF DISABLED SCHOOL CHILDREN TO PARTICIPATE IN SPORTS

Do school aged children with disabilities have a right to participate in organized sports?

Section 504 of the Rehabilitation Act indicates students with disabilities have the rights to an equal opportunity to participate in schools' extracurricular activities.

According to Education Secretary Arne Duncan, "Sports can provide invaluable lessons in discipline, selflessness, passion and courage, and this guidance will help schools ensure that students with disabilities

---

[7] "The IPC suspends the Russian Paralympic Committee with immediate effect," Press Release of International Paralympic Committee, July 8, 2016.

have an equal opportunity to benefit from the life lessons they can learn on the playing field or on the court."[8]

In 2010 a report by the Government Accountability Office (GAO) found that students with disabilities participated in athletics at significantly lower rates than students without disabilities.[9]

Largely in response to the GAO report, the U.S. Department of Education in 2013 issued orders to all schools receiving federal funds about dealing with the rights of disabled students to participate in sports. School districts were informed that they were now required to provide disabled students with the opportunity to participate in sports equal to that of students without disabilities.

The Department of Education issued guidelines in 2013 for elementary and high schools to make reasonable changes to their sports programs to provide opportunities for disabled students to compete or to create separate teams for them. Using the power of the purse, the Department of Education indicated that participating in school athletics is a civil right for disabled students and that schools that do not meet their obligation to provide an opportunity for disabled athletes to compete in school sports could risk losing federal funding. Although these rules only apply to student athletes up through high school, it is not a stretch of the imagination to see these rules extended to collegiate athletes as well.

But just what is a reasonable change to a sport to accommodate a disabled athlete and how can these changes be made without fundamentally changing the sports or providing an unfair advantage to the disabled athlete? Certainly a visual cue of some sort to signal a deaf track athlete of the start of his or her race is something that can

---

8    U.S. Department of Education, Press Release, "U.S. Department of Education Clarifies Schools' Obligation to Provide Equal Opportunity to Students with Disabilities to participate in Extracurricular Athletics" January 25, 2013.

9    United States Government Accountability Office, "Students with Disabilities: More Information and Guidance Could Improve Opportunities in Physical Education and Athletics" GAO–10–519, June 2010.

be readily done without any problem, however, all accommodations would not be that easy to implement or as economical to accomplish.

Underscoring these rules is the recognition that participation in sports is about more than sports, as the Department of Education rules indicated, some of the benefits include "socialization, improved teamwork and leadership skills, and fitness." According to Education Secretary Arne Duncan, "Sports can provide invaluable lessons in discipline, selflessness, passion and courage." The rules, she said would provide guidance to schools to "ensure that students with disabilities have an equal opportunity to benefit from the life lessons they can learn on the playing field or no the court."

In a letter dated January 25, 2013 Seth Galanter, Acting Assistant Secretary for Civil Rights wrote:

"Dear Colleague: Extracurricular athletics—which include club, intramural, or interscholastic (e.g., freshman, junior varsity, varsity) athletics at all education levels—are an important component of an overall education program. The United States Government Accountability Office (GAO) published a report that underscored that access to, and participation in, extracurricular athletic opportunities provide important health and social benefits to all students, particularly those with disabilities. These benefits can include socialization, improved teamwork and leadership skills, and fitness. Unfortunately, the GAO found that students with disabilities are not being afforded an equal opportunity to participate in extracurricular athletics in public elementary and secondary schools.

To ensure that students with disabilities consistently have opportunities to participate in extracurricular athletics equal to those of other students, the GAO recommended that the United States Department of Education (Department) clarify and communicate schools' responsibilities under Section 504 of the Rehabilitation Act of 1973 (Section 504) regarding the provision of extracurricular athletics. The Department's Office for Civil Rights (OCR) is responsible for enforcing Section 504, which is a Federal law designed to protect the rights of individuals with disabilities in programs and activities (including traditional public schools and charter schools) that receive Federal financial assistance.

In response to the GAO's recommendation, this guidance provides an overview of the obligations of public elementary and secondary schools under Section 504 and the Department's Section 504 regulations, cautions against making decisions based on presumptions and stereotypes, details the specific Section 504 regulations that require students with disabilities to have an equal opportunity for participation in nonacademic and extracurricular services and activities, and discusses the provision of separate or different athletic opportunities. The specific details of the illustrative examples offered in this guidance are focused on the elementary and secondary school context. Nonetheless, students with disabilities at the postsecondary level must also be provided an equal opportunity to participate in athletics, including intercollegiate, club, and intramural athletics.

I.    Overview of Section 504 Requirements

To better understand the obligations of school districts with respect to extracurricular athletics for students with disabilities, it is helpful to review Section 504's requirements. Under the Department's Section 504 regulations, a school district is required to provide a qualified student with a disability an opportunity to benefit from the school district's program equal to that of students without disabilities. For purposes of Section 504, a person with a disability is one who (1) has a physical or mental impairment that substantially limits one or more major life activities; (2) has a record of such an impairment; or (3) is regarded as having such an impairment. With respect to public elementary and secondary educational services, "qualified" means a person (i) of an age during which persons without disabilities are provided such services, (ii) of any age during which it is mandatory under state law to provide such services to persons with disabilities, or (iii) to whom a state is required to provide a free appropriate public education under the Individuals with Disabilities Education Act (IDEA).

Of course, simply because a student is a "qualified" student with a disability does not mean that the student must be allowed to participate in any selective or competitive program offered by a school district; school districts may require a level of skill or ability of a student in order for that student to participate in a selective or competitive program or activity, so long as the selection or competition criteria are not discriminatory.

Among other things, the Department's Section 504 regulations prohibit school districts from:

• denying a qualified student with a disability the opportunity to participate in or benefit from an aid, benefit, or service;

• affording a qualified student with a disability an opportunity to participate in or benefit from an aid, benefit, or service that is not equal to that afforded others;

• providing a qualified student with a disability with an aid, benefit, or service that is not as effective as that provided to others and does not afford that student with an equal opportunity to obtain the same result, gain the same benefit, or reach the same level of achievement in the most integrated setting appropriate to the student's needs;

• providing different or separate aid, benefits, or services to students with disabilities or to any class of students with disabilities unless such action is necessary to provide a qualified student with a disability with aid, benefits, or services that are as effective as those provided to others; and

• otherwise limiting a qualified individual with a disability in the enjoyment of any right, privilege, advantage, or opportunity enjoyed by others receiving an aid, benefit, or service.

A school district must also adopt grievance procedures that incorporate appropriate due process standards and that provide for prompt and equitable resolution of complaints alleging violations of the Section 504 regulations.

A school district's legal obligation to comply with Section 504 and the Department's regulations supersedes any rule of any association, organization, club, or league that would render a student ineligible to participate, or limit the eligibility of a student to participate, in any aid, benefit, or service on the basis of disability. Indeed, it would violate a school district's obligations under Section 504 to provide significant assistance to any association, organization, club, league, or other third party that discriminates on the basis of disability in providing any aid, benefit, or service to the school district's students. To avoid violating their Section 504 obligations in the context of extracurricular athletics, school districts should work with their athletic associations to ensure that students with disabilities are not denied an equal opportunity to participate in interscholastic athletics.

## II.   Do Not Act On Generalizations and Stereotypes

A school district may not operate its program or activity on the basis of generalizations, assumptions, prejudices, or stereotypes about disability generally, or specific disabilities in particular. A school district also may not rely on generalizations about what students with a type of disability are capable of—one student with a certain type of disability may not be able to play a certain type of sport, but another student with the same disability may be able to play that sport.

Example 1: A student has a learning disability and is a person with a disability as defined by Section 504. While in middle school, this student enjoyed participating in her school's lacrosse club. As she enters the ninth grade in high school, she tries out and is selected as a member of the high school's lacrosse team. The coach is aware of this student's learning disability and believes that all students with the student's particular learning disability would be unable to play successfully under the time constraints and pressures of an actual game. Based on this assumption, the coach decides never to play this student during games. In his opinion, participating fully in all the team practice sessions is good enough.

Analysis: OCR would find that the coach's decision violates Section 504. The coach denied this student an equal opportunity to participate on the team by relying solely on characteristics he believed to be associated with her disability. A school district, including its athletic staff, must not operate on generalizations or assumptions about disability or how a particular disability limits any particular student. Rather, the coach should have permitted this student an equal opportunity to participate in this athletic activity, which includes the opportunity to participate in the games as well as the practices. The student, of course, does not have a right to participate in the games; but the coach's decision on whether the student gets to participate in games must be based on the same criteria the coach uses for all other players (such as performance reflected during practice sessions).

III. Ensure Equal Opportunity for Participation

A school district that offers extracurricular athletics must do so in such manner as is necessary to afford qualified students with disabilities an equal opportunity for participation. This means making reasonable modifications and providing those aids and services that are necessary to ensure an equal opportunity to participate, unless the school district can show that doing so would be a fundamental alteration to its program. Of course, a school district may adopt bona fide safety standards needed to implement its extracurricular athletic program or activity. A school district, however, must consider whether safe participation by any particular student with a disability can be assured through reasonable modifications or the provision of aids and services.

Schools may require a level of skill or ability for participation in a competitive program or activity; equal opportunity does not mean, for example, that every student with a disability is guaranteed a spot on an athletic team for which other students must try out. A school district must, however, afford qualified students with disabilities an equal opportunity for participation in extracurricular athletics in an integrated manner to the maximum extent appropriate to the needs of the student. This means that a school district must make reasonable modifications to its policies, practices, or procedures whenever such modifications are necessary to ensure equal opportunity, unless the school district can demonstrate that the requested modification would constitute a fundamental alteration of the nature of the extracurricular athletic activity.

In considering whether a reasonable modification is legally required, the school district must first engage in an individualized inquiry to determine whether the modification is necessary. If the modification is necessary, the school district must allow it unless doing so would result in a fundamental alteration of the nature of the extracurricular athletic activity. A modification might constitute a fundamental alteration if it alters such an essential aspect of the activity or game that it would be unacceptable even if it affected all competitors equally (such as adding an extra base in baseball). Alternatively, a change that has only a peripheral impact on the activity or game itself might nevertheless give a particular player with a disability an unfair advantage over others and, for that reason, fundamentally alter the character of the competition. Even if a specific modification would constitute a fundamental alteration, the school district would still be required to determine if other modifications might be available that would permit the student's participation.

To comply with its obligations under Section 504, a school district must also provide a qualified student with a disability with needed aids and services, if the failure to do so would deny that student an equal opportunity for participation in extracurricular activities in an integrated manner to the maximum extent appropriate to the needs of the student.

Example 2: A high school student has a disability as defined by Section 504 due to a hearing impairment. The student is interested in running track for the school team. He is especially interested in the sprinting events such as the 100 and 200 meter dashes. At the tryouts for the track team, the start of each race was signaled by the coach's assistant using a visual cue, and the student's speed was fast enough to qualify him for the team in those events. After the student makes the team, the coach also signals the start of races during practice with the same visual cue. Before the first scheduled meet, the student asks the district that a visual cue be used at the meet simultaneously when the starter pistol sounds to alert him to the start of the race. Two neighboring districts use a visual cue as an alternative start in their track and field meets. Those districts report that their runners easily adjusted to the visual cue and did not complain about being distracted by the use of the visual cue.

After conducting an individualized inquiry and determining that the modification is necessary for the student to compete at meets, the district nevertheless refuses the student's request because the district is concerned that the use of a visual cue may distract other runners and trigger complaints once the track season begins. The coach tells the student that although he may practice with the team, he will not be allowed to participate in meets.

Analysis: OCR would find that the school district's decision violates Section 504.

While a school district is entitled to set its requirements as to skill, ability, and other benchmarks, it must provide a reasonable modification if necessary, unless doing so would fundamentally alter the nature of the activity. Here, the student met the benchmark requirements as to speed and skill in the 100 and 200 meter dashes to make the team. Once the school district determined that the requested modification was necessary, the school district was then obligated to provide the visual cue unless it determined that providing it would constitute a fundamental alteration of the activity.

In this example, OCR would find that the evidence demonstrated that the use of a visual cue does not alter an essential aspect of the activity or give this student an unfair advantage over others. The school district should have permitted the use of a visual cue and allowed the student to compete.

Example 3: A high school student was born with only one hand and is a student with a disability as defined by Section 504. This student would like to participate on the school's swim team. The requirements for joining the swim team include having a certain level of swimming ability and being able to compete at meets. The student has the required swimming ability and wishes to compete. She asks the school district to waive the "two-hand touch" finish it requires of all swimmers in swim meets, and to permit her to finish with a "one-hand touch." The school district refuses the request because it determines that permitting the student to finish with a "one-hand touch" would give the student an unfair advantage over the other swimmers.

Analysis: A school district must conduct an individualized assessment to determine whether the requested modification is necessary for the student's participation, and must determine whether permitting it would fundamentally alter the nature of the activity. Here, modification of the two-hand touch is necessary for the student to participate. In determining whether making the necessary modification—eliminating the two-hand touch rule—would fundamentally alter the nature of the swim competition, the school district must evaluate whether the requested modification alters an essential aspect of the activity or would give this student an unfair advantage over other swimmers.

OCR would find a one-hand touch does not alter an essential aspect of the activity. If, however, the evidence demonstrated that the school district's judgment was correct that she would gain an unfair advantage over others who are judged on the touching of both hands, then a complete waiver of the rule would constitute a fundamental alteration and not be required.

In such circumstances, the school district would still be required to determine if other modifications were available that would permit her participation. In this situation, for example, the school district might determine that it would not constitute an unfair advantage over other swimmers to judge the student to have finished when she touched the wall with one hand and her other arm was simultaneously stretched forward. If so, the school district should have permitted this modification of this rule and allowed the student to compete.

Example 4: An elementary school student with diabetes is determined not eligible for services under the IDEA. Under the school district's Section 504 procedures, however, he is determined to have a disability. In order to participate in the regular classroom setting, the student is provided services under Section 504 that include assistance with glucose testing and insulin administration from trained school personnel. Later in the year, this student wants to join the school-sponsored gymnastics club that meets after school. The only eligibility requirement is that all gymnastics club members must attend that school. When the parent asks the school to provide the glucose testing and insulin administration that the student needs to participate in the gymnastics club, school personnel agree that it is necessary but respond that they are not required to provide him with such assistance because gymnastics club is an extracurricular activity.

Analysis: OCR would find that the school's decision violates Section 504. The student needs assistance in glucose testing and insulin administration in order to participate in activities during and after school. To meet the requirements of Section 504 FAPE, the school district must provide this needed assistance during the school day.

In addition, the school district must provide this assistance after school under Section 504 so that the student can participate in the gymnastics club, unless doing so would be a fundamental alteration of the district's education program. Because the school district always has a legal obligation under IDEA to provide aids or services in its education program to enable any IDEA-eligible students to participate in extracurricular Page 11—Students with disabilities in extracurricular athletics activities, providing these aids or services after school to a student with a disability not eligible under the IDEA would rarely, if ever, be a fundamental alteration of its education program. This remains true even if there are currently no IDEA-eligible students in the district who need these aids or services.

In this example, OCR would find that the school district must provide glucose testing and insulin administration for this student during the gymnastics club in order to comply with its Section 504 obligations. The student needs this assistance in order to participate in the gymnastics club, and because this assistance is available under the IDEA for extracurricular activities, providing this assistance to this student would not constitute a fundamental alteration of the district's education program.

IV.   Offering Separate or Different Athletic Opportunities

As stated above, in providing or arranging for the provision of extracurricular athletics, a school district must ensure that a student with a disability participates with students without disabilities to the maximum extent appropriate to the needs of that student with a disability. The provision of unnecessarily separate or different services is discriminatory. OCR thus encourages school districts to work with their community and athletic associations to develop broad opportunities to include students with disabilities in all extracurricular athletic activities.

Students with disabilities who cannot participate in the school district's existing extracurricular athletics program—even with reasonable modifications or aids and services—should still have an equal opportunity to receive the benefits of extracurricular athletics. When the interests and abilities of some students with disabilities cannot be as fully and effectively met by the school district's existing extracurricular athletic program, the school district should create additional opportunities for those students with disabilities.

In those circumstances, a school district should offer students with disabilities opportunities for athletic activities that are separate or different from those offered to students without disabilities. These athletic opportunities provided by school districts should be supported equally, as with a school district's other athletic activities. School districts must be flexible as they develop programs that consider the unmet interests of students with disabilities. For example, an ever-increasing number of school districts across the country are creating disability-specific teams for sports such as wheelchair tennis or wheelchair basketball. When the number of students with disabilities at an individual school is insufficient to field a team, school districts can also: (1) develop district-wide or regional teams for students with disabilities as opposed to a school based team in order to provide competitive experiences; (2) mix male and female students with disabilities on teams together; or (3) offer "allied" or "unified" sports teams on which students with disabilities participate with students without disabilities. OCR urges school districts, in coordination with students, families, community and advocacy organizations, athletic associations, and other interested parties, to support these and other creative ways to expand such opportunities for students with disabilities.

V.   Conclusion

OCR is committed to working with schools, students, families, community and advocacy organizations, athletic associations, and other interested parties to ensure that students with disabilities are provided an equal opportunity to participate in extracurricular athletics. Individuals who believe they have been subjected to discrimination may also file a complaint with OCR or in court.

For the OCR regional office serving your area, please visit: http://wdcrobcolp01.ed.gov/CFAPPS/OCR/contactus.cfm, or call OCR's Customer Service Team at 1-800-421-3481 (TDD 1-877-521-2172). Please do not hesitate to contact us if we can provide assistance in your efforts to address this issue or if you have other civil rights concerns. I look forward to continuing our work together to ensure that students with disabilities receive an equal opportunity to participate in a school district's education program.

Sincerely, /s/ Seth M. Galanter Acting Assistant Secretary for Civil Rights"[10]

A number of states have already passed laws to provide opportunities for disabled students in sports.

These rules only apply to K–12, but could lead to changes in colleges in the future.

## QUESTIONS

1.   Should the anti-discrimination rules enabling greater participation in sports by people with disabilities be broadened to apply to colleges?

2.   How great a role should financial concerns play in requiring schools to increase opportunities for disabled athletes?

3.   Should legal attention to the rights of disabled athletes be considered secondary to the rights of women athletes?

4.   Should schools be required to establish separate athletic teams for disabled athletes if they cannot be integrated into the regular varsity and intramural sports programs?

5.   To what extent must a school adapt the rules of its varsity sports programs to enable a disabled athlete to participate? What are reasonable accommodations and how are they determined for each sport?

6.   Should the optimum goal be to integrate disabled athletes into the existing varsity and intramural sports programs or to establish separate, but equal alternative programs?

# SYNOPSIS

1.   Participation in sports offers substantial advantages to disabled individuals.

2.   The history of organized sports for disabled people goes back to 1911.

---

[10]   United States Department of Education, Office for Civil Rights, Letter to Colleagues, Seth M. Galanter, Acting Assistant Secretary for Civil Rights, January 25, 2013.

3.    The Paralympics has ten defined levels of impairment used to evaluate athletes.

4.    A key element of the Paralympic standards for impairment is that the impairment and disability must be of a permanent nature.

5.    Disabled athletes may not compete in the Olympics if they have a prosthesis that provides them with a competitive advantage.

6.    Financial support for training of American Paralympians by the United States Olympic Committee is not equal to the financial support to athletes competing in the regular Olympics.

7.    The entire Russian Paralympic team was banned from the 2016 Rio Paralympic Games.

8.    Public schools from kindergarten through high school receiving federal funds have a federal duty to provide access to sports to disabled students.

# CHAPTER TEN

# Intellectual Property

## TRADEMARK

A Trademark is a distinctive sign used by a business to uniquely identify itself and distinguish itself from others. It can be a name, word, phrase, logo, symbol, design, image or any combination thereof. A trademark is established through its use or registration with the trademark office. Registering a trademark provides exclusive rights to use and prevents unauthorized use by others in relation to similar services or products. The law prohibits trademarks that are deceptive or cause confusion with other registered trademarks as well as those that are generic names for goods or services.

The federal trademark law is found in the Lanham Act in 15 USC Section 1127 which reads in part:

"The term 'trademark' includes any word, name, symbol, or device, or any combination thereof—

(1)   used by a person, or

(2)   which a person has a bona fide intention to use in commerce and applies to register on the principal register established by this chapter, to identify and distinguish his or her goods, including a unique product, from those manufactured or sold by others and to indicate the source of the goods, even if that source is unknown.

The term 'service mark' means any word, name, symbol, or device, or any combination thereof—

(1)   used by a person, or

(2)   which a person has a bona fide intention to use in commerce and applies to register on the principal register established by this chapter, to identify and distinguish the services of one person, including a unique service, from the services of others and to indicate the source of the services, even if that source is unknown. Titles, character names, and other distinctive features of radio or television programs may be registered as service marks notwithstanding that they, or the programs, may advertise the goods of the sponsor."

It is important to note that the courts have consistently said that the language of the Lanham Act is not to be considered restrictive, but rather should be interpreted broadly in determining whether something can be trademarked.

# CATCHPHRASES

Athletes often try to cash in on their popularity by trademarking a catch phrase or a nickname with which they are associated. In 2013, three years after applying NFL cornerback Darrelle Revis was awarded a trademark for the name "Revis Island" for use on t-shirts, sweat pants, hats, footwear, sleepwear and swimwear. Trademark applications generally cost between $275 and $375 for each business category. The term Revis Island referred to the area of the football field where cornerback Darelle Revis would cover opposing receivers who, Revis argued, would be marooned there and left out of the play.

Former NFL star Michael Strahan's trademarked, "Stomp You Out." Talented, but often erratic baseball player Manny Ramirez trademarked "Manny being Manny" only to later abandon the trademark. Jeremy Lin trademarked the word "Linsanity" when he played for the New York Knicks of the NBA.

Heisman Trophy winning football player and devoutly religious, Tim Tebow obtained a trademark for the phrase and the visual of what has come to be known as "Tebowing" where he knelt, head down with his clenched fist to his forehead in prayer. In Tebow's case, he said he trademarked the movement and phrase because he wanted to control how it was used to make sure it was used in, what he considered, the correct manner rather than for financial gain.[1]

Trademarking athletic related catch phrases is not a new phenomenon. Legendary professional basketball coach Pat Riley smartly trademarked the phrase "three peat" following the 1988 NBA season in which he coached the Los Angeles Lakers to their second consecutive NBA title. In fact, to cover all bases, Riley trademarked "three peat," "threepeat," "3-peat" and "3peat." Ironically, although Riley's Lakers failed to win the 1989 NBA title, Riley's licensing of the term provided him with royalties when the Chicago Bills completed three peats in 1993 and 1998.

Sometimes athletes will turn over the rights to use their name to the companies with which they have endorsement contracts. For instance Nike owns the right to "LeBron". LeBron James signed with Nike fresh out of high school and before playing a minute of professional basketball and assigned the trademark right to his name at that time.

## QUESTION

1.    What phrases that you would associate with particular athletes do you think should be trademarked?

# WASHINGTON REDSKINS

The now controversial NFL's Redskins name and logo was adopted in 1933 when the team was based in Boston. Previously the team had been known as the Braves. The team said that the name Redskins was chosen in honor of its then coach William Henry "Lone Star Dietz" a

---

[1]    "Jets' Tebow trademarking 'Tebowing' " Associated Press, October 19, 2012.

Native American. Or was he? Dietz was actually convicted of falsely registering as a Native American in order to avoid the draft during World War I.

The Redskins name was originally trademarked in 1967 and since that time the trademark had been renewed every ten years as required by law. However, in 1999 the Trademark Trial and Appeal Board cancelled the Trademark in response to a legal challenge by a group of Native Americans pursuant to the Lanham Act, which reads:

"§ 2 (15 U.S.C. § 1052). Trademarks registrable on the principal register; concurrent registration

No trademark by which the goods of the applicant may be distinguished from the goods of others shall be refused registration on the principal register on account of its nature unless it—(a) Consists of or comprises immoral, deceptive, or scandalous matter; or matter which may disparage or falsely suggest a connection with persons, living or dead, institutions, beliefs, or national symbols, or bring them into contempt, or disrepute;"

The challenge to the Redskins trademark was ultimately denied in the appeals courts based primarily on the issue of laches which is a defense based upon an unreasonable delay in bringing the initial legal challenge. By ruling in this manner the appeals courts avoided dealing with the issue of whether or not the Redskins trademark was disparaging and violated the law.

In order to eliminate laches as a basis for avoiding ruling on the issue, a younger group of Native Americans filed a new case challenging the Redskins trademark in a case entitled Blackhorse v. Pro-Football, Inc. and the Trademark Trial and Appeal Board again ruled that the trademarks were disparaging. Their decision is presently on appeal.

If the Redskins logo and name were not allowed to continue to be registered trademarks, this would not actually prevent the team from using the name and logo, however, most significantly, by losing trademark protection the team would be unable to legally prevent anyone else from using the name and logo and would, therefore render their trademark worthless as anyone would then be able to use the name and logo without being licensed or paying a royalty.

In a case entitled In re Simon Shiao Tam, in 2015 the U.S. Court of Appeals overturned the denial by a three judge panel of the Court of Appeals that upheld a previous decision of the Patent and Trademark Office not permitting an Asian-American rock band, the Slants to trademark their name. The court ruled that the First Amendment "forbids government regulators to deny registration because they find the speech likely to offend others." The court went on to say that "It is a bedrock principle underlying the First Amendment that the government may not penalize private speech merely because it disapproves of the message it conveys. The ruling of the 11th Circuit overturned the seventy year old provision of the Lanham Act not allowing disparaging or offensive trademarks. This case was watched closely as to how it related to the ongoing controversy as to the use of the Washington Redskins trademark.[2]

This decision in the In re Simon Shiao Tam case was of the Eleventh Circuit Court of Appeals and therefore was not legally binding on the Fourth Circuit Court of Appeals where the Redskins appeal was being heard.

Meanwhile the Tam case was appealed to the Supreme Court where in 2017, a unanimous court ruled that the disparagement provision of the Lanham act was an unconstitutional limitation of free speech as protected by the First Amendment. Judge Alito wrote in the majority opinion that "Speech that demeans on the basis of race, ethnicity, gender, religion, age, disability or any other similar ground is hateful; but the proudest boast of our free speech jurisprudence is that we protect the freedom to express 'the thought that we hate.' "[3]

---

[2]    In Re Simon Shiao Tam, United States Court of Appeals for the Federal Circuit, 2014–1203, December 22, 2015.

[3]    Matal v. Tam, 137 S. Ct. 1744 (2017).

In response to arguments that trademarks do not receive the full protection of the First Amendment, but the lesser protection under the First Amendment of commercial speech which has been recognized by a series of cases, most notably the Supreme Court's decision in the case of Central Hudson Gas and Electric Corp. v. Public Service Commission, 447 U.S. 557 (1980) in which the Court recognized that commercial speech did not receive the same level of protection under the First Amendment as other forms of speech such as political or artistic speech, Judge Alito wrote:

"Commerce we are told is disrupted by trademarks that 'involve disparagement of race, gender, ethnicity, national origin, religion, sexual orientation, and similar demographic classification. . . Such trademarks are analogized to discriminatory conduct, which has been recognized to have an adverse effect on commerce. . . .

A simple answer to this argument is that the disparagement clause is not 'narrowly drawn' to drive out trademarks that support invidious discrimination. The clause reaches any trademark that disparages any person, group, or institution. It applies to trademarks like the following: 'Down with racists,' 'Down with sexists,' 'Down with homophobes.' It is not an anti-discrimination clause; it is a happy-talk clause. In this way, it goes much further than is necessary to serve the interest asserted.

The clause is far too broad in other ways as well. The clause protects every person living or dead as well as every institution. Is it conceivable that commerce would be disrupted by a trademark saying: 'James Buchanan was a disastrous president' or 'Slavery is an evil institution?'

There is also a deeper problem with the argument that commercial speech may be cleansed of any expression likely to cause offense. The commercial market is well stocked with merchandise that disparages prominent figures and groups, and the line between commercial and non-commercial speech is not always clear, as this case illustrates. If affixing the commercial label permits the suppression of any speech that may lead to political or social 'volatility,' free speech would be endangered."

Judge Alito concluded by saying, "For these reasons, we hold that the disparagement clause violates the Free Speech Clause of the First Amendment."

With the position of the Supreme Court abundantly clear, the long battle over the trademark of the Washington Redskins was finally concluded with the NFL team's trademark right recognized. However, merely because the right to use the Washington Redskins logo was recognized by the Supreme Court does not mean that those opposing the use of the name will cease their efforts to galvanize public opinion to sway the team's ownership to change the name as a business decision.

# NCAA AND NATIVE AMERICAN MASCOTS

Since 1970 many colleges and universities have dropped Native American references in team names and mascots For example, the UMass Redmen became the Minutemen. The Dartmouth Indians became the Big Green. The Stanford Indians became the Cardinals and the Miami University Redskins became the Redhawks.

In 2005 the NCAA governing board recommended that eighteen schools remove "hostile or abusive" racial/ethnic/national origin nicknames or mascots.[4]

The schools contained on the list were the following:

Alcorn State University (Braves)

Central Michigan University (Chippewas)

Catawba College (Indians)

Florida State University (Seminoles)

Midwestern State University (Indians)

---

[4]  "NCAA Executive Committee Issues Guidelines for Use of Native American Mascots at Championship Events," NCAA News Release, August 5, 2005.

University of Utah (Utes)

Indiana University–Pennsylvania (Indians)

Carthage College (Redmen)

Bradley University (Braves)

Arkansas State University (Indians)

Chowan College (Braves)

University of Illinois–Champaign (Illini)

University of Louisiana–Monroe (Indians)

McMurry University (Indians)

Mississippi College (Choctaws)

Newberry College (Indians)

University of North Dakota (Fighting Sioux)

Southeastern Oklahoma State University (Savages)

A number of the schools complied with the NCAA advisory, however two weeks after the list came out, Florida State University whose teams are known as the Seminoles was removed from the list after the Seminoles tribe notified the NCAA that their connection with Florida State University was a positive relationship that celebrated their culture. The use of the Seminole name and logo is officially sanctioned by the Seminole tribe. The NCAA then modified its initial ruling such that if individual tribes had no objections to teams using their names, the NCAA would comply with their wishes.

The NCAA does not actually have the direct authority to compel a school to refrain from using a particular mascot or name, however the NCAA discourages hostile or abusive names or mascots through actions such as banning schools using such mascots or nicknames from hosting NCAA championship competitions. In addition, such teams may not wear uniforms with hostile or abusive references at NCAA competitions. The University of Iowa and the University of

Wisconsin have gone so far as to refuse to compete with schools that use Native American nicknames or mascots.

# NORTH DAKOTA FIGHTING SIOUX

The University of North Dakota "Fighting Sioux" nickname and logo was one of those deemed by the NCAA to be hostile and abusive. Wealthy alumni and former University of North Dakota hockey player Ralph Engelstad had previously donated one hundred million dollars to the University for the hockey arena named after him which opened in 2001. One of his conditions of the gift was that the University retain the nickname Fighting Sioux. In an attempt to keep the name without being sanctioned by the NCAA, the North Dakota Board of Higher Education sued to prevent the NCAA from penalizing the University for maintaining the Fighting Sioux name and logo. In 2006 the UND obtained a preliminary injunction to prevent the NCAA from enforcing the rule against the University. A year later the UND and the NCAA settled the case through an agreement that gave the University three years to gain support from the state's Sioux tribes in order to continue to use the name and logo, however, if after the end of three years they were unable to get sufficient support, the University agreed to stop using the name and logo. Unable to get approval from the state's Sioux tribes and following 67.35% of voters in a state wide referendum voting against the name and logo, the State Board of Higher Education voted to retire the name and logo. Following a vote of students, alumni faculty, staff, donors and season ticket holders the name Fighting Hawks was chosen as the new name and logo.

# COPYRIGHT

The authority of Congress to enact copyright laws is found in the Constitution and the first copyright laws in the United States were enacted in 1790. Since that time, there have been numerous amendments and expansions of copyright laws.

Copyrights protect creative literary works, music, plays, choreography, pantomimes, pictures, graphics and sculptures, photographs and paintings, computer software, maps, architectural designs, recordings, movies, radio and television shows. This list is not meant to be limiting but only examples of creative productions covered. It does not protect ideas, but it does protect the manifestation of ideas.

In order to be copyrightable the work has to be original in nature and fixed in a tangible medium. To be original it must be creative, but the level of creativity required is little. Feist Publications, Inc. v. Rural Tel. Serv. Co., 499 U.S. 340, 345 (1991).

The owner of a copyright has specific rights as indicated below. Anyone else must pay the copyright holder to use the work unless the use qualifies as fair use, such as when the material is used for teaching purposes, news reporting, parody or used in a transformative fashion to make a new work which will be discussed later in this chapter.

# FEDERAL COPYRIGHT LAW

17 USC section 106 (2012)

Subject to sections 107 through 122, the owner of copyright under this title has the exclusive rights to do and to authorize any of the following:

**(1)** to reproduce the copyrighted work in copies or phonorecords;

**(2)** to prepare derivative works based upon the copyrighted work;

**(3)** to distribute copies or phonorecords of the copyrighted work to the public by sale or other transfer of ownership, or by rental, lease, or lending;

**(4)** in the case of literary, musical, dramatic, and choreographic works, pantomimes, and motion pictures and other audiovisual works, to perform the copyrighted work publicly;

**(5)** in the case of literary, musical, dramatic, and choreographic works, pantomimes, and pictorial, graphic, or sculptural works, including the individual images of a motion picture or other audiovisual work, to display the copyrighted work publicly; and

**(6)** in the case of sound recordings, to perform the copyrighted work publicly by means of a digital audio transmission

# COPYRIGHTING ATHLETIC PERFORMANCES

Can athletes copyright specific athletic performances?

In the case of Baltimore Orioles, Inc. v. Major League Baseball Players Association, 805 F. 2d 663 (7th Cir. 1986) the issue was whether professional baseball teams owned the exclusive right to the televised athletic performances of players in televised games. The dispute that led to the lawsuit was the players' union argument that individual players had intellectual property rights in their performances and that the teams for which they played televised games without the players' permission in violation of those rights.

The trial court and later the appellate court ruled against the players, concluding that the players were employees and their televised performances were done in the course of their employment, however, most significantly, the court suggested that the individual athletic performances by players were copyrightable because they had the sufficient level of creativity necessary for copyright protection, which sets the stage for players to copyright their particular athletic performances. While the trademarking of catch phrases by players is now commonplace, we have yet to seen the copyrighting of athletic works.

# COPYRIGHT PROTECTIONS FOR SPORTS MOVES

The creative aspects of figure skating, gymnastics, synchronized swimming and diving certainly could be considered as choreographic works which would qualify for copyright registration but what about football formations or basketball offenses. Couldn't coaches and players copyright these?

The requirement for copyright protection that the work be fixed is easily met through a videotape of the performance and it would be a simple task to come up with the minimum levels of creativity required to qualify for copyright.

Touchdown celebration moves are a fan pleasing part of the game, particular when athletes such as Rob Gronkowski of the NE Patriots or Victor Cruz formerly of the New York Giants are doing them. For years the NFL enforced rules against what it deemed excessive celebrations, however, quite possibly in response to fans' enjoyment of these celebrations, in 2017 the NFL considerably loosened its rules for touchdown celebrations.

Many touchdown celebrations could be classified for copyright purposes as choreography or pantomime, which are areas of creative expression that can be copyrighted.

While it would seem that a player who may copyright his touchdown or sack celebration movement would have the right under copyright law to prevent others from performing the same movement without his permission, the fair use rules would, as an exception to the copyright rules, permit another player to do a similar dance as a parody of the copyright holding player. Indeed as a psychological tactic, players already mock the athletic celebrations of particular athletes by performing the movements with which the other player may be identified as a form of trash talking. Notably, in 2011 Carlos Rogers parodied Victor Cruz' Salsa dance when he intercepted a pass intended for Cruz.

Parody, which is described as an imitation of the copyrighted work for comic effect or to ridicule is protected as a fair use exception to the copyright laws.

Although no touchdown dances have been copyrighted yet, these movements appear to have all of the necessary requirements for copyright protection.

---

## QUESTIONS

1. What would be the repercussions if an athlete or coach could copyright a particular movement or offensive or defensive scheme?

2. Would it be fair for that person to control and restrict its use in sport?

3. Should players be able to copyright their touchdown or sack celebrations?

# RIGHT OF PUBLICITY

The first case to utilize the term "right of publicity" was Haelan Laboratories, Inc. v. Topps Chewing Gum, Inc. which dealt with the rights of baseball players to their photographs on bubble gum trading cards.

Judge Frank wrote, at 202 F.2d 866 (2d Cir. 1953):

"We think that, in addition to and independent of that right of privacy (which in New York derives from statute), a man has a right in the publicity value of his photograph, *i. e.*, the right to grant the exclusive privilege of publishing his picture, and that such a grant may validly be made "in gross," *i. e.*, without an accompanying transfer of a business or of anything else. Whether it be labelled a "property" right is immaterial; for here, as often elsewhere, the tag "property" simply symbolizes the fact that courts enforce a claim which has pecuniary worth. This right might be called a "right of publicity." For it is common knowledge that many prominent persons (especially actors and ball-players), far from having their feelings bruised through public exposure of their likenesses, would feel sorely deprived if they no longer received money for authorizing advertisements, popularizing their countenances, displayed in newspapers, magazines, busses, trains and subways. This right of publicity would usually yield them no money unless it could be made the subject of an exclusive grant which barred any other advertiser from using their pictures."

The right of publicity evolved from the right to control the financial exploitation of one's image. It was first recognized by the Supreme Court in the case of Zacchini v. Scripps-Howard Broadcasting Co., 433 U.S. 562 (1977) a case involving a human cannonball whose act in its entirety was shown on a local television news show in violation of this right to control the showing of his act.

## O'BRIEN V. PABST SALES, CO.

In an earlier case before the right of publicity was recognized, O'Brien v. Pabst Sales, Co., 124 F. 2d 167 (5th Cir. 1941) David "Davey" O'Brien a college and NFL star sued the Pabst Sales Co. the makers of Pabst Blue Ribbon Beer for using his photo in a 1939 advertising calendar. He had never endorsed any beer and was actually active in a group urging teenagers not to drink alcoholic beverages. Unfortunately, he lost his case when the court ruled that if he did not object to the publicity he received in the sports pages of newspapers, the dominant form of media at the time, he could not object to the publicity he got from the calendar. In a view consistent with what the law would evolve into, the dissenting judge's opinion disagreed saying that athletes should have control over their image when used for commercial purposes.

## FANTASY SPORTS DATA

In 2005, the Major League Baseball's players' union sold their rights to Major League Baseball (MLB) to use players' names and data for all interactive media including most prominently, fantasy baseball. CBC Distribution and Marketing, Inc, which operated a fantasy baseball program refused to pay licensing fees arguing that using players' names and statistics did not infringe upon their right of publicity. The court ruled in favor of CBC indicating that there was no violation of intellectual property law because all of the information was readily available in the public domain and that baseball players were highly paid from salaries and endorsements. Having their statistics available would have little impact on them. C.B.C. Distribution & Marketing, Inc. v. Major League Baseball Advanced Media, L.P., 505 F. 3d 818 (8th Cir. 2007).

# ATHLETES RIGHTS VS. ARTISTS' RIGHTS

While an athlete has his or her right to publicity, artists have the right to use the athlete's image to create art and so these competing First Amendment interests must be balanced. The test used by the courts has been whether the art is transformative and uses the athlete's image to create something with new meaning, in which case the use of the image is allowed and is not a violation of the rights of the athlete. As a practical matter this standard can be difficult to interpret and leaves judges and juries in the role of art critics.

A major case dealing with the balancing of the publicity rights and other intellectual property rights of individual athletes with the right of artists to create new works using the images of particular athletes is ETW Corporation v. Jireh Publishing Inc. This case involved a challenge by golfer Tiger Woods through the company that handled his intellectual property against the artist Rick Rush who had created a work entitled "The Masters of Augusta" which commemorated Tiger Wood's record twelve stroke victory in the 1997 Masters tournament. In the painting, Woods is seen as joining a pantheon of golfing legends from the Masters including Arnold Palmer and Jack Nicklaus. The case dealt with the issues of trademark infringement and the right of publicity.

## ETW Corporation v. Jireh Publishing, Inc.

United States Court of Appeals, Sixth Circuit

332 F.3d 915 (2003)

### OPINION

Graham, District Judge.

Plaintiff-Appellant ETW Corporation ("ETW") is the licensing agent of Eldrick "Tiger" Woods ("Woods"), one of the world's most famous professional golfers. Woods, chairman of the board of ETW, has assigned to it the exclusive right to exploit his name, image, likeness, and signature, and all other publicity rights. ETW owns a United States trademark registration for the mark "TIGER WOODS" (Registration No. 2,194,381) for use in connection with "art prints, calendars, mounted photographs, notebooks, pencils, pens, posters, trading cards, and unmounted photographs."

Defendant-Appellee Jireh Publishing, Inc. ("Jireh") of Tuscaloosa, Alabama, is the publisher of artwork created by Rick Rush ("Rush"). Rush, who refers to himself as "America's sports artist," has created paintings of famous figures in sports and famous sports events. A few examples include Michael Jordan, Mark McGuire, Coach Paul "Bear" Bryant, the Pebble Beach Golf Tournament, and the America's Cup Yacht Race. Jireh has produced and successfully marketed limited edition art prints made from Rush's paintings.

In 1998, Rush created a painting entitled *The Masters of Augusta,* which commemorates Woods's victory at the Masters Tournament in Augusta, Georgia, in 1997. At that event, Woods became the youngest player ever to win the Masters Tournament, while setting a 72-hole record for the tournament and a record 12-stroke margin of victory. In the foreground of Rush's painting are three views of Woods in different poses. In the center, he is completing the swing of a golf club, and on each side he is crouching, lining up and/or observing the progress of a putt. To the left of Woods is his caddy, Mike "Fluff" Cowan, and to his right is his final round partner's caddy. Behind these figures is the Augusta National Clubhouse. In a blue background behind the clubhouse are likenesses of famous golfers of the past looking down on Woods. These include Arnold Palmer, Sam Snead, Ben Hogan, Walter Hagen, Bobby Jones, and Jack Nicklaus. Behind them is the Masters leader board.

The limited edition prints distributed by Jireh consist of an image of Rush's painting which includes Rush's signature at the bottom right hand corner. Beneath the image of the painting, in block letters, is its title, "The Masters Of Augusta." Beneath the title, in block letters of equal height, is the artist's name, "Rick Rush," and beneath the artist's name, in smaller upper and lower case letters, is the legend "Painting America Through Sports."

Here, ETW claims protection under the Lanham Act for any and all images of Tiger Woods. This is an untenable claim. ETW asks us, in effect, to constitute Woods himself as a walking, talking trademark. Images and likenesses of Woods are not protectable as a trademark because they do not perform the trademark function of designation. They do not distinguish and identify the source of goods. They cannot function as a trademark because there are undoubtedly thousands of images and likenesses of Woods taken by countless photographers, and drawn, sketched, or painted by numerous artists, which have been published in many forms of media, and sold and distributed throughout the world. No reasonable person could believe that merely because these photographs or paintings contain Woods's likeness or image, they all originated with Woods.

We hold that, as a general rule, a person's image or likeness cannot function as a trademark. Our conclusion is supported by the decisions of other courts which have addressed this issue. In *Pirone v. MacMillan, Inc.,* 894 F.2d 579 (2nd Cir.1990), the Second Circuit rejected a trademark claim asserted by the daughters of baseball legend Babe Ruth. The plaintiffs objected to the use of Ruth's likeness in three photographs which appeared in a calendar published by the defendant. The court rejected their claim, holding that "a photograph of a human being, unlike a portrait of a fanciful cartoon character, is not inherently 'distinctive' in the trademark sense of tending to indicate origin." *Id.* at 583. The court noted that Ruth "was one of the most photographed men of his generation, a larger than life hero to millions and an historical figure[.]" *Id.* The Second Circuit Court concluded that a consumer could not reasonably believe that Ruth sponsored the calendar:

[A]n ordinarily prudent purchaser would have no difficulty discerning that these photos are merely the subject matter of the calendar and do not in any way indicate sponsorship. No reasonable jury could find a likelihood of confusion.

*Id.* at 585. The court observed that "[u]nder some circumstances, a photograph of a person may be a valid trademark—if, for example, a particular photograph was consistently used on specific goods." *Id.* at 583. The court rejected plaintiffs' assertion of trademark rights in every photograph of Ruth.

Here, ETW does not claim that a particular photograph of Woods has been consistently used on specific goods. Instead, ETW's claim is identical to that of the plaintiffs in *Pirone,* a sweeping claim to trademark rights in every photograph and image of Woods. Woods, like Ruth, is one of the most photographed sports figures of his generation, but this alone does not suffice to create a trademark claim.

The district court properly granted summary judgment on ETW's claim of trademark rights in all images and likenesses of Tiger Woods.

E.   Application of the Law to the Evidence in this Case

The evidence in the record reveals that Rush's work consists of much more than a mere literal likeness of Woods. It is a panorama of Woods's victory at the 1997 Masters Tournament, with all of the trappings of that tournament in full view, including the Augusta clubhouse, the leader board, images of Woods's caddy, and his final round partner's caddy. These elements in themselves are sufficient to bring Rush's work within the protection of the First Amendment. The Masters Tournament is probably the world's most famous golf tournament and Woods's victory in the 1997 tournament was a historic event in the world of sports. A piece of art that portrays a historic sporting event communicates and celebrates the value our culture attaches to such events. It would be ironic indeed if the presence of the image of the victorious athlete would deny the work First Amendment protection. Furthermore, Rush's work includes not only images of Woods and the two caddies, but also carefully crafted likenesses of six past winners of the Masters Tournament: Arnold Palmer, Sam Snead, Ben Hogan, Walter Hagen, Bobby Jones, and Jack Nicklaus, a veritable pantheon of golf's greats. Rush's work conveys the message that Woods himself will someday join that revered group.

In regard to the Ohio law right of publicity claim, we conclude that Ohio would construe its right of publicity as suggested in the RESTATEMENT (THIRD) OF UNFAIR COMPETITION, Chapter 4, Section 47, Comment d., which articulates a rule analogous to the rule of fair use in copyright law. Under this rule, the substantiality and market effect of the use of the celebrity's image is analyzed in light of the informational and creative content of the defendant's use. Applying this rule, we conclude that Rush's work has substantial informational and creative content which outweighs any adverse effect on ETW's market and that Rush's work does not violate Woods's right of publicity.

We further find that Rush's work is expression which is entitled to the full protection of the First Amendment and not the more limited protection afforded to commercial speech. When we balance the magnitude of the speech restriction against the interest in protecting Woods's intellectual property right, we encounter precisely the same considerations weighed by the Tenth Circuit in *Cardtoons*. These include consideration of the fact that through their pervasive presence in the media, sports and entertainment celebrities have come to symbolize certain ideas and values in our society and have become a valuable means of expression in our culture. As the Tenth Circuit observed "[c]elebrities . . . are an important element of the shared communicative resources of our cultural domain." *Cardtoons,* 95 F.3d at 972.

In balancing these interests against Woods's right of publicity, we note that Woods, like most sports and entertainment celebrities with commercially valuable identities, engages in an activity, professional golf, that in itself generates a significant amount of income which is unrelated to his right of publicity. Even in the absence of his right of publicity, he would still be able to reap substantial financial rewards from authorized appearances and endorsements. It is not at all clear that the appearance of Woods's likeness in artwork prints which display one of his major achievements will reduce the commercial value of his likeness.

While the right of publicity allows celebrities like Woods to enjoy the fruits of their labors, here Rush has added a significant creative component of his own to Woods's identity. Permitting Woods's right of publicity to trump Rush's right of freedom of expression would extinguish Rush's right to profit from his creative enterprise.

After balancing the societal and personal interests embodied in the First Amendment against Woods's property rights, we conclude that the effect of limiting Woods's right of publicity in this case is negligible and significantly outweighed by society's interest in freedom of artistic expression.

Finally, applying the transformative effects test adopted by the Supreme Court of California in *Comedy III,* we find that Rush's work does contain significant transformative elements which make it especially worthy of First Amendment protection and also less likely to interfere with the economic interest protected by Woods' right of publicity. Unlike the unadorned, nearly photographic reproduction of the faces of The Three Stooges in *Comedy III,* Rush's work does not capitalize solely on a literal depiction of Woods. Rather, Rush's work consists of a collage of images in addition to Woods's image which are combined to describe, in artistic form, a historic event in sports history and to convey a message about the significance of Woods's achievement in that event. Because Rush's work has substantial transformative elements, it is entitled to the full protection of the First Amendment. In this case, we find that Woods's right of publicity must yield to the First Amendment.

---

## QUESTIONS

1.   What is or should be the definition of transformative art?

2.   Can commercial speech qualify as transformative art?

# UNIVERSITY OF ALABAMA V. NEW LIFE ART, INC.

A later landmark case dealing with similar intellectual property issues is the case of University of Alabama vs. New Life Art, Inc.

Daniel Moore is an artist who specializes in sports art. One of his most famous works is a painting entitled "The Sack" which shows University of Alabama quarterback Steve Beurlein being tackled by Notre Dame defensive player Cornelius Bennett in 1986. The painting was reproduced not just in prints, but on coffee cups, calendars and other merchandise. The University of Alabama objected to Moore's commercialization of what they referred to as the University's "famous crimson and white color scheme" in violation of their intellectual property rights.

The case balanced the interests of a trademark owner against the right of free speech of artists to be able to comment on the trademark. Generally, this and similar cases revolve around whether consumers are likely to be confused as to who is producing the particular work and whether artists add something meaningful to the work that makes it transformative in nature by infusing it with a new meaning as was the central issue in Tiger Woods' lawsuit against the artist Rick Rush.

Moore had been painting famous scenes from Alabama football for almost twenty years when he was first told in 2000 by the University to stop using their trademarks. In 2005, after five years of failed negotiations, the University filed a lawsuit against Moore to prohibit him from using Alabama's trademarked colors and logos.

In 2009 a federal court judge ruled in Moore's favor that he did not need a license from the University of Alabama to do paintings depicting scenes of University of Alabama football games. In his decision, the judge wrote, "The court concludes that the depiction of the uniforms in the paintings is incidental to the purpose and expression of the paintings; that is, to artistically depict and preserve notable football plays in the history of University of Alabama football."[5]

On appeal, the University of Alabama argued that Moore's paintings were actually too realistic and did not transform the original scenes sufficiently to qualify as artistic expression that would be protected by the First Amendment, however, the appeals court disagreed, indicating that the very reality of the paintings was necessary to describe what was being shown and that it added to the artistry.

## UNIVERSITY OF ALABAMA BOARD OF TRUSTEES V. NEW LIFE ART, INC.

United States Court of Appeals, Eleventh Circuit
683 F.3d 1266 (2012)

Before MARTIN and ANDERSON, CIRCUIT JUDGES, and SCHLESINGER, DISTRICT JUDGE.

ANDERSON, CIRCUIT JUDGE.

Since 1979, Daniel A. Moore has painted famous football scenes involving the University of Alabama (the "University" or "Alabama"). The paintings feature realistic portrayals of the University's uniforms, including helmets, jerseys, and crimson and white colors. Moore has reproduced his paintings as prints and calendars, as well as on mugs and other articles.

---

5    *Univ. of Alabama Board of Trustees v. New Life Art Inc.*, CV 05–UNAS–PT–585–W (N.D. Ala. Nov. 2, 2009).

In 2002, the University told Moore that he would need permission to depict the University's uniforms because they are trademarks. Moore contended that he did not need permission because the uniforms were being used to realistically portray historical events. The parties could not reach a resolution, and in March 2005, the University sued Moore in the Northern District of Alabama for breach of contract, trademark infringement, and unfair competition.

## I. FACTS

From 1979 to 1990, Moore painted historical Alabama football scenes without any kind of formal or informal relationship with the University. From 1991 to 1999, Moore signed a dozen licensing agreements with the University to produce and market specific items, which would often include additional Alabama trademarks on the border or packaging, or would come with a certificate or stamp saying they were officially licensed products.

From 1991 to 2002, Moore produced other Alabama-related paintings and prints that were not the subject of any licensing agreements. He also continued to sell paintings and prints of images that had originally been issued before 1991. He did not pay royalties for any of these items, nor did the University request that he do so. Moore said that he would enter into a licensing agreement if he felt that it would help increase the sales of that particular product, or if he wanted the University—his alma mater—to benefit from royalties.

During this time, the University issued Moore press credentials so he could obtain material for his work. The University also asked Moore to produce an unlicensed painting on live television during a football game.

However, in January 2002, the University told Moore that he would need to license all of his Alabama-related products because they featured the University's trademarks. In particular, the University asserted that Moore needed permission to portray the University's uniforms, including the jersey and helmet designs and the crimson and white colors.

Moore contended that he did not need permission to paint historical events and that there was no trademark violation so long as he did not use any of the University's trademarks outside of the "image area" of the painting (i.e., outside the original painting). Despite this disagreement, the University still sold Moore's unlicensed calendars in its campus stores for several years. It also displayed unlicensed paintings at its Bryant Museum and athletic department office.

## B.  Trademark Claims

Because we find that the licensing agreements were not intended to prohibit Moore's depiction of the University's uniforms in unlicensed paintings, prints, or calendars, we proceed to address the University's trademark claims with respect to these items. The University's claim is that Moore's unlicensed paintings, prints, and calendars infringe on the University's trademarks because the inclusion in these products of the University's football uniforms (showing the University's crimson and white colors) creates a likelihood of confusion on the part of buyers that the University sponsored or endorsed the product.

The University argues that its uniforms are "strong" trademarks and that its survey provides strong evidence of confusion sufficient to establish a likelihood of confusion to sustain a Lanham Act violation by Moore. See 15 U.S.C. § 1125(a); Two Pesos, Inc. v. Taco Cabana, Inc., 505 U.S. 763, 769, 112 S. Ct. 2753, 2758 (1992). Contrary to the University's argument, the district court concluded there was a "weak mark and [merely] some likelihood of confusion." And contrary to the University's argument that its trademarks triggered the sales of Moore's products, the district court concluded with respect to the paintings and prints that "the plays and Moore's reputation established during a period when his art was agreeably not licensed are what predominantly trigger the sales." Similarly, with respect to the University's survey upon which the University relies to support likelihood of confusion, the district court concluded "that the survey lacks strength because of its manner of taking, the form of the questions, the nature of the surveyed customers, and the number of responders. It involved only one print. The questions are loaded with suggestions that there is a 'sponsor' other than the artist." We note that Moore's signature was prominent on the paintings, prints, and calendars, clearly telegraphing that he was the artist who created the work of art. We also note that the one print used in the survey was in fact specifically licensed, and thus had an actual, historical sponsorship association with the University. Although we are in basic agreement with the district court's evaluation of the mark and the degree of confusion as to the source and sponsorship of the paintings, prints, and calendars, we need not in this case settle upon a precise evaluation of the strength of the mark or the degree of likelihood of confusion. As our discussion below indicates, we conclude that the First Amendment interests in artistic expression so clearly outweigh whatever consumer confusion that might exist on these facts that we must necessarily conclude that there has been no violation of the Lanham Act with respect to the paintings, prints, and calendars.

The First Amendment's protections extend beyond written and spoken words. "[P]ictures, films, paintings, drawings, and engravings . . . have First Amendment protection[.]" Kaplan v. California, 413 U.S. 115, 119–20, 93 S. Ct. 2680, 2684 (1973); see also Hurley v. Irish-Am. Gay, Lesbian & Bisexual Grp. of Bos., 515 U.S. 557, 569, 115 S. Ct. 2338, 2345 (1995) ("[T]he Constitution looks beyond written or spoken words as mediums of expression.").

The University argues that Moore's paintings, prints, and calendars "are more commercial than expressive speech and, therefore, entitled to a lower degree" of First Amendment protection. See Cent. Hudson Gas & Elec. Corp. v. Pub. Serv. Comm'n of N.Y., 447 U.S. 557, 562–63, 100 S. Ct. 2343, 2350 (1980) ("The Constitution . . . accords a lesser protection to commercial speech than to other constitutionally guaranteed expression."). However, these items certainly do more than "propos[e] a commercial transaction." Id. at 562, 100 S. Ct. at 2349. Naturally, Moore sells these items for money, but it "is of course no matter that the dissemination [of speech] takes place under commercial auspices." Smith v. California, 361 U.S. 147, 150, 80 S. Ct. 215, 217 (1959). Like other expressive speech, Moore's paintings, prints, and calendars are entitled to full protection under the First Amendment. Accord ETW Corp. v. Jireh Pub., Inc., 332 F.3d 915, 925 (6th Cir. 2003).

Thus, we must decide whether Moore's First Amendment rights will give way to the University's trademark rights. We are not the first circuit to confront this issue. In 1989, the Second Circuit decided Rogers v. Grimaldi, 875 F.2d 994 (2d Cir. 1989), which is the landmark case for balancing trademark and First Amendment rights. In Rogers, the defendant created a film about two fictional Italian dancers who were called "Ginger and Fred," which was the film's title. Id. at 996–97. Ginger Rogers, a famous dancer who often worked with Fred Astaire, sued under § 43(a) of the Lanham Act, 15 U.S.C. § 1125(a), arguing that the film's title falsely implied that she was endorsing or featured in the film. Rogers, 875 F.2d at 997.

The court noted that the purchaser of artistic works, "like the purchaser of a can of peas, has a right not to be misled as to the source of the product." Id. at 997–98. However, the court concluded that the Lanham Act should be read narrowly to avoid impinging on speech protected by the First Amendment. Id. at 998–1000. Thus, the court adopted a balancing test:

We believe that in general the Act should be construed to apply to artistic works only where the public interest in avoiding consumer confusion outweighs the public interest in free expression. In the context of allegedly misleading titles using a celebrity's name, that balance will normally not support application of the Act unless the title has no artistic relevance to the underlying work whatsoever, or if it has some artistic relevance, unless the title explicitly misleads as to the source of the work.

Under the facts of Rogers, the court concluded that "the slight risk that such use of a celebrity's name might implicitly suggest endorsement or sponsorship to some people is outweighed by the danger of restricting artistic expression." Id. at 1000. Accordingly, the court ruled in favor of the movie's producers because the title was artistically relevant to the film, there had been no evidence of explicit misleading as to source, and the risk of confusion was "so outweighed by the interests in artistic expression as to preclude application of the Lanham Act." Id. at 1001.

Circuit courts have also applied Rogers in cases where trademark law is being used to attack the content—as opposed to the title—of works protected by the First Amendment. In Cliffs Notes, Inc. v. Bantam Doubleday Dell Publishing Group, 886 F.2d 490 (2d Cir. 1989), the defendant published humorous versions of "Cliffs Notes" study books and had imitated the plaintiff's trademarked black and yellow covers. Id. at 492. The court held that the Rogers test was "generally applicable to Lanham Act claims against works of artistic expression" and found that the parody books were protected by the First Amendment because the defendant had not explicitly misled consumers as to the source or content of the books. Id. at 495–96.

In ESS Entertainment 2000, Inc. v. Rock Star Videos, Inc., 547 F.3d 1095 (9th Cir. 2008), a scene in the defendant's video game featured the trademark of the plaintiff's entertainment club located in Los Angeles. Id. at 1096–98. The Ninth Circuit held that there "is no principled reason why [Rogers] ought not also apply to the use of a trademark in the body of the work." Id. at 1099. The court found that the defendant's use of the trademark did not explicitly mislead as to the source or content of the video game, and thus the First Amendment protected the defendant's use of the plaintiff's trademark. Id. at 1099–101.

In the case perhaps most similar to the one sub judice, the Sixth Circuit addressed a claim of false endorsement under the Lanham Act where an artist had painted a collage of Tiger Woods images. ETW Corp. v. Jireh Publ'g, Inc., 332 F.3d 915, 918–19 (6th Cir. 2003). Woods's publicity company sued the artist, and the court applied the Rogers balancing test and found that Woods's image on the painting had artistic relevance to the underlying work and did not explicitly mislead as to the source of the work. Id. at 936–37. As a result, the painting was protected by the First Amendment against a claim of false endorsement. Id. at 937.

The University contends that none of those cases are analogous to our current set of facts. It argues that Cliffs Notes and ESS Entertainment are not applicable because those cases involved parody, whereas Moore's paintings do not. However, neither Rogers nor ETW dealt with parody, yet the courts in those cases still read the Lanham Act narrowly to avoid First Amendment concerns. See Rogers, 875 F.2d at 999–1000; ETW, 332 F.3d at 937. Additionally, courts adopting Rogers have noted that it is "generally applicable to works of artistic expression," not just parodies. Cliffs Notes, 886 F.2d at 495; see also ESS Entm't, 547 F.3d at 1099 ("artistic works"); ETW, 332 F.3d at 937 ("artistic works").

The University responds by saying that we should not consider Rogers or ETW because those cases dealt with rights of publicity, which the University contends are much weaker than trademark rights. However, Rogers and ETW both dealt also with Lanham Act false endorsement claims, and we have never treated false endorsement and trademark infringement claims as distinct under the Lanham Act. See Tana v. Dantanna's, 611 F.3d 767, 777 n.9 (11th Cir. 2010) ("[W]e have . . . never recognized a separate claim of false endorsement, distinct from trademark infringement under § 43(a) . . . ."); see also Landham v. Lewis Galoob Toys, Inc., 227 F.3d 619, 626 (6th Cir. 2000) ("A false designation of origin claim . . . under § 43(a) of the Lanham Act . . . is equivalent to a false association or endorsement claim . . . .").

Therefore, we have no hesitation in joining our sister circuits by holding that we should construe the Lanham Act narrowly when deciding whether an artistically expressive work infringes a trademark. This requires that we carefully "weigh the public interest in free expression against the public interest in avoiding consumer confusion." Cliffs Notes, 886 F.2d at 494. An artistically expressive use of a trademark will not violate the Lanham Act "unless the use of the mark has no artistic relevance to the underlying work whatsoever, or, if it has some artistic relevance, unless it explicitly misleads as to the source or the content of the work." ESS Entm't, 547 F.3d at 1099 (quotations and alterations omitted); see also Rogers, 875 F.2d at 999.

In this case, we readily conclude that Moore's paintings, prints, and calendars are protected under the Rogers test. The depiction of the University's uniforms in the content of these items is artistically relevant to the expressive underlying works because the uniforms' colors and designs are needed for a realistic portrayal of famous scenes from Alabama football history. Also there is no evidence that Moore ever marketed an unlicensed item as "endorsed" or "sponsored" by the University, or otherwise explicitly stated that such items were affiliated with the University. Moore's paintings, prints, and calendars very clearly are embodiments of artistic expression, and are entitled to full First Amendment protection. The extent of his use of the University's trademarks is their mere inclusion (their necessary inclusion) in the body of the image which Moore creates to memorialize and enhance a particular play or event in the University's football history. Even if "some members of the public would draw the incorrect inference that [the University] had some involvement with [Moore's paintings, prints, and calendars,] . . . that risk of misunderstanding, not engendered by any overt [or in this case even implicit] claim . . . is so outweighed by the interest in artistic expression as to preclude" any violation of the Lanham Act. Rogers, 875 F.2d at 1001.

Because Moore's depiction of the University's uniforms in the content of his paintings, prints, and calendars results in no violation of the Lanham Act, we affirm the district court with respect to paintings and prints, and reverse with respect to calendars.

## IV. CONCLUSION

As evidenced by the parties' course of conduct, Moore's depiction of the University's uniforms in his unlicensed paintings, prints, and calendars is not prohibited by the prior licensing agreements. Additionally, the paintings, prints, and calendars do not violate the Lanham Act because these artistically expressive objects are protected by the First Amendment, by virtue of our application of the Rogers balancing test. The uniforms in these works of art are artistically relevant to the underlying works, Moore never explicitly misled consumers as to the source of the items, and the interests in artistic expression outweigh the risk of confusion as to endorsement. Accordingly, we affirm the judgment of the district court with respect to the paintings and prints, and reverse with respect to the prints as replicated on calendars.

---

**QUESTIONS**

1.   What are the reasons in favor of and against being able to trademark color schemes as was done by the University of Alabama?

2.   How should transformative art be defined?

# SYNOPSIS

1.   Catch phrases associated with particular athletes have been trademarked.

2.   The NCAA has taken action to discourage the use of Native American names as mascots for college teams.

3.   Athletes have a right of publicity in their names.

4.   An athlete's right of publicity in his own image does not extend to preventing an artist from creating "transformative art" using that image.

5.   An athlete's distinctive "moves" might be able to be copyrighted as choreography.

# CHAPTER ELEVEN

# Drugs and Sports

## HISTORY

The use of performance enhancing drugs is as old as athletic competition itself. Athletes in ancient Greece took mushrooms they thought would increase their athletic prowess. Competitors in the original Olympic Games ate sheep testicles in an effort to increase their testosterone.

The term doping comes from the Dutch word "dop" which was the name of an alcoholic beverage made of grape skins that was used by South African Zulu warriors to enhance their strength.

In the early 20th century Styrchnine, hashish, cola plants, cocaine, alcohol and a wide range of other substances that were thought to have performance enhancing qualities were used by athletes.

Thomas Hicks, a marathon runner at the 1904 Summer Olympic Games in St. Louis took multiple doses of strychnine mixed with brandy. He won the race, collapsing at the finish line. Interestingly, in a foreshadowing of the infamous 1980 Boston Marathon race in which women's winner Rosie Ruiz was found to have cheated by taking the subway for part of the race, in the 1904 marathon, Hicks was actually beaten in the race by Fred Lorz, who was quickly disqualified when it was discovered that he had ridden in a car for 11 miles of the 26 mile race and probably would have ridden further had the car in which he was riding not broken down at mile 20.

The use of performance enhancing drugs was neither a major public concern nor a major concern of the organizations regulating athletics until the latter part of the 20th century. Although the International Amateur Athletic Federation (IAFF) first attempted to ban doping in 1928 and other international organizations followed suit, the bans had little effect because of the lack of tests for performance enhancing drugs. It wasn't until the death of a Danish Olympic cyclic competitor, Knut Jensen at the 1960 Rome Olympics that the discussion of the use in sports of performance enhancing drugs and possible harm caused by these substances began in earnest. An autopsy of Jensen found the presence of amphetamines in his body. The death of British cyclist Tom Simpson in the 1967 Tour de France whose death was viewed on television brought even greater attention to the problems of performance enhancing drugs in sports in general and specifically in cycling. Three tubes of amphetamines were found in Simpson's jersey at the time of his death.

The International Olympic Committee's Medical Commission started testing for performance enhancing drugs and instituted a program to educate athletes as to the dangers inherent in the taking of such substances. The 1968 Mexico City Olympics were the first to require drug testing in each event and the first to disqualify an athlete, Hans-Gunnar Liljenvall, a Swedish pentathlete who was stripped of his Bronze medal for of all things, alcohol, which although a banned substance could hardly have been considered a performance enhancing drug.

In 1967 the IOC Medical Commission issued the first extensive list of banned substances. The 1972 Olympics in Munich were the first Olympics to include comprehensive testing at an international sporting competition of all participating athletes rather than limiting the number of athletes tested in each event. However, it was not until the 1976 Montreal Olympics that anabolic steroids were added to the banned substances list. The delay was related to there finally being a dependable test for determining the presence of anabolic steroids. Of the eleven athletes disqualified for drug use in the 1976 Olympics, eight of them were for the use of steroids. It was not until 1988, that the sale of steroids for non-medical use was made illegal in the United States.

The tests for steroids at that time were not terribly sophisticated and the East German Olympic team in particular was able to evade detection of the steroids administered to their male and female athletes through a state sponsored and administered program. In particular, the East German women's swim team dominated the 1976 Montreal Olympics with women who appeared to show many of the physical side effects of steroid use such as facial hair and lower voices.

One of the greatest Olympic swimmers of all time was American Shirley Babashoff who was the fastest clean swimmer in the world at the time of the 1976 Montreal Olympic Games in which she won four silver medals in individual events, losing in each instance to a later disgraced East German steroid taking swimmer. The East German women's swimmers won eleven of the thirteen swimming events after failing to win a single gold medal just four years earlier. While American swimmer Mark Spitz parlayed his seven gold medals and seven world records from the 1972 Munich Olympics into a lucrative career of endorsements and public speaking, Shirley Babashoff who openly complained of perceived cheating by the East Germans, but was considered a poor sport, ended up living on unemployment compensation and then her job as a mail carrier.

In one of the most famous Olympic steroid disqualifications of all time, Canadian sprinter Ben Johnson was stripped of his gold medal in the 1988 Seoul, South Korea Olympic one hundred meter dash with the gold medal being awarded instead to American sprinter Carl Lewis who had finished second to Johnson in the race. Johnson tested positive for the banned steroid Stanozolol.

The International Olympic Committee formed the World Anti-Doping Agency (WADA) in 1999 to centralize the anti-doping movement in international sports.

In the 2008 Beijing Olympics four competitors flunked drug tests, but only three of them were human. One was a horse.

None of the participants in the 1980 Moscow Olympics were found to have used performance enhancing drugs at the time, however, years later, retests on preserved urine samples found numerous violations. Urine samples are routinely preserved for later testing using newer techniques to catch violations that had previously gone undetected.

The next step in the battle against performance enhancing drugs came when the IOC Medical Commission began banning substances that were not in and of themselves performance enhancing drugs, but rather were substances that would render the use of other performance enhancing drugs undetectable under then used tests. These drugs are referred to as masking agents.

Major League Baseball has had a long history of drug use with a number of notorious performance enhancing drug users, such as Mark McGwire. In 1991, Commissioner Fay Vincent sent a memorandum to both the players union and all of the team owners indicating that possession, sale or use of any illegal drugs were banned by Major League Baseball. However, this ban had no real strength since terms for testing of players had not been agreed upon in a collective bargaining agreement at that time.

Under pressure from the public, as a part of the 2002 collective bargaining agreement, the players agreed to a program by which the players would submit to anonymous drug testing. Only if positive results exceeded 5% of the total players taking the test would a punitive anti-drug program be agreed to by the players' union. The results showed between 5% and 7% of the tests were positive for banned substances. It was generally thought that the true results would have been even higher and that the number of players who were caught understated the number of players actually using the banned substances because the tests were given during the off season providing the players taking banned substances such as steroids with ample time to stop taking the drugs and have evidence of their use no longer present in their systems.

The Bay Area Laboratory Co-Operative, better known by the acronym BALCO provided legal supplements to a myriad of athletes, but also produced and provided its own steroids including the infamous "cream" used by Barry Bonds. In 2003 law enforcement investigators found in the records of BALCO not merely information about its development of steroids that could avoid detection under then currently used tests, but also the list of its customers using such substances including Barry Bonds, Jason Giambi and track and field champion Marion Jones.

In 2005, under public and governmental pressure the MLB Commissioner hired former Senator George Mitchell to head an investigation into performance enhancing drugs in baseball. Following a twenty-one month investigation, Mitchell issued his report which included the names of offending players such as Roger Clemens and Andy Pettitte.

Tony Bosch the founder of the Florida based Biogenesis of America clinic where he falsely represented that he was a licensed physician while he provided performance enhancing drugs to a large number of Major League Baseball players including, most notably, Alex Rodriguez was sued civilly by Major League baseball in addition to facing criminal charges. Bosch who had initially vigorously denied all charges both agreed to cooperate with Major League Baseball in its investigation and plead guilty to conspiring to distribute testosterone. Bosch, who was initially sentenced to four years in prison in 2014 had his sentence reduced by 16 months in return for his extensive cooperation with federal prosecutors.

# ANABOLIC STEROIDS

Anabolic (muscle building) steroids are synthetic versions of the male hormone testosterone. They can be taken as pills, a cream, a gel or by injections. The drugs themselves are not illegal and are prescribed by physicians for patients with low testosterone levels. In addition AIDS patients suffering from weight loss and muscle deterioration have been prescribed steroids as have been burn victims due to the ability of steroids to speed up healing. Even asthma inhalers are a version of steroids. However, like nearly all medications they come with side effects, which for steroids may include acne, hair growth and possible increase in cholesterol and high blood pressure. Although abuse of steroids taken in excessive amounts and not under a doctor's supervision can be dangerous, there has been much unsupported hysteria demonizing steroids such as occurred following the death of NFL defensive lineman Lyle Alzado who died of brain tumors that Alzado blamed on his long term use of steroids. There is no scientific support, however, for any connection between steroid abuse and brain cancer.

## HOW STEROIDS WORK

In and of themselves steroids will not increase muscle mass or stamina, however athletes using these substances are able to train harder and recover faster due to the ability of these substances to improve muscle growth and repair which is why they are prescribed to burn victims.

Athletic training consists of heavy exercise that actually breaks down muscle. It is in the resting recovery phase that muscles adapt and grow back stronger and with more stamina. The use of anabolic steroids does not create muscle or stamina merely by taking the drugs; however, what they do is permit the athlete to recover significantly faster following intense athletic training and competition thereby allowing the athlete to achieve a greater level of performance in a shorter time. Particularly at the Olympic Games where the athletes may intensely compete in a relatively short period of days, steroids enabled athletes to maintain a higher level of fitness despite the stress of intense competition.

# HUMAN GROWTH HORMONE

Human Growth Hormone (HGH) is naturally produced by the human pituitary gland and aids and stimulates cell growth and healing. As people age, the amount of HGH that the body produces decreases. Many older Americans take HGH both legally and illegally to achieve a more youthful body. Although some studies have found HGH to have an anabolic effect, other studies have found no such effect. In any event, HGH is banned by the NCAA, WADA and all of the professional sports leagues.

# PURPOSE OF DRUG POLICIES

Although performance enhancing drugs have been uniformly banned by sports governing organizations and professional sports leagues, the justification has not been particularly clear. The standard for determining whether or not to ban a specific substance may be based upon the legitimate standard of whether the substance is determined to threaten the health of the athlete or the more amorphous standard of whether use of the substance is deemed to be against the spirit of sport, whatever that may mean. Sometimes the justification is stated as being done for the integrity of the sport without indicating why a particular substance is considered a performance enhancing drug and thereby detrimental to the integrity of the sport while a supplement or a medical procedure such as an eye operation is permissible and not considered to negatively affect the integrity of the sport.

Many athletes, most notably, NBA star LeBron James and PGA star Tiger Woods had Lasik eye surgery that improved their vision.

Ulnar collateral ligament reconstruction, commonly described as Tommy John surgery after an early user of this surgery involves the removal of a tendon from one part of the body and the transplanting of it into the elbow thereby enabling, a pitcher unable to pitch due to a ligament injury to pitch again. In fact, a number of baseball pitchers have found that they were able to throw harder and faster following the surgery than they were able to do previously before their injuries.

A basic question that hardly appears to be asked is the reason for having anti-doping rules and the inconsistencies in allowing certain performance enhancing substances and procedures while banning others. The World Anti-Doping Association (WADA) avoids this question by merely defining doping as the presence of a prohibited substance in the athlete's body. Whether the substance actually increased the athlete's performance or even whether the athlete actually intended to take such a substance is irrelevant in determining whether or not the anti-doping rules have been violated. Vitamins are not banned, yet in excessive amounts can cause serious negative side effects. Creatine is an allowed supplement that is purported to enhance muscle growth. A standard for determining why a particular substance is banned or allowed has never been established.

# SLEEP SUPPLEMENTS

Every little edge is to be exploited toward athletic success and with major professional sports teams playing long seasons with large amounts of travel in which the players need to adjust to different time zones, the restorative element of sleep is of primary concern. The San Jose Sharks of the NHL worked with Cheri Mah a researcher at the University of California, San Francisco to arrive at sleep protocols that include chamomile, lavender and tart cherry juice while also utilizing zinc, magnesium and other legal supplements as a way of steering clear of prescription sleep aids such as Ambien that may have significant drawbacks particularly when used extensively. According to Mah, better quality and quantity of sleep improved speed, stamina strength and naturally raised levels of testosterone. Yet the question still remains, what is it that distinguishes an illegal performance enhancing drug from a permitted supplement?

# ARGUMENTS AGAINST PERFORMANCE ENHANCING DRUGS

Potential physical or mental harm to the athlete posed by performance enhancing drugs are also given as reasons for banning their use although, in the past, the dangers of specific performance enhancing drugs, particularly anabolic steroids that might be given under a physician's supervision have been significantly exaggerated. Blood doping by which an athlete merely receives a transfusion of his or her own blood carries little risk of adverse side effects. In addition, there is the question of just as smokers have the right to make choices as to what they do that may affect their health, whether athletes should be able to choose to take performance enhancing drugs. This argument is strengthened when you consider that the detrimental health effects of steroid use could be significantly reduced if the use of such drugs, which are prescribed by physicians for a range of patients, were to be regulated and monitored. The use of performance enhancing drugs under a physician's supervision would be safer and discourage resorting to black market dealers where quality control is non-existent and the temptation to over use the drugs is greater.

The Draconian nature of the response of various sports governing bodies to violations of performance enhancing drug policies is typified by the case of Zach Lund, an American skeleton racer who was banned for a year from participating in international competitions preventing him from being able to compete in the 2006 Winter Olympic Games in Torino, Italy due to the fact that he tested positive for Finasteride, a drug found in Propecia, a common hair growth product. Although he had been using Propecia for seven years without it being a problem for anti-doping authorities, Finasteride was added to the list or prohibited substances in 2005 not for its ergogenic capabilities, but rather because it was determined to be a masking agent for anabolic steroid use. Although on appeal, the Court of Arbitration determined that Lund did not intentionally take the drug to mask steroid use, his one year suspension from competition was still upheld.

What is the purpose of the banning of excessive alcohol use? Alcohol is generally not considered a substance that will increase athletic performance. Irish swimmer, Michelle Smith won three gold medals and a bronze medal in the Atlanta Olympics, but was banned from international competition for four years for having a high level of whiskey in a urine test. There was significant suspicion that Michelle Smith had been using performance enhancing drugs although she passed all of her drug tests at the 1996 Atlanta games. However, two years later, an unannounced drug test provided a urine sample that appeared to be contaminated with a high level of whiskey whereupon she was banned from international competition for four years. Her use of alcohol was believed to have been to mask the use of performance enhancing drugs. Suspicions had arisen regarding Smith because as recently as three years before the Atlanta Olympics she was not ranked within the top 25 swimmers in any stroke. In addition, her Olympic medals were won at the old age for a swimmer of 26 when instead of regressing; she managed to knock off an astounding 21 seconds from her best time in the 400 meter medley during her gold medal performance. Suspicion was increased because in the two years prior to the Atlanta Olympics she moved to Holland to be with her future husband Eric de Bruin, a Dutch discus thrower who was serving a four year suspension for the use of performance enhancing drugs.

# UNINTENTIONAL VIOLATIONS

American swimmer Rick DeMont was stripped of his gold medal in the 1972 Olympics because his asthma medication contained the banned substance Ephedrine. Did it enhance his performance? Probably not. Should it be relevant that he took the substance for a medically required reason?

Kansas City Royal's minor league infielder Raul A. Mondesi was suspended in May of 2016 for fifty games following a positive test for the banned substance Clenbuterol. His original suspension of eighty games, the standard penalty for first time offenders was reduced to fifty games by an arbitration panel that determined that Mondesi had not intentionally taken the Clenbuterol as a performance enhancing drug, but rather had taken an over the counter cold and flu medication in the Dominican Republic that contained the substance without checking with his team trainer. Due to the fact that many legitimately available over the counter medicines and supplements contain banned substances, athletes are advised to always read the labels and check with their trainers before taking anything. Clenbuterol, while routinely used as a decongestant and a treatment for asthma is also used to increase aerobic capacity and is thereby a banned substance.

# RECREATIONAL DRUGS

Should recreational drugs such as cocaine or marijuana be banned?

While all sports at the amateur and professional level ban certain performance enhancing drugs, recreational drugs are also banned. Marijuana is a banned substance by the NCAA and all of the professional sports leagues despite the fact that it is legalized in a number of states both for medicinal and recreational purposes. Many NFL players have argued that marijuana is more effective a pain killer with fewer side effects than the prescription pain killers often provided to them.

American judo competitor Olympian Nicholas Delpopolo was sent home from the 2012 London Olympic Games following a drug test showing the presence of marijuana that he attributed to unknowingly eating food with marijuana baked into it.

## QUESTIONS

1.   What is the reason for the banning of recreational drugs by the NCAA and professional sports leagues?

2.   What is the justification behind permitting body altering surgery, such as Tommy John surgery or Lasik eye surgery, but outlawing the use of performance enhancing drugs that are otherwise legal?

3.   Why are certain supplements such as Creatine permitted to be used, but other substances deemed to be impermissible performance enhancing drugs?

4.   Are the rules against anabolic steroids warranted?

5.   Are these drugs inherently dangerous and unhealthy? If so, why are they routinely given to burn victims?

# PRESENT DAY DRUG USE

What is old can become new again. In 2016, MLB players Daniel Stumpf of the Phillies and Chris Colabello of the Blue Jays were suspended for using the steroid Turinabol, an older generation steroid developed in the 1960s by the East German pharmaceutical company Jenapharm. This anabolic steroid was used extensively by East German athletes during that country's run as an Olympic power in the 1970s and 1980s during which time it was administered to young athletes who at times did not even know they were taking a performance enhancing drug and were told that the pills they took were merely vitamins.

Turinabol is now available online and has even turned up as a labeled and unlabeled ingredient in supplements sold by legitimate supplement dealers, which leads to the problem of some athletes unknowingly taking the drug.

While Turinabol, like all anabolic steroids enables an athlete to recover faster and build muscle following intense workouts, it is relatively easily detected by newly developed tests which have led to an increase in the number of positive tests.

# OLYMPIC DRUG POLICY

The Olympics have been a hotbed for performance enhancing drug cheating. The Olympic standards for punishment are among the strongest in all of sport. Olympic athletes may be tested randomly any time of day, any day of the year. An athlete testing positive for a banned substance is banned for two years from all Olympic competitions and a second offense results in a permanent lifelong ban from Olympic competition.

Drug testing is done most commonly through a urine sample although blood samples are also taken now for testing of HGH. Samples are contained in two bottles, designated Sample A and Sample B. The bottles do not carry the name of the athlete on the bottle, but rather contain a bar code or serial number in order to make the test totally anonymous. Sample A is tested and only if the test is positive is the second bottle tested to confirm the results. Only if both samples test positive for a banned substance is the athlete disqualified.

A new technique for drug detection is the biological passport where baseline blood samples are used to track changes such as changes in red blood counts to determine if illegal drugs were used without ever finding evidence of the use of a specific banned substance.

The executive summary of the May 18, 2012 report to the WADA Executive Committee on the Lack of Effectiveness of Testing Programs outlined the problems encountered in enforcing an effective drug policy:

"To date, testing has not proven to be particularly effective in detecting dopers/cheats. The primary reason for the apparent lack of success of the testing programs does not lie with the science involved. While there may well be some drugs or combinations of drugs and methods of which the anti-doping community is unaware, the science now available is both robust and reliable. The real problems are the human and political factors. There is no general appetite to undertake the effort and expense of a successful effort to deliver doping-free sport. This applies (with varying degrees) at the level of athletes, international sport organizations, national Olympic committees, NADOs and governments. It is reflected in low standards of compliance measurement (often postponed), unwillingness to undertake critical analysis of the necessary requirements, unwillingness to follow-up on suspicions and information, unwillingness to share available information and unwillingness to commit the necessary informed intelligence, effective actions and other resources to the fight against doping in sport."[1]

# WEIGHT LIFTING

A sport such as weight lifting in which pure power is the most essential element of the sport would seem to be a prime candidate for problems with abuse of anabolic steroids.

Prior to the 2016 Summer Olympic Games in Rio, individual weight lifters from ten countries, Azerbaijan, Armenia, Cyprus, Kazakhstan, Moldova, North Korea, Romania, Turkey, Ukraine and Uzbekistan were banned from participating in the 2016 Rio Summer Olympic Games while the entire teams of Russia and Bulgaria were also prohibited from participating in the games when the International Weightlifting Federation Executive Board ruled that National Federations confirmed to have produced three or more anti-doping rule violations from the reanalyzed tests from the 2008 and 2012 games were suspended for a year from international competition.

In addition, at the 2015 world weight lifting championships twenty four athletes failed drug tests. Making the problem even worse was the fact that when urine tests of athletes who had passed drug tests from the 2008 Beijing Olympics and 2012 London Olympics were retested using more up to date procedures 20 more drug samples

---

[1]   Report to WAD Executive Committee on "Lack of Effectiveness of Testing Programs" prepared by Working Group Established Following Foundation Board Meeting of 18 May 2012.

showed the presence of performance enhancing drugs. Included among these failing the drug tests were three Chinese gold medal winning weight lifters from the 2008 Beijing Olympics., Cao Lei, Chen Xiexia and Liu Chun as well as Ilya Ilyin of Kazakhstan who won the gold medal in both 2008 and 2012. All in all, forty-eight weight lifters from the 2008 and 2012 Olympic Games tested positive for banned substances during retesting of samples preserved at the times of their competitions.

At the 2012 Summer Olympic Games in London, Polish weight lifter Tomasz Zielinski was awarded the bronze medal when six of the weight lifters who had beaten him were all disqualified for drug violations. Then at the 2016 Summer Olympic Games in Rio, Zielinski joined the ranks of disgraced athletes when he failed his drug test as well.

Russia, Kazakhstan and Belarus were also banned by the IWF from international competitions for one year following the Olympics. The situation has gotten so bad that the IOC has threated to remove weight lifting as a sport in the 2024 Olympics if the International Weightlifting Federation is not able to reign in its serious drug problem.

# WADA REPORT OF JULY 18, 2016 ON RUSSIAN STATE SPONSORED DOPING PROGRAM

In 2016 WADA ordered an investigation into claims of Russian doping in 28 Olympic sports. What prompted the report was a 60 Minutes television story and later New York Times reporting of allegations of the Russian government operation of a doping program during the Sochi 2014 Winter Games. The allegations were based primarily on the whistle blowing of Dr. Grigory Rodchenkov, the former Director of the Moscow and Sochi doping control laboratories. These revelations prompted WADA to appoint an independent investigator to look into the charges. Canadian lawyer and law professor Richard H. McLaren, also the CEO of McLaren Global Sports Solutions Inc. was hired to investigate the charges.

Due to the extreme importance of the charges coupled with the impending Rio Olympic games only a few months away, Professor McLaren was given a short and compressed time of only 57 days in which to complete his investigation resulting in, as the report indicated, "This Report reflects the work of the IP, but it must be recognized that we have only skimmed the surface of the extensive data available."

According to the report, Russia's Deputy Minister of Sports Uri Nagornykh ordered employees of the Russian anti-doping laboratory as to which positive samples to process and which to hide. Russian internal security services the FSB, formerly the KGB, also participated in the conspiracy. According to McLaren 312 positive results of 577 positive testing samples were hidden and relabeled. More than half of these were from track and field and wrestling, however other implicated sports included swimming, rowing, snowboarding and, strange as it may seem, table tennis.

In the Executive Summary of his report, the key findings were listed as:

"1. The Moscow Laboratory operated, for the protection of doped Russian athletes, with a State-dictated failsafe system, described in the report as the Disappearing Positive Methodology.

2. The Sochi laboratory operated a unique sample swapping methodology to enable doped Russian athletes to compete at the Games.

3. The Ministry of Sport directed, controlled and oversaw the manipulation of athlete's analytical results or sample swapping, with the active participation and assistance of the FSB, CSP and both Moscow and Sochi Laboratories."

The CSP is the Center of Sports Preparation of the national teams of Russia.

The report found that:

"The IC uncovered a system within Russia for doping athletes directed by senior coaching officials of Russian athletics. That was accomplished by the corruption of Doping Control Officers (DCO) working under the direction of RUSADA. The coaches were also able to achieve their objectives of doping athletes under their direction by knowing the wash out periods for various performance enhancing drugs (PED). They would be assisted in that regard by various informed medical personnel. The coaches were using the well-known and tried system of doping with anabolic steroids without understanding that what they were accomplishing with the PED's program. This was starting to show up in the Athlete Biological Passport (ABP), which was legally recognized in 2011 but not well understood in Russian sporting circles for at least another full year. As the problem became more acute, the corruption of both Russian and international Athletics officials was used as a method of slowing down and otherwise distorting the reporting of positive results by use of the ABP. . . .

What the IP investigation adds to the bigger picture is how the WADA accredited laboratory was controlled by the state and acted as the failsafe mechanism to cover up doping. If all other steps were unsuccessful in covering up or manipulating the doping control system then the laboratory's role was to make an initial finding of a positive result disappear. With the additional evidence available to the IP, this Report provides facts and proof beyond that of the IC and describes a larger picture of Russian doping activity and the sports involved beyond merely Athletics."

"1.6   Overall Outcomes of the Independent Investigation

Upon embarking on its investigation the IP quickly found a wider means of concealing positive doping results than had publically described for Sochi. The Sochi Laboratory urine sample swapping scheme was a unique standalone approach to meet a special set of circumstances. Behind this lay a greater systematic scheme operated by the Moscow Laboratory for false reporting of positive samples supported by what the IP termed the disappearing positive methodology. What emerged from all the investigative sources was a simple but effective and efficient method for direction and control under the Deputy Minister of Sport to force the Laboratory to report any positive screen finding as a negative analytical result. The disappearing positive!

The Disappearing Positive Methodology was used as a State directed method following the very abysmal medal count by the Russian Olympic athletes participating in the 2010 Winter Olympic Games in Vancouver. At that time, Sochi had already been designated as the next Winter Olympic venue. A new Deputy Minister of Sport, Yuri Nagornykh, was appointed in 2010 by Executive Order of the then Prime Minister Vladimir Putin. Nagornykh, also a member of the Russian Olympic Committee (ROC), reports to the Minister of Sport, Vitaly Mutko. Minister Mutko has continuously held this appointment since the Presidential Order of President Medvedev in May 2008. He is also the chairman of the organizing committee for the 2018 FIFA World Cup in Russian and is a member of the FIFA Executive Committee.

Deputy Minister Nagornykh was critical to the smooth running of the Disappearing Positive Methodology. Representing the State, he was advised of every positive analytical finding arising in the Moscow Laboratory from 2011 onwards. Nagornykh, as the Deputy Minister of Sport decided who would benefit from a cover up and who would not be protected.

In total violation of the WADA International Standard for Laboratories (ISL) all analytical positives appearing on the first sample screen at the Moscow laboratory were reported up to the Deputy Minister after the athlete's name had been added to the information to be supplied. The order would come back from the Deputy Minister 'SAVE' or "QUARANTINE". If the order was a SAVE the laboratory personnel were required to report the sample negative in

WADA's Anti-Doping Management System (ADAMS). Then the laboratory personnel would falsify the screen result in the Laboratory Information Management System (LIMS) to show a negative laboratory result. The athlete benefited from the cover up determined and directed by the Deputy Minister of Sport and could continue to compete dirty.

The Disappearing Positive Methodology worked well to cover up doping except at international events where there were independent observers such as the IAAF World Championships held in Moscow in 2013 and the Winter Olympics and Paralympics in Sochi in 2014.

Through the efforts of the FSB, a method of surreptitiously removing the caps of tamper evident sample bottles containing the urine samples of doped Russian athletes had been developed for use at Sochi. The IP has developed forensic evidence that establishes beyond a reasonable doubt some method was used to replace positive dirty samples during the Sochi Games. The bottle opening method was used again in December 2014 to cover up some dirty samples, which WADA had advised would be removed from the Moscow Laboratory for further analysis.

Unlike the method used during the Sochi Games, the Disappearing Positive Methodology was in operation at IAAF World Championships (IAAF Championships). The IP also has evidence that sample swapping occurred after the IAAF Championships in respect of positive samples.

The IP investigation, assisted by forensic experts, has conducted its own experiments and can confirm, without any doubt whatsoever, that the caps of urine sample bottles can be removed without any evidence visible to the untrained eye. Indeed, this was demonstrated in front of Professor Richard McLaren. As will be noted later in this report, evidence of tapering could be detected on bottle caps from Sochi and the December 2014 sample seizure by WADA with the use of microscopic technology.

The fundamental building block of the Sochi scheme was in place. The FSB was intricately entwined in the scheme to allow Russian athletes to compete while dirty. The FSB developed a method to surreptitiously open the urine bottles to enable sample swapping. This keystone step cleared the way for the development of a clean urine bank as a source from which to draw urine samples for swapping. The coordinating role for this aspect of the State run system was that of Irinia Rodionova. Rodionova currently sits as the Deputy Director of the Center of Sports Preparation of National Teams of Russia (CSP) (in Russian LICII) which is a subordinate organization of the Russian Ministry of Sport. She was a staff member of the Russian Olympic Committee (ROC) during the Sochi 2014 Games as the head of the Monitoring and Management of Medical Anti-Doping Programs Department and also on the ROC staff for the London 2012 Games as the head of the Medical and Research Department.

Athletes, on instruction, would collect what were thought to be clean urine samples outside of the wash out periods for any PEDs they were using. Rodionova would receive these samples from athletes and arrange for their freezer storage at the CSP. Dr. Rodchenkov would test some of these clean urine samples to ensure they were in fact not positive.

Once the clean urine bank was fully populated by the chosen athletes, the samples were then secretly transported by the FSB from Moscow to the FSB storage freezer in the FSB building located next to the Sochi Laboratory. The bank of clean urine sat in storage awaiting the swapping program at Sochi when required.

The swapping occurred largely as described in The New York Times article. Dr. Rodchenkov provided credible evidence that the A and B bottles would pass through the 'mouse hole' from the aliquoting room inside the secure perimeter of the Sochi Laboratory into an adjacent operations room, outside the secure perimeter. From there, FSB officer Evgeny Blokhin would take the B bottles and leave the operations room. In the meantime, clean urine from the athletes who had given their sample at a Sochi doping control venue would be withdrawn from the freezer at the FSB building and brought over to the operations room to complete its thawing there. The B sample bottle would be returned to the operations room by FSB Blokhin, open and with the cap removed. The dirty urine disposed of and replaced by clean urine would be put in the A and B bottles. The stopper replaced in the A bottle and the B bottle cap screwed back into place; the bottles would be passed back through the mouse hole thereby reentering the secure perimeter of the laboratory aliquoting room ready for clinical bench work the following morning.

Dr. Rodchenkov's role in the sample swapping scheme included ensuring that the substituted sample was manipulated to match as closely as possible the Specific Gravity (SG) indicated on the original Doping Control Form (DCF) taken at the Sochi venue. This adjustment was accomplished by adding table salt to raise the clean urine SG or distilled water to dilute the clean urine sample so as to closely match the SG number on the DCF.

The veracity of Dr. Rodchenkov's statements to The New York Times article is supported by the forensic analysis of the IP which included laboratory analysis of the sale content of samples selected by the investigative team. The London WADA accredited Laboratory, at the request of the IP, advised that of the forensically representative samples tested, 6 had salt contents higher than what should be found in urine of a healthy human. The forensic examination for marks and scratches within the bottle caps confirmed that they had been tampered with. Both findings support the evidence of Dr. Rodchenkov.

The Sochi sample swapping methodology was a unique situation, required because of the presence of the international community in the Laboratory. It enabled Russian athletes to compete dirty while enjoying certainty that their anti-doping samples would be reported clean. Following the Winter Olympics, the scheme to cover up State sponsored doping returned to the Disappearing Positive Methodology described previously.

The first ARD documentary aired in early December of 2014. The concerns of the international sporting community led to the appointment of the IC, one of the Commissioners of whom was subsequently to become the IP. In connection with the creation of the IC, but not by way of direction for the IC, Dr. Olivier Rabin from WADA asked the Moscow laboratory to prepare for a visit during which the samples stored in the laboratory would be packed up and shipped out of the country for storage and further analysis.

The anxiety level of personnel in the laboratory rose because of the pending WADA visit. The Disappearing Positive Methodology was used during the summer of 2014. As a consequence, Dr. Rodchenkov knew that he would have dirty B samples from that period. A number of dirty samples had been collected and reported as negative, and were stored in the laboratory. The solution to the problem in part was to destroy thousands of samples obtained and stored prior to 10 September 2014, being the minimal 90-day period of storage as prescribed under the ISL. However, the massive destruction of samples only got rid of part of the problem. Still to be dealt with were the samples between 10 September 2014 and 10 December 2014.

Dr. Rodchekov prepared a schedule of 37 athletes whose samples were potentially a problem if another accredited laboratory were to analyze them. A meeting was held with deputy Minister Nagornykh in which the jeopardy of the laboratory was discussed were something not done to deal with the selected samples. The upshot of that meeting was that Deputy Minister Nagornykh resoled to call in the 'magicians'. That night the FSB visited the laboratory and the next day sample bottles were in the laboratory without their caps. The IP found that these samples all had negative findings recorded on ADAMS.

The IP forensic examination of these bottles found evidence of scratches and marks confirmed tampering. A urine examination of 3 of the samples showed that the DNA was not that the athlete involved."

The report concluded that:

"The IC exposed State involvement in the manipulation of the doping control program operated by Russian Anti-Doping Agency (RUSADA) and within Russian Athletics. The IC Report detailed the in the field regime for doping athletes and the corruption surrounding it. The outcomes of the IP add a deeper understanding of this scheme and show proof of State directed oversight and corruption of the entirety of the Moscow laboratory's analytical work.

The State implemented a simple failsafe strategy. If all the operational precautions to promote and permit doping by Russian athletes proved to have been ineffective for whatever reason, the laboratory provided a failsafe mechanism. The State had the ability to transform a positive analytical result into a negative one by ordering that the analytical process of the Moscow Laboratory be altered. The Ministry of Sport (MofS), RUSADA and the Russian Federal Security Service (the FSB) were all involved in this operation."[2]

## STEROID COCKTAIL

The report also described the earlier method for administering PEDs. Prior to 2010, although doping was rampant, it was not done in a unified manner overseen by the Ministry of Sports. Rather it was accomplished through individual Russian athletes receiving advice as to PEDs directly from their coaches. This became problematic because the coaches were providing PEDs of questionable quality to the athletes as well as doing so without knowing the time periods necessary to have the PEDs not show up in drug tests, an essential element of any illegal PED program to be effectively operated.

However, once Dr. Rodchenkov became the laboratory director, he took over the responsibility for improving the international

---

[2]    WADA Investigation of Sochi Allegations, Richard H. McLaren, July 18, 2016.

performance of Russian athletes through the use of PEDs and the covering up of their use. He developed what became known as a steroid cocktail nicknamed "Duchess" after a traditional Russian beverage that when used as directed would avoid detection. The first version of the cocktail was made up of the PEDs Oral Turinabol, Oxandrolone and Methasterone. These steroids were dissolved in Chivas brand Scotch whiskey for the male athletes and vermouth for the women athletes. The mixture was swished around in the athletes' mouths in order to be more effectively absorbed by the buccal membrane and then spit out. Dr. Rodchenkov's research had determined that administering the PEDs in this manner would render the PEDs undetectable by the tests used at the time after between three and five days, which was an improvement over PEDs administered either by way of injections or swallowing.

The cocktail evolved as detection procedures improved. Oral Turinabol was replaced by Trenbolone due to its ability to avoid long term detection better than Oral Turinabol. Russian athletes using the initial cocktail recipe were able to avoid detection at the time of the 2012 London Olympic Games, however, preserved samples of eight Russian athletes who had tested negative at the Olympics for PEDs were retested in 2016 and found to contain evidence of Oral Turinabol through the use of more sophisticated testing than was available in 2012.

# IOC RESPONSE TO THE MCLAREN REPORT

The follow up to the McLaren report was swift as it had to be with the 2016 Rio Olympics looming. On July 24, 2016, a mere twelve days before the Rio Olympics, the fifteen member International Olympic Committee Executive Board unanimously ruled that "Under these exceptional circumstances, Russian athletes in any of the 28 Olympic summer sports have to assume the consequences of what amounts to a collective responsibility in order to protect the credibility of the

Olympic competitions, and the 'presumption of innocence' cannot be applied to them. On the other hand, according to the rules of natural justice, individual justice, to which every human being is entitled, has to be applied. This means that each affected athlete must be given the opportunity to rebut the applicability of collective responsibility in his or her individual case."[3]

# RUSSIAN RESPONSE TO THE MCLAREN REPORT OF A STATE SPONSORED PERFORMANCE ENHANCING DRUG PROGRAM

The Russian government initially denied that it was involved with a government sponsored doping program and called Rodchenkov's accusations "groundless." However, later, Viataly Mutko Russia's Minister of Sport publicly apologized and acknowledged that Russian athletes and coaches had violated the rules pertaining to performance enhancing drugs, saying, "Let us be clear. We are ashamed of them." He went on to say, "We are very sorry that athletes who tried to deceive us, and the world, were not caught sooner. We are very sorry because Russia is committed to upholding the highest standards in sport and is opposed to anything that threatens the Olympic values."[4]

# CONDITIONS FOR RUSSIAN PARTICIPATION IN THE 2016 RIO OLYMPICS

In the wake of the July 2016 McLaren report the IOC established conditions to be met for a Russian athlete to be eligible to participate in the 2016 Rio Olympic Summer Games. Among the conditions were that the athlete would have to provide evidence to the full satisfaction of the particular International Federation governing his or

---

[3]  Press Release, "Decision of the IOC Executive Board Concerning the Participation of Russian Athletes in the Olympic Games Rio 2016" July 24, 2016.

[4]  "Russia 'sorry' for doping" Jon Ungoed-Thomas, The Sunday Times, May 15, 2016.

her support including an analysis of the doping record of the particular athlete "taking into account only reliable adequate international tests." Even then, the IOC further required that the ruling of the athlete's particular International Federation allowing a particular athlete to compete would then be subject to the further approval of an expert from the Court of Arbitration for Sport (CAS) list of arbitrators. Then in an unprecedented move, the IOC ruled that no Russian athlete who had ever been sanctioned for doping even if he or she had served their sanction would be eligible for the Rio Olympics.

In addition, the IOC ruled that any Russian athlete managing to meet these stiff conditions would be subject to "rigorous additional out-of-competition testing programme in coordination with the relevant IF and WADA. Any non-availability for this programme will lead to the immediate withdrawal of the accreditation by the IOC."

Prior to making its determination, the IOC Executive Board provided the Russian Olympic Committee (ROC) with the opportunity to be heard on this matter. Alexander Zhukov, the President of the ROC began by guaranteeing the full cooperation with all international organizations to "shed light on the issue in every respect." He also guaranteed the commitment of the ROC to a "complete and comprehensive restructuring of the Russian anti-doping system. In this context he stressed that the ROC is committed to clean sport and would work towards guaranteeing clean sport in Russia."

In defense of the particular athletes seeking to compete in the Rio Games, he indicated that every one of them had been tested for the previous six months by non-Russian, foreign laboratories. Urine samples were taken by foreign doping control officers and analyzed in foreign laboratories. The total number of samples analyzed was more than 3,000 and, according to Zhukov, the "vast majority of the results were negative."

The IOC was not convinced although it did note that the report of McLaren did not make any specific findings of wrong doing by the

ROC. Ultimately, the IOC determined that "all Russian athletes seeking entry to the Olympic Games Rio 2016 are considered to be affected by a system subverting and manipulating the anti-doping system."

The IOC could have avoided the problem by leaving it totally up to the individual international sports federations for each sport to make its own decision, but instead took the middle of the road approach of leaving specific determinations to the international sports federations subject to the conditions as set out by the IOC, but subject to review by the IOC. It also could have made a blanket rule banning all Russian competitors.

Before making its ruling, the IOC waited to see what the IAAF would do.

Prior to the IOC decision, the International Association of Athletics Federations, the international governing organization for track and field had already banned the entire Russian Olympic track and field team from competing at the Rio Olympics due to its state-sponsored doping program. This decision was later upheld by the Court of Arbitration for Sport, which is the final determiner of international sports disputes. Due to the closeness of the 2016 Rio Olympics, when the CAS made its decision on July 14th, it only released its verdict without the reasons for its determination. It did, however, note that the ruling to ban the Russian track and field team from the Rio Olympics was unanimous. In its decision, however the IAAF did leave open the opportunity for Russian athletes who had been living and training outside of Russia and who regularly tested negatively for performance enhancing drug use to be able to petition to be permitted to compete in the 2016 Summer Olympic Games. Using those criteria, two athletes were initially declared eligible to compete in Rio. They were Darya Klishina and Yuliya Stepanova, a middle distance runner, both of whom had lived and trained in the United States and had regularly passed drug tests.

The last thing dealt with by the IOC dealt in its ruling was the request by Russian 800 Meter runner Yuliya Stepanova to be declared eligible to compete as a "neutral athlete." Mrs. Stepanova had already declined to compete as a member of the Russian Olympic. Stepanova who left Russia to live in the United States had competed as an individual athlete in the European Track and Field Championships in Amsterdam two months before the Olympics. A number of factors made her request unique.

According to the IOC:

"Mrs. Stepanova is basing her request on her role as a 'whistle-blower' with regard to the manipulation of the anti-doping system and corruption involving the WADA-accredited Moscow Anti-Doping Laboratory, the All-Russia Athletic Federation (ARAF) and the IAAF. The Ethics Commission applauds the contribution of Mrs. Stepanova to the fight against doping. It put this contribution into the perspective of Mrs. Stepanova's own long implication of at least five years, in this doping system and the timing of her whistle-blowing, which came after the system did not protect her any longer following a positive test for which she was sanctioned for doping for the first time.

After a careful evaluation of the arguments, the Ethics Commission gave the following advice to the IOC EB:

'While it is true that Mrs. Stepanova's testimony and public statements have made a contribution to the protection and promotion of clean athletes, fair play and the integrity and authenticity of sport, the Rules of the Olympic Charter related to the organization of the Olympic Games run counter to the recognition of the status of neutral athlete. Furthermore, the sanction to which she was subject and the circumstances in which she denounced the doping practices which she had used herself, do not satisfy the ethical requirements for an athlete to enter the Olympic Games."

The IOC EB accepted the advice of the IOC Ethics Commission, also taking into consideration its above-mentioned decision not to allow any Russian athlete who has ever been sanctioned for doping to participate in the Olympic Games Rio 2016. Therefore, the IOC will not enter Mrs. Stepanova as a competitor in the Olympic Games Rio 2016.

However, the IOC EB would like to express its appreciation for Mrs. Stepanova's contribution to the fight against doping and to the integrity of sport. Therefore the IOC invites Mrs. Stepanova and her husband to the Olympic Games Rio 2016. Furthermore, the IOC is ready to support Mrs. Stepanova so that she can continue her sports career and potentially join a National Olympic Committee."[5]

Her husband, Vitaly Stepanov, it should be noted was a former Russian anti-doping official who had joined his wife in exposing the Russian PED program.

The IOC's position that no Russian athlete who had been found to have violated the anti-doping rules in the past and had received a sanction for such violations could participate in the Rio Games immediately disqualified world 100 meter breaststroke champion Yulia Efimova, 2012 Olympic silver medalist weight lifter Tatyana Kashirina, and two-time Olympic bronze medalist cyclist Olga Zabelinskaya.

# THERAPEUTIC EXCEPTIONS TO OLYMPIC DRUG POLICY

In September of 2016 following the 2016 Summer Olympics in which the Russian Track and Field team was barred due to violations of the Olympic drug rules, a data breach occurred at WADA attributed to Russian hackers in which the medical records of American athletes Venus Williams, Serena Williams, Elena Delle Donne and Simone Biles were released by the hackers showing the use by them of banned substances, however, in all four cases the use of the drugs was legal under WADA's Therapeutic Use Exemptions which permits the use

---

[5] Press Release, "Decision of the IOC Executive Board Concerning the Participation of Russian Athletes in the Olympic Games Rio 2016" July 24, 2016.

of otherwise banned substances when there is a legitimate medical reason for the particular athletes use of such substances. In the case of Simone Biles, she took Ritalin to control her ADHD which in no way served as a performance enhancing drug.

Bradley Wiggins of the UK a top level international cyclist who won the 2012 Tour de France was another person whose medical records with the WADA were made public following the hacking of the WADA. Wiggins also benefited from a therapeutic use exemption. In his case, he was allowed to use the otherwise banned substance triamcinolone acetonide, which is a corticosteroid that functions as an anti-inflammatory helpful to long distance cyclists. Leaked WADA records showed that Wiggins was permitted to use the substance to control asthma and hay fever that was not susceptible to being controlled through conventional antihistamines.

A concern is the possibility that athletes will use real or otherwise medical conditions as the grounds for turning their illnesses, real or imagined, into an avenue for being able to take performance enhancing drugs to provide an edge in high level international competitions.

Russian President Vladimir Putin even went so far as to suggest that athletes using otherwise banned drugs through a therapeutic use exemption only be allowed to compete against similar situated athletes rather than being allowed to compete against totally drug free athletes.

# FINAL MCLAREN REPORT

In December of 2016 a more detailed follow up report was issued by the committee headed by Richard McLaren which stated:

"Chapter 1: Executive Summary of 2nd IP Report Key Highlights of 2nd Report

Institutionalised Doping Conspiracy and Cover Up

1. An institutional conspiracy existed across summer and winter sports athletes who participated with Russian officials within the Ministry of Sport and its infrastructure, such as the RUSADA, CSP and the Moscow Laboratory, along with the FSB for the purposes of manipulating doping controls. The summer and winter sports athletes were not acting individually but within an organised infrastructure as reported on in the 1st Report.

2. This systematic and centralised cover up and manipulation of the doping control process evolved and was refined over the course of its use at London 2012 Summer Games, Universiade Games 2013, Moscow IAAF World Championships 2013, and the Winter Games in Sochi in 2014. The evolution of the infrastructure was also spawned in response to WADA regulatory changes and surprise interventions.

3. The swapping of Russian athletes' urine samples further confirmed in this 2nd Report as occurring at Sochi, did not stop at the close of the Winter Olympics. The sample swapping technique used at Sochi became a regular monthly practice of the Moscow Laboratory in dealing with elite summer and winter 2 athletes. Further DNA and salt testing confirms the technique, while others relied on DPM.

4. The key findings of the 1st Report remain unchanged. The forensic testing, which is based on immutable facts, is conclusive. The evidence does not depend on verbal testimony to draw a conclusion. Rather, it tests the physical evidence and a conclusion is drawn from those results. The results of the forensic and laboratory analysis initiated by the IP establish that the conspiracy was perpetrated between 2011 and 2015.

The Athlete Part of Conspiracy and Cover Up

5.    Over 1000 Russian athletes competing in summer, winter and Paralympic sport, can be identified as being involved in or benefiting from manipulations to conceal positive doping tests. Based on the information reported to International Federations through the IP to WADA there are 600 (84%) summer athletes and 95 (16%) winter athletes.

London Summer Olympic Games

6.    Fifteen Russian athlete medal winners were identified out of the 78 on the London Washout Lists. Ten of these athletes have now had their medals stripped.

IAAF Moscow World Championships

7.    Following the 2013 IAAF Moscow World Championships, 4 athletics athletes' samples were swapped. Additional target testing is in progress.

Sochi Winter Olympic Games

8.    Sample swapping is established by 2 female ice hockey players' samples with male DNA.

9.    Tampering with original sample established by 2 [sport] athletes, winners of four Sochi Olympic Gold medals, and a female Silver medal winner in [sport] with physiologically impossible salt readings.

10.  Twelve medal winning athletes (including the above 3) from 44 examined samples had scratches and marks on the inside of the caps of their B sample bottles, indicating tampering.

11.  Six winners of 21 Paralympic medals are found to have had their urine samples tampered with at Sochi."[6]

The follow up report detailed a program of institutional doping for years that reached its apex at the Sochi Games at an unprecedented

---

    6    WADA Investigations of Sochi Allegations, Independent Person 2nd Report, Richard H. McLaren, December 9, 2016.

level beyond even the state sponsored doping by Eastern Bloc countries such as East Germany during the 1970s.

In the wake of the December 2016 report after long denying responsibility, Russia admitted that the accusations contained in the McLaren report were accurate and agreed to retesting of all drug test samples given by Russian athletes at both the 2012 London and 2014 Sochi Olympics. The one accusation which Russian officials continue to deny is that President Vladimir Putin or his closest associates had any involvement with the state sponsored doping program.

# RETESTING

The Swiss Laboratory for Doping Analyses (LAD) is one of thirty-four labs in the world accredited by the World Anti-Doping Agency to perform drug testing. This lab stores the urine and blood samples from the 2008, 2012 and 2016 Olympic Games and is where samples were retested under the updated tests.

Following urine sample retesting from the 2008 Beijing and 2012 London Summer Olympic games more than 75 athletes were found to have violated the rules on doping. At least 40 of those disqualified were medalists resulting in finishers as low as sixth place in Olympic events being declared medal winners. The largest numbers of drug violations were found in track and field and weight lifting competitions. Almost all of the violations related to the use of the anabolic steroid Turinabol, which had previously been used as long ago as the 1970s. Newer testing procedures able to detect smaller residual amounts of the drugs have led to the disqualifications.

# NFL DRUG POLICY

The National Football League bans both illegal drugs and certain prescription drugs. Among the drugs tested for are cocaine, marijuana, amphetamines, morphine, codeine and PCP. The NFL first initiated a banned substance policy in 1987 and has been often considered the toughest in American professional sports. The league first began testing in 1987 and has been doing year round random testing since 1990. The NFL performs random drug testing throughout the year and every player in the league is tested at least once a year. A player can be tested as many as six times during the off season while during the season there is no limit to the number of tests to which an athlete may be subjected or the timing of the tests which can even be done on the day of a game. The penalty for a first drug offense is a four game suspension without pay. A second offense carries an eight game suspension without pay and a third offense, a one year suspension without pay. The NFL not only tests for performance enhancing drugs, but also masking agents which although in and of themselves are benign, enable the athlete to hide the taking of the performance enhancing drugs.

The NFL became the first professional league to test for Human Growth Hormone, which is significant since unlike the other tests for substances such as anabolic steroids, HGH is only tested for through a blood test. Human Growth Hormone enables an injured body to heal faster and is a legal prescription drug.

The league also has specific provisions for players convicted of operating a vehicle under the influence of alcohol or testing positive for marijuana use. In both instances, first time offenders are required to attend the league's substance abuse program. Second offenses are punished by a $25,000 fine and a two game suspension; third offenses result in a four game suspension without pay while fourth offenses bring a ten game suspension without pay. A fifth violation results in a full one year suspension. Among the notable NFL player suspended for the use of marijuana is Cleveland Wide Receiver Josh Gordon who subsequently also was suspended for alcohol use.

The NFL's policy on the use of marijuana has been criticized in particular by a number of former players on an unusual basis. Their concern was not with the recreational use of the drug, but rather with its medicinal use to aid players deal with the chronic pain suffered by many players. As legendary football coach Duffy Daugherty once said, "Football is not a contact sport; Football is a collision sport. Dancing is a contact sport." Those collisions come at a price and the price for many players is chronic pain. The argument that marijuana is safer, less addictive and more effective in managing pain then the opioids often prescribed for players is an interesting argument. Presently twenty-four states provide for the legal use of medical marijuana.

The NFL, recognizing the difference between performance enhancing drugs and banned recreational drugs, tests them differently. Tests for recreational drugs are done with advance warning. No punishment is meted out to a player who tests positive the first time for recreational drug use.

---

## QUESTIONS

1.    Should medicinal marijuana be permitted by the NFL?

2.    What is the justification of classifying HGH as a performance enhancing drug when it is a legal drug that merely quickens the healing process?

3.    What is the justification for the NFL banning recreational drug use?

# NBA DRUG POLICY

The NBA put its initial drug policy into effect in 1983. Under this policy, players are subject to random tests based on "reasonable cause" during the pre-season while first year players are subject to three tests on a random basis throughout the regular season.

A first time offender of the league drug policy receives a five game suspension and is required to attend the league's anti-doping counseling program. Second offenders receive a ten game suspension and are also required to attend counseling; third time offenders receive a twenty-five game suspension with mandatory counseling and four time offenders receive a minimum of two years suspension from the league.

The NBA now tests for HGH through blood tests. MLB has been testing for it since 2011 and the NFL now tests for it as well.

While the NBA tests its athletes for performance enhancing drugs throughout the year, they only test for marijuana and other nonperformance enhancing drugs during the season.

## MLB DRUG POLICY

In the spring of 2006 an agreement between the Major League Baseball Players Association (MLBPA) and the Treatment Office of the Commissioner's office was negotiated. This started the Joint Drug Prevention and Treatment agreement which set the standards for testing and setting penalties for the use of PEDs in MLB.

All major league players can be tested for PEDS which include steroids, stimulants and other listed drugs under the Joint Drug Prevention and Treatment Program. Major League managers, coaches and other clubhouse personnel can be tested. This testing began in 2008. The tests are administered by Independent Private Administrators (IPA) and penalties are meted out by the commissioner.

Until 2014, player testing for steroids and drugs of abuse were administered by urine testing. Since then the MLBPA and MLB have agreed to blood testing which is the only way to test for HGH. These tests can take place between Spring training and the end of the season but penalties can cross over to the following season.

Among the substances banned by major league baseball are 70 different types of steroids and 50 types of stimulants. In addition, drugs labeled as "drugs of abuse" including THC, hashish and marijuana are also banned.

The "Drugs of Abuse" are:

THC, Hashish and Marijuana.

Synthetic THC & Cannabimimetics.

Cocaine

LSD

Opiates: Heroin, Morphine, Oxycodone & Codeine.

Ecstasy

GHB

PCP

There are three separate categories for MLB penalties:

1) Failure to comply with the treatment program

2) Positive steroid test

3) Conviction for using prohibited substances

PENALTIES

**Failure to comply with treatment programs**

First noncompliance: 15–25 game suspension and or fine of $10,000.

Second incidence: 25–50 game suspension and or fine of $25,000.

Third: 50–75 game suspension and or fine of $50,000.

Fourth: One year suspension plus a $100,000 fine.

**Positive Steroid testing result**

First incidence: 50 game suspension

Second incidence: 100 game suspension

Third incidence: Lifetime ban

Penalized players receive no pay during the term of their suspensions.

It is also interesting to note that in the 2016 CBA the use of smokeless tobacco, often referred to as chewing tobacco was banned for new players entering the major leagues. This is part of a transition that was begun when smokeless tobacco use was first banned in the minor leagues. In addition, the CBA also recognizes that the use of smokeless tobacco in baseball stadiums is banned when local laws or ordinances so provide.

The drug policy negotiated in the 2016 CBA also was made tougher in regard to the number of random urine tests being expanded during the season from 3,200 to 4,800 and the number of off-season random urine tests increased from 350 to 1,550 in order to make sure that every MLB player is tested at least once during the off season. Random testing for HGH, was also increased during the baseball season from 260 to 500 tests and off season from 140 to 400 tests. The 2016 CBA also increased the suspension time for offenders. While those caught using stimulants for the first time only receive a warning along with increased testing, second time stimulant violators are suspended for fifty games, third time offenders for 100 games and fourth time violators can receive a permanent suspension from baseball. A major victory for the players in the 2016 CBA, however came with increased authority of arbitrators to reduce the suspension times mandated by the CBA based upon mitigating circumstances.

In 2016 Mets relief pitcher Jenrry Mejia became the first player in MLB history to be banned from baseball for life due to a third failed drug test for performance enhancing drugs. Each of his three convictions was for taking anabolic steroids. Two of the infractions involved the use of Boldenone, a steroid that has been used on horses although it also has been used by baseball players and major league soccer players.

Although Mejia was banned for life, he does have the ability to appeal for reinstatement after two years.

Once a player has failed a test for performance enhancing drugs, he is also subject to six unannounced urine tests and three unannounced blood tests each year for the rest of his major league baseball career.

## QUESTION

1.   What are the reasons for and against the banning of smokeless tobacco use by MLB players?

# NHL DRUG POLICY

The National Hockey League did not institute a drug testing policy until 2005 and its policy provides for random tests for performance enhancing drugs no more than three times during the year with testing done only during off days during the regular season and no testing during the playoffs or during the off season. The penalties for violating the league's drug policy are a twenty game suspension without pay for a first offense; a sixty game suspension without pay for a second offense and a lifetime ban for a third offense.

# NCAA MARIJUANA RULES

In 2009 the NCAA released the findings of an anonymous survey of more than 20,000 NCAA athletes that indicated that 22.6% of college athletes polled admitted to using marijuana during the previous year. While 16.9% of Division I athletes admitted to using marijuana during the previous year, this number rose to 28.3% at the Division III level. Perhaps indicating a concern about prospects for future professional basketball and football contracts, the male Division I athletes playing these sports admitted using marijuana at a lesser rate than those of other sports with Men's Lacrosse having the highest level of marijuana usage at 48.5%. Among female college athletes, 35.7% of field hockey players admitted using marijuana.

A 2014 report of the NCAA about substance use habits of Student Athletes found 22% used marijuana in the last twelve months with usage levels of 29% for Division III athletes, 20% for Division II athletes and 16% for Division I athletes.[7]

# BLOOD DOPING

Blood doping is another banned practice used by cyclists, marathoners and other endurance athletes. Red blood cells help give an athlete greater endurance, which is a tremendous advantage in a sport such as long distance cycling. The more red blood cells the athlete has, the better equipped he or she is to fight fatigue during competition. One type of blood doping involves the athlete having his or her own blood drawn in the months preceding a competition and then receiving a transfusion of his or her own blood shortly before the competition thereby increasing the number of red blood cells in his or her body. This can be difficult to trace by testing since the athlete's body merely contains his or her own blood.

Another type of blood doping commonly used involves the use of Erythropoietin (EPO) a synthetic substance that stimulates the athlete's body to increase the production of red blood cells. It works similarly to blood doping with the athlete's own blood but in this case artificially induces the production of large amounts of red blood cells and greater oxygen carrying capabilities to the muscles.

Rita Jeptoo, of Kenya a three time winner of the Boston Marathon failed a test for EPO. Previously, Kenya did not have strong anti-doping testing, but now is a part of a regional anti-doping agency made up of a number of different countries that do not have sufficient funds to establish and maintain effective national anti-doping testing on their own, but in recent years have banded together to make drug testing more effective.

Cycling which had been among the sports with the greatest use of performance enhancement drugs has taken the lead in trying to

---

[7]   NCAA National Study of Substance Use Habits of College Student-Athletes, Final Report July 2014, Revised August 2014, compiled by Markie Rexroat, Assistant Direction of Research, NCAA Research.

aggressively identify and punish violators. In 2009 the International Cycling Union (ICU) initiated the first biological passports by which over a year the ICU took 8,000 blood samples from its 800 riders through unannounced testing both within the competitive season and during the off season to be used to establish a blood profile that would make it easier to track the use of EPO and other substances that might be used to increase the red blood cells of the athlete. The biological passports measure eight different blood markers which are then used to determine the statistical probability of an athlete using performance enhancing substances. Thus the specific performance enhancer used to increase red blood cells would not even need to be identified. Merely by recognizing an uncharacteristic higher level of red blood cells, the athlete would be determined to be in violation of the rules. Under the ICU rules all cyclists are required to provide notice to the ICU as to exactly where they will be at all times and they are subject to random testing on a mere one hour's notice.

During the first three years that the biological passport was used by the ICU, 26 riders tested positive for EPO. The use of the biological passport has spread to other sports. The International Association of Athletics Federations also started its biological passport program in 2009 and first used it as the basis of the suspension of an athlete in 2012 when Portuguese marathoner Helder Ornelas became the first track and field athlete to receive a suspension based upon evidence obtained through the biological passport.

The biological passport was also used in February of 2017 by the Court of Arbitration for Sport (CAS) to strip Russian middle distance runner Mariya Savinova-Farnosova of her 2012 Olympic gold medal in the 800 meter event leaving controversial runner Caster Semenya who had received the silver medal as the winner. The Court of Arbitration for Sport (CAS) also banned Savinova-Farnosova from all competition for a period of four years.

# FG-4592

Athletes are always looking for the newest performance enhancing drug and this is typified by FG-4592 which is an experimental drug that increases production of red blood cells. The problem is that it has not been approved for use by humans. However, resourceful athletes are getting it by simply ordering it online from chemical supply companies. The catch is that it is supposed to be sold only to researchers so the athlete has to have documentation that he or she is a researcher and the drug has to be sent to a university or research lab.

The World Anti-Doping Agency has designated it as a banned substance and tests for it. More than 600 sports organizations including the IOC use the list of the WADA to determine which substances are banned.

## GENE DOPING

Athletic training has become tremendously sophisticated over the years, however the standard for determining when a training method or supplement crosses the line into illegal performance enhancement is not clear. In many instances it is akin to Justice Potter Stewart's response when having to come up with a definition of hard core pornography when he wrote that he could not define it, but he knew it when he saw it.

Having eye surgery to better a biathlete's eyesight is legal, but surgery to create webbing on the hands of a swimmer would not be.

Gene therapy is the latest frontier in either athletic training or illegal cheating, depending upon your perspective. Gene therapy has been a legitimate source of medical research and inquiry for years. Gene therapy can be used to fight muscle wasting diseases. One of the genes being studied is Myostatin a gene that inhibits muscle growth. Removal of this gene leads to an increase in muscle size and power.

The IGF-1 gene was able to be inserted into the muscles of mice in the 1990s to increase muscle growth and slow the ageing process.

Scientists are able to produce a synthetic gene to secrete a particular protein that is involved in muscle growth and repair. This gene is attached to a harmless virus and introduced into the patient's body thereby enabling the patient to repair damaged muscle from various diseases. This is a legitimate medical use, but it raises the possibility of introducing a synthetic gene into the body of an elite athlete which would enable the athlete to train harder and recover quicker following an injury.

Lab rats were able to use such gene doping to increase muscle mass by 15% and the effects were long lasting. Studies are being done now to develop the targeting of specific muscles through injections.

Making a permanent change to the genome is very complicated, but the EPO gene can also be obtained on the Internet and injected into the muscle directly which can provide a temporary result rather than the permanent change made by manipulating the genome. This type of temporary injection would be very difficult to detect.

Anti-doping agencies will have even less of a chance of catching athletes who move beyond drugs and hormones to "gene doping"— inserting genes in their DNA that could increase strength and endurance without leaving telltale chemicals in the bloodstream.

In June of 2001, Theodore Friedmann and Johann Olav Koss published a paper first warning about the dangers of gene doping.

Research published in 2002 described how a gene therapy called Repoxygen delivered EPO as a treatment for anemia, however, it also could be used to increase athletic performance. The Erythropoietin gene can be artificially produced and then introduced into the body of an athlete. This is the same EPO used by Lance Armstrong to assist him in winning seven consecutive Tour de France races before he was stripped of his titles for use of this and other performance enhancing drugs.

The World Anti-Doping Agency (WADA) banned gene doping in 2003 before it even was being done.

Presently there are significant and potentially even deadly side effects to gene doping. Jesse Gelsinger died in a gene therapy clinical trial from a massive inflammatory reaction to the drug. However as the process becomes more developed and safer and if the benefits of slowing muscle deterioration were able to be legally and safely done through such therapy, shouldn't such therapies be able to be utilized by athletes?

Research in 2004 showed mice could be given gene therapy to double their endurance and were referred to as marathon mice.

In 2012 Glybera a gene therapy for a rare genetic disorder became the first gene therapy to be approved for clinical use in the United States.

The risks are still considerable, but must, like all medical treatments, be balanced against the dangers of a particular disease. Gene therapy can produce an immune reaction to the protein that could create a massive inflammatory response, cancer or death. When used as an alternative to a debilitating or deadly disease the risk may be worth taking, but what are the ethics of using such gene therapy on a healthy athlete? Should the decision be up to athletes to make the decisions for themselves as to whether the risk was worth taking.

Detecting the use of gene therapy might primarily be done through examination of bodily changes and differences between natural occurring proteins and those introduced into the body, but it is difficult to determine which anomalies are proof of gene doping and which are just naturally occurring, but unusual biological properties of particular athletes. Eero Mantyranta an Olympic cross country skier had a naturally occurring mutation in his genes by which his body naturally produced abnormally high amounts of red blood cells.

According to Raymond McCauley, a biotechnology scientist:

"Genetic engineering techniques are now cheap and widespread enough that any knowledgeable individual can order every material they need off the Internet and download the software to do their own experiments on themselves. Everyone in citizen science and the biohacker community has stories of being contacted by trainers, coaches, and athletes. There is absolutely no way to regulate it, and if you tried to it would be like stemming the tide with a fork."[8]

The athlete of the future may largely be a factor of the mapping of the human genome and the increasing ability to manipulate genes to alter physical abilities and traits.

# GENES AFFECTING ATHLETIC PERFORMANCE

Scientists have already discovered 220 individual genes that contribute to athletic performance. Some of the specific genes that can be manipulated to dramatically increase athletic performance are ACTN3, ACE, SCN9A, MSTN and PEPCK.

ACTN3 is a gene that can strongly increase sprinting performance in athletes. One study finding this was described in the American Journal of Human Genetics.[9]

EpoR is a gene which results in increased red blood cell count which provides dramatically aids in endurance sports.

SCN9A, is a pain inhibiting gene which would enable an athlete to more effectively compete without succumbing to pain.

MSTN is a gene which when deactivated enables increased muscle mass.

Myostatin inhibitors are being tested on laboratory animals, but are not yet legally available for human use. However, experimental myostatin inhibitors are already being sold on the black market.

---

[8]    The Future of Sports Report, USA Today, September 2015.

[9]    "ACTN3 Genotype Is Associated with Human Elite Athletic Performance," American Journal of Human Genetics, 2003 September 73(3) 627–631, Nan Young.

PEPCK is a gene which promotes better processing of fatty acids for energy without producing lactic acid which would enable an athlete to run faster for a longer distance. Manipulating PEPCK would permit an athlete to use fatty acid for energy without producing fatigue inducing lactic acid and enable an athlete to run at top speed for 60% longer than an athlete whose PEPCK was not manipulated.

LRP5 is a gene which when manipulated can improve bone density and strength.

While gene manipulation offers much promise in treating diseases and increased health, the use of this science to increase athletic performance is a tremendous lure and is difficult to detect.

## CATCHING VIOLATORS

Anti-doping forces are always on the defensive, responding to new types of PEDs, many of which may be difficult to identify. Drug testing has only had limited success as evidenced by the fact that using recently developed sophisticated tests on urine samples retained of athletes who had passed state of the art tests in the recent past have found that cheating had occurred. Recent PED abuse has been discovered more by whistleblowers than drug tests, which is a further indication of the ineffectiveness of drug testing in reducing the use of PEDs.

Sometimes the pharmaceutical companies will warn WADA about legitimate new drugs about to the made available to the public that they believe may have the potential to be abused by athletes as PEDs. This was done by Roche Holding AG, the makers of a new drug used to fight anemia called Micera or CERA which is a new version of EPO stimulating substances that can increase red blood cells. WADA then was able to create a test for CERA. Using the test WADA analyzed previous samples from the 2008 Summer Olympics and found six athletes who had previously been determined not to have violated drug tests testing positive for CERA. This group included two medal winning athletes.

According to physicist Yoseph Bar-Cohen, as reported in an article in the Smithsonian Magazine,

"Embedded technologies, such as artificial muscles or hidden motors, could someday give athletes another way to cheat, assuming they could mask them in their bodies or equipment. Electroactive polymers (EAPs) bend and stretch like real muscle fiber in response to an electrical charge; clothing woven with EAPs might augment an athlete's muscle power."[10]

How would these adaptations be detected?

# GENETIC TESTING

As genetic testing becomes more precise will college recruiting and professional sports teams' evaluation or prospects include genetic testing? Will it be considered the equivalent of a height measurement, weight measurement, weight lifting test, sprinting test or agility test or will it be considered a violation of the athlete's personal privacy?

# ARGUMENTS IN FAVOR OF DOPING

In an article in the journal Lancet, Bengt Kayser, a professor of exercise physiology at the University of Geneva stated, "The need for rules in sports cannot be dismissed. But the anchoring of today's antidoping regulations in the notion of fair play is misguided, since other factors that affect performance—e.g. biological and environmental factors—are unchecked. Getting help from one's genes—by being blessed with a performance-enhancing genetic predisposition—is acceptable. Use of drugs is not. Yet both types of advantage are underserved. Prevailing sports ethics is unconcerned with this contradiction."

He went on to say "legalization of doping, we believe would encourage more sensible, informed use of drugs in amateur sport,

---

[10] "The Future of Cheating in Sports" Smithsonian Magazine July 2012, Christie Aschwanden.

leading to an overall decline in the rate of health problems associated with doping. Finally by allowing medically supervised doping, the drugs used could be assessed for a clearer view of what is dangerous and what is not."

In the article Globalization of Anti-Doping: The Reverse Side of the Medal by Bent Kayser and Aaron C.T. Smith BMJ: British Medical Journal, Vol 337, No. 7661 (Jul 12, 2008) pp 85–87 Professor Kayser states:

"Rules and sampling procedures associated with testing protocols impinge on athletes' privacy to an unreasonable degree and violate basic notions of personal freedom and self regulation."

"Four reasons are conventionally advanced in favour of anti-doping; the need to ensure a 'level playing field'; the need to protect the health of athletes; the need to preserve the integrity of sport; and the need to set a good example. All four assumptions have at their core a need for moral certainty and all four are flawed.

The level playing field argument does not take into account the difficulties associated with competitive parity in sport or the inevitable differences between individuals arising from different environments (training technology, economic means) and talent (genotype and phenotype). In reality innumerable factors unfairly advantage some athletes.

The athlete health argument is paternalistic and at odds with the unhealthy aspects and risks inherent to elite sport practice.

The integrity argument is based on the claim that taking drugs to enhance sports performance is inappropriate because it compromises the ethical foundation and social authenticity of sport. The idea that all sport is bound by common values and customs ignores the cultural histories and evolution of different sports and impact of science, technology, and commercialization on their structure and operation.

The role argument is naïve in that it expects elite athletes to be model citizens judged against criteria that are not imposed on any other category of admired citizen."

"A consequence of prohibition (the third problem) is that users of drugs like anabolic steroids find it difficult to obtain medical advice. Athletes who self-medicate may use higher doses than are safe or necessary. In these instances, punitive policies relying on intensive policing and punishments may have increased the harms associated with drug use while doing little to curtail usage.

A fourth problem of existing policy is its claim to uphold parity by ensuring a level playing field. Current policy exacerbates inequity because the rapid development of science and medicine in sport serves only privileged athletes with access to the latest technological and pharmacological inventions."

"As the use of performance enhancing substances in the general population is increasing, doping is not just a problem affecting elite sports and does not justify a sport-only approach. International organized crime has quickly understood the potential of this market and has cultivated markets in anabolic steroids, erythropoietin, human growth hormone and other substances. Prohibition sends users of these substances often of dubious quality into hiding in medically unsupervised practice. Dangerous practices, such as the sharing of syringes, lead to the risk of HIV or hepatitis virus infection with considerable impact on public health."

"Secondly, the evidence related to the adverse effects of anabolic steroids and similar drugs is not clear. Most reports are from clinical populations or case studies and rarely deal with the supra-therapeutic regimens and complex pharmacology used by many individuals."

"In competitive sport, harm reduction would not necessarily imply abandoning drug testing altogether. If performance enhancing drugs were legal athletes would be more likely to use doping techniques to maintain their competitive positions. An alternative policy might involve making legal the use of drugs associated with low harm and testing health rather than testing for drugs. Implicit in this argument is that more athletes would use performance enhancing drugs if they were both legal and safe, thereby obviating both the moral and level playing field problems. This view holds that if health is safeguarded it does not matter how performance is supplemented."[11]

In the British Medical Journal in 2008, more than 30 scholars signed a statement supporting Dr. Kayser's position that the present system outlawing performance enhancing drugs is a failure and should be replaced. The article also criticized the medical establishment for "prophylactic lies" that exaggerated the dangers of drugs like anabolic steroids based "on scant evidence tainted by a misguided moralistic motivation to protect sports."[12]

## QUESTIONS

1.    What should be the standard for legal performance enhancement in sport?

2.    Should genetic manipulation for purposes of increased sports performance be permitted?

3.    Does genetic manipulation that provides for more efficient healing from injuries constitute unethical performance enhancement?

4.    If genetic manipulation is permitted for prevention or treatment of disease should it be permitted for purposes of increased athletic performance?

5.    Should regulation in sports of genetic manipulation be abandoned because it would be too difficult to enforce?

6.    If there are adverse side effects to particular genetic manipulations for purposes of increased sports performance, should athletes be able to

---

[11]    "Viewpoint: Legislation of performance-enhancing drugs" The Lancet, Volume 366, Special Issue, S21, December 2005, Professor Bengt Kayser, MD.

[12]    "Globalization of anti-doping: the reverse side of the medal," British Medical Journal, 2008 July 12; 337(7661): 85–87, Bengt Kayser and Aaron C.T. Smith.

make the informed choice for themselves as to whether or not to partake of genetic manipulation?

7.  Should sports in the future be divided between competitions between legally enhanced athletes and separate division for "natural" athletes?

# SYNOPSIS

1.  Performance enhancing drugs are uniformly banned throughout amateur and professional sports yet there is no accepted definition of what makes something an illegal performance enhancing drug.

2.  Recreational drugs are also banned by the NCAA and professional sports leagues.

3.  The history of the use of performance enhancing drugs and substances is as old as athletic competitions.

4.  Agents that may serve no anabolic purpose, but would mask the use of performance enhancing drugs are also banned.

5.  Anabolic steroids will not in and of themselves grow muscle, but will enable an athlete to train harder and recover faster thus creating increased muscle growth.

6.  For years Russia had been involved in a large scale doping program for its athletes.

7.  All of the professional sports leagues have their own rules against drug use that were arrived at through collective bargaining agreements. These drug policies relate to both performance enhancing drugs and recreational drugs.

8.  Blood doping is used by endurance athletes and is being dealt with through the use of biological passports.

9.  Gene therapy was banned even before it was ever used.

10. Retesting of preserved drug samples from previous Olympics using more advanced testing procedures has uncovered previously undiscovered drug violations.

# CHAPTER TWELVE

# Violence in Sports

## CIVIL AND CRIMINAL ACTIONS

Violence tied to sporting events can be subject to civil tort law, criminal law or both. The violence can involve participants in the sporting events, but it can also involve spectators, as well.

Torts are civil actions that do not involve contracts. Examples of torts are assault and battery libel or negligence. Torts like all civil actions are proven in court by the standard of preponderance of the evidence. The preponderance of the evidence standard means that in order to be successful in a civil lawsuit, the plaintiff must only show that it is more likely than not that the facts are as he or she alleges. If put into percentages, the plaintiff must merely show that his or her version of the case is 51% more likely to be true.

Torts can be classified as intentional torts where there is an intent to cause injury or negligent torts where there is no intention to do harm, but harm resulted through a breach of a duty of care causing injury to someone.

Responsibility for what would otherwise be tortious actions can be mitigated in accordance with the legal theories of contributory negligence, comparative negligence and assumption of the risk.

Under the theory of contributory negligence, if a plaintiff is even partially responsible through his or her own negligence for the injuries he or she sustained, he or she is not entitled to a judgment against someone else whose negligence may have contributed to his or her injury. Assumption of risk is a subset of contributory negligence by which someone assumes and accepts the risk associated with a particular activity and is not entitled to a judgment against someone else whose negligence may have contributed to injuries suffered by the person who assumes the risk of such injury.

The more modern legal theory is that of comparative negligence by which the negligence, if any, of the injured party is compared to the negligence of the other person or entity whose negligence is alleged to have contributed to the injury of the plaintiff. If the negligence of the person being sued is more than that of the harmed individual, that plaintiff is entitled to a judgment on his or her behalf. However, the amount of money to be awarded to the plaintiff is reduced by a percentage that corresponds to the court determined percentage of the plaintiff's negligence.

For example, if a plaintiff is determined by a jury to have suffered injuries valued by the jury at $1,000,000 and the jury also determines that the plaintiff was 40% negligent while the defendant was 60% negligent, the award to the plaintiff would be reduced by 40% which in this example would result in the plaintiff being awarded $600,000.

Tort laws apply not only to individuals, but also the makers of products used in sports, such as football helmets. Here potential tort liability is determined under product liability laws.

Criminal actions are brought by the government and use the stricter standard of proof requiring guilt be proven beyond a reasonable doubt and to a moral certainty. It is not unusual for the same conduct, such as assault and battery to qualify for both civil and criminal sanctions.

Many sports, such as football, hockey and, of course, boxing contain levels of violent, physical contact that would not be allowed outside of the sporting venue, but are within the rules of the particular sport consented to by the participants in the context of the sport. However, even these sports have levels of violence that go beyond what is consented to as "part of the game" and rise to a level of a civil tort, a crime or both. A good example is Mike Tyson's biting off of a piece of the ear of Evander Holyfield during a heavyweight boxing match in 1997. No criminal charges were brought, primarily because Holyfield refused to file a criminal complaint. Nor did Holyfield bring a civil action against Tyson although he certainly had sufficient grounds for such an action. The boxing authorities did, however, suspend Tyson's license to box for a period of seventeen months and fined him three million dollars.

Actions that would be undoubtedly considered civil or criminal assaults off of the playing field may merely result in a penalty during the game, a league imposed fine or in egregious circumstances a suspension. Only the most serious assaults ever result in civil or criminal penalties.

# ALBERT HAYNESWORTH

During a game in 2006 between the NFL's Tennessee Titans and the Dallas Cowboys, following a Dallas touchdown, Tennessee Titans defensive player Albert Haynesworth stomped on the head of Cowboys' Center Andre Gurode while he was on the ground. Haynesworth received a penalty for his actions and was also ejected from the game. Gurode required 30 stitches to close the wound below his right eye. The NFL suspended Haynesworth for five games without pay, but no legal action was taken against Haynesworth by Nashville law enforcement authorities, primarily because Gurode did not wish criminal charges to be brought.

## QUESTION

1. Should prosecutors bring criminal charges against particularly egregious and violent violations of the rules by a participant in a sporting event even when the injured party does not desire to be part of a criminal prosecution?

# AUTHORITY OF COURTS OVER SPORTS VIOLENCE

Perhaps the most significant case to deal with the authority of the courts to deal with violence during sporting events is Hackbart v. Cincinnati Bengals and Charles Clark.

Dale Hackbart was a defensive back for the Denver Broncos. During a game against the Cincinnati Bengals in 1973 a pass was intercepted by a Bronco defensive player and during the runback Hackbart attempted to block Cincinnati player Boobie Clark. In anger and frustration, Clark struck Hackbart on the head and neck while Hackbart was kneeling on the ground. No penalty was called because no referee saw what had occurred, however, film of the game clearly showed Clark improperly hit Hackbart. As a result of the assault on Hackbart suffered a broken neck.

Hackbart sued Clark and the Bengals civilly, however, despite the fact that the blow to Hackbart was intentional, the trial court judge ruled that professional football is a violent game and that Clark assumed the risk of such an injury.

The trial court ruled that such acts of violence and brutality were reasonably foreseeable. The judge also ruled that it was difficult for participants in a professional football game to control their anger and that such confrontations were merely a part of the game. On appeal, however, the Appeals Court ruled that extent of the harm and intentional striking of Hackbart was outside of the realm of the sport as a matter of degree. The court determined that there was no principle of law that allows a court to rule out certain tortious conduct by reason of general roughness of the game or difficulty of administering such rules.

## HACKBART V. CINCINNATI BENGALS, INC.

United States Court of Appeals, Tenth Circuit
601 F.2d 516 (1979)

Before DOYLE, MCKAY and LOGAN, CIRCUIT JUDGES.

WILLIAM E. DOYLE, CIRCUIT JUDGE.

The question in this case is whether in a regular season professional football game an injury which is inflicted by one professional football player on an opposing player can give rise to liability in tort where the injury was inflicted by the intentional striking of a blow during the game.

The injury occurred in the course of a game between the Denver Broncos and the Cincinnati Bengals, which game was being played in Denver in 1973. The Broncos' defensive back, Dale Hackbart, was the recipient of the injury and the Bengals' offensive back, Charles "Booby" Clark, inflicted the blow which produced it.

By agreement the liability question was determined by the United States District Court for the District of Colorado without a jury. The judge resolved the liability issue in favor of the Cincinnati team and Charles Clark. Consistent with this result, final judgment was entered for Cincinnati and the appeal challenges this judgment. In essence the trial court's reasons for rejecting plaintiff's claim were that professional football is a species of warfare and that so much physical force is tolerated and the magnitude of the force exerted is so great that it renders injuries not actionable in court; that even intentional batteries are beyond the scope of the judicial process.

Clark was an offensive back and just before the injury he had run a pass pattern to the right side of the Denver Broncos' end zone. The injury flowed indirectly from this play. The pass was intercepted by Billy Thompson, a Denver free safety, who returned it to mid-field. The subject injury occurred as an aftermath of the pass play.

As a consequence of the interception, the roles of Hackbart and Clark suddenly changed. Hackbart, who had been defending, instantaneously became an offensive player. Clark, on the other hand, became a defensive player. Acting as an offensive player, Hackbart attempted to block Clark by throwing his body in front of him. He thereafter remained on the ground. He turned, and with one knee on the ground, watched the play following the interception.

The trial court's finding was that Charles Clark, "acting out of anger and frustration, but without a specific intent to injure * * * stepped forward and struck a blow with his right forearm to the back of the kneeling plaintiff's head and neck with sufficient force to cause both players to fall forward to the ground." Both players, without complaining to the officials or to one another, returned to their respective sidelines since the ball had changed hands and the offensive and defensive teams of each had been substituted. Clark testified at trial that his frustration was brought about by the fact that his team was losing the game.

Due to the failure of the officials to view the incident, a foul was not called. However, the game film showed very clearly what had occurred. Plaintiff did not at the time report the happening to his coaches or to anyone else during the game. However, because of the pain which he experienced he was unable to play golf the next day. He did not seek medical attention, but the continued pain caused him to report this fact and the incident to the Bronco trainer who gave him treatment. Apparently he played on the specialty teams for two successive Sundays, but after that the Broncos released him on waivers. (He was in his thirteenth year as a player.) He sought medical help and it was then that it was discovered by the physician that he had a serious neck fracture injury.

Despite the fact that the defendant Charles Clark admitted that the blow which had been struck was not accidental, that it was intentionally administered, the trial court ruled as a matter of law that the game of professional football is basically a business which is violent in nature, and that the available sanctions are imposition of penalties and expulsion from the game. Notice was taken of the fact that many fouls are overlooked; that the game is played in an emotional and noisy environment; and that incidents such as that here complained of are not unusual.

The trial court spoke as well of the unreasonableness of applying the laws and rules which are a part of injury law to the game of professional football, noting the unreasonableness of holding that one player has a duty of care for the safety of others. He also talked about the concept of assumption of risk and contributory fault as applying and concluded that Hackbart had to recognize that he accepted the risk that he would be injured by such an act.

## THE ISSUES AND CONTENTIONS

1. Whether the trial court erred in ruling that as a matter of policy the principles of law governing the infliction of injuries should be entirely refused where the injury took place in the course of the game.

## WHETHER THE EVIDENCE SUPPORTED THE JUDGMENT

The evidence at the trial uniformly supported the proposition that the intentional striking of a player in the head from the rear is not an accepted part of either the playing rules or the general customs of the game of professional football. The trial court, however, believed that the unusual nature of the case called for the consideration of underlying policy which it defined as common law principles which have evolved as a result of the case to case process and which necessarily affect behavior in various contexts. From these considerations the belief was expressed that even *intentional* injuries incurred in football games should be outside the framework of the law. The court recognized that the potential threat of legal liability has a significant deterrent effect, and further said that private civil actions constitute an important mechanism for societal control of human conduct. Due to the increase in severity of human conflicts, a need existed to expand the body of governing law more rapidly and with more certainty, but that this had to be accomplished by legislation and administrative regulation. The judge compared football to coal mining and railroading insofar as all are inherently hazardous. Judge Matsch said that in the case of football it was questionable whether social values would be improved by limiting the violence.

Thus the district court's assumption was that Clark had inflicted an intentional blow which would ordinarily generate civil liability and which might bring about a criminal sanction as well, but that since it had occurred in the course of a football game, it should not be subject to the restraints of the law; that if it were it would place unreasonable impediments and restraints on the activity. The judge also pointed out that courts are ill-suited to decide the different social questions and to administer conflicts on what is much like a battlefield where the restraints of civilization have been left on the sidelines.

We are forced to conclude that the result reached is not supported by evidence.

## WHETHER INTENTIONAL INJURY IS ALLOWED BY EITHER WRITTEN RULE OR CUSTOM

Plaintiff, of course, maintains that tort law applicable to the injury in this case applies on the football field as well as in other places. On the other hand, plaintiff does not rely on the theory of negligence being applicable. This is in recognition of the fact that subjecting another to unreasonable risk of harm, the essence of negligence, is inherent in the game of football, for admittedly it is violent. Plaintiff maintains that in the area of contributory fault, a vacuum exists in relationship to intentional infliction of injury. Since negligence does not apply, contributory negligence is inapplicable. Intentional or reckless contributory fault could theoretically at least apply to infliction of injuries in reckless disregard of the rights of others. This has some similarity to contributory negligence and undoubtedly it would apply if the evidence would justify it. But it is highly questionable whether a professional football player consents or submits to injuries caused by conduct not within the rules, and there is no evidence which we have seen which shows this. However, the trial court did not consider this question and we are not deciding it.

Contrary to the position of the court then, there are no principles of law which allow a court to rule out certain tortious conduct by reason of general roughness of the game or difficulty of administering it.

Indeed, the evidence shows that there are rules of the game which prohibit the intentional striking of blows. Thus, Article 1, Item 1, Subsection C, provides that:

All players are prohibited from striking on the head, face or neck with the heel, back or side of the hand, wrist, forearm, elbow or clasped hands.

Thus the very conduct which was present here is expressly prohibited by the rule which is quoted above.

The general customs of football do not approve the intentional punching or striking of others. That this is prohibited was supported by the testimony of all of the witnesses. They testified that the intentional striking of a player in the face or from the rear is prohibited by the playing rules as well as the general customs of the game. Punching or hitting with the arms is prohibited. Undoubtedly these restraints are intended to establish reasonable boundaries so that one football player cannot intentionally inflict a serious injury on another. Therefore, the notion is not correct that all reason has been abandoned, whereby the only possible remedy for the person who has been the victim of an unlawful blow is retaliation.

## WAS IT LEGALLY JUSTIFIABLE FOR THE TRIAL COURT TO HOLD, AS A MATTER OF POLICY, THAT JURISDICTION SHOULD NOT BE ASSUMED OVER THE CASE IN VIEW OF THE FACT THAT IT AROSE OUT OF A PROFESSIONAL FOOTBALL GAME?

Whether the theory of judicial restraint applies.

It is a well-settled principle of federal jurisdiction that where a federal court does not have a discretion to accept or reject jurisdiction, if it does not have jurisdiction, it will not take it; but it is ruled, on the other hand, that if it has jurisdiction it must take it. This principle has been expressed many times with perhaps one of the best expressions being found in an early opinion, that of Mr. Chief Justice Marshall in *Cohens v. Virginia,* 19 U.S. (6 Wheat.) 264, 404, 5 L.Ed. 257 (1821):

It is most true, that this court will not take jurisdiction if it should not: but it is equally true, that it must take jurisdiction, if it should. The judiciary cannot, as the legislature may, avoid a measure, because it approaches the confines of the constitution. We cannot pass it by, because it is doubtful. With whatever doubts, with whatever difficulties, a case may be attended, we must decide it, if it be brought before us. We have no more right to decline the exercise of jurisdiction which is given, than to usurp that which is not given. The one or the other would be treason to the constitution. Questions may occur, which we would gladly avoid; but we cannot avoid them. All we can do is, to exercise our best judgment, and conscientiously to perform our duty. In doing this, on the present occasion, we find this tribunal invested with appellate jurisdiction in all cases arising under the constitution and laws of the United States. We find no exception to this grant, and we cannot insert one.

Much more recently the Supreme Court in the case of *Willcox v. Consolidated Gas Co.,* 212 U.S. 19, 40, 29 S.Ct. 192, 195, 53 L.Ed. 382 (1909), speaking through Mr. Justice Peckham, stated that where a federal court is appealed to in the case over which it has by law jurisdiction, it is its duty to take such jurisdiction.

The spirit and the letter of the decisions are that if jurisdiction to hear or determine cases exists, as it does in the case at bar, the cause is to be tried on its merits.

The position which was adopted by the trial court in this case was then directly contrary to all of the law dealing with the exercise of jurisdiction by federal courts.

## IS THE STANDARD OF RECKLESS DISREGARD OF THE RIGHTS OF OTHERS APPLICABLE TO THE PRESENT SITUATION?

The Restatement of Torts Second, § 500, distinguishes between reckless and negligent misconduct. Reckless misconduct differs from negligence, according to the authors, in that negligence consists of mere inadvertence, lack of skillfulness or failure to take precautions; reckless misconduct, on the other hand, involves a choice or adoption of a course of action either with knowledge of the danger or with knowledge of facts which would disclose this danger to a reasonable man. Recklessness also differs in that it consists of intentionally doing an act with knowledge not only that it contains a risk of harm to others as does negligence, but that it actually involves a risk substantially greater in magnitude than is necessary in the case of negligence. The authors explain the difference, therefore, in the degree of risk by saying that the difference is so significant as to amount to a difference in kind.

Subsection (f) also distinguishes between reckless misconduct and intentional wrongdoing. To be reckless the *act* must have been intended by the actor. At the same time, the actor does not intend to cause the harm which results from it. It is enough that he realized, or from the facts should have realized, that there was a strong probability that harm would result even though he may hope or expect that this conduct will prove harmless. Nevertheless, existence of probability is different from substantial certainty which is an ingredient of intent to cause the harm which results from the act.

Therefore, recklessness exists where a person knows that the act is harmful but fails to realize that it will produce the extreme harm which it did produce. It is in this respect that recklessness and intentional conduct differ in degree.

In the case at bar the defendant Clark admittedly acted impulsively and in the heat of anger, and even though it could be said from the admitted facts that he intended the act, it could also be said that he did not intend to inflict serious injury which resulted from the blow which he struck.

In ruling that recklessness is the appropriate standard and that assault and battery is not the exclusive one, we are saying that these two liability concepts are not necessarily opposed one to the other. Rather, recklessness under § 500 of the Restatement might be regarded, for the purpose of analysis at least, a lesser included act.

Assault and battery, having originated in a common law writ, is narrower than recklessness in its scope. In essence, two definitions enter into it. The assault is an attempt coupled with the present ability to commit a violent harm against another. Battery is the unprivileged or unlawful touching of another. Assault and battery then call for an intent, as does recklessness. But in recklessness the intent is to do the act, but without an intent to cause the particular harm. It is enough if the actor knows that there is a strong probability that harm will result. Thus, the definition fits perfectly the fact situation here. Surely, then, no reason exists to compel appellant to employ the assault and battery standard which does not comfortably apply fully in preference to the standard which meets this fact situation.

In sum, having concluded that the trial court did not limit the case to a trial of the evidence bearing on defendant's liability but rather determined that as a matter of social policy the game was so violent and unlawful that valid lines could not be drawn, we take the view that this was not a proper issue for determination and that plaintiff was entitled to have the case tried on an assessment of his rights and whether they had been violated.

The cause is reversed and remanded for a new trial in accordance with the foregoing views.

# TED GREEN—WAYNE MAKI

In a 1969 pre-season exhibition hockey game between the Boston Bruins and the St. Louis Blues, Bruins player Ted Green slashed Blues' player Wayne Maki who responded by hitting Green over the head (prior to the era in which players were required to wear helmets) causing extensive brain damage. Criminal charges were brought independently against both players in Canada where the game had taken place and each was acquitted. Each judge determined the other player was the instigator of the fight and ruled that the incident was merely a part of the game and players assumed the risk of such harm.

In the Maki case Regina v. Maki, 3 O.R. 780, 782 (Canada) the judge did rule, however that "there is a question of degree involved, and no athlete should be presumed to accept malicious, unprovoked or overtly violent attack." In the Green case, 1 O.R. 591, 594 (Canada) the judge acquitted Green stating, "There is no doubt that the players who enter the hockey arena consent to a great number of assaults on their person, because the game of hockey as it is played in the National Hockey League, which is the league I am dealing with, could not possibly be played at the speed at which it is played and with the force and vigour with which it is played, and with the competition that enters into it, unless there were a great number of what would in normal circumstances be called assaults, but which are not heard of. No hockey player enters on to the ice of the National Hockey League without consenting to and without knowledge of the possibility that he is going to be hit in one of many ways once he is on that ice."

# PEOPLE V. SCHACKER

In the 1998 case of People v. Schacker, 670 N.Y.S.2d 308, 309–310 (Dist. Ct. 1998) the court went so far as to say that "In order to allege a criminal act which occurred in a hockey game, the factual portion of the information must allege acts that show that the intent was to inflict physical injury and was unrelated to the athletic competition. Although play may have terminated, the information herein does not show that the physical contact had no connection with the competition." The court made this ruling despite evidence that the defendant hit another player from behind after the whistle had blown and play was over. This expansive view of permissible violence essentially legitimizes almost any level of violence occurring during a game. This is not, however, the dominant view of courts today.

---

## QUESTION

1.   Would the possibility of criminal charges being brought against an athlete for conduct during a game with emotions running high deter intense play necessary for success?

# STEVE MOORE—TODD BERTUZZI

During a 2004 game between the Vancouver Canucks and the Colorado Avalanche, Steve Moore of the Avalanche injured Vancouver player Markus Naslund with a hard, but within the rules, check that Naslund never saw coming. No penalty was called. As a result of his injury, Naslund missed five games. Three weeks later the Canucks and Avalanche played again and Todd Bertuzzi, in his role as an "enforcer" for the Canucks continually tried to taunt Moore into a fight, which Moore repeatedly avoided. Finally, Bertuzzi skated up behind Moore, punched him on the side of the head, knocked him to the ice and repeatedly beat Moore. Criminal charges were brought against Bertuzzi and he pleaded guilty to criminal assault causing bodily harm. He was sentenced to a year's probation and eighty hours of community service. The NHL suspended him for fifteen months. Moore suffered a concussion, three fractured vertebra and never played another minute in the NHL. Moore sued Bertuzzi civilly and ultimately settled for an undisclosed amount.

---

## QUESTIONS

1.   How does a judge determine the level of violence permissible in a particular sport?

2.   Fighting in hockey is so much a part of the game, there are even rules for it. When should those fights be subject to criminal or civil sanctions?

# ASSUMPTION OF THE RISK

Jose Avila was a college baseball player who in 2001 was hit in the head by a pitched ball during a game and sued the pitcher civilly. However, the California Supreme Court ruled that even though it is a violation of the rules of baseball for a player to intentionally throw at a player's head, that fact did not make the pitcher's action a tort. According to the court, that particular action was a part of the game and a "fundamental and inherent risk of the sport of baseball." The court also noted it was not the function of the court to police such conduct.

## AVILA V. CITRUS COMMUNITY COLLEGE DISTRICT

Supreme Court of California
38 Cal.4th 148 (2006)

During an intercollegiate baseball game at a community college, one of the home team's batters is hit by a pitch. In the next half-inning, the home team's pitcher allegedly retaliates with an inside pitch and hits a visiting batter in the head. The visiting batter is injured, he sues, and the courts must umpire the dispute.

Factual and Procedural Background

Jose Luis Avila, a Rio Hondo Community College (Rio Hondo) student, played baseball for the Rio Hondo Roadrunners. On January 5, 2001, Rio Hondo was playing a preseason road game against the Citrus Community College Owls (Citrus College). During the game, a Roadrunners pitcher hit a Citrus College batter with a pitch when Avila came to bat in the top of the next inning, the Citrus College pitcher hit him in the head with a pitch, cracking his batting helmet. Avila alleges the pitch was an intentional "beanball" thrown in retaliation for the previous hit batter or, at a minimum, was thrown negligently.

Avila staggered, felt dizzy, and was in pain. The Rio Hondo manager told him to go to first base. Avila did so, and when he complained to the Rio Hondo first base coach, he was told to stay in the game. At second base, he still felt pain, numbness, and dizziness. A Citrus College player yelled to the Rio Hondo dugout that the Roadrunners needed a pinch runner. Avila walked off the field and went to the Rio Hondo bench. No one tended to his injuries. As a result, Avila suffered unspecified serious personal injuries.

## II.   The Duty of Care Owed College Athletes

### A.   Primary Assumption of the Risk and the Duty Not to Increase Risks Inherent in a Sport

The District asserted as an alternate basis for demurrer that it owed Avila no duty of care. To recover for negligence, Avila must demonstrate, inter alia, that the District breached a duty of care it owed him. Generally, each person has a duty to exercise reasonable care in the circumstances and is liable to those injured by the failure to do so. (Rowland v. Christian (1968) 69 Cal.2d 108, 112, 70 Cal.Rptr. 97, 443 P.2d 561.) By statute, the Legislature has extended this common law standard of tort liability to public employees (§ 820, subd. (a); Hoff v. Vacaville Unified School Dist. (1998) 19 Cal.4th 925, 932, 80 Cal.Rptr.2d 811, 968 P.2d 522) and has extended liability for public employees' negligent acts to public entity defendants (§ 815.2, subd. (a); Hoff, at p. 932, 80 Cal.Rptr.2d 811, 968 P.2d 522).

The existence of " ' "[d]uty" is not an immutable fact of nature " 'but only an expression of the sum total of those considerations of policy which lead the law to say that the particular plaintiff is entitled to protection.' " ' " (Parsons v. Crown Disposal Co. (1997) 15 Cal.4th 456, 472, 63 Cal.Rptr.2d 291, 936 P.2d 70.) Thus, the existence and scope of a defendant's duty is an issue of law, to be decided by a court, not a jury. (Kahn v. East Side Union High School Dist. (2003) 31 Cal.4th 990, 1004, 4 Cal.Rptr.3d 103, 75 P.3d 30.) When the injury is to a sporting participant, the considerations of policy and the question of duty necessarily become intertwined with the question of assumption of risk.

The traditional version of the assumption of risk doctrine required proof that the plaintiff voluntarily accepted a specific known and appreciated risk. (Prescott v. Ralph's Grocery Co. (1954) 42 Cal.2d 158, 161–162, 265 P.2d 904, citing Rest., Torts, § 893.) The doctrine depended on the actual subjective knowledge of the given plaintiff (Shahinian v. McCormick (1963) 59 Cal.2d 554, 567, 30 Cal.Rptr. 521, 381 P.2d 377) and, where the elements were met, was an absolute defense to liability for injuries arising from the known risk (Quinn v. Recreation Park Assn. (1935) 3 Cal.2d 725, 731, 46 P.2d 144).

California's abandonment of the doctrine of contributory negligence in favor of comparative negligence (Li v. Yellow Cab Co. (1975) 13 Cal.3d 804, 119 Cal.Rptr. 858, 532 P.2d 1226) led to a reconceptualization of the assumption of risk. In Knight v. Jewett (1992) 3 Cal.4th 296, 11 Cal.Rptr.2d 2, 834 P.2d 696 (Knight), a plurality of this court explained that there are in fact two species of assumption of risk: primary and secondary. (Id. at pp. 308–309, 11 Cal.Rptr.2d 2, 834 P.2d 696 (plur. opn. of George, J.).) Primary assumption of the risk arises when, as a matter of law and policy, a defendant owes no duty to protect a plaintiff from particular harms. (Ibid.) Applied in the sporting context, it precludes liability for injuries arising from those risks deemed inherent in a sport; as a matter of law, others have no legal duty to eliminate those risks or otherwise protect a sports participant from them. (Id. at pp. 315–316, 11 Cal.Rptr.2d 2, 834 P.2d 696.) Under this duty approach, a court need not ask what risks a particular plaintiff subjectively knew of and chose to encounter, but instead must evaluate the fundamental nature of the sport and the defendant's role in or relationship to that sport in order to determine whether the defendant owes a duty to protect a plaintiff from the particular risk of harm. (Id. at pp. 313, 315–317, 11 Cal.Rptr.2d 2, 834 P.2d 696.) A majority of this court has since embraced the Knight approach. (Kahn v. East Side Union High School Dist., supra, 31 Cal.4th at pp. 1004–1005, 4 Cal.Rptr.3d 103, 75 P.3d 30; Cheong v. Antablin (1997) 16 Cal.4th 1063, 1067–1068, 68 Cal.Rptr.2d 859, 946 P.2d 817.)

B.   Application

We consider next whether Avila has alleged facts supporting breach of the duty not to enhance the inherent risks of his sport. Though it numbers them differently, Avila's complaint in essence alleges four ways in which the District breached a duty to Avila: by (1) conducting the game at all; (2) failing to control the Citrus College pitcher; (3) failing to provide umpires to supervise and control the game; and (4) failing to provide medical care. The District's demurrer was properly sustained if, and only if, each of these alleged breaches, assumed to be true, falls outside any duty owed by the District and within the inherent risks of the sport assumed by Avila.

With respect to the first of these, conducting the game, Avila cites unspecified "community college baseball rules" prohibiting preseason games. But the only consequence of the District's hosting the game was that it exposed Avila, who chose to participate, to the ordinary inherent risks of the sport of baseball. Nothing about the bare fact of the District's hosting the game enhanced those ordinary risks, so its doing so, whether or not in violation of the alleged rules, does not constitute a breach of its duty not to enhance the ordinary risks of baseball. Nor did the District owe any separate duty to Avila not to host the game.

The second alleged breach, the failure to supervise and control the Citrus College pitcher, is barred by primary assumption of the risk. Being hit by a pitch is an inherent risk of baseball. (Balthazor v. Little League Baseball, Inc. (1998) 62 Cal.App.4th 47, 51–52, 72 Cal.Rptr.2d 337; see also Mann v. Nutrilite, Inc. (1955) 136 Cal.App.2d 729, 734, 289 P.2d 282 [same re being hit by thrown ball].) The dangers of being hit by a pitch, often thrown at speeds approaching 100 miles per hour, are apparent and well known: being hit can result in serious injury or, on rare tragic occasions, death.

Being intentionally hit is likewise an inherent risk of the sport, so accepted by custom that a pitch intentionally thrown at a batter has its own terminology: "brushback," "beanball," "chin music." In turn, those pitchers notorious for throwing at hitters are "headhunters." Pitchers intentionally throw at batters to disrupt a batter's timing or back him away from home plate, to retaliate after a teammate has been hit, or to punish a batter for having hit a home run. (See, e.g., Kahn, The Head Game (2000) pp. 205–239.) Some of the most respected baseball managers and pitchers have openly discussed the fundamental place throwing at batters has in their sport. In George Will's study of the game, Men at Work, one-time Oakland Athletics and current St. Louis Cardinals manager Tony La Russa details the strategic importance of ordering selective intentional throwing at opposing batters, principally to retaliate for one's own players being hit. (Will, Men at Work (1990) pp. 61–64.) As Los Angeles Dodgers Hall of Fame pitcher Don Drysdale and New York Giants All Star pitcher Sal "The Barber" Maglie have explained, intentionally throwing at batters can also be an integral part of pitching tactics, a tool to help get batters out by upsetting their frame of mind. Drysdale and Maglie are not alone; past and future Hall of Famers, from Early Wynn and Bob Gibson to Pedro Martinez and Roger Clemens, have relied on the actual or threatened willingness to throw at batters to aid their pitching. (See, e.g., Kahn, The Head Game, at pp. 223–224; Yankees Aced by Red Sox, L.A. Times (May 31, 2001) p. D7 [relating Martinez's assertion that he would even throw at Babe Ruth].)

While these examples relate principally to professional baseball, "[t]here is nothing legally significant about the level of play" in this case. (West v. Sundown Little League of Stockton, Inc. (2002) 96 Cal.App.4th 351, 359–360, 116 Cal.Rptr.2d 849; see Balthazor v. Little League Baseball, Inc., supra, 62 Cal.App.4th at pp. 51–52, 72 Cal.Rptr.2d 337; Mann v. Nutrilite, Inc., supra, 136 Cal.App.2d at p. 734, 289 P.2d 282.) The laws of physics that make a thrown baseball dangerous and the strategic benefits that arise from disrupting a batter's timing are only minimally dependent on the skill level of the participants, and we see no reason to distinguish between collegiate and professional baseball in applying primary assumption of the risk.

It is true that intentionally throwing at a batter is forbidden by the rules of baseball. (See, e.g., Off. Rules of Major League Baseball, rule 8.02(d); National Collegiate Athletic Assn., 2006 NCAA Baseball Rules (Dec.2005) rule 5, § 16(d), p. 62.) But "even when a participant's conduct violates a rule of the game and may subject the violator to internal sanctions prescribed by the sport itself, imposition of legal liability for such conduct might well alter fundamentally the nature of the sport by deterring participants from vigorously engaging in activity that falls close to, but on the permissible side of, a prescribed rule." (Knight, supra, 3 Cal.4th at pp. 318–319, 11 Cal.Rptr.2d 2, 834 P.2d 696.) It is one thing for an umpire to punish a pitcher who hits a batter by ejecting him from the game, or for a league to suspend the pitcher; it is quite another for tort law to chill any pitcher from throwing inside, i.e., close to the batter's body-a permissible and essential part of the sport-for fear of a suit over an errant pitch. For better or worse, being intentionally thrown at is a fundamental part and inherent risk of the sport of baseball. It is not the function of tort law to police such conduct.

In Knight, supra, 3 Cal.4th at page 320, 11 Cal.Rptr.2d 2, 834 P.2d 696, we acknowledged that an athlete does not assume the risk of a coparticipant's intentional or reckless conduct "totally outside the range of the ordinary activity involved in the sport." Here, even if the Citrus College pitcher intentionally threw at Avila, his conduct did not fall outside the range of ordinary activity involved in the sport. The District owed no duty to Avila to prevent the Citrus College pitcher from hitting batters, even intentionally. Consequently, the doctrine of primary assumption of the risk bars any claim predicated on the allegation that the Citrus College pitcher negligently or intentionally threw at Avila. The dissent suggests primary assumption of the risk should not extend to an intentional tort such as battery and that Avila should have been granted leave to amend to allege a proper battery claim. (Conc. & dis. opn.post, 41 Cal.Rptr.3d at pp. 317–319, 131 P.3d at pp. 398–402.) Amendment would have been futile. Absence of consent is an element of battery. (Barouh v. Haberman (1994) 26

Cal.App.4th 40, 45–46, 31 Cal.Rptr.2d 259.) "One who enters into a sport, game or contest may be taken to consent to physical contacts consistent with the understood rules of the game." (Prosser & Keeton, Torts (5th ed.1984) § 18, p. 114; see also Knight, supra, 3 Cal.4th at p. 311, 11 Cal.Rptr.2d 2, 834 P.2d 696 ["It may be accurate to suggest that an individual who voluntarily engages in a dangerous activity 'consents to' or 'agrees to assume' the risks inherent in the activity"]; Ritchie-Gamester v. City of Berkley (1999) 461 Mich. 73, 597 N.W.2d 517, 524 ["The act of stepping onto the field may be described as 'consent to the inherent risks of the activity' "].) Thus, the boxer who steps into the ring consents to his opponent's jabs; the football player who steps onto the gridiron consents to his opponent's hard tackle; the hockey goalie who takes the ice consents to face his opponent's slapshots; and, here, the baseball player who steps to the plate consents to the possibility the opposing pitcher may throw near or at him. The complaint establishes Avila voluntarily participated in the baseball game; as such, his consent would bar any battery claim as a matter of law.

Disposition

For the foregoing reasons, we reverse the judgment of the Court of Appeal.

The dissenting judge, however, had an interesting point in regard to intentionality when he wrote:

"My third concern is that the majority's application of the no-duty-for-sports rule to include pitches intentionally thrown at a batter's head is an ill-conceived expansion of that rule into intentional torts. In Knight, the plaintiff alleged only that the defendant acted negligently (Knight v. Jewett, supra, 3 Cal.4th at p. 318, 11 Cal.Rptr.2d 2, 834 P.2d 696), and the plurality there justified the no-duty-for-sports rule with the comment that a baseball player should not be held liable "for an injury resulting from a carelessly thrown ball or bat during a baseball game" (ibid., italics added). Here, however, the majority applies that rule to hold that the trial court properly sustained the District's demurrer to Avila's cause of action alleging an intentional tort, in which he alleged that the pitch that hit him "was thrown in a deliberate retaliatory fashion, with reckless disregard for the safety of plaintiff." Even if I were to accept the majority's misguided no-duty-for-sports rule, I would apply it only to causes of action for negligence, not for intentional torts."

# CONCUSSIONS

In recent years much attention has been focused on the dangers of concussions particularly in the sport of football as it relates to the condition known as Chronic traumatic encephalopathy (CTE).

# CTE

Chronic traumatic encephalopathy (CTE) is thought to come about as a result of repeated head trauma that harms brain cells in sections of the brain that control mood, emotions and executive functioning. CTE symptoms, which can be confused with Alzheimer's disease symptoms, include cognitive impairment, dementia, depression, memory loss, confusion, tremors and more.

According to Dr. Ann McKee, the Director of the Boston University CTE Center, even impacts less than required to bring about a concussion are dangerous. Dr. McKee said, "The science has evolved. All the work to date is that concussions don't correlate with CTE, rather it's the length of playing, the years of exposure to trauma, and the subconcussive impacts that correlate to severity and the risk of CTE."[1]

According to a study from 2011:

"Risk and Protective Factors

Clearly, CTE research is in its infancy, and decades of research are likely necessary to move the field to the point where CTE can be

---

[1]  "Scientific and medical jargon aside, Kevin Turner died from playing football," Boston Globe, Christopher L. Gasper, November 5, 2016.

diagnosed early in its course using a combination of clinical tools and biomarkers. However, the research that has currently been conducted has profound implications for current practice by medical professionals, athletic trainers, and related specialists, as well as policy makers in both government and athletic organizations. CTE is the only known neurodegenerative dementia with a specific identifiable cause; in this case, the cause is head trauma. It is unknown whether a single blow to the head is sufficient to initiate the metabolic cascade that precedes the clinical and neuropathological changes characteristic of CTE, as all confirmed cases of CTE to date have had a history of multiple head injuries. Therefore, the most obvious way to prevent CTE is, in theory, to prevent repetitive head injuries from occurring. In some sports, such as boxing and American football, it may be impossible to prevent repetitive head injuries, especially the repeated subconcussive blows that are characteristic of the impacts felt by offensive and defensive linemen in football on nearly every play. In sports where repeated blows to the head are unavoidable, proper concussion assessment and management may be paramount for preventing long-term consequences. At the present time, it is unknown whether returning to play while symptomatic from a previous concussion, or sustaining a second concussion while symptomatic, is a risk factor for developing CTE. However, other strategies to reduce the number and severity of head trauma are possible, such as limiting full-contact practices, implementing rules of play which diminish the likelihood of repeated head trauma (e.g., removing the three-point stance in football), or increasing the use of newer protective headgear aimed at absorbing force and thus diminishing the impact to the brain.

Along these same lines, there are many potential variables surrounding head trauma in athletes that may be important for preventing CTE later in life. The sport played and the position played within each sport may be relevant; for instance, boxers receive a greater proportion of rotational forces to the head, while American football players receive a greater proportion of linear forces to the head. Even within the same sport, athlete exposure to head injuries can differ considerably. In the case of American football, some positions such as wide receiver may receive occasional severe blows with the potential to cause unconsciousness, while other players, such as linemen, may take hundreds of small impacts per season, most of which are not, in and of themselves, forceful enough to cause symptoms. It is unknown whether CTE is more likely to occur following a small number of severe head injuries, a large number of subconcussive injuries, or other forms of head trauma. Currently, investigations are ongoing that attempt to quantify the force of head impacts across different sports and positions. These findings will play an important role in understanding the specific head injury variables that influence CTE risk.

The age at which an athlete suffers his or her head injuries may also influence future CTE risk. At younger ages, the brain may be more vulnerable to injury. On the other hand, the increased plasticity of the young brain may be better able to compensate for specific difficulties such as behavioral dysfunction It is also not clear whether particular lifestyle factors may be protective against CTE in the context of repetitive head injuries. In other neurodegenerative diseases such as AD, the neuropathology is thought to precede the clinical symptoms, possibly by several decades. The same may be true for CTE, as evidenced by the presence of CTE neuropathology in asymptomatic individuals studied at autopsy. Conceivably, health and medical factors that are absent or present during this preclinical stage may influence the extent of neurodegeneration or the brain's ability to compensate for any neurodegeneration. For instance, the presence of chronic inflammation, such as that which accompanies medical conditions such as obesity, hypertension, diabetes mellitus, atherosclerosis, and heart disease, may facilitate neurodegeneration and NFT formation. In addition, as with other neurodegenerative diseases like AD, some individuals may have greater 'cognitive reserve,' thus increasing the threshold for the clinical manifestation of the underlying neuropathological condition.".[2]

# COLLEGE FOOTBALL AND CONCUSSIONS

Concussions are not limited to NFL players. In 2016, the Concussion Legacy Foundation announced that the brains of more than a hundred former college football teams were diagnosed as having CTE.

In 2016 Federal Judge John Z. Lee gave preliminary approval to a 75 million dollar class action against the NCAA regarding concussions. If final approval is granted, the NCAA will set up a fifty year medical monitoring program for college athletes and fund research into the prevention and treatment of concussions. The medical monitoring program will apply to both current and prior NCAA athletes without regard to the sport they played. The settlement also provided for new concussion protocols for schools to follow in regard to testing and return to play. The settlement does not apply to individual concussion cases brought by individual players, most notably Ray Griffin, the brother of two time Heisman Trophy winner Archie Griffin which will proceed on their own through the courts. Griffin sued the NCAA and the Big 10 although, interestingly not Ohio State University for whom he played defensive back from 1974 through 1977.

# YOUTH FOOTBALL CONCUSSIONS

The NFL supported and promoted the Heads-Up Football program, which is an online course that teaches youth football coaches about safety procedures in order to increase the safety of young football

    2    Gavett BE, RA Stern; AC McKee, Chronic traumatic encephalopathy: a potential late effect of sport-related concussive and subconcussive head trauma, Clinics In Sports Medicine, Jan 01, 2011; Vol. 30, No. 1.

players. The NFL has touted an independent 2015 study[3] that they said proved that the program reduced injuries by 76 percent and concussions by 30 percent. However, a 2016 review of the program by the NY Times[4] showed no demonstrable effect on injuries including concussions. Participation in youth football has dropped from 3 million children in 2010 to 2.2 million in 2015. This drop is largely attributed to concerns of parents about concussions and other injuries.

# POP WARNER LAWSUITS

In 2016 a class action was filed against Pop Warner which operates a tackle football program for children as young as five years old who can participate in its tiny-mite division up to age fifteen in its varsity program. The class action also was brought against USA Football and the organization creating safety standards for football helmets for failing to protect children from the dangers of brain trauma and ignoring medical research as to the dangers of football. The class action was brought by mothers of two deceased former Pop Warner players who were found to have CTE when they died prematurely. More than 250,000 children play Pop Warner football around the country each year. The class action alleges that Pop Warner and the other defendants misled parents as to the dangers of youth football. The lawsuit alleges that the defendants misrepresented the safety of football, the safety of the equipment and the training of their coaches. Previously Pop Warner had settled lawsuits brought by parents of a boy with degenerative brain disease who had played Pop Warner

[3] "Comprehensive Coach Education and Practice Contact Restriction Guidelines Result in Lower Injury Rates in Youth American Football," The Orthopaedic Journal of Sports Medicine, 3(7) Zachary Y. Kerr, 2015.

[4] "NFL-Backed Youth Program Says It Reduced Concussions. The Data Disagrees." NY Times, Alan Schwarz, July 27, 2016.

football and later committed suicide as well as with the mother of Donnovan Hill a paralyzed player.[5]

## QUESTION

1. Should young children be permitted to play tackle football and, if so, should the rules be changed to reduce the level of concussive and subconcussive impacts?

# OTHER SPORTS AND CONCUSSIONS

While football has the highest incidents of concussions with women's soccer the second highest, brain injuries occur in many other sports as well including synchronized swimming.

According to Bill Boreau, the managing director for sports medicine for the U.S. Olympic Committee 50% of the synchronized swimmers he supervised had suffered concussions. Synchronized swimmers may swim as close as eight inches to each other and kicks in the head are not uncommon.[6]

# NFL AND CONCUSSIONS

For many years the NFL and its Mild Traumatic Brain Injury Committee which was established in 1994 downplayed the risks of head injuries and concussions. The Committee was led by Dr. Elliott J. Pellman, the team physician for the New York Jets who had no training in neurology, but was listed as the primary author of many papers published in the Journal of Neurosurgery between 2003 and 2006 that were at odds with the increasing recognition of the serious dangers posed by concussions.

---

[5] Kimberly Archie et al. v. Pop Warner Little Scholars, Inc., United States District Court, Central District of California, Western Division, Case. No. 2.16–cv–6603, Class Action Complaint.

[6] "Synchronized Swimmers Find Danger Lurking Below Surface: Concussions" NY Times, Ken Belson, July 18, 2016.

In 2005 independent neurologists studying the problem concluded that multiple concussions had a direct relationship to problems such as dementia and depression. Autopsies on former NFL players found CTE occurring as a result of multiple concussions. The response of the NFL's Concussion committee was to not only deny any relationship between concussions, CTE and other brain diseases, but to even request that the article describing the research be removed from the scientific journal in which it had been published. The studies were done by neuropathologists while there was not a single neuropathologist on the NFL's Concussion committee.

For the next few years the NFL continued to debunk the research into CTE and denied any link to concussions. However, in 2009 the NFL sponsored a study at the University of Michigan that found that former NFL players suffered from Alzheimer's disease and similar memory damaging brain diseases 19 times more often than the general public for men of the same age group.

It wasn't until late in 2009 that the NFL actually conceded that concussions posed long term health risks.[7]

During a hearing before the House Judiciary Committee on October 28, 2009 the NFL's position regarding the dangers of concussions from football was compared to the denials of the tobacco industry in years past to health issues posed by cigarette smoking. For years the NFL had taken positions similar to the tobacco industry by first denying any connection and then indicating that there was not sufficient research to indicate a connection between concussions and long term harm to players.

In 2010, the NFL appointed two neurology specialists, Dr. H. Hunt Batjer, the chairman of neurological surgery at Northwestern Memorial Hospital and Dr. Richard G. Ellenbogen, the chief of neurological surgery at Harborview Medical center to be in charge of its new NFL Head, Neck and Spine Medical Committee.

---

[7] "NFL Acknowledges Long-Term Concussion Effect, NY Times, Alan Schwarz, December 20, 2009.

In the years since then, the NFL has taken positive steps to deal with head trauma including new protocols for evaluation of concussed players and numerous rules intended to reduce the likelihood of head trauma.

In 2011, a number of retired players suffering concussion related illnesses sued the NFL. They alleged that the NFL knew of the dangers and hid them from the players and the public just as years earlier the tobacco industry knew about, yet hid the extreme health risks of smoking.

Here are copies of the original complaint's allegations: from the Plaintiff's Amended Master Administrative Long Form Complaint In Re: National Football League Players' Concussion Injury Litigation—United Sates District Court—Eastern District of Pennsylvania No. 2:12–md–02323–AB MDL No. 2323:

"2. This action arises from the pathological and debilitating effects of mild traumatic brain injuries (referenced herein as "MTBI") caused by the concussive and sub-concussive impacts that have afflicted former professional football players in the NFL. For many decades, evidence has linked repetitive MTBI to long-term neurological problems in many sports, including football. The NFL, as the organizer, marketer, and face of the most popular sport in the United States, in which MTBI is a regular occurrence and in which players are at risk for MTBI, was aware of the evidence and the risks associated with repetitive traumatic brain injuries virtually at the inception, but deliberately ignored and actively concealed the information from the Plaintiffs and all others who participated in organized football at all levels.

3. The published medical literature, as detailed later in this Complaint, contains studies of athletes dating back as far as 1928 demonstrating a scientifically observed link between repetitive blows to the head and neuro-cognitive problems. The earliest studies focused on boxers, but by the 1950s and 1960s, a substantial body of

medical and scientific evidence had been developed specifically relating to neuro-cognitive injuries in the sport of football.

4. Since the NFL's inception in the first half of the 20th Century, the NFL has been aware of the growing body of scientific evidence and its compelling conclusions that professional football players who sustain repetitive MTBI during their careers are at greater risk for chronic neurocognitive illness and disabilities both during their football careers and later in life.

5. Notwithstanding that it was aware of this body of scientific evidence, the NFL ignored, minimized, disputed, and actively suppressed broader awareness of the link between subconcussive and concussive injuries in football and the chronic neuro-cognitive damage, illnesses, and decline suffered by former players, including the Plaintiffs.

6. Since its inception, the NFL has recognized, acknowledged and acted in a monopolistic manner, intent on controlling and regulating every aspect of the game of professional football, particularly with respect to player safety and health. The NFL has used this authority to compel all NFL players and participants to follow the policies, rules, and regulations the NFL has enacted and imposed. As the governing body of professional football, the NFL has held itself out as the guardian and authority on the issue of player safety and has unilaterally shouldered for itself a common law duty to provide players with rules and information that protect them as much as possible from short-term and long-term health risks.

7. The NFL's role as the guardian of player health and safety began in the 1930s, continued throughout the 1940s, 1950s and 1960s, and continues up through the present day. The NFL has exercised that role through its unilateral decisions to issue rules to improve upon NFL football's public acceptance, to make a profit, and to address issues of player safety. During these decades, the NFL voluntarily provided teams and players with information and regulations that

directly affected the short and long term health of NFL players, including the Plaintiffs.

8. Despite the NFL's assumption of this responsibility, the NFL was negligent and failed to carry out this duty in that it failed to inform NFL players of the risks associated with MTBI and/or it was willfully blind to the medically proven fact that repetitive MTBI would lead to neuro-cognitive injuries in many NFL players, including the Plaintiffs. Further, the NFL actively suppressed and kept secret information about MTBI it knew would change the economics of the game and the health of players such as the plaintiffs.

9. The NFL, like the sport of boxing, was aware of the health risks associated with repetitive blows producing sub-concussive and concussive results and the fact that some members of the NFL player population were at significant risk of developing long-term brain damage and cognitive decline as a result. Despite its knowledge and controlling role in governing player conduct on and off the field, the NFL turned a blind eye to the risk and failed to warn and/or impose safety regulations governing this health and safety problem.

10. While the NFL has assumed voluntarily its role as the unilateral guardian of player safety, and NFL players and their families, including the Plaintiffs, have looked to the NFL for guidance on player safety issues, the NFL has exacerbated the health risk to players by promoting the game's violence and lauding players for returning to play despite being rendered unconscious and/or disoriented due to their exposure to sub-concussive and concussive forces.

11. In its supervisory role, as well as in its position as arbiter of all aspects of professional football, the NFL has, since its inception, unilaterally and voluntarily chosen how to spend its funds to investigate and regulate many different circumstances affecting player health and safety, including, but not limited to, requiring players to wear certain equipment, designating some player gear as illegal, and ultimately deciding what helmet brand should be recognized as the official equipment of the NFL.

12. During the decades of the 1970s and 1980s, the NFL was aware of publications in the medical science community that established that concussive and sub-concussive injuries to athletes and the general population were a significant risk factor for short-term and long-term neuro-cognitive health complications, both as single incidents and particularly as repetitive impacts. During these decades, the NFL voluntarily participated, albeit inadequately, in the work of various entities studying the performance and effectiveness of safety gear to reduce the risk of neurological injury. The NFL's participation in these activities was voluntary and a continuance of the historic duty it had assumed in the first half of the twentieth century.

13. By the early 1990s, the consensus among experts in the scientific community forced the NFL to take a different approach to the growing problem of MTBI among existing and former NFL players. In or around 1992, the NFL knew that many football players, including, by way of example, Al Toon, a Pro Bowl receiver for the New York Jets, had developed brain injuries, including chronic severe headaches, malaise, intolerance of loud noises, depression, and emotional lability as a consequence of multiple "dings," sub-concussive injuries, and concussions. The NFL was aware that Mr. Toon retired in 1992 because of these chronic problems.

14. In 1994, the NFL, through its own initiative and voluntary undertaking, took its historic duty and unilateral authority regarding player health and safety one step further. The NFL created and/or decided to fund the NFL's so-called Mild Traumatic Brain Injury Committee (the "MTBI Committee") ostensibly to research and study MTBI affecting NFL players. Notwithstanding this purported purpose, and despite clear medical evidence that on-field subconcussive and concussive injuries can produce MTBI with tragic results, the NFL (a) failed to inform its current and former players of the true risks associated with MTBI and (b) purposefully misrepresented and/or concealed medical evidence on that issue.

15. Through its MTBI Committee, the NFL gratuitously and voluntarily inserted itself into the scientific research and discussion concerning the link between sub-concussive and concussive impacts sustained by NFL players and short-term and long-term impairment of the brain. By voluntarily inserting itself into the MTBI research and public discourse, the NFL gratuitously undertook a responsibility (a) to make truthful statements; (b) not to wrongfully advance improper, biased, and falsified industry-generated studies; (c) not to discredit well-researched and credible studies that came to a conclusion that did not comport with the NFL's financial and political interests; and, (d) to inform all former players, all current players, and the football-playing public, including young people and their families, regarding the risks of MTBI in football.

16. At the same time, the NFL and its agents continued to market, as it had in the past, the ferocity and brutality of the sport that, in part, gives rise to the latent and debilitating neuro-cognitive conditions and injuries from which Plaintiffs now suffer.

17. After voluntarily assuming a duty to investigate, study, and truthfully report the medical risks associated with MTBI in football, the NFL produced industry-funded, biased, and falsified research that claimed that concussive and sub-concussive head impacts in football do not present serious, life-altering risks.

18. For sixteen years, the NFL actively and continuously denied any link between MTBI sustained by former NFL players in NFL games and practices and the neurological symptoms and problems (such as headaches, dizziness, loss of memory, dementia and ALS) from which they now suffer. The NFL made its biased and falsified position known by way of gratuitous press releases, publications in scientific literature, and other communications.

19. Consistent with its historic role as the guardian of player health and safety, the NFL intended for the general public, NFL players, the Plaintiffs, and participants at every level of the game to rely on the misinformation it propagated.

20. During the same time period, the NFL actively sought to suppress the findings of other members of the medical communities that showed the link between on-field sub-concussive and concussive head impacts and post-career neuro-cognitive damage, illness and decline.

21. The NFL's active and purposeful concealment and misrepresentation of the severe neurological risks of repetitive MTBI exposed players to dangers they could have avoided had the NFL provided them with truthful and accurate information. Many of the players, including the Plaintiffs, sustained repetitive MTBI while in the NFL and now suffer from latent neurodegenerative disorders and diseases, all of which, in whole or in part, were caused by the NFL's acts and/or omissions.

22. The NFL caused or contributed to the injuries and increased risks to Plaintiffs through its acts and omissions by, among other things: (a) historically ignoring the true risks of MTBI in NFL football; (b) failing to disclose the true risks of repetitive MTBI to NFL players; and (c) since 1994, deliberately spreading misinformation concerning the cause and effect relationship between MTBI in NFL football and latent neurodegenerative disorders and diseases.

23. On information and belief, the NFL's motive to ignore and misrepresent the link between MTBI sustained in NFL play and neuro-cognitive injury and decline was economic. The NFL knew or suspected that any rule changes that sought to recognize that link and the health risk to NFL players would impose an economic cost that would significantly and adversely change the profit margins enjoyed by the NFL and its teams."

# SETTLEMENT DEVELOPMENTS

Eventually the class action lawsuit was settled. By settling the lawsuit with the players the NFL managed to avoid not only any admissions of liability, but also was able to keep many of its records private. The players initially settled for an amount that the judge considered inadequate and refused to accept the settlement.

Here is an edited version of Judge Brody's opinion in which she would not approve the initially proposed settlement:

## IN RE NATIONAL FOOTBALL LEAGUE PLAYERS' CONCUSSION INJURY LITIGATION

United States District Court, E.D. Pennsylvania
961 F.Supp.2d 708 (2014)

### *MEMORANDUM*

ANITA B. BRODY, DISTRICT JUDGE.

Plaintiffs, through their proposed Co-Lead Class Counsel, Class Counsel, and Subclass Counsel, and Defendants National Football League and NFL Properties LLC (collectively, the "NFL Parties") have negotiated and agreed to a Class Action Settlement ("Settlement") that will resolve all claims against the NFL Parties in this multidistrict litigation and Related Lawsuits. To that end, proposed Co-Lead Class Counsel, Class Counsel, and Subclass Counsel have filed a Motion for Preliminary Approval and Class Certification ("Motion"). This Motion is unopposed by the NFL Parties. In light of my duty to protect the rights of all potential class members and the insufficiency of the current record, I will deny the Motion without prejudice.

### I.   BACKGROUND

In July 2011, Retired NFL Football Players filed the first lawsuit against the NFL Parties alleging, *inter alia,* that the NFL Parties breached their duties to the players by failing to take reasonable actions to protect players from the chronic risks created by concussive and sub-concussive head injuries and that the NFL Parties concealed those risks. Since then, more than 4,500 former players have filed substantially similar lawsuits. These lawsuits have been consolidated before me as a multidistrict litigation ("MDL"), pursuant to 28 U.S.C. § 1407. *See* Panel on Multidistrict Litigation Transfer

Order, Jan. 31, 2012, ECF No. 1, 842 F.Supp.2d 1378. As the transferee judge, I exercise authority over any coordinated or consolidated pretrial proceedings, including settlement proceedings. *See In re Patenaude*, 210 F.3d 135, 144–45 (3d Cir.2000); 15 Charles Alan Wright et al., *Federal Practice & Procedure* § 3866 (4th ed. 2013) ("The transferee judge inherits the entire pretrial jurisdiction that the transferor court could have exercised had the case not been transferred.").

On July 8, 2013, I directed the parties to mediation before retired U.S. District Judge Layn Phillips. Order, July 8, 2013, ECF No. 5128. During the course of the mediation, "[t]he Settling Parties met with multiple medical, actuarial, and economic experts to determine, develop and test an appropriate settlement framework to meet the needs of Retired NFL Football Players suffering from, or at risk for, the claimed injuries." Pl. Mem. Law 36, Jan. 6, 2014, ECF No. 5634. "The parties' economists and actuaries assisted in modeling the likely disease incidence and adequacy of the funding provisions and benefit levels contained in the proposed settlement." Pl. Mot. Ex. D, Phillips Decl. ¶ 8, Jan. 6, 2014, ECF No. 5634. On August 29, 2013, Judge Phillips informed me that the Plaintiffs and the NFL Parties had signed a term sheet incorporating the principal terms of a settlement. Order, Aug. 29, 2013, ECF No. 5235. On December 16, 2013, pursuant to Federal Rule of Civil Procedure 53, I appointed Perry Golkin as Special Master to assist me in analyzing the financial aspects of the Settlement. Order Appointing Special Master, Dec. 16, 2013, ECF No. 5607. Plaintiffs filed their Class Action Complaint on January 6, 2014. Class Action Compl., *Turner v. Nat'l Football League,* No. 14–29 (E.D.Pa. Jan. 6, 2014), ECF No. 1.

## II. THE PROPOSED CLASS ACTION SETTLEMENT

### A. The Proposed Settlement Class

The Settlement provides for a nationwide Settlement Class consisting of three types of claimants: (1) Retired NFL Football Players; (2) authorized representatives, ordered by a court or other official of competent jurisdiction, of deceased or legally incapacitated or incompetent Retired NFL Football Players ("Representative Claimants"); and (3) close family members of Retired NFL Football Players or any other persons who properly assert, under applicable state law, the right to sue by virtue of their relationship with the Retired NFL Football Player ("Derivative Claimants"). Based on the records of the NFL Parties, there are more than 20,000 Settlement Class Members. Pl. Mem. Law 41, Jan. 6, 2014, ECF No. 5634.

The Settlement Class consists of two Subclasses: Subclass 1 is defined as Retired NFL Football Players who were not diagnosed with a Qualifying Diagnosis prior to the date of the Preliminary Approval and Class Certification Order, and their Representative Claimants and Derivative Claimants; and Subclass 2 is defined as Retired NFL Football Players who were diagnosed with a Qualifying Diagnosis prior to the date of the Preliminary Approval and Class Certification Order and their Representative Claimants and Derivative Claimants, and the Representative Claimants of deceased Retired NFL Football Players who were diagnosed with a Qualifying Diagnosis prior to death or who died prior to the date of the Preliminary Approval and Class Certification Order and who received a post-mortem diagnosis of chronic traumatic encephalopathy ("CTE"). A Qualifying Diagnosis is defined as Level 1.5 Neurocognitive Impairment (early Dementia), Level 2 Neurocognitive Impairment (moderate Dementia), Alzheimer's Disease, Parkinson's Disease, amyotropic lateral sclerosis ("ALS"), and/or Death with CTE.

B.   The Proposed Settlement

As explained in the Plaintiffs' Memorandum of Law accompanying the Motion, the NFL Parties will make payments totaling $760 million over a period of 20 years to create three potential sources of benefits for Settlement Class Members.

First, the Settlement provides for a $75 million Baseline Assessment Program ("BAP") that will offer eligible Retired NFL Football Players baseline neuropsychological and neurological evaluations to determine the existence and extent of any cognitive deficits. In the event that retired players are found to suffer from moderate cognitive impairments, they may receive certain BAP Supplemental Benefits in the form of specified medical treatment and/or evaluation, including counseling and pharmaceutical coverage.

Second, the Settlement provides for a $675 million Monetary Award Fund that will award cash to Retired NFL Football Players who already have a Qualifying Diagnosis or receive one in the future. Representative Claimants and Derivative Claimants related to such players will also be eligible for cash awards. The Qualifying Diagnoses and their maximum Monetary Award levels are as follows: Level 1.5 Neurocognitive Impairment ($1.5 million); Level 2 Neurocognitive Impairment ($3 million); Alzheimer's Disease ($3.5 million); Parkinson's Disease ($3.5 million); ALS ($5 million); Death with CTE ($4 million). These awards may be reduced based on a retired player's age at the time of diagnosis, the number of NFL seasons played, and other applicable offsets outlined in the Settlement Agreement.

Third, the Settlement establishes a $10 million Education Fund to fund education programs promoting safety and injury prevention with regard to football players, including safety-related initiatives in youth football. This Fund will also educate Retired NFL Football Players regarding the NFL's medical and disability programs.

In addition, the NFL Parties will pay up to $4 million in notice expenses. The NFL Parties will also pay attorneys' fees and costs, which Plaintiffs' Co-Lead Counsel will seek in an amount not to exceed $112.5 million. These amounts are in addition to the $760 million for the BAP, the Monetary Award Fund, and the Education Fund.

The Settlement includes a complex system of administration to manage the distribution of benefits. A Special Master, appointed for a five-year term, will oversee the work of a BAP Administrator, a Claims Administrator, and other administrative staff. The NFL Parties have agreed to pay one-half of the compensation of the

Special Master, which is capped at $200,000 per year. The BAP Fund will pay the compensation and reasonable costs and expenses of the BAP Administrator. The Monetary Award Fund will pay the compensation and reasonable costs and expenses of the Claims Administrator; the reasonable costs and expenses of the Special Master; and the other half of the Special Master's compensation.

In exchange for the benefits provided in the Settlement, Settlement Class Members and their related parties will release all claims and dismiss with prejudice all actions against, and covenant not to sue, the NFL Parties and others in this litigation and all Related Lawsuits in this Court and other courts. Settlement Class Members who receive Monetary Awards will also be required to dismiss pending and/or forebear from bringing litigation relating to cognitive injuries against the National Collegiate Athletic Association ("NCAA") and any other collegiate, amateur, or youth football organizations and entities.

## III. DISCUSSION

### B. Preliminary Approval of the Proposed Settlement

Under Federal Rule of Civil Procedure 23(e), the settlement of a class action requires court approval, which may issue only "on finding that [the settlement] is fair, reasonable, and adequate." Fed. R.Civ.P. 23(e)(2). Review of a proposed class action settlement typically proceeds in two stages. At the first stage, the parties submit the proposed settlement to the court, which must make "a preliminary fairness evaluation." *Manual for Complex Litigation (Fourth)* § 21.632 (2004) [hereinafter, *MCL*]. If the proposed settlement is preliminarily acceptable, the court then directs that notice be provided to all class members who would be bound by the proposed settlement in order to afford them an opportunity to be heard on, object to, and opt out of the settlement. *See* Fed. R.Civ.P. 23(c)(3), (e)(1), (e)(5); *see also Grunin v. Int'l House of Pancakes*, 513 F.2d 114, 120 (8th Cir.1975) ("[D]ue process requires that notice of a proposed settlement be given to the class."). At the second stage, after class members are notified of the settlement, the court holds a formal fairness hearing where class members may object to the settlement. *See* Fed.R.Civ.P. 23(e)(1)(B). If the court concludes that the settlement is "fair, reasonable and adequate," the settlement is given final approval. At this time, Plaintiffs request only that I grant preliminary approval.

b.  Analysis

Counsel for the Plaintiffs and the NFL Parties have made a commendable effort to reach a negotiated resolution to this dispute. There is nothing to indicate that the Settlement is not the result of good faith, arm's-length negotiations between adversaries. Nonetheless, on the basis of the present record, I am not yet satisfied that the Settlement "has no obvious deficiencies, grants no preferential treatment to segments of the class, and falls within the range of possible approval." *Cordy v. USS-Posco Indus.,* No. 12–553, 2013 WL 4028627, at *3 (N.D.Cal. July 31, 2013).

I am primarily concerned that not all Retired NFL Football Players who ultimately receive a Qualifying Diagnosis or their related claimants will be paid. The Settlement fixes the size of the Monetary Award Fund. It also fixes the Monetary Award level for each Qualifying Diagnosis, subject to a variety of offsets. In various hypothetical scenarios, the Monetary Award Fund may lack the necessary funds to pay Monetary Awards for Qualifying Diagnoses. More specifically, the Settlement contemplates a $675 million Monetary Award Fund with a 65-year lifespan for a Settlement Class of approximately 20,000 people. Retired NFL Football Players with a Qualifying Diagnosis of Parkinson's Disease, for example, are eligible for a maximum award of $3.5 million; those with a Qualifying Diagnosis of ALS may receive up to $5 million. Even if only 10 percent of Retired NFL Football Players eventually receive a Qualifying Diagnosis, it is difficult to see how the Monetary Award Fund would have the funds available over its lifespan to pay all claimants at these significant award levels.

The parties are responsible for supplementing the record to provide the court with the information needed to evaluate the fairness or adequacy of a proposed settlement. *MCL* at § 21.632. *See Martin v. Cargill, Inc.*, 295 F.R.D. 380, 383–84 (D.Minn.2013) (holding that the evidence submitted by the parties was insufficient to support preliminary approval of the class settlement where the parties' submissions provided almost no information enabling the court to gauge the value of the proposed class' claims); *Custom LED, LLC v. eBay, Inc.*, No. 12–350, 2013 WL 4552789, at *9 (N.D.Cal. Aug. 27, 2013) (denying a motion to preliminarily approve settlement where, *inter alia*, the parties "provided the Court with no information as to the class members' potential range of recovery"); *Galloway v. Kansas City Landsmen, LLC,* No. 11–1020, 2013 WL 3336636, at *4 (W.D.Mo. July 2, 2013) (denying a motion for preliminary approval where the court remained concerned that the amended settlement offered insufficient value for class members' claims and the record was insufficient to determine the approximate value of the class members' claims and the amended settlement); *Sobel v. Hertz Corp.,* No. 06–545, 2011 WL 2559565, at * 10 (D.Nev. June 27, 2011) (finding the court could not "even begin th[e] inquiry" where "the parties ha[d] failed to provide . . . evidence of . . . the total amount of . . . fees that were charged to the class members, let alone potential ranges of recovery and the chances of obtaining it").

The current record does not sufficiently address my concerns. The Declaration from Judge Phillips refers to "analyses conducted by the independent economists or actuaries retained by the parties" to justify his belief that the $760 million to be paid by the NFL Parties "is fair and reasonable and will be sufficient to fund the benefits to which the parties have agreed." Pl. Mot. Ex. D, Phillips Decl. ¶ 20, Jan. 6, 2014, ECF No. 5634. Plaintiffs allege that their economists conducted analyses to ensure that there would be sufficient funding to provide benefits to all eligible Class Members given the size of the Settlement Class and projected incidence rates, and Plaintiffs' counsel "believe" that the aggregate sum is sufficient to compensate all Retired NFL Football Players who may receive Qualifying Diagnoses. Pl. Mem. Law 22, Jan. 6, 2014, ECF No. 5634. Unfortunately, no such analyses were provided to me in support of the Plaintiffs' Motion. In the absence of additional supporting evidence, I have concerns about the fairness, reasonableness, and adequacy of the Settlement.

## IV. CONCLUSION

I will deny the Motion for Preliminary Approval and Class Certification without prejudice. As a first step toward preliminary approval, I will order the parties to share the documentation referred to in their submissions with the Court through the Special Master.

# SETTLEMENT APPROVAL

Finally, after the amount that the NFL would pay was increased to be as high as a billion dollars, Judge Brody approved the class action settlement and dismissed the lawsuit as it pertained to the NFL. Some people criticized the settlement as not being for a sufficiently high amount. Others criticized the settlement for not being sufficiently inclusive. The present settlement unfortunately does not provide for lifetime payments for CTE which cannot be definitively diagnosed prior to death.

Actuaries retained by the NFL provided data to Judge Brody to assist in the determination of whether to approve the settlement. Their figures tended to show that both the players and the NFL only expected several dozen former players to obtain payments of up to 5 million dollars for diagnoses of Parkinson's disease. The majority will receive payments of more than 800 million dollars for Alzheimer's disease and for advanced dementia. The NFL's figures estimated 28% of former players would come down with brain damage sufficient to qualify for the settlement.[8]

A major incentive for the players to approve the settlement was the difficult burden of proof they would have had to meet in their lawsuit to support their allegations that their brain injuries were caused by

---

[8] "Brain Trauma to Affect One in Three Players, NFL Agrees" NY Times, Ken Belson, September 12, 2014.

playing football in the NFL rather than in a lifetime of playing youth, high school and college football. The incentive of the NFL to settle was to avoid having to disclose what it knew about the dangers of concussions and when they knew it. The allegation that the NFL may have known about the significant dangers posed by concussions, but hid this fact from the players would be quite damning to the NFL on many levels if proven. By settling the players' lawsuit, the NFL avoided having to go through the discovery phase of the lawsuit during which their records would be scrutinized and their management subject to intense depositions.

Or did they?

The funds necessary to pay for the settlement as well as the legal fees involved in defending the players' lawsuit was to be paid by the thirty insurance companies insuring the NFL. These companies refused to honor the policies on the basis that they were unable to determine whether the NFL committed fraud, which they allege would relieve them of the obligation to pay under the terms of the insurance policies. The much avoided discovery of NFL records may still occur as part of an order by Judge Jeffrey Oing of the New York Supreme Court in 2016 to allow such discovery although his order was appealed. Another possible alternative is that the NFL may well settle its dispute with the insurance companies by reducing its demand for funds from their insurance policies in an effort to maintain the confidentiality of its records.

A number of former NFL players objected to the settlement and petitioned the court to have the settlement overturned in the hope that the parties would negotiate a settlement more favorable to the former players but both the 3rd Circuit Court of Appeals and the Supreme Court refused to overturn the settlement.

In June of 2017 the first two claims were approved under the settlement. One former player received 5 million dollars for his diagnosis of amyotrophic lateral sclerosis, sometimes referred to as Lou Gehrig's Disease while the family of a deceased player who suffered from CTE was paid 4 million dollars. Because CTE can only be definitively diagnosed through an autopsy, players afflicted with CTE cannot receive compensation pursuant to the settlement during their lifetimes.

About two hundred players opted out of the NFL settlement in order to bring their own lawsuits.

## NHL AND CTE

In 2016 Commissioner Gary Bettman denied a link between concussions and CTE, which has been diagnosed in at least six deceased NHL players as of 2016. In response to questions put to him by Senator Richard Blumenthal of Connecticut, Bettman blamed the media for misleading the public about the dangers of CTE. Bettman's 24 page response was filed in federal court as a part of a concussion lawsuit against the NHL. According to Bettman:

"Ultimately the most concerning aspect of the current public dialogue about concussions in professional sports (as well as youth sports) is the implicit premise that hundreds of thousands—if not millions—of individuals who have participated in contact sports at the high school, collegiate and/or professional levels are not only at a high level of risk for, but actually more than likely to develop, a degenerative, irreversible brain disease (i.e., C.T.E.) and that they should be informed as such. The NHL chooses to be guided on this very serious subject by the medical consensus of experts examining the science, not the media hype driven in part by plaintiffs' counsel."

"The relationship between concussions and the asserted clinical symptoms of C.T.E. remains unknown."[9]

The first NHL player to be definitively diagnosed hockey player with CTE was Reggie Fleming who died in 2009 at age 73. Fleming played in the NHL between 1959 and 1974 and experienced many hockey

---

[9] "NHL Commissioner Gary Bettman Continues to Deny C.T.E. Link" NYTimes, John Branch, July 26, 2016.

fights during his NHL career which preceded the era in which NHL players wore helmets.

Inching its way through the courts since 2014 is a class action against the NHL that in many ways mirrors the NFL case although in the case of the NHL it was a league that also encouraged fighting.

# CHRIS BOSH AND PLAYER SAFETY

Chris Bosh was an NBA All Star eleven times and won two NBA Championships with the Miami Heat, however, his playing career has apparently ended due to recurring problems with blood clots and while often professional teams have been accused of hiding medical dangers both generally and as to specific players due to a desire to have those players continue to play, the situation was reversed in the case of Chris Bosh who wanted to continue his NBA career while the Miami Heat did not want him to compete again.

Bosh first experienced painful cramps, muscle spasms and difficulty breathing in February of 2015. He initially tried to hide the symptoms from the team. Eventually he was hospitalized for nine days after a blood clot in his leg moved to his lungs causing a pulmonary embolism, which could have been fatal. Bosh missed the remainder of the 2014–2015 NBA season.

In many instances, blood clots can be treated with blood-thinning drugs. In fact, Bosh has appeared in a television commercial for a particular blood thinning drug. However, the effectiveness of blood thinning medications are diminished by the physical contact that is a part of playing in the NBA along with the long season with few days off that would make it difficult for the clot thinning drugs to be fully flushed from Bosh's system as required for the optimum use of the drugs.

Bosh was cleared by the Miami Heat medical staff to play in the 2015–2016 season and played without incident for the first half of the season, however, shortly before the mid-season All Star Game he began experiencing muscle soreness that upon further investigation was found to be due to the return of blood clot problems. Team doctors made the determination to end his season.

Bosh's desire to play again in the 2016–2017 NBA season was also thwarted by team physicians. Regardless of whether he plays another minute of an NBA game, Bosh's contract which would pay him $75.8 million dollars over the next three seasons remains an obligation of the team although the expense would be covered by insurance if Bosh is deemed unable to play due to his medical condition. However, in order to have the amount paid to Bosh not countable for salary cap purposes, Bosh will be required to be determined physically unable to play by a physician chosen jointly by the NBA and the National Basketball Players Association. It is interesting to note that even if the physician agrees with the Miami Heat that Bosh's condition is career ending, it does not mean that another team that is willing to take the risk of harm to Chris Bosh could not hire him to play for them. It only would mean that the Heat would not have his salary counted in salary cap determinations.

## QUESTIONS

1.    Is the obligation of team doctors to the players they treat or the teams for which the players play? What ethical issues do they face?

2.    Should a player be allowed to play professional sports if team doctor determines that there exists a substantial health risk to the player or should this be the individual player's decision?

# PRODUCT LIABILITY

The history of the football helmet was described in the lawsuit of NFL Hall of Fame running back Paul Hornung against Riddell, the maker of football helmets used in the NFL as follows:

"In 1893, U.S. Naval Academy Midshipman, Joseph M. Reeves, made a protective device out of mole skin for his use in that year's Army-Navy game after having been advised that another kick to his head would result in "instant insanity" or even death. Most believe this was the first time a helmet was used in the game of football. In 1939, the Riddell Company of Chicago, Illinois started manufacturing plastic helmets under the guise that plastic helmets would be safer than those made of leather."[10]

Riddell, the company that makes the football helmets used in the NFL was sued alleging that it deceptively marketed its helmets as being able to prevent or reduce concussions by as much as 31%.

Hall of Famer Paul Horning sued Riddell alleging that the company knew about the dangers of concussions and that their helmets provided no protection from these injuries and the resulting brain damage. A week later, a group of fourteen former NFL players led by former Pro Bowl receiver from the Pittsburgh Steelers, Yancey Thigpen filed a similar lawsuit against Riddell.

In his lawsuit, Hornung alleged in paragraph 9 of his complaint:

"9. Prior to, during, and after PAUL HORNUNG's NFL football career, RIDDELL knew of the harmful long-term effects of brain traumas sustained by football players while wearing RIDDELL's supposed protective equipment; however, it misrepresented and concealed these facts from PAUL HORNING."

In their lawsuits, Horning and the other players allege that Riddell, much like the cigarette manufacturers of a different era chose to ignore scientific evidence of the dangers of concussions for as long as eighteen years until 2002 at which point a warning was put on the helmets. The players' lawsuits allege that Riddell knew of the dangers and its failure to warn was a direct cause of the players' injuries. They also allege that Riddell was negligent in its testing, assembly, manufacture and marketing of helmets which contributed to the dangers of concussions while using their helmets.

---

[10] Paul Hornung and Angela Hornung v. BRG Sports, LLC et al. collectively Riddell, Circuit Court of Cook County, Illinois, Law division 2016–L–006686, Complaint, July 7, 2016.

Riddell had been the official helmet of the NFL between 2002 and 2013. NFL players now can use any helmet they wish that complies with league standards. Some players continue to use Riddell helmets while others use helmets made by companies such as Schutt, Xenith and Rawlings.

## OTHER RIDDELL LEGAL ACTIONS

Riddell was also a co-defendant along with the NFL in the concussion class action lawsuit filed by former NFL players who alleged that the company and the NFL knew about the dangers of concussions, but hid that fact from the players. While the NFL settled the lawsuit with the players, Riddell has not settled.

Riddell has been sued other times in the past. In the case of Edward Acuna v. Riddell, Inc., case number LC090924, in the Superior Court of California, County of Los Angeles (2014) the company was sued on behalf of a young man who suffered serious brain damage as a 17 year old high school football player which occurred when he suffered a rotational blow to his head leading to brain damage. A rotational blow twists the head from side to side as contrasted with a direct linear blunt force hit. The plaintiff's lawyers argued that the front pad of the helmet was defectively designed and that different material should have been used. Defense counsel argued that the front pad met or exceeded all applicable standards for absorbing impact energy. During the trial, on cross examination a Plaintiff's expert witness admitted that no football helmet could protect against rotationally induced head injuries. After a four week trial, the jury ruled in favor of Riddell, accepting their argument that its helmet met all applicable safety standards.

Riddell lost a 3.1 million dollar verdict involving a high school football player in Colorado who suffered permanent brain damage, but not on the grounds that the helmet was defectively designed, but on the ground that the helmet maker did not properly warn about the risk of concussion. Ridolfi v. Begano.[11]

# HELMET DISCLAIMERS

Helmet makers include written warnings on all helmets in an attempt to disclaim liability.

Here is the warning presently being used on Riddell helmets.

**"NO HELMET CAN PREVENT SERIOUS HEAD OR NECK INJURIES A PLAYER MIGHT RECEIVE WHILE PARTICIPATING IN FOOTBALL.**

Do not use this helmet to butt, ram or spear an opposing player. This is in violation of the football rules and such use can result in severe head or neck injuries, paralysis or death to you and possible injury to your opponent. Contact in football may result in CONCUSSION-BRAIN INJURY which no helmet can prevent. Symptoms include: loss of consciousness or memory, dizziness, headache, nausea or confusion. If you have symptoms, immediately stop playing and report them to your coach, trainer and parents. Do not return to a game or practice until all symptoms are gone and you have received medical clearance. Ignoring this warning may lead to another and more serious or fatal brain injury."

The helmet warning of Schutt, another helmet manufacturer, even goes so far as to say that to avoid concussions you shouldn't play football, where it states in capital letters, "NO HELMET SYSTEM CAN PROTECT YOU FROM SERIOUS BRAIN AND/OR NECK INJURIES INCLUDING PARALYSIS OR DEATH. TO AVOID THESE RISKS. DO NOT ENGAGE IN THE SPORT OF FOOTBALL."

---

[11]  Ridolfi v. Begano, No. 2010–cv–58 (Colo. Dist. Ct. of Las Animas Cnty. verdict entered Apr. 13, 2013).

## QUESTION

1.    Should such a warning be sufficient to absolve the helmet maker of tort liability and its duty to make a safe product?

# SAFER FOOTBALL HELMETS

Using the latest technology, helmets containing sensors can measure the impacts the helmet takes and send that data in real time to coaches and other sideline staff. The goal is to be able to measure the impact and the helmet's use to determine whether a player should be removed from the game. The developing of standards will be critical to the success of this tool.

Riddell developed technology starting in 2002 which it calls its HITS system which stands for the Head Impact Telemetry System that measures the severity and number of head impacts a player receives; however, critics believe that this system does not properly consider the dangers of low impact blows to the head. More research is required to determine the danger of repeated sub-concussive blows to the head. Preliminary research does tend to indicate that sub-concussive blows pose a significant danger.

Some of the things being considered for increased player safety are protocols that require a player suffering a concussion to not be allowed to play for a specifically determined period of time thereby taking the pressure off of a player who wishes to keep on playing disregarding the risk. Greater use of sensors to gather data and correlate it to injuries would be helpful, but only in the long run as it will take much time to analyze the information particularly as to effects that may not be apparent until much later following the concussion.

One major unanswered question is how many concussions it takes to become a problem. Also is it possible to make a safe helmet? In 2014, researchers from UCLA and Architected Materials won the Head Health Challenge which is sponsored by the National Football

League, General Electric and Under Armour. The UCLA and Architected Materials group are working on microlattice material to better absorb the energy that results from a head blow better than the foam presently used. The Architechted Lattise has many advantages including being light, improved as to shock absorbing and can even be enhanced with the capability to measure and send data about head blows to be used for further research.

## QUESTIONS

1.  Do football helmet makers have a duty to make their helmets as safe as possible regardless of the cost of doing so?

2.  If it is determined that sub-concussive blows create a risk of CTE, should football be banned as a sport or could the sport be made safer?

3.  How would the amount of an acceptable risk of brain damage be determined?

# DUTY TO SPECTATORS

Teams and stadium owners have a duty to provide a reasonably safe place for spectators at sporting events although the rules regarding that responsibility may differ from state to state. While spectator injuries are perhaps most common in baseball, other sports including hockey have also seen significant numbers of spectator injuries.

Lawsuits seeking to hold stadiums responsible for injuries suffered from foul balls hit into the stands go back as early as 1913 in the case of Crane v. Kansas City Baseball & Exhibition Co., 168 Mo. App. 301 (1913). In that case the court determined that the stadium was not negligent for failing to provide netting around the entire stadium and emphasized both that the spectator was aware of the risk of being hit by a foul ball and could have chosen to purchase a seat behind home plate where protective netting was provided.

Gradually, as the law developed, some jurisdictions adopted the rule of assumption of the risk as a total defense to lawsuits brought by injured spectators, while other jurisdictions adopted the more modern approach of comparative negligence, whereby the relative negligence of the injured spectator is compared with the negligence of the stadium owner to determine whether or not compensation would be awarded. If the spectator's negligence was determined to be more than the negligence of the stadium owner, no compensation would be awarded, however, if the stadium owner was deemed more negligent and the negligence contributed to the injuries suffered by the spectator, the spectator would be successful in his or her lawsuit against the stadium owner.

Most courts have ruled that as our national pastime, the dangers inherent in attending a game are apparent and well known by spectators. This has come to be known as the "Baseball Rule." Such dangers include the risk of being hit by a foul ball or a splintered bat while attending a baseball game and represent risks spectators voluntarily assume. However, even if a particular spectator was unaware of the nature of the game, his or her ignorance would not be a factor in his or her favor in such a lawsuit.[12]

In the case of Yates v. Chicago National League Ball Club, 595 N.E. 2d 570 (Ill. 1992) a child, attending a Cubs game accompanied by her father, was hit by a foul ball suffering serious injuries. A jury awarded the family $67,500. On appeal, the court upheld the verdict indicating that baseball stadiums must provide adequate screening sufficient to protect those spectators desiring such protection. Also of significance was the fact that the appeals court did not find the standard disclaimer of liability appearing on the back of the tickets sufficient to avoid liability.

In recent years, attention has been focused on whether protective netting at baseball stadiums which had previously been limited to the area behind home plate should be extended to the areas behind the home and visiting dugouts on both sides of the field. Generally, however, spectators choosing to watch the game from unprotected

---

[12]   Gunther v. Charlotte Baseball Inc., 854 F.Supp. 424, 427 (D.S.C. 1994).

areas have been deemed to have assumed the risk of being hit by a foul ball.

While spectators may assume the risk of being hit by a ball or a bat while attending a baseball game, do spectators assume the risk of being hit in the eye by a hot dog while attending a game? This was the situation presented when Kansas City Royals fan, John Coomer was hit in the eye by a hotdog launched into the air by the Royals' mascot "Sluggerrr." Ultimately, the Missouri Supreme Court ruled that this was not an inherent risk of the game assumed by spectators and the Royals owed their fans a duty to use reasonable care in conducting their Hotdog Launch and could be liable for breach of that duty. Coomer v. Kan. City Royals Baseball Corp., 437 S.W. 3d 184 (Mo. 2014).

Hockey is another sport in which spectators are in danger of being hit by flying projectiles, in this case a puck during the course of a game This is an obvious risk inherent in attending a hockey game. However, it is also one that stadium owners are required to be aware of and mitigate in a reasonable fashion. Just as in baseball, fans are presumed to be aware of the dangers that are an integral part of attending a hockey game, however, stadium owners also have a responsibility to make the rinks as safe as reasonably possible, which generally has been interpreted as installing plexiglass around the perimeter of the rink and netting to catch wayward pucks behind the goals where statistically most pucks enter the seating area.

Following the death in 2002 of Brittanie Cecil, a thirteen year old girl who died from injuries sustained when she was hit in the head by a deflected puck while watching an NHL game in Columbus, Ohio, the NHL mandated all teams have protective netting behind the goals at both ends of the rink. Cecil's family sued the NHL and settled out of court for 1.2 million dollars.

In the case of Rosa v. County of Nassau, 544 N.Y.S.2d 652 (N.Y. Ct. App. 1989) the court recognized that although netting around the entire seating area would provide greater protection to spectators, it would be an undue burden upon the stadium owners to require this and that merely having netting behind the goals was sufficient to meet the stadium owner's burden of making the stadium reasonably safe.

Spectator injuries at golf tournaments present a unique situation because the game is played in a wide open golf course instead of the narrower confines of a stadium. As with all sporting events there is a duty of the golf course to reasonably maintain a safe venue for spectators with appropriate seating and screening as well as written warnings, however, the law assumes that spectators are aware of the dangers and have a corresponding duty to protect themselves while at a golf tournament. Grisim v. Tapemark Charity Pro-Am Golf Tournament, 394 N.W. 2d 261 (Minn. Ct. App. 1986).

The danger posed by attendance at an automobile racing event, such as a NASCAR, are both obvious and serious, namely the danger of pieces of automobile flying into the viewing stands. Therefore it is the duty of the race track owner to both provide and maintain sufficient protective netting to offset this danger.

Professional wrestling matches present an unusual set of circumstances as the danger to spectators can include being hit by a wrestler thrown from the ring as well as possible assaults on spectators perpetrated by the wrestlers themselves. Reynolds. v. Deep South Sports, Inc. 211 So. 2d 37 (Fla. Ct. App. 1968). The courts have generally held that wrestling promoters are responsible for foreseeable harm and that the possibility of being attacked by a wrestler going into the audience is a foreseeable risk. Pierce v. Murnick, 145 S.E. 2d 11 (N.C. 1965).

## QUESTION

1.   What is the level of responsibility of sports venues for the safety of their fans and how should that level of responsibility be determined?

# ALCOHOLIC BEVERAGES

The sale of alcoholic beverages is a significant source of revenue to stadium owners and teams, however, with increased drinking of alcoholic beverages, particularly in an emotionally charged sports venue comes the risk of fan violence and danger to innocent spectators. Police have reported that where beer sales are limited or reduced, arrests and ejections from the event dramatically went down. Bishop v. Fair Lanes Ga. Bowling, Inc., 803 F. 2d. 1548 (11th Cir. 1986).

---

### QUESTION

1.    If excessive alcohol use is generally considered a precipitating factor in spectator violence among fans, does the stadium have an obligation to reduce sales of alcoholic beverages and are stadiums owners responsible for the actions of inebriated fans?

# BRAWLS IN THE STANDS

The most notorious example of a brawl involving both athletes and spectators occurred on November 19, 2004 at the end of an NBA game between the Indiana Pacers and Detroit Pistons. With less than a minute remaining in the game and Indiana leading by fifteen points, Pacer Ron Artest flagrantly fouled Detroit's Ben Wallace as he went in for a layup. A shoving match ensued that grew to involve the teams. A spectator, John Green then threw a cup of beer at Ron Artest, who went into the stands to seek out the person who had thrown the beer on him. Artest ended up punching another spectator, Mike Ryan, who Artest mistakenly thought had thrown the beer. The brawl escalated between players and fans.

As a result of the altercation, the NBA suspended nine players for a total of 146 games with Ron Artest receiving the harshest penalty, being suspended for the remainder of the season which consisted of

73 regular season games and 13 playoff games. This suspension cost him $4,995,000 in lost salary.

In addition, five players were prosecuted criminally for assault. All five pleaded no contest and were sentenced to a year's probation and community service. Legal actions, however, were not limited to the players. Five fans were banned for life from attending future Pistons' games and prosecuted criminally, the most prominently being John Green who was convicted of assault and battery. He was sentenced to thirty days in jail and two years of probation. The event also served as the impetus to the NBA to limit the size of beer containers, limit the number of beers an individual could purchase at one time and stop the sale of alcoholic beverages after the completion of the third quarter of games.

## SYNOPSIS

1.    Torts are civil actions that do not involve contracts and include assault and battery.

2.    An action, such as assault and battery can be considered both a civil tort and a criminal act.

3.    Torts can be intentional or unintentional, such as when they involve negligence.

4.    Responsibility for tortious action may be mitigated by contributory negligence.

5.    Responsibility for tortious action may be mitigated by the injured party's assumption of the risk.

6.    Comparative negligence is often used in determining legal liability and the amount of money a tortfeasor will be ordered by a court to pay his or her victim.

7.    Product liability law is a subsection of tort law.

8.    Criminal cases require guilt to be determined beyond a reasonable doubt.

9. Civil actions require responsibility to be determined by a preponderance of the evidence (51%).

10. Many sports contain levels of violence that would be considered unlawful outside of the sport, but are consented to by participants in the sport.

11. In its settlement of the class action brought by NFL players regarding liability for concussions, the NFL did not admit liability.

12. In settling their class action against the NFL regarding concussion liability, the players considered the difficulty of proving that the harm they suffered due to concussions was due to concussions incurred while playing professional football and not from concussions that had occurred earlier in their football playing amateur careers.

13. Spectators in many instances have been held to assume the risk of harm that occurs when watching a sporting event.

14. Criminal charges can be brought in egregious cases of violence on the playing field.

# CHAPTER THIRTEEN

# Sports and Social Media

Social media such as Facebook, Twitter and Instagram are a major part of the lives of everyone and athletes, both professional and collegiate amateurs are no exception. According to a Pew Research Poll in 2013, 73% of adults use social media. (Social Media Update 2013 Pew Research Center December 30, 2013.) The history of social media can largely be traced back to 2006 when Facebook broadened its availability from college students to the general public and Twitter was born.

Social media is used by athletes to not just communicate with friends, but also to connect with their fan base. In addition, it serves as a major source of marketing of the athlete personally and for the products he or she endorses. Both college and professional sports teams also make extensive use of social media for marketing and public relations purposes.

The Commissioners of the various professional sports leagues generally are vested with the authority to regulate social media because unlike essential elements of collective bargaining such as wages and other terms of employment, social media is not required to be negotiated as a part of a collective bargaining agreement although it may be a permissive topic for collective bargaining. To date, the use of social media has not been a major part of the collective bargaining negotiations between players' unions and management in any of the major professional sports in America with the exception of the NHL.

Thus the authority by default has largely passed to the respective commissioners of the NBA, MLB, and NFL.

# FIRST AMENDMENT RIGHTS

The First Amendment of the Constitution protects the right of free speech, but only against limitations placed by federal, state or local governments and their agencies. The First Amendment does not apply to private corporations and organizations which may and often do put restrictions on the speech of their employees.

# CORPORATE SOCIAL MEDIA RESTRICTIONS

In the corporate world it is common for companies to formulate social media policies and include them in official employee handbooks. Such regulations generally permit social media use by employees, but limit certain types of actions on social media such as those characterized as harassment, intimidation or threats. While employees may be required as a condition of employment to comply with corporate social media rules, the National Labor Relations Board (NLRB) has recognized the rights of workers to discuss workplace conditions on social media.

# NBA

NBA teams first began using Twitter in 2008 and individual players have millions of Twitter followers led by LeBron James with more than 33 million Twitter followers.

The NBA commissioner is empowered to enact reasonable rules governing players' conduct at games which includes not just conduct on the court, but in the locker room or anywhere in the stadium both prior to the game and after the game. While the Commissioner does not have specific authority to promulgate rules regarding player conduct away from the stadium, he does have broadly written authority to "promulgate and enforce reasonable rules governing conduct that are reasonably related to 'preservation of the integrity of, or the maintenance of public confidence in the game." The NBA Constitution permits the commissioner to discipline a player "for any statement he makes or endorses which is prejudicial or detrimental to the best interests of basketball and to fine the player for conduct that is detrimental to the NBA," which includes conduct that does not conform "to standards of morality and fair play;" which has been reasonably construed to include the power to regulate and punish comments made through social media.

The NBA prohibits players from using social media 45 minutes before a game, during the game and until traditional media interviews have been completed after the game. Although there are no specific content rules pertaining to social media content, the individual teams and the league maintain the ability to regulate and punish what it considers inappropriate tweets and social media content under the broad category of actions detrimental to the NBA and basketball.

Some teams such as the Milwaukee Bucks and the Los Angeles Clippers ban use of any social media at arenas during games or practices. This is legally permissible and would not be considered an unfair labor practice because it is merely a regulation of conduct during working time. Unlike state colleges and universities that may have a duty to recognize a right to free speech pursuant to the First Amendment, as a private organization a professional sport team has a right to restrict the use of social media by its employees.

NY Knicks player Amare Stoudemire was fined $50,000 for tweeting anti-gay and obscene language to a fan in 2012 in response to a benignly critical tweet from the fan. Stoudemire issued an apology for his comments.

# MLB

Similar to the NBA commissioner's authority, the Commissioner of MLB may take actions in the broadly stated best interests of baseball. However, the MLB CBA requires new rules that "significantly affect terms and conditions of employment" must be negotiated between the Major League Baseball Players Association (MLBPA) and the Commissioner. If no agreement is reached, the Commissioner may not put such rule change into effect until the end of the next baseball season.

MLB rules state that "all social media messages must stop 30 minutes prior to the first pitch, and they can resume after the game at the individual club's discretion."

MLB, through its Major League Baseball Advanced Media subsidiary organization, operates Facebook and Twitter accounts for all its teams. Cognizant of the power of social media, all players are required to meet with MLB media specialists prior to the season to discuss the effects of social media.

Chicago White Sox manager Ozzie Guillen was the first MLB employee to be disciplined for violating its social media rules following a tweet he sent out criticizing an umpire after Guillen was ejected in the first inning of a game against the Yankees in 2011. Guillen was suspended for two games and fined $20,000.

# NFL

Social media usage has not been a matter included in collective bargaining in the NFL. While the NFL Commissioner must give the National Football League Players Association (NFLPA) notice of all proposed rule changes, the NFLPA's rights are limited unless the proposed rule change is deemed by the NFLPA to have a negative impact on the safety and health of players. Even in the event that the NFLPA deems a rule change to adversely affect players' health and safety, their only option in that event is to request an advisory decision by arbitrators and even then the arbitrator's decision is not binding on the NFL which is still able to enforce such rules.

Although the NFL encourages its players to use social media, the NFL's policy also restricts players from using social media at the stadium for a period beginning ninety minutes before the start of a game and ending when the post-game traditional locker room interviews have been completed. Other than that, individual teams are allowed to make their own restrictions.

Kansas City Chiefs running back Larry Johnson was suspended and ultimately released after he used an anti-gay slur, criticized his coach and mocked a fan on Twitter in 2009.

Antonio Cromartie was fined $2,500 by the San Diego Chargers for referring to training camp food in 2009 as "nasty."

The league gives individual teams the authority to develop social media guidelines for players and employees. The guidelines should address four points, according to a statement from NFL spokesman Brian McCarthy. The league says statements on social media should be "professional, accurate, and consistent with the NFL and club's mission values" and should not reveal game strategy, injury information or personal information about a player. The guidelines also say statements displaying obscenity or criticism of officiating, opposing players, owners, coaches, fans or threatening comments are subject to discipline. However, the amount of possible fines is never mentioned. Though it has been acceptable for players to criticize each other through social media without consequence, some teams ask players to refrain from speaking out on current affairs matters.

# NHL

The commissioner with the greatest restrictions on his authority is the NHL commissioner. According to the terms of the NHL CBA all rules regarding personal conduct must be collectively bargained with the National Hockey League Players Association. Social media policy is a part of the NHL CBA. Like the other professional sports there is a period on game days during which social media may not be used which for NHL games begins two hours before the game begins and ends similar to the other professional sports when post-game traditional media interviews are completed.

All of the players' unions for all of the professional sports are cognizant of protecting the rights of players to be relatively free of restrictions during their own free time both during the season and in the off season. The topic of social media use away from the stadium on game day and during the off season would seem to be a topic for future negotiations during collective bargaining because it regulates the terms and conditions of employment when athletes are not performing essential job functions.

## QUESTIONS

1.    Should the use of social media away from the arena and during the off season be a topic of collective bargaining?

2.    If a professional athlete is using social media for his or her personal use unrelated to his or her sport, is it appropriate for a team to restrict such usage?

# EUROPE

In the UK the social media messages by professional soccer players are routinely examined. Teams hire cybersecurity companies to monitor the social media accounts of their players. Out of a concern for the reputation of the team, the cybersecurity firms have lists of as many as a thousand problematic words dealing with drugs, racist terms and criminal behavior as well as hate speech which is against the law in the UK. Players have been fined for using offensive terms on social media.

# JOHN ROCKER

Even though players may be using social media during their own free time, it can legitimately be a subject of league discipline because it affects the perception of the team and the league in businesses where public relations concerns are significant. Although the comments were made in a pre-Twitter world, Atlanta Braves pitcher John

Rocker was fined $20,000, suspended for thirty days and required to attend diversity training following a 1999 magazine interview that included homophobic and racist comments. The actions of the Commissioner were challenged by the MLBPA on behalf of John Rocker and although the suspension and fine were reduced following an arbitration hearing, the authority of the Commissioner to punish for offensive speech was recognized. Punishing for actions not in the best interests of baseball was again recognized.

Arbitrator Shyam Das wrote that although free speech as misconduct requires special consideration due to the "customary norms of free expression[,] . . . [a]n individual's First Amendment right to speak his . . . mind regardless of the offensive or hateful nature of the speech does not, under a just cause standard, necessarily preclude an employer from taking appropriate disciplinary action where such speech, even if off-duty, it has a negative impact on the employer's business." He reasoned that even though Rocker's Sports Illustrated interview took place out of uniform during the off-season, Rocker knew he was being interviewed as a baseball player and he should have known that whatever was published would be associated not only with him, but also reflect on the Atlanta Braves and MLB.[1]

In the Rocker case, the MLBPA may have been more successful in charging the Commissioner with violating the CBA by way of an unfair labor practice for unilaterally implementing a penalty that affects a mandatory term of collective bargaining. Perhaps, if players start getting penalized frequently for the content of their tweets, the players' unions will challenge the imposition of discipline as an unfair labor practice. Conversely, the players may also attempt to negotiate guidelines on acceptable social media conduct and content as part of the future CBAs.

---

[1]   "In the Matter of Arbitration between the Major League Baseball Players Association and The Commission of Major League Baseball" Panel Decision No. 104, John Rocker, Grievance No. 2000–3.

# COLLEGE LIMITATIONS

In Tinker v. Des Moines Independent Community School District, 393 U.S. 503, 506 (1969) the Supreme Court ruled in regard to the First Amendment rights of high school students protesting the Vietnam war that "it can hardly be argued that either students or teachers shed their constitutional rights to freedom of speech or expression at the schoolhouse gate." Three years later, in the case of Healy v. James, 408 U.S. 169, 180 (1972) the Supreme Court extended the recognition of the rights of students to First Amendment protections to college students.

In the case of Texas v. Johnson, 491 U.S. 397, 414 (1989) in which the court determined that flag burning was a protected form of free speech, the Supreme Court indicated that "if there is a bedrock principle underlying the First Amendment, it is that the government may not prohibit the expression of an idea simply because society finds the idea itself offensive or disagreeable."

The First Amendment applies to government limitations on freedom of speech, not those of private institutions. Consequently, while private colleges are free to make whatever rules they wish limiting free speech, state colleges and universities definitely fall under the classification of a governmental unit subject to the First Amendment.

At public colleges and universities which are subject to First Amendment protections, it is questionable whether students may have their rights of expression limited for being inappropriate or offensive. A starting point for many schools in their regulation of the use of social media by their student-athletes is their position that participation in intercollegiate athletics is a privilege and not a right. Fundamental Constitutional rights may be limited by governments only if there is a compelling state interest and no less intrusive way of accomplishing the goal. However, a privilege may have reasonable restrictions imposed so long as the restrictions advance a positive governmental or societal goal.

Colleges and universities generally justify their limitations on social media use by student-athletes due to concerns as to the reputation of the particular school.

Another reason given for monitoring student athlete social media postings is to identify possible activities that would violate NCAA rules such as recruiting violations. While the NCAA does not require schools to monitor its athletes' social media postings, such an action might be considered to be a part of the school's duty to investigate when it has reason to believe there may be rules violations.

Social media restrictions, however, impede upon the free speech rights of student-athletes under the First Amendment of the U.S Constitution and raise constitutional concerns. The NCAA strongly limits all manner of communications including social media by colleges and universities with high school students who are being recruited to play for particular schools. However, the NCAA is uncharacteristically silent as to regulation of social media use by student-athletes while attending NCAA member colleges and universities. The NCAA does, however, require colleges to monitor social media use by its athletes for purposes of insuring compliance with NCAA rules.

The NCAA sanctions universities that fail to "adequately and consistently" monitor social media. After the University of North Carolina removed player Marvin Austin from the football team after his receipt of improper benefits in violation of NCAA rules was disclosed on Twitter, the NCAA fined UNC $50,000 and took away 15 football scholarship from UNC alleging that UNC failed to "adequately and consistently monitor social networking activity that visibly illustrated potential amateurism violations within the football program."

College athletic programs fear that social media may cause distractions that affect athletic performance, disclose game-day strategies, generate negative attention or expose violations of the NCAA rules of conduct. Consequently, several Division I programs have placed restrictions on student-athlete access to social media by placing bans on Facebook and Twitter.

Some schools have different social media policies for different teams. Ultimately the individual coaches have much discretion in setting and enforcing social media rules.

Student athletes are subject to codes of conduct in addition to those required by other students including mandatory drug testing, rules against gambling and special academic standards. Limitations on rights of free speech are included in those codes of conduct.

However, for public institutions whose students' Constitutional rights are protected, treating student athletes differently than other students may present problems for public colleges and universities. The Fourteenth Amendment's right of equal protection of the law would seem to prohibit student-athletes from being treated differently from other students in exercising their First Amendment rights of free speech through the use of social media. The high threshold that the colleges and universities would have to meet in order to justify such disparate treatment of student athletes would have to include a compelling reason for limiting the free speech rights of student athletes. Had the right being limited not been a basic Constitutionally protected right, all the colleges and universities would have to prove to justify such restrictions of the rights of student athletes was that such a restriction would advance a legitimate college interest.

Some schools totally ban social media use by their athletes such as Boise State and Clemson University which bans the use of social media by its football team during the season. The University of Connecticut women's basketball team and the University of Louisville's men's basketball team have similar bans.

Other schools hire companies to monitor the student athletes' use of social media, which the athletes must agree to. The athletes are also required to provide their passwords and usernames.

Schools such as the University of Kentucky, LSU, Baylor and others use software to monitor social media activities of their athletes. The software necessary to do the monitoring must be agreed to be used by the athletes who are required by the schools to assent. The software monitors for specific words the schools have deemed to be unacceptable. Here is a list of common unacceptable words:

Agent

Benjamins

Cocaine

KKK

White Power

Dime bag

Doobie

Glock

Marijuana

Meth

Murder

Shoot

Strip Club

Suicide

Beer

Scotch

Tequila

Amphetamine

Bong

Juiced

Breasts

Gzongas

Queer

Rape

Whore

Common prohibited themes are agents and improper payments that may violate NCAA rules, alcohol, violence and sex. Some schools even prohibit the names of specific sports agents from athletes' social media postings.

Missouri State University's Social Networking & New Media Policy prohibits sexual content, alcohol content, tobacco content, drug content and "comments, information, photos, video(s), comments or other representations of inappropriate behavior (For example, threats of violence, derogatory comments) or which contain offensive or foul language that could embarrass or ruin the reputation of yourself, your family, your team, the athletic department or Missouri State University."

The Florida State University policy specifically indicates that students are not restricted from using social media; however, their usage is monitored. In regard to possible NCAA violations, the policy states "Do not post or participate in any endorsement of commercial (for profit) products, services or local establishments via social media. Such behavior constitutes an NCAA violation and will impact your eligibility to participate."

The Florida State University policy also specifically warns students, "Do not have a false sense of security about your rights to freedom of speech. Understand that freedom of speech is not unlimited. The on-line social network sites are NOT a place where you can say and do whatever you want without repercussions."

The actual prohibitions in the Florida State policy are broadly stated as "The FSU Department of Athletics prohibits malicious and reckless behavior when using public media outlets."

Indiana University holds its student athletes to a higher standard in its guidelines for student athletes:

Statement of Principles on the Conduct of Participants in Student Athletic Programs

"2.4 Participants' conduct shall reflect the fact that, by virtue of their participation in student athletic programs sponsored by Indiana University, they are public representatives of the University. Accordingly, they are expected to exhibit a higher standard of behavior and maturity than might be displayed by other students, staff, and faculty. They should always avoid conduct that could be perceived as improper or unfitting of a University representative."

A Kent State University wrestler tweeted anti-gay remarks and epithets regarding University of Missouri football player Michael Sam when he publicly announced that he was gay. The wrestler was indefinitely suspended for his tweets.

According to the Student-Athlete Conduct Policy Regarding Involvement in Internet based Social Networking Communities for Kent State University:

"Participation in intercollegiate athletics at Kent State University is a privilege, not a right. Athletic Department conduct policy currently states, 'Student-athletes shall conduct themselves in a manner befitting highly visible members of the university community at all times and abide by all rules established by the university, department, and head coach.' While the athletic department does not prohibit student-athlete involvement with internet-based social networking communities, this Department reserves the right to take action against any currently enrolled student-athlete engaged in behavior that violates University, department, or team rules, including, such behavior that is evidenced in postings on the internet. This action may include education, counseling, team suspension, termination from the varsity team and reduction or non-renewal of any athletic scholarships. Athletes are prohibited from blocking coaches or athletic department staff from viewing their sites."

QUESTIONS

1.    Is the Florida State University social media prohibition too vague to be enforceable?

2.    Are the social media regulations of state universities of their student-athletes an invasion of the privacy of student-athletes?

3.    Are the social media regulations of state universities of their student-athletes a violation of the First Amendment rights of the student-athletes?

4.    Are social media regulations discriminatory that only apply to student-athletes, but not other students?

---

In the Fall of 2016 within a span of just a few weeks, Princeton suspended its men's swimming and diving team, Harvard cancelled the remainder of its men's soccer team, Columbia suspended members of its wrestling team and Amherst College suspended its men's cross country team for a variety of sexually explicit and in some instances racist comments electronically communicated through emails and social media.

There is little case law on the First Amendment rights of athletes which may in part be due to the fact that cases take so long to make their way through the courts that college athletes with short careers may not wish to jeopardize those careers while litigation is pending.

# PROTECTION OF THE PRIVACY OF STUDENT ATHLETES

Some states such as Maryland, Delaware and California have passed specific laws that prevent colleges from infringing upon the rights of privacy of student athletes.

The California law reads as follows:

**SB–1349 Social media privacy: postsecondary education.** (2011–2012)

## SECTION 1.

The Legislature finds and declares that quickly evolving technologies and social media services and Internet Web sites create new challenges when seeking to protect the privacy rights of students at California's postsecondary educational institutions. It is the intent of the Legislature to protect those rights and provide students with an opportunity for redress if their rights are violated. It is also the intent of the Legislature that public postsecondary educational institutions match compliance and reporting requirements for private nonprofit and for-profit postsecondary educational institutions imposed by this act.

## SEC. 2.

Chapter 2.5 (commencing with Section 99120) is added to Part 65 of Division 14 of Title 3 of the Education Code, to read:

**CHAPTER 2.5.   Social Media Privacy**

**99120.**

As used in this chapter, "social media" means an electronic service or account, or electronic content, including, but not limited to, videos or still photographs, blogs, video blogs, podcasts, instant and text messages, email, online services or accounts, or Internet Web site profiles or locations.

**99121.**

(a)   Public and private postsecondary educational institutions, and their employees and representatives, shall not require or request a student, prospective student, or student group to do any of the following:

(1)   Disclose a user name or password for accessing personal social media.

(2) Access personal social media in the presence of the institution's employee or representative.

(3) Divulge any personal social media information.

(b) A public or private postsecondary educational institution shall not suspend, expel, discipline, threaten to take any of those actions, or otherwise penalize a student, prospective student, or student group in any way for refusing to comply with a request or demand that violates this section.

(c) This section shall not do either of the following:

(1) Affect a public or private postsecondary educational institution's existing rights and obligations to protect against and investigate alleged student misconduct or violations of applicable laws and regulations.

(2) Prohibit a public or private postsecondary educational institution from taking any adverse action against a student, prospective student, or student group for any lawful reason.

**99122.**

A private nonprofit or for-profit postsecondary educational institution shall post its social media privacy policy on the institution's Internet Web site.

# NORTHWESTERN UNIVERSITY AND THE NLRB

In August 2015, the NLRB's five-member national board ruled that Northwestern University football players could not attempt to unionize. The decision ended the case, though the board punted on the essential question about whether Northwestern players are employees. Instead, the NLRB concluded that it wouldn't assert jurisdiction because doing so would create chaos for public and private universities abiding by different NCAA rules since private school players would be able to collectively bargain and public schools would not be able to collectively bargain.

In a related matter, also in August of 2015, David Rosenfeld, a labor lawyer with the firm of Weinberg Roger & Rosenfeld in Alameda, California filed a complaint with the NLRB alleging that Northwestern was guilty of "unfair labor practices" in its treatment of football players in regard to its social media policy and other aspects of Northwestern's rules for football players. Section 8(a)(1) of the National Labor Relations Act (NLRA) makes it an unfair labor practice for employers to "interfere with, restrain or coerce employees in the exercise of the rights guaranteed" which has been interpreted to apply to the use of social media for the discussion of work conditions. Although Rosenfeld had absolutely no connection with Northwestern or its football players, the law allows anyone to bring to the attention of the NLRB unfair treatment of employees.

In response to Rosenfeld's complaint, the NLRB issued an "advice memorandum" on September 22, 2016 in Case 13–CA–157467 that described the Northwestern team rules as "unlawfully overbroad." The NLRB dismissed the charges against Northwestern once Northwestern changed some of its communications policies in accordance with the advice memorandum to allow players to more freely use social media, discuss health issues and speak with the media.

It could be expected that this opinion of the NLRB will form the basis for future challenges of the social media policies of other private colleges and universities. The opinion is unlikely to affect the social media policies of public colleges and universities because the NLRB's authority is limited to private employers and has no power over public colleges and universities.

For many, the most relevant part of the Sept. 22, 2016 memo, from NLRB Associate General Counsel Barry J. Kearney was the first footnote: which stated: "We assume, for purposes of this memorandum, that Northwestern's scholarship football players are statutory employees." Northwestern while objecting to the assumption that the players were employees modified its social media policy to comply with the memorandum.

Prior to the charges being brought by Rosenfeld, Northwestern's team handbook formerly contained a provision indicating that social media may be regularly monitored, but after the Rosenfeld complaint, Northwestern removed the provision for regular monitoring of social media. The university also removed a sentence stating concern about protecting its image in regard to social media posts by players.

While formerly the Northwestern rules broadly and vaguely prohibited the posting of inappropriate or embarrassing material, under the modification offered by Northwestern and agreed to by the NLRB, the new social media rule for Northwestern student athletes states that postings "can be seen" and cautions against posting "harassing, unlawful or dangerous behaviors such as full or partial nudity (of yourself or another) sex, racial or sexual epithets, underage drinking, drugs, weapons, or firearms, hazing, harassment, unlawful activity or any content that violates Northwestern University, Athletics Department or student-athlete codes of conduct and/or state or federal laws."

Another previous handbook rule informed Northwestern players that they "should never agree to an interview (with the media) unless the interview has been arranged by the athletic communications office," and that the players must be "positive when talking about your teammates, coaches and team." Responding to the NLRB's conclusions that the rule was an infringement on player freedoms, Northwestern abandoned the rule, rewriting it to provide that players "may directly speak with members of the media if (they) choose to do so."

In its revised handbook, the school suggested to players that, in interviews, they should "share credit for your success by talking about the contributions of your teammates and use their names." Players were also admonished to remember that "every great running back needs a good offensive line" and "talking about the great work of others shows you have confidence in your own role and the value of your own contributions, so you're not afraid of letting someone else have their moment of glory, too."

The handbook previously instructed players: "Never discuss any aspects of the team, the physical condition of any players, planned strategies, etc. with anyone. The team is a family and what takes place on the field, in meetings or in the locker room stays with the family." The new rule limits the ban to individual medical conditions, due to medical privacy laws. It allows players to discuss "on a no-names basis about vital health and safety issues impacting themselves, their teammates, and fellow collegiate football players."[2]

# SYNOPSIS

1.   The First Amendment of the Constitution protects the right of free speech, but only against limitations placed by federal, state or local governments and their agencies. The First Amendment does not apply to private corporations and organizations which may and often do put restrictions on the speech of their employees.

2.   In the corporate world it is common for companies to formulate social media policies and include them in official employee handbooks.

3.   The National Labor Relations Board (NLRB) has recognized the rights of workers to discuss workplace conditions on social media.

4.   The NBA Constitution permits the commissioner to discipline a player "for any statement he makes or endorses which is prejudicial or detrimental to the best interests of basketball and to fine the player for conduct that is detrimental to the NBA," which includes conduct that does not conform "to standards of morality and fair play." This

---

[2]   Advice Memorandum from Barry J. Kearney, Associate General Counsel NLRB to Peter Sung Ohr, Regional Director NLRB Region 13, regarding Northwestern University, Case 13–CA–157467, September 22, 2016.

has been construed to include power to regulate and punish comments made through social media.

5.    Similar to the NBA commissioner's authority, the Commissioner of MLB may take actions in the broadly stated best interests of baseball.

6.    While the NFL encourages its players to use social media, the NFL's policy also restricts players from using social media at the stadium for a period beginning ninety minutes before the start of a game and ending when the post-game traditional locker room interviews have been completed. Other than that, individual teams are allowed to make their own restrictions.

7.    According to the terms of the NHL CBA all rules regarding personal conduct must be collectively bargained with the National Hockey League Players Association. Social media policy is a part of the NHL CBA.

8.    In the case of Healy v. James, 408 U.S. 169, 180 (1972) the Supreme Court extended the recognition of the rights of free speech to college students.

9.    The First Amendment applies to government limitations on freedom of speech not private institutions. However, while private colleges are free to make whatever rules they wish limiting free speech, state colleges and universities fall under the classification of a governmental unit subject to the First Amendment.

10.    Some states such as Maryland, Delaware and California have passed specific laws that prevent colleges from infringing upon the rights of privacy of student athletes.

11.    Some schools totally ban social media use by their athletes. Other schools hire companies to monitor the student athletes' use of social media, which the athletes must agree to and are required to provide their passwords and usernames.

# CHAPTER FOURTEEN

# Fantasy Sports

Participants in fantasy sports assemble imaginary teams of individual real players from professional sports such as basketball, baseball, hockey and, perhaps most popular, football to compete against the imaginary teams of other participants. Statistics based points determined by the performance of the individual players in real competitions are totaled and the winner is the person with the highest number of points.

## HISTORY

The roots of fantasy sports can be traced back to as early as 1960 when Sociology Professor William Gamson started the first National Baseball Seminar, a fantasy baseball game which has operated continually since then. Only four statistics, earned run average, games won, runs batted in and batting average were used to determine points as compared to the more modern fantasy sports of today that often include many more statistics in determining the overall points for competing teams.

Fantasy sports are also often referred to as Rotisserie sports. The term Rotisserie sports is derived from a fantasy baseball league referred to as Rotisserie League Baseball begun in 1980 which took the name Rotisserie from the restaurant where founder Daniel Okrent and the other participants would meet to play.

These privately operated fantasy sports leagues generally start the season with the participating players drafting players, much like professional sports drafts where participants in the draft take turns choosing players for their respective teams. Early fantasy sports competitions were primarily season long events where each participants' players individual game statistic derived points were compiled over the course of a long professional sports league season, such as the NFL's season and the participant with the most points at the end of the season would receive a cash prize based upon the entrance fees of the participants. The entrance fees for these informal fantasy leagues, which generally had around a dozen competitors, were usually small, such as $50, however, in 2008 the Wall Street Journal reported about a fantasy football league that had been operating since 2002 comprised of ten financial industry titans where the entrance fee was $100,000 per person with the winner receiving a top prize of $600,000, the second place entrant receiving $300,000 and the third place entrant receiving $100,000.[1]

As with so many other aspects of society, advancements in computer technology and the Internet dramatically increased the popularity of fantasy sports as tremendous amounts of sports statistics became readily available online. From small personal groups of fantasy players, fantasy sports evolved through the Internet with big companies getting involved such as Yahoo which began offering large scale fantasy sports in 1999 and the World Championship of Fantasy Football which started in 2008 and offered a one million dollar cash prize its season long winner.

The landscape of fantasy sports changed forever with the advent of daily fantasy sports which began in 2014. Instead of season long competitions, daily fantasy sports offered single game or single week options providing instant gratification. Rather than being operated by the informal groups first offering seasonal fantasy sports or even the

---

[1] "Wall Street's $1 Million Fantasy League," Jon Weinbach, Wall Street Journal, October 17, 2008.

large companies such as Yahoo and ESPN offering large scale seasonal competitions, daily fantasy sports were offered by a small number of companies, most prominently Fan Duel and Draft Kings which advertised big prizes derived from entrance fees of large numbers of participants with the companies sponsoring the competition making its profit from a small percentage, generally around 10% of the amounts bet, following the business model of legal Nevada sports books.

While as originally practiced season long fantasy sports competitions were generally small affairs at little cost to entrants and later grew to include large online contests sponsored by Yahoo and others at little or no cost to entrants, the business of daily fantasy sports quickly grew into a five billion dollar industry with 35 million participants as early as 2014.[2]

The stakes are indeed high when it comes to daily fantasy sports because not only is the daily fantasy sports industry a big business in and of itself, but television ratings for NFL games increased with the advent of daily fantasy sports which is to some extent attributable to fantasy sports participants watching games in which their players are participating. Increased viewers translates into increased advertising revenues for the networks and cable companies carrying such games.

## LEGALITY OF FANTASY SPORTS

The groundwork for daily fantasy sports was laid in the Unlawful Internet Gambling Enforcement Act (UIGEA), a law passed by Congress with little debate or discussion that was tacked on as an amendment to the SAFE PORT ACT in 2006. This law was intended to criminalize the transfer of funds to illegal Internet based gambling companies. While strictly speaking the law did not make it illegal for individuals to gamble online, the effect of preventing the transfer of

---

[2]    Robert M. Crawford & David J. Apfel, Welcome to Fantasy Island, Betting on the Growth of Fantasy Sports in the U.S., A Gamble with many Risks, Casino International Magazine, October 2014.

funds by wire, credit card or otherwise to companies operating Internet gambling websites was the same. However, the UIGEA contains a specific exception for fantasy sports, which, at the time of the enactment of the law, was generally done as season long competitions.

The exception reads and applies to:

**"(ix)** participation in any fantasy or simulation sports game or educational game or contest in which (if the game or contest involves a team or teams) no fantasy or simulation sports team is based on the current membership of an actual team that is a member of an amateur or professional sports organization (as those terms are defined in section 3701 of title 28) and that meets the following conditions:

**(I)** All prizes and awards offered to winning participants are established and made known to the participants in advance of the game or contest and their value is not determined by the number of participants or the amount of any fees paid by those participants.

**(II)** All winning outcomes reflect the relative knowledge and skill of the participants and are determined predominantly by accumulated statistical results of the performance of individuals (athletes in the case of sports events) in multiple real-world sporting or other events.

**(III)** No winning outcome is based—

**(aa)** on the score, point-spread, or any performance or performances of any single real-world team or any combination of such teams; or

**(bb)** solely on any single performance of an individual athlete in any single real-world sporting or other event."

31 U.S. Code Section 5362.

_____

As applied toward both season long fantasy sports and daily fantasy sports, the conditions for the exception provided by the UIGEA appear to have been met because, entries are not submitted based on the performance of either amateur or professional teams, but rather the achievement level of individual players. The prizes, as well, are set by the companies in advance of the game and the winning is not dependent on the number of entries. The issue, however, of skill as a factor would appear to be strongly indicated by the fact that, as practiced, players with the best skill and knowledge appear to dominate the contests. It is an important distinction to note, however, that the UIGEA does not specifically legalize fantasy sports, but rather merely states that fund transfers done as a part of fantasy sports are allowed.

## QUESTIONS

1. For purposes of the law, should season long fantasy sports be considered differently than daily fantasy sports?

2. What elements of fantasy sports make it a game of skill rather than chance?

3. Are the elements of skill different for season long fantasy sports compared to daily fantasy sports?

# DAILY FANTASY SPORTS

Daily fantasy sports began in 1999 with the creation of FanDuel in Scotland, followed three years later by DraftKings in 2002. These companies dominate the field of daily fantasy sports and now are attempting to merge.

The growth of daily fantasy sports was enhanced by its being embraced by the NBA, MLB and individual NFL teams. The NBA is a part owner of FanDuel. MLB and the NHL have partnered with DraftKings in operations. In 2015 the NFL Players Association entered into a contract that provided for active NFL players to be included in DraftKings advertising and promotional material. The relationship with daily fantasy sports by the NFL is particularly interesting in the light of its extreme position against gambling in any form.

Daily fantasy sports as dominated by DraftKings and FanDuel initially appeared to come out of nowhere to immediate prominence due to a barrage of television advertising in 2015. A key date in the development of daily fantasy sports was September 27, 2015 when an employee of DraftKings, Ethan Haskell inadvertently made public information that could have provided him with an advantage in his own playing of a daily fantasy sports competition on FanDuel in which he won $350,000. The public uproar was immediate and the questioning of the inherent fairness of the games was widely debated. An investigation determined that information posted by Haskell was obtained by him after he had actually submitted his fantasy sports entry and that he had not used any special access to information for his own personal gain, but public questioning continued. Following this incident, both DraftKings and FanDuel banned their employees from playing daily fantasy sports anywhere.

Over the next few months, Nevada, Arizona, Illinois, Iowa, Louisiana, Montana and Washington banned daily fantasy sports. New York went a step further and New York Attorney General Eric Schneiderman not only issued cease and desist orders to both FanDuel and DraftKings to stop operations in New York, but also filed lawsuits against the two companies seeking reimbursement to New York players who lost money playing with these two companies.

The response in New York, where daily fantasy sports are particularly popular, to the actions of Attorney General Schneiderman shutting down FanDuel and DraftKings was the swift action by the state legislature to legalize fantasy sports with the passage of S 8153 which provides in its introduction:

"(A) INTERACTIVE FANTASY SPORTS ARE NOT GAMES OF CHANCE BECAUSE THEY

CONSIST OF FANTASY OR SIMULATION SPORTS GAMES OR CONTESTS IN WHICH THE FANTASY OR SIMULATION

SPORTS TEAMS ARE SELECTED BASED UPON THE SKILL AND KNOWLEDGE OF THE PARTICIPANTS AND NOT BASED ON THE CURRENT MEMBERSHIP OF AN ACTUAL TEAM THAT IS A MEMBER OF AN AMATEUR OR PROFESSIONAL SPORTS ORGANIZATION;

(B) INTERACTIVE FANTASY SPORTS CONTESTS ARE NOT WAGERS ON FUTURE CONTINGENT EVENTS NOT UNDER THE CONTESTANTS' CONTROL OR INFLUENCE BECAUSE CONTESTANTS HAVE CONTROL OVER WHICH PLAYERS THEY CHOOSE AND THE OUTCOME OF EACH CONTEST IS NOT DEPENDENT UPON THE PERFORMANCE OF ANY ONE PLAYER OR ANY ONE ACTUAL TEAM. THE OUTCOME OF ANY FANTASY SPORTS CONTEST DOES NOT CORRESPOND TO THE OUTCOME OF ANY ONE SPORTING EVENT. INSTEAD,

THE OUTCOME DEPENDS ON HOW THE PERFORMANCES OF PARTICIPANTS' FANTASY ROSTER CHOICES COMPARE TO THE PERFORMANCE OF OTHERS' ROSTER CHOICES.

2. BASED ON THE FINDINGS IN SUBDIVISION ONE OF THIS SECTION, THE LEGISLATURE DECLARES THAT INTERACTIVE FANTASY SPORTS DO NOT CONSTITUTE GAMBLING IN NEW YORK STATE AS DEFINED IN ARTICLE TWO HUNDRED TWENTY-FIVE OF THE PENAL LAW.

3. THE LEGISLATURE FURTHER FINDS THAT AS THE INTERNET HAS BECOME AN INTEGRAL PART OF SOCIETY, AND INTERACTIVE FANTASY SPORTS A MAJOR FORM OF ENTERTAINMENT FOR MANY CONSUMERS, ANY INTERACTIVE FANTASY SPORTS ENFORCEMENT AND REGULATORY STRUCTURE MUST BEGIN FROM THE BEDROCK PREMISE THAT PARTICIPATION IN A LAWFUL AND LICENSED INTERACTIVE FANTASY SPORTS INDUSTRY IS A PRIVILEGE AND NOT A RIGHT, AND

THAT REGULATORY OVERSIGHT IS INTENDED TO SAFEGUARD THE INTEGRITY OF THE GAMES AND PARTICIPANTS AND TO ENSURE ACCOUNTABILITY AND THE PUBLIC TRUST."

---

By designating the participation in daily fantasy sports as a privilege rather than a right, the ability of the New York legislature to regulate became easier to accomplish. When an activity is classified as a right, regulations can only be done if there exists a compelling state interest while if it is a privilege, the activity can be regulated merely when there is a reasonable relation of the regulation to a legitimate governmental interest.

## SHARKS VS. FISHES

A major problem with the daily fantasy sports businesses as operated primarily by DraftKings and FanDuel is that despite television advertising that would make it appear that anyone playing had an equal chance of winning substantial prizes, the truth is that daily fantasy sports were dominated by a relatively few high-volume players who would enter up to thousands of entries prepared using sophisticated computer software and algorithms that helped them assimilate tremendous amounts of data providing these high-volume players with a significant advantage in winning prizes.

In a study reported in the Sports Business Journal in 2015, it was shown that during the first half of the 2015 MLBB season 91% of the daily fantasy baseball profits were won by only 1.3% of the players, who are often referred to as the sharks, while the small, less sophisticated players referred to as the minnows who made up 98.7% of the players won only 9% of the daily fantasy baseball winnings.[3]

---

[3] "For Daily Fantasy Sports Operators, the Curse of Too Much Skill," Ed Miller and Daniel Singer, Sports Business Journal, July 27, 2015.

For FanDuel and DraftKings these high-volume players posed a problem. By dominating the competitions, it was not a level playing field for the millions of ordinary players that these companies needed to maintain the high level of customers needed to operate profitably. On the other hand, they also needed these high-volume players to indeed submit large numbers of entries in order to increase the size of the prizes and the profits for the companies. When this first became public knowledge, even in the states where daily fantasy sports were not considered to be illegal gambling, there were no regulations in place to protect ordinary consumers from being taken advantage of in this manner.

Interestingly, the domination of the daily fantasy sports business poses both an advantage and a disadvantage to the legal status of companies such as FanDuel and DraftKings because while the fact that the games are consistently dominated by a few players points to fantasy sports being a game of skill more akin to chess than a gambling activity, the more important fact was that daily fantasy sports as then operated could be considered to be inherently unfair to the smaller, less sophisticated players which could and did jeopardize the unregulated legal standing of the activity.

## QUESTIONS

1. Does the fact that sharks are able to win more often than minnows reinforce the argument that daily fantasy games are games of skill rather than chance?

2. Does the advertising of daily fantasy sports misrepresent the chances of the average player winning?

3. Should states enact regulations to protect the "minnows" in playing daily fantasy sports?

# USE OF PLAYER STATISTICS

Fantasy sports are entirely dependent for their existence on the names of the specific players and the standard statistical measures of their performance, such as the number of catches by an NFL receiver, being available to fantasy sports players. This is the life blood of fantasy sports. The legal issue that arose early in the development of fantasy sports was whether players had an intellectual property right in their names and statistics when used in fantasy sports. Initially, unions such as the Major League Baseball Players' Association, on behalf of its individual members, licensed the use of their names and statistics to specific companies to exclusively use this information for purposes of operating fantasy sports operations, however, CBC a company that operated a fantasy sports operation sued arguing that the use of players' names and publicly available statistics for purposes of fantasy sports was a "fair use" exception to the intellectual property laws.

In the case of C.B.C. Distribution and Marketing, Inc. v. Major League Baseball Advanced Media, L.P., 505 F. 3d 818 (2007) the appeals court ruled that the players' names and statistics were available at no cost to anyone using them for fantasy sports.

In this case the court ruled:

"CBC argues that the first amendment nonetheless trumps the right-of-publicity action that Missouri law provides. Though this dispute is between private parties, the state action necessary for first amendment protections exists because the right-of-publicity claim exists only insofar as the courts enforce state-created obligations that were "never explicitly assumed" by CBC. *See Cohen v. Cowles Media Co.*, 501 U.S. 663, 668, 111 S.Ct. 2513, 115 L.Ed.2d 586 (1991).

The Supreme Court has directed that state law rights of publicity must be balanced against first amendment considerations, *see Zacchini v. Scripps-Howard Broad.*, 433 U.S. 562, 97 S.Ct. 2849, 53 L.Ed.2d 965 (1977), and here we conclude that the former must give way to the latter. First, the information used in CBC's fantasy baseball games is all readily available in the public domain, and it would be strange law that a person would not have a first amendment right to use information that is available to everyone. It is true that CBC's use of the information is meant to provide entertainment, but "[s]peech that entertains, like speech that informs, is protected by the First Amendment because '[t]he line between the informing and the entertaining is too elusive for the protection of that basic right.'" *Cardtoons, L.C. v. Major League Baseball Players Ass'n*, 95 F.3d 959, 969 (10th Cir. 1996) (quoting *Winters v. New York*, 333 U.S. 507, 510, 68 S.Ct. 665, 92 L.Ed. 840 (1948)); *see also Zacchini*, 433 U.S. at 578, 97 S.Ct. 2849. We also find no merit in the argument that CBC's use of players' names and information in its fantasy baseball games is not speech at all. We have held that "the pictures, graphic design, concept art, sounds, music, stories, and narrative present in video games" is speech entitled to first amendment protection. *See Interactive Digital Software Ass'n v. St. Louis County, Mo.*, 329 F.3d 954, 957 (8th Cir.2003). Similarly, here CBC uses the "names, nicknames, likenesses, signatures, pictures, playing records, and/or biographical data of each player" in an interactive form in connection with its fantasy baseball products. This use is no less expressive than the use that was at issue in *Interactive Digital*.

Courts have also recognized the public value of information about the game of baseball and its players, referring to baseball as "the national pastime." *Cardtoons*, 95 F.3d at 972. A California court, in a case where Major League Baseball was itself defending its use of players' names, likenesses, and information against the players' asserted rights of publicity, observed, "Major league baseball is followed by millions of people across this country on a daily basis ... The public has an enduring fascination in the records set by former players and in memorable moments from previous games ... The records and statistics remain of interest to the public because they provide context that allows fans to better appreciate (or deprecate) today's performances." *Gionfriddo v. Major League Baseball*, 94 Cal.App.4th 400,

411, 114 Cal.Rptr.2d 307 (2001). The Court in *Gionfriddo* concluded that the "recitation and discussion of factual data concerning the athletic performance of [players on Major League Baseball's website] command a substantial public interest, and, therefore, is a form of expression due substantial constitutional protection." *Id.* We find these views persuasive.

In addition, the facts in this case barely, if at all, implicate the interests that states typically intend to vindicate by providing rights of publicity to individuals. Economic interests that states seek to promote include the right of an individual to reap the rewards of his or her endeavors and an individual's right to earn a living. Other motives for creating a publicity right are the desire to provide incentives to encourage a person's productive activities and to protect consumers from misleading advertising. *See Zacchini,* 433 U.S. at 573, 576, 97 S.Ct. 2849; *Cardtoons,* 95 F.3d at 973. But major league baseball players are rewarded, and handsomely, too, for their participation in games and can earn additional large sums from endorsements and sponsorship arrangements. Nor is there any danger here that consumers will be misled, because the fantasy baseball games depend on the inclusion of all players and thus cannot create a false impression that some particular player with "star power" is endorsing CBC's products."

## STATE LEGISLATION

While sports gambling is specifically made illegal by the federal Professional and Amateur Sports Protection Act (PASPA), the individual states each have the legal authority to determine whether or not fantasy sports constitute a game of skill, in which case it is not gambling or a game of chance, in which it is determined to be illegal gambling. The standard for determining whether an activity is a game of chance or skill differs from state to state with some states using the dominant factor test which designates the activity as a game of chance or skill dependent upon whether skill or chance is the dominant factor in the game. Alaska and California are two states that use the dominant factor standard.

The case of Morrow v. State of Alaska, 511 P. 2d 127 (1973) describes the four conditions that make up the dominant factor test as follows:

"The following aspects are requisite to a scheme where skill predominates over chance. (1) Participants must have a distinct possibility of exercising skill and must have sufficient data upon which to calculate an informed judgment. The test is that without skill it would be absolutely impossible to win the game. (2) Participants must have the opportunity to exercise the skill, and the general class of participants must possess the skill. Where the contest is aimed at the capacity of the general public, the average person must have the skill, but not every person need have the skill. It is irrelevant that participants may exercise varying degrees of skill. Johnson v. Phinney, 218 F.2d 303, 306 (5th Cir.1955). The scheme cannot be limited or aimed at a specific skill which only a few possess. "[W]hether chance or skill was the determining factor in the contest must depend upon the capacity of the general public—not experts—to solve the problems presented." State ex inf. McKittrick v. Globe-Democrat Publishing Co., 341 Mo. 862, 110 S.W.2d 705, 717 (1937). (3) Skill or the competitors' efforts must sufficiently govern the result. Skill must control the final result, not just one part of the larger scheme. Commonwealth v. Plissner, 295 Mass. 457, 4 N.E.2d 241 (1936). Where "chance enters into the solution of another lesser part of the problems and thereby proximately influences the final result," the scheme is a lottery. State ex inf. McKittrick v. Globe-Democrat Publishing Co., *supra*. Where skill does not destroy the dominant effect of chance, the scheme is a lottery. Horner v. United States, 147 U.S. 449, 459, 13 S.Ct. 409, 37 L.Ed. 237, 241 (1893). (4) The standard of skill must be known to the participants, and this standard must govern the result. The language used in promoting the scheme must sufficiently inform the participants of the criteria to be used in determining the results of the winners. The winners must be determined objectively."

Other states use the stricter categorizing of an activity as illegal gambling if there is any element of chance in the activity. Using this standard, Texas ruled that fantasy sports constituted illegal gambling. The considerable difference in state laws has resulted in daily fantasy sports being declared illegal in numerous states. Meanwhile, due to the extreme popularity of the activity and the subtle difference between fantasy sports and sports gambling on the outcomes of specific athletic events, legislation is being proposed in numerous states where fantasy sports have been determined to be illegal gambling to legalize the activity. It can be expected to be years before this matter is resolved throughout the country. Some states have ruled that the fantasy sports are legal, but have enacted regulations to protect consumers participating in fantasy sports. This nationwide patchwork of differing regulations from state to state complicates the business of companies such as FanDuel and DraftKings and makes it expensive for smaller companies to compete in the daily fantasy sports business.

Notably, Nevada, the only state to have full sports gambling declared daily fantasy sports to be a form of gambling subject to state gambling regulations.

In his opinion, the Attorney General of Nevada concluded:

"Upon extensive review of pay-to-play daily fantasy sports, we conclude that they constitute sports pools under NRS 463.0193 and gambling games under NRS 463.0152. Daily fantasy sports may also constitute illegal lotteries under NRS 462.105(1) depending on the legal question of whose skill is being assessed and the factual question of whether skill or chance is dominant. If the skill being assessed is that of the actual players rather than that of the fantasy sports team owners, then daily fantasy sports constitute illegal lotteries. If the skill being assessed is that of the owners, then there is a factual question as to whether the skill in selecting lineups predominates over chance."[4]

---

4    Memorandum of Nevada Attorney General "Legality of Daily Fantasy Sports Under Nevada Law," October 16, 2015.

In his opinion the Texas Attorney General indicated that daily fantasy sports were illegal under Texas law, but also ruled that season long fantasy sports would not be subject to prosecution. He wrote:

"Under section 47.02 of the Penal Code, a person commits an offense if he or she makes a bet on the partial or final result of a game or contest or on the performance of a participant in a game or contest. Because the outcome of games in daily fantasy sports leagues depends partially on chance, an individual's payment of a fee to participate in such activities is a bet. Accordingly, a court would likely determine that participation in daily fantasy sports leagues is illegal gambling 'under section 47.02 of the Penal Code. Though participating in a traditional fantasy sports league is also illegal gambling under section 47.02, participants in such leagues may avail themselves of a statutory defense to prosecution under section 47.02(b) of the Penal Code when play is in a private place, no person receives any economic benefit other than personal winnings, and the risks of winning or losing are the same for all participants."[5]

Texas applied the stricter test of any element of chance made the activity constitute illegal gambling, such that injuries, weather and even the level of officiating could all affect the outcome of a sporting event.

## VIRGINIA PASSES THE FIRST FANTASY SPORTS REGULATIONS

The first state to enact a law pertaining to daily fantasy sports was Virginia in early 2016. Title 59.1 Chapter 51. Fantasy Contests Act. The law included a $50,000 registration fee for daily sports fantasy companies seeking to do business in Virginia which discourages

---

[5]    Opinion No. KP–0057 of the Texas Attorney General "The Legality of Fantasy Sports Leagues Under Texas Law," January 19, 2016.

competition by smaller startup companies. In addition, the law also unnecessarily lumped in season long fantasy sports for regulation along with daily fantasy sports.

The law defined fantasy sports subject to regulation as follows:

"Fantasy contest" includes any online fantasy or simulated game or contest with an entry fee in which (i) the value of all prizes and awards offered to winning participants is established and made known to the participants in advance of the contest; (ii) all winning outcomes reflect the relative knowledge and skill of the participants and shall be determined by accumulated statistical results of the performance of individuals, including athletes in the case of sports events; and (iii) no winning outcome is based on the score, point spread, or any performance of any single actual team or combination of teams or solely on any single performance of an individual athlete or player in any single actual event."

The Virginia law also restricted participation in fantasy sports to people over the age of 18 and, in an effort to limit the disproportionate power of technically supported major players dominating contests with huge numbers of entries, provided operators must:

"6. Disclose the number of entries a single fantasy contest player may submit to each fantasy contest and take reasonable steps to prevent such players from submitting more than the allowable number;"

## MASSACHUSETTS REGULATIONS

In April of 2016 Massachusetts became the eighth state to authorize daily fantasy sports with laws that essentially mirrored regulations put into effect by its Attorney General Maura Healey who had earlier ruled that daily fantasy sports did not constitute illegal gambling, but could be regulated.

Some of the key elements of the regulations 940 C.M.R. 34 include requirements that:

1.    Employees of daily fantasy sports companies may not play daily fantasy sports;

2.    Advertising must be truthful and not misleading;

3.    Sites must offer specific games limited to participation by beginners and highly experienced players must be identified.

4.    Users cannot use unauthorized third party computer scripts that automatically without any interaction by the player receive and convert data into new lineups providing a considerable edge to those employing these scripts. This has been a major factor in the sharks being able to dominate contests. Under the Massachusetts regulations unauthorized third party scripts may not be used to enter or alter entries and all scripts used must not only be authorized by the daily fantasy sports website, but it must be made available to all players. Whether this regulation is enforceable or avoidable by particular players is open to question.

Highly experienced players are defined under the Massachusetts regulations as:

"Highly-Experienced Player: Any DFS player who has 1) entered more than 1,000 contests offered by a single DFSO; or 2) has won more than three DFS contest Prizes valued at $1,000 or more. Once a DFS player is classified as Highly-Experienced Player, a player will remain classified as such."

5.    The number of entries a single player may enter is limited in a single contest to the lesser of 150 entries or 3% of all entries with limited exceptions.

6.    All players must be over 21 years of age.

# SYNOPSIS

1.  Season long fantasy sports go back to 1960.

2.  Daily fantasy sports began with the creation of Fan Duel in Scotland in 1999.

3.  Fantasy sports were recognized as a legal activity in the Unlawful Internet Gambling Enforcement Act enacted by Congress in 2006.

4.  Daily fantasy sports became popular in the United States in 2014 and provided a way for individual players to win significant amounts of cash.

5.  In September of 2015 when a Draft Kings employee won a large amount of money playing on Fan Duel, much public attention was focused on daily fantasy sports and a number of states outlawed daily fantasy sports as illegal gambling.

6.  The names and performance statistics of professional athletes used in fantasy sports are deemed to be in the public domain.

7.  A major concern of legislators when authorizing fantasy sports is the advantage of the "sharks" over the "minnows."

# CHAPTER FIFTEEN

# Sports and Gambling

With the exception of legal sports betting in Nevada, which in 2015 totaled 4.2 billion dollars, the actual amount bet on sporting events in the United States is largely unknown. It is difficult to estimate the true level of how much is bet with estimates ranging from 100 billion dollars bet illegally to as much as 149 billion dollars. The Superbowl alone accounted for an estimated 47 billion dollars of illegal bets in 2016.

As long ago as 1999 the National Gambling Impact Study Commission estimated that amount of money illegally bet on sports gambling in the United States was between 80 billion dollars and 380 billion dollars annually.[1]

According to the Gambling Compliance Research Service, if sports betting were legal in the United States, gambling revenues would reach 11.9 billion dollars which would dwarf that of the UK which brings in annual revenues of 2.8 billion dollars.

Much of the sports gambling done by Americans today is done via the Internet on websites based in jurisdictions outside of the United States. Sports wagering is generally done through people referred to as bookmakers who make their profit by taking a percentage of the money bet as a vigorish or vig. Many legal bookmakers, such as in the

---

[1]    National Gambling Impact Study Commission Report June 18, 1999.

UK operate outside of the United States and are not subject to American regulations.

# ONLINE SPORTS GAMBLING

The Internet has revolutionized much of modern daily life and the effect of the Internet on sports gambling has been profound. It has been estimated that Americans spend 2.6 billion dollars annually on illegal websites headquartered off shore, often in the Caribbean.[2]

Offshore gambling websites using the latest Internet technology do business on line with bettors anywhere in the world. Some of the websites are operated by organized crime while others are run by ordinary businessmen. Europe has had legal sports betting largely without incident for many years tending to disprove the arguments of the NFL and others who say that sports gambling would affect the integrity of the game. The NFL's argument ignores two important facts. The first is that people already bet on games and the second is that through legalization and increased use of analytics sports, gambling could be effectively regulated to protect consumers who presently have no legal protection.

In a stunning reversal of policy, in 2011 the Justice Department ruled that federal online gambling laws only prohibited wagering on sporting events and left it up to the states to determine their own laws regarding other forms of online gambling.[3]

Prior to 2011, horseracing was the only online gambling allowed by federal law. At that time the laws were changed to allow online poker and casino games to be played legally online, however the federal government kept the restriction against online sports gambling.

---

    [2]  "Policymakers must get on board with online gambling," Las Vegas Review Journal, Geoff Freeman, September 19, 2013.

    [3]  "Whether Proposals by Illinois and New York to use the Internet and out-of-state Transaction Processors to Sell Lottery Tickets to in-state Adults Violate the Wire Act," Memorandum Opinion for the Assistant Attorney General, Criminal Division, Virginia A. Seitz, Assistant Attorney General, September 20, 2011.

# BLACK SOX SCANDAL

In the early twentieth century professional baseball players were not particularly well paid. Chicago White Sox owner, Charles Comiskey was considered to be particularly frugal when it came to paying his players although all of the owners were able to and did keep salaries low by the use of the reserve clause which bound a player to his team for his entire career thereby eliminating the possibility of free agency and competition among team owners to obtain the services of highly skilled ballplayers.

With a record of 88 wins and 52 losses, the Chicago White Sox were by far the best team in baseball in 1919 and a clear favorite to win the World Series against the Cincinnati Reds. During the summer of 1919 one or two White Sox players initiated a meeting with two groups of gamblers led by Joseph Sullivan, Bill Burns and Billy Maharg to discuss the idea of intentionally losing the World Series in return for $100,000 in payments to the players. Adjusted for inflation, $100,000 in 1919 would have been the equivalent of approximately 1.5 million dollars in 2016. The scheme to fix the World Series was bankrolled by New York gambler, Arnold Rothstein. The Reds went on to win the 1919 World Series over the White Sox 5 games to 3 with the play in some of the games appearing to be somewhat suspicious. At that time the World Series was a best of nine games event.

Rumors quickly spread that the White Sox had thrown the World Series. The National Commission, a three person committee which governed professional baseball between 1903 and 1920 initially publicly discounted the possibility that the World Series had been fixed, but as the rumors continued, the National Commission, concerned about the public perception of the game of professional baseball, appointed federal Judge Kenesaw Mountain Landis to investigate the matter. The owners wanted Landis to head up a revised National Commission to govern professional baseball however, Landis was adamant that the only way he would be involved was as the sole commissioner with tremendous powers. One of the first things that Landis did upon being named the first Commissioner of Baseball was to ban all eight players implicated in, what now was being called, the Black Sox Scandal, for life.

Meanwhile, a Grand Jury was convened in September of 1920 to do its own investigation. As a result of the Grand Jury investigation, eight players, Shoeless Joe Jackson, Eddie Cicotte, Oscar Happy Felsch, Claude Lefty Williams, Arnold Chick Gandil, Fred McMullin, Charles Swede Risberg and George Buck Weaver were indicted and later put on trial. After less than three hours of deliberation, the jury found all of the players not guilty, but they were still widely considered by the public to have committed the crimes of which they were accused. On August 3, 1921, the day after the players were found not guilty, Landis made his position clear that the jury's verdict would have no effect on his ruling when he said, "Regardless of the verdict of juries, no player who throws a ball game, no player who undertakes or promises to throw a ball game, no player who sits in confidence with a bunch of crooked ballplayers and gamblers, where the ways and means of throwing a game are discussed and does not promptly tell his club about it will ever play professional baseball."[4]

# TIM DONAGHY

The biggest betting scandal in NBA history involved a referee, Tim Donaghy, who had refereed in the NBA for nine years. Donaghy was convicted in 2008 of conspiracy to engage in wire fraud and transmitting betting information to gamblers through interstate commerce for his role in providing gamblers with inside information about NBA games including ones in which he acted as a referee. He now is out of prison and has a website where he provides his knowledge of the NBA, particularly the tendencies of particular referees to gamblers. His success rate in predicting the winners of

---

[4]  "The Black Sox Trial," University of Missouri, Kansas City, Faculty Project, Douglas Linder, 2010.

games 60% of the time is about 5% higher than most professional gamblers which is a significant advantage in the long run.[5]

# THE POINT SPREAD

Famed sportswriter Grantland Rice may have said that it didn't matter whether you won or lost, but rather how you played the game, but for sports bettors this famous quote could be rewritten to read that it doesn't matter whether you win or lose, what matters is the point spread.

The point spread is a number established by bookmakers designating the number of points by which a team favored to win would need to defeat an underdog team for a person betting on the favorite to win his or her bet. Correspondingly, in order to win his or her bet, someone betting on an underdog team in the same contest would merely have to not lose by more than the point spread in order to win the bet. Point spreads are established to encourage equal betting on both teams playing a particular game in order to make the bookmaker more profitable since if the betting is particularly lopsided favoring one team, the bookmaker runs the risk of having to absorb steep losses if a large majority of the money bet is bet on the winning team.

# CONTROVERSIAL GAMES INVOLVING THE POINT SPREAD

During the 2015 March Madness Sweet 16 game between Duke and Utah when the final buzzer sounded, it appeared that Duke had beaten Utah by a score of 62–57. The point spread at the sports books at the casinos in Las Vegas at Caesars Palace, MGM and the Wynn all had Duke as a five point favorite, which, had the score stood, would have left the game a "push" meaning that no one betting on that game would have won any money. Winning and losing for betting purposes requires that the score be either above or below

---

5    "Does This Ex-Con, Ex-Referee Know the NBA Better than LeBron" New York Magazine, Pat Jordan, June 14, 2015.

the established point spread. It is for this reason that you often find point spreads that contain ½ points which are found in no sport. For instance, a bettor who bets on a winner that is a 6 ½ point favorite would be required to have his or her team win by 7 points in order to win the bet.

In the Duke/Utah game, while the players were heading into the locker room after the apparent end of the game, the referees were reviewing the final play in which a Utah player was attempting to foul a Duke player in order to prolong the game although for all intents and purposes the game had been decided because even if Duke were to miss its free throws and a Utah player were to hit a three point shot and be fouled and make the foul shot, all in the span of .06 of a second, Utah would have fallen a point short of a tie necessary to send the game into overtime. Regardless, the referees determined that indeed the Utah player had committed a foul so the game was resumed and Quinn Cook of Duke made one of two foul shots making the final score 63–57 thereby covering the point spread for bettors who had bet on Duke to win and making losers of those betting on Utah.

Perhaps the most outrageous instance of this type of what is referred to as a "backdoor cover" occurred during the early weeks of the 2012 NFL season during which time the regular NFL referees were on strike and replacement referees were working in their place. A close game between the Green Bay Packers and the Seattle Seahawks was decided on the final play of the game when the underdog Seahawks completed a long pass into the end zone that was ruled a catch and a touchdown by the replacement referee, in a highly disputed ruling. It was estimated by Las Vegas bookmakers that 300 million dollars changed hands on that one controversial referee's decision. The public uproar following that game brought pressure that led to a quick resolution of the labor dispute between the referees and the league.

In 2008, the Pittsburgh Steelers beat the San Diego Chargers by a score of 11–10, however the Las Vegas bookmakers had made the Steelers 4 point favorites so that those people who bet on the Steelers lost their bet despite the Steelers having won the game. However, at the end of the game, Steeler strong safety Troy Polamalu scored a touchdown that would have made the final score 17–10 enabling the Steelers to "cover" the spread. The referees mistakenly nullified the touchdown. Although the mistake was later acknowledged by the referee, the official score did not change, making many gamblers losers when they should have been winners.

The most common misconception about the point spread is that it is that it represents the oddsmakers' prediction of by how many points the favorite will win. This is not correct. The intent of the point spread is to attract equal betting action on both sides. It is not uncommon for people to bet emotionally or for the fans in large numbers of a particular city's teams to bet on their team to win which will result in an adjustment of the point spread by bookmakers that has no relationship to the points by which their team is likely to win or lose.

Point spreads may also change as more information becomes available, such as the likelihood of a particular athlete to play or not play in a game due to injury. Bookmakers want to create a line that will entice equal betting on both teams as much as possible. The bookmaker makes his profit primarily by his 10% vig. Equally divided betting means the sport book is guaranteed a profit on a game because of this fee charged to the bettor. Lopsided betting by a majority of bettors on one team that ends up beating the point spread and winning the bet translates to a loss for the bookmaker.

## THE LAW

It is against the law for Internet websites to take bets on sporting events, but the act of betting itself by individual bettors is not illegal.

# THE WIRE ACT OF 1961

The Wire Act of 1961 was enacted by Congress primarily to prohibit sports betting using the telephone. In 1961 Las Vegas was the only place in the United States that legal sports betting could be done in any manner. The Internet had not even been invented yet.

The applicable portion of this law referred to as 18 USC Section 1084 provides:

"Whoever being engaged in the business of betting or wagering knowingly uses a wire communication facility for the transmission in interstate or foreign commerce of bets or wagers or information assisting in the placing of bets or wagers on any sporting event or contest, or for the transmission of a wire communication which entitles the recipient to receive money or credit as a result of bets or wagers, or for information assisting in the placing of bets or wagers, shall be fined under this title or imprisoned not more than two years, or both."

Obviously since the law was written prior to the creation of the Internet, the term "wire communication" was not intended to apply to online gambling. The law has not been enforced against online gamblers.

# PASPA

The Professional and Amateur Sports Protection Act (PASPA) sometimes referred to as the Bradley Act was passed by Congress in 1992. According to the law, found in 28 USC section 3702 It shall be unlawful for

"(1) a governmental entity to sponsor, operate, advertise, promote, license, or authorize by law or compact, or

(2) a person to sponsor, operate, advertise, or promote, pursuant to the law or compact of a governmental entity, a lottery, sweepstakes, or other betting, gambling, or wagering scheme based, directly or indirectly (through the use of geographical references or otherwise),

on one or more competitive games in which amateur or professional athletes participate, or are intended to participate, or on one or more performances of such athletes in such games."

---

The purpose of the law was to limit sports betting with a few exceptions. There was concern that the integrity of the games would be threatened by sports betting as well as concerns as to increased gambling, particularly by teenagers. At the time, thirteen states were considering some form of sports gambling which in theory could provide a significant source of new state tax revenues. Already existing sports lotteries in Oregon, Delaware and Montana were "grandfathered" which means that they were allowed to continue their sports lotteries at the level they were doing at the time the law went into effect on January 1, 1993. In addition, the law did not affect Nevada's extensive sports betting.

All of the professional sports leagues were consulted in regard to the drafting of the law and strongly supported it at the time.

In 2009, Delaware, one of the states grandfathered by PASPA, passed legislation to allow betting on individual NFL games, however, the law was struck down in court because the level of sports betting grandfathered by PASPA was limited to a level no more expansive than was in place at the time of the passage of PASPA leaving Delaware with its sports betting limited to multigame wagers on NFL games.

In 2011, in a New Jersey state referendum, 64% of the voters voted in favor of amending the New Jersey Constitution to permit sports gambling. In response to the referendum, the New Jersey legislature enacted the Sports Wagering Act in 2012 to establish a regulatory scheme for sports gambling in New Jersey. The NCAA and all of the major professional sports leagues sued New Jersey to prevent the law from going into effect. Since that time, the matter has been repeatedly before the courts, most recently in the summer of 2016 when the Third Circuit Court of Appeals ruled against New Jersey thereby preventing legal sports gambling in New Jersey. NCAA et al. v. Governor of the State of New Jersey et al., 832 F. 3d 389 (2016).

## NATIONAL COLLEGIATE ATHLETIC ASSOCIATION V. GOVERNOR OF NEW JERSEY
United States Court of Appeals, Third Circuit
832 F.3d 389 (2016)

After a lengthy discussion of PASPA, the Appeals Court wrote in its opinion:

"IV. Conclusion

The 2014 Law violates PASPA because it authorizes by law sports gambling. We continue to find PASPA constitutional. We will affirm."

However, and perhaps more telling, are the dissenting opinions which would have allowed individual sports betting in New Jersey and form the basis of further appeal to the United States Supreme Court.

Here is the dissenting opinion of Judge Fuentes:

In November 2011, the question of whether to allow sports betting in New Jersey went before the electorate. By a 2–1 margin, New Jersey voters passed a referendum to amend the New Jersey Constitution to allow the New Jersey Legislature to "authorize by law" sports betting. Accordingly, the Legislature enacted the 2012 Sports Wagering Act ("2012 Law"). The Sports Leagues challenged this Law, claiming that it violated the Professional and Amateur Sports Protection Act's ("PASPA") prohibition on states "authoriz[ing] by law" sports betting. In *Christie I,* we agreed with the Sports Leagues and held that the 2012 Law violated and thus was preempted by PASPA. We explained, however, that New Jersey was free to repeal the sports betting prohibitions it already had in place. We rejected the argument that a repeal of prohibitions on sports betting was equivalent to authorizing by law sports betting. When the matter was brought to the Supreme Court, the Solicitor General echoed that same sentiment, stating that, "PASPA does not even obligate New Jersey to leave in place the state-law prohibitions against sports gambling that it had chosen to adopt prior to PASPA's enactment. To the contrary, New Jersey is free to repeal those prohibitions in whole or in part."

So New Jersey did just that. In 2014, the New Jersey Legislature repealed certain sports betting prohibitions at casinos and gambling houses in Atlantic City and at horse racetracks in the State ("2014 Repeal"). In addition to repealing the 2012 Law in full, the 2014 Repeal stripped New Jersey of *any* involvement in sports betting, regulatory or otherwise. In essence, the 2014 Repeal rendered previous prohibitions on sports betting non-existent.

But the majority today concludes that the New Jersey Legislature's efforts to satisfy its constituents while adhering to our decision in *Christie I* are still in violation of PASPA. According to the majority, the "selective" nature of the 2014 Repeal *amounts to* "authorizing by law" a sports wagering scheme. That is, because the State retained certain restrictions on sports betting, the majority *infers* the authorization by law. I cannot agree with this interpretation of PASPA.

PASPA restricts the states in six ways—a state cannot "sponsor, operate, advertise, promote, license, or *authorize by law* or compact" sports betting. The only one of these six restrictions that includes "by law" is "authorize." None of the other restrictions say anything about *how* the states are restricted. Thus, I believe that Congress gave this restriction a special meaning—that a state's "authoriz[ation] by law" of sports betting cannot merely be inferred, but rather requires a specific legislative enactment that affirmatively allows the people of the state to bet on sports. Any other interpretation would be reading the phrase "by law" out of the statute.

Indeed, we stated exactly this in *Christie I*—that all PASPA prohibits is "the affirmative 'authoriz[ation] *by law*' of gambling schemes." Thus, we explained, nothing prevented New Jersey from repealing its sports betting prohibitions, since, "in reality, the lack of an affirmative prohibition of an activity does not mean it is *affirmatively* authorized by law." As we noted, "that the Legislature needed to enact the [2012 Law] itself belies any contention that the mere repeal of New Jersey's ban on sports gambling was sufficient to 'authorize [it] by law.' " The Legislature itself "saw a meaningful distinction between repealing the ban on sports wagering and authorizing it by law, undermining any contention that the amendment alone was sufficient to affirmatively authorize sports wagering—the [2012 Law] was required." In short, we explained that there was a false equivalence between repeal and authorization.

With the 2014 Repeal, the New Jersey Legislature did what it thought it was permitted to do under our reading of PASPA in *Christie I*. The majority, however, maintains that the 2014 Repeal "authorizes" sports wagering at casinos, gambling houses, and horse racetracks simply because other sports betting prohibitions remain in place. According to the majority, "[a]bsent the 2014 Law, New Jersey's myriad laws prohibiting sports gambling would apply to the casinos and racetracks," and thus "the 2014 Law provides the authorization for conduct that is otherwise clearly and completely legally prohibited." But I believe the majority is mistaken as to the impact of a partial repeal.

A repeal is defined as an "abrogation of an existing law by legislative act." When a statute is repealed, "the repealed statute, in regard to its operative effect, is considered as if it had never existed." If a repealed statute is treated as if it never existed, a partially repealed statute is treated as if the repealed sections never existed. The 2014 Repeal, then, simply returns New Jersey to the state it was in before it first enacted those prohibitions on sports gambling. In other words, after the repeal, it is as if New Jersey *never* prohibited sports wagering at casinos, gambling houses, and horse racetracks. Therefore, with respect to those locations, there are no laws governing sports wagering. Contrary to the majority's position, the permission to engage in such an activity is not affirmatively granted *by virtue of* it being prohibited elsewhere.

To bolster its position, the majority rejects our reasoning in *Christie I,* stating that "[t]o the extent that in *Christie I* we took the position that a repeal cannot constitute an authorization, we now reject that reasoning." I continue to maintain, however, that the 2014 Repeal *is not* an affirmative authorization by law. It is merely a repeal—it does not, and cannot, authorize by law anything.

In my view, the majority's position that the 2014 Repeal "selectively grants permission to certain entities to engage in sports gambling" is simply incorrect. There is no explicit grant of permission in the 2014 Repeal for any person or entity to engage in sports gambling. Rather, the 2014 Repeal is a self-executing deregulatory measure that repeals existing prohibitions and regulations for sports betting and requires the State to abdicate *any* control or involvement in sports betting. The majority fails to explain why a partial repeal is equivalent to a grant of permission (by law) to engage in sports betting.

Suppose the State did exactly what the majority suggests it could have done: repeal completely its sports betting prohibitions. In that circumstance, sports betting could occur anywhere in the State and there would be no restrictions as to age, location, or whether a bettor could wager on games involving local teams. Would the State violate PASPA if it later enacted limited restrictions regarding age requirements and places where wagering could occur? Surely no conceivable reading of PASPA would preclude a state from *restricting* sports wagering in this scenario. Yet the 2014 Repeal comes to the same result.

The majority also fails to illustrate how the 2014 Repeal results in sports wagering *pursuant to state law* when there is effectively no law in place as to several locations, no scheme created, and no state involvement. A careful comparison with the 2012 Law is instructive. The 2012 Law lifted New Jersey's ban on sports wagering and created a licensing scheme for sports wagering pools at casinos and racetracks in the State. This comprehensive regime required close State supervision and regulation of those sports wagering pools. For instance, the 2012 Law required any entity that wished to operate a "sports pool lounge" to acquire a "sports pool license." To do so, a prospective operator was required to pay a $50,000 application fee, secure Division of Gaming Enforcement ("DGE") approval of all internal controls, and ensure that any of its employees who were to be directly involved in sports wagering obtained individual licenses from the DGE and the Casino Control Commission ("CCC"). In addition, the betting regime required entities to, among other things, submit extensive documentation to the DGE, adopt new "house" rules subject to DGE approval, and conform to DGE standards. This, of course, violated PASPA in the most basic way: New Jersey developed an intricate scheme that both "authorize[d] *by law*" and "license[d]" sports gambling. The 2014 Repeal eliminated this entire scheme. Moreover, all state agencies with jurisdiction over state casinos and racetracks, such as the DGE and the CCC, were stripped of any sports betting oversight.

The majority likewise falters when it analogizes the 2014 Repeal to the exception Congress originally offered to New Jersey in 1992. The exception stated that PASPA did not apply to "a betting, gambling, or wagering scheme . . . conducted exclusively in casinos[,] . . . but only to the extent that . . . any commercial casino gaming scheme was in operation . . . throughout the 10-year period" before PASPA was enacted. Setting aside the most obvious distinction between the 2014 Repeal and the 1992 exception—that it contemplated a *scheme* that the 2014 Repeal does not authorize—the majority misses the mark when it states: "If Congress had not perceived that sports gambling in New Jersey's casinos would violate PASPA, then it would not have needed to insert the New Jersey exception." Congress did not, however, perceive, or intend for, private sports wagering in casinos to violate PASPA. Instead, Congress prohibited sports wagering undertaken pursuant to state law. That the 2014 Repeal might bring about an increase in the amount of private, legal sports wagering in New Jersey is of no moment, and the majority's reliance on such a possibility is misplaced. The majority is also wrong in a more fundamental way.

The exception Congress offered to New Jersey was exactly that: an *exception* to the ordinary prohibitions of PASPA. That is to say, with this exception, New Jersey could have "sponsor[ed], operate[d], advertise[d], promote[d], license[d], or authorize[d] by law or compact" sports wagering. Under the 2014 Repeal, of course, New Jersey cannot and does not aim to do any of these things.

Because I do not see how a partial repeal of prohibitions is tantamount to authorizing by law a sports wagering scheme in violation of PASPA, I respectfully dissent."

---

New Jersey appealed the decision to the United States Supreme Court where five states, Arizona, Louisiana, Mississippi, West Virginia and Wisconsin have all filed briefs in support of New Jersey. In addition, the Pennsylvania legislature passed a resolution urging Congress to repeal PASPA.

# UIGEA

The Unlawful Internet Gaming Enforcement Act of 2006 (UIGEA) was enacted by Congress in an effort to stop American banks and financial institutions from processing payments related to online gambling. While the actual making or attempting to make a bet was not criminalized, Congress attempted to reduce online gambling including sports gambling by making it difficult for gamblers to deposit funds and receive winnings from online betting sites.

The initial section of the UIGEA is found in 31 USC section 5361 which reads;

(a) FINDINGS.—Congress finds the following:

(1) Internet gambling is primarily funded through personal use of payment system instruments, credit cards, and wire transfers.

(2) The National Gambling Impact Study Commission in 1999 recommended the passage of legislation to prohibit wire transfers to Internet gambling sites or the banks which represent such sites.

**(3)** Internet gambling is a growing cause of debt collection problems for insured depository institutions and the consumer credit industry.

**(4)** New mechanisms for enforcing gambling laws on the Internet are necessary because traditional law enforcement mechanisms are often inadequate for enforcing gambling prohibitions or regulations on the Internet, especially where such gambling crosses State or national borders.

It is interesting to note that this law was not passed independently, but rather added as a last minute addition to an unrelated bill that dealt with the security of American ports. The law did not apply to gambling on horse racing which is specifically allowed under earlier law. Also, specifically exempted was what is commonly referred to as day trading, which although protected by the law, is an implicit recognition of the gambling nature of such investments. Most notably, however, was a specific exclusion for fantasy sports where the law reads.

**"(ix)** participation in any fantasy or simulation sports game or educational game or contest in which (if the game or contest involves a team or teams) no fantasy or simulation sports team is based on the current membership of an actual team that is a member of an amateur or professional sports organization (as those terms are defined in section 3701 of title 28) and that meets the following conditions:

**(I)** All prizes and awards offered to winning participants are established and made known to the participants in advance of the game or contest and their value is not determined by the number of participants or the amount of any fees paid by those participants.

**(II)** All winning outcomes reflect the relative knowledge and skill of the participants and are determined predominantly by accumulated statistical results of the performance of individuals (athletes in the case of sports events) in multiple real-world sporting or other events."

The UIGEA goes on to describe its relation to horse racing in 31 USC section 5362 which reads:

**"(D) Interstate horseracing.—**

**(i) In general.—**

The term "unlawful Internet gambling" shall not include any activity that is allowed under the Interstate Horseracing Act of 1978 (15 U.S.C. 3001 et seq.).

**(ii) Rule of construction regarding preemption.—**

Nothing in this subchapter may be construed to preempt any State law prohibiting gambling.

**(iii) Sense of congress.—**

It is the sense of Congress that this subchapter shall not change which activities related to horse racing may or may not be allowed under Federal law. This subparagraph is intended to address concerns that this subchapter could have the effect of changing the existing relationship between the Interstate Horseracing Act and other Federal statutes in effect on the date of the enactment of this subchapter. This subchapter is not intended to change that relationship. This subchapter is not intended to resolve any existing disagreements over how to interpret the relationship between the Interstate Horseracing Act and other Federal statutes."

Here is the text of the Interstate Horse Racing Act referred to in the UIGEA:

"15 U.S.C. 3001, *et seq.*

*Last visited Jan. 26, 2005*

§ 3001. Congressional findings and policy

(a) The Congress finds that—

(1) the States should have the primary responsibility for determining what forms of gambling may legally take place within their borders;

(2) the Federal Government should prevent interference by one State with the gambling policies of another, and should act to protect identifiable national interests; and

(3)   in the limited area of interstate off-track wagering on horseraces, there is a need for Federal action to ensure States will continue to cooperate with one another in the acceptance of legal interstate wagers.

(b)   It is the policy of the Congress in this chapter to regulate interstate commerce with respect to wagering on horseracing, in order to further the horseracing and legal off-track betting industries in the United States."

Thus horse racing is treated differently from other forms of sports gambling and is afforded special treatment federally, leaving it up to the individual states to determine whether or not to allow online or phone gambling.

## QUESTIONS

1.   What are the reasons supporting legalizing sports gambling?

2.   What is the justification for permitting online horse racing betting, but not other sports wagering?

# LEGAL SPORTS BETTING IN THE UK

There is an extensive history of sports betting in the United Kingdom where sports betting has long been legal and where the highest level professional soccer league even operates its own legal betting business. In one of the earliest rule books for Cricket in the 1800s there was even a section about gambling on the game. More than 2.5 billion dollars' worth of tax revenue was generated by taxes on the gambling industry between 2012 and 2015.[6]

---

[6]   Jordan Meddy, Switch Hitters: How League Involvement in Daily Fantasy Sports Could End the Prohibition of Sports Gambling 10 Brook J. Corp Fin & Com L Volume 20 Issue 2 (2016).

# BETTING AT THE OLYMPICS

While betting on a myriad of sports events is legal in Las Vegas on both amateur and professional sporting events, international companies such as Ladbrokes offered betting on almost every event at the 2016 Summer Olympic Games. Ladbrokes is an international online gambling company based in the UK that can trace its roots as a business back to 1886. It evolved into a gambling company in 1961 when betting shops were legalized in the UK. Much of its present business is done online, taking bets on any and every sport imaginable even Snooker. The odds for American swimmer Katie Ledecky at the 2016 Summer Olympic Games were a startling 1–50 in the 400 and 800 meter freestyle races which was an accurate assessment by the oddsmakers of her eventual victories in those events. Ladbrokes even takes bets on politics such as American and British elections.

# TENNIS

Among professional athletes the lower pay of some tennis players may be a factor in rumors of fixed tennis matches that have dogged the sport in recent years. According to a report in the New York Times, an international group of players and match fixers, many of whom had played professional tennis themselves, used their experience and connections to recruit players to participate in fixed matches. Many of the matches fixed were alleged to be at the lower Futures level where the prize money is significantly lower than the ATP and WTA tours. According to the Times article, players at the Futures level were paid as little as $2,000 to throw a match, while at the higher level of the ATP and WTA tours, the cost for throwing a match was around $100,000.[7]

Part of the problem is that while top tennis professional earn millions in prize money and endorsements, lower level professionals earn far less and become tempting targets for bribes to lose a match.

---

[7] "An Invitation Into the Shadowy World of Match Fixing" NY Times, Ben Rothernberg, January 27, 2016.

However, even tennis star Novak Djokovic indicated that he was offered and refused $100,000 to lose a match in 2007. A report published by the BBC in 2016 alleged that sixteen players ranked in the top fifty players during the last ten years were implicated in match fixing. Suspicion of match fixing is most often generated by unusual betting patterns with legal betting businesses.

The sportsbook, Pinnacle Sports suspended betting on a mixed doubles match at the Australian Open in 2015 due to concerns of match fixing when large amounts of money were bet on the match between low ranked players that would generally not attract much attention by the betting public.

Professional Tennis has had its own Tennis Integrity Unit to investigate and adjudicate allegations of fixing of tennis matches since 2008 which works with the cooperation of the legal bookmaking community through Memorandums of Understanding according to which the betting industry will notify the TIU of unusual betting patterns on professional tennis matches. The TIU is funded by the International Tennis Federation, the Association of Tennis Professionals (ATP), the Women's Tennis Association (WTA), Australian Open, French Open, Wimbledon and the U.S. Open.

In 2011, Daniel Koellerer became the first professional tennis player to be banned for life for attempting to fix matches. In 2009, he achieved his highest ranking of 55 in the world. In 2016 four tennis officials received lifetime bans as did South African player Joshua Chetty for match fixing. A total of eleven cases were prosecuted in 2016 of which nine players and officials were sanctioned which is the most for any year since the founding of the TIU. While the TIU was alerted by the betting industry to only 292 suspicious tennis matches out of more than 114,000 matches played, professional tennis still takes the issue of the fixing of tennis matches very seriously.

# E-SPORT GAMBLING

Even e-sports, the current name for video game competitions, are involved in sports gambling. With stadium crowds such as the 40,000 people who packed the World Cup Stadium in Seoul, South Korea watching the 2014 League of Legends World Championships while upwards of 32 million people watched online or in theaters, the popularity of highly competitive e-sports is tremendous. This has translated into interest in gambling on the outcomes of such contests. In 2015 the company Unikrn instituted betting on League of Legends games and other e-sports played in professional tournaments. Although with the exception of Nevada, this type of sports betting is largely illegal in the United States, betting on sports such as basketball and soccer is legal throughout much of the rest of the world. As with just about everything there is even a mobile app, Luxbet to make such gambling easier on your smartphone.

# DANGERS OF SPORTS GAMBLING

The primary concern in regard to legalizing sports gambling continues to be the fear of games being "thrown" by players or referees taking bribes to affect the outcome of the game to benefit corrupt gamblers. The relatively lower pay of professional athletes that can lead, as shown by the Black Sox Scandal of 1919, to bribe taking, affecting the integrity and honesty of the games played is less of an issue in today's sports world of spiraling salaries. The risk of being caught would not seem to warrant the benefit derived by taking a bribe to affect the outcome of a game. Even referees who are certainly lower paid and can affect a game's outcome, particularly in basketball, would be unlikely candidates to be involved with bribes due to the tremendous use of instant replay which could lead to an uncovering of any such plan. Even at lower levels of pay, referees of today are still paid significant amounts that would lessen the risk of taking a bribe that would be more readily discovered with modern investigative techniques. Increased analytics and statistical analysis would also make it less likely for a cheater to succeed without being caught.

# BENEFITS OF LEGALIZED SPORTS GAMBLING

The benefits of sports betting are many and obvious including increased jobs, increased revenues and money saved in decriminalizing an activity participated in illegally by so many otherwise law abiding citizens who see nothing wrong in sports betting. The fact that mainstream media publicizes each day the point spread on sporting events is recognition of how accepted sports betting is.

Congressman Fran Pallone Jr. of New Jersey has said that present federal gambling laws need updating. "The laws need a wholesale review to see how they can actually work together and create a fairer playing field for all types of gambling, both online and offline, including sports betting and daily fantasy sports." Congressman Pallone is a member of the House Energy and Commerce Committee which is reviewing the sports betting legislation.[8]

The move toward legalizing sports gambling is gathering momentum. New Jersey, Pennsylvania and California have already seen efforts started to legalize sports betting and NBA Commissioner Adam Silver has even said that the time is coming for legalized sports betting.

Another important benefit of legalizing sports gambling is that online gambling has been used by organized crime to launder money and make illegally obtained funds appear to be from a legitimate source. Were online gambling to be legalized and regulated, it could be monitored more closely to defeat such money laundering.

---

[8]   "Congress reviewing 'obsolete' federal gambling laws, to introduce new legislation," ABC News, ESPN, David Purdum, October 21, 2016.

# NBA AND GAMBLING

Bob Dylan wrote, "You don't need a weatherman to know which way the wind blows" and it is apparent that NBA Commissioner Adam Silver indeed knows that the wind is blowing toward legalization of sports gambling. In a 2014 editorial in the New York Times, Silver wrote, "Betting on professional sports is currently illegal in most of the United States outside of Nevada. I believe we need a different approach."

Silver recognized the reality of the situation that people are gambling on sports whether it is legal or not and argued for a combination of legalization and comprehensive regulation to insure the integrity of the games.

According to Silver, "But despite legal restrictions, sports betting is widespread. It is a thriving underground business that operates free from regulation or oversight. Because there are few legal options available, those who wish to bet resort to illicit bookmaking operations and shady offshore websites. There is no solid data on the volume of illegal sports betting activity in the United States, but some estimate that nearly $400 billion is illegally wagered on sports each year."

Silver also noted, "Outside of the United States, sports betting and other forms of gambling are popular, widely legal and subject to regulation. In England, for example, a sports bet can be placed on a smartphone, at a stadium kiosk or even using a television remote control. In light of these domestic and global trends, the laws on sports betting should be changed. Congress should adopt a federal framework that allows states to authorize betting on professional sports, subject to strict regulatory requirements and technological safeguards. These requirements would include: mandatory monitoring and reporting of unusual betting-line movements; a licensing protocol to ensure betting operators are legitimate; minimum-age verification measures; geo-blocking technology to ensure betting is available only where it is legal; mechanisms to identity and exclude people with gambling problems; and education about responsible gaming."[9]

All of Silver's arguments make sense and don't even get into the matter of increased tax revenues in the future when sports gambling inevitably becomes legal.

# REGULATION

Any system of regulation would include intensive monitoring of betting patterns to identify anomalies for investigation. The use of modern big data analytics would make this a relatively easy thing to do, particularly in a highly regulated legal environment requiring extensive record keeping. The experience of regulated sports betting in the UK has shown that regulated sports betting can be successful.

# THE FUTURE OF SPORTS GAMBLING IN THE UNITED STATES

The combination of public support for legalized sports gambling and state legislators in a number of states including New Jersey, Pennsylvania, New York and California seeking to legalize sports gambling dramatically increases the likelihood of legalized sports gambling beyond Nevada. But what will the future of legal sports gambling look like? We may have already seen the prototype for the future of legalized gambling in the United States through "exchange wagering" which is already being done in thoroughbred horse racing in the United States through the efforts of a British company, Betfair. While the century's old pari-mutuel betting system is still the dominant betting system for horse racing here in the United States and throughout the world, exchange wagering uses advanced technology to match bettors much like eBay matches buyers and sellers. Bets are made in real time with bettors posting odds and prices to be accepted or rejected by others online. Betfair which

---

[9]    "Legalize and Regulate Sports Betting," NY Times, OpEd, Adam Silber, November 13, 2014.

began in 2000 is the pioneer of this type of betting which it uses worldwide for betting on sports in addition to horse racing in other parts of the world, but is presently limited in the United States to thoroughbred horseracing. Betfair's exchange wagering has been used since 2016 at New Jersey racetracks where customers can not only use exchange wagering to bet on races in New Jersey, but also on any twenty other tracks around the country participating in Betfair's exchange wagering plan.

Additionally, Betfair also owns two television channels that broadcast 40,000 horse races annually to more than 40 million homes in the United States as well as the online betting website TVG that already takes in a billion dollars of legal horse racing bets in the United States each year.

Using split second technology, exchange wagering as practiced by Betfair, even permits bettors to match bets as the races are being run. While there is still much room for exchange wagering on horse racing to grow and attract the much sought younger demographic bettor to horse racing with its technological advances in betting, the business model created by Betfair in horse racing could easily be duplicated for exchange betting on professional sports such as baseball, football, hockey and basketball if and when legalized gambling on these sports becomes more widespread throughout the United States. It is easy to foresee a time when a bet could be made during a particular game as to whether a particular player will strike out, hit a home run, make a free throw or successfully kick a field goal.

---

## QUESTION

1.    How might computer technology change sports gambling in the future?

# SYNOPSIS

1.    Much of the sports gambling done by Americans today is done via the Internet on websites based in jurisdictions outside of the United States.

2.    Sports wagering is generally done through people referred to as bookmakers who make their profit by taking a percentage of the money bet as a vigorish or vig.

3.    The point spread is a number established by bookmakers predicting the number of points by which a favored team is expected to defeat an underdog team. The favored team must win by more than the point spread in order for a person betting on that team to win his or her bet.

4.    Point spreads are established to encourage equal betting on both teams playing a particular game in order to make the bookmaker more profitable.

5.    The Wire Act of 1961 was enacted by Congress to primarily prohibit sports betting using the telephone.

6.    The Professional And Amateur Sports Protection Act (PASPA) sometimes referred to as the Bradley Act was passed by Congress in 1992 in an attempt to outlaw sports betting with some exceptions.

7.    The Unlawful Internet Gaming Enforcement Act of 2006 (UIGEA) was enacted by Congress in an effort to stop American banks and financial institutions from processing payments related to online gambling. It does not apply to horse racing and fantasy sports.

8.    The Justice Department has interpreted the gambling laws to permit gambling online with the exception of sports gambling.

9.    Exchange wagering is changing the way many people bet on horse races and may change the way sports betting in the future is done.

# CHAPTER SIXTEEN

# Analytics and Technology

## TECHNOLOGY

Technology has been an important part of sports for many years. In 1937 gears to switch speeds on bicycles were first permitted at the Tour de France. In 1965 the first metal tennis racket was patented by French tennis player, Rene Lacoste. The first aluminum tennis rackets were sold in 1968. Medal rackets rapidly replaced wooden tennis rackets due to the greater "sweet spot" for hitting and greater power. It wasn't until 1981 that the International Tennis Federation enacted rules and standards for tennis rackets. Titanium drivers that are lighter and enable a faster and more powerful golf swing along with a larger "sweet spot" became popular with amateur and professional golfers in the 1990s. In 2008 new form fitting bodysuits made of spandex, nylon and polyurethane were used in the Beijing Olympics and were worn by 98% of the medal winning swimmers. Within a year of their introduction, 97 world records fell to swimmers wearing the drag reducing suits that were in July of 2009 determined to present an unfair advantage and were banned by the international swimming federation. More recently, Nike developed a high tech running shoe used by leading marathon runners including all three medalists in the men's marathon at the 2016 Rio Summer Olympic Games. The new Nike shoe contains a carbon-fiber plate that stores and releases energy with each stride. The International Association of Athletics Federations (IAAF) has not yet ruled as to whether the shoe violates

IAAF Rule 143 which indicates that shoes "must not be constructed so as to give an athlete any unfair additional assistance, including by the incorporation of any technology which will give the wearer any unfair advantage." The question is what qualifies as an "unfair advantage?"

---

## QUESTION

1.   What should be the standard as to when technology should be allowed in regard to sporting equipment and when it should be banned?

---

Technological advances have not been limited, however, to equipment. Instant replay to review specific plays was first introduced in the National Football League in 1986 with all of the other professional sports leagues soon following suit. In 2006 tennis introduced ball tracking technology to accurately review disputed calls as to whether or not a ball is out of bounds or not. In Major League Baseball, technology is used to provide instant replay and review of every umpire decision in games with the glaring exception of the calling of balls and strikes where technology could provide the most precise determination as to whether a pitch is a ball or a strike. Baseball had an early version of an electronic umpire to call balls and strikes in 1950 and now has a pitch tracking system installed in every MLB stadium called PITCHf/x which accurately can determine balls and strikes, but is not used to call balls and strikes during a game, but rather only available as a resource for umpires to review their calls after the game and is rarely used by umpires for that purpose. The reticence to use available and reliable technology to call balls and strikes is disconcerting when the data, as shown by researchers Noah Davis and Michael Lopez, indicates that 14% of the time and often in crucial situations, umpires make incorrect calls.[1]

---

[1]   "Umpires Are Less Blind Than They Used to Be," Noah Davis and Michael Lopez, FiveThirtyEight, August 19, 2015.

Subconscious biases as described by Etan Green and David P. Daniels in their paper entitled "What Does it Take to Call a Strike? Three Biases in Umpire Decision Making" presented at the MIT Sloan Sports Analytics Conference in 2014 can affect the calls by umpires. In their paper, Green and Daniels concluded that "Contrary to their formal role as unbiased arbiters of balls and strikes, umpires are biased by the state of the at-bat when deciding whether a pitch intersects the strike zone."[2]

## QUESTION

1.  Why does Major League Baseball resist using technology to call balls and strikes when it is proven to be more accurate then human umpires?

# ANALYTICS

Analytics are computerized programs that gather and analyze data. They are used throughout industry to help businesses make better business decisions. Analytics are now being used in sports, particularly professional sports to make informed decisions and obtain an edge in competition through enhanced utilization of the data to achieve a competitive advantage and increase the level of performance. Analytics are also used to organize data in evaluating players as to whether or not to draft them or sign them to free agent contracts.

At the heart of any analytics program is the gathering of accurate and helpful data. Where many sports decisions in the past were guided by mere hunches, coaches and general managers using analytics can determine effective strategies as well as analyze both their players and opposing players to identify strengths and weaknesses. Predictive analytics can be a tremendous aid to a coach in allowing the coach to go beyond his or her own instincts and make strategic or personnel moves based on scientific evidence and applied data.

---

[2]  "What Does it Take to Call a Strike? Three Biases in Umpire Decision Making" MIT Sloan Sports Analytic Conference, Eric Green, David P. Daniels, 2014.

Analytics are used to analyze tendencies of opposing coaches in particular situations or the likelihood of success of particular plays, something that perhaps Seattle Seahawks coach Pete Carroll might have considered in the 2015 Super Bowl in which he chose a pass play at the New England Patriots goal line only to have the pass intercepted. Hindsight, as the old saying goes, is 20/20 and perhaps the element of surprise might have enhanced the chances of success of a pass play that ended badly for the Seahawks, but it would have been helpful for the coach to have had more than just a hunch to determine the advisability of a particular play. Perhaps this is what we will see in the future although there is always room for the personal human element.

The NBA has been using analytics to calculate the value of players in recent years through the use of the RPM which stands for Real Plus-Minus. This statistic measures how much a team outscores or falls behind its opponent while the particular player is on the court playing. Obviously, players who play with stars such as LeBron James or Stephen Curry can expect to score highly in this statistic; however, advanced analytic techniques are able to adjust for the effects of both teammates of the player and those of opposing players. As always, the more data you have to work with, the better your statistical analysis should be and the RPM model uses data compiled from more than 230,000 possessions in each NBA season. The RPM is able to quantify how may points a particular player may add or subtract from his team's scoring for every one-hundred possessions to a simple figure that provides an easy basis for comparing the value of players whose intangibles might not be calculated by simpler statistics such as points scored, rebounds or steals. The RPM is further refined to provide separate figures for the offensive and defensive ends of the court.

Analytics can be used to perform predictive analysis to project the value of players and strategies and the likelihood of success of particular strategies as well as help determine what factors best contribute to success on the field and how to measure those matters.

# ESTABLISHING ANALYTICS

The first step in analytics is to determine what information you want to gather and then develop the systems for both gathering and analyzing that data.

It is important to remember, however, as Astronomer Clifford Stoll has said, "Data is not information, information is not knowledge, knowledge is not understanding, understanding is not wisdom." The important thing is to determine what information is relevant and then determine how to effectively use that information.

While data itself is valuable, data alone does not provide helpful conclusions. The true value of the data is found in the ability of people to analyze the data to better understand and predict behavior and occurrences. Throughout history it has not been unusual for the most advanced scientific theories of the times to be later proven to be false for many reasons including new data as well as false assumptions and interpretations of the data. And so it will be with analytics. Analytics may start with raw data without any bias, but how that data is interpreted is determined by people who give meaning to the data which is something that cannot be assumed to be accurate.

Analytics will have a tremendous effect on the game not only in how it is played, but in determining the value of particular players which in turn will have an effect on salaries, particularly during free agency. For the first time teams, using analytics such as the RPM, will be able to show a correlation between defensive prowess and team success or failure.

The history of statistical analysis to aid in decision making in sports predates the wide availability of advanced computers to analyze data. An article by G.R. Lindsey entitled "Statistical Data Useful for the operation of a Baseball Team," was published in Volume 7 Number 2 of the Operations Research March-April 1959 pages 197–207 which dealt with statistical analysis to help make decisions as to when to relieve a pitcher, when to sacrifice bunt and when to replace a stronger hitting, but weaker fielding player with a weaker hitting, but stronger fielding player once a lead had been established in a game.

# BASEBALL

Analytics have been used in baseball longer than in other professional sports. An example of the type of data analysis used in baseball can be found in a 2016 paper entitled "Opposite Hand Advantage and the Overrepresentation of Left-Handed Players in Major League Baseball," by C.Y. Cyrus Chu, Ted Chang and John Chu in the Academia Economic Paper 44:2 June 2016 Volume 44 which quantified the conventional baseball wisdom that batters have an advantage when facing an opposite-handed pitcher. Using statistics on more than 1.3 million incidents between 2000 and 2012 the advantage was quantified as a strategic advantage 7.15% of the time.

However, until recently, the analytics used in baseball primarily have related to offensive skills and performance rather than defensive play. BAM is changing that. BAM is a program developed by Major League Baseball Advanced Media which is a company owned collectively by all of the MLB franchises. BAM uses radar systems that follow pitches along with multiple cameras that are able to observe and record all of the movements that occur on the field and convert those images into digital data. Thus fielding is now able to be precisely measured. The data is then made available to each of the MLB teams. However, having access to such data is not the same as being able to readily translate that data into useful information capable of evaluating player performance as well as predicting positive game decision strategies based upon the data. Until now, however, such statistical analysis of defensive prowess was lacking although even old baseball purists instinctively knew the value of a highly skilled fielding shortstop or an outfielder who managed to cover exceptional amounts of the outfield effectively.

While it is commonly believed that Abner Doubleday invented baseball in 1839, most scholars agree that this is not accurate and that baseball had been played in some forms for many years prior to Doubleday's involvement. Regardless, of where and when baseball started, written statistics played a major part of this statistic heavy game from as early as the 1860s when Henry Chadwick applied statistical measurements of hits, at bats and putouts to measure the performance of players. From these early measurements, batting averages, earned run averages and other statistical measurements evolved into a major part of the game.

In 1977 Bill James wrote the first edition of "The Bill James Baseball Abstract" which contained his theories of applying statistical data which he called sabermetrics, a term he created referring to the Society for American Baseball Research, to analyze the game of baseball, how it was played and how it should be played. James created his statistics through time consuming gathering and analysis of box scores of MLB games. Among the new measurements created by James was the Runs Created, a statistic used to measure a player's contributions to runs scored by his team using hits, walks and plate appearance data. A proponent of James' theories was Billy Beane, the General Manager of the Oakland Athletics who effectively used these theories including an emphasis of on-base percentage rather than batting average to gauge the effectiveness of a particular player as a hitter. Beane's story was chronicled in the book "Moneyball" by Michael Lewis which later became a popular movie. Beane understood that scoring the most runs was the key to winning baseball games and the best way to do that was to have a higher on-base percentage than the other team and while home run hitters thrill fans, these big swinging hitters often strike out. Beane's team would draw far more walks than strike outs. The idea behind Moneyball was to identify particular players who might not necessarily fit the traditional mold of a great player, but would be able to substantially contribute to the success of the ball club at a reduced price.

Following the surprising success of Beane, all of the other major league baseball teams started using statistical analysis and analytics to measure performance and guide decision making. As for the pioneer

Bill James, he went to work for the Boston Red Sox and contributed his knowledge toward three World Series championships in 2004, 2007 and 2013.

# NATIONAL FOOTBALL LEAGUE

Analytics have been slower to show their potential in football when compared to baseball due to fundamental differences in how the games are played. The MLB season will typically have 677,000 plays from which data can be extracted providing a great sampling of data to be used for analysis and prediction while an NFL season will have only 43,000 plays. In addition, the MLB plays are more narrowly constructed with fewer factors involved with each play consisting of a pitcher throwing to a batter, a batter hitting and a fielder fielding while a typical football play will involve all 22 players on the field in complex interactions. Gleaning which data is significant is a difficult, but not impossible task that will take more time.

In football, data is primarily gathered through small sensors mounted on the player's shoulder pads that use Radio Frequency Identification (RFID) chips technology that monitor the player's movements and the speed of those movements. It then sends that information to computers within the stadium. Turning that information into usable data is another story, however, and NFL teams are still in the early stages of finding ways to productively utilize this information. This information could be helpful in diagnosing injuries or determining whether a player is tired such that his training could be adjusted for his greater health and efficiency, but it also could be used as a weapon by the team during contract negotiations to indicate a reduction in the player's skills and abilities. In addition, to achieve a performance bonus in his contract, a player wish to mask an injury to enable him to play while injured. Should he be required to provide this personal information to the team through sensors or does he have a right to privacy? This is an important legal question that has not been previously considered.

Analytics can also be used to analyze a team's tendencies on both offense and defense to help coaches determine the most effective plays to call and the players to utilize in specific situations.

According to Brian Burke of Advanced Football Analytics, which did an analysis of the wisdom of not punting on fourth down, NFL teams are successful doing an offensive play rather than punting on fourth and one yard to go for a first down almost 70% of the time. Yet NFL coaches, particularly in championship games continue to be more conservative than statistics indicate they should be. According to David Leonhardt of the New York Times, "The shortest explanation revolves around a football cliché: Turnovers can kill a team. A punt is a voluntary turnover. Coaches punt nonetheless because they think the change in field position is more valuable than the chance to keep the ball. They also know they are more likely to face postgame criticism for a failed risk than for excessive caution."[3]

# NATIONAL BASKETBALL ASSOCIATION

Is it a coincidence that the Golden State Warriors, the NBA champions in 2015 and again in 2017 were also the winners of the Best Analytics Organization award at the 2016 MIT Sloan Sports Analytics Conference? Not necessarily, however, analytics certainly do not guarantee success. Among the franchises most committed to analytics is the NBA Philadelphia 76ers whose performance has been quite abysmal in recent years.

The other finalists for the Best Analytics Organization award were the Chicago Blackhawks who won the Stanley Cup in 2015; the Houston Astros, a perennial losing MLB team that had a dramatic turnaround in its success in 2015 and FC Midtjylland, a successful, but not championship caliber Danish professional soccer team.

The Warriors were among the first teams in the NBA to commit to the value of analytics using SportVu cameras to monitor players'

---

[3] "The Worst 4th-Down Decisions in Super Bowl History" NY Times, David Leonhardt, January 29, 2015.

movements continually during games producing data later compiled and analyzed. SportVu cameras are able to detect the intensity of a player's movements as well as the speed with which they move which may help detect fatigue which can often lead to injuries as well as a drop off in production. The Warriors also use wearable technology during practices to monitor the activity of their players which can identify fatigue and predict the likelihood of injuries.

During March of 2015 with the Warriors holding an insurmountable lead in the NBA's Western Conference standings, Coach Steve Kerr rested two of his best players, Stephen Curry and Klay Thompson despite criticism from some disappointed fans who wanted to see their star players perform. The information provided from the use of analytics monitoring the players' movements indicated fatigue on the part of these players, which led to Kerr's decision to rest the players rather than risk injury by playing them at that time.

According to the SportVu software website, teams in the NBA are now using six cameras installed in the catwalks of arenas to track the movements of every player on the court and the basketball 25 times per second. The data collected provides a plethora of innovative statistics based on speed, distance, player separation and ball possession. Some examples include how fast a player moved, how far he traveled during a game, how many times he touched the ball, how many passes he made, how many rebounding opportunities he had, and much more. The information is available to fans on NBA.com and NBA TV. While technologies like "Player Tracking" seem like the wave of the future, turning this massive amount of data into information that will help players and coaches gain an advantage is not simple. With so much data being gathered, again the key question is to determine what data is relevant and then determine how it will be used in evaluating players or adapting team strategies.

Twelve NBA teams use technology created by the Australian company Catapult that fit into the linings of the compression shirts worn by NBA players during practices which monitor their movements. These monitors use GPS technology combined with gyroscopes, magnometers and microprocessors to measure the player's movements and transmit data to a computer for the coach or trainer to observe. Half of NBA teams also require their players to wear heart monitors that can measure the player's response to various training exercises.

Zephyr Technology Corp makes a BioHarness that is built into compression shirts that use GPS and other monitoring technologies to measure heart rate, breathing rate, posture, activity levels, peak acceleration, speed and distance and transmits that data instantly to computers of trainers or coaches.

P3 is another company that has developed advanced sensors and analytics used by NBA teams at the draft combine where prospective players are worked out in the presence of NBA scouts prior to the draft to measure and analyze movement patterns for efficiencies or weaknesses that could predict possible susceptibility to injury. P3's equipment utilizes force plates and a 3-D motion analysis system that tracks and analyzes thousands of data points of a player going through conditioning practice drills.

The sheer volume of data created has not been used yet to create predictive analytics that can infallibly predict injuries, but as more data becomes available and analysis of the data becomes more refined, improvements will occur. And while statistics are not fully available and translatable as to the specific value of using such data to conclusively predict and prevent injuries, anecdotally, teams such as the Toronto Raptors which had been among the teams suffering the most injuries over the course of a season dramatically improved their team health after using the Catapult technology.

An example of the data being used to make more efficient players is exemplified by teams such as the Raptors who determined that 80% of players' movements in practice were lateral rather than moving forward. This caused the Raptors to change the emphasis in practices from forward movements to lateral movements. Catapult's data confirmed this observation in the measurement of minor league basketball games where forward movements only occurred 15.5% of the time during a game.

A new question is arising as to how much information should a team have a right to know about a player's health and conditioning and how much is an invasion of the player's privacy rights? This could be an issue in upcoming collective bargaining agreements. No team in the NBA presently is permitted to use such wearable technology in actual games despite the fact that such data would be tremendously useful.

During the negotiations in 2016 that resulted in a new CBA, the players and the league agreed to the formation of a joint advisory committee to deal with the issues of the use and limits of wearable technology. The NBA has been particularly interested in heart monitoring and heart health as the unusual size of NBA players may have a relation to heart health. The deaths from heart disease in recent years of a number of former NBA players such as Moses Malone at age 60 and Darryl Dawkins at age 58 have increased concern.

# WEARABLE TECHNOLOGY

Wearable technology provides data about players including the amount of energy being expended by the player and the need for hydration. The promise of analytics is that they can provide data that can more precisely monitor players and lead to more efficient training regimens, knowing when players should be rested as well as help avoid injuries or recognize injuries at earlier, more treatable stages.

Wearable technology is not limited to professional athletes. Many people use wearable technology such as Fitbit or Adidas' miCoach to measure various bodily functions and monitor fitness activities. However, the sophistication of the wearable technology created for professional sports teams can provide a greater range of data to measure players' speed, respiration, heart rate, acceleration, hydration levels and force.

Certainly no technology or analytics can possibly measure the important intangibles that go into making a successful athlete or team, however, analytics can provide compelling, insightful knowledge that might not otherwise be available to athletes and teams to assist in achieving higher levels of performance.

Technology that measures body movements of a player and compares that data with historical data gathered about a particular player can enable injuries and potential injuries to be discovered earlier and dealt with sooner. In football the possibility of diagnosing concussions earlier is something that future technology and analytics can improve upon.

Wearable technology that contains sensors that can track a player's movements as well as measure various body functions have been used by NFL coaches. As further developments occur, the ability of this information to be provided to coaches to determine when a player is fatigued and should be rested and measure the amount of force in a particular tackle to prompt possible inquiry into a concussion or other injury possibility will be more commonplace. Motion sensors in the shoes of a skill position player, such as a wide receiver can be used to determine the precision with which a player runs his pass route. Measurements of body temperature can be used to determine when a player may be in danger of overheating and need water or rest.

Wearables can also measure the direction a player may be leaning when he moves, jumps or lands as well as whether he is favoring a certain side which can be an indication of either an injury or a precursor to an injury, which can be remedied through training, rest or treatment.

The issues involved with wearable technology have developed so fast and so recently that there is little guidance in the collective bargaining agreements as to its use. However, any rule requiring a player to use wearable technology either in practice or at a game as a condition of employment would seem to be within the items properly subject to collective bargaining.

The 2011 NFL CBA dealt with this issue primarily for purposes of adding a new dimension to broadcasts of games, but it goes beyond the microphones players can be required to wear to wearables where it reads:

"The NFL may require all NFL players to wear during games and practices equipment that contains sensors or other nonobtrusive tracking devices for purposes of collecting information regarding the performance of NFL games, including players' performances and movements, as well as medical and other safety-related data."

However, the NFL 2011 CBA also requires the NFLPA's consent prior the use of any sensors for "health or medical purposes."

In 2015 the NFLPA filed a grievance against the NFL regarding the use by NFL teams of sleep measuring wearables that were not approved by the NFLPA prior to implementation. The grievance was settled and the NFLPA approval of any programs was agreed to be required before such programs would be implemented in the future. Presently only the Seattle Seahawks are using the technology.

The MLBPA negotiated with MLB for more than a year about the limits on use of wearables before agreeing to the use during the 2016 MLB baseball season of two wearable technology devices during games. The data gathered may not be used in salary arbitration. The two devices were the Zephyr BioHarness which measures a player's breathing and heart rate and the Motus sleeve used on pitchers to be able to measure arm angles and force on ligaments and the elbow. Under the rules agreed upon with MLB the pitcher's team will not have access to the data generated by the Motus sleeve although the player and his agent will have access to this information. In addition, by measuring the stress on the elbow, the Motus sleeve could possibly negate the necessity of serious Tommy John type surgeries by identifying issues that could possibly be corrected by changing the pitcher's motion.

Heart monitors are used in MLB and the data is available to the teams. Changes in heart rate can be an indicator of stress and could be useful information for a team to help determine the optimum amount of rest and proper practice loads for pitchers.

The importance of this issue as a subject to be covered by collective bargaining is magnified because the medical data collected is not protected as medical records under federal HIPAA medical privacy laws.

## QUESTIONS

1.    Should players be required to sign waivers for teams to measure their biological functioning and what should be the repercussions if they should fail to do so?

2.    Should the use of wearable technology be a mandatory subject of collective bargaining?

3.    Are there limits as to the information about a player that a team should be permitted to gather through wearable technology? Everything about a player's lifestyle can affect his ability to perform including the amount of sleep he gets, the foods he eats and the beverages he drinks. Should all of this information be available to the team?

4.    When would the use of wearables represent a conflict of interest between the player and the team?

5.    Does a team have the right to monitor the player and his activity when not in practice or during a game?

6.    If the teams can regulate the players for curfew can they use GPS?

7.    Could a team be deemed negligent and legally responsible for not properly evaluating health data received through wearable technology that resulted in harm to a player?

# WEARABLE TECHNOLOGY FOR COLLEGE ATHLETES

The issue of wearable technology involves not just professional athletes, but college athletes as well. As a part of its multi-million dollar endorsement contracts with the University of Michigan and the University of Tennessee, Nike is permitted to use wearable technology on these colleges' athletes to gather a wide range of data to be used by Nike for further development of its athletic apparel products. It should be emphasized that while the Nike contracts with the University of Michigan and the University of Tennessee permit the gathering of such data and do not limit the uses of such data, Nike has not, as of yet, exercised those rights. While the contracts with these schools do indicate that the data collected will be anonymous and will comply with all applicable laws, there are few, if any, laws that do apply to the collection of this data so the area is essentially unregulated. For instance, while the Health Insurance Portability and Accountability Act (HIPAA) provides privacy protection for medical records, the information gathered through wearables does not qualify as medical information subject to the protective provisions of HIPAA. Because the information to be gathered by Nike would be used for purposes of further product development, Nike, unlike professional sports teams would have no need or use for the data to identity individual players, however, this information could, if leaked or hacked, have an effect on the professional draft status of individual players. Additionally, while professional athletes have unions to protect their privacy interests in the personal data provided by wearable technology, there is no union or other organization to protect the rights of college athletes in regard to wearable technology.

## QUESTIONS

1.   Should amateur college athletes have the right to refuse to be monitored through wearable technology?

2.    Should regulations be enacted to protect the security of such data? If so, who should make those regulations?

3.    Would the hacking of such data provide an edge to college sports gamblers?

# WEARABLE TECHNOLOGY FOR HORSES

Wearable technology is not just for humans. The Equimetre technology invented by a French company is a device that fits into the strap used to hold the saddle of race horses. It is used to measure various physical functions of the horse such as heart rate and respiratory rate as well as measuring the horse's acceleration and speed which can be used to detect injuries and inflammation earlier thereby enabling earlier medical intervention or adjusted training all to the benefit of the horse.

# SLEEP

Sleep is an important factor in athletic performance and the problem of getting good sleep is magnified by teams traveling around the country for games frequently changing time zones. Some teams have hired sleep specialists such as Cheri Mah of the University of California, San Francisco who developed a protocol for the NHL San Jose Sharks that includes natural substances, chamomile, lavender, zinc, magnesium and tart cherry juice. But teams have also shown an interest in gathering data on the individual sleep habits of their players to use through analytics to develop more effective sleep strategies as well as glean useable data from the sleep habits of their players.

The importance of sleep for optimum performance is well established and professional sports teams are interested in this. Sleep science used to be complex and only done in sleep labs with expensive equipment. Now wearable monitors can be used to provide sophisticated data about the length and quality of an athlete's sleep. When he coached the Philadelphia Eagles, Chip Kelly attempted to put in a sleep monitoring program with the Eagles, but the plan never got off the ground due to privacy objections by the NFLPA.

Wearable technology worn by 230 minor league baseball players in 2016 measured exertion, recovery and sleep throughout the day except during games showed that pitchers who were better rested and more recovered pitched faster and hitters hit with more velocity. The data indicated that lesser quality sleep translated to a slower recovery while traveling. Teams are still learning what to do with this data such as providing for naps and adjusting travel times.

Sleep science is still in early stages and while players are amenable to information that can help them get better sleep, they are resistant to sleep information being used against them, such as in contract negotiations.

## QUESTIONS

1.    Does a team have a right to know all of the body measurements that go into sleep measurement?

2.    How could information derived from sleep data be used by a team against the best interests of a player?

3.    Who owns the information about a player's sleep habits gathered through wearable technology?

# MENTAL EVALUATIONS

Look for the next analytical breakthrough to come in the areas of predicting how a player's mental makeup will adjust to the rigors of professional sports and how the emotional aspect of the player correlates to on field performance. Teams need an analytic that predicts behavioral response. Being able to recognize early the psychological problems in a player such as former New England Patriots player Aaron Hernandez who was convicted of murder and committed suicide would save teams large amounts of money.

For years the National Football League has given a 50 question, twelve minute intelligence test at the annual NFL combine at which prospective draftees are subjected to physical strength, speed and agility tests. However, in 2013, the NFL started also doing hour long psychological assessments of players with the intention of identifying players with the best psychological makeup to succeed in professional football. The test attempts to gauge their personalities, cognitive abilities and measure sixteen factors deemed to be harbingers of success in professional football. Many industries use such personality tests.

## QUESTIONS

1.   Is there a point where a psychological test can be considered an invasion of privacy?

2.   Does the player have any rights to protect him from being harmed professionally by a test that may or may not be accurate?

3.   Could future tests be used to disqualify athletes without a scientific basis and no appeal?

4.   Can analytics be applied to mental states of players?

# DATA SECURITY

While Bill James and the early proponents of statistical analysis as well as numerous academic scholars writing on this topic made their works public and available to anyone, teams are becoming more and more protective of the data and the analytics they use in an effort to get a competitive edge on their competition.

Just as companies are often victims of industrial espionage through the stealing of secrets by competitors in the business world so it is in the business world of sports as well. In 2007 The International Automobile Federation (IAF), the governing body of Formula One automobile racing fined the McLaren Mercedes racing team 100 million dollars for spying on its primary rival, the Ferrari racing team.

At the time of the fine, McLaren Mercedes was the leading team in the Formula One Championship. Along with the fine, McLaren Mercedes forfeited all of its championship points for the 2007 racing season. Data stolen from Ferrari was used, according to the IAF to improve McLaren Mercedes' race cars.

The proprietary data and evaluations of players is such that teams are quite secretive in protecting their own specific analytics and data as a way of maintaining that slight edge that can lead to increased chances of success in competition. The advantage held by Billy Beane in his emphasis of the on-base percentage was lost when other teams became aware of the statistic regardless of not having his specific data. It is for this reason that teams jealously guard their data. However, as shown by the hacking of the St. Louis Cardinals data in 2014, cyberespionage within the world of sports is not unheard of and could be anticipated to increase.

After a prolonged investigation, Christopher Correa of the St. Louis Cardinals pleaded guilty in January of 2016 to hacking the private online data base of the Astros called Ground Control that contained tremendous amounts of confidential data including scouting reports and statistics on baseball players. In April of 2016 Correa was sentenced to 46 months in prison and ordered to pay restitution of $279,038.65.

At the time he did the hacking, Correa was the Director of Baseball Development for the St. Louis Cardinals. Correa was fired by the Cardinals when he first became a suspect in the hacking of the Astros. A current Astros employee had worked previously for the Cardinals and Correa was able to easily guess the password used by him to access Ground Control by merely using variations of the password the Astro employee had used when he worked for the Cardinals. Armed with this password, Correa stole data from Ground Control for use by the Cardinals.

In January of 2017 MLB Commissioner Rob Manfred banned Correa for life from participating in any manner with Major League Baseball.

In addition, Manfred ordered the Cardinals to pay the Astros two million dollars and forfeit to the Astros the Cardinals' top two picks in the June 2017 amateur draft despite the fact that Manfred determined that no one in the Cardinals' organization other than Correa knew about or participated in the crime.

---

## QUESTION

1.   Should matters of data security be subject to the exclusive jurisdiction of law enforcement authorities or should professional sports leagues also be empowered to make regulations regarding data security and determine punishment for violations of such rules?

# SYNPOSIS

1.   Technological advances have occurred in sports for many years; however, certain technological advances have been banned, such as drag resistant swim suits.

2.   Technology is available to accurately call balls and strikes in baseball games, but has not been used although the infallibility of MLB umpires has been proven.

3.   Analytics, the management of compiled data to enable predictive analysis through enhanced utilization of the data to achieve a competitive advantage and increase the level of performance is being done throughout sports.

4.   The use of wearable technology by professional athletes is generally considered subject to each league's Collective Bargaining Agreement.

5.   Wearable technology has the ability to improve the health and safety of players, but has the risk to the player that such information could be used by the team against the player's interest.

6.   Psychological tests are used by professional teams and players are required to take such tests.

7.   Data security and industrial espionage have become issues in professional sports.

8.   College athletes are now subject to being required to use wearable technology at some colleges as part of the school's endorsement contracts for athletic apparel and equipment.

# CHAPTER SEVENTEEN

# Stadiums

Sports stadiums in the United States have changed tremendously since the construction of early baseball stadiums such as Fenway Park in Boston, built in 1912 for the Boston Red Sox and still used today to the construction of Levi's stadium in Santa Clara, California the home of the NFL's San Francisco 49ers. Even adjusted for inflation, the stadiums of today are far more expensive to build and cost fans far more to attend events than earlier stadiums.

New stadiums are regularly being built. In the past twenty years 75% of professional sports teams have built or substantially remodeled their stadiums, often with the primary focus of adding luxury suites. Catering to corporate clients able to pay the large fees for corporate suites is a big reason for the building of new stadiums such as the new Yankee Stadium which cost 1.5 billion dollars. In fact, many new stadiums are being built, not because they have become physically out of date, but because their lack of luxury suites makes them financially out of date with the business model of many professional sports teams.

## STADIUM ECONOMICS

Prices for suites at Dallas' AT&T Stadium for Cowboys' games range from $14,000 to $24,000 per game. The prices vary according to the particular opponent. The suite will rent out for more when a popular team, such as the New England Patriots comes to Dallas than a less popular team, such as the Jacksonville Jaguars. Prices go up also depending on the location of the suite. The Dallas Cowboy's stadium has three hundred luxury suites.

Luxury suites offer perks that appeal to the corporations and wealthy individuals that buy them including comfortable theater type seating, large high definition flat screen televisions as well as televisions in the mirrors in the private bathrooms included with the suite, exclusive entrances to the stadium, premium food and liquor and even the possibility to attend special events provided by the team for its luxury suite ticket holders. While the cost of the suites are large, it could be said that the cost is subsidized to some extent by other regular ticket holders as well as the rest of the tax paying public because corporations are able to deduct up to 50% of their costs for the suites used for business purposes such as marketing.

While upper level nose bleed seats at AT&T stadium could be had for $82.83 in 2013, premium seats on the fifty yard line not only cost $500 per seat, but, if obtained through season tickets, required the fan to purchase a Personal Seat License which is a one-time fee paid by the fan for the privilege of being able to purchase season tickets. The PSL goes up depending on where the seats are located in the stadium with 50 yard line seats costing the fan $150,000 merely for the right to purchase season tickets for these particular seats. The Dallas Cowboys provide loans with interest to finance the cost of the PSL. The average PSL for Dallas Cowboys season ticket holders in 2013 was $29,100. The license also requires the fan to buy ten tickets for not only the eight regular season games, but also for two preseason games every year for the next thirty years. If the license holding fan fails to meet his or her obligations pursuant to the PSL agreement, the license can be revoked by the Cowboys and the fan forfeits all funds already paid toward the license. Of course, these costs do not include parking and refreshments.

But it isn't just the Cowboys. This business model of PSLs is used by 15 other teams and can be expected to be incorporated into the ticketing for all new stadiums.

# NAMING RIGHTS

Naming rights of stadiums are an important source of revenue to professional teams. It is common for teams to sell naming rights as in the NFL's New England Patriots, Gillette Stadium; Dallas Cowboys, AT&T Stadium and the Carolina Panthers Bank of America Stadium. Citibank paid 400 million dollars for the naming rights to the new stadium of the New York Mets baseball team for twenty years and MetLife paid more than 400 million dollars for the naming rights of the former New Meadowlands Stadium used by the NFL's Giants and Jets. When contrasted to the cost of three million dollars for a thirty second television advertisement during the Super Bowl, this may look like a justifiable marketing expense although there is little or no evidence that the name recognition for these companies has a correlation to corporate profits. Times change and names change as when the name of the stadium for the Houston Astros baseball team was changed from the tainted and infamous Enron Field to Minute Maid Park.

Between naming rights and luxury suites, two-thirds of a team's revenues can come from corporations rather than everyday individual fans.

While the upscale high priced stadiums are a boon to the teams that play in them, the NFL has found that ticket sales to regular fans have gone down in recent years. There are many reasons for this including the increased cost of attending games, but the inconvenience of crowds and the fact that fans can more conveniently watch games on their own large screen televisions at home at far less cost are also relevant factors. Therefore it is now up to the NFL to come up with incentives to get fans to attend the games in person. Special apps available to those attending games to provide experiences not able to be achieved at home can be expected to be experimented with. Using the fan's smartphone as the vehicle for delivering video of games around the league and other content that the at-home viewer cannot readily receive can well be a factor in the future. The NFL already has a channel called NFL Red Zone which shows all of the plays inside the twenty yard line in other games being played around the league. While it is now shown on stadium screens, it can be expected to make its way to the fans' smartphones soon as well. Already in Australia, a cricket stadium provides commentary to fans on their smartphones which cannot be obtained outside of the stadium. Greater access to camera views not available on television and the possible ability to hear audio of coaches and players speaking during the games are all being considered. Even the possibility of holographic replays at the stadium is being developed.

# NOTABLE STADIUMS

Candlestick Park in San Francisco was built at a cost of 120 million dollars in 1960. It served as the home of the San Francisco Giants in baseball and the San Francisco 49ers in football. Notably it was also the venue of the last concert of the Beatles in 1966.

The Houston Astrodome, once called the Eighth Wonder of the World was built at a cost of 262 million dollars in 1960 and was the first multi-purposed domed sports stadium.

AT&T Stadium, the home of the Dallas Cowboys was built in 2009 at a cost of 1.1 billion dollars with the 160 foot long high definition video screen hanging in the middle of the stadium itself costing more than 35 million dollars which is more than the cost of the Cowboy's entire former stadium.

Levi's Stadium the home of the San Francisco 49ers was built at a cost of 1.3 billion dollars in 2014 and ushered in a new era of high technology stadiums.

# HISTORY

In the early 1900s professional sports franchises, primarily baseball franchises paid for the cost of their own stadium construction at places such as Wrigley Field in Chicago, Ebbets Field in Brooklyn and Fenway Park, in Boston which still stands. Fenway Park was built at a cost of $650,000 in 1912, which even with inflation would only be 16 million dollars today.

In the following decades larger stadiums were built, such as the iconic Los Angeles Memorial Coliseum built in 1923 which was used for many events including two Olympic Games. It was built with public funds, but at a dramatically low cost of less than a million dollars which adjusted for inflation today would only be 14 million dollars. The Cleveland Municipal Stadium constructed in 1931 was also built with public funds. It originally cost a million dollars which adjusted for inflation would be 64.8 million dollars today.

With the dramatic expansion of the number of professional sports franchises in the 1960s and 1970s, cities competed to become the host cities for these new franchises. Cities also attempted to lure existing franchises from cities in which they were already established with newer stadiums, offers of free land, public stadium financing or tax incentives. These stadiums, as exemplified by Cincinnati's Riverfront Stadium were often the homes for both professional baseball and football teams. They were, however, largely Spartan in design and did not provide for the luxury boxes that have come to dominate the designs of modern day stadiums. The costs, however, were not particularly exorbitant. Cincinnati's Riverfront Stadium was built in 1970 at a cost of 45 million which adjusted for inflation today would be 275 million dollars which while a great leap from the adjusted for inflation costs of stadiums built earlier in the century is dwarfed by the costs of stadium construction today.

The first of the new concept stadiums was Camden Yards in Baltimore, which is the home of the Baltimore Orioles. The park was designed solely for baseball and the sight lines are fan friendly. It was built in 1992 at a cost of 110 million dollars which adjusted for inflation would be 186 million dollars today. The design for a single sport rather than using the stadium for both football and baseball made for a better fan experience at the game, but also necessitated the building of additional stadiums to house the other professional sport teams in cities with both NFL and MLB franchises. Camden Yards was also used to revitalize the downtown area in which it was sited.

Fearful of losing the Baltimore Orioles as they had lost the NFL's Baltimore Colts in 1984, the State of Maryland created a new state agency, the Maryland Stadium Authority to be in charge of the construction and management of new stadiums in the state. The Maryland Stadium Authority obtained the money to construct stadiums through the sale of tax-free municipal bonds. In 1992 the Baltimore Orioles signed a complicated thirty year lease in which the Maryland Stadium Authority receives 7% of net admission revenues, some concession funds, some parking revenues, some advertising revenues and between 7 and 10% of luxury suite revenues. In addition, Maryland levies a 10% state admission tax on all tickets with the funds derived from this allocated to the Maryland Stadium Authority. Most of this money is used to pay the debt on the municipal bonds used to initially fund the stadium as well as increased costs of maintenance of an aging structure. The question, however, becomes whether even if the arrangement does not lose money for the state and its taxpayers, is this the best use of taxpayer funds and tax free municipal bonds issued by the state or should they be used for other purposes, such as schools, hospitals and essential infrastructure? Whether or not the rent paid by the Orioles for the use of Camden Yards is fair is difficult to determine as the Baltimore Orioles are not required to publicly provide full financial statements.

# STADIUM FINANCING

The public financing of stadiums for use by professional sports teams through tax-exempt municipal bonds provides a direct benefit to the teams playing in these stadiums but deprives taxpayers of the federal income taxes on the millions of dollars of bonds issued in order to finance the construction of such stadiums.

While some cities, such as Seattle, in recent years have gone on record as being against the public financing of new stadiums, numerous cities including Houston, Miami and New York have followed the long standing path of financing stadiums for professional teams through tax-exempt municipal bonds and tax increases.

The Santa Clara Stadium Authority is a public agency created for the purpose of building and managing the 49ers new stadium but also to protect the City from financial liability for stadium costs. It is run by the Santa Clara City Council and responsible for as much as 950 million in construction loans to be paid back from revenue generated by the stadium including naming rights for which it received a 154 million dollar share of the 220 million dollar naming rights contract with Levi's, the sale of seat licenses which range from $2,000 to $250,000 and the right to buy 49ers season tickets. The 49ers were responsible for construction costs overruns on the stadium and the annual rent is 24.5 million dollars for each year of the 40 year lease.

Incidental costs sometimes get overlooked when analyzing the funding that goes into a new stadium. The City of Santa Clara, California paid millions to move an electrical substation necessary for the functioning of the new Levi's Stadium. The total 1.31 billion dollars price tag for the construction of the new stadium was paid partially with 200 million dollars from the 49ers which amount, in turn, was obtained through a loan from the NFL. However 9% of the cost of the new stadium was still borne by the City of Santa Clara for a total of 114 million dollars made up of 42 million dollars from the Santa Clara Redevelopment Agency, 20 million dollars as the cost to Silicon Valley Power to move and upgrade the electrical substation, 17 million dollars from the stadium's share of previously sold bonds to build a parking garage and 35 million dollars in the form of a new 2% tax on hotel guests at eight hotels close to the stadium. This 2% tax is on top of a regular hotel tax bringing the total tax paid by a hotel visitor at one of these hotels to 11.5% whether or not they are attending a game. It is often an easier choice for taxpayers to put the financial burden of stadium construction on tourists. The stadium itself is owned by the Stadium Authority which paid for the rest of the cost with loans from banks and seat licenses of 312 million dollars. Naming rights and seat licenses have become crucial parts of stadium financing.

## LAS VEGAS RAIDERS

The NFL's Raiders franchise which originated in Oakland, moved to Los Angeles and then back to Oakland in 2017 obtained NFL permission by a vote of 31–1 to move the franchise to Las Vegas. Funding for a new 65,000 seat stadium, which, particularly due to weather concerns, would be a domed stadium carries an estimated price tag of 1.98 billion dollars. The cost of the stadium includes payments of 500 million dollars from the Raiders themselves and 750 million dollars from the State of Nevada which agreed to an increase in the Clark County hotel room tax to cover the cost. This 750 million dollar in public funding represents the largest taxpayer subsidy in the history of the NFL. While it would appear that the public funding through an increased hotel tax would come from the pockets of tourists rather than the citizens of Nevada, the hotel room tax has generally been used to fund state education costs which will be more difficult to raise if the tax is already being used to cover stadium costs. In addition, the hotel tax is quite vulnerable to bringing in lower revenues if there is a downward movement in the economy that reduces tourism.

Although the stadium would be used both by the Raiders and the football team of the University of Nevada Las Vegas, the financial benefit of a new stadium to the citizens of Nevada is not clear, particularly since they will not share in stadium profits.

# REVENUE ACT OF 1913

The Revenue Act of 1913 was the first law to provide that interest income earned from state or municipal bonds would not be subject to federal income taxes. In 1968 this law was amended by the Revenue and Expenditure Control Act of 1968 to provide that the income tax exclusion would not apply if 25% of the property secured by the bond was used by a non-governmental entity and 25% of the payments of interest and principal were secured by property used by private, non-governmental entities. However, these provisions specifically did not apply to the use of such bonds to finance sports stadiums. This clarification of the law enabled not only cities and states to fund with taxpayers' money the construction of stadiums to be used by professional sports teams, but also served to remove from the federal income tax coffers interest earned on these bonds that would otherwise have been subject to federal income tax. Backlash to the public funding of stadiums being built for use by professional sports teams resulted in the Tax Reform Act of 1986 which removed the 1968 exemption for stadium construction from the bond laws except for projects already started. Further, the 25% figure used in the 1968 law was reduced to 10% which could have been expected to reduce the amount of public financing of stadium construction. However, rather than dissuade states and municipalities from stadium construction, it just made the financing more complicated for these states and municipalities seeking to be the hosts of professional sports teams. Under the Tax Reform Act of 1986 states and municipalities now had to be responsible for at least 90% of the financing and were not able to rely on ticket, concession, parking and other revenue from the stadium to produce up to 25% of the carrying costs. States and municipalities turned to funding the bonds from the general tax revenues to avoid the federal law. Between 1990 and 2001, American taxpayers contributed as much as ten billion dollars toward the cost of stadium construction.

The purpose of tax exempt bonds as provided for in the federal tax law was to raise funds for important infrastructure such as airports, roads, utilities and sewage facilities which are generally too expensive for private companies to finance without government help. It is questionable whether a professional sport stadium serves an equivalent public purpose for which the public should pay through higher taxes. Cities can operate without a sports team, but not without essential infrastructure such as an airport. In essence there are far more worthy projects for public bond funding than sports stadiums, particularly when the cost of tickets to attend many professional sporting events is priced too high for many taxpayers to afford. Expensive tickets and cost of attending events make it impossible for much of the population to attend sporting events at stadiums, yet their tax dollars are still used to finance the stadiums.

While public support may wane for necessary improvements such as airports, many times the public has been convinced that there is a need for public funding for stadiums that benefit private owners of professional sports teams. Out of a perhaps realistic fear of losing their teams, municipalities use public money to pay for a stadium that provides little tangible public use when contrasted with greater needs of schools and infrastructure. Stadium construction presents limited rewards to local taxpayers compared to using the money for more tangible improvements for the citizenry, but voters are often convinced to vote for such funding and sometimes, they don't even get the opportunity to vote for municipal or state funding of stadiums and their elected officials make the decisions for them.

In 2015 President Obama proposed to close the loophole that allowed cities and states to use tax exempt bonds for stadium construction. Even that would not, however, have prevented the cities and states from borrowing money to build stadiums, but the money would have had to be borrowed at a higher rate making it a less attractive option for the municipalities. Unfortunately, the proposal never got past Congress.

Stadium funding is rarely totally privately funded by the team occupying the stadium with a few notable exceptions such as the New England Patriots. Generally, municipalities and states provide the financing for new stadiums and take control of a large depreciating asset, the stadium, while team owners pay favorable rents because the law doesn't permit the bonds to be tax-exempt if the income is more than 10% of the funding. Thus a professional team paying a high rent would jeopardize the tax exempt status of the municipal bonds used to finance the project.

29 of 31 NFL stadiums have received public funds for construction or improvements. Taxpayers have spent almost 7 billion dollars on stadiums for the NFL which had 10 billion dollars in revenue in 2014.

A 2012 Bloomberg analysis found new stadiums had contributed to a doubling of team values in professional sports. Even when the NFL puts in its own moneys it does so out of revenue sources such as luxury suites, personal seat licenses and naming rights that would not even exist without the new stadium. The public takes the risk and the profits go to the teams.

---

**QUESTION**

1. Is the building of sports stadiums an appropriate use of governmental funds?

# PROPERTY TAXES AND OTHER SOURCES OF REVENUE

Property taxes have long been a major source of income for municipalities. The potential property taxes on a stadium are large, however, abatements of such property taxes have been a strategy used by municipalities to make themselves more attractive to teams locating in the particular city. However the commitment to exempt properties from property taxes is often limited by law, such as in New York where property taxes may not be abated for more than ten years. In response, municipalities have turned to Payment In Lieu of Taxes (PILOT) bonds. These permit teams to make payments toward public bonds used for their benefit in lieu of paying property taxes.

PILOT bonds used in the funding of the new Yankee Stadium took payments from the team that would have been used to pay for local property taxes that would have paid for police and schools and other municipal services and used those funds exclusively to pay off the bonds.

To tax those who are using the stadiums, some municipalities put taxes on the tickets, concessions and parking. Increasing a general sales tax spreads the tax burden for the new stadium throughout the population, but targeted taxes such as on tickets, concessions and parking put more of the burden of the building of stadiums on the people using the stadium.

Hotel and rental car taxes have been used to also help fund stadiums as was done in Houston and Miami with these taxes often being considered to be most highly applied to tourists who are not in a position to vote on the particular tax that will affect them.

Tobacco and alcohol taxes have also been used to fund stadiums, but have become less of a source of revenue as smoking has gone down in recent years.

The argument in favor of states and municipalities paying for new stadiums for professional teams is that they attract tourist dollars media coverage and increases in business. However, often stadiums are not located near many other businesses that would benefit from increased traffic. Proponents of state and municipal funding of stadiums often say that they spur the local economy, create jobs and increase tourism, but these claims are largely exaggerated. Stadiums and arenas are poor investments for economic development.

Stadiums, particularly indoor arenas, however, can be used for multiple purposes including conventions which can bring in more revenue than large stadiums the use of which is more limited to big sporting events and concerts.

## QUESTIONS

1.  Is a stadium as necessary today for the public who will by and large watch the sport on television and other electronic media?

2.  The federal government and by extension all taxpayers lose money when tax exempt bonds are used to finance sports stadiums. What are the advantages and disadvantages to using public funds to pay for the cost of stadiums primarily used by professional sports teams?

# TAXPAYERS PROTECTION ALLIANCE

In September of 2015, the Taxpayers Protection Alliance issued a report entitled "Sacking Taxpayers: How NFL Stadium Subsidies Waste Money and Fall Short on Their Promises of Economic Development."

Some of the startling conclusions in the report indicated:

"Since 1995, a staggering 29 of the 31 stadiums that house NFL teams received public subsidies for construction, renovation or both. Between 1995 and today, taxpayers have been forced to spend nearly $7 billion subsidizing NFL stadium construction and renovation projects.

The subsidies amount to little more than crass corporate welfare. After all, the handouts for stadium construction and renovation projects amount to money being taken from struggling taxpayers by politicians, then funneled to the billionaire owners of the teams in order to reduce their overhead cost and increase their profits.

While government leaders and team officials argue that publicly subsidized stadiums are justified because the projects encourage economic growth by generating wealth and creating jobs.

In an effort to determine the economic impact of taxpayer-financed NFL stadiums on the people who pay the taxes that fund the construction of most NFL stadiums, the Taxpayers Protection Alliance compared median household income and poverty rates in counties with NFL stadiums before and after tax dollars were used to subsidize the stadiums.

Data revealed that median income decreased and poverty rose substantially in counties with publicly funded NFL stadiums.

Taxpayers funded more than half the construction cost of 12 stadiums from 1995–2013. During that time, national median household income rose 0.3 percent across the United States, adjusted for inflation. In the dozen counties in which an NFL stadium was built using more than 50 percent public funds, however, median household income plummeted 5.7 percent during the same time.

Twenty-six counties in America are home to an NFL stadium that received tax dollars between 1995 and 2013. In an astonishing 17 of those 26 counties, the median household income actually decreased in constant dollars after the stadium received public money for construction or renovation. Taxpayer-financed NFL stadiums didn't just appear to decrease median income, they also apparently contributed to increasing the number of people living in poverty.

In the 12 counties in which taxpayers funded more than half the cost of a new stadium between 1995 and 2013, the percentage of the total population living in poverty rose from 16 percent to 18.7 percent. That poverty rate increase is a 26.3 percent greater increase in poverty over other counties that are home to NFL stadiums, and an increase of more than 231 percent the national average, which rose from 13.8 to 14.5 percent during that time."

The report indicated that through a combination of hotel taxes, rental car taxes, sales taxes and bonds, the following teams received taxpayers' funds as follows:

Arizona Cardinals 308 million dollars

Chicago Bears 387 million dollars

Cincinnati Bengals 424.8 million dollars

Cleveland Browns 200 million dollars

Dallas Cowboys 444 million dollars

In addition, the report shows that the 289 million dollars in public funding used to improve Sports Authority Field at Mile High Stadium of the Denver Broncos included a six-county sales tax increase that provided 72% of the cost of the stadium renovations which the average family in the six counties affected around Denver having to approximately pay an additional $1,100 in sales taxes.[1]

A glimmer of hope though is provided in the report describing the 400 million dollars of renovations done to Sun Life Stadium the home of the NFL's Miami Dolphins in 2016 with the Dolphins ownership paying for the cost privately along with a 200 million dollar loan from the NFL through its program that loans money to teams that fund their improvements privately. Not that the taxpayers come out totally unscathed. The Miami-Dade County commission is providing payments to the stadium owners pursuant to Performance-Based Marquee Event (PBME) Grants by which the stadium owners are paid specific funds for attracting major events to the stadium that can provide short term economic benefit to the area. A Super Bowl or World Cup final would bring a payment of 4 million dollars, a college football championship or World Cup soccer match 3 million dollars and a college football national championship semifinal game $750,000. Making the payment even more tax payer friendly is the provision that payments of the grants will only be made from funds earned through the Convention Development Tax funds and the county is not obligated to make payments until December 31, 2024 although the county may choose to make payments earlier if funds are available. In addition, there is an annual cap of no more than 5 million dollars in PBME grant funds being earned in any year with a total

---

[1]   http://protectingtaxpayers.org/assets/files/NFL-Subsidies-report-Sept2015.pdf

earned and payable of no more than 30 million dollars in PBME for all events up to the year 2024.

There are, however, an increasing number of stadiums that are being built without public money. The NFL's St. Louis Rams move to Inglewood outside of Los Angeles was accomplished with no public funding being used toward the construction costs of a new 1.9 billion dollar stadium. Also, legislators in San Diego refused to give in to the demands of its longtime NFL franchise, the Chargers to come up with hundreds of millions of public funds to pay for a replacement for its aging Qualcomm Stadium. A 2016 referendum in San Diego to fund a new stadium for the Chargers through a new hotel tax failed when it was supported by only 43% of the voters when it needed a two-thirds majority to pass. The NBA's Golden State Warriors are also planning a billion dollar basketball arena to be built without public funding.

# TECHNOLOGY

Levels of technology have increased dramatically in recent years bringing with it new entertainment, options and greater convenience along with greater incursions into the privacy of many fans of which they not be aware.

Levi's Stadium is an example of the creative use of technology to improve the fan's experience on many levels. The stadium's mobile app performs multiple functions including providing assistance in locating parking spaces, finding seats, concession stands and uncrowded restrooms. In addition, food and beverages can be ordered using the app for delivery to the fan's seat or available for pickup. During the game, instant replays from multiple angles are available to the fan. The cost alone of the technological features for Levi's Stadium was approximately 125 million dollars. The stadium WIFI network also tracks the movements and usage of fans and provides greater data to the stadium operators that can provide greater awareness of the individual needs and desires of its fans, however this comes at a cost of decreased privacy with many fans not being aware that their movements and network usage are being tracked and used.

# SYNOPSIS

1.   Stadiums for professional sports teams were originally built by and paid for by the teams themselves, such as the Red Sox building and paying for Fenway Park.

2.   The modern day stadiums of today are filled with high end technology with pricing of seats such that average families are priced out of attending games.

3.   Municipalities and other governmental units have taken on much of the financial burden of construction of modern stadiums.

4.   Stadium funding is often done by municipalities and other governmental units through bonds and increased taxes.

5.   The Revenue Act of 2013 provided the mechanism for the issuance of tax-free bonds to finance public projects.

6.   Luxury suites and stadium naming rights have become major revenue streams for professional sports teams.

7.   Projected financial benefits of having a municipality or other governmental unit build a stadium for professional sports teams rarely occur.

8.   Recently teams have taken on more of the financial burden of stadium construction.

# Glossary

**Agent:** An agent is someone who is legally authorized to act on behalf of someone else.

**Anabolic steroids:** Anabolic (muscle building) steroids are synthetic versions of the male hormone testosterone. They can be taken as pills, a cream, a gel or by injections.

**Analytics:** Analytics are computerized programs that gather and analyze data.

**Assumption of the risk:** Assumption of risk is a subset of contributory negligence by which someone assumes the risk associated with a particular activity and is not entitled to a judgment against someone else whose negligence may have contributed to injuries suffered by the person who assumed the risk of such injury.

**Clayton Act:** The Clayton Act of 1914 is a federal law that exempts labor unions from being considered monopolies.

**Collective bargaining:** Collective bargaining requires management and unions to negotiate in good faith on matters of compensation and working conditions.

**Collective Bargaining Agreement (CBA):** A contract negotiated between an employer and a union that provides for the terms and conditions of employment.

**Comparative negligence:** A legal theory by which the negligence, if any, of the injured party is compared to the negligence of the other person or entity whose negligence is alleged to have contributed to the injury of the plaintiff and if the negligence of the person being sued is more than that of the harmed individual, that person is entitled to a judgment on his or her behalf. However, the amount of money to be awarded to that person is reduced by a percentage that corresponds to the court determined percentage of the plaintiff's negligence.

**Contributory negligence:** Under the theory of contributory negligence, if a plaintiff is even partially responsible through his or her own negligence for the injuries he or she sustained, he or she is not entitled to a judgment against someone else whose negligence may have contributed to his or her injury.

**Copyright:** Copyright law protect creative literary works, music, plays, choreography, pantomimes, pictures, graphics and sculptures, photographs and paintings, computer software, maps, architectural designs, recordings, movies, radio and television shows.

**CTE:** Chronic traumatic encephalopathy (CTE) is a brain disorder that comes about as a result of repeated head trauma that harms brain cells in sections of the brain that control mood, emotions and executive functioning. CTE symptoms which can be confused with Alzheimer's disease symptoms include cognitive impairment, dementia, depression, memory loss, confusion, tremors and more.

**Fantasy sports:** Participants in fantasy sports assemble imaginary teams of individual real players from professional sports such as basketball, baseball, hockey and, perhaps most popular, football to compete against the imaginary teams of other participants. Statistics based points determined by the performance of the individual players in real competitions are totaled and the winner is the person with the highest number of points. Fantasy sports can be done on a season-long basis or individual day basis.

**Fiduciary relationship:** It is a special relationship of trust and confidence where the agent owes the highest standard of loyalty to his or her client and must avoid any conflict of interest.

**Franchise player:** A provision of the NFL CBA which provides for the designation of a player as a Franchise Player who is required to sign a one year contract with his team for the greater of either the average of the top five salaries in the league for the position he plays or 120% of his prior salary.

**Gelding:** A Gelding is a neutered male racehorse.

**HGH:** Human Growth Hormone (HGH) is a hormone that is naturally produced by the human pituitary gland that aids and stimulates cell growth and healing.

**Hyperandrogenism:** Hyperandrogenism is a condition whereby female athletes have high levels of naturally occurring testosterone.

**Independent contractor:** A worker is considered an independent contractor rather than an employee if the person paying the worker has the right to control or direct only the result of the work and not what will be done and how it will be done.

**Liability waiver:** A provision in an athlete's endorsement contract by which the endorsing athlete waives his or her right to bring legal action against the company whose products he or she is endorsing if the player suffers some harm due to use of the endorsed product.

**Moral turpitude:** Actions considered by society to be morally reprehensible, which may or may not be violations of civil or criminal law.

**Morality clause:** A provision in a player's contract that enables the team to terminate the contract for conduct not related to the player's performance as an athlete that puts the athlete into disrepute. It is also found in endorsement contracts and enables the company to terminate the athlete's endorsement contract.

**National Labor Relations Act:** The National Labor Relations Act is a federal law enacted in 1935 designed to protect the rights of employees, encourage collective bargaining and respond to unfair labor practices. It is enforced by the National Labor Relations Board.

**NCAA:** The National Collegiate Athletic Association (NCAA) is the organization that regulates intercollegiate athletics. It has more than 1,200 member schools. The NCAA regulates 89 different championships in 23 sports across its three divisions.

**Negligence:** The failure of someone with a duty of care to exercise such care as a reasonably prudent person would exercise thereby causing harm to someone to whom the duty of care is required.

**No Trade Clause:** A No Trade Clause is a provision in a professional athlete's contract that limits the ability of the team to trade the player to another team without the permission of the player.

**Norris-LaGuardia Act:** Norris-LaGuardia Act of 1932 permits employees to organize as a collective bargaining unit without violating anti-trust law.

**Paralympics:** The Paralympics is an international sporting competition for physically and intellectually disabled people governed by the International Paralympic Committee which oversees 176 national Paralympic committees and various international disabled sports federations.

**Pari-mutuel betting:** The pari-mutuel system of betting on horse races originated in France in the 1860s. Under this system the odds of winning are calculated, after the track takes its fee, based upon the relative amounts bet on the horses with the more money bet on a particular horse lowering the odds and the payouts to winners.

**Per se rule:** Under the *per se* rule, a labor practice is considered a violation of anti-trust law if it is an inherently unreasonable restraint of trade.

**PILOT bonds:** Payment In Lieu of Taxes (PILOT) bonds are used by professional sports teams to make payments toward public bonds used for their benefit in lieu of paying property taxes.

**Point spread:** The point spread is a number established by bookmakers designating the number of points by which a favorite team would need to defeat an underdog team for a person betting on the favorite to win his bet. The point spread is a number established by bookmakers designating the number of points by which a favorite team would need to defeat an underdog team for a person betting on the favorite to win his bet.

**Revenue Act of 1913:** The Revenue Act of 2013 was the first law to provide for interest income earned from state or municipal bonds would not be subject to federal income taxes. These bonds have been used to finance stadium construction.

**Salary cap:** The salary cap is an amount determined through a Collective Bargaining Agreement that limits the total amount of compensation paid by a team to its players.

**Sherman Act:** Sherman Anti-Trust Act of 1890 prohibits monopolies that harmed consumers. The law prohibits agreements or practices that unduly restricted free competition between businesses.

**SPARTA:** The Sports Agent Responsibility and Trust Act of 2004 commonly referred to as SPARTA is the federal law that deals with sports agency.

**Title IX:** Title IX of the 1972 Education Amendments provides that no one shall on the basis of sex be excluded from participation in or denied the benefit of or discriminated against in any education program that receives federal financial assistance. Although the language of the law speaks of education programs, its primary focus has been on equal opportunity for women in the area of athletics.

**Torts:** Torts are civil actions that do not involve contracts. Examples of torts are assault and battery libel or negligence.

**Trademark:** A Trademark is a distinctive sign used by a business to uniquely identify itself from others. It can be a name, a word, phrase, logo, symbol, design, image or combination thereof.

**Transition player:** This designation for an NFL player provides the team with a right to match the offer of any other team that makes an offer to the player. Unlike with restricted free agency, if the player designated as a Transition Player signs with another team and his former team decides not to match the offer of the new team, the former team does not receive any form of compensation from the new team.

**UAAA:** The Uniform Athletes Agents Act (UAAA) was drafted in 2000 by the National Conference of Commissioners on Uniform State Laws, a non-profit organization made up of commissioners from each of the states to develop laws to provide uniformity in specific areas of the law, such as the Uniform Commercial Code. In this case, the UAAA deals with athlete agency law.

**UIGEA:** The Unlawful Internet Gambling Enforcement Act (UIGEA) is a federal law a law that criminalizes the transfer of funds to illegal Internet based gambling companies. The law contains a specific exemption for fantasy sports.

**Vigorish:** Sports wagering is generally done through people referred to as bookmakers who make their profit by taking a percentage of the money bet as a vigorish or vig.

**WADA:** The World Anti-Doping Association is the organization that oversees drug testing for international sports such as the Olympics.

**Wire Act of 1961:** The Wire Act of 1961 was enacted by Congress to prohibit sports betting using the telephone.

# Index